BLACK MARXISM

THE MAKING
OF THE BLACK
RADICAL
TRADITION

ACK MARX-ISM

CEDRIC J. ROBINSON

FOREWORD BY ROBIN D. G. KELLEY

WITH A NEW PREFACE BY THE AUTHOR

THE UNIVERSITY OF NORTH CAROLINA PRESS

CHAPEL HILL & LONDON

Foreword and preface copyright © 2000
The University of North Carolina Press

First published 1983 by Zed Press, 57 Caledonian Road,
London N1 9DN; reprinted 2000 by the University of
North Carolina Press.

Designed by April Leidig-Higgins
Set in Minion type by Keystone Typesetting, Inc.
Manufactured in the United States of America

The paper in this book meets the guidelines for perma-
nence and durability of the Committee on Production
Guidelines for Book Longevity of the Council on Library
Resources.

Library of Congress Cataloging-in-Publication Data
Robinson, Cedric J. Black marxism: the making of the
Black radical tradition / Cedric J. Robinson; foreword by
Robin D. G. Kelley; with a new preface by the author.
p.   cm. Includes bibliographical references and index.
ISBN 0-8078-4829-8 (pbk.: alk. paper)
1. Communism—Africa.   2. Communism—Developing
countries.   3. Afro-American communists.   I. Title.
HX436.5.R63 2000   335.43'0917'496—dc21   99-30995 CIP

04 03 02 01 00   5 4 3 2 1

For Leonard and Gary,
for whom there was not enough time

CONTENTS

FOREWORD

When black scholars hear the call to equal opportunity in darkness,
they must remember that they do not belong in the darkness of an
American culture that refuses to move toward the light. They are not
meant to be pliant captives and agents of institutions that deny light
all over the world. No, they must speak the truth to themselves and to
the community and to all who invite them into the new darkness. They
must affirm the light, the light movement of their past, the light
movement of their people. They must affirm their capacities to move
forward toward new alternatives for light in America.
—Vincent Harding, "Responsibilities of the Black Scholar to
Community"

I can say, without a trace of hyperbole, that this book changed my life. Like a specter,
it has haunted me from the day I pulled it out of its brown padded envelope over
sixteen years ago to the moment I agreed to write this foreword. The long hours,
weeks, and months I agonized over this essay proved as exhilarating and frustrating
and anxiety-ridden as my first encounter with Cedric J. Robinson's *magnum opus*
during my first year in graduate school. It arrived out of the blue in the form of a
review copy sent to *Ufahamu*, a graduate student journal published by UCLA's African
Studies Center. The book's appearance caught me off guard; none of my colleagues
had mentioned it, and I do not recall seeing any advertisements for it in any of the
scholarly journals with which we were familiar. Nevertheless, for me the timing was
fortuitous, if not downright cosmic. Just a few months into graduate school, I was
toying with the idea of writing a dissertation on the South African Left. The inspiration was hardly academic; I was more interested in becoming a full-time Communist
than a full-time scholar. I could not have cared less about historiography or the
current academic debates about social movements. I wanted to know how to build a
left-wing movement among people of color so that we could get on with the ultimate
task of making revolution.

So when I saw the title, *Black Marxism: The Making of the Black Radical Tradition*, I
could hardly contain myself. I had never heard of Cedric J. Robinson despite the fact
that he was a faculty member and director of the Center for Black Studies at the

neighboring University of California at Santa Barbara. Whoever he was, I thought to myself, he was certainly well read: his footnotes could have been a separate book altogether. Indeed, I was shocked at the size of the text (just shy of 500 pages and with tiny, almost unreadable print to boot!) given my own futile search for materials on the history of the Black Left, not just in Africa but throughout the Diaspora. I quickly stuffed this unusually dense paperback into my bag and took it upon myself to read it in my capacity as book review editor for *Ufahamu*.

When I finally got around to opening the book, I realized why it was so big. *Black Marxism* is far more ambitious than its modest title implies, for what Cedric Robinson has written extends well beyond the history of the Black Left or Black radical movements. Combining political theory, history, philosophy, cultural analysis, and biography, among other things, Robinson literally rewrites the history of the rise of the West from ancient times to the mid-twentieth century, tracing the roots of Black radical thought to a shared epistemology among diverse African people and providing a withering critique of Western Marxism and its inability to comprehend either the racial character of capitalism and the civilization in which it was born or mass movements outside Europe. At the very least, *Black Marxism* challenges our "common sense" about the history of modernity, nationalism, capitalism, radical ideology, the origins of Western racism, and the worldwide Left from the 1848 revolutions to the present. shift

Perhaps more than any other book, *Black Marxism* shifts the center of radical thought and revolution from Europe to the so-called "periphery"—to the colonial territories, marginalized colored people of the metropolitan centers of capital, and those Frantz Fanon identified as the "wretched of the earth." And it makes a persuasive case that the radical thought and practice which emerged in these sites of colonial and racial capitalist exploitation were produced by cultural logics and epistemologies of the oppressed as well as the specific racial and cultural forms of domination. Thus Robinson not only decenters Marxist history and historiography but also what one might call the "eye of the storm."

Yet for all of Robinson's decentering, he begins his story in Europe. While this might seem odd for a book primarily concerned with African people, it becomes clear very quickly why he *must* begin there, if only to remove the analytical cataracts from our eyes. This book is, after all, a critique of Western Marxism and its failure to Critique understand the conditions and movements of Black people in Africa and the Diaspora. Robinson not only exposes the limits of historical materialism as a way of understanding Black experience but also reveals that the roots of Western racism took hold in European civilization well before the dawn of capitalism. Thus, several years before the recent explosion in "whiteness studies," Robinson proposed the idea that Whiteness the racialization of the proletariat and the invention of whiteness began within Europe itself, long before Europe's modern encounter with African and New World labor. Such insights give the "Dark Ages" new meaning. Despite the almost axiomatic tendency in European historiography to speak of early modern working classes in national terms—English, French, and so forth—Robinson argues that the "lower orders" usually were comprised of immigrant workers from territories outside the nations in which they worked. These immigrant workers were placed at the bottom of a racial hierarchy. The Slavs and the Irish, for example, were among Europe's first "niggers," and what appears before us in nineteenth-century U.S. history as their struggle to achieve whiteness is merely the tip of an iceberg several centuries old.[1]

Robinson not only finds racialism firmly rooted in premodern European civilization but locates the origins of capitalism there as well. Building on the work of the Black radical sociologist Oliver Cromwell Cox, Robinson directly challenges the Marxist idea that capitalism was a revolutionary negation of feudalism.[2] Instead, Robinson explains, capitalism emerged within the feudal order and grew in fits and starts, flowering in the cultural soil of the West—most notably in the racialism that has come to characterize European society. Capitalism and racism, in other words, did not break from the old order but rather evolved from it to produce a modern world system of "racial capitalism" dependent on slavery, violence, imperialism, and genocide. So Robinson not only begins in Europe; he also chips away at many of the claims and assertions central to European historiography, particularly of the Marxist and liberal varieties. For instance, Robinson's discussion of the Irish working class enables him to expose the myth of a "universal" proletariat: just as the Irish were products of popular traditions borne and bred under colonialism, the "English" working class of the colonizing British Isles was formed by Anglo-Saxon chauvinism, a racial ideology shared across class lines that allowed the English bourgeoisie to rationalize low wages and mistreatment for the Irish. This particular form of English racialism was not invented by the ruling class to divide and conquer (though it did succeed in that respect); rather, it was there at the outset, shaping the process of proletarianization and the formation of working-class consciousness. Finally, in this living feudal order, socialism was born as an alternative bourgeois strategy to combat social inequality. Directly challenging Marx himself, Robinson declares: "Socialist critiques of society were attempts to further the bourgeois revolutions against feudalism."[3]

There is yet another reason for Robinson to begin in the heart of the West. It was there—not Africa—that the "Negro" was first manufactured. This was no easy task, as Robinson reminds us, since the invention of the Negro—and by extension the fabrication of whiteness and all the policing of racial boundaries that came with it—required "immense expenditures of psychic and intellectual energies in the West" (4). Indeed, a group of European scholars expended enormous energy rewriting of the history of the ancient world. Anticipating Martin Bernal's *Black Athena: The Afroasiatic Roots of Classical Civilization, Vol. I* (1987) and building on the pioneering scholarship of Cheikh Anta Diop, George G. M. James, and Frank Snowden, Robinson exposes the efforts of European thinkers to disavow the interdependence between ancient Greece and North Africa. This generation of "enlightened" European scholars worked hard to wipe out the cultural and intellectual contributions of Egypt and Nubia from European history, to whiten the West in order to maintain the purity of the "European" race. They also stripped all of Africa of any semblance of "civilization," using the printed page to eradicate African history and thus reduce a whole continent and its progeny to little more than beasts of burden or brutish heathens. Although efforts to reconnect the ancient West with North Africa have recently come under a new wave of attacks by scholars like Mary Lefkowitz, Robinson shows why these connections and the debates surrounding them are so important.[4] It is not a question of "superiority" or the "theft" of ideas or even a matter of proving that Africans were "civilized." Rather, *Black Marxism* reminds us again today, as it did sixteen years ago, that the exorcising of the Black Mediterranean is about the fabrication of Europe as a discrete, racially pure entity solely responsible for modernity, on the one hand, and the fabrication of the Negro, on the other. In this respect, Robinson's intervention parallels that of Edward Said's *Orientalism*, which argues that the European study of and romance with the "East" was primarily about constructing the Occident.[5]

At the very same moment European labor was being thrown off the land and herded into a newly formed industrial order, Robinson argues, African labor was being drawn into the orbit of the world system through the transatlantic slave trade. European civilization, either through feudalism or the nascent industrial order, did not simply penetrate African village culture. To understand the dialectic of African resistance to enslavement and exploitation, in other words, we need to look outside the orbit of capitalism—we need to look West and Central African culture. Robinson observes, "Marx had not realized fully that the cargoes of laborers also contained African cultures, critical mixes and admixtures of language and thought, of cosmology and metaphysics, of habits, beliefs, and morality. These were the actual terms of their humanity. These cargoes, then, did not consist of intellectual isolates or deculturated Blacks—men, women, and children separated from their previous universe. African labor brought the past with it, a past that had produced it and settled on it the first elements of consciousness and comprehension" (121).

Therefore, the first waves of African New World revolts were governed not by a critique of Western society but rather a total rejection of the experience of enslavement and racism. More intent on preserving a past than transforming Western society or overthrowing capitalism, they created maroon settlements, ran away, became outliers, and tried to find a way home, even if it meant death. However, with the advent of formal colonialism and the incorporation of Black labor into a more fully governed social structure, a more direct critique of the West and colonialism emerged—a revolt set on transforming social relations and revolutionizing Western society rather then reproducing African social life. The contradictions of colonialism produced the native bourgeoisie, more intimate with European life and thought, whose assigned task was to help rule. Trained to be junior partners in the colonial state, members of this bourgeoisie experienced both racism from Europeans and a deep sense of alienation from their native lives and cultures. Their contradictory role as victims of racial domination and tools in the empire, as Western educated elites feeling like aliens among the dominant society as well as among the masses, compelled some of these men and women to revolt, thus producing the radical Black intelligentsia. It is no accident that many of these radicals and scholars emerged both during the First World War, when they recognized the vulnerability of Western civilization, and the second world crisis—the international depression and the rise of fascism.

The emergence of this Black radical intelligentsia is the focus of the third and final section of *Black Marxism*. Examining the lives and selected works of W. E. B. Du Bois, C. L. R. James, and Richard Wright, Robinson's engagement with these three thinkers extends far beyond intellectual biography and critique. Taking us on a journey through two centuries of U.S. and Diaspora history, Robinson revisits the revolutionary processes of emancipation that caught the eyes of these men. He demonstrates how each of these figures came through an apprenticeship with Marxism, was deeply affected by the crisis in world capitalism and the responses of workers' and anticolonial movements, and produced, in the midst of depression and war, important books that challenged Marxism and tried to grapple with the historical consciousness embedded in the Black Radical Tradition. Du Bois, James, and Wright eventually revised their positions on Western Marxism or broke with it altogether and, to differing degrees, embraced Black radicalism. The way they came to the Black Radical Tradition was more of an act of recognition than invention; they did not create the theory of Black radicalism as much as found it, through their work and study, in the mass movements of Black people.[6]

I finally completed my first reading of *Black Marxism* about two months after I took it home. The book so overwhelmed me that I suffered a crisis in confidence. I never wrote the review—thus contributing unwittingly to the conspiracy of silence that has surrounded the book since its publication. Instead, I phoned Professor Robinson and virtually begged him to take me on as his student. He agreed and played a formative role in shaping my dissertation (which, coincidentally, was published by the University of North Carolina Press a decade ago as *Hammer and Hoe: Alabama Communists during the Great Depression*) and all of my work thereafter.

Although his book scared me to death, Cedric the teacher turned out to be remarkably humble, straightforward, down-to-earth, and generous with his time and energy. A demanding reader, to be sure, he ranks among the warmest, funniest characters one could ever meet in this profession—and his subtle sense of humor finds its way even into *Black Marxism*'s most difficult passages. What also amazes me is that Professor Robinson was still in his thirties when he published *Black Marxism*, a book which would have compelled even the great Du Bois to take a seat and listen.

Like Du Bois and the other subjects of his book, Robinson's political work on behalf of Black liberation sent him to the library in search of the Black Radical Tradition. His ideas evolved directly out of the social movements in which he took part and the key social and political struggles that have come to define our era. For example, as an undergraduate at the University of California at Berkeley during the mid-1960s, Robinson was active in the Afro-American Association, a radical nationalist student group based in California's East Bay and led by Donald Warden. Founded in 1962, the Association became the basis for the California chapter of the Revolutionary Action Movement (RAM); some of its members, including Huey Newton, went on to form the Black Panther Party. This small but militant group of Bay-area Black intellectuals drew many of their ideas from Malcolm X and other Black nationalists, and they were deeply influenced by revolutions in Africa, Asia, and Latin America. Although they directed their attention to domestic problems such as urban poverty, racism, education, police brutality, and Black student struggles, they understood the African American condition through an analysis of global capitalism, imperialism, and Third World liberation.[7]

It is hard not to see the links between *Black Marxism* and Robinson's formative experiences in the Afro-American Association. One of the key documents circulating among this group was Harold Cruse's 1962 essay, "Revolutionary Nationalism and the Afro-American," which argued that Black people in the United States were living under domestic colonialism and that their struggles must be seen as part of the worldwide anticolonial movement. "The failure of American Marxists," he writes, "to understand the bond between the Negro and the colonial peoples of the world has led to their failure to develop theories that would be of value to Negroes in the United States." Cruse reversed the traditional argument that the success of socialism in the developed West is key to the emancipation of colonial subjects and the development of socialism in the Third World. Instead, he saw the former colonies as the vanguard of the new socialist revolution, with Cuba and China at the forefront: "The revolutionary initiative has passed to the colonial world, and in the United States is passing to the Negro, while Western Marxists theorize, temporize and debate."[8] Robinson took up Cruse's challenge to develop new theories of revolution where Marxism failed, but he moved well beyond Cruse's positions. Eventually, Robinson came to the conclusion that it is not enough to reshape or reformulate Marxism to fit the needs of Third World revolution; instead, he believed all universalist theories of political and social order had to be rejected. In fact, Robinson's first book, *The Terms of Order: Political Science and the Myth of Leadership*, critiques the Western presumption—rooted as much in Marxism as in liberal democratic theory—that mass movements reflect social order and are maintained and rationalized by the authority of leadership.[9]

The chaotic international political situation at the time Robinson was completing *Black Marxism* was enough to dispel the myth of order. It was, after all, the last decade of the Cold War, the era of Reaganism and Thatcherism and new imperialist wars in the Middle East, Grenada, and the Falkland Islands. Yet the late 1970s and early 1980s were also a new age of revolution. Dictatorships in Africa, Asia, and Latin America were being challenged by radical movements from El Salvador to Zaire and Nicaragua to South Africa. Political violence, torture, and assassinations seemed to proliferate in the early 1980s; the casualties included the great Guyanese historian Walter Rodney, an intellectual Robinson would certainly situate squarely within the Black Radical Tradition. Let us not forget that under Reagan, the United States invaded Grenada in 1983 precisely because it had undergone its own socialist revolution four years earlier. Closer to home, deindustrialization, the flight of American corporations to foreign lands, and the displacement of millions of workers across the country created further turmoil in the metropolitan centers of global capital. Permanent unemployment, underemployment, and homelessness became a way of life. And despite the growing presence of African Americans in political office, city services declined, federal spending on cities dried up, and affirmative action programs came under assault. Racism was also on the rise, resulting in urban rebellions from Liberty City, Florida, to the English (and predominantly Black) suburbs of Bristol and Brixton. In the United States, the Ku Klux Klan tripled its membership and waged a campaign of terror and intimidation against African Americans. In Mississippi in 1980 (not 1890), at least twelve African Americans were lynched, and at least forty racially motivated murders occurred in cities as different as Buffalo, New York, Atlanta, Georgia, and Mobile, Alabama. The era, in fact, saw police killings and nonlethal acts of brutality emerge as central political issues among Black people on both sides of the Atlantic. Overall, the Reagan and Thatcher years ushered in a new era of corporate wealth and callous disregard for the poor and people of color.

This rightward drift did not go unchallenged, however. *Black Marxism* appeared during a crucial period of political organizing, just a few years after the founding of the National Black United Front (NBUF) and the National Black Independent Political Party (NBIPP). Black nationalism was on the rise in this period, following a decade in which an increasing number of Black radicals turned to Marxism-Leninism and Maoism as alternatives to liberal integrationism and "race first" capitalism. During the 1970s, Black radicals took factory jobs to reach the working classes, sought to free political prisoners and build prison movements, threw their energies behind building a socialist Africa, and continued the long tradition of community-based organizing. Meanwhile, Afrocentrism and cultural nationalism captured the imagination of various segments of the Black community across class lines. Independent Black schools flourished; kinte cloth and red, black, and green medallions adorned brown bodies; Afrocentric literature finally found its market. On the other hand, we had reason to be pessimistic. By the 1980s the jobs disappeared, the most progressive African nations were as unstable as ever, and the Black prison population was growing by leaps and bounds thanks to mandatory sentencing policies for possession of crack cocaine.

So there I and other young radicals stood, at a political and cultural crossroads, ready for action but unsure where the world was heading. We needed analyses of social movements that had made a difference. We needed to know how we built communities and kept ourselves whole in the midst of slavery and Jim Crow. We needed to figure out who our friends and enemies were, past and present. We needed new histories willing to adopt a more global perspective. In short, we needed a clearer, more radical understanding of the past in order to chart the way forward. And *Black Marxism* was one of several books written by Black radical intellectuals in the late 1970s and early 1980s to meet these challenges. Among the others were Chinweizu's *The West and the Rest of Us* (1975), Angela Davis's *Women, Race, and Class* (1981), Vincent Harding's *There Is a River* (1983), V. P. Franklin's *Black Self-Determination* (1984), Manning Marable's *Blackwater* (1981) and *How Capitalism Underdeveloped*

Black America (1982), and Cornel West's *Prophesy Deliverance* (1982). For Black folk with radical leanings, these were the new prophets of the era, and it seemed as if everyone kept their ragged, marked up copies close to them. To the rest of the world, however, these books barely existed. With few exceptions, they were initially ignored in the mainstream, and sales fell below expectations. Even books published by commercial publishing houses, such as Chinweizu's biting and witty critique of Western imperialism and its alliance with the African bourgeoisie, received very few reviews.[10]

Black Marxism, in particular, garnered no major reviews and very little notice in scholarly publications. The few reviews it did receive were mainly from left-leaning publications or very specialized journals, and the only substantial review essays that dealt with the book at length were written by Cornel West and the radical Black philosopher Leonard Harris, with both published several years after the book appeared.[11] West, whose very critical yet respectful essay in the socialist *Monthly Review* was a deliberate effort to generate renewed interest *Black Marxism*, suggested that the book "fell through the cracks" in large part due to the state of the academic Left, which was lost in "jargon-ridden discourses in which race receives little or no attention," and the Black Left, which was simply too weak and disorganized to cultivate and sustain a "high-level critical exchange."[12]

Whatever the reasons for the silence surrounding *Black Marxism*, the results have been unfortunate. The Europeanists, whose historical scholarship Robinson challenges head-on, have never, to my knowledge, responded to his criticisms. Even the new generation of scholars examining race and Black movements have paid scant attention to Robinson's insights. The 1990s witnessed the proliferation of scholarship on Black radicalism, the African Diaspora, the origins of Western racism, and the writings of Du Bois, James, and Wright, yet very few of these studies cite Robinson's work. One startling example is Winston James's *Holding Aloft the Banner of Ethiopia: Caribbean Radicalism in Early Twentieth Century America* (1998). While Robinson's book is much broader in chronology and scope, a portion of *Black Marxism* covers the same ground as James's text. Robinson, like James, discusses the overwhelming Caribbean presence in U.S.-based Black radical movements, examining groups like the African Blood Brotherhood and the Universal Negro Improvement Association and intellectuals including Hubert Harrison and Cyril Briggs. In some respects, Robinson's arguments prefigure some of James's claims; in other respects, the two are at odds. Yet as prodigious and carefully researched as *Holding Aloft the Banner of Ethiopia* is (it is over 400 pages), Robinson is neither mentioned nor cited.[13]

Paul Gilroy's much acclaimed *The Black Atlantic: Modernity and Double Consciousness* (1993) is also surprisingly quiet about *Black Marxism*. While Gilroy at least acknowledges Robinson in his text,[14] Gilroy's lack of an extensive engagement or dialogue with Robinson's work is quite jarring, since they explore much the same ground. I think it is fair to say that parts of *Black Marxism* anticipate Gilroy's argument, for Robinson had established the centrality of African people in the creation of the modern and premodern world. And he set the stage, in some respects, for Gilroy's notion of Black Atlantic culture as a "counterculture of modernity." "The rebellious slaves," writes Robinson, "vitalized by a world-consciousness drawn from African lore and composing their American experience into a rebellious art, had constituted one of the crucial social bases in contradiction to bourgeois society" (314). Robinson continued the earlier legacy of Diaspora studies but also developed a conception of the Black Mediterranean as a precondition to the Black Atlantic and the making of Europe itself. As for Gilroy's emphasis on the double consciousness and cultural hybridity of New World Black intellectuals such as Wright and Du Bois, this recognition is fundamental to Robinson's argument about the radical petit bourgeoisie. Indeed, drawing on the writings of Amilcar Cabral and the various musings of C. L. R. James, Aimé Césaire, and others, Robinson demonstrates that their imbibing of Western Civilization and their hybrid cultural lives were key to their radicalization. When confronted with the limits of democracy under racial capitalism and colonialism and with the uprisings of the Black masses whose access to bourgeois European culture was limited, the Black petit bourgeoisie was forced to choose sides. Abandoning the West was never an option, Robinson argues, but critiquing and challenging it was.

Yet while Robinson and Gilroy grapple with many of the same questions, they do have different agendas. Gilroy's point, and one of his most important critical interventions, is to show the analytical limits of cultural nationalism and ethnic absolutism. He demonstrates that Black people are products of the modern world, with a unique historical legacy rooted in slavery; Blacks are hybrid people with as much claim to the Western heritage as their former slave masters. Robinson, on the other hand, takes the same existential condition but comes to different conclusions: slavery did *not* define the Black condition because we were Africans first, with world views and philosophical notions about life, death, possession, community, and so forth that are rooted in that African heritage. And once we understand how to define ourselves in terms of this collective identity, Robinson implies, then perhaps we can understand the persistence of nationalism and various forms of race consciousness (which have never been fully contained under the limited rubric of "nationalism"). *Black Marxism* is less interested in whether or not these collective forms of struggle and consciousness are "essentialist." Instead, Robinson wants to know where they come from and why they continue. Moreover, he is attempting to discover how these mass movements shaped the thinking and actions of the Black middle strata, the most direct recipients of Western "civilization."

All this is to say that Gilroy and Robinson are indeed examining the same issues, but each brings his own brilliant insights and challenging questions to the history of Europe and the African Diaspora. I am not at all suggesting, then, that one is right and the other wrong, or that any work that ignores Robinson's interventions ought to be discounted. My main point, instead, is that an opportunity for conversation has been missed. The disappearance of such a powerful, provocative book as *Black Marxism* from the landscape of Black cultural and political studies—not to mention the vast literature on the rise of the West, capitalism, imperialism, colonialism, nationalism, transnationalism, Diaspora studies, race, labor, and intellectual history—was a genuine tragedy.

Thanks to the University of North Carolina Press, this tragedy should prove to be temporary. Not unlike the music of Thelonious Monk, *Black Marxism* remains as fresh and insightful as when it was first composed, still productively engaged with the central questions posed by histories of the African Diaspora. For example, the book attempts to address the important matter of how extensively Black people reproduced an "African" culture in the New World. This age-old question was first raised provocatively by scholars such as Melville Herskovits and Lorenzo Turner,[15] but it has returned with a vengeance in the recent work of Michael Mullin, Gwendolyn Midlo Hall, Carolyn Fick, Margaret Washington, Michael Gomez, and Joao Reis. These newer studies, despite their emphasis on documenting and acknowledging African "ethnic" diversity, reinforce Robinson's thesis that African resistance to New World slavery was profoundly shaped by the influence of slaves' West and Central African roots.[16] Also, *Black Marxism* questioned what was then the existing scholarship on both the Haitian Revolution and Brazil's "Male Uprising" in Bahia, anticipating some of the arguments proposed by the abovementioned authors. Robinson suggested, for instance, as Carolyn Fick would later, that historians of Haiti need to pay more attention to the role of the Maroons. Indeed, Robinson even took C. L. R. James's *Black Jacobins* to task for not paying enough attention to the mass uprising.

Yet while Robinson's thesis finds confirmation in much of this new work, the manner in which he makes his case is bound to draw criticism from scholars resistant to the idea of "authentic" African culture or cultures. In our current era of extreme antiessentialism, Robinson's controversial chapter, "The Nature of the Black Radical Tradition," strikes a discordant note. The idea that all Africans share certain understandings of the world and their place in it, and that these shared understandings shaped virtually all encounters between Black people and their European masters, will invariably come across to some readers as a kind of nationalist fiction. But careful readers will recognize that Robinson's argument is deeply historical and powerfully supported by evidence. He does not claim that Africans possess some kind of fixed essence, for as he points out, the characteristics of the Black Radical Tradition are more clearly evident in Africans less assimilated into a common New World identity. Moreover, Robinson is broadly speaking of general ideas and belief systems—ways of seeing, ways of worshipping. Few bat an eye when confronted with similarly broad notions such as "Western thought," "Western civilization," and "Western philosophy."

The most important benefit of the return of *Black Marxism*, however, is not its confirmation of and challenges to recent scholarship but rather its ability to point scholars in new directions and encourage them to take up where Robinson left off. He opened up many roads we have yet to travel, roads that might bring us closer to understanding and even enacting the real agenda Robinson had in mind: liberation. How, for instance, have gender and sexuality shaped Black revolt? How do we interpret the fact that Black women were often invested with great spiritual powers, or that

Black men tended to have more opportunities to travel? Who else deserves a place in the pantheon of Black radical intellectuals, and who will tell their stories? How does Robinson's framework challenge the familiar narratives of Black radicalism after 1960? What do we make of radicals who are neither black nor white, militants such as Harlem's Yuri Kochiyama or Detroit's Grace Lee Boggs or the many South Asians in England and elsewhere who cast their lot with the Black Radical Tradition? Are there other avenues besides Marxism that have brought Black radical intellectuals face to face with the Black Radical Tradition?[17]

Let us briefly take up the last question. When we consider the lives and works of Black radical intellectuals such as Aimé Césaire, Suzanne Césaire, Wifredo Lam, Etienne Léro, Jayne Cortez, Simone and Pierre Yoyotte, René Dépestre, René Ménil, and even Richard Wright, I think it could be argued that surrealism served as a bridge between Marxism and the Black Radical Tradition. All of these thinkers were either active in the surrealist movement or expressed an interest in surrealism. A revolutionary movement whose official origins can be traced to post–World War I Paris, surrealism drew on Marx and Freud while remaining critical of Marxism. What is surrealism? The Chicago Surrealist group offers one of the most eloquent definitions:

Surrealism is the exaltation of freedom, revolt, imagination and love. . . . [It] is above all a revolutionary movement. Its basic aim is to lessen and eventually to completely resolve the contradiction between everyday life and our wildest dreams. . . . Beginning with the abolition of imaginative slavery, it advances to the creation of a free society in which everyone will be a poet—a society in which everyone will be able to develop his or her potentialities fully and freely.[18]

Although the surrealist movement was led by European writers and artists such as André Breton, Paul Éluard, and Benjamin Péret, one could see in their pronouncements why surrealism would attract the radical Black petit bourgeoisie. Surrealists explicitly called for the overthrow of bourgeois culture, identified with anticolonial movements in Africa and Asia, and turned to non-European cultures as a source of ideas and inspiration in their critique of Western civilization. In 1925 the Paris surrealist group asserted in no uncertain terms, "We profoundly hope that revolutions, wars, colonial insurrections, will annihilate this Western civilisation whose vermin you defend even in the Orient." And seven years later, amid economic crisis and the spread of fascism, the group issued a document titled "Murderous Humanitarianism" (1932) that consisted of a relentless attack on colonialism, capitalism, the clergy, hypocritical liberals, and even the Black bourgeoisie. They also declared war: "we Surrealistes pronounced ourselves in favour of changing the imperialist war, in its chronic and colonial form, into a civil war. Thus we placed our energies at the disposal of the revolution, of the proletariat and its struggles, and defined our attitude towards the colonial problem, and hence towards the colour question."[19]

For these Black intellectuals and activists, their dissatisfaction with socialist realism had to do with the suppression of key elements of Black culture that surrealism embraced: the unconscious, the spirit, desire, magic, and love. That most Black radicals did not jump headlong onto the surrealist bandwagon, ironically, has to do with its similarity to the revolutionary core that was recognized as having always existed in African and Black diasporic life. To paraphrase Cedric Robinson, surrealism was not the path to inventing a theory of Black radicalism, but it might have been a path to recognition. ~~Surrealism to blk thought~~

The Afro-Chinese Cuban painter Wifredo Lam says he was drawn to surrealism because he already knew the power of the unconscious having grown up in the Africanized spirit world of Santeria. Aimé Césaire insists that surrealism merely brought him back to African culture. In a 1967 interview he explained, "Surrealism provided me with what I had been confusedly searching for. I have accepted it joyfully because in it I have found more of a confirmation than a revelation." Surrealism also helped him to summon up powerful unconscious forces: "This, for me, was a call to Africa. I said to myself: it's true that superficially we are French, we bear the marks of French customs; we have been branded by Cartesian philosophy, by French rhetoric; but if we break with all that, if we plumb the depths, then what we will find is fundamentally black." Likewise, Richard Wright, who began studying surrealist writings in the late 1930s, discussed its impact on his thinking in his unpublished essay titled "Memories of my Grandmother." Surrealism, he claimed, helped him clarify the "mystery" of his grandmother, and by extension, the character and strengths of African American folk culture. He gained a new appreciation for the metaphysical as well as for cultural forms that do not follow the logic of Western rationality.[20] The artist Cheikh Tidiane Sylla is even more explicit about how surrealism reveals what is already familiar in African culture. "In the ecologically balanced tribal cultures of Africa," he writes, "the surrealist spirit is deeply embedded in social tradition. The 'mysticism' prevalent in all Black African philosophy presupposes a highly charged psychic world in which every individual agrees to forget himself or herself in order to concentrate on the least known instances of the mind's movement—a thoroughly emancipatory experience." He further asserts that in Africa, the practice of poetry was always a way of life, whereas in the West, surrealism was the product of a long philosophical and political struggle "to recover what the traditional African has never lost."[21]

In many respects, the assertions of Sylla and other Black surrealists resonate powerfully with Robinson's description of the nature of the Black Radical Tradition. For the Africans whom Robinson identified as the progenitors of this tradition in the New World, he insists that the focus of their revolt "was [always] on the structures of the mind. Its epistemology granted supremacy to metaphysics not the material" (169). One can easily surmise from *Black Marxism* that surrealism might have been, at least for some, the missing link that brought Black intellectuals (especially in the Francophone world) face to face with the Black radical tradition. The connection between surrealism and Black radicalism certainly deserves greater exploration.

Of course, other missing links and roads not taken might shed greater light on the history and meaning of Black radicalism. It is precisely because Robinson has written such an ambitious, bold, and provocative book that it is bound to stimulate an endless array of questions and challenges. And *Black Marxism* is as politically important and relevant now as it was seventeen years ago. The crises faced in the early 1980s have hardly abated. We enter the new millennium with fewer well-paying jobs, fewer protections for the rights of oppressed people, poorer health care, more prisons, more wealth for fewer people, more racist backlash, more misery. In these cases, we end the twentieth century almost where we ended the last one. Here, in the 1990s, so-called legitimate intellectual circles openly proclaim a link between race and intelligence; some, in very serious tones, are proposing the return of formal colonialism as a way of solving Africa's problems; the United States continues to wage imperialist wars; and the problem of the color line as Du Bois saw it at the dawn of our century is still with us.

Yet, amidst crisis and defeat, during the middle and late 1990s we witnessed well over a million Black men and women, young and old, willing to march on Washington or through Harlem in the name of atonement, freedom, self-determination, even revolution. And in June 1998, several thousand of us gathered in Chicago to launch the Black Radical Congress. The people drawn to these movements are looking for direction, trying to find their bearings in a world where Black existential suffering is as much an internal, psychic, spiritual, and ideological crisis as it is a crisis of the material world. We debate these tensions constantly—structure versus culture, spirituality versus materiality. They are tensions Cedric Robinson explores in *Black Marxism*, which is why the Black radical movement needs this book as much as the academy.

I have no doubt that the return of *Black Marxism* will have as great an impact on current and future generations of thinkers as it had on me almost two decades ago. I am also confident that this time around, it will reach a much larger audience and will be widely discussed in classrooms, forums, and publications that take both the past and the future seriously. Why? Because for all of its illuminating insights, bold proclamations, subtle historical correctives, and fascinating detours along paths still unexplored, *Black Marxism*'s entire scaffolding rests on one fundamental question: where do we go from here? It is the question that produced this remarkable book in the first place, and it is the question that will bring the next generation to it.

Robin D. G. Kelley

Notes

1. On the construction of "whiteness," see Theodore W. Allen, *The Invention of the White Race*, vol. 1, *Racist Oppression and Social Control* (London: Verso, 1994); David R. Roediger, *The Wages of Whiteness* (London: Verso, 1991), and *Toward the Abolition of Whiteness: Essays on Race, Politics, and Working Class History* (London: Verso, 1994); Alexander Saxton, *The Rise and Fall of the White Republic: Class Politics and Mass Culture in Nineteenth Century America* (London: Verso, 1990); Noel Ignatiev, *How the Irish Became White* (New York: Routledge, 1995); Eric Lott, *Love and Theft: Blackface Minstrelsy and the American Working Class* (New York: Oxford University Press, 1993); Matthew Frye Jacobson, *Whiteness of a Different Color: European Immigrants and the Alchemy of Race* (Cambridge, Mass.: Harvard University Press, 1998).

Two important texts that appeared after Robinson's work and that trace European racialism back at least to the early Enlightenment are George L. Mosse, *Toward the Final Solution: A History of European Racism* (Madison: University of Wisconsin Press, 1985); and David Theo Goldberg, *Racist Culture: Philosophy and the Politics of Meaning* (London: Basil Blackwell, 1993).

2. In addition to discussing Cox in chapter 1 of *Black Marxism*, Robinson makes a more explicit

connection between his work and Cox's in note 47 of chapter 4, below. Robinson further develops his analysis of Cox's contribution to a critique of Marxist historiography in his essay, "Oliver Cromwell Cox and the Historiography of the West," *Cultural Critique* 17 (Winter 1990/91): 5–20; also see Oliver C. Cox, *Capitalism as a System* (New York: Monthly Review Press, 1964).

3. See Robinson, 00, below. Henceforth, references to this edition of *Black Marxism* are cited parenthetically in the text.

4. Martin Bernal, *Black Athena: The Afroasiatic Roots of Classical Civilization*, vol. 1, *The Fabrication of Ancient Greece, 1785–1985* (New Brunswick: Rutgers University Press, 1987); Mary Lefkowitz, *Not Out of Africa: How Afrocentrism Became an Excuse to Teach Myth as History* (New York: Basic Books, 1996). For the sources Robinson draws on, see notes 53–129 of chapter 4, below. A recent and insightful intervention on this question is Wilson Jeremiah Moses, *Afrotopia: The Roots of African American Popular History* (Cambridge: Cambridge University Press, 1998).

5. Edward Said, *Orientalism* (New York: Pantheon, 1978).

6. Of course, Robinson in no way is saying that these three men are the only ones to have confronted and eventually embraced the Black Radical Tradition. He is merely offering an opening, locating three figures whose lives and works clearly embody these ideas. One can extend his analysis to Amilcar Cabral, Frantz Fanon, Claudia Jones, Aimé and Suzanne Césaire, Wifredo Lam, "Queen Mother" Audley Moore, Martin Delany, the historian Vincent Harding, musician/composer/playwright Archie Shepp, and many others.

7. Ernest Allen, phone interview by author, April 7, 1996; Huey P. Newton, *Revolutionary Suicide* (New York: Harcourt Brace Jovanovich, 1973), 71–72; Donald Warden, "The California Revolt," *Liberator* 3, no. 3 (March 1963): 14–15. Perhaps it is worth noting that one of Robinson's first scholarly publications was a study of Malcolm X; see Robinson, "Malcolm Little as a Charismatic Leader," *Afro-American Studies* 3 (1972): 81–96.

8. Harold Cruse, "Revolutionary Nationalism and the Afro-American," in *Rebellion or Revolution?* (New York: Morrow, 1968), 74–75; originally published in *Studies on the Left* 2, no. 3 (1962): 12–25.

9. Robinson, *The Terms of Order: Political Science and the Myth of Leadership* (Albany: State University of New York Press, 1980).

10. Chinweizu, *The West and the Rest of Us: White Predators, Black Slavers, and the African Elite* (New York: Vintage, 1975); Angela Davis, *Women, Race, and Class* (New York: Random House, 1981); Vincent Harding, *There Is a River: The Black Struggle for Freedom in America* (New York: Random House, 1983); V. P. Franklin, *Black Self-Determination: A Cultural History of the Faith of Our Fathers* (Westport: Greenwood Press, 1984); Manning Marable, *Blackwater: Historical Studies in Race, Class Consciousness, and Revolution* (Dayton, Ohio: Black Praxis Press, 1981), and *How Capitalism Underdeveloped Black America* (Boston: South End Press, 1982); Cornel West, *Prophesy Deliverance: An Afro-American Revolutionary Christianity* (Philadelphia: Westminster, 1982).

I am indebted to V. P. Franklin for his insight into the publicity problems that surrounded these and similar books. He told me an interesting story about his efforts to find a publisher for *Black Self-Determination*. He had written Toni Morrison, then editor at Random House and the person most responsible for their publication of several Black radical books, about possibly sending the manuscript to her for consideration. Random House had published Chinweizu's *The West and the Rest of Us*, which received almost no notice or reviews, so Morrison warned Franklin about the difficulty of publishing Black radical scholarship. He eventually published with Greenwood Press and, to his disappointment, *Black Self-Determination*—like *Black Marxism* and others—received the same treatment. (Franklin's book has since been reprinted as *Black Self-Determination: A Cultural History of African American Resistance* [Brooklyn: Lawrence Hill Books, 1992].) Aware of this conspiracy of silence, Franklin took it upon himself to promote this body of radical scholarship; his efforts included a lengthy review of *Black Marxism*, a shorter version of which was published in *Phylon* 47, no. 3 (1986): 250–51. V. P. Franklin, conversation with author, October 24, 1998; V. P. Franklin, letter to author, November 2, 1998.

11. See, for example, Cornel West, "Black Radicalism and the Marxist Tradition," *Monthly Review* 40, no. 4 (September 1988): 51–56; and Leonard Harris, "Historical Subjects and Interests: Race, Class, and Conflict," in *The Year Left 2: An American Socialist Yearbook*, ed. Mike Davis, Manning Marable, et al. (London: Verso, 1987), 90–105. Most of the reviews were short summaries with a few passing critical remarks. See V. P. Franklin's review in *Phylon* 3, no. 3 (1986): 250–51; Charles Herrod, *Canadian Review of Studies in Nationalism* 15, nos. 1–2 (1988): 153; Erroll Lawrence, *Race and Class* 26, no. 2 (Autumn 1984): 100–102.

12. West, "Black Radicalism and the Marxist Tradition," 51.

13. Winston James, *Holding Aloft the Banner of Ethiopia: Caribbean Radicalism in Early-Twentieth Century America* (London: Verso, 1998). James sets out to explain the overwhelming presence of West Indians in Black radical movements and the American Left. His explanation lies in the peculiarities of Caribbean history and the profiles of the migrants themselves. This early wave of West Indian migrants were generally "race" men and women with superior education, white collar occupations, protected legal status as British subjects, experience as international travelers and sojourners, political experience in the Caribbean, little or no commitment to Christianity, and a tendency for direct confrontation rather than

retreat. For these reasons, James argues, they were predisposed to radicalism. A careful reading of *Black Marxism*, however, suggests that many of these characteristics, especially with regard to education and political experience, can be found among members of the U.S.-born radical Black petit bourgeoisie. Indeed, building on the insights of Amilcar Cabral, Robinson had already identified the key role of colonial education in the formation of a radical Black intelligentsia, but whereas James emphasizes the "love of reading" as a unique Caribbean cultural characteristic, Robinson suggests a more structural explanation tied to the imperatives of empire. Colonial rulers, especially in the British and French empires, very consciously sought to nurture a class of functionaries—a Black petit bourgeoisie willing and able to run things on behalf of the imperial order. After all, the love of reading was equally intense among U.S.-born Black people, as was argued in Du Bois's *Black Reconstruction*, and more recently, V. P. Franklin's *Black Self-Determination*.

More significantly, Robinson's findings call into question James' generalizations that West Indians adopted a tradition of "frontal assault" on forces of oppression while Blacks in North America adopted dissimulation, or "wearing the mask." Robinson identifies a tendency on the part of New World Africans to avoid direct confrontation and the use of violence in the Caribbean and North America; instead, these New World Africans sought to recreate village life on foreign soil. Indeed, Robinson places great emphasis on the absence of violence throughout the Diaspora and the critical importance of spiritual and psychic well-being. While I do not believe these positions are in direct contradiction, I do think Robinson's insights, developed almost two decades ago, might have enriched or complicated James's discussion.

Furthermore, while Robinson acknowledges the large numbers of Caribbean radicals in New York during World War I and the immediate postwar period—the period and place of James's incredibly rich and detailed study—because Robinson's scope extends globally and across a longer time span, he is able to locate the impulse toward Black radicalism throughout the Diaspora. Even if we were simply to limit our scope to the continental United States, once we get out of New York City and explore the South, the Midwest (especially Oklahoma), and the West Coast, the West Indians are not so prominent in radical movements.

14. Paul Gilroy, *The Black Atlantic: Modernity and Double Consciousness* (Cambridge, Mass.: Harvard University Press, 1993). Surprisingly, *The Black Atlantic* only mentions Robinson once to level a criticism based on what appears to be a misreading of the text. Gilroy disputes Robinson's use of the term "Black Radical Tradition" because "it can suggest that it is the radical elements of this tradition which are its dominant characteristics . . . and because the idea of tradition can sound too closed, too final, and too antithetical to the subaltern experience of modernity which has partially conditioned the development of these cultural forms" (122). Robinson, however, does not use "radical" as a way of closing off other characteristics of black life, thought, and struggle—on the contrary, the term is a way of specifying the source of opposition to slavery, Jim Crow, and various other modes of oppression born of racial capitalism, colonialism, and imperialism. By "tradition" he is simply signaling the need for a long view, because his argument rests on his point that the logic of slavery and capitalism does not explain Black opposition, nor its particular nature; rather, Robinson explains, we need to trace resistance back to who Africans were at the moment of their incorporation into the world capitalist system. The Black Radical Tradition is not conceived as a static thing but as a process, one borne not only of African life and thought but also of European life and thought, one linked directly to premodern forms of European racialism and the subsequent invention of the Negro.

15. Melville Herskovits, *The Myth of the Negro Past* (New York: Harper and Brothers, 1941), and *The New World Negro: Selected Papers in Afro-American Studies* (Bloomington: Indiana University Press, 1966); Leonard Barrett, *Soul-Force: African Heritage in Afro-American Religion* (Garden City, N.Y.: Anchor Press, 1974); Roger Bastide, *African Civilisations in the New World* (London: C. Hurst, 1971), and *The African Religions of Brazil: Toward a Sociology of the Interpretation of Civilisations* (Baltimore: Johns Hopkins University Press, 1978); Winifred Vass, *The Bantu Speaking Heritage of the United States* (Los Angeles: Center for Afro-American Studies, University of California, 1979); Sidney Mintz and Richard Price, *The Birth of African American Culture: An Anthropological Perspective*, 2d ed.(Boston: Beacon Press, 1992); Richard Price, *First Time: The Historical Vision of an Afro-American People* (Baltimore: Johns Hopkins University Press, 1983).

16. Gwendolyn Midlo Hall, *Africans in Colonial Louisiana: The Development of Afro-Creole Culture in the Eighteenth Century* (Baton Rouge: Louisiana State University Press, 1992); Carolyn Fick, *The Making of Haiti: The Saint-Domingue Revolution from Below* (Knoxville: University of Tennessee Press, 1990); Michael Mullin, *Africa in America: Slave Acculturation and Resistance in the American South and the British Caribbean, 1736–1831* (Urbana: University of Illinois Press, 1992); João José Reis, *Slave Rebellion in Brazil: The Muslim Uprising of 1835 in Bahia* (Baltimore: Johns Hopkins University Press, 1995). See also Robert Farris Thompson, *Flash of the Spirit: African and Afro-American Art and Philosophy* (New York: Vintage, 1983); Margaret Washington Creel, *"A Peculiar People": Slave Religion and Community-Culture among the Gullahs* (New York: New York University Press, 1988); Sandra T. Barnes, ed., *Africa's Ogun: Old World and New* (Bloomington: Indiana University Press, 1989); George Brandon, *Santeria from Africa to the New World:*

The Dead Sell Memories (Bloomington: Indiana University Press, 1993); Joseph Holloway and Winifred Vass, The African Heritage of American English (Bloomington: Indiana University Press, 1993); Joseph Murphy, Santeria: African Spirits in America (Boston: Beacon Press, 1993), and Working the Spirit: Ceremonies of the African Diaspora (Boston: Beacon Press, 1994); Karen Fog Olwig, Cultural Adaptation and Resistance on St. John: Three Centuries of Afro-Caribbean Life (Gainesville: University of Florida Press, 1985); and Jim Wafer, The Taste of Blood: Spirit Possession in Brazilian Candomble (Philadelphia: University of Pennsylvania Press, 1991).

Among these newer books, the one that I think shares the deepest affinity with Black Marxism is Sterling Stuckey's Slave Culture: Nationalist Theory and the Foundations of Black America (New York: Oxford University Press, 1987), which focuses on the ring shout as a key element in the construction of a black culture and oppositional ideology. Published just four years after Black Marxism, Slave Culture also recognizes the African roots of black folk opposition to racial capitalism, demonstrating how the ring shout's conception of community—as a metaphor and practice—shaped black thinkers as diverse as David Walker, Henry Highland Garnet, W. E. B. Du Bois, and Paul Robeson.

17. Numerous scholars—Black radical intellectuals, for the most part—have taken up these and other questions related to themes in Black Marxism. While I do not have the space to cite all of the exciting work of which I am aware, let me offer just a small sampling. Aside from the texts cited above and below (not to mention Robinson's own work, which continues to explore Black radical movements, intellectuals, and culture), see Rod Bush, We Are Not What We Seem: Black Nationalism and Class Struggle I the American Century (New York: New York University Press, 1999); Hazel Carby, Reconstructing Black Womanhood (New York: Oxford University Press, 1987), and Race Men (Cambridge, Mass.: Harvard University Press, 1998); Angela Y. Davis, Blues Legacies and Black Feminism: Gertrude "Ma" Rainey, Bessie Smith, and Billie Holiday (New York: Pantheon, 1998); Kevin Gaines, Uplifting the Race: Black Leadership, Politics, and Culture in the Twentieth Century (Chapel Hill: University of North Carolina Press, 1996); Farah Jasmine Griffin, Who Set You Flowin'?: The African-American Migration Narrative (New York: Oxford University Press, 1995); Michael Hanchard, Orpheus and Power: The Movimento Negro of Rio de Janeiro and Sao Paulo, Brazil, 1945–1988 (Princeton: Princeton University Press, 1994); Gerald Horne, The Fire This Time: The Watts Uprising and the 1960s (Charlottesville: University Press of Virginia, 1995); Tera Hunter, To 'Joy My Freedom: Southern Black Women's Lives and Labors after the Civil War (Cambridge, Mass.: Harvard University Press, 1997); Lewis Gordon, Her Majesty's Other Children: Sketches of Racism From a Neo-Colonial Age (Lanham, Md.: Rowman and Littlefield, 1997), and Fanon and the Crisis of European Man: An Essay on Philosophy and the Human Sciences (New York: Routledge, 1995); Joy James, Transcending the Talented Tenth: Black Leaders and American Intellectuals (New York: Routledge, 1997); Robin D. G. Kelley, Hammer and Hoe: Alabama Communists during the Great Depression (Chapel Hill: University of North Carolina Press, 1990), and Race Rebels: Culture, Politics, and the Black Working Class (New York: Free Press, 1994); George Lipsitz, A Life in the Struggle: Ivory Perry and the Culture of Opposition (Philadelphia: Temple University Press, 1988); Brenda Gayle Plummer, Rising Wind: Black Americans and U.S. Foreign Affairs, 1935–1960 (Chapel Hill: University of North Carolina Press, 1996); Tricia Rose, Black Noise: Rap Music and Black Culture in Contemporary America (Hanover: Wesleyan University Press, 1994); Timothy B. Tyson, Radio Free Dixie: Robert Williams and the Roots of Black Power (Chapel Hill: University of North Carolina Press, 1999); Penny von Eschen, Race against Empire (Ithaca: Cornell University Press, 1997); Komozi Woodard, A Nation within a Nation (Chapel Hill: University of North Carolina Press, 1998); Clyde Woods, Development Arrested: Race, Power, and the Blues in the Mississippi Delta (London: Verso, 1998); as well as forthcoming books by Barbara Bair, Elsa Barkley Brown, Nahum Chandler, Cathy Cohen, Gina Dent, Brent Edwards, Grant Farred, Ruth Wilson Gilmore, Adam Green, Jonathan Holloway, Peniel Joseph, Chana Kai Lee, Wahneema Lubiano, Tony Monteiro, Jeffery Perry, Vijay Prashad, Barbara Ransby, Nikhil Singh, Tracye Matthews, Genna Rae McNeil, Tiffany R. L. Patterson, Linda Reed, Ula Taylor, Akinyele Umoja, and Cynthia Young, to name a few.

18. Quote from "Surrealism and Blues," Living Blues 25 (Jan.–Feb. 1976): 19.

19. Franklin Rosemont, ed., Andre Breton: What Is Surrealism?: Selected Writings (New York: Pathfinder, 1978), 37; The Surrealist Group of France, "Murderous Humanitarianism," Race Traitor (Special Issue—Surrealism: Revolution against Whiteness) 9 (Summer 1998): 67–69, originally published in Negro: An Anthology, ed. Nancy Cunard (London: Wishart and Company, 1934); also see Michael Richardson, ed., Refusal of the Shadow: Surrealism and the Caribbean (London: Verso, 1996).

20. Max-Pol Fouchet, Wifredo Lam, 2d ed. (Barcelona: Ediciones Polgrafa, S.A., 1989), 38, 192, 196; Aimé Césaire, Discourse on Colonialism, trans. by Joan Pinkham (New York: Monthly Review Press, 1972), 67; Eugene E. Miller, Voice of a Native Son: The Poetics of Richard Wright (Jackson: University Press of Mississippi, 1990), 78–85.

21. Cheikh Tidiane Sylla, "Surrealism and Black African Art," Arsenal: Surrealist Subversion 4 (1989): 128–29.

PREFACE TO THE 2000 EDITION

The workers in the advanced nations have done all they could, or intended, to do—which was always something short of revolution.
—Oliver C. Cox, *Capitalism as a System*

There is much to be admired in those who have struggled under the inspiration of Marxism. And no recitation of their courage and sacrifice would be adequate or sufficiently eloquent to capture their awesome achievements—or unhappy failures. But the same may be said of diverse other social movements over the centuries, equally inspired by particular constructions of human experience. What such historical spectacles of human endeavor share, of course, is the magnificence of the human spirit: the inextinguishable resolve to refashion society according to some powerful but imperfect moral vision.

Myths and theories of liberation have been constants in the long record of human experience. They are the bracing concomitants to impositions of domination and oppression, whatever the form of a particular regime. And even when the recorder of the moment was unsympathetic or downright hostile to even the most fugitive and muted affirmation of human integrity, there has been almost inevitably at least a trace—a hint—of the desire for a just order. Solon, Aristophanes, Plato, Isocrates, and Aristotle, notwithstanding their unrelieved identifications with the propertied classes of ancient Athens, all could not entirely conceal or effectively dismiss the moral challenges of the poor (*demos*), slaves, and women.[1] Among these writers were some of the most clever weavers of aristocratic flummery. So it is not surprising that if the moral authority spawned in the quest for freedom confounded their gifts for eloquent argument, the same would be repeated over the next two thousand years in the works of their seemingly inexhaustible line of heirs. The medieval inquisition, with its vast clerical intelligentsia and uncontested access to lethal force, never achieved the extinction of the urban Waldensian, Franciscan, and Cathar rebellions against poverty, or the largely rural communisms which bubbled up from among the peasants and the Church's own convents and monasteries.[2] And half a millennium later, though the sheer volume of three centuries of legislation, literature, and state force in support of slavery in Africa and the New World might have appeared daunting, history proves otherwise—the liberationist agenda of antislavery triumphed.[3]

These three examples from ancient Athens, medieval Europe, and the modern New World are merely instances, moments, in the extraordinary historical index of liberation. Presently one might surmise that more attention is being given to liberation's record than at any previous moment in Western historiography. At least in part, this is a legacy of Marxism. The more substantial inspiration, however, is the present state of the world. For the vast majority of the planet's peoples, the global economy publicizes itself in human misery. Thus, the simple fact is that liberationist movements abound in the real world—a reason for attention far more weighty than the self-serving conceits of capitalist triumphalism and the incessant chants of globalism which followed upon the disintegration of the Soviet Union.

As Foucault recounted, neither Marx nor Engels were particularly audacious when they characterized the capitalist mode of production as voraciously exploitative. As far back as the eighteenth century, David Ricardo, Adam Smith, and numerous other nonradical predecessors in the emerging field of political economy had expressed similar doubts and unease.[4] Hegel's economic observations of industrial capitalism were even more immediate to the studies conducted by Engels and Marx. In the late eighteenth century, with uncharacteristic brevity and specificity, Hegel recorded: "Complete mercilessness. Factories, manufacturing, base their subsistence on the misery of one class."[5] What was stunning in the writings of Marx and Engels, then, was not their mere recognition of class struggle but rather their sympathies in that struggle. While Kant and Hegel threw their support to the bureaucrats as that stratum which constituted what Hegel designated as the "universal class," Marx and Engels proposed the industrial proletariat, wage laborers. But quite possibly that was less an error in judgment (as Cox supposed) than a deceit: even in their own times, notwithstanding their different historical contexts and their specific political maneuvers, it should have been obvious that Kant, Hegel, Marx, and Engels all concealed their faith in philosophy. As Marx put it in 1844: "The weapon of criticism cannot, of course, supplant the criticism of weapons; material force must be overthrown by material force. But theory, too, will become material force as soon as it seizes the masses."[6] Given the miserable social and political chaos of their era (and of our own), we should have little difficulty in sympathizing with the impulse to seek political refuge—that is, a social agenda—in the illusory order and power of pure logic and speculation.[7]

The "masses" whom Marx presumed would be "seized" by theory were European male wage laborers and artisans in the metropoles of Western Europe, Britain, and the United States. Here both theory and Marx's casting of historical materialism betrayed him. Instead of the anarchic globalism of modern capitalist production and exchange, Marx imagined a coherent ordering of things: congruous imperial sites from which cohorts of capitalists cultivated, directed, and dominated satellite societies. For Marx, capitalism consisted of a geometric whole whose elementary and often hidden characteristics (price, value, accumulation, and profit) could be discovered with arithmetic means and certainty.

Who's left out of theory

Driven, however, by the need to achieve the scientific elegance and interpretive economy demanded by theory, Marx consigned race, gender, culture, and history to the dustbin. Fully aware of the constant place women and children held in the workforce, Marx still deemed them so unimportant as a proportion of wage labor that he tossed them, with slave labor and peasants, into the imagined abyss signified by precapitalist, noncapitalist, and primitive accumulation.[8] And how, can we suppose, was Marx's conception of the mode-specific, internal development of European productive forces to accommodate the technological borrowings from China, India, Africa, and the Americas which propelled the West into industrialism and imperialism?[9] As Andre Gunder Frank declares:

> the original sin of Marx, Weber, and their followers was to look for the "origin," "cause," "nature," "mechanism," indeed the "essence" of it [capitalism, development, modernization] all essentially in European exceptionalism instead of in the real world economy/system.[10]

Marx's conceit was to presume that the theory of historical materialism explained history; but, at worst, it merely rearranged history. And at its best (for it must be acknowledged that there are some precious insights in Marxism), historical materialism still only encapsulated an analytical procedure which resonated with bourgeois Europe, merely one fraction of the world economy.

Eurocentrism and secular messianism, however, were not the only ideological elements which worked to constrict Marx's imaginary. There was an obvious genealogy and a striking parallel between Aristotle's treatments of slaves and slavery and those of Marx. Aristotle saw slavery as necessary for the self-sufficiency of the *polis*, and in only rare instances were slaves expected to achieve a virtuous life. Given their marginal intelligence and development, Aristotle found no compelling reason for inquiry into the ethics, consciousness, or desires of slaves, content to state that "the slave is in a sense a part of his master, a living but separate part of his body."[11] Marx, though he found slavery abhorrent, similarly recessed slaves from his discourse on human freedom: "The slave only works swayed by fear, and it is not his existence itself which is at stake, since it is guaranteed to him even if it does not belong to him."[12] Their role in capitalist production, Marx believed, was an embarrassing residue of a precapitalist, ancient mode of production, which disqualified them from historical and political agency in the modern world. And this is not the only evidence that Marx had been substantially influenced by Aristotle. As much as on his own immediate predecessors (Kant, Hegel, etc.), Marx also had drawn on Aristotle for his notions of class and class conflict, the latter most frequently signified by ancient Greek writers as *stasis*. Moreover, in *Capital*, Marx had acknowledged the genius of Aristotle, whose discussion of use-value and exchange-value in the *Politics* had predated by one and three-quarters millenia any economic system which Marx was willing to acknowledge as capitalist.[13]

How and by what Marx and Engels were seduced into these misapprehensions is explored in Part I of the following study. But of equal and perhaps greater interest are the efforts of renegade radical thinkers to determine what those seductions were and how to recouperate radical theory from its blunders. These particular critics of Marxism were products of other histories, other intellectual traditions, and other, neglected participants in the world economy. When I took up this work, I was interested specifically in those radical thinkers who had emerged from what I have termed the Black Radical Tradition; how some of the most illustrious and perceptive of them came to terms with Marxism is explored in Part III. Rather than belonging to the mercantile, bureaucratic, or technical classes of Western Europe, their foreparents had been the slaves and freedpersons of the West Indies and North America. More accurately, their predecessors had been human beings who happened to be slaves. And so in Part II, in lieu of simply locating these foreparents in some passive, residual economic category, it was critical to explore the histories of their cultures and then how these enslaved people responded to and reacted against the violence which instigated and patrolled their slave statuses. Only through such an interrogation was it possible to demonstrate their roles in the initiation of the Black Radical Tradition.

Ironically, to Black radicals of the twentieth century, one of the most compelling features of Marxism was its apparent universalism. Unlike the dominant historical discourses of the nineteenth century, historical materialism was inflected by an internationalism and a scientific rigor which plainly transcended the obnoxious and sinister claims for destiny exhibited by such conceits as German nationalism, British imperialism, the racism of the "White Man's Burden," and so forth. For a time, then, Marxism might have seemed an effective antidote to contemporary discourse. But Marxism's internationalism was not global; its materialism was exposed as an insufficient explanator of cultural and social forces; and its economic determinism too often politically compromised freedom struggles beyond or outside of the metropole. For Black radicals, historically and immediately linked to social bases predominantly made up of peasants and farmers in the West Indies, or sharecroppers and peons in North America, or forced laborers on colonial plantations in Africa, Marxism appeared distracted from the cruelest and most characteristic manifestations of the world economy. This exposed the inadequacies of Marxism as an apprehension of the modern world, but equally troubling was Marxism's neglect and miscomprehension of the nature and genesis of liberation struggles which already had occurred and surely had yet to appear among these peoples.

The Black Radical Tradition was an accretion, over generations, of collective intelligence gathered from struggle. In the daily encounters and petty resistances to domination, slaves had acquired a sense of the calculus of oppression as well as its overt organization and instrumentation. These experiences lent themselves to a means of preparation for more epic resistance movements. The first organized revolts in the slave castles in Africa, and on board slave ships, were generally communal in the terms of their Old World kinships (Bambara, Ganga, Yoruba, etc.). These rebellions sought return to African homelands and a repair of the discontinuity produced by enslavement and transportation. Later, in the colonial settlements, when conditions were favorable, revolts often took the form of marronage, a concession to the relocation of slavery and to the new, syncretic cultural identities emergent from the social cauldron of slave organization. Newly transported "outlaw" Africans and creole Blacks, and sometimes Native Americans and European slaves, withdrew beyond the patrolled presence of exploitation to forge egalitarian societies.

With each historical moment, however, the rationale and cultural mechanisms of domination became more transparent. Race was its epistemology, its ordering principle, its organizing structure, its moral authority, its economy of justice, commerce, and power. Aristotle, one of the most original aristocratic apologists, had provided the template in Natural Law. In inferiorizing women ("[T]he deliberative faculty of the soul is not present at all in the slave; in a female it is present but ineffective" [*Politics*, 1260a12]), non-Greeks, and all laborers (slaves, artisans, farmers, wage workers, etc.: "[T]he mass of mankind are evidently quite slavish in their tastes, preferring a life suitable to beasts" [*Nicomachean Ethics*, 1095b20]), Aristotle had articulated an uncompromising racial construct. And from the twelfth century on, one European ruling order after another, one cohort of clerical or secular propagandists following another, reiterated and embellished this racial calculus.[14] As the Black Radical Tradition was distilled from the racial antagonisms which were arrayed along a continuum from the casual insult to the most ruthless and lethal rules of law; from the objectifications of entries in marine cargo manifests, auction accountancy, plantation records, broadsheets and newspapers; from the loftiness of Christian pulpits and biblical exegesis to the minutia of slave-naming, dress, types of food, and a legion of other significations, the terrible culture of race was revealed. Inevitably, the tradition was transformed into a radical force. And in its most militant manifestation, no longer accustomed to the resolution that flight and withdrawal were sufficient, the purpose of the struggles informed by the tradition became the overthrow of the whole race-based structure.

In the studies of these struggles, and often through engagement with them, the Black Radical Tradition began to emerge and overtake Marxism in the work of these Black radicals. W. E. B. Du Bois, in the midst of the antilynching movement, C. L. R. James, in the vortex of anticolonialism, and Richard Wright, the sharecropper's son, all brought forth aspects of the militant tradition which had informed successive generations of Black freedom fighters. These predecessors were Africans by origins, predominantly recruited from the same cultural matrices, subjected to similar and interrelated systems of servitude and oppression, and mobilized by identical impulses to recover their dignity. And over the centuries, the liberation projects of these men and women in Africa, the Caribbean, and the Americas acquired similar emergent collective forms in rebellion and marronage, similar ethical and moral articulations of resistance; increasingly, they merged as a function of what Hegel might have recognized as the negation of the negation in the world system. Hegel's "cunning of history," for one instance, was evident when in the late eighteenth and early nineteenth centuries, Franco-Haitian slaveowners fled to Louisiana, Virginia, and the Carolinas with as many slaves as they could transport, thereby also transporting the Haitian Revolution. The outrage, courage, and vision of that revolution helped inspire the Pointe Coupee Conspiracy in 1795 in Louisiana, the Gabriel-led rebellion in 1800 in Virginia, and the rebellion organized by Denmark Vesey in 1822 outside of Charleston.[15] And, in turn, Denmark's movement informed the revolutionary tract, *APPEAL in Four Articles; Together with a Preamble, to the Coloured Citizens of the World, But in Particular, and Very Expressly, to Those of the United States of America*, penned by David Walker in Boston in 1829.

Du Bois drew on Hegelian dialectics and Marx's notions of class struggle to correct the interpretations of the American Civil War and its subsequent Reconstruction period grown dominant in American historiography (for instance, Woodrow Wilson's *A History of the American People* [1908]) and popular culture (Thomas Dixon's and D. W. Griffith's *Birth of a Nation* [1915]).[16] Undaunted by the fact that he was already on forbidden terrain in the thinking of Hegel, Marx, and his own American contemporaries, Du Bois ventured further, uncovering the tradition. Almost simultaneously, James discovered the tradition in the Haitian Revolution. And only a little later, Wright contributed his own critique of proletarian politics from the vantage point of the Black Radical Tradition. For Du Bois, James, and Wright, Marxism became a staging area for their immersion into the tradition. Black Marxism was not a site of contestation between Marxism and the tradition, nor a revision. It was a new vision centered on a theory of the cultural corruption of race. And thus the reach and cross-fertilization of the tradition became evident in the anticolonial and revolutionary struggles of Africa, the Caribbean, and the Americas.

As a culture of liberation, the tradition crossed the familiar bounds of social and historical narrative. Just as in the eighteenth and early nineteenth centuries, to take one instance, African marronage infected Native American and African settlements in Florida to produce the Black Seminoles who fought against the United States for three decades, the tradition has effused in myriad forms and locations. For some sense of the diversity, one might examine how the tradition insinuated itself quite unexpectedly into the writings of Harriet Beecher Stowe when she authored *A Key to Uncle Tom's Cabin* (1853), and particularly *Dred, a Tale of the Great Dismal Swamp* (1856); into the Blacks who volunteered during the Civil War, and those in the American military who sent letters of outrage from the Philippines during the Spanish-American War; into Pentecostalism in the early twentieth century; into the blues composed by Rainey and all the women named Smith; and into the filmic work of Oscar Micheaux during the silent film era. Reviewing this list, I suspect the Black Radical Tradition extends into cultural and political terrains far beyond my competence to relate.

In short, as a scholar it was never my purpose to exhaust the subject, only to suggest that it was there.

Notes

1. See my forthcoming study of the history of Western socialism, *The Anthropology of Marxism* (Hanover, N.H.: University Press of New England); and Cynthia Farrar, *The Origins of Democratic Thinking* (New York: Cambridge University Press, 1988).

2. See R. I. Moore, *The Formation of a Persecuting Society: Power and Deviance in Western Europe, 950–1250* (New York: Blackwell, 1987); and the classic work of Norman Cohn, *Pursuit of the Millennium* (New York: Oxford University Press, 1961).

3. See my *Black Movements in America* (New York: Routledge, 1997).

4. Michel Foucault, *The Order of Things* (London: Tavistock Publications, 1970), 255ff.

5. Leo Rauch, ed., *Hegel and the Human Spirit* (Detroit: Wayne State University Press, 1983), 166.

6. Karl Marx, "Towards a Critique of Hegel's Philosophy of Right: Introduction." In *Karl Marx: Selected Writings*, ed. David McLellan (New York: Oxford University Press, 1977), 69.

7. Sheldon Wolin, *The Politics and Vision* (Boston: Little, Brown, 1960).

8. See Marx's rather perfunctory comments on women and children in *Capital*, where he suggests they constitute part of the reserve army employed episodically to retard the falling rate of profit, and compare with the implications of his research into parliamentary investigations of child labor which describe a more constant exploitation of child laborers. Earlier, in *The German Ideology* (1844), Marx had implied that the control over female reproduction in tribal society had inaugurated the first division of labor in human history.

9. Andre Gunder Frank, *ReOrient: Global Economy in the Asian Age* (Berkeley: University of California Press, 1998). Frank comments: "[Joseph] Needham lists not only the well-known Chinese inventions of gunpowder, paper and printing, and the compass. He also examines co-fusion and oxygenation iron and steel technology, mechanical clocks, and engineering devices such as drive-belts and chain-drive methods of converting rotary to rectilinear motion, segmental arch and iron-chain suspension bridges, deep-drilling equipment; and paddle-wheel boats, foresails and aft sails, watertight compartments and sternpost rudders in navigation, and many others" (193). He goes on to state that "Indian mathematics and astronomy were sufficiently advanced for Europeans to import astronomical tables and related works from India in the seventeenth and eighteenth centuries. In medicine, the theory and practice of inoculation against smallpox came from India." Frank then continues with a survey of more recent studies of "[t]he export of Indian science and technology relating to shipbuilding, textiles, and metallurgy" (194).

10. Ibid., 336.

11. Aristotle, *Politics*, 1255b12.

12. See Marx's "sixth" chapter of *Capital*, in *Karl Marx: Selected Writings*, 512.

13. On Marx's debt to Aristotle, see chapters 1 and 2 of G. E. M. de Ste. Croix, *The Class Struggle in the Ancient Greek World* (Ithaca: Cornell University Press, 1981); and Scott Meikle, *Aristotle's Economic Thought* (Oxford: Clarendon, 1995).

14. For some recent Aristotelians, see Thomas K. Lindsay, "Was Aristotle Racist, Sexist, and Anti-Democratic?," *The Review of Politics* 56 (Winter 1994): 127–51; Peter Garnsay, *Ideas of Slavery from Aristotle to Augustine* (New York: Cambridge University Press, 1996), which traces the influence of Aristotle into the first 400 years of Christianity; and Sir Moses Finley, *Ancient Slavery and Modern Ideology* (London: Penguin, 1986), which traces Aristotle into the modern age.

15. Robinson, *Black Movements in America*, 32–36.

16. See Robinson, "In the Year 1915: D. W. Griffith and the Whitening of America," *Social Identities* 3 (June 1997): 161–92.

PREFACE

It is always necessary to know what a book is about, not just what has been written in it but what was intended when it was written.

This work is about our people's struggle, the historical Black struggle. It takes as a first premise that for a people to survive in struggle it must be on its own terms: the collective wisdom which is a synthesis of culture and the experience of that struggle. The shared past is precious, not for itself, but because it is the basis of consciousness, of knowing, of being. It cannot be traded in exchange for expedient alliances or traduced by convenient abstractions or dogma. It contains philosophy, theories of history, and social prescriptions native to it. It is a construct possessing its own terms, exacting its own truths. I have attempted here to demonstrate its authority. More particularly, I have investigated the failed efforts to render the historical being of Black peoples into a construct of historical materialism, to signify our existence as merely an opposition to capitalist organization. We are that (because we must be) but much more. For the younger brothers and sisters, and for those who identify with the Black struggle who are tempted by the transubstantiation of Black history to European radical theory, this book is a challenge. I humbly submit this work to you—and to the others with whom the project had its beginnings: Mary Agnes Lewis, Margot Dashiell, Frederick Douglas Lewis, Welton Smith, Sherman Williams, Nebby-Lou Crawford, Jim Lacy, Gopalan Shyamala, Jay Wright, J. Herman Blake, Don Hopkins, Henry Ramsey, Donald Warden . . . and the others I met along the way.

ACKNOWLEDGMENTS

This work was begun while I was teaching in Binghamton, New York. By the time it was finished, my family and I had moved to the Santa Barbara region of California. In between we had spent a year in the small English village of Radwinter, south of Cambridge. In sum this covered a period of almost six years. During this time support for the research and writing was extended to me by the SUNY-Binghamton Foundation, the University of California at Santa Barbara, and the National Research Council and Ford Foundation program of Post-Doctoral Fellowships for Minorities.

Such support was important. But even more important was that extended by the staff at the Center for Black Studies at UC–Santa Barbara, headed by Alyce Whitted, its administrative assistant and heart. They constituted a second family within which it was possible to work on matters of seriousness and purpose. In England, this support was augmented by my friends at the Institute of Race Relations, A. Sivanandan, Jenny Bourne, Colin Prescod, Hazel Walters, Paul Gilroy, Lou Kushnick, Danny Reilly, Harsh Punja, and Tony Bunyan. I am also deeply indebted to my editors at Zed Press, Robert Molteno and Anna Gourlay. To them is owed any coherence which might exist in the work that follows.

Among the number of scholars to whom an intellectual acknowledgement is owed, I must distinguish St. Clair Drake. Both his patience and example are reflected in the body of the work. He carries his knowledge with wisdom and grace.

The last word is reserved for my family: Elizabeth, who read the first writings and suggested their worth; and Najda, who will some day, I hope, share that opinion. Six of her first eight years are at stake. I expect she will, if for no other reason than the authority of her mother, who read every line of this manuscript (and suggested some). To the two of them I extend my deepest appreciation.

BLACK MARXISM

INTRODUCTION

This study attempts to map the historical and intellectual contours of the encounter of Marxism and Black radicalism, two programs for revolutionary change. I have undertaken this effort in the belief that in its way each represents a significant and immanent mode of social resolution, but that each is a particular and critically different realization of a history. The point is that they may be so distinct as to be incommensurable. At issue here is whether this is so. If it is, judgments must be made, choices taken.

The inquiry required that both Marxism and Black radicalism be subjected to interrogations of unusual form: the first, Marxism, because few of its adherents have striven hard enough to recognize its profound but ambiguous indebtedness to Western civilization; the second, Black radicalism, because the very circumstance of its appearance has required that it be misinterpreted and diminished. I have hoped to contribute to the correction of these errors by challenging in both instances the displacement of history by aeriform theory and self-serving legend. Whether I have succeeded is for the reader to judge. But first it may prove useful to outline the construction of the study.

In Western societies for the better part of the past two centuries, the active and intellectual opposition of the Left to class rule has been vitalized by the vision of a socialist order: an arrangement of human relations grounded on the shared responsibility and authority over the means of social production and reproduction. The variations on the vision have been many, but over the years of struggle the hardiest tradition has proven to be that identified with the work and writings of Karl Marx, Friedrich Engels, and V. I. Lenin. Obviously here the term "tradition" is used rather loosely since the divergencies of opinion and deed between Marx, Engels, and Lenin have been demonstrated by history to be as significant as their correspondence. Nevertheless, in common as well as in academic parlance, these three activist-intellectuals are taken to be the principal figures of Marxist or Marxist-Leninist socialism. Marxism was founded on the study of the capitalist expropriation and exploitation of labor as first taken up by Engels, then elaborated by Marx's "material theory of history," his recognition of the evolving systems of capitalist production and the inevitability of class struggle, and later augmented by Lenin's conceptions of imperialism, the state, the "dictatorship of the proletariat," and the role of the revolutionary party. It has provided the ideological, historical, and political vocabulary for much of the radical and revolutionary presence emergent in modern Western societies. Elsewhere, in lands economically parasitized by the capitalist world system, or in those rare instances where its penetration has been quarantined by competing historical formations, some sorts of Marxism have again translated a concern with fundamental social change.

However, it is still fair to say that at base, that is at its epistemological substratum, Marxism is a Western construction—a conceptualization of human affairs and historical development that is emergent from the historical experiences of European peoples mediated, in turn, through their civilization, their social orders, and their cultures. Certainly its philosophical origins are indisputably Western. But the same must be said of its analytical presumptions, its historical perspectives, its points of view. This most natural consequence though has assumed a rather ominous significance since European Marxists have presumed more frequently than not that their project is identical with world-historical development. Confounded it would seem by the cultural zeal that accompanies ascendant civilizations, they have mistaken for universal verities the structures and social dynamics retrieved from their own distant and more immediate pasts. Even more significantly, the deepest structures of "historical materialism," the foreknowledge for its comprehension of historical movement, have tended to relieve European Marxists from the obligation of investigating the profound effects of culture and historical experience on their science. The ordering ideas that have persisted in Western civilization (and Marx himself as we shall see was driven to admit such phenomena), reappearing in successive "stages" of its development to dominate arenas of social ideology, have little or no *theoretical* justification in Marxism for their existence. One such recurring idea is racialism: the legitimation and corroboration of social organization as natural by reference to the "racial" components of its elements. Though hardly unique to European peoples, its appearance and codification, during the feudal period, into Western conceptions of society was to have important and enduring consequences.

In the first part of this study, I have devoted three chapters to explicating the appearance and formulation of racial sensibility in Western civilization and its social and ideological consequences. Chapter 1 reconstructs the history of the emergence of racial order in feudal Europe and delineates its subsequent impact on the organization of labor under capitalism. Racism, I maintain, was not simply a convention for ordering the relations of European to non-European peoples but has its genesis in the "internal" relations of European peoples. As part of the inventory of Western civilization it would reverberate within and without, transferring its toll from the past to the present. In contradistinction to Marx's and Engels's expectations that bourgeois society would rationalize social relations and demystify social consciousness, the obverse occurred. The development, organization, and expansion of capitalist society pursued essentially racial directions, so too did social ideology. As a material force, then, it could be expected that racialism would inevitably permeate the social structures emergent from capitalism. I have used the term "racial capitalism" to refer to this development and to the subsequent structure as a historical agency. The second chapter, as it rehearses the formation of the working classes in England, looks precisely at this phenomenon. Since the English working classes were the social basis for Engels's conceptualization of the modern proletariat, and conjoined with the *sans-culotte* of the French Revolution to occupy a similar place in Marx's thought, their evolving political and ideological character is of signal importance in reckoning the objective basis for Marxist theory. Of particular interest is the extent to which racialism (and subsequently nationalism) both as ideology and actuality affected the class consciousness of workers in England. In the intensely racial social order of England's industrializing era, the phenomenology of the relations of production bred no objective basis for the extrication of the universality of class from the particularisms of race. Working-class discourse and politics remained marked by the architectonic possibilities previously embedded in the culture.

But the appearance of European socialism and its development into a tradition was, as well, somewhat at odds with socialism's subsequent historiography and orthodoxies. The third chapter pursues among the middle classes the obscured origins of socialism and the contradictions that weakened its political and ideological expressions. It was indeed nationalism, a second "bourgeois" accretion, that most subverted the socialist creation. Nationalism, as a mix of racial sensibility and the economic interests of the national bourgeoisies, was as powerful an ideological impulse as any spawned from these strata. As an acquired temper and as a historical force met on the fields of social and political revolution, nationalism bemused the founders of historical materialism and those who followed them. It was to overtake both the direction of capitalist development and eventually the formative structures of socialist societies as they appeared in the present century. The historical trajectories of those developments, again, were almost entirely unexpected in a theoretical universe from which it had been discerned that ideology and false consciousness were supposedly being expelled. When in its time Black radicalism became manifest within Western society as well as at the other junctures between European and African peoples, one might correctly expect that Western radicalism was no more receptive to it than were the apologists of power.

Part II takes up this other radical tradition, Black radicalism, the conditions of its historical emergence, its forms, and its nature. This exposition begins in chapter 4 with the reinvestigation of the past relations between Europeans and Africans, a past that has been transformed by Europeans and for Europeans into a grotesque parody, a series of legends as monstrously proportioned as Pliny's *Blemmyae* "whose heads / Do grow beneath their shoulders." The obscuring of the Black radical tradition is seated in the West's suppression of Europe's previous knowledge of the African (and its own) past. The denial of history to African peoples took time—several hundreds of years—beginning with the emergence of Western Europeans from the shadow of Muslim domination and paternalism. It was also a process that was to transport the image of Africa across separate planes of dehumanization latticed by the emerging modalities of Western culture. In England, at first gripped by a combative and often hysterical Christianity—complements of the crusades, the "reconquests," and the rise of Italian capitalism—medieval English devouts recorded dreams in which the devil appeared as "a blacke moore," "an Ethiope." This was part of the grammar of the church, the almost singular repository of knowledge in Europe. Centuries later the Satanic gave way to the representation of Africans as a different sort of beast: dumb, animal labor, the benighted recipient of the benefits of slavery. Thus the "Negro" was conceived. The Negro—whose precedents could be found in the racial fabrications concealing the Slavs (*the* slaves), the Irish and others—substantially eradicated in Western historical consciousness the necessity of remembering the significance of Nubia for Egypt's formation, of Egypt in the development of Greek civilization, of Africa for imperial Rome, and more pointedly of Islam's influence on Europe's economic, political, and intellectual history. From such a creature not even the suspicion of tradition needed to be entertained. In its stead there was the Black slave, a consequence masqueraded as an anthropology and a history.

The creation of the Negro was obviously at the cost of immense expenditures of psychic and intellectual energies in the West. The exercise was obligatory. It was an effort commensurate with the importance Black labor power possessed for the world economy sculpted and dominated by the ruling and mercantile classes of Western Europe. As chapter 5 indicates, the Atlantic slave trade and the slavery of the New World were integral to the modern world economy. Their relationship to capitalism was historical and organic rather than adventitious or synthetic. The Italian financiers and merchants whose capital subsidized Iberian exploration of the Atlantic and Indian oceans were also masters of (largely "European") slave colonies in the Mediterranean. Certainly slave labor was one of their bases for what Marx termed "primitive accumulation." But it would be an error to arrest the relationship there, assigning slave labor to some "pre-capitalist" stage of history. For more than 300 years slave labor persisted beyond the beginnings of modern capitalism, complementing wage labor, peonage, serfdom, and other methods of labor coercion. Ultimately, this meant that the interpretation of history in terms of the dialectic of capitalist class struggles would prove inadequate, a mistake ordained by the preoccupation of Marxism with the industrial and manufacturing centers of capitalism; a mistake founded on the presumptions that Europe itself had produced, that the motive and material forces that generated the capitalist system were to be wholly located in what was a fictive historical entity. From its very foundations capitalism had never been—any more than Europe—a "closed system."

Necessarily then, Marx's and Engels's theory of revolution was insufficient in scope: the European proletariat and its social allies did not constitute *the* revolutionary subject of history, nor was working-class consciousness necessarily *the* negation of bourgeois culture. Out of what was in reality a rather more complex capitalist world system (and one to which Marx in his last decade paid closer attention), other revolutionary forces emerged as well. Informed as they were by the ideas and cultures drawn from their own historical experiences, these movements assumed forms only vaguely anticipated in the radical traditions of the West. In the terms of capitalist society they were its negation, but that was hardly the source of their being. And among them was the persistent and continuously evolving resistance of African peoples to oppression. The sixth chapter rehearses the history of this Black radical tradition in the African diaspora and to some extent in the African continent itself. As both this and the seventh chapter attempt to demonstrate, the record of resistance for four centuries or more, from Nueva Espana to Nyasaland, leaves in no doubt the specifically African character of those struggles. Resistances were formed through the meanings that Africans brought to the New World as their cultural possession; meanings sufficiently distinct from the foundations of Western ideas as to be remarked upon over and over by the European witnesses of their manifestations; meanings enduring and powerful enough to survive slavery to become the basis of an opposition to it. With Western society as a condition, that tradition almost naturally assumed a theoretical aspect as well.

The third and final section of this study traces the social and intellectual backgrounds of the processes that led to the theoretical articulation of Black radicalism. The conditions for modern Black theory were present first in the African diaspora. Far from Africa and physically enveloped by hostile communities, Black opposition acquired a penetrative comprehension. But it was a social and political as well as a historical process that nurtured theory. In the pursuit of that process I have identified three seminal Black radical intellectuals: William Edward Burkhardt Du Bois, Cyril Lionel Robert James, and Richard Nathaniel Wright. They have been chosen for detailed treatment not only because they made substantial contributions to the theoretical text, but because their lives and circumstances were prisms of the events impending on and emanating from the Black radical tradition. Their reactions to their confrontation with Black resistance, the very means used for their expression were distinct but related, characterized by circumstance, temperament, and training. Though their lives were very dissimilar—only Wright could be said to have been directly produced by the Black peasant and working classes—they all came to that tradition late (and hesitantly, as I will argue with respect to Du Bois and James). For all three, though, Marxism had been the prior commitment, the first encompassing and conscious experience of organized opposition to racism, exploitation, and domination. As Marxists, their apprenticeships proved to be significant but ultimately unsatisfactory. In time, events and experience drew them toward Black radicalism and the discovery of a collective Black resistance inspired by an enduring cultural complex of historical apprehension. In these concluding chapters I have attempted to demonstrate how and why this was so. Taken together, the efforts of Du Bois, James, and Wright consisted of a first step toward the creation of an intellectual legacy that would complement the historical force of Black struggle. Their destiny, I suggest, was not to create the idea of that struggle so much as to articulate it. Regardless, the Black opposition to domination has continued to acquire new forms. In a very real sense then, the present study follows.

PART I

THE EMERGENCE AND LIMITATIONS OF EUROPEAN RADICALISM

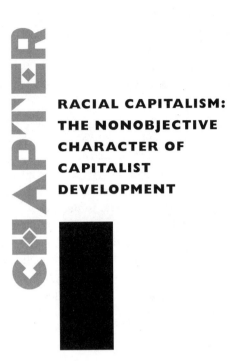

RACIAL CAPITALISM: THE NONOBJECTIVE CHARACTER OF CAPITALIST DEVELOPMENT

The historical development of world capitalism was influenced in a most fundamental way by the particularistic forces of racism and nationalism. This could only be true if the social, psychological, and cultural origins of racism and nationalism both anticipated capitalism in time and formed a piece with those events that contributed directly to its organization of production and exchange. Feudal society is the key. More particularly, the antagonistic commitments, structures, and ambitions that feudal society encompassed are better conceptualized as those of a developing civilization than as elements of a unified tradition.

The processes through which the world system emerged contained an opposition between the rationalistic thrusts of an economistic worldview and the political momenta of collectivist logic. The feudal state, an instrument of signal importance to the bourgeoisie, was to prove to be as consistently antithetical to the commercial integration represented by a world system as it had to the idea of Christendom. Neither the state nor later the nation could slough off the particularistic psychologies and interests that served as contradictions to a global community. A primary consequence of the conflict between those two social tendencies was that capitalists, as the architects of this system, never achieved the coherence of structure and organization that had been the promise of capitalism as an objective system.[1] On the contrary, the history of capitalism has in no way distinguished itself from earlier eras with respect to wars, material crises, and social conflicts. A secondary consequence is that the critique of capitalism, to the extent that its protagonists have based their analyses upon the presumption of a determinant economic rationality in the development and expansion of capitalism, has been characterized by an incapacity to come to terms with the world system's direction of developments. Marxism, the dominant form that the critique of capitalism has assumed in Western thought, incorporated theoretical and ideological weaknesses that stemmed from the same social forces that provided the bases of capitalist formation.

The creation of capitalism was much more than a matter of the displacement of feudal modes and relations of production by capitalist ones.[2] Certainly, the transformation of the economic structures of noncapitalist Europe (specifically the Mediterranean and western European market, trade, and production systems) into capitalist forms of production and exchange was a major part of this process. Still, the first appearance of capitalism in the fifteenth century[3] involved other dynamics as well. The social, cultural, political, and ideological complexes of European feudalisms contributed more to capitalism than the social "fetters"[4] that precipitated the bourgeoisie into social and political revolutions. No class was its own creation. Indeed, capitalism was less a catastrophic revolution (negation) of feudalist social orders than the extension of these social relations into the larger tapestry of the modern world's political and economic relations. Historically, the civilization evolving in the western extremities of the Asian/European continent, and whose first signification is medieval Europe,[5] passed with few disjunctions from feudalism as the dominant mode of production to capitalism as the dominant mode of production. And from its very beginnings, this European civilization, containing racial, tribal, linguistic, and regional particularities, was constructed on antagonistic differences.

Europe's Formation

The social basis of European civilization was "among those whom the Romans called the 'barbarians.'"[6] Prior to the eleventh or twelfth centuries, the use of the collective sense of the term "barbarian" was primarily a function of exclusion rather than a reflection of any significant consolidation among those peoples. The term signified that the "barbarians" had their historical origins beyond the civilizing reach of Roman law and the old Roman imperial social order. The "Europe" of the ninth century for which the Carolingian family and its minions claimed paternity was rather limited geopolitically[7] and had a rather short and unhappy existence. Interestingly, for several centuries following the deaths of Charlemagne and his immediate heirs (the last being Arnulf, d.899), both the Emperor and Europe were more the stuff of popular legend and clerical rhetoric than manifestations of social reality.[8] The idea of Europe, no longer a realistic project, was transferred from one of a terrestrial social order to that of a spiritual kingdom: Christendom.

In fact, those peoples to whom the Greeks and the Romans referred collectively as barbarians were of diverse races with widely differing cultures.[9] The diversity of their languages is, perhaps, one measure of their differences. But in using this measure, we must be cautious of the schemes of classification of those languages that reduce the reality of their numbers to simple groupings like the Celtic, the Italic, the Germanic, the Balto-Slavonic, and Albanian languages.[10]

Direct and indirect evidence indicates that a more authentic mapping of the languages of the proto-Europeans would be much more complex. For instance, H. Munro Chadwick, as late as 1945, could locate extant descendants of those several languages among the Gaelic, Welsh, and Breton languages of Great Britain and France; the Portuguese, Spanish, Catalan, Provençal, French, Italian, Sardinian, Alpine, and Rumanian languages and dialects of southern and western Europe; the English, Frisian, Dutch, German, Danish, Swedish, Norwegian, and Icelandic languages of England, Scotland the Netherlands, Germany, and Scandinavia; the Russian, Bulgarian, Yugoslavian, Slovenian, Slovakian, Czech, Polish, and Lusitian languages and dialects of central and eastern Europe; and the Latvian and Lithuanian languages of northern Europe.[11] But even Chadwick's list was of merely those languages that had survived "the millennium of Europe." The list would lengthen considerably if one were to consider the languages which existed in this area at the beginning of this era and are no longer spoken (for example, Latin, Cornish, and Prusai), along with those languages of peoples who preceded the migrations from the north and east of Rome's barbarians (for example, Basque, Etruscan, Oscan, and Umbrian).[12]

The Ostrogoth, Visigoth, Vandal, Suevi, Burgundi, Alamanni, and Frank peoples—that is the barbarians—whose impact on the fortunes of the Late Roman Empire from the fifth century was quick and dramatic,[13] were in fact a small minority of thousands among the millions of the decaying state. Henri Pirenne, relying on the estimates of Emile-Felix Gautier and L. Schmidt, reports that the Ostrogoths and Visigoths may have numbered 100,000 each, the Vandals 80,000, and the Burgundi 25,000.[14] Moreover, the warrior strata of each kingdom are consistently estimated at about 20 percent of their populations. On the other hand, the Empire that they invaded contained as many as 50–70 million persons.[15] Pirenne cautiously concludes:

> All this is conjecture. Our estimate would doubtless be in excess of the truth if, for the Western provinces beyond the *limes*, we reckoned the Germanic element as constituting 5 percent of the population.[16]

More importantly, the vast majority of the barbarians "came not as conquerors, but exactly as, in our own day, North Africans, Italians, Poles cross into Metropolitan France to look for work."[17] In a relatively short time, in the southern-most European lands that were bounded by the Western Roman Empire, these peoples were entirely assimilated by the indigenous peoples as a primarily slave labor force.[18] The pattern was already a familiar one within the dying civilization of the Mediterranean[19] with which they desired and desperately needed to join.[20] It is also important to realize that with respect to the emerging European civilization whose beginnings coincide with the arrivals of these same barbarians, slave labor as a critical basis of production would continue without any significant interruption into the twentieth century.[21]

From the *familia rustica* that characterized Roman and even earlier Greek (*doulos*) rural production within vast estates, through the *manucipia* of the *colonicae* and *mansi* land-holdings of Merovingian (481–752) and Carolingian eras, the feudal villains of western medieval Europe and England, and the *sclavi* of the Genoese and Venetian merchants who dominated commercial trade in the Mediterranean from the thirteenth to the sixteenth century, slave labor persisted as an aspect of European agrarian production up to the modern era.[22] Neither feudal serfdom, nor capitalism had as their result the elimination or curtailment of slavery.[23] At the very most (it is argued by some), their organization served to relocate it.[24]

Despite the "Romanization" of the southern Goths, or seen differently because of it, the Germanic tribes did establish the general administrative boundaries that were to mark the nations of modern western Europe. The kingdoms that they established, mainly under the rules of Roman *hospitalitas* and in accordance with Roman administration,[25] were in large measure the predecessors of France, Germany, Spain, and Italy.

Still, we must not forget that in historical reconstruction, a medieval age is to be intervened between these two ages. Medieval Europe, though still agricultural in economy, was a much cruder existence for slave, peasant, farmer, artisan, land-owner, cleric, and nobility alike than had been the circumstance for their predecessors in the Empire. Urban life declined, leaving the old cities in ruins,[26] long-distance trade, especially by sea routes, decayed dramatically.[27] Latouche summarizes:

> The balance-sheet of the Merovingian economy is singularly disappointing. The now fashionable, if unpleasant, word "rot" describes it to perfection. Whether in the sphere of town life, commerce, barter, currency, public works, shipping, we find everywhere the same policy of neglect, the same selfish refusal to initiate reform. From this disastrous, drifting laissez-faire which left men and things as they had always been, pursuing unchanged their traditional way of life, there sprang the illusion that the ancient world still lingered on; it was, in fact, no more than a facade.[28]

The Carolingian Empire did little to repair the "rot" that anticipated the restructuring of Europe in feudal terms. The Muslim conquests of the Mediterranean in the seventh and eighth centuries had deprived the European economies of the urban, commercial, productive, and cultural vitality they required for their reconstruction. Pirenne put it boldly:

> The ports and the cities were deserted. The link with the Orient was severed, and there was no communication with the Saracen coasts. There was nothing but death. The Carolingian Empire presented the most striking contrast with the Byzantine. It was purely an inland power, for it had no outlets. The Mediterranean territories, formerly the most active portions of the Empire, which supported the life of the whole, were now the poorest, the most desolate, the most constantly

menaced. For the first time in history the axis of Occidental civilization was displaced toward the North, and for many centuries it remained between the Seine and the Rhine. And the Germanic peoples, which had hitherto played only the negative part of destroyers, were now called upon to play a positive part in the reconstruction of European civilization.[29]

Latouche, though he differed with Pirenne on many of the particulars of the Carolingian response to the loss of the Mediterranean, finally concurred:

[T]he Empire broke up less than half a century after its creation, and Charlemagne did nothing to prevent, and did not even attempt to delay, the development of feudal institutions, so heavy with menace for the future . . . a world in which there were no great business concerns, no industries, and in which agricultural activity was predominant.[30]

Urban life, trade, and market systems incorporating the goods of long-distance trade did not return to Europe until the end of the eleventh century at the earliest, and most probably during the twelfth century.[31] By then, the depth to which the degradation of European life had fallen is perhaps best expressed by the appearance of commercialized cannibalism.[32]

The First Bourgeoisie

Into this depressed land where few were free of the authority of an intellectually backward and commercially unimaginative ruling class, where famine and epidemics were the natural order of things, and where the sciences of the Ancient World had long been displaced as the basis of intellectual development by theological fables and demonology,[33] appeared the figure to which European social theorists, Liberal and Marxist, attribute the generation of Western civilization: the bourgeoisie. The merchant was as alien to feudal society as the barbarian invaders had been to the Empire. Unlike the Mediterranean tradesmen,[34] the origins of the western European bourgeoisie are obscured. No doubt this is largely due to the fact that historical documentation is inevitably sparse where civilization in the formal sense of urban culture has largely disappeared, and where life is recorded by an elite of land and church largely preoccupied with its own experience while hostile to commerce.[35] Nevertheless, it is clear that the western European merchant class—"a class of deracines"[36]—crystallized within a social order for which it was an extrinsic phenomena.

The economic organization of demesne production was characterized by Pirenne as a "closed domestic economy one which we might call, with more exactitude, the economy of no markets."[37] In fact, there were markets, local ones, but their function and existence had no part in the development of the markets of long-distance trades that were the basis of the merchant class's development. The *mercati*, whose existence predates the bourgeoisie, dealt not in trade but foodstuffs at the retail level.[38] The one factor "internal" to the feudal order that did contribute to the rise of the bourgeoisie was the eleventh century's population growth. This increase had ultimately placed significant strains on feudal production:

It had as a result the detaching from the land an increasingly important number of individuals and committing them to that roving and hazardous existence which, in every agricultural civilization, is the lot of those who no longer find themselves with their roots in the soil. It multiplied the crowd of vagabonds. . . . Energetic characters, tempered by the experience of a life full of the unexpected, must have abounded among them. Many knew foreign languages and were conversant with the customs and needs of diverse lands. Let a lucky chance present itself . . . they were remarkably well equipped to profit thereby. . . . Famines were multiplied throughout Europe, sometimes in one province and sometimes in another, by that inadequate system of communications, and increased still more the opportunities, for those who knew how to make use of them, of getting rich. A few timely sacks of wheat, transported to the right spot, sufficed for the realizing of huge profits. . . . It was certainly not long before nouveaux riches made their appearance in the midst of this miserable crowd of impoverished, bare-foot wanderers in the world.[39]

In the beginning, before they could properly be described as bourgeoisie, these merchants traveled from region to region, their survival a matter of their mobility and their ability to capitalize on the frequent ruptures and breakdowns of the reproduction of populations sunk into the manorial soil. Their mobility may have also been occasioned by the fact that many of them were not free-born and thus sought respite from their social condition by flight from their lords: "By virtue of the wandering existence they led, they were everywhere regarded as foreigners."[40] For security they often traveled in small bands—a habit that would continue into their more sedentary period. It was not long before they began to establish *porti* (storehouses or transfer points for merchandise) outside the *burgs* (the fortresses of the Germanic nobles) bishoprics and towns that straddled the main routes of war, communications, and later, international trade. It was these *porti*, or merchant colonies, that founded, in the main, the medieval cities of Europe's hinterland. It was at this point that the merchants of Europe became bourgeoisies (*burgenses*). By the beginnings of the twelfth century, these bourgeoisies had already begun the transformation of European life so necessary for the emergence of capitalism as the dominant organization of European production.

The western European bourgeoisie re-established the urban centers by basing them upon exchange between the Mediterranean, the East, and northern Europe:

[In the tenth century] there appears in Anglo-Saxon texts the word "port," employed as a synonym for the Latin words *urbs* and *civitas*, and even at the present day the term "ports" is commonly met with in the names of cities of every land of English speech.

Nothing shows more clearly the close connection that existed between the economic revival of the Middle Ages and the beginnings of city life. They were so intimately related that the same word which designated a commercial settlement served in one of the great idioms of Europe to designate the town itself.[41]

Elsewhere, Pirenne puts it more succinctly: "Europe 'colonized' herself, thanks to the increase of her inhabitants."[42] Flanders—geographically situated to service the commerce of the northern seas, and economically critical because of the Flemish cloth industry—was the first of the major European merchant centers. Close behind Flanders came Bruges, Ghent, Ypres, Lille, Douai, Arras, Tournai, Cambrai, Valenciennes, Liege, Huy, Dinant, Cologne, Mainz, Rouen, Bordeaux, and Bayonne.[43] Cloth, which both Pirenne[44] and Karl Polanyi[45] identify as the basis of European trade, originally a rural industry, was transformed by the bourgeoisie in Flanders into an urban manufacture "organized on the capitalistic basis of wage labour."[46] The urban concentration of industry was thus initiated:

> The increase of the population naturally favored industrial concentration. Numbers of the poor poured into the towns where cloth-making, the activity of which trade grew proportionately with the development of commerce, guaranteed them their daily bread. . . .
>
> The old rural industry very quickly disappeared. It could not compete with that of the town, abundantly supplied with the raw material of commerce, operating at lower prices, and enjoying more advanced methods. . . .
>
> [W]hatever might be the nature of industry in other respects, everywhere it obeyed that law of concentration which was operative at such an early date in Flanders. Everywhere the city groups, thanks to commerce, drew rural industry to them.[47]

It is also true that the bourgeoisie, in so doing, came to free some portions of the serfs[48] only to re-enslave them through wage labor. For with urban industry came the successful attack on feudal and seigniorial servitude:

> Freedom, of old, used to be the monopoly of a privileged class. By means of the cities it again took its place in society as a natural attribute of the citizen. Hereafter it was enough to reside on city soil to acquire it. Every serf who had lived for a year and a day within the city limits had it by definite right: the statute of limitations abolished all rights which his lord exercised over his person and chattels. Birth meant little. Whatever might be the mark with which it had stigmatized the infant in his cradle, it vanished in the atmosphere of the city.[49]

With the flourishing of long-distance trade and the development of urban centers in western Europe came some specializations in rural production. Though open-field agriculture dominated Europe as a whole in the thirteenth, fourteenth, and fifteenth centuries, specialized grain production could be found in Prussia (corn), Tuscany and Lombardy (cereals), England (wheat), and north Germany (rye). By the late fifteenth century, viticulture had appeared in Italy, Spain, France, and southwest Germany. In the Baltic and North Seas, fishing and salt made up a significant part of the cargoes of Hanseatic shippers. And in England and Spain, meat production for export had begun to emerge.[50]

In northern Europe, these exports joined wool and woolen cloth as the major bases of international trade. In southern Europe—more precisely the Mediterranean—the long-distance trade in cloth (wool, silk, and later cotton), grains, and wines came to complement a significant trade in luxury goods:

> The precious stuffs from the east found their way into every rich household, and so did the specialities of various European regions: amber and furs from the countries bordering on the Baltic; *objets d'art* such as paintings from Flanders, embroidery from England, enamels from Limoges; manuscript books for church, boudoir or library; fine armor and weapons from Milan and glass from Venice.[51]

Still, according to Iris Origo, the most precious cargo of the Mediterranean tradesmen was slaves:

> European and Levantine traders sold Grecian wines and Ligurian figs, and the linen and woolen stuffs of Champagne and Lombardy, and purchased precious silks from China, carpets from Bokhara and Samarkand, furs from the Ural Mountains, and Indian spices, as well as the produce of the rich black fields and forests of the Crimea. But the most flourishing trade of all was that in slaves—for Caffa was the chief slave-market of the Levant.[52]

Tartar, Greek, Armenian, Russian, Bulgarian, Turkish, Circassian, Slavonic, Cretan, Arab, African (*Mori*), and occasionally Chinese (Cathay) slaves[53]—two-thirds of whom were female[54]—were to be found in the households of wealthy and "even relatively modest Catalan and Italian families."[55]

From the thirteenth century to the beginnings of the fifteenth century, the primary function of these predominantly European slaves in the economics of southern Europe was domestic service.[56] Nevertheless, in Spain (Catalan and Castile) and in the Italian colonies on Cyprus, Crete, and in Asia Minor (Phocaea) and Palestine, Genoese and Venetian masters used both European and African slaves in agriculture on sugar plantations, in industry, and for work in mines:

> This variety of uses to which slaves were put illustrates clearly the degree to which medieval colonial slavery served as a model for Atlantic colonial slavery. Slave manpower had been employed in the Italian colonies in the Mediterranean for all the kinds of work it would be burdened with in the Atlantic colonies. The only important change was that the white victims of slavery were replaced by a much greater number of African Negroes, captured in raids or bought by traders.[57]

In an unexpected way, this trade in slaves would prove to be the salvation of the Mediterranean bourgeoisie. In the thirteenth and early fourteenth centuries, however, it appeared that the merchants of the European hinterland would inevitably overshadow those of Italy's city-states. They, unlike the Italians, were undeterred, as

Giuliano Procacci points out, by the peninsula's small but densely packed populations; the increasingly unfavorable ratios of townsmen to countrymen (Florence could only survive on the produce of its countryside for five months of the year, Venice and Genoa had to be almost entirely supplied by sea); and the rapid deforestation of the countryside that aggravated the destruction of the autumn and spring floods.[58]

However, it was the fate of this nascent bourgeoisie not to thrive. Indeed, for one historical moment, even the further development of capitalism might be said to have been in question. The events of the fourteenth and fifteenth centuries intervened in the processes through which feudalism was ultimately displaced by the several forms of capitalism.[59] The consequence of those events were to determine the species of the modern world: the identities of the bourgeoisies that transformed capitalism into a world system; the sequences of this development; the relative vitalities of the several European economies; and the sources of labor from which each economy would draw.

The momentous events of which we speak were: the periodic famines that struck Europe in this period, the Black Death of the mid-fourteenth century and subsequent years, the Hundred Years War (1337–1453), and the rebellions of peasants and artisans.[60] Together they had a devastating impact on western Europe and the Mediterranean—decimating the populations of cities and countryside alike, disrupting trade, collapsing industry and agricultural production—leveling, as it were, the bulk of the most developed regions of western European bourgeois activity. Denys Hay has summed it up quite well:

> The result of prolonged scarcity, endemic and pandemic plague, the intermittent but catastrophic invasions of ruthless armies, and the constant threat in many areas from well-organized robber bands, was seen not only in a dwindling population but in roads abandoned to brambles and briars, in arable land out of cultivation and in deserted villages. Contraction in the area of cultivation in its turn made dearth the more likely. There was in every sense a vicious circle. A sober estimate suggests that "in 1470 the number of households was halved in most European villages compared with the start of the fourteenth century"; the reconquest of forest and waste of the arable is "an episode equal in importance to the drama of the earlier clearings."[61]

This general economic decline in Europe of the fourteenth and fifteenth centuries was marked in a final and visible way by social disorders much more profound than the territorial wars. Such wars, after all had been in character with feudal society. The appearance of peasant movements was not:

> In the boom condition of the thirteenth century there had been in rural areas a degree of over-population which made many peasants—day labourers, poor serfs—very vulnerable. Now the countryside was more sparsely occupied and a better living was possible for those who remained. . . . What was new in the slump

conditions of the fourteenth century was a bitterness in the lord's relations with the villagers.[62]

As Hay indicates, the most intense of the peasant rebellions occurred in Flanders (1325–28), northern France (the Jacquerie of 1358), and England (1381). But such movements erupted over much of western Europe during the fourteenth, fifteenth, and sixteenth centuries. In France, and especially Normandy (precipitated surely by the final savaging of the peasants by the forces of the Hundred Years War), in Catalonia (1409–13 and later), in Jutland (1411), in Finland (1438), and in Germany (1524), peasants arose, seizing land, executing lords, clergy, and even lawyers, demanding an end to manorial dues, petitioning for the establishment of wage-labor, and insisting on the dissolution of restrictions on free buying and selling.[63]

Within the vortex of these disturbances, long-distance trade declined drastically. In England, the export of wool and cloth, and subsequently their production, fell well below thirteenth-century levels.[64] In France (Gascony), the export of wine was similarly affected.[65] Hay remarks that "Florentine bankruptcies in the first half of the fourteenth century are paralleled by similar troubles in Florence at the end of the fifteenth century,"[66] while P. Ramsey notes the precipitous fall of "the great merchant bankers of southern Germany."[67] Further north, the Hansa League disintegrated,[68] while to the west, the Flemish cloth industry collapsed.[69] Finally, even the northern Italian city-states found their bourgeoisie in decline. The rise of the Ottoman Empire, at first disruptive to the Italian merchant houses, would dictate new accommodations to Islam and commerce, eventually persuading some of the Italians to relocate as capitalist colonists in the Iberian peninsula.[70] For the moment, however, the foundations of the European civilization, still figuratively embryonic, appeared to be crumbling.

The Modern World Bourgeoisie

Henri Pirenne, however, provided a key to one of the mysteries of the emergence of the modern era in the sixteenth century from the chaos and desperation of the fourteenth and fifteenth centuries: the "survival" of the bourgeoisie. Pirenne also anticipated the somewhat rhetorical question put by K. G. Davies in the heat of the debate revolving around the historical authenticity of the phrase: the rise of the middle class. Davies queried:

> What, after all, is wrong with the suggestion that the *bourgeoisie*, not steadily but by fits and starts, improved its status over many centuries, a process that began with the appearance of towns and has not yet been finally consummated?[71]

Forty years earlier, Pirenne had already replied:

> I believe that, for each period into which our economic history may be divided, there is a distinct and separate class of capitalists. In other words, the group of capitalists of a given epoch does not spring from the capitalist group of the preceding epoch. At every change in economic organization we find a breach of con-

tinuity. It is as if the capitalists who have up to then been active recognize that they are incapable of adapting themselves to conditions which are evoked by needs hitherto unknown and which call for methods hitherto unemployed.[72]

Both Pirenne and Davies understood that the biological metaphor of a bourgeoisie emerging out of the Middle Ages, nurturing itself on the "mercantilisms" and administrations of the Absolute Monarchies of the traditional period between feudalism and the capitalism, and on the lands and titles of impoverished nobilities, then finally achieving political and economic maturity and thus constituting industrial capitalism, is largely unsupported by historical evidence. Rather it is a historical *impression*, a phantom representation largely constructed from the late eighteenth century to the present by the notional activity of a bourgeoisie as a dominant class. This history of "the rise of the middle class" is an amalgam of bourgeois political and economic power, the self-serving ideology of the bourgeoisie as the ruling class and thus an intellectual and political preoccupation—mediated through the constructs of evolutionary theory:

> From Darwin has descended the language of error, a language that has locked up historical thinking and imposed slovenly and imprecise conclusions even upon scholarly and sensible researchers. Words like "growth," "decline," "development," "evolution," "decay," may have started as servants but they have ended as masters: they have brought us to the edge of historical inevitability.[73]

Hegel's dialectic of *Aufhebung*, Marx's dialectic of class struggle and the contradictions between the mode and relations of production, Darwin's evolution of the species and Spencer's survival of the fittest are all forged from the same metaphysical conventions. The declining European bourgeoisies of the fourteenth and fifteenth centuries were not, for the most part, the lineal antecedents of those that appeared in the sixteenth century. The universality of capitalism is less a historical reality than a construct of this "language of error."[74] These "distant and separate class[es] of capitalists" were less the representatives of an immanent, rational, commercial order than extensions of particular historical dynamics and cultures. They were not the "germ" of a new order dialectically posited in an increasingly confining host—feudalism—but an opportunistic strata, willfully adaptive to the new conditions and possibilities offered by the times. Not only did different western European bourgeoisies appear in the sixteenth century, but these new bourgeoisie were implicated in structures, institutions, and organizations that were substantively undeveloped in the Middle Ages.

For one, the focus of long-distance trade in Europe gravitated from the Mediterranean and Scania areas to the Atlantic. The most familiar forms of this extension of trade to the south and west of the European peninsula were merchant voyages and colonization. Second, "expanded bureaucratic state structures"[75] became the major conduits of capitalist expansion: determining the direction of investment, establishing political security for such investments, encouraging certain commercial networks and relations while discouraging others:

In these conditions, in fact, may be seen the matrix of modern capitalism: like nationalism, less the creator than the creation of the modern state. It had many antecedents, but its full emergence required a conjunction of political and moral as well as strictly economic factors. This emergence could take place within the intricate framework of one type of western state then evolving; it may be doubted whether it could have done so under any other circumstances that we know of in history; at any rate it never did.[76]

The city, the point of departure for the earlier bourgeoisies and their networks of long-distance trade and productive organization, proved to be incapable of sustaining the economic recovery of those bourgeoisies situated where the merchant town had reached its highest development: northern Italy, western Germany, the Netherlands, and the Baltic.[77] The Absolutist State, under the hegemony of western European aristocracies, brought forth a new bourgeoisie. The territories of Castile (Spain), the Ile de France, the Home Counties and London (England), the expansionist and colonial ambitions and policies of their administrations, and the structures of their political economies organized for repression and exploitation, these constituted the basis of this bourgeois' formation.

The bourgeoisies of the sixteenth century accumulated in the interstices of the state. And as the state acquired the machinery of rule—bureaucracies of administrative, regulatory, and extractive concerns, and armies of wars of colonial pacification, international competition, and domestic repression[78]—those who would soon constitute a class, settled into the proliferating roles of political, economic, and juridical agents for the state. And as the state necessarily expanded its fiscal and economic activities,[79] a new merchant and banking class parasitized its host: State loans, state monopolies, state business became the vital centers of its construction.

> So while the territorial states and empires acquired lands in plenty, they were unable to exploit unaided the resultant huge economic units. This incapacity again opened the door to the towns and the merchants. It was they, who, behind the facade of subordination were making their fortunes. And even where the states could most easily become masters, in their own territory with their own subjects, they were often obliged to make shifts and compromises.[80]

It is still debatable whether this was a result of what Adam Smith and Eli Heckscher after him termed the "system" of *mercantilism*,[81] or the consequence of what other historians describe as the ideology of *statism*.[82] Nevertheless, it is clear that by the seventeenth century, the new bourgeoisies were identified with political attitudes and a trend in economic thought that was pure mercantilism:

> [I]mplicit in the "tragedy of mercantilism" was the belief that what was one man's or country's gain was another's loss. . . . It was, after all, a world in which population remained remarkably static; in which trade and production usually grew only very gradually; in which the limits of the known world were expanded slowly and with great difficulty; in which economic horizons were narrowly limited; and in

which man approximated more closely than today to Hobbes' vision of his natural state: for most men most of the time, life was "poor, nasty, brutish and short."[83]

The parochialism of the town, which had so much characterized the perspective of the bourgeoisie of the Middle Ages, was matched in this second era of Western civilization by a parochialism of the state. Heckscher commented that:

> The collective entity to [peoples of the sixteenth and seventeenth centuries] was not a nation unified by common race, speech, and customs: the only decisive factor for them was *the state*. . . . Mercantilism was the exponent of the prevailing conception of the relationship between the state and nation in the period before the advent of romanticism. It was the state and not the nation which absorbed its attention.[84]

Again, the particularistic character of the formations of these bourgeoisies[85] withheld, from what would be called capitalism, a systemic structure. The class that is so consistently identified with the appearance of industrial capitalism was inextricably associated with specific "rational" structures—a relationship that profoundly influenced bourgeois imaginations and realizations. Political economies,[86] that is national economies, enclosed them, and thus the bourgeoisie perceived what later analysis argues in retrospect is the beginnings of a world system as something quite different: an international system.[87] The bourgeoisies of early modern capitalism were attempting to destroy or dominate each other.

The Lower Orders

Just as the western European middle classes were suspended in webs of state parochialisms, so too was that vast majority of European peoples: the lower orders. The class that ruled, the nobility, by its orchestration of the instrumentalities of the state, imprinted its character on the whole of European society. And since much of that character had to do with violence,[88] the lower orders were woven into the tapestry of a violent social order. By the nature of hierarchical societies, the integration of the lower classes—wage laborers, peasants, serfs, slaves, vagabonds, and beggars—into the social, political, and economic orders of the Absolute State was on the terms of the clients of the latter. The function of the laboring classes was to provide the state and its privileged classes with the material and human resources needed for their maintenance and further accumulations of power and wealth. This was not, however, a simple question of the dominance of a ruling class over the masses.

The masses did not exist as such. As earlier, Greek and Roman thinkers had created the totalizing construct of the barbarians, the feudal nobilities of western Europe had inspired and authored a similar myth. Friedrich Hertz has reported that:

> In the Middle Ages and later, the nobility, as a rule, considered themselves of better blood than the common people, whom they utterly despised. The peasants were supposed to be descended from Ham, who, for lack of filial piety, was known to have been condemned by Noah to slavery. The knightly classes of many lands, on

the other hand, believed themselves to be the descendants of the Trojan heroes, who after the fall of Troy were said to have settled in England, France and Germany. This theory was seriously maintained not only in numerous songs and tales of knightly deeds, but also in many scholarly works.[89]

It was a form of this notion that Count Gobineau revived in the mid-nineteenth century, extending its conceptualization of superiority so as to include elements of the bourgeoisie.[90] The nobilities of the sixteenth century, however, proved to be more circumspect about "the masses" than their genealogical legends might imply. They did not become victims of their own mythic creations. When it came to the structures of the state, their knowledge of the social, cultural, and historical compositions of the masses was exquisitely refined. Perhaps this is no more clearly demonstrated than in one of the most critical areas of state activity: the monopolization of force.

The Absolutist State was a cause and effect of war. Its economy was a war economy, its foreign trade was combative,[91] its bureaucracy administered the preparations and prosecutions of war.[92] Such a state required standing armies (and, eventually, navies). But for certainly political and sometimes economic reasons, soldiers could not be recruited easily from, in V. G. Kiernan's phrase, "the mass of ordinary peasants and burghers." Kiernan puts the situation most simply for France, though it was the same all over Europe: "Frenchmen were seldom eager to serve their king, and their king was not eager to employ Frenchmen."[93] Loyalty to the state of the monarchy from the exploited ranks of the lower classes was rare. In any case, not one state of the sixteenth or seventeenth century was reliant on such an identification between the masses and their rulers. The soldiers of the armies of France, Spain, England, Holland, Prussia, Poland, Sweden, and at first Russia, were either alien to the states for which they fought and policed or very marginal to them:

> European governments . . . relied very largely on foreign mercenaries. One of the employments for which they were particularly well suited was the suppression of rebellious subjects, and in the sixteenth century, that age of endemic revolution, they were often called upon for this purpose. . . . Governments . . . had to look either to backward areas for honest, simple-minded fellows untainted by political ideas . . . or to foreigners.[94]

Depending then on changing fortunes, the "identities" of the combatants, the geo-politics of wars, and the mission, mercenaries were drawn from among the Swiss, the Scots, Picardians, Bretons, Flemings, Welsh, Basques, Mavarrese, Gallowayians, Dalmatians, Corsicans, Burgundians, Gueldrians, the Irish, Czechs, Croatians, Magyars, and from Gascony, Allgaeu, Norway, and Albania. Since one function and result of the work of these mercenaries was the suppression of subject peoples, the degree of their success is directly indicated by their own absence, for the most part, from the political geography of modern Europe. The Absolute State (or its direct successors), the instrument that propelled them into prominence in the sixteenth and seventeenth centuries (for France, into the late eighteenth century), ultimately absorbed the autonomous sectors from which the mercenaries originated.

In the armies of the sixteenth century, native recruits distributed among the foreign mercenaries were also chosen with an eye to minimizing the political and social risks of the monarchy and its allied nobility. In France, the army "drew its volunteers from the least 'national,' most nondescript types, the dregs of the poorest classes," Kiernan informs us.[95] In Spain, the hills of Aragon and the Basque provinces served a similar function. In Britain, until the mid-eighteenth century, the Scottish Highlands were the most frequent sites of recruitment; and the Welsh soldier's skills became legendary.[96]

Important as the formation of these armies was for the construction of the states that dominated Europe for more than 200 years, we must not be diverted from their more historical importance by the romantic richness of the social and political drama to which they contributed. Louis XI's innovation in 1474, of organizing a "French infantry without Frenchmen"[97] was revolutionary in scale, not in character.[98] The tactic of composing armies from mercenaries and from marginal peoples and social strata extended back into the Middle Ages and earlier. Imperial armies, republican armies, bandit armies, invading armies and defending armies, the armies of rebellious slaves, of nobles, and even of the chauvinist medieval cities, all laid claim to, or incorporated to some extent, souls for whom they had at best few considerations in less intense times.[99] More significantly, in reviewing this phenomenon for the sixteenth and later centuries, the point is not that mercenaries were recruited from the outside and from among those least secure internally; this is simply the best documented form of a more generalized pattern of structural formation and social integration.

The important meaning is that this form of enlisting human reserves was not peculiar to military apparatus but extended throughout Europe to domestic service, handicrafts, industrial labor, the ship- and dock-workers of merchant capitalism, and the field laborers of agrarian capitalism. There has never been a moment in modern European history (if before) that migratory and/or immigrant labor was not a significant aspect of European economies.[100] That this is not more widely understood seems to be a consequence of conceptualization and analysis: the mistaken use of the *nation* as a social, historical, and economic category; a resultant and persistent reference to national labor "pools" (e.g., "the English working class"); and a subsequent failure of historical investigation. Wallerstein, in his otherwise quite detailed study of the origins of the capitalist world system, can devote a mere page to this phenomenon, including a single paragraph on the ethnic divisions of sixteenth-century immigrant labor. And though compelled to acknowledge that "not much research seems to have been done on the ethnic distribution of the urban working class of early modern Europe," he goes on to speculate that Kazimiery Tymimecki's description of systematic ethnic distinctions of rank within the working class "in the towns of sixteenth-century East Elba . . . [is] typical of the whole of the world economy."[101] Despite the paucity of studies there are historical records that tend to confirm this view. We discover in them Flemish cloth workers in early sixteenth-century London; and later in the sixteenth and in the seventeenth century, Huguenot refugees (40,000–80,000 of them), many of them handloom weavers, fleeing France and settling in Spitalfields in London's East End and thus, establishing England's silk industry.[102] In the eighteenth and nineteenth centuries, Irish workers "formed the core of the floating armies of labourers who built canals, the docks, the railways and transformed the face of England."[103] And again on the European Continent, as German farm workers and peasants were drawn to urban and industrial sectors of central and western Germany, Polish labor was used to fill the vacuum in eastern Germany.[104] France and Switzerland also recruited heavily from Poland, Italy, and Spain.[105] And, of course, the formation of industrial cores in the United States before the Civil War located immigrant workers from northern Italy, Germany, Scotland, and Ireland; and after the Civil War from southern Italy, and the lands of eastern, northern, and central Europe: Russia, Finland, Poland, Greece, and the Balkans.[106] (Perhaps the only unique aspect of north American industrial recruitment was the appearance of Asian workers beginning in the late nineteenth century, from China, Japan, and the Philippines.)[107]

We begin to perceive that the nation is not a unit of analysis for the social history of Europe. The state is a bureaucratic structure, and the nation for which it administers is more a convenient construct than the historical, racial, cultural, and linguistic entity that the term "nation" signifies.[108] The truer character of European history resides beneath the phenomenology of nation and state. With respect to the construction of modern capitalism, one must not forget the particular identities, the particular social movements and societal structures that have persisted and/or have profoundly influenced European life:

> Altogether western Europe had acquired a greater richness of forms, of corporate life, a greater crystallization of habits into institutions, than any known elsewhere. It had a remarkable ability to forge societal ties, more tenacious than almost any others apart from those of the family and its extensions, clan or caste; ties that could survive from one epoch to another, and be built into more elaborate combinations. But along with fixity of particular relationships went a no less radical instability of the system as a whole.[109]

European civilization is not the product of capitalism. On the contrary, the character of capitalism can only be understood in the social and historical context of its appearance.

The Effects of Western Civilization on Capitalism

The development of capitalism can thus be seen as having been determined in form by the social and ideological composition of a civilization that had assumed its fundamental perspectives during feudalism. The patterns of recruitment for slave and mercenary we have reviewed held true for bourgeoisies and proletariats. According to Robert Lopez, in the Carolingian Empire long-distance trade was dominated by Jews and Italians.[110] In medieval Europe, Lopez and Irving Raymond have documented the importance of Mediterranean traders at international fairs, and the development of foreign merchant houses in the towns of the hinterland.[111] Fernand Braudel amplifies:

[M]any financial centres, *piazze*, sprang up in Europe in towns that were of recent origin. But if we look more closely at these sudden, and quite considerable developments, we shall find that they were in fact ramifications of Italian banking that had by then become traditional. In the days of the fairs of Champagne it was already the bankers from Sienna, Lucca, Florence, or Genoa who held the moneychanger's scales; it was they who made the fortune of Geneva in the fifteenth century and later those of Antwerp, Lyons, and Medina del Campo. . . .

In short, throughout Europe a small group of well-informed men, kept in touch by an active correspondence, controlled the entire network of exchanges in bills or specie, thus dominating the field of commercial speculation. So we should not be too taken in by the apparent spread of "finance."[112]

For Spain under Charles V (1516–56) and Philip II (1556–98), the German Fuggers, the Genoese, and other "international merchant firms" organized the state revenues, exploited mines, and administered many of the most important estates.[113] And at Constantinople, Genoese, Venetian, and Ragusan bankers and merchants shepherded the trade and financial relations between Europe and the Ottoman Empire.[114] For the Mediterranean towns of the sixteenth century, Braudel has observed the functions of the "indispensable immigrant." To Salonica, Constantinople and Valona, Italian and Spanish Jews, as merchants and artisans, brought new trades to further broaden an already multicultured bourgeoisie.

There were other valuable immigrants, itinerant artists for instance attracted by expanding towns which were extending their public buildings; or merchants, particularly the Italian merchants and bankers, who activated and indeed created such cities as Lisbon, Seville, Medina del Campo, Lyons and Antwerp.[115]

And in Venice:

A long report by the *Cinque Savii*, in January, 1607, indicates that all "capitalist" activity, as we should call it, was in the hands of the Florentines, who owned houses in the city, and the Genoese, who provided silver, between them controlling all exchanges.[116]

Just as Nuremberg had ravaged Bohemia, Saxony, and Silesia, Braudel asserts, it was the Genoese who "blocked the development of Spanish capitalism."[117] It was, too, the "indispensable immigrant" who complemented the urban proletariat incapable of maintaining itself "let alone increas[ing] without the help of continuous immigration."[118] In Ragusa it was the *Morlachi*; in Marseilles, the Corsicans; in Seville, the

Moriscos of Andalusia; in Algiers, the Aragonese and the Berbers; in Lisbon, Black slaves; and in Venice, the immigrant proletariat was augmented by *Romagnoli, Marchiani*, Greeks, Persians, Armenians and Portuguese Jews.[119]

The bourgeoisie that led the development of capitalism were drawn from particular ethnic and cultural groups; the European proletariats and the mercenaries of the leading states from others; its peasants from still other cultures; and its slaves from entirely different worlds. The tendency of European civilization through capitalism was thus not to homogenize but to differentiate—to exaggerate regional, subcultural, and dialectical differences into "racial" ones. As the Slavs became the natural slaves, the racially inferior stock for domination and exploitation during the early Middle Ages, as the Tartars came to occupy a similar position in the Italian cities of the late Middle Ages, so at the systemic interlocking of capitalism in the sixteenth century, the peoples of the Third World began to fill this expanding category of a civilization reproduced by capitalism.[120]

As a civilization of free and equal beings, Europe was as much a fiction in the nineteenth century (and later) as its very unity had been during the Merovingian and Carolingian eras. Both the church and the more powerful nobilities of the Holy Roman Empire and its predecessor had been the source of the illusion in those earlier periods. From the twelfth century forward, it was the bourgeoisie and the administrators of state power who initiated and nurtured myths of egalitarianism while seizing every occasion to divide peoples for the purpose of their domination.[121] The carnage of wars and revolutions precipitated by the bourgeoisies of Europe to sanctify their masques was enormous.

Eventually, however, the old instruments gave way to newer ones, not because they were old but because the ending of feudalism and the expansion of capitalism and its world system—that is the increasingly uneven character of development among European peoples themselves and between Europeans and the world beyond—precipitated new oppositions while providing new opportunities and demanding new "historical" agents. The Reformations in western Europe and then England that destroyed the last practical vestiges of a transcendent, unified Christendom, were one manifestation of this process of disequilibrium.

In England, as an instance, representatives of the great landowners, and agrarian capitalism, in pursuit of their own social and financial destinies disciplined first the church and then the monarchy and finally "the masses" through enclosures, the Poor Laws, debtors' prisons, "transportation" (forced emigration), and the like.[122] The contrasts of wealth and power between labor, capital, and the middle classes had become too stark to sustain the continued maintenance of privileged classes at home and the support of the engines of capitalist domination abroad. New mystifications, more appropriate to the times, were required, authorized by new lights. The delusions of medieval citizenship, which had been expanded into shared patrimony and had persisted for five centuries in western Europe as the single great leveling principle, were to be supplanted by race and (to use the German phrase) *Herrenvolk*, in the seventeenth and eighteenth centuries.[123] The functions of these latter ideological constructions were related but different. Race became largely the rationalization for the domination, exploitation, and/or extermination of non-"Europeans" (including Slavs and Jews). And we shall have occasion in Part II to explore its applications beyond Europe and particularly to African peoples more closely. But while we remain on European soil, it is *Herrenvolk* that matters. In eighteenth-century England, Reginald Horsman sees its beginnings in the "mythical" Anglo-Saxonism that was flown as an ideological pennant by the Whig intelligentsia.[124] In France (for example, Paul de Rapin-Thoyras and Montesquieu, and before them François Hotman and Count Henri de Boulainvilliers), in Germany (Herder, Fichte, Schleiermacher, and Hegel), in north America (John Adams and Thomas Jefferson), "bourgeois" ideologists displayed the idea of the heroic Germanic race.[125] And the idea swept through nineteenth-century Europe, gathering momentum and artifice through such effects as Sir Walter Scott's historical novels and Friedrich von Schlegel's philological fables. Inevitably, of course, the idea was dressed in the accoutrement of nineteenth-century European science. *Herrenvolk* explained the inevitability and the naturalness of the domination of some Europeans by other Europeans. Though he reconstructed the pieces back to front, Louis Snyder, for one, recognized the effect.

> Racialists, not satisfied with merely proclaiming the superiority of the white over the coloured race, also felt it necessary to erect a hierarchy within the white race itself. To meet this need they developed the myth of the Aryan, or Nordic, superiority. The Aryan myth in turn became the source of other secondary myths such as Teutonism (Germany), Anglo-Saxonism (England and the United States), and Celticism (France).[126]

Then, in the nineteenth century, modern nationalism appeared.

The emergence of nationalism[127] was again neither accidental nor unrelated to the character that European capitalism had assumed historically. Again, the bourgeoisie of particular cultures and political structures refused to acknowledge their logical and systemic identity as a class. Instead, international capitalism persisted in competitive anarchy—each national bourgeoisie opposing the others as "natural" enemies. But as powerful as the bourgeoisie and its allies in the aristocracy and bureaucracy might be in some ways, they still required the co-optation of their "rational" proletariat in order to destroy their competitors. Nationalism mobilized the armed might they required to either destroy the productive capacities of those whom they opposed, or to secure new markets, new labor, and productive resources.[128] Ultimately, the uneven developments of national capitalisms would have horrifying consequences for both Europe and the peoples under European dominations.

In Germany and Italy, where national bourgeoisies were relatively late in their formation, the marshaling of national social forces (peasants, farmers, workers, clerics, professional classes, the aristocracy, and the state) was accomplished by the ideological phantasmagoria of race, *Herrenvolk,* and nationalism. This compost of violence, in its time, became known under the name of fascism.[129] With the creation of fascism, the bourgeoisie retained the full range of its social, political, and economic prerogatives. It had the cake of the total control of its national society, an efficient instrument for expanding its domination and expropriation to the Third World, and the ultimate means for redressing the injuries and humiliations of the past. Again, not unexpectedly, slavery as a form of labor would reappear in Europe.[130]

But this goes far beyond our immediate purposes. What concerns us is that we understand that racialism and its permutations persisted, rooted not in a particular era but in the civilization itself. And though our era might seem a particularly fitting one for depositing the origins of racism, that judgment merely reflects how resistant the idea is to examination and how powerful and natural its specifications have become. Our confusions, however, are not unique. As an enduring principle of European social order, the effects of racialism were bound to appear in the social expression of every strata of every European society no matter the structures upon which they were formed. None was immune. And as we shall observe in the next two chapters, this proved to be true for the rebellious proletariat as well as the radical intelligentsias. It was again, a quite natural occurrence in both instances. But to the latter—the radical intelligentsias—it was also an unacceptable one, one subsequently denied. Nevertheless, it insinuated itself into their thought and their theories. And thus, in the quest for a radical social force, an active historical subject, it compelled certain blindnesses, bemusements that in turn systematically subverted their analytical constructions and their revolutionary project. But this is still to be shown. To that end we will now turn to the history of the English working classes. Since these workers were one of the centerpieces for the development by radical intelligentsias of the notion of the proletariat as a revolutionary class, an inquiry into the effects of racialism on their consciousness forms the next step in the demonstration of the limits of European radicalism.

CHAPTER 3

THE ENGLISH WORKING CLASS AS THE MIRROR OF PRODUCTION

Until quite recently much of what was generally known about the appearance of the industrial working classes in England and presumed about the development of class consciousness among them was enveloped by ideological mists and historical simplifications. This may be because the creators of heroic sagas of tragedy and triumph—whether of the liberal or radical sort—frequently find close attention to history confining. Historical inquiry, however, does have its rewards, often unexpected ones. Nevertheless, no small amount of historical consideration had been given to the English working classes. From these abundant materials we will attempt a comprehension of the material and social factors that impinged on the development of working-class consciousness—the mirror of production—and the forms it assumed in the eighteenth and nineteenth centuries. We shall be guided, hopefully, less by what we have been led in the abstract to expect *should* have occurred than by what *did*. Expropriation, impoverishment, alienation, and the formations of class consciousness and expression will be treated not as abstractions or the residual effects of a system of production but as living categories. We are concerned with how real men and women (and children) experienced dislocation, poverty, and the exploitation of their labor and reacted to them; how they employed the intellectual and emotional inventories available to them to come to terms with their experience. For that purpose I shall endeavor to keep this inquiry to the framing declarations about the English working class made by E. P. Thompson twenty years ago: "[T]he working class made itself as much as it was made." Further, he summarized:

Class consciousness is the way in which the experiences are handled in cultural terms: embodied in traditions, value-systems, ideas and institutional forms. If the experience appears as determined, class consciousness does not. . . . [C]lass is defined by men as they live their own history, and, in the end, this is its only definition.[1]

And since I have argued that among these "cultural terms" was racialism, I shall hold Thompson to his word.[2] But first it is important to lay aside certain beliefs about the circumstances in which the English industrial working classes made their appearance.

When one reviews the appearance of socialism in the nineteenth century, we are repeatedly informed by its historians that the movement and its ideologies began with the Industrial Revolution and the French Revolution.[3] However, the ease by which so many students of socialism have arrived at this association between a multifaceted ideal and the twinned catalysts of modernity is somewhat dissipated by a closer look at the more concrete realities that lay behind these abstractions of sudden, irreversible change. The Industrial Revolution, for one, was never quite the phenomenon it has become in the hands of some of its historians and in the popular mind. Much has been questioned since the popularization of the phrase in Arnold Toynbee's *Industrial Revolution* (1884). Still the legend lingers.

One might begin by noting that the large-scale [technical] economic and social changes of the late eighteenth and early nineteenth centuries,[4] which are now most frequently referred to as the Industrial Revolution, affected the whole of Britain's Empire as well as parts of western Europe. This suggests that to comprehend the scale on which this "revolution" operated requires a sense that it involved more than the introduction of new techniques of production. The recruitment, training, and disciplining of labor, the transportation of goods and raw materials, the political and legal structures of regulation and trade, the physical and commercial apparatus of markets, the organization and instrumentation of communication, the techniques of banking and finance, these too would have already had to be of a character that could accommodate increased commodity production. Their appearance was hardly instantaneous. On the contrary, their formation was organically determined by the economic developments of previous centuries. Moreover, it is probable, as A. E. Musson has argued, that the appearance of industrial production was neither revolutionary (in the sense of a sudden, catastrophic change) nor uniquely British:

From a technological point of view . . . it may be said that the eighteenth century witnessed little that was really revolutionary, and that the early Industrial Revolution was, in fact, based largely on . . . previous advances; even the steam engine was a product of sixteenth and seventeenth century scientific theory and experiment, while in other fields older techniques, such as water-powered machinery, were developed and extended.

The majority of these technological developments from the late Middle Ages onwards appear to have been introduced into England from the Continent.[5]

Musson's interpretation is not generally shared, nor are the facts[6] he marshals to support his argument generally known. This is in large part a consequence of the tendency of most historians and analysts of the processes of industrialization to proceed along national (and much less frequently, subcontinental, i.e., western European) lines. Indeed, it is by no means rare for the reader to encounter in otherwise very careful studies, the statement—in some form—that *the* Industrial Revolution occurred in England: a popular proposition, which appears to stem from the confusion of the points of origin of technical rationalization for the sake of production with practical mechanical invention; and a further confusion of a national economy with the ultimate impact of practical invention on an economic system already extensively characterized by international production (e.g., English cotton, sugar). Regardless, the systematic and detailed study of the technical and social consequences of industrial production is still largely located in the historiography of late eighteenth- and early nineteenth-century Britain (though one should note that E. J. Hobsbawm is certainly correct that it would be more accurate to envision several industrial revolutions occurring subsequent to the initial period of the Industrial Age).[7]

Poverty and Industrial Capitalism

For the working classes in Great Britain, the immediate and terrible consequences of the Industrial Age are generally, if not precisely, known.[8] In purely economic terms, there is the direct evidence of the workhouses that began in the eighteenth century but achieved their more permanent character in the two decades following Rev. Robert Lowe's experiment in deterrent welfare in 1818 at Bingham.[9] Though pauperism (which Hobsbawm defines as "the permanent core of poverty"[10]) as we have suggested earlier was by no means a new phenomenon in England or western Europe before the eighteenth and nineteenth centuries, in England, at least, the numbers of paupers increased somewhat rapidly during this latter period. This seems to have been the direct result of both the interruption of rural life by the adoption of reaping and threshing machines, and by the policy of land enclosures inspired by agricultural capitalism that, between 1760 and 1810, included five million acres of common fields.[11] Elsewhere, in the industrial cores, unemployment accompanied the severe business cycles of the period.[12] The workhouse, whose truest function was to act as asylums of last resort for the poor, was one response of the ruling classes. Characteristically, this response was the rationalization of an almost total misperception of the basis of pauperism: the presumption that the dispossessed and unemployed lacked work discipline.[13]

The recurring cycles of unemployment in the first half of the nineteenth century were of a scale to give any observer pause. Hobsbawm's comments on the slump of 1826, and Henry Mayhew's observations of the rise of unemployment that would persist from 1847 to 1851 are instructive. Hobsbawm found the figures so startling that they can bear a good deal of deflation. They suggest that in the hard-hit areas of Lancashire between 30 and 75 per cent of the total population might have been destitute in the course of this slump; in the woollen areas of Yorkshire, between 25 per cent and 100 per cent; in the textile areas of Scotland, between 25 per cent and 75 per cent. In Salford, for instance, half the population was wholly or partly out of work, in Bolton about one third, in Burnley at least 40 per cent.[14]

Yet what Hobsbawm as a historian found difficult to accept, Mayhew as a contemporary observer (described by E. P. Thompson as "incomparably the greatest social investigator in the mid-century")[15] found matters of fact:

> [E]stimating the working classes as being between four and five million in number, I think we may safely assert—considering . . . particular times, seasons, fashions, and accidents, and the vast quantity of over-work and scamp-work . . . the number of women and children . . . continually drafted into the different handicrafts . . . there is barely sufficient work for the *regular* employment of half of our labourers, so that only 1,500,000 are fully and constantly employed, while 1,500,000 more are employed only half their time, and the remaining 1,500,000 wholly unemployed, obtaining a day's work *occasionally* by the displacement of some of the others.[16]

Moreover, when we are informed by Hobsbawm that paupers housed in the purposely punitive workhouses of the nineteenth century, though themselves victims of the applied disgust of their social and economic superiors, probably ate substantially better than significant proportions of farm-laborers and urban workers,[17] we are chastened from the too easily presumed distinctions between employed and unemployed labor and pauperism. All three constituted an underclass that extended into the ranks of skilled workers.[18]

Further evidence for the Industrial Age's impact on the British working class and the poor is to be found in the studies of housing (the term would presumably apply to conditions of survival ranging from the makeshift night shelters in the doorways, alleys, cellars, and streets of the towns and in the open fields beside village roads, the parish and union workhouses themselves and the worker cottages—structures quite different concretely and subjectively from the benign pastoralism now associated with the term),[19] morbidity, mortality, child-labor, the physical conditions of labor, and food consumption.[20] In general, the more reliable the data, the more firm is the impression of a progressively depressed population during the period under discussion. Still, all these figures are in some sense superficial to (though helpful for sensing) the real issue that is the *experience* of the men, women, and children who made up the English poor and working classes. Just what did they make of their lives?

Much of what can be measured is merely the conditions of their lives and not their social, moral, and ideological contents. The objective conditions, rhythms, and patterns of the proletarianization of English labor frame that experience, but do not determine it, thus the social eruptions of that class have persistently resisted a monotonic correlation.[21] In 1930, J. L. Hammond, who along with his colleague Barbara Hammond contributed so much to the history of British labor, put this point well enough to be repeated:

> [I]f we are considering the kind of social life that was created by the Industrial Revolution, we find that in one sense no class of work-people escaped the Industrial Revolution. For all workers alike there was the same want of beauty, the same want of playing fields or parks, the same want of pageants or festivals, the same speeding up of industry, the same absence of anything calculated to create what Sophocles called "the temper that buildeth a city's wall" . . . the ugliness of the new life, with its growing slums, its lack of beautiful buildings, its destruction of nature and its disregard of man's deeper needs, affected not this or that class of workers only, but the entire working-class population.[22]

In terms of the "happiness and unhappiness of men and women," Hammond would write elsewhere, "if you look at the life of the age of the Industrial Revolution . . . you are struck at once by its extraordinary poverty."[23]

The Reaction of English Labor

Hammond's view of the sort of concerns that focused the minds of the laboring classes as they came face to face with the dislocations of the industrial world is in part substantiated by the political and social movements among the underclass that so distressed the upper and middle classes of the earliest moments of this period. (In 1831, James Mill had written to an associate, "Nothing can be conceived more mischievous than the doctrines which have been preached to the common people.")[24] One quite obvious expression of working-class anger toward the impoverishment of their social lives and, as Hammond called it, "Imagination," is the movement to which Hobsbawm refers as the "machine breakers."[25] Distinguishing between those movements where attacks on private property and machinery were tactics designed to force concessions from employers, and those movements energized by workers "concerned, not with technical progress in the abstract, but with the practical twin problems of preventing unemployment and maintaining the customary standard of life, which included nonmonetary factors such as freedom and dignity,"[26] Hobsbawm linked the revolts that echoed the ideals initially recorded among the Spitalfields weavers in 1675. Hobsbawm tells us of successive generations of weavers at Spitalfields rioting in 1719 ("against wearers of printed calicoes"), in 1736, and again, in the 1760s, against machines; in 1778–80, machine-breakers appeared in Lancashire. Luddism, proper, appeared in 1802, peaked in the 1811–13 period (spinningjennys), before largely disappearing after the suppression of the farm labor machine-breakers in 1830 in the southern counties, in East Anglia, and the Midlands.[27] More interestingly, these Luddite movements not only reflected a resistance to the machine as a tool of capitalist production on the part of workers, but also served to reveal the existence of a broader social hostility to capitalist industry:

The fully developed capitalist entrepreneurs formed a small minority. . . . The small shop-keeper or local master did not want an economy of limitless expansion, accumulation and technical revolution. . . . His ideal was the secular dream of all "little men," which has found periodic expression in Leveller, Jeffersonian or Jacobin radicalism, a small-scale society of modest property-owners and comfortably-off wage-earners, without great distinctions of wealth or power. . . . It was an unrealizable ideal, never more so than in the most rapidly evolving societies. Let us remember, however, that those to whom it appealed in early nineteenth-century Europe made up the majority of the population, and outside such industries as cotton, of the employing class.[28]

A more critical confirmation of Hammond's thesis on the significance that must be attached to the subversion of the social and cultural integument of feudal society in Britain by the imposition of industrial production, is suggested elsewhere. It would appear that the ideological and social response of the English working classes to the immanent domination by a new social order was not restricted to class-specific or economistic behaviors. The class consciousness of English workers did not strictly adhere to the logic of working-class formation premised on capitalist exploitation and modeled by Marx from the histories of the French and English bourgeoisies.[29] Indeed, the more profound reaction to an industrial capitalist order found among English "producers" in the eighteenth and nineteenth centuries, largely deterred those political and social consequences of proletarianization that had already become the dogma of English radical thought and expectation in the years immediately following the Great Revolution in France. The development of Anglo-Saxon chauvinism, the earliest form of English nationalism, and the appearance of rather extreme forms of racism among the English working class determined the form and characteristics that English working-class consciousness assumed. The parochialisms of ethnocentrism and race hostility constituted a response that was both a native of and a consequence to the loss of precapitalist social integrations. Of the first, Anglo-Saxon chauvinism, George Rude would note:

[O]ne of the most remarkably persistent beliefs of all was that perfect "Liberties" had existed under the Saxon Kings and that these had been filched, together with their lands, from "freeborn" Englishmen by the invading Norman knights under William the Bastard in 1066. This myth of the "Norman Yoke" persisted until Chartist times [1840s] and was handed down by generations of Levellers, Whigs reared on "revolution principles," London eighteenth-century radicals and democrats nurtured on the more recent doctrines of "popular sovereignty" and the "rights of man."[30]

The existence of this "constantly recurring theme in popular ideology" in English social history eventually took the form of nationalism, but more particularly as a nationalism incorporating a virulent xenophobia. The processes behind the appearance of a racially conscious working-class nationalism require some rather close attention, if for no other reason than that they have been obscured in radical English histories written appropriately as responses to works less sympathetic to and less comprehensive of the conditions and struggles of the English industrial working classes.[31]

English society was the first to have developed an industrial proletariat among its working classes.[32] Yet well before the peaks of Luddite and Chartist protests and during the heyday of the earlier Owenite socialism, the supranationalist class identity that Thompson has noted among English workers and in the "heroic culture" they produced between the French Revolution and the defeat of Chartism (while demonstrating its erratic course) had begun its retreat before protonationalism.[33] This was one aspect of the "lost vision" of the English working classes in the 1830s, and one that Thompson was forced to reluctantly recognize:

> It is easy enough to say that this culture was backward-looking or conservative. True enough, one direction of the great agitations of the artisans and outworkers, continued over 50 years, was to *resist* being turned into a proletariat. When they knew that this cause was lost, yet they reached out again, in the Thirties and Forties, and sought to achieve new and only imagined forms of social control.[34]

It would reappear in the mid-1860s, but by then what would become the general labor union movement (replacing an earlier and explicit consciousness of a class struggle for political power) had so progressed as to be so much under the sway of labor bureaucrats that not even the direct intervention of Marx was sufficient to more than briefly deflect English working-class consciousness from nationalism.[35] Despite the evidence that in 1864, the year of the founding of the International Working Men's Association (the I.W.M.A., or First International), spokesmen for British labor addressed themselves publicly to what Royden Harrison characterizes as the "national liberation and unification movements in America, Italy and Poland," by 1871 the more persistent thrust of trade unionism was once more dominant:

> In 1871 Marx was opposed to an attempt at a proletarian revolution in Paris. But when it was made, his loyalty to the working class and his own past record left him no choice but to give it his unflinching support. By identifying the International with the Commune, Marx occasioned the break with the majority of English labour leaders and sealed the fate of the I.W.M.A., a course of action from which there was no honourable release. . . . Marx and the English trade union leaders disowned each other.[36]

The formulation of an explanation for the revival and dominance of trade-union consciousness among the English working classes is not a simple task. For one, it must take account of what Thompson terms the "counter-revolution" of the dominant classes that struck such decisive blows to working-class radicalism in 1834, 1835, and 1848;[37] it must also encompass the historical processes by which industrial forms of production were established in England, including the patterns of labor recruitment from the villages and countryside of England (and the subsequent forms of work discipline established to proletarianize the recruits), and the divisions of labor that characterized the international structure of British capitalism.[38] But perhaps most important to the understanding of the evolution of working-class nationalism in Britain, and more to the issue here, is the role another nationalism—Irish nationalism—played in the formative period of English working-class development and its concomitant construction of English working-class culture. Moreover, the part played by Irish workers in the revolts of English labor in the late eighteenth and early nineteenth centuries being the social and historical expression of Irish nationalism, must also be noted.

The Colonization of Ireland

As far as the English ruling classes might have been concerned, the nineteenth century was inaugurated by the Irish Rebellion of 1798.[39] Having already survived the American and French Revolutions, the "immovable object," Ireland and what the English termed "the Irish Question," became "the biggest issue in late-Victorian politics, as perhaps it had been for most of the century."[40] In any case, their response to what they perceived as a particularly pernicious manifestation of Jacobin conspiracy and French interference was to dissolve what had passed for an Irish parliament and to declare in 1800 an Act of Union between Ireland and the United Kingdom.[41] In effect, the English state was setting aside the ineffective structures and instrument of indirect rule for those of a more direct and familiar domination.[42] This substitution of one set of institutions for another, in the long view, proved to be indifferent for the purposes of the English state though it logically followed the evident interests of English capital and Anglo-Saxonist ideology.[43] The Irish Question became much more a part of the nineteenth century than it had been for the eighteenth. It would appear, however, that its character had been fixed long before.

James Anthony Froude, in his history of *The English in Ireland*, provides his reader with what is both a detailed political history and a demonstration of the extent and sort of images of the Irish that had become fixed in the minds of Englishmen. Froude began by informing his reader that when the "military aristocracy" of the Normans invaded Ireland in the twelfth century, "the Irish . . . were, with the exception of the clergy, scarcely better than a mob of armed savages."[44] Having defeated the defenders of the island, Froude continues, the Normans had three courses of action toward the conquered peoples: extermination, armed occupation, or armed colonization.[45] The Normans, Froude laments, chose an entirely different path:

> The Normans in occupying both England and Ireland were but fulfilling the work for which they were specially qualified and gifted. . . . They did not destroy the Irish people; they took the government of them merely, as the English have done in India, dispossessing the chiefs, changing the loose order of inheritance into an orderly succession, giving security to life and property, and enabling those who cared to be industrious to reap the fruits of their labours without fear of outrage

and plunder. Their right to govern lay in their capability of governing and in the need of the Irish to be governed.[46]

The end result was an unfortunate one for the civilizing mission of the Normans. Instead of extending "English" civilization to the inhabitants of the island, the conquered people absorbed their Norman rulers racially, culturally, and politically.[47] By the second half of the fourteenth century, England having undergone the disasters detailed above, judicial, and political attempts at ensuring a specifically Anglo-Norman presence in the four counties of the English Pale (Dublin, Meath, Kildare, and Louth) were in actuality indications of the futility of the designs that had followed the conquest. Indeed, the term "conquest" was a conceit of English political history. With respect to their political relations with England, Ireland, and more precisely the Pale, staggered between indirect rule and home rule, depending on the resources of the English state, the preoccupations of English feudal society, and the capacities and proclivities of various feudal lords in Ireland to command national or English loyalties. In brief, such was the situation until the sixteenth century. In economic, and often in political terms, feudal Ireland was almost entirely independent from England.

This mode of English sovereignty in Ireland was to be initially pierced during the reign of Henry VII (1485–1509), and finally reshaped altogether during that of Henry VIII (1509–47). Between these first two kings of the Tudor Dynasty (1485–1603), English policy toward Ireland managed to produce a bizarre series of results: an administrative unification of Ireland under the Earl of Kildare (a Celticized Norman family); the fomenting of a rebellion led by Kildare as the champion of Catholicism following the rupture of the English state with the Papacy; and with the suppression of rebellion and the execution of some of its leaders, a new subjugation of Ireland and its most powerful families. The stabilization of the English feudal monarchy had brought with it the possibility of transforming Ireland into an English colony.[48]

Once Elizabeth I (1533–1603) was established on the English throne—following the brief and chaotic reigns of her siblings, Edward VI (1547–53) and Mary I (1553–58)— English policy toward Ireland, not for the first or last time, changed dramatically:

> The English set upon the plan of putting Ireland to plantation as the best means to subdue the island. The most extensive of these plantations was to be that in Londonderry, established in 1608, and roughly contemporaneous to the Virginia Plantation. Englishmen and lowland Scotsmen were lured to Ireland by the promise of free land. Their job was to drive the Irish into the woods and fortify their own villages.[49]

The suppression of the rebellions that followed (the major rebellions were led by Shane O'Neill in 1559, the Fitzgeralds of Desmond between the years 1568–83, and by O'Neill, the former earl of Tyrone, and O'Donnell from 1594–1603),[50] required such extensive expenditures that at least one historian, R. D. Edwards, surmises that "the poverty of the crown, which was a serious factor in the seventeenth-century conflict with parliament, was at least in part due to commitments over Ireland."[51] Whether this was the case or not, a more lasting pacification of Ireland was not achieved until the final years of Elizabeth's reign, despite the persistence of legends which put it otherwise:

> The reputation of the Elizabethan settlers, won for the most part in other fields, remains; but their Irish enterprise, lacking all sustained sense of purpose, proved deservedly transient. And so in succeeding centuries the sombre tale of Plantation, of rebellion, of Cromwellian violence, of civil and religious war, of the Penal Code, mocked the illusion of a final Elizabethan settlement.[52]

Though it was Elizabeth's administration that had initiated the policy, it was under James I (1603–25) that the colonization of Ireland by planters and farmers from Scotland and the western counties of England assumed significant proportions (first in Ulster, and then proceeding to the alienation of Irish lands in north Wexford, Longford, and Leitrim). By 1641, that is in the midst of the reign of James's successor, Charles I (1625–49), William Petty, the seventeenth-century English economist and statistician, would estimate that there were 260,000 Undertakers (as the Protestant colonists were called) among the one and a half million people living in Ireland.[53] It was also in this year that the Irish rebelled again, mounting the most serious and lethal effort to reject English rule since the Conquest. In English historiography, this rebellion became known as the massacre of 1641. This rebellion was to last for 11 years, a fire that ultimately had to be attended to by Cromwell himself. What followed was what Froude, with inadvertent irony, would have us know as the Penal Era (1652–1704).[54] It would be during this latter period that Ireland assumed the characteristics that typified the Irish experience until the early twentieth century:[55] colonized, absentee land ownership; Catholic persecution and Protestant privilege; the land alienation of its laboring classes; the corrupt and punitive administrations and official terror. It was again during this Penal Era that much of the restrictive legislation written by the English parliament would appear to complete the derationalization of the Irish economy:[56] acts against the marketing of Irish cattle in England, 1681; against Irish woolens and colored linens, 1699; and against glass, 1746. Once these policies had accomplished their purpose, free trade could be re-established:

> By 1801, free trade between Great Britain and Ireland was a reality; however, Irish industry, with one exception—linen, could not withstand English competition. After the Union, Ireland, therefore, became more rural, more agricultural, more economically specialized than it had been previously.[57]

Ireland had been transformed into a dependent sector of the English economy. Such were the historical experiences that informed Irish nationalism in the eighteenth, nineteenth, and twentieth centuries. The psychic and intellectual characters of the Irish workers who emigrated to England in the eighteenth and nineteenth centuries to complement the labor of the emergent English proletariat were determined to a large extent by these same events. Certainly, the social and political relations of the immigrant Irish workers with their English counterparts were severely constrained by a past consisting of almost unmitigated hostility between the interests that had come to be identified with their respective national entities.

English Working-Class Consciousness and the Irish Worker

The Irish immigrant was an important element in the industrial English working class (by 1841, 400,000 Irish-born immigrants were living in Great Britain).[58] He was, as Thompson describes the Irish worker of the early nineteenth century, "the cheapest labour in Western Europe."[59] Irish workers were recruited and used to fill

> the heavy manual occupations at the base of industrial society [which] required a spendthrift expense of sheer physical energy—an alternation of intensive labour and boisterous relaxation which belongs to preindustrial labour-rhythms, and for which the English artisan or weaver was unsuited both by reason of his weakened physique and his Puritan temperament.[60]

Still Thompson's explanation for the need to complement the English working classes was not the rationale that prevailed at the time. Engels was much closer to the English manufacturing class, and perhaps more accurate in his assessment of their motives when he observed that "the Irish have . . . discovered the minimum of the necessities of life, and are now making the English workers acquainted with it."[61] For whatever it is worth, it would have been inconsistent with the tenets of Anglo-Saxonism to detach the English worker from a racial hierarchy that was quite adequate in locating the deficiencies of the Irish "race."[62] The Irish worker having descended from an inferior race, so his English employers believed, the cheap market value of his labor was but its most rational form.

Setting aside for the moment popular prejudices, the English working classes, especially those at the industrial cores of English industry, had more occasion than their superiors to form very different attitudes toward their Irish counterparts. Indeed, in the early nineteenth century, the opportunities for the formation of successful social movements built on Irish and English workers were frequent and seemed promising. Irish labor leaders took prominent roles in working-class agitation in England (in the Chartist movement for example)[63] and it is a widely held belief that working class movements and organizations in England in general were modeled from Irish organizational methods.[64] The extent to which the direction of a unified and radical working-class movement had been realized and subsequently so easily dispatched in the early nineteenth century, has troubled at least one historian of the period so deeply that it has occasioned uncharacteristic speculation. E. P. Thompson, reviewing the observations that Engels had made on the positive (revolutionary) effects consequent to the mixture of the two "races" in the working class ("the more facile, excitable, fiery Irish temperament with the stable, reasoning, persevering English"),[65] himself paused to reflect on the political possibilities that English capitalist production had inevitably produced:

> It was an advantage to the employers, at a time when precision engineering co-existed with tunnelling by means of shovel and pick, to be able to call upon both types of labour. But the price which had to be paid was the confluence of sophisticated political Radicalism with a more primitive and excitable revolutionism. This confluence came in the Chartist movement. . . . Once before, in the 1790s . . . it seemed possible that English Jacobinism and Irish nationalism would engage in a common revolutionary strategy. If O'Connor had been able to carry Ireland with him as he carried the north of England, then the Chartist and "Young Ireland" movements might have come to a common insurrectionary flash-point.[66]

Chartism, however, proved to be the high point of cooperation between the Irish and English elements of the working classes in England.[67] This movement, organized behind a People's Charter, the platform of universal suffrage, annual parliaments, and parliamentary salaries; and represented by demonstrations, petitions, riots, and rebellions, though neither politically nor ideologically homogeneous, had once held the promise of an enduring organization. Instead, it collapsed totally, from within and without. After the late 1840s, the tentative efforts that might have resulted in a politically significant class solidarity were frustrated by events of both political and economic character.

In England itself, the defeat of the Chartist protests came with the extent and kind of reaction of the English ruling classes aptly recounted by Thompson:

> [I]t was the organ of middle-class Radicalism, *The Times*, which led the outcry for examples of severity. The advice was followed: "On the 9th of January [1831], judgment of death was recorded against twenty three prisoners, for the destruction of a paper machine in Buckingham; in Dorset, on the 11th, against three, for extorting money, and two for robbery; at Norwich, fifty-five prisoners were convicted of machine-breaking and rioting; at Ipswich, three, for extorting money; at Petworth, twenty-six for machine-breaking and rioting; at Gloucester, upwards of thirty; at Oxford, twenty-nine; and at Winchester, out of upwards of forty convicted, six were left for execution. . . . At Salisbury, forty-four prisoners were convicted."

And it was a Whig Ministry again that sanctioned, three years later, the transportation of the laborers of Tolpuddle in Dorsetshire, who had had the insolence to form a trade union.[68]

Following this era of overt class warfare and its accompanying persecution, the English working class, as we have seen, turned toward trade unionism as its primary form of activity. In part, this was also a reflection of the social consequences concomitant to the growth of English trade and production. The English worker in the second half of the nineteenth century began to enjoy certain of the perquisites of a labor aristocracy in a world system.[69]

In Ireland, the late 1840s was the time of the great harvest disasters that came to be known as the Potato Famine or the Great Hunger. Its immediate consequences were both the momentous emigration from Ireland to the United States and the precipitation of an even more extreme nationalism among Irishmen both home and abroad.[70]

Together, these political and economic setbacks—on the one hand to English and Irish industrial workers, and on the other to Irish farmers, peasants, and industrial workers in Ireland—resulted in both an ideological and physical drifting apart of the two "races." From the mid-nineteenth century on, among English workers, the ideology of English nationalism gained ascendancy over the counterideology of international class solidarity and socialist hopes. This was a part of a conservative reaction (trade unionism) to political defeat and economic growth, but it also had to do with the radical directions the Irish working classes (and the nationalist Irish middle class) had taken.[71] As Marx had often stated in one fashion or another: "The English working class will *never accomplish anything* before it has got rid of Ireland."[72] Early on, of course, it had been the presence of the Irish immigrant as a distorting and depressive element in the labor market that had produced markedly anti-Irish sentiment among English workers. This hostility had merely confirmed and complemented the racial feeling extant among England's ruling classes, the historical bases of which we traced above. Later, from the 1850s on, the development of sympathy among English workers toward Irish nationalism became even more remote with the appearances of Irish Radical (middle-class) nationalism—the Home Rule movement—and the more radical peasant and working-class nationalist movement that assumed the form of a revolutionary agrarian movement.[73] By the end of the nineteenth century, the English people were at one with respect to the Irish Question. Wherever exceptions existed, they were associated with political weakness and inconsequentiality.

The Proletariat and the English Working Class

The terms "English" and "Irish" have been used in the preceding discussion for convenience. It would have been most difficult to be both precise while treating the subject at an appropriate length. One hopes, however, that such conveniences have not escaped the reader's attention, given the consistent emphases here on ethnic and cultural conservaticisms and their importance. Though Ireland is but a small island, the integration of the Irish peoples was by no means an accomplished fact by the time of the Great Famine and the major emigrations from Ireland in the nineteenth century. Indeed, some students of the emigrations are quite specific as to the regions, local cultures, dialect groups, and occupations from which successive emigrants were drawn and how these particularities influenced historical movements.[74] The Irish peoples had been in the process of achieving a national identity and a national culture since the Norman-led conquest. They had not done so when the time came for the mass relocation that has marked their collective history for the past 200 years. Theirs is, then, a national identity deeply marked by the Irish dispersion.

But even more to the point, we have seen that the generic terms "the English working class" or "the English proletariat" mask the social and historical realities that accompanied the introduction of industrial capitalism in England and its Empire. Social divisions and habits of life and attitude that predated capitalist production continued into the modern era and extended to the working classes located in Britain specific social sensibilities and consciousness. The English working class was never the singular social and historical entity suggested by the phrase. An even closer study of its elements—for we have merely reviewed the more extreme case with the Irish— would reveal other social divisions, some ethnic (Welsh, Scottish, and more recently West Indian and Asian),[75] some regional, and others essentially industrial and oc- cupational. The negations resultant from capitalist modes of production, relations of production, and ideology did not manifest themselves as an eradication of opposi- tions among the working classes. Instead, the dialectic of proletarianization disci- plined the working classes to the importance of distinctions: between ethnics and nationalities; between skilled and unskilled workers; and, as we shall see later in even more dramatic terms, between races. The persistence and creation of such opposi- tions within the working classes were a critical aspect of the triumph of capitalism in the nineteenth century.

Neither Marx nor Engels were unaware of the proletariat's failure to become a uni- versal class.[76] Both studied the Irish Question closely, were active in the attempt to resolve its destructive impact on the historical processes of English working-class formation, and commented on its import for future proletarian organization.[77] Nev- ertheless, the impact of their *experience* with the English proletariat on their *theory* of the proletariat's historical role appears to have been slight. Shlomo Avineri ob- serves that:

> The universalistic nature of the proletariat does not disappear in Marx's later writings, when his discussion concentrates mainly on the historical causes of the emergence of the proletariat. What was at the outset a philosophical hypothesis is verified by historical experience and observation: the universalistic nature of the proletariat is a corollary of the conditions of production in a capitalist society, which must strive for universality on the geographical level as well.[78]

This would appear to confirm one of Engels's more famous estimations of their work:

> Marx and I are ourselves partly to blame for the fact that the younger people sometimes lay more stress on the economic side than is due to it. We had to emphasize the main principle *vis-a-vis* our adversaries, who denied it, and we had not always the time, the place or the opportunity to allow the other elements involved in the interaction to come into their rights. But when it was a case of

presenting a section of history, that is, of a practical application, it was a different matter and there no error was possible.[79]

Engels was absolutely correct, though the instance to which he was immediately responding might deceive.

The distinction that Engels was making here between history[80] and theory can, at one level, be read as an attempt to differentiate between the functions of the publicist and the scientific philosopher. Such an interpretation would in fact trivialize Engels's intent. Like Marx, Engels understood that their attempt to construct a total system of "the materialist conception of history" would bear the imprint of their historical moment.[81] Not only ideology and philosophy but all human activity was of such a nature:

> We make our history ourselves, but, in the first place, under very definite assumptions and conditions. Among these the economic ones are ultimately decisive. But the political ones, etc., and indeed even the traditions which haunt human minds also play a part, although not the decisive one.[82]

What history demonstrated to Marx and Engels was that dialectical change was never a total negation of the conditions from which it generated, but a transformation of the meaning, intent, and directionality of the elements and forces of the preexisting whole. This meant that their work, itself the critique of "bourgeoise society" and industrial capitalism, would some day—when the material forces of society had progressed beyond their stage of development in the nineteenth century—be subject to criticism (negation). That which was ideological ("partial consciousness") in their study of history would be transcended by a *necessarily* higher form of social thought corresponding to its historical moment.

Perhaps the most obvious of the ideological constructs that appear in the work of Marx and Engels (and most of the Marxists who have followed them) are the notions of the proletariat as the revolutionary subject, and the class struggle between the proletariat and the bourgeoisie. They persist in Marxian thought in precisely the terms suggested by Isaiah Berlin:

> [T]he Marxist doctrine of movement in dialectical collisions is not a hypothesis liable to be made less or more probable by the evidence of facts, but a pattern, uncovered by a non-empirical historical method, the validity of which is not questioned.[83]

To comprehend this "haunting" of radical European thought, and its Eurocentrism, it becomes appropriate to review the socialist tradition from which Marx and Engels emerged and that had for its historical setting the late eighteenth century and the early nineteenth century. Here we will discover the groundings of the pattern that thrust European Marxism into an era for which it was not prepared: the modern world.

CHAPTER 3

SOCIALIST THEORY AND NATIONALISM

Scientific socialists have become accustomed to locating the source of their observational point on the modern era in the nineteenth century. But in truth it is the scientism of the nineteenth century to which they refer. It was the political and intellectual critique of capitalism—the opposition to the alienation of labor and the ordering of social life according to the dictates and requirements of private property that could be traced to nineteenth-century sources. On the other hand, their socialism had its ideological, analytical, and theoretical beginnings in even earlier times. As such, the beginnings of modern socialism, though likewise committed to the ultimate rationalization of society, were informed by a fundamentally different conception of the project than that socialism that resulted from the ideology's collision with German materialism industrial production, and the revolutionary events of the early nineteenth century.[1]

Prior to the nineteenth century, what has sometimes been referred to as the socialist vision was a species of the moral and architectonic traditions that had penetrated European thought in the form of ethical systems and considerations preserved from the civilizations of Egypt, ancient Greece, and Asia Minor. Norman Cohn states:

> Like the other phantasies which have gone to make up the revolutionary eschatology of Europe, egalitarian and communistic phantasies can be traced back to the ancient world.[2]

Christianity, of course, was an important conduit in the intervening ages. But interestingly enough, the growing power, wealth, and human properties of the church, an important focus of medieval socialism, did not obviate the retention and enunciation of communistic doctrine.[3] For more than a millennium and a half, often based upon specious ecclesiastical authority,

> it became a commonplace amongst canonists and scholastics that in the first state of society, which had also been the best state, there had been no such thing as private property because all things had belonged to all people.[4]

Indeed, the communal life was taught and practiced among both the monastic and lay lower orders of the church. The church thus incorporated the oppositions of feudal privilege and Christian dogma. Eventually, this contradiction would erupt, informing the heresies of the fourteenth century and beyond as well as the revolutionary eschatology of the numerous peasant revolts that occurred in the last Middle Ages.[5] Both the doctrine of primitive communalism and the movements of insurrection would become a part of the socialist tradition.[6] Surveying the history of feudal Europe, Marx and Engels recognized the predecessors of socialist praxis in such movements as the sixteenth-century Anabaptists in Germany, and in seventeenth-century England, the Levellers; Engels had called them forerunners of the "modern proletariat."[7] On their part, the historians of nineteenth-century socialist constructions place their points of origin quite firmly on French soil and among the sons and daughters of the most politically and intellectually mobile elements of the Third Estate: the bourgeoisie, the petit bourgeoisie, and the artisans.[8] Moreover, these historians of the socialist movement unanimously assert that the French Revolution (an event upon which there is less agreement among them) was the more dramatic of the two moments that spurred the development of socialist ideas. As we have already noted, somewhat peculiarly, the Industrial Revolution, that is, the appearance of a technologically vigorous and mechanically imaginative industrial capitalism as the second moment that allowed for the subsequent development of socialist thought, has been seen as an English phenomenon.

Socialist Thought:
Negation of Feudalism or Capitalism?

Just as the historical character of capitalist development and the working classes associated with that development can be better understood through the medieval civilization in which they were created, a similar task applies to the history of socialism. Socialism as an articulated opposition to social inequality and poverty was first addressed to the adaptation of bourgeois society to feudal structures. Socialist critiques of society were attempts to further the bourgeois revolutions against feudalism. It possessed then a moral character:

> The critique of property that arose with the liberalism of eighteenth-century France was not . . . geared to the industrial system at all. Aside from advocating that private property be eliminated, it had no economic orientation. Rather, the concern of

such a characteristic communist thinker of the era as Morelly was entirely moral, and the abolition of private ownership was for him simply the focal point of a rationalized social and political structure that would then bring about the moral regeneration of man.[9]

As Marx and Engels made obvious in *The Communist Manifesto* (as polemicists, their intention was to emphasize their differences with those socialist traditions that had preceded them, not to identify with them), the socialism with which they were contemporaries was generally founded on the attempt to distinguish and preserve the rights of property (bourgeois) from the wrongs of property (feudalism).[10] Socialism was an expression of the social and intellectual liberation and enlightenment of a strata of European societies for which the terrors of feudalism and the power of the Absolute State were no longer natural, immediate, or inevitable. As an ideology committed to the historical and providential force of science, reason, and rationality, it was largely an obviation of those ideologies and structures that had served to legitimate the manifold forms of feudal and imperial authority: caste hierarchies, aristocratic privilege, the absolute power of the prince (later, the state) over the peasantry, the authority and wealth of the church, and finally, the poverty and powerlessness of the masses.[11] The cause to which early socialism was addressed was the freeing of the secularized soul:

> The highest point attained by *contemplative* materialism, that is, materialism which does not comprehend sensuousness as practical activity, is the contemplation of single individuals in "civil society."[12]

To accept the notion, so frequently put forth, that early socialist thought was the ideological and theoretical negation of capitalist society (industrial capitalism during the stages of competitive and monopoly capitalism) is to presume a historical relationship that is not in evidence. As Schumpeter has so cleverly cautioned:

> [T]he question arises whether the economic interpretation of history is more than a convenient approximation which must be expected to work less satisfactorily in some cases than it does in others. An obvious qualification occurs at the outset. Social structures, types and attitudes are coins that do not readily melt. Once they are formed they persist, possibly for centuries, and since different structures and types display different degrees of this ability to survive, we almost always find that actual group and national behaviour more or less departs from what we should expect it to be if we tried to infer it from the dominant forms of the productive process. . . . Such facts Marx did not overlook but he hardly realized all their implications.[13]

The initial appearances of modern socialism and its forms are more closely related to feudal society than is suggested by the later shapes socialist thought would assume. Socialism began as one expression of the bourgeois society and the bourgeoisie that it came to oppose explicitly.

The materialist historicism of socialism is thus mistaken. That "nature" of socialism to which scholars like George Lichtheim[14] have devoted so much attention is a philosophical-ideological construct—an interpretation of the history of socialist *thought* that fixes on that variant of the tradition which was a response to the revolutionary failures of the mid-nineteenth century. Combined with the persistent thrust of Marx's materialism toward a positive science—the critique of the capitalist mode of production, and the political-historical myths of Leninist revolution, the dominant legend of the socialist tradition replaces a history of socialism. The function of the alternative "history" of socialism is to obscure the obvious: that the origins of socialist thought are not with the European proletariat but the middle classes.[15]

> It was not the working classes in Germany who were at the origin of socialist ideas. . . . [S]ocialist ideas were spread by a party of the intellectual elite, who saw the proletarian masses as a possible instrument of social renewal.[16]

Indeed, the history of European socialism is dotted by a consistent opposition to the practical activity and consciousness of proletarian classes. As Marx and Engels themselves declared:

> The question is not what goal *is envisaged* for the time being by this or that member of the proletariat, or even by the proletariat as a whole. The question is *what is the proletariat* and what course of action will it be forced historically to take in conformity with its own *nature*.[17]

The intelligentsia was by far the stratum most likely to discern that course of action. Of course, Lenin, in substituting the revolutionary party for the conscious proletariat, agreed with Marx and Engels, both theoretically and programmatically.[18] Unfortunately, neither of them recalled to any significant political purpose, Marx's warning, in 1851, of the nature of their own class as it was demonstrated in Paris of 1848:

> [O]ne must not form the narrow-minded notion that the petty bourgeoisie, on principle, wishes to enforce an egoistic class interest. Rather, it believes that the *special* conditions of its emancipation are the *general* conditions under which modern society can alone be saved and the class struggle avoided.
> . . . [T]he democrat, because he represents the petty bourgeoisie, therefore a *transition class*, in which the interests of two classes are simultaneously deadened, imagines himself elevated above class antagonism generally.[19]

As a class whose historical character included the ideological and administrative mediation of bourgeois rule and domination, the petit bourgeoisie tended to produce political and conceptual lattice-works from which its inevitably derivative authority might extend and absorb the whole of society.[20] So as utilitarianism and functionalism had served as bases for those elements of the petit bourgeoisie enveloped by bureaucracy, commerce, and the professions—that is, the mainstream of a capitalist social order—socialism became the pennant of those members of the petit bourgeoisie appalled by the cruel lack of restraint and the chaotically foreshortened vision of the bourgeoisie.

From Babeuf to Marx:
A Curious Historiography

The industrial working classes constituted a minority of the workers of England and France at the moments when modern socialism began to take form.[21] Indeed, much of the revolutionary agitation that marked this period was pushed forward by crowds dominated by artisans and shopkeepers. (Albert Soboul, for instance, indicates that though the most powerful element of the Third Estate of the French Revolutionary period was bourgeois, two-thirds of the order, that is its Jacobin wing, were artisans and shopkeepers.)[22] England and France (the latter as the most industrialized economy in continental Europe) were still essentially agrarian societies when their working-class movements assumed class-specific ideological and organizational forms in the 1830s and 1840s. Even then, for example, Rude speaks of the importance of "the survival of traditional ideas and values" in movements that were to come so close to power.[23] The relationship between the social movements of the lower classes and the socialist intelligentsia was at least ambiguous.

Students of socialism generally argue that the socialist tradition that would come to be closely identified with an industrial proletariat begins in 1795 with the Conspiracy of Equals in which François-Noel (Gracchus) Babeuf was so prominent.[24] G. D. H. Cole, with apparent approval, notes that:

> Babeuf's Conspiracy continued to be regarded by revolutionary Socialists, and is to-day regarded by Communists, as the first plain manifestation of the proletariat in revolutionary action, proclaiming from afar the new revolution which was destined to complete the work begun in 1789.[25]

Lichtheim, quite naturally, makes an identical remark before proceeding to the declaration of a direct legacy from Babeuf to Lenin:

> Babeuf and his associates appear as the precursors of nineteenth-century radicals like Blanqui and, at a remove, of the Russian revolutionary Populists of the 1860s and 1870s whose heritage was subsequently assumed by the Bolsheviks.[26]

Though Lichtheim's lineage may be problematic, certain similarities are obvious between the moments at which the Babeufists and the Bolsheviks emerged from their respective revolutionary situations. Since it is the Conspiracy of Equals that is likely to be the lesser known, some detail might be appropriate to demonstrate this apparent similarity.

By 1794, that is Year II of the French republic, the most radical of the several bourgeois-dominated governments established in Paris had been overthrown and its leading citizens (most prominently Robespierre) had been executed, exiled, or forced to flee to the countryside and beyond.[27] The reaction that followed, under the Directory, had abolished the radical legislation and the egalitarian policies of a directed economy decreed the year before.[28] The limitations on prices (the *maximum*), the taxation of the wealthy classes, national assistance to the poor, free and compulsory education, the confiscation and distribution to the poor of emigre property, were either repealed or discontinued in practice. As had been the case on several previous occasions since the aristocracy's power had been challenged, the revolutionary crowds of France's towns and cities, and the peasants in the countryside began to suspect that the Revolution was being betrayed.[29] This time the traitors were the reactionary bourgeoisie, those members of the class whose wealth and power the Revolution had already secured. The executions of the leaders of the Jacobin "left wing" of the Convention, removed from the Parisian *sans-culottes* those elements (the Montagnard) which had been most responsive to its demands. Those members of the left wing that had survived its repression had gone underground, frequently organizing themselves into secret societies and clubs. One such group was the remnant of the *Union du Pantheon*: the Conspirators. While Babeuf and his comrades were negotiating in 1796 with the Jacobin underground, they were betrayed by a military associate, Crisel, acting as a spy for the Directory.[30] At their subsequent trial in Year V (1797), the intent of the Conspiracy of Equals was revealed for the first time:

> [T]hey had projected a seizure of power by a small revolutionary group of leaders, who were then to establish a revolutionary government based on their following among the Parisian local societies, with the intention of summoning as speedily as possible a National Assembly, to be elected under the democratic franchise of the abortive Constitution of 1793, which had never been allowed to come into force.
>
> Pending the bringing into action of this Constitution, Babeuf and his followers proposed to establish a temporary dictatorship, based mainly on the Paris workers; but they had no theory of revolutionary—much less of proletarian—dictatorship as more than an expedient of transition over a short period to a fully democratic Constitution based on manhood suffrage. They did, however, propose to proceed immediately . . . to large measures of expropriation and redistribution of property holdings on a basis of communal appropriation and enjoyment of all goods.[31]

Such were the beginnings of the notion of proletarian dictatorship in European socialism. It is a heritage that tends to confirm Marx's later characterizations of the petit bourgeoisie while suggesting some of the political forms and consequence of such presumptions. It is also useful to note that at no point had the conspiracy become a popular or mass movement. Cole observes

> that Babeuf's movement [n]ever really took shape as a nationwide revolutionary campaign. It found its support, as the Jacobins had done, mainly in the larger towns and pre-eminently in Paris, where its following was attracted to it mainly by the conditions of scarcity and unemployment that followed upon the reluctance of emancipated peasants to keep the towns supplied with the necessaries of life. Nor

did it ever command more than a small fraction even of the urban proletariat. It was a conspiracy of a few who aimed at drawing after them the large elements of urban discontent arising mainly out of sheer hunger.[32]

It would be another thirty years before a working-class movement gave evidence of its influence, and much longer than that before the principles of a socialist society became dominant in European social movements.[33]

Following the execution of Babeuf and his co-conspirators, it is not until almost mid-century, the years noted for the appearance of Marx and Engels, that thinkers in the socialist tradition became actively engaged in working-class politics. The historians of socialist thought take this period for what it was, in relationship to their subject, and unanimously commit themselves to exegeses. The literary, pamphleteering, and historical works of forgotten and dimly remembered writers, with the rare interruptions of a Buonarroti, Blanqui, or Blanc, are sequenced to form the tapestry of socialist thought. It is a period dominated by eccentrics, visionaries, and didacts. The wistful trails of Godwin, Paine, Fourier, Saint-Simon, Cabet, Pecqueur, lesser and grander lights, preoccupy the historians, along with the most often short-lived utopian communities associated with some of them. The agitations, rebellions, riots, and struggles of artisans, wage laborers, peasants, and slave laborers are largely irrelevant to the tradition in the early nineteenth century and mostly constitute a background "noise" in this the era of the socialist writer. The "historical" issues that arise are each writer's contribution to socialist theory, and whether or not the "systems" that were constructed should properly be categorized as "socialist." This is a particularly telling historical project since so many of the historians, the Coles, Lichtheims, Beers, are themselves sympathetic to the tradition they reconstruct. Their work becomes a demonstration of the independence of socialist theory and social movements from one another. When once again they collide, in the 1840s, 1870s, and early 1900s, each had assumed forms and prerogatives only slightly tolerable to those of the other. While the movements of the working classes tended toward an accommodation with capitalism in the form of trade unionist demands, abandoning revolutionary initiatives to those whose social origins were, most often, the peasant and petit bourgeois classes, socialist theory became more and more dominated by the figure of the revolutionary proletariat.

Marx, under the influence both of his readings of Hegel and his intense encounters with a number of intellects of his own generation who had identified themselves as Hegelians (David Strauss, Bruno Bauer, Karl Koppen, Moses Hess, Lorenz von Stein, and Ludwig Feuerbach),[34] had sought to construct an epistemological system founded on materialism as a metatheoretic; the currency underneath social structures and forms:

> My inquiry led me to the conclusion that neither legal relations nor political forms could be comprehended whether by themselves or on the basis of a so-called general development of the human mind, but that on the contrary they originate in the material conditions of life . . . that the anatomy of this civil society . . . has to be sought in political economy.[35]

History, for Marx, became the antagonistic play of the relations of living social categories whose existence was predicated on the particular characters of production and property that had been the basis of social life.[36] Political economy was thus the most fundamental of historical inquiries. The materialist conception of history situated the objective and necessary forces of a society, distinguishing their significance from those categories of human activity that were the result of pure speculation (idealism) and ideology. As Marx's theoretical work proceeded, the progressive tendency to place the study of capitalist forms of production, exchange, and distribution at the center of his work became more and more pronounced. By 1847, capitalism had become his primary subject. His infrequent sojourns into the study of revolutions were dictated by their occurrence (he would write in 1850 articles later published as *The Class Struggles in France* and, in 1851, *The Eighteenth Brumaire of Louis Bonaparte* as studies of the 1848 revolutionary movement in France, and, in 1871, *The Civil War in France* as a statement of the Paris Commune of the same year) and the degree to which Marx believed them to be important testaments to the political and methodological efficacy of the materialist conception of history.[37]

Marx, Engels, and Nationalism

The bulk of the almost two decades that Marx spent on his "Economics," largely sandwiched between the revolutions of 1848 and the appearance of the rather more ambiguous "International" in 1864, though substantially marked by intensive research, writing, mathematical training, and theoretical development, was also a period of extreme frustration. Plagued by what he constantly referred to as "bourgeois" troubles (indebtedness, familial demands, and disruptions) and debilitating illnesses (carbuncles and boils),[38] Marx's celebrated temper and sometimes mean preoccupations propelled him into drawn quarrels, some petty but no less vicious (with Karl Vogt; Ferdinand Lassalle, "the dirty Breslaw Jew"; Giuseppe Mazzini; and even one, probably the only one, with Engels following the death of Mary Burns);[39] most the result of Marx's proprietary attitude toward a "party" (the Communist League), which he himself in 1860 had declared defunct since 1852.[40] One of these disputes, however, is particularly instructive here for it reveals in dramatic terms the ideological restraints and theoretical bounds that placed Marx and Engels at an especial disadvantage in their confrontation with the form of nationalism beginning to surface by the mid-nineteenth century. Because nationalism is the most important ideology of our time, its treatment by Marx and Engels and later Marxists can be informative both with respect to the essence of Marxist thought as well as the nature of ideology.

The nationalism in question was German, a nation from which Marx and Engels had been in enforced exile for several years. Exile, however, is hardly a satisfactory defense in this instance since Marx and Engels, as leaders of the German democratic (socialist) movement, were in almost daily touch with German correspondents. It is true that as émigrés from Germany, Marx and Engels can be expected to have drawn increasingly distant from the ambitions and moods of working-class organizations at home. Franz Mehring, one of Marx's most sympathetic biographers, notes that in Marx's and Engels's argument with Lassalle over the consequences for the German revolutionary struggle of a war between Germany (Prussia and the German League) and Italy (the Kingdom of Sardinia) and France, "the two friends had to pay for having lost touch with conditions in Germany for so long."[41] Given the world-historical scope that Marx and Engels attempted to achieve in their work, however, Mehring's intervention by interpretation appears excessively apologetic and not particularly instructive. He failed to come to terms with the political-ideological effect that Marx's notion of the logic of capitalist development would incur.

In brief, the situation was this. Neither Italy, Germany, or France (and for that matter Austria) had yet achieved territorial configurations that conformed to the ambitions of their ruling and military elites, nor the natural (ethnic and linguistic) affections of their nationalistic citizenry. Cavour, the Prime Minister of the Sardinian kingdom, had gradually been converted from a repressive antinationalist to an extremely skilled unificationist by the persistent development and growth of nationalist sympathy and organization both on the Italian peninsula and among the exiles his government had been so instrumental in relocating.[42] By the outbreak of the Crimean War in 1854, Cavour had become convinced that the French army would be the critical tool for the expulsion of Austria from central Italy and the achievement of a decisive advantage for Piedmont (continental Sardinia) over the Papal States (Cavour appears to have presumed the Kingdom of the Two Sicilies beyond his reach). Cavour saw to it that Sardinian troops accompanied the British and French armies when they invaded Russia in 1854. The Crimean War ultimately resulted in the weakening of both Austria and Russia, and at the peace conference in Paris (1856), Austria's Italian possessions (Venetia and Lombardy) became a matter for discussion as a breach of the Vienna settlement (1815). It appears that diplomatic considerations and the brutal and continuing suppression of Italian rebels by Austria had joined to make Austria's position in Italy untenable. By July 1858, Napoleon III, convinced on the one hand, as a Bonaparte, that Italy was ancestral country,[43] and on the other that French power required a larger destiny than that bounded by the defeat of his imperial uncle, had met secretly with Cavour[44] and agreed on a joint venture against Austria: Piedmont was to lure Austria into a declaration of war. The French army would intervene against the aggressor Austria. France would be rewarded by the ceding of the Savoy and Nice provinces; Sardinia, by incorporating Lombardy, Venetia, and the central Duchies, would become the Kingdom of North Italy. Mehring continues the story:

On New Year's Day, 1859, Bonaparte received the Austrian Ambassador in audience and informed him of the French intentions, whilst a few days later the King of Sardinia announced to the world that he was not deaf to the heart-rending appeals of the Italian people. These threats were perfectly understood in Vienna . . . the Austrian government was clumsy enough to let itself be manoeuvred into the role of attacker. Half-bankrupt, attacked by France and threatened by Russia, it was in a difficult position . . . so it therefore sought to win the support of the German League. . . . [I]t tried to persuade the League that the maintenance of Austrian oppression in Italy was a matter of vital national importance for Germany.[45]

In order to comprehend the response of Marx and Engels to this situation it is first necessary to know more about the Germany from which they came, and the Germany to which Austria appealed.

The defeat of the Napoleonic armies and the 1815 settlement of Vienna that followed, had not resulted in the reunification of Germany. The "Holy Alliance" of the Reich, whose most recent manifestation was an alliance between Prussia, the Confederation of the Rhine, and Austria, which had been dissolved in 1806, was entirely frustrated by a statesmanship whose architect was Austria's Metternich and that was dominated by the interests of Austria, Russia, and Great Britain. Between 1815 and 1866, Germany—the *Deutscher Bund*—consisted of 39 states or principalities (including the four free cities of Hamburg, Bremen, Lubeck, and Frankfurt).[46] Even during the War of Liberation (1812–15), the particularisms of the German principalities had been persistent, causing Johann Friedrich Bohmer's father to write to his son, the future historian, "Unhappily, those fighting for the great patriotic cause are not so much Germans as Bavarians, Wurttemberger, Hessians, Saxons, Nassauer, Wurzburger and even subjects of the petty state of Ysenburg."[47] Within the *Bund* (or League), Prussia emerged as the most powerful competitor to Austria on the basis of its army and its bureaucracy (a legacy of French rule).[48]

W. O. Henderson indicates that Germany, at the beginning of the nineteenth century, was much less industrialized than France. The industrialization of Germany really began in the 1830s and 1840s with the introduction of steam-powered machinery and the importation of skilled artisans from England (to operate mule-jennys in the cotton mills of Saxony, build textile machinery and steam-ships, and inaugurate power loom weaving in Lower Silesia).[49] Up through the mid-nineteenth century, however, Germany was still overwhelmingly agricultural. And despite an estimated 38 percent rise in population between 1815 and 1845,

> the proportions of town and country dwellers remained virtually unchanged. Few towns had recovered from the effects of the Thirty Years War and the stagnation of the eighteenth century, and at the beginning of the nineteenth century the total population of all the free cities and university towns of Germany was scarcely the equivalent of the population of Paris. Hence neither industrial capitalists nor industrial workers existed as a serious political force, and the towns were still, as in the eighteenth century, dominated by a professional and bureaucratic middle-class, which had little to gain by radical political change.[50]

Still, it was largely out of this middle class that early nineteenth-century liberalism and nationalism found their social base.[51] Barraclough, indeed, expressed some surprise that "radical and national feeling" would persist so long in Germany as to achieve popular support in the German revolutions of 1848. Yet when crowds of artisans and workers rose in Vienna and Berlin in that year, the liberal elements of the middle classes were not enthusiastic, choosing politically to abdicate their momentary advantage rather than provide any further momentum to the revolutions.[52] We shall see that Marx and Engels, as members of that generation and class that had committed themselves to the democratization and reunification of Germany, were thus deeply implicated and consequently ambivalent toward the events that affected these interests between the liberal defection of 1849 and the assumption of power in Prussia by Bismarck in 1862. Lichtheim is quite correct to observe that:

> Neither the Marxian theory of democracy nor the Marxian view of national evolution is fully comprehensible unless it is remembered that they took shape on the morrow of the worst defeat democracy and nationalism had yet suffered in Europe.[53]

When the liberal parliamentarians abandoned the attempt at democratic reforms in May 1849, the future of German liberalism and nationalism was remanded into the hands of the Prussian Junker class. The first, liberalism, was to be destroyed as a threat to that class, the second retained as a weapon of that class against Austrian ambitions:

> Bismarck . . . realized that, despite the setback of 1848–1849, German liberalism and nationalism supported by Austria were still a serious threat to Prussian particularism and Prussian aristocratic privilege. . . . Liberalism was fatal to the social order for which Bismarck stood; but nationalism, carefully handled, could be made to subserve the purposes of Prussia. . . . He separated German national aspirations from the liberal background which, from 1813 to 1848 and in centuries past, had given them meaning. Nationalism had grown strong as an instrument of liberal reform, as an essential means of breaking the stranglehold of particularist interest over the German people. . . . [H]e offered the German people unity, but at the expense of the radical reform which alone made unity worth while.[54]

Bismarck, as we know, was successful, but not on the basis of sheer energy or diplomatic acumen. The economic prosperity, between 1850 and 1871, of an industrializing Germany had made radical (that is liberal) reform less urgent,[55] while the ubiquitous international machinations and the persistent hostility of Napoleon III to German unity underscored the logic of nationalism. As we return to the first months of the war, these dynamics and their history should be kept in mind. And though the era of Bismarck takes us beyond the moment of the Italian war, some familiarity with these later events is useful since they indicate the momentum of certain social processes more clearly evident to Lassalle than to Marx or Engels.

Engels's reaction to the outbreak of war in 1859 between Austria, Sardinia, and France, and to the German nationalist movement that had attended the prelude of war, was to publish a pamphlet entitled *Po und Rhein*.[56] Lassalle acted for Engels as his German agent with Franz Duncker, while Marx gave his enthusiastic support to the project. In his pamphlet, Engels argued that though the Po river boundary was of no military significance to Germany (in these terms, Engels added, France's claims were more defensible), politically, the French encroachment on the Po was the beginning of an attempt to recapture the Rhine frontier. On this basis, Engels insisted, the Po was where Germany must make its stand with Austria. The pamphlet was published in Germany, anonymously, on the advice of Marx so as to give the impression that the author was probably a Prussian general—a stratagem that was apparently quite successful, to Marx's great satisfaction. He wrote to Engels, congratulating him on the fact that in his induced identity he was now being celebrated in their homeland as a military expert.[57] The intent of Marx and Engels, their "ulterior motive" as they put it, has been reconstructed by Mehring:

> First of all both Marx and Engels believed that the national movement in Germany was a really genuine one. . . . The instinct of the people demanded war against Louis Bonaparte as the representative of the traditions of the First French Empire, and this instinct was right.
>
> Secondly, they assumed that Germany was really seriously threatened by the Franco-Russian alliance. . . .
>
> And finally . . . [i]n their opinion the German governments needed goading on by the national movement, and what they then expected was described by Engels in a passage of a letter to Lassalle . . . : "Long live a war in which we are attacked simultaneously by the French and the Russians, for in such a desperate situation with disaster immediately threatening, all parties, from those which are now ruling to Zitz and Blum, would exhaust themselves, and the nation would then finally turn to the most energetic party in order to save itself."[58]

But what Mehring did not recognize as an important element of both Engels's and Marx's position was a fundamental historicism. Engels had made clear in *Po und Rhein* that the logic of capitalist development supported German nationalism but not Italian nationalism:

> All changes (in the map of Europe), if they are to last, must in general start from the effort to give the large and viable European nations more and more their true national boundaries, which are determined by language and sympathies, while at the same time the ruins of peoples, which are still found here and there and which are no longer capable of a national existence, are absorbed by the larger nations and either become a part of them or maintain themselves as ethnographic monuments without political significance.[59]

We shall return to the implications of this theme more than once.

Lassalle, we know already, disagreed with Marx and Engels. He quickly responded to Engels's essay by writing a pamphlet of his own, *The Italian War and Prussia's Task*. In it he urged the Prussian government to side with France and Italy against Austria on the grounds that "the complete destruction of Austria was the preliminary condition of German unity."[60] As he would inform Marx by letter, he wrote in this way so as to appeal to a public mentality (which he believed Marx and Engels to be unaware of) in order to discredit a policy (Prussian defense of Austria) that he believed inevitable:

> My dear Marx, You simply cannot conceive the idiocy of opinion here which is all for war with France, and which threatens to sweep away in its current even those democrats who are not thoroughly independent. I should regard the *popularity* of the war as a much greater misfortune than the war itself—and there can be no doubt that at the present moment a war would be extremely popular.
>
> . . . I have pointed out to the government an extremely national and popular way, which *in abstracto* it could very well follow, but which *in concreto* would prove utterly impracticable. For the very reason that the government will *not* take this course, it seems to me that I have found a means of making it fundamentally *unpopular*. I do not know whether you have read enough of the German news-papers to be well informed concerning the popular mood. The press is in full blast for the *devouring of all Frenchmen* and voices an *unqualified Gallophobia.* (Napoleon is a mere pretext; the underlying ground is the revolutionary development of France) . . . a war supported by a blind uprush of popular feeling would be most prejudicial to our democratic development.[61]

Lassalle, whose pamphlet was described by Marx as "an enormous blunder"[62] and "monstrously false,"[63] prompting Marx to observe to Engels that "we must now absolutely insist on party discipline or everything will be in the soup,"[64] was decidedly more insightful as to the nature of German nationalism than either Marx or Engels.[65] Mehring, largely free of the restraints that bound Lassalle to a solicitous concern for Marx's feelings, presented Lassalle's thesis with less discretion than Lassalle and in language much more appropriate:

> In his eyes a Franco-German war in which the two greatest Continental peoples would rend each other for mere nationalist delusions, a really popular war against France not prompted by any vital national interest, but nourished by pathologically irritated nationalism, high-flown patriotism and childish anti-Gallicism, was a tremendous danger to European culture and to all really national and revolutionary interests.[66]

Thus the dispute between Lassalle, Marx, and Engels had not merely raised questions as to the nature of the political relationship between them (that is whether Lassalle had the right to disagree publicly with an anonymously authored position) or the extent to which Marx and Engels were themselves victims of a Germanic chauvinism.[67] Certainly these were important issues, but they could just as well be understood as the inevitable excesses of personality and political ambition to which intellectuals such as Marx and Engels in the midst of a workers' movement fall prey.[68] More important, however, is the effect that political economy, the central analytical tool of their materialist conception of history, had on their ability to conceptualize correctly the ideological character of industrial social movements.

In Marx's historical view, the "genesis of the industrial capitalist" was inextricably tied to the development of the state. It was by means of the state that the proletariat came into being, transformed as producers from peasants to wage laborers,

> Thus were the agricultural people, first forcibly expropriated from the soil, driven from their homes, turned into vagabonds, and then whipped, branded, tortured by laws grotesquely terrible, into the discipline necessary for the wage system.[69]

and as consumers into the home market.

> The many scattered customers, whom stray artisans until now had found in the numerous small producers working on their own account, concentrate themselves now into one great market provided for by industrial capital. Thus, hand in hand with the expropriation of the self-supporting peasants, with their separation from their means of production, goes the destruction of rural domestic industry, the process of separation between manufacture and agriculture. And only the destruction of rural domestic industry can give the internal market of a country that extension and consistence that the capitalist mode of production requires.[70]

Having secured the home market, the further expansion of capitalism required of the state that it assume new forms and additional functions. "National debts, i.e. the alienation of the state—whether despotic, constitutional or republican—marked with its stamp the capitalistic era."[71] First in Holland, and subsequently in England (but with precedents in Genoa, Venice, Spain, and Portugal), the primitive accumulation of capital that was the basis for manufacturing had been accomplished through the agencies of a "colonial system, public debts, heavy taxes, protection, commercial wars, etc."[72]—all the attributes of state structures. Marx conceived the triumph of bourgeois society over feudalism as a victory won by the most extraordinary instrument of class struggle: the state. He was inclined, then, as we have already noted in Engels,[73] to see the nation (the manifest form of the state in the nineteenth century) as a sine qua non of bourgeois rule.[74] In turn, bourgeois rule and capitalist production were necessary for the development of the socialized production that the immanent society required.[75]

> The development of the industrial proletariat is, in general, conditioned by the development of the industrial bourgeoisie. Only under its rule does the proletariat gain that extensive national existence that can raise its revolution to a national one, and only thus does the proletariat itself create the modern means of production, which becomes just so many means of its revolutionary emancipation. Only bourgeois rule tears up the material roots of feudal society and levels the ground on which alone a proletarian revolution is possible.[76]

Marx had initially presumed (with an enthusiasm of youth, according to Lichtheim) that the bourgeoisie would reproduce itself everywhere, "In one word, it creates a world after its own image."[77] However, while Marx clearly envisioned the historical role of the bourgeoisie in world-historical terms,[78] he also maintained the contradictory view of its historical development as occurring in national terms.[79] The expansion of the bourgeoisie meant the extension of the nation-state:

The bourgeoisie keeps more and more doing away with the scattered state of the population, of the means of production, and of property. It has agglomerated population, centralized means of production, and has concentrated property in a few hands. . . . Independent, or but loosely connected provinces, with separate interests, laws, governments and systems of taxation, became lumped together into one nation, with one government, one code of laws, one national class-interest, one frontier and one customs tariff.[80]

It may be that at this stage of Marx's development, his universe consisting of western Europe might dissolve this contradiction through the vision of an immanent pan-European formation. It may be that his ideas demonstrated an unresolved strain between his predilection as an idealist-trained philosopher-theorist and his processes of inquiry as a social and historical analyst. Further, Marx may have already begun the tendency, much more obvious in his later work, to confuse and confound his theory of historical change by extrapolating from French social history a sense of the ultimate character of *class struggle* in capitalist society (in spite of the rather primitive development of industrial capitalism in France, the dominance of a maritime bourgeoisie, the presence of a capitalist aristocracy, and a working class more peasant and artisan than industrial proletariat) while determining the nature of *capitalism* from the more industrially developed England.[81] Last, as a propagandist, he may simply have been more concerned with the political impact of rhetoric on his audience than with analytical precision. Whichever of these explanations one chooses, none really reconciles the existence in the early work of two opposing views of the nature and character of bourgeois society. In time, Marx would relinquish one for the other.

Interestingly enough, Marx's disavowal of the genesis of capitalism in western Europe as a general "historico-philosophic theory" is best illustrated by letters written to Russian Marxists who, from the 1870s on, became engaged in controversies concerning the process of industrialization and social development that Russia should assume in order to achieve a social revolution. In November 1877, Marx drafted a letter (never sent) to the editors of the Russian socialist journal, *Otechestvenniye Zapiski*. He meant to object to the use a *Narodnik* author, N. K. Mikhailovsky, had made of his work in an attack on Marx's sympathizers in Russia. Marx wrote:

The chapter on primitive accumulation does not pretend to do more than trace the path by which, in Western Europe, the capitalist order of economy emerged from the womb of the feudal order of economy. . . . That is all. But that is too little for my critic. He feels he absolutely must metamorphose my historical sketch of the genesis of capitalism in Western Europe into a historico-philosophic theory of the general path every people is fated to tread, whatever the historical circumstances in which it finds itself, in order that it may ultimately arrive at the form of economy which ensures, together with the greatest expansion of the productive powers of social labour, the most complete development of man. But I beg his pardon. (He is both honouring and shaming me too much.)[82]

Four years later, in a letter written to Vera Zusulich, the Russian revolutionary who would later work with Lenin in London, Marx would quote from the French edition of *Capital* as a response to her inquiries on "the agrarian question" in Russia: "The 'historical necessity' of this movement is thus explicitly restricted to the *countries of Western Europe*. The reason for this restriction is indicated . . . in chapter XXXII."[83]

Yet the historical figure of the nation, conceived in terms of its historic role in the development of capitalist production, remained an aspect of the acceptance or rejection of nationalist movements by Marx and Engels. Nationalism was acceptable if its success resulted in the construction of a "viable" industrial nation. In the same vein, it was unacceptable ("nonsense," "impracticable," "fanatical") for nationalist movements to threaten what Engels had termed "true [i.e. productive] national boundaries" in *Po und Rhein*.[84] As late as 1888, Engels was still giving his blessing to German nationalism on this basis:

> One can see from all this that the desire for a united "Fatherland" had a very material foundation. It was no longer the dim impulse of the students of the Wartburg days, when "strength and courage burned in German souls," . . . neither was it any longer the much more down-to-earth call for unity advanced by the lawyers and other bourgeois ideologists of the Hambach Festival . . . no, it was the demand arising from the immediate commercial needs of practical businessmen and industrialists for the elimination of all the historically out-dated rubbish which obstructed the free development of trade and industry, for the removal of all the unnecessary irritations, which all his competitors had overcome, and which the German businessman had to put an end to at home if he wished to play a part on the world market.[85]

Though Marx and Engels substantially agreed about the historical elements and characteristics of European nations extant in the mid-nineteenth century, there were some differences between them respecting the nationalism, or what they came to call the national question (the difference was linked in all probability with whatever it was behind Engels's contempt for the Slavs).[86] In *The Communist Manifesto* and *The German Ideology*, Marx had stressed proletarian internationalism over nationalism, observing, as we have seen, that it was in the nature of the bourgeoisie to have national interests and retain them, but in the nature of capitalism to dissolve national interests both politically (through the formation of an international class: the proletariat) and economically (through the creation of a world system). Later on, as noted, particularly in his considerations of Ireland[87] Marx began to deal with the question of national liberation more deliberately, and, perhaps, realistically. Here Marx came to insist that national liberation was the precondition for proletarian internationalism and simultaneously the destruction of bourgeois economic, political, military, and ideological hegemony.[88] He did not, however, extend this analysis to India, Mexico, or Italy.[89] Engels, on the other hand, tended to recognize and emphasize a counterrevolutionary tendency of national liberation movements, which he had sensed since observing the social upheavals of 1848–49. Including the Scots,

Bretons, and Basques with the Southern Slavs, Engels had declared these peoples "non-historic nations,"

> remnants of a nation, mercilessly crushed, as Hegel said, by the course of history, this *national refuse*, is always the fanatical representative of counterrevolution and remains so until it is completely exterminated or de-nationalized, as its whole existence is in itself a protest against a great historical revolution.[90]

Michael Lowy's observation that Marx's treatment of national liberation tended toward economism,[91] while Engels's was legalistic[92] is a bit simplistic, if not entirely incorrect. Their habits of thought tended toward the recognition of different forces if not configurations in human experience. The familiar, in the instance of Marx, was of things philosophically dialectical and reflective, with Engels it was the mundane and the practical instincts of the market place. While Marx tended, at the level of the historical epic, to discover the forces of the new world disguised in epiphenomenal forms, Engels's commitment to the revolutionary vision determined for him ultimately, the uses of history (and science). With respect to nationalism, Marx was the more likely to recognize that as an ideology its historical significance was ambiguous at worst, and Engels that such ambiguity constituted an unacceptable threat.

As analysts of nationalism, their legacy then was ambiguous. It appears that with respect to the actual nationalist movements of their time, in Germany, Poland, eastern, or southern Europe, neither Marx nor Engels achieved an extraordinary comprehension or fully escaped the parochialisms of the day. Rather, their historical method provided them with a means of supporting their predispositions on the historical worth of peoples and the varying capacities of the several European national movements. Their own nationalism whether "unconscious or subconscious," as Davis is forced to concede,[93] or otherwise, made them generally unsympathetic to the national liberation movements of peoples (e.g., the Russians and other Slavs) that historically threatened what Marx and Engels believed to be the national interests of the German people. An opposition to movements such as these could be rationalized by their failure to accord with the practical requirements of a viable political economy. On the other hand, certain European peoples were destined to be unified by the state and capitalist development. For the time being, in the interests of socialism, the proletariat of such societies were best advised to support their bourgeoisie. Germany, they argued, fitted that circumstance:

> For some other countries, nationalism still meant struggling for national unification, as with the East European countries from Poland to the Balkans; or fighting for national independence against the imperialist powers, as with the Irish, the Czechoslovaks, and the oriental and African peoples. Marxism had still to answer the questions of how far these nationalist movements were justified, how far they were a legitimate concern of the working class, and what attitude the proletariat of all countries should take to them. Was there a general principle involved? If so, Marx and Engels had not clearly enunciated it.[94]

Marxism and Nationalism

After Marx and Engels, the most significant contributors to the national question were the Bolsheviks, the Radical Left (Luxemburg, Pannekoek, Strasser, and Trotsky), and the Austro-Marxists (Karl Renner and Otto Bauer). Luxemburg attacked the notion of the right of self-determination as abstract, metaphysical, bourgeois, and utopian.[95] Her argument was based largely on both the economistic strain in Marx's thought, which underscored the cultural element of national divisions, and on Engels's characterization of "non-historic nations." Both Anton Pannekoek and Josef Strasser[96] saw the nation as an ideology comparable to religion, which disappears with the advent of socialism. Opposing Otto Bauer's position, which identified the national question in psychocultural terms,[97] Pannekoek and Strasser rejected the theory of a national culture that could be appropriated for its own interest by the working class.

The permutations were (and are) seemingly endless, each evidently possessing its own rationales. In the characterization of nationalism by Marxist theorists, presumably general principles of historical or objective nature were opposed to factors of special and short-term significance; but every debate responded to contemporary events by attempting to encompass the evidences of new sciences, new events, and the effects of immediate political and ideological struggles. And the antagonists often reversed their opinions with the appropriate shows of "new understanding." Unfortunately, the relegation of consciousness in the Marxian logic to a reflex of the relations of production and the frequent preoccupation with capitalism as a system determined by its own objective laws and *the* motivating force of historical change, most consistently led to the conclusion that nationalism among working classes was contrary to the historical movement of modern societies. In this sense, nationalism was a backward ideology, often a means of deflecting the class struggle into imperialist wars, and in any case not a fit subject for serious study in its own right since it was merely a politically convenient conduit of other forces and interests. Franz Borkenau would rejoin:

> In the political field, nationalism is the fact against which the Marxist theory breaks itself. Here is a force which has proved definitely stronger in the modern world than the class struggle which for orthodox Marxists makes the essence of history. The natural result was that the Marxists constantly tended to underestimate a force which did not easily fit into their ideas, and which at the same time was clearly contrasted with the ideals of the class-struggle. It became almost a mark of an orthodox Marxist to despise every nationalist feeling.[98]

The dismissal of culture, that is, a transmitted historical consciousness, as an aspect of class consciousness, did not equip the Marxian movement for the political forces that would not only erupt in Europe and the Third World but within the movement itself. For many Marxists it would be left to the new ideological and political order instituted by the Bolshevik triumph in the Russian Revolution, and not received theory, to sort out a Marxist orthodoxy on the national question. Ultimately the resolution was a political one clothed only partially by theory. Here we need only to sketch its politically authoritative form since we will return to more closely inspect its development in Part III.

Trotsky, though early on committed to the idea that nations had the right to self-determination,[99] was also of the opinion that the "centralizing needs of economic development" would ultimately lead to the dissolution of the nation-state. "The nation, divorced from the economy and freed from the old framework of the state, would have the right to self determination . . . in the sphere of 'cultural development.' "[100] Trotsky's formulations seemed to be entirely borrowed first from Marx and later from Lenin.

Lenin, indeed, seems to have done most to extend Marxist theory on the national question. Lowy writes:

> Lenin understood better than his comrades of the revolutionary left the dialectical relationship between internationalism and the right of national self-determination. He understood, firstly, that only the *freedom* to secede makes possible *free* and voluntary union. . . . Secondly, that only the recognition by the workers' movement in the oppressor nation of the right of the oppressed nation to self-determination can help to eliminate the hostility and suspicion of the oppressed, and unite the proletariat of both nations in the international struggle against the bourgeoisie.[101]

Of course, Lenin's prominence as an architect of the October Revolution, as leader of the Soviet State and a founder of the Third International, gave his opinions the requisite authority to become dogma. Nevertheless, the complex and rather voluminous character of his writings on the national question left his ideas vulnerable to simplification. In the course of things, it was Lenin's successor, Stalin, who would supply the most simple and authoritative proclamations on the national question. In 1913, with the instruction of Lenin, Stalin wrote his now famous pamphlet, *Marxism and the National Question*. In his article, Stalin took it upon himself to define a nation ("A nation is a historically evolved, stable community of language, territory, economic life, and psychological make-up manifested in a community of culture. . . . It is only when all these characteristics are present that we have a nation.[102] He also declared his support for the right of national self-determination ("The right of self determination means that a nation can arrange its life according to its own will. It has the right to arrange its life on the basis of autonomy. It has the right to enter into federal relations with other nations. It has the right to complete secession. Nations are sovereign and all nations are equal.")[103] It was Stalin's formulae that would dominate discourse on the national question for at least three decades after Lenin's death. This is particularly unfortunate since it was precisely during this period that socialist organization and thought came to the most persistent encounters with the ideology of nationalism.

What the Marxists did not understand about the political and ideological phenomenon of nationalism is that it was not (and is not) a historical aberration (of proletarian internationalism). Nor is it necessarily the contrary: a developmental stage of internationalism. Nationalism defeated the Marxism of the Second International (World War I), but ironically, was a basis of the Marxism of the Third International (the Russian revolutions; Stalin's socialism in one country; the conditions for membership in the Comintern), yet its primary world-historical significance was denied. It remained for most northern Marxists a secondary phenomenon (to the class struggle). As I have indicated, Lenin saw its character as principally political, Luxemburg as principally cultural. The error resided less in the mythic, analytic, or theoretical treatments of nationalism, than in "a defective grasp of the overall nature and depth of capitalist development."[104]

> The unforeseeable, antagonistic reality of capitalism's growth into the world is what the general title "uneven development" refers to. . . .
>
> In the traditional philosophical terminology, this amounts of course to a "contradiction." The contradiction here is that capitalism, even as it spread remorselessly over the world to unite human society into one more or less connected story for the first time, *also* engendered a perilous and convulsive new fragmentation of that society. The socio-historical cost of this rapid implantation of capitalism into world society was "nationalism." . . .
>
> The world market, world industries and world literature predicted with such exultation in *The Communist Manifesto* all conducted, in fact, to the world of nationalism.[105]

The consequence of the hegemony of capitalism, that is, the social and political reactions to capitalism, have seldom held to those conjectured by a logic bound by the laws of "capitalism." It is not that those reactions have been illogical, but that they have failed to conform to the political economic code emergent from capitalist society. It is this same code that still influences—maintains, as it were—the epistemological boundaries of radical social theory.

> It generalizes the economic mode of rationality over the entire expanse of human history, as the generic mode of human becoming. It circumscribes the entire history of man in a gigantic simulation model. It tries somehow to turn against the order of capital by using as an analytic instrument the most subtle ideological phantasm that capital has itself elaborated.[106]

It is in no way unusual for Marxian thinkers to declare, as Alex Callinicos did recently: "The role of philosophy is that of the theoretical reflection of proletarian class positions."[107] It does not seem to matter that this tradition placed Trotsky and Bukharin in Brooklyn only weeks before the revolution against Tsarist Russia.[108] We are again reminded of Engels's warning to the Marxist generation of his last years:

> Marx and I are ourselves partly to blame for the fact that the younger people sometimes lay more stress on the economic side than is due to it. . . . Unfortunately, however, it happens only too often that people think they have fully understood a

new theory and can apply it without more ado from the moment they have mastered its main principles, and even those not always correctly.[109]

This criteria might well have been extended to the more mature, and ultimately more responsible, members of later generations of Marxists. It would have to be deepened, however, to fathom the structure of Marxian theory.

With respect to Marxism's failure in determining the historical force and character of ideology as nationalism, another of Engels's remarks is apropos:

[O]nce an historic element has been brought into the world by other, ultimately economic causes, it reacts, can react on its environment and even on the causes that have given rise to it.[110]

Just as the expansion of capitalism has resulted in the preservation of certain aspects of non- ("pre-") capitalist modes of production, there is also evidence that nationalism in many places has assumed forms largely organized through ideational systems indigenous to those peoples exploited by the world market. It is not entirely accurate to argue as Tom Nairn has recently that:

Nationalism defeated socialism in the zone of high development, forcing it outwards into successive areas of backwardness where it was bound to become part of their great compensatory drive to catch up—an ideology of development or industrialization, rather than one of post-capitalist society.[111]

Nairn suggests the transfer of a socialism bred in the historical conditions at the center of industrial capitalism. This is a socialism capable of changing place without changing character! However, no single model of socialist industrialization or development has resulted from the revolutionary social orders of the Soviet Union, the People's Republic of China, Cuba, Vietnam, Kampuchea, Mozambique, or Angola. That is because each of these revolutionary orders is informed by political, moral, and ideological presumptions with priorities that precede their envelopment into the modern world system. Again, it may not be the case that we have seen "the full historical potential of 'nationalism.'"[112]

Conclusion

Among the several curious and unhappy legacies in Western civilizations of those centuries nearest to us are the system of capitalism and the beliefs in rationalism and science. But perhaps in some sense the term "legacy" is inappropriate, not the least for its suggestions of fatality, for none of these has passed away. Capitalism, rationalism, and scientism are not merely forms of activity (production) and reflexives of that activity. Each became a momentous historical force, providing substantially the character of the present industrial world—its character, but not necessarily its historical direction. This has been, of course, a frustrating disappointment to some—particularly those who believed that through the movement of capitalism they had discovered the nature, that is, the basis for historical change. For them, perhaps, the most disturbing social phenomenon of our time has been the "re-emergence" of ideology—what Marx called partial consciousness—to its prescientific, prerational prominence in the affairs of humankind. Ideology, especially in the twentieth century, has come to play a discordant role within the body of modern social thought, somewhat akin to that which slavery assumed among the rationalistic analytical frameworks concomitant to the rise of capitalism. Ideology, simply, is a negation of those strains of contemporary social inquiry that have become dominant. Its "intrusions" in our century and the one that preceded it have helped to abort those social and historical processes believed to be necessary and inevitable; have catalyzed rebellions and revolutions in often unlikely circumstances and among unlikely peoples; and have assisted in extraordinary historical achievement where failure was "objectively" immanent. As an ally of historical forces only poorly understood, ideology has exposed Western thought both in its form as mechanical Marxism for its reductionism,[113] and, in an entirely different way, liberal thought for its reifications.[114]

The limits of Western radicalism as demonstrated in Marxist theory, the most sustained critique of the modern era, are endemic to Western civilization. Those limitations relate directly to the "understanding" of consciousness, and the persistence of racialism in Western thought was of primary importance. It would have been exceedingly difficult and most unlikely that such a civilization in its ascendancy as a significant power in the world would produce a tradition of self-examination sufficiently critical to expose one of its most profound terms of order. Racialism, as I have tried to show, ran deep in the bowels of Western culture, negating its varying social relations of production and distorting their inherent contradictions. The comprehension of the particular configuration of racist ideology and Western culture has to be pursued historically through successive eras of violent domination and social extraction that directly involved European peoples during the better part of two millennia. Racialism insinuated not only medieval, feudal, and capitalist social structures, forms of property, and modes of production, but as well the very values and traditions of consciousness through which the peoples of these ages came to understand their worlds and their experiences. Western culture, constituting the structure from which European consciousness was appropriated, the structure in which social identities and perceptions were grounded in the past, transmitted a racialism that adapted to the political and material exigencies of the moment. In the medieval and feudal social orders of the European hinterland and the Mediterranean, racialism was substantiated by specific sets of exploitation through which particular caste or classes exploited and expropriated disparate peoples.

At the very beginnings of European civilization (meaning literally the reappearance of urban life at the end of the first Christian millennium), the integration of the Germanic migrants with older European peoples resulted in a social order of domination from which a racial theory of order emerged; one from which the medieval nobilities would immerse themselves and their power in fictional histories, positing distinct racial origins for rulers and the dominated. The extension of slavery and the application of racism to non-European peoples as an organizing structure by first the ruling feudal strata and then the bourgeoisies of the fourteenth, fifteenth, and sixteenth centuries retained this practical habit, this social convention. And as we shall soon see in Part II, from the seventeenth century on, English merchant capital (to cite an important example) incorporated African labor in precisely these terms, that is, the same terms through which it had earlier absorbed Irish labor. Moreover, European racialism was to undergo a kind of doubling onto itself, for in between the era of intra-European racism that characterized the first appearance of European consciousness and the predatory era of African enslavement, is the almost entirely exogenous phenomenon of Islamic domination of the Mediterranean—the eventual fount of European revitalization and recivilization. Independent of the historical meshings of European development but profoundly restricting that development—first in literally retarding European social development by isolating it from civil life, science, speculative thought, and so on, and then, after four centuries, by accelerating its recovery from the twelfth century onward—Muslim civilization mapped the contours of the European cultural renaissance. These events were to leave tell-tale marks on Western consciousness: the fear and hatred of "blackamoors"; the demonization of Islam; the transfiguration of Muhammad the Prophet into the anti-Christ. Not surprisingly, Europeans, that is "Christendom," still experience recurrences of antipathy toward what became their shared phantasmagoria.

In short, there were at least four distinct moments that must be apprehended in European racialism; two whose origins are to be found within the dialectic of European development, and two that are not:

1. the racial ordering of European society from its formative period, which extends into the medieval and feudal ages as "blood" and racial beliefs and legends.
2. the Islamic (i.e., Arab, Persian, Turkish, and African) domination of Mediterranean civilization and the consequent retarding of European social and cultural life: the Dark Ages.
3. the incorporation of African, Asian, and peoples of the New World into the world system emerging from late feudalism and merchant capitalism.
4. the dialectic of colonialism, plantocratic slavery, and resistance from the sixteenth century forward, and the formations of industrial labor and labor reserves.

It is now a convention to begin the analysis of racism in Western societies with the third moment; entirely ignoring the first and second and only partially coming to terms with the fourth. As we shall observe in the next section of this study, the results have been rather bizarre: some students of racism have happily reiterated the premise of a sort of mass psychology of chromatic trauma in which European reactions to darker-skinned peoples are seen as natural; others, including Marxists, have argued for a simplistic "empiricism" where the inevitable consequences of slavery and domination are the rationalizations of racial superiority and inferiority. In each instance, the root of the methodological and conceptual flaws is the same: the presumption that the social and historical processes that matter, which are determinative, are European. All else, it seems, is derivative. (On this score the preoccupation of Western radicalism with capitalism as a system has served the same purpose. Marxists have often argued that national liberation movements in the Third World are secondary to the interests of the industrial proletariat in the capitalist metropoles, or that they need to be understood only as the social efflux of world capitalism. Such movements require fitting in at the margins of the model for socialist revolution.) What is least defensible though, is how scant the attention paid to intra-European racialism has been.

We have now given consideration to the first moment of European racialism; it is time to explore the other three. This we shall do, but with a difference. History will no longer be left to revolve around European peoples or to originate from Europe as its center. In Part II, in particular respecting African peoples and the African diaspora, we will explore the foundations of the modern era as they were forged or enhanced by the activities of other peoples. In focusing on the history of the struggles of Black peoples for a different social order, we will of course, be reminded again of the limitations of Western radicalism, but more importantly we shall be preparing ourselves for a more profound understanding of the Black radical tradition. When in turn we have concluded that preparation, we shall then examine the pioneering efforts of Black radical theorists. This, too, will provide us with some insight into the problems of Western radicalism. The basis of Part III will be the thought of three Black ideologists, Du Bois, James, and Wright, who became conscious of their own positions and that of Black struggles in Western civilization and thought. Their attempts to reconcile their social consciousness to the priorities of "historical materialism" led to a critique of the very tradition in which they sought relief, and finally to a radical Black consciousness. Most important, however, is their eventual encounter with the Black radical tradition. The result was the first theoretical articulation of a revolutionary tradition whose nature was founded on a very different historical role for consciousness than was anticipated in Western radicalism. The object informing this study is to synthesize the elements of that emergent Black tradition into a coherent schema so that its remarkable insights and its historical project might assume their most authentic significance.

PART

THE ROOTS OF
BLACK RADICALISM

CHAPTER 4

THE PROCESS AND CONSEQUENCES OF AFRICA'S TRANSMUTATION

In the 500 years that have led directly to our moment, the destinies of African peoples have been profoundly affected by the development of economic structures and political institutions among European peoples. Moreover, it has been the nature of these relationships between Africans and Europeans that both Western civilization and the cultures of African peoples have been increasingly contorted and perverted as the years have accumulated. For the West, the appropriation of the means and forces of African reproduction have had unintended and unacceptable significance. The psychic, intellectual, and cultural consequences of Europe's intrusion into African history have served to accelerate the formulation of the mechanisms of self-destruction inherent in Western civilization, exacerbating its native racisms, compelling further its imperatives for power and totalitarian force, while subverting the possibilities of the rationalization of its states, its diverse cultural particularities, and its classes. Everywhere one turns or cares to look, the signs of a collapsing world are evident; at the center, at its extremities, the systems of Western power are fragmenting. Thus the British Empire at the beginning of the twentieth century, the German Empire in the middle years of this century, and the American empire today are simultaneously forewarnings, witnesses, and the history of this dissolution; and the development of each testified to the characteristic tendency of capitalist societies to amass violence for domination and exploitation and a diminishing return, a dialectic, in its use. "Things fall apart; the centre cannot hold." My subject, however, is not primarily the modern Western world and its contortions. Rather, I intend to focus here on the centuries of the modern world's adolescence, and on the formation and emergence of African peoples.

The Diminution of the Diaspora

Before the African and New World Black liberation movements of the post–Second World War era, few Western scholars of the African experience had any conception of the existence of an ideologically based or epistemologically coherent historical tradition of Black radicalism. The presence of such a tradition, the possibilities and conditions of its existence were literally and configuratively alien to these observers. Given the presumptions these students of Africa and its diaspora made about the bases of the identities, cultures, ethnicities, and group formations of these various African peoples, neither space nor time, geography nor periodicity, led them to suspect the presence of such a tradition. In its stead, these observers reconstructed social and ideological movements among Blacks to conform to the exigencies of specific locales and of immediate social causes.[1] If in their minds such movements occasionally were allowed some resemblance to one another, this followed from the fact of a general racial order shared by most Blacks, whether as slaves or ex-slaves, rather than the presence of a historical or political consciousness or a social tradition among Blacks. An ideological connective was presumed remote between the African mutineers on the *Amistad* or the captors of the *Diane*; the maroon settlements in Pernambuco, Florida, Virginia, Jamaica, the Guianas, and the Carolinas; the slave revolutionists of the Revolution in Haiti; the slave insurrectionists of the Caribbean and early nineteenth-century America; the Black rebels of the regions of the Great Fish River, the Limpopo and the Zambezi in southern Africa; the Black emigrationists of the American antebellum period; the untolled wars across the African landscape in the 1800s and 1900s; and their twentieth-century successors in Africa and the diaspora.

These events were seen as geographically and historically bounded acts, episodes connected categorically by the similarity of their sociological elements (e.g., slave or colonial societies) but evidently unrelated in the sense of any emerging social movement inspired by historical experience and a social ideology.[2] Such scholarship, of course, was either inspired or at least influenced by the ideological requirement that modern Western thought obliterate the African. As an ideological current, its adherents were not always Europeans. It permeated the intellectual culture and even compromised the work of some of those Africans' descendants. The pioneering work of Black scholars such as C. L. R. James and W. E. B. Du Bois was obviously unacceptable to orthodox Anglo-American scholastic establishment.[3]

The difference was not one of interpretation but comprehension. The makings of an essentially African response, strewn across the physical and temporal terrain of societies conceived in Western civilization, have been too infrequently distinguished. Only over time has the setting for these events been integrated into the tradition. The social cauldron of Black radicalism is Western society. Western society, however, has been its location and its objective condition but not—except in a most perverse fashion—its specific inspiration. Black radicalism is a negation of Western civilization, but not in the direct sense of a simple dialectical negation. It is certain that the evolving tradition of Black radicalism owes its peculiar moment to the historical interdiction of African life by European agents. In this sense, the African experience of the past five centuries is simply one element in the mesh of European history: some of the objective requirements for Europe's industrial development were met by the physical and mental exploitation of Asian, African, and native American peoples. This experience, though, was merely the condition for Black radicalism—its immediate reason for and object of being—but not the foundation for its nature or character. Black radicalism, consequently, cannot be understood within the particular context of its genesis. It is not a variant of Western radicalism whose proponents happen to be Black. Rather, it is a specifically African response to an oppression emergent from the immediate determinants of European development in the modern era and framed by orders of human exploitation woven into the interstices of European social life from the inception of Western civilization:

> [T]he similarity of African survivals in the New World points not to tribal peculiarities but to the essential oneness of African culture. That culture was the shield which frustrated the efforts of Europeans to dehumanize Africans through servitude. The slave may have appeared in a profit and loss account as an "item," and "thing," a piece of "property," but he faced his new situation as an African, a worker, and a man. At this level of perception, it is quite irrelevant to enquire from which tribe or region a particular African originated.[4]

As we shall see, in slave society such a signification of African culture was accessible for practical and ideological reasons only in a most grotesque form, that is, racism. Racist ideologues observed that all Blacks were identical and supplied the content of that identity. More important, though, few of the proponents of the philosophical, epistemological, or historical traditions of Western culture have found the authentic reality easy to grasp. For longer than the African slave trades to the old or new worlds, the Eurocentric traditions of Western civilization have categorically erred. And though he appeared rather late in this process, Hegel, perhaps somewhat crudely, spoke for these traditions when he declared, "The true theatre of History is therefore the temperate zone"; and further:

> The peculiarly African character is difficult to comprehend, for the very reason that in reference to it, we must quite give up the principle which naturally accompanies all *our* ideas—the category of Universality. . . . Another characteristic fact in reference to the Negroes is Slavery. Negroes are enslaved by Europeans and sold to America. Bad as this may be, their lot in their own land is even worse, since there a slavery quite as absolute exists; for it is the essential principle of slavery, that man has not yet attained a consciousness of his freedom, and consequently sinks down to a mere Thing—an object of no value. . . .
> At this point we leave Africa, not to mention it again. For it is no historical part

of the World; it has no movement or development to exhibit. Historical movements in it—that is in its northern part—belong to the Asiatic or European World.[5]

Except, perhaps, in its form of expression, the Eurocentrism that Hegel displays in
these passages has proven to be neither anachronistic nor idiosyncratic. He would be
echoed by legions of European scholars (and their non-European epigony) in a
myriad of ways into the present century.[6] The tradition persisted and permutated.

Such was the character of the world consciousness that dominated thought in
Western Europe. Its origins, as we have seen in Part I, were intra-European rather
than a reflex of encounters between Europeans and non-Europeans. Indeed, the
social base to which this conception was a response assumed its sociological forms
more than a millennium before the advent of an extensive European trade in African
workers and they were not easily displaced even by the eighteenth century.[7] This
cultural tradition of a moral and social order that rested on racial distinctions was
nevertheless readily available for the extension to Asian, African, and other non-
European peoples when it became appropriate. With respect to the African, that
occasion presented itself in the trade that saw its most bountiful fruition in the
New World.

The Primary Colors of
American Historical Thought

In the summer of 1856, the pro-slavery apologist's argument for the inferiority of
African peoples was most eloquently summarized in an article appearing in the
fledgling but prestigious American literary magazine, *Putnam's Monthly*:

> The most minute and the most careful researches have, as yet, failed to discover a
> history or any knowledge of ancient times among the negro races. They have
> invented no writing; not even the rude picture-writing of the lowest tribes. They
> have no gods and no heroes; no epic poem and no legend, not even simple tradi-
> tions. There never existed among them an organized government; there never
> ruled a hierarchy or an established church. Might alone is right. They have never
> known the arts; they are ignorant even of agriculture. The cities of Africa are vast
> accumulations of huts and hovels; clay walls or thorny hedges surround them, and
> pools of blood and rows of skulls adorn their best houses. The few evidences of
> splendour or civilization are all borrowed from Europe; where there is a religion or
> creed, it is that of the foreigners; all knowledge, all custom, all progress has come to
> them from abroad. The negro has no history—he makes no history.[8]

This anonymous writer's tortuously comprehensive characterization of the history
and social integrity of Black peoples had appeared in print midway between two
desperate acts in American history: the enactment of the Fugitive Slave Law of 1850 by
a Congress panicked into legislating martial law to defend slavery as a property right,
and the desperate resoluteness of John Brown's final bloody and radical blow against

slavery in 1859.[9] It was not, however, some sort of mathematical mean between the political sentiments, economic interests, and moral consciousness that inspired these two mutually contradictory but historically complementary public acts (each in its own way, of course, proved to be a necessary condition for the Civil War that followed). The division of opinion among whites and the European immigrant (who perhaps too would be "white" someday) could not be neatly correlated in arrangements of paired and equivalent moral postures: Black inferiority/pro-slavery; Black equality/anti-slavery. On the contrary, this confident declaration from the bleached bowels of mid-nineteenth-century American intelligentsia, wrenching history and historical consciousness from Black peoples, was the dominant ideological rationalization of racial oppression in the United States.[10] Its arrogant and specious historiography, itself the immediate and mangled product of 300 years of systemic African slavery in the New World, was both an absolute imperative as a cornerstone for the rationalization of a slave society[11] and a logical development of an errant civilization served so long by racial orders. By the middle of the nineteenth century, Western civilization, both at the strata of intellectual and scientific thought and that of popular opinion and mythology, had effectively sealed the African past.[12] The undercurrent that gave some recognition to the African's and the Black slave's humanity, and that had been used to nurture much of the earliest anti-slavery sentiment and literature, had been overwhelmed by the more constant and morally profound tradition of racism.[13]

The denial of the African's social order and history was not simply a question of Europe's or colonial America's ignorance of Africa. David Brion Davis, while reconstructing the descent of the African's image in eighteenth-century European thought, has sifted through materials that indicate that at least in this instance knowledge had not been cumulative:[14]

> It was known two centuries ago that Negroes lived in settled, agriculture societies; that they cultivated a variety of crops, raised large herds of cattle, and planted groves of shade trees. It was known that they were highly skilled in the use of iron and copper, in the making of jewelry and pottery, and in the weaving of fine cotton textiles.
>
> . . . It was known that Africans lived in neat and spacious villages which allowed privacy to the individual while preserving an intricate system of class and family distinctions. . . . Numerous books told of the Negroes' polite manners, their well-established patterns of trade, their knowledge of the planets and constellations.[15]

European travelers and tradesmen, their lives and fortunes so often dependent upon practical knowledge of African peoples, had frequently published such informed accounts, detailing social relations with which they had become familiar. Why such understanding had not persisted in European thought, Davis is at a loss to explain. Having come to the proposition that slavery had always been problematic to Western culture,[16] Davis, like Jordan,[17] resorted to mystery: "For reasons that can perhaps never be fully explained, it was the African's colour of skin that became his defining characteristic, and aroused the deepest response in Europeans."[18] Davis in conforming to racial convention has inherited its tautology: racial distinctions are the basis of racial sensibilities. He would have been better served by a less presumptuous inquiry into the ideological traditions resident in Western history. Then he might have realized that after some centuries of racial indulgences the substratum of Western thought was unprepared for anything else. Even the shift in eighteenth-century and nineteenth-century Western thought from a basis of a religious and philosophical epistemology to that of modern science had made little difference.[19] In point of fact, it had merely served to extend the terms and rationales for the fantasy of racial inferiority (for the Jews, Irish, Slavs, and Asians as well as for Blacks).[20] Western scientific thought simply took its place as the latest formal grammar for the expression of a racial metaphysics to which its most natural response was acquiescence. Indeed, during much of the nineteenth century, one of the most persistent projects for which Western science was employed was the attempt to demonstrate what was already understood to be the natural order of the races.[21]

In America, the accommodation of Western historical consciousness to racial ideologies created a particular chain of social misperceptions and historical distortions that endured into the present century. Not only was popular thought affected but the very foundations of that American academic thought which first began to mature in the nineteenth century was suffused with racialist presumptions. The emerging American bourgeoisie, in its mercantile, manufacturing, and plantocratic aspects, was purposefully and progressively achieving its first stages of ideological coherence. This intellectual grounding came to absorb the past of those peopling America as well as their present. The result was the construction of the historical legends that obscured the origins and character of the republic and the social relations upon which it rested.[22] The hard edges of class divisions, rooted in the European socioeconomic traditions of English gentry and continental European aristocracies and their lower classes, were softened and obscured by a mythical racial unity. The existence of land-rich elites, the social and political prerogatives of mercantile capital and agrarian property, even the genesis of a southern American aristocracy, all this was inundated by paeans to the political enlightenment that—culling from Europe the "best" of its moral traditions—had presumably conducted the people to independence, constructed near-perfect instruments of governance, and provided to the individual rights guaranteed by formal legal codes.[23] Even the long, vociferous, and sometimes violent opposition of "American Democracy" (the Democratic Party that had dominated federal policy and federal offices in the second quarter of the nineteenth century) to social democracy or "mob rule" (to its opponents)—both symptomatic of the truer character of the social order and one of its last overt manifestations—was faded and forgotten in the wake of an emergent racial consensus.[24] John Brown, closer to the artisanal origins associated with English working-class radicalism a quarter of a century earlier, was a suggestion of a certain strata not entirely mesmerized by the still novel variant of Western hierarchical systems.

One could discern the character and direction of historical distortion much earlier of course. Some of the realities of colonial America were hardly the stuff from which national legend could be easily formed. By the eighteenth century, American ideologists, already exempted by colonial victory, pacification and an established slave system from the challenges of the non-Western peoples their narratives would abuse, had begun to construct alternative realities. It would be some time before their machinations were no longer tolerable fictions. More recently, while reviewing these beginnings, Edmund Morgan, reconstructing the relations of the earliest Virginian colonists with native peoples, summarized the collective psychic state that he felt must have accompanied the cycle of atrocities that would extend ultimately into the present century:

> If you were a colonist, you knew that your technology was superior to the Indians'. You knew that you were civilized, and they were savages. It was evident in your firearms, your clothing, your housing, your government, your religion. The Indians were supposed to be overcome with admiration and to join you in extracting riches from the country. But your superior technology had proved insufficient to extract anything. The Indians, keeping to themselves, laughed at your superior methods and lived from the land more abundantly and with less labor than you did. They even furnished you with the food that you somehow did not get around to growing enough of yourselves. To be thus condescended to by heathen savages was intolerable. And when your own people started deserting in order to live with them, it was too much. . . . So you killed the Indians, tortured them, burned their villages, burned their cornfields. It proved your superiority.[25]

Yet as early as 1751, Benjamin Franklin, a most deliberate ruling-class colonial intellectual whose ultimate influence on American society would be vast in ideological, financial, and territorial terms, was already immersed in a quite different record of these relationships:

> The Europeans found America as fully settled as it well could be by Hunters; yet these having large Tracks, were easily prevailed on to part with Portions of Territory to the new Comers, who did not much interfere with the Natives in Hunting, and furnish'd them with many Things they wanted.[26]

The violent event of colonial aggression and its corollary of "Indian" slavery had already been transmuted in Franklin's neo-nativistic "American" mind into a relationship of supplication secured by an economic rationale; indeed, the dependence of "new Comers" on natives already reversed. The curtain of supremacist ideology had by now begun its descent on American thought, obscuring from the historically unconscious generations of descendants of colonialists and later immigrants the oppressive violence and exploitation interwoven in the structure of the republic.

The emigrant indentured servant, whose origins were most frequently and casually traced to England, was another of the labor forces upon which the colonial settlements of the seventeenth century depended. They would fare little better than the native American in the traditions being shaped in American historiography by ruling-class ideologues. Of course, it is now generally presumed that the "white servant" as a class had soon disappeared in the English mainland colonies as a result of the trade in African workers that had begun to reach substantial numbers beginning in the late seventeenth century.[27] This, however, was not the case. Richard Hofstadter tells us: " 'The labor of the colonies,' said Benjamin Franklin in 1759, 'is performed chiefly by indentured servants brought from Great Britain, Ireland, and Germany, because the high price it bears cannot be performed in any other way.' "[28] And as late as the years immediate to the American Revolution, servants still constituted approximately 10 percent of the two and one-half million people occupying the rebellious colonies. Like the slave, legally chattel to be sold at the discretion of a master, often the subject of cruel punishments, and without the rights to property, to marry without the permission of the master, or to drink in a public tavern, the white servant joined the vast excluded majority of the young republic's population:[29]

> Had Lockean dicta been applied to all the human beings in British North America on the eve of the Revolution, and had all been permitted to enjoy the natural and legal rights of freemen, it would have been necessary to alter the status of more than 85 per cent of the population. In law and in fact no more than 15 per cent of the Revolutionary generation was free to enjoy life, liberty, and the pursuit of happiness unhampered by any restraints except those to which they had given their consent.
>
> The unfree of Revolutionary America may be conveniently considered in five categories: Negroes, white servants, women, minors, and propertyless adult white males.[30]

The privileges of democracy were illusory for most.[31] White servants themselves were no closer to liberation at the end of the eighteenth century than were their distracted predecessors who had joined with the rankly ambitious Indian-killer Bacon in a desperate attempt to redraw the boundaries of power and wealth of colonial society in the seventeenth century.[32] Nevertheless, the tragic experiences of these generations of working poor were seldom transliterated into heroic saga. Even Abbot E. Smith, whose studies would prove to be so important to the reclamation of this class's historical role, found that an appropriate instrument was difficult to construct. While he fiddled with the calculation that the actual importance of the servant class to those who organized the settlements might be measured by their proportions of the colonial populations (indentured servants amounted to "at least half, and perhaps two-thirds, of all immigrants to the colonies south of New York"),[33] Smith would ultimately insist in bemused concord with his less than objective primary sources that such a measure was finally inflationary:

> [M]odern writers have generally viewed them with generous tolerance, and magnified their virtues either out of patriotic pride or out of a wish to demonstrate how grievously worthy persons were exploited by economic overlords in the bad old

days. But almost with one accord their own contemporaries, who knew them and saw them, denounced them as next to worthless.

... [A]fter making due allowances for middle-class arrogance and the necessities of argument, there cannot remain the slightest doubt that in the eyes of contemporaries, indentured white servants were much more idle, irresponsible, unhealthy and immoral than the generality of good English laborers. Common sense, without evidence, would in fact indicate much the same thing.[34]

Smith would have little of this "tolerance" for the servant class. Nor would Hofstadter. White servitude was a gathering of the inevitable effluence of "casual workers, lumper-proletarians, and criminals" of an England characterized by Hofstadter as a "backward economy . . . moving toward more modern methods in industry and agriculture."[35] Only vaguely understood was the fact that white servants, held to be virtually silent on their experiences by the majority of American historians,[36] were drawn from those redundant sectors of English and continental European societies whose economic and political displacements constituted the basis for the judgment of "overpopulation." Even quite good historians could be smitten by the ideological prerogatives of their class predecessors.

As might be expected, the white servant class drew to itself the social categories that had long been a basic currency for Western culture. Smith recorded the points of observation of the contemporaries of these "white" servants. He noted the attempts made to characterize the colonial lower class in racial and national terms:[37]

Franklin said the Germans were stupid. . . . Rarely was any criticism levelled against the Scots. . . . Even though they had been rebels or vagabonds at home, they were looked upon as universally ambitious, industrious, and intelligent. . . . Irish were least favored, and some colonies taxed or even forbade their importation. This was partly because of their religion, which was held to be politically dangerous, but mainly because of their tendency to be idle and to run away. [Christopher] Jefferson wrote that many of them were "good for nothing but mischief"; we read that they "straggled" in Bermuda, that they rioted in Barbados, that they would never settle down to an obedient servitude, satisfactory to their masters. Welsh were highly esteemed.[38]

Smith's inventory, however, was far from complete. It was, as well, somewhat deceptive, since neither the Welsh nor the Scots were as numerous as the Irish or Germans among seventeenth- and eighteenth-century immigrants.[39] Not surprisingly, given the history of Ireland since the sixteenth century, the Irish were the primary source of indentured and forced immigrants. In the eighteenth century, for example, perhaps as many as 10,000 men, women, and children were "transported" from Ireland to the New World as convicts.[40] And again between 1745 and 1775, according to the Naval Officer's Returns for the Maryland port of Annapolis, 5,835 servants emigrated from Ireland compared to a total for Great Britain (London, Bristol, and "other ports") of

4,725, some of whom were doubtlessly Irish.[41] As significant as the numbers, is the role that the colonization of Ireland had played in the development of English colonization of the New World:

> The adventurers to Ireland claimed that their primary purpose was to reform the Irish and . . . "to reduce that countrey to civilitie and the maners of England." It is evident, however, that no determined effort was ever made to reform the Irish, but rather that at the least pretext—generally resistance to the English—they were dismissed as a "wicked and faythles peopoll" and put to the sword. This formula was repeated in the treatment of the Indians in the New World. . . . We also find the same indictments being brought against the Indians, and later the blacks, in the New World that had been brought against the Irish. It was argued that the Indians were an unsettled people who did not make proper use of their land and thus could be justly deprived of it by the more enterprising English. Both Indians and blacks, like the Irish, were accused of being idle, lazy, dirty, and licentious, but few serious efforts were made to draw any of them from their supposed state of degeneracy.[42]

The Irish were, then, the prototype for the white servant. And as their own impressive numbers were increased, and the servant class augmented by immigrants from Germany and other refugees from the political upsets of European society and their socioeconomic aftershocks in the late seventeenth and eighteenth centuries, the vise of intra-European racialism, religious oppression, and class contempts was lifted to embrace most of them.[43] This enveloping racial social order was an ideological accommodation for ignoring or obfuscating the real origins and the more authentic categories of the developing white working class. If they were poor, it was because they had been victims of massive thefts by states and ruling classes; if they were rude and unruly, it was a consequence of the wholesale violations to which they had been subject. Little of this was ideologically convenient when it was comprehended by that infinitesimally small colonial capitalist class that was to use them as laborers, as buffer settlements at the frontiers, or as instruments of discipline for the African populations. It was enough to know that they were "the middling and the poor that emigrated," as Crèvecoeur put it.[44] That, of course, was the barest outline of the tale.

By the eighteenth century, the racial mist of European civilization had settled over the social topography of the English colonies, its blanket scattering the realities of domination and remixing their elements into familiar hues. However, in the lower orders, where the mist was thickest and where received wisdom has taught us to expect Blackness, the contemporary spectrum was more complex: the natives of the New World obtained a savage red, European labor a mottled gray. Above their heads it was a simpler matter: the ruling classes stood in dramatic, white relief. But between ourselves and the specter of that American past are the historical and racial fables that obscure the related exploitations and oppressions of African, European, Asian, and Amerindian peoples during the intervening 200 years. As a means of obliterating these events, the myth of white solidarity arose and came to dominate American sensibility. It was for the most part a lie but a terribly seductive one. By the end of the nineteenth century it had already substantially displaced the past and mystified the relations of the day. It remains in place.

The Destruction of the African Past

For many reasons, however, it is fair to say that the most significant of the obliterations of the New World's past was that which affected the African. The African became the more enduring "domestic enemy,"[45] and consequently the object around which a more specific, particular, and exclusive conception of humanity was molded. The "Negro," that is the color black, was both a negation of African and a unity of opposition to white. The construct of Negro, unlike the terms "African," "Moor," or "Ethiope" suggested no situatedness in time, that is history, or space, that is ethno- or politico-geography. The Negro had no civilization, no cultures, no religions, no history, no place, and finally no humanity that might command consideration.[46] Like his eastern, central, and western European prototypes, in their time, and the French peasants, the Slavs, the Celtic peoples, and more recently the American "Indians," the Negro constituted a marginally human group, a collection of things of convenience for use and/or eradication. This was, of course, no idle exercise in racial and moral schemata since it directly related to a most sizable quantum of labor disciplined and applied in a most extraordinary way. Slave labor in the New World, as we have seen in the precapitalist societies of Europe, was an inextricable element in the material, commercial, and capital development that took place. Leaving little to the imagination, Marx, in a letter to P. V. Annenkov, had argued:

> Direct slavery is as much the pivot of our industrialism today as machinery, credit, etc. Without slavery no cotton; without cotton no modern industry. Slavery has given value to the colonies; the colonies have created world trade; world trade is the necessary condition of large-scale machine industry. . . . Slavery is therefore an economic category of the highest importance.[47]

Though Marx's declaration was even then a slight over-simplification, it did make the point that has not only endured but to some extent dominated attempts to characterize the relationship of slave labor to industrialization:[48] the creation of the Negro, the fiction of a dumb beast of burden fit only for slavery, was closely associated with the economic, technical, and financial requirements of Western development from the sixteenth century on.[49] Slave labor, the slave trade, and their associated phenomena—markets for cheap commodities; shipbuilding and outfitting; mercantile and military navies; cartography; forestry; banking; insurance; technological improvements in communication, industrial production (e.g., metallurgy)—profoundly altered the economies of those states directly or indirectly involved in colonization and production by slave labor.[50] And nowhere was the trade between Europe, Africa, and the New World more significant than in England:

The triangular trade . . . gave a triple stimulus to British industry. The Negroes were purchased with British manufactures; transported to the plantations, they produced sugar, cotton, indigo, molasses and other tropical products, the processing of which created new industries in England; while the maintenance of the Negroes and their owners on the plantations provided another market for British industry, New England agriculture and the Newfoundland fisheries. By 1750 there was hardly a trading or a manufacturing town in England which was not in some way connected with the triangular or direct colonial trade. The profits obtained provided one of the main streams of that accumulation of capital in England which financed the Industrial Revolution.[51]

Still England was not alone, nor the English unique in having arrived at a point where the appearance of representatives of the "Negro race" was convenient. One simple measure of the importance of African labor that lay behind the construction of this creature is that "before the nineteenth century . . . for 300 years more Africans than Europeans crossed the Atlantic each year."[52] Only the accumulated interests and mercantile activities of the ruling classes and bourgeoisies of Portugal, Spain, France, Belgium, the Netherlands, Italy, and Britain could have accomplished such a massive scale of exploitation.

This "Negro" was a wholly distinct ideological construct from those images of Africans that had preceded it. It differed in function and ultimately in kind. Where previously the Blacks were a fearful phenomenon to Europeans because of their historical association with civilizations superior, dominant, and/or antagonistic to Western societies (the most recent being that of Islam), now the ideograph of Blacks came to signify a difference of species, an exploitable source of energy (labor power) both mindless to the organizational requirements of production and insensitive to the subhuman conditions of work. In the more than 3,000 years between the beginnings of the first conception of the "Ethiopian" and the appearance of the "Negro," the relationship between the African and European had been reversed.

Premodern Relations between Africa and Europe

Because one's sense of the past is so often conceptually distorted by a consciousness whose natural world of things and relationships is the present, it is important to recall that the collisions of the Black and white "races" began long before the events of the fifteenth and sixteenth centuries that prefigured modern African slavery.[53] The obliteration of the African past from European consciousness was the culmination of a process a thousand years long and one at the root of European historical identity.

More than a millennium before the beginning of the Christian era, civilizations of the eastern and northern Mediterranean had encountered at least one of the "high civilizations" of Africa.

The Mediterranean:
Egypt, Greece, and Rome

Ancient Egypt was a land primarily of peasants and farmers whose chief preoccupations centered on the Nile's beneficence. It appears quite likely that the state emerged as a direct result of the administrative requirements involved in planning and controlling the waters the Nile brought or did not bring during its periods of inundation. Reservoirs, dikes, canals, and dams became the means of preserving the land during the frequent periods of drought. Once institutionalized, the state became the basis of the first world system, extending Egyptian civilization down the Nile into eastern and northern Mediterranean lands.[54] As early as the Egyptian nineteenth dynasty (1320–1200 B.C.) the Lukku (Lycians), and Teresh (Tarsians) and the Akaiawasha (the Achaeans), as either mercenaries or allies of the Hittites (and most probably the former) had been recorded on the stele of Merneptah (1236–23 B.C.) as among the enemies of Egypt which he had defeated.[55] Greek traditions themselves speak of the founding of Egyptian colonies (Attica, Argolis) in Greece in the fifteenth and fourteenth centuries.[56] Seven hundred years passed before the historical evidence as it is presently preserved reveals another encounter. In the seventh and sixth centuries B.C., Ionian and Carian mercenaries served the Pharaohs Psamtik I (663–609 B.C.) and Psamtik II (594–88 B.C.).[57] Among other duties, they were used to man the garrison at the Pelusian Daphnae (now the western Sinai), and along with Greek merchant traders encouraged to settle at Naucratis near the capital of Sais in the western Nile delta. The settlement of Greeks at Naucratis is interesting, since before this time they had been forbidden residence in Egypt. This dependence on foreign mercenaries to defend its borders was one symptom of the weakness of an Egyptian state that would succumb to the Assyrians less than half a century later.[58] In the fifth century B.C., Herodotus, the first of Europe's historians, traced Egyptian colonial settlements as far as the northern Black Sea region. Herodotus described a Black people, the Colchians ("they are black skinned and have woolly hair")[59] living in what at present is Soviet Georgia. Herodotus believed that the Colchians were descendants of an Egyptian army under "King Sesostris" (believed to be a composite of Sety I, 1313–1301 B.C., and Rameses II, 1301–1234 B.C.).[60] He also noted the participation of Ethiopian soldiers under Xerxes in the Persian wars.[61] Herodotus' references to Black peoples may be taken quite literally since his Egyptian travels (around 440 B.C.) took him up the Nile as far as Elephantine (an island opposite modern Aswan), fully acquainting him with the people whom he called Ethiopians.

From the pre-Christian seventh century on, Egyptian law, science, religion, and philosophy began to have dramatic impacts on the development of Ionian and Greek thought.[62] The Egyptian Mysteries, expelled from Greece 300 or 400 years earlier in the struggle against Egyptian imperialism, once again became the basis of Greek development. Now the spoils of a crumbling state, this time the Mysteries served to advance intellectual and scientific development rather than a technology extended for purposes of imperialist exploitation.[63] Two centuries later, Plato in his *Timaeus*, while reconstructing the legend of Atlantis (presumably told to Solon by Egyptian priests during the statesman's visit to Egypt), seems to have accepted in his stride the notion of Egyptians as mentors of the Greeks.[64] As Margaret Stefana Drowser has put it "The Greeks felt that their own civilization was new and inexperienced in comparison with the age-old traditions and skills of this ancient land where the past still lived in the present."[65]

As for the origins of Egyptian civilization itself, both Egyptian and non-Egyptian sources of the ancient period agree. Chiekh Anta Diop has observed that:

> Egyptians themselves—who should surely be better qualified than anyone to speak of their origin—recognize without ambiguity that their ancestors came from Nubia and the heart of Africa. The land of the Amam, or land of the ancestors . . . the whole territory of Kush south of Egypt, was called land of the gods by the Egyptians.[66]

Diodorus Siculus (of Sicily), writing in the first century B.C., came to a similar conclusion (a conclusion for the most part only quite recently accepted by Western archaeologists and Egyptologists):

> The civilized Ethiopians . . . according to Diodorus, were the first to honor the gods whose favor their [*sic*] enjoyed, as evidenced by the fact that they had been free from foreign invasion. These Ethiopians were not only pioneers in religion, Diodorus informs us, but also originators of many customs practiced in Egypt, for the Egyptians were colonists of the Ethiopians. From these Ethiopians the Egyptians derived, for example, beliefs concerning their kings, burial practices, shapes of statues, and forms of letters.[67]

As one might anticipate, during the more than 3000 years of Egyptian pre-Christian history, the relationship between Lower and Upper Egypt was never a stable one. First one or the other of the two kingdoms was dominant. During the eighth and seventh centuries, perhaps for the last time, the south (Upper Egypt, Nubia, or Ethiopia) reasserted its dominance, conquering and ruling Lower Egypt until the defeat by the Assyrians in 671–61 B.C.[68] Unquestionably, Western Egyptologists of the eighteenth, nineteenth, and early twentieth centuries found the next 2000 years more palatable to their racial cosmologies and ethnocentrism than Egypt's more ancient past.

The Romans, of course, succeeded the Greeks as the dominant civilization in the northern Mediterranean. As their empire far exceeded the dimensions of Hellenic adventure, their knowledge of Africa was much more extensive. And much like the Greeks, it was those most integral to Rome's imperialist apparatus—its military command, its administrative and colonialist bureaucrats, and its intelligentsia responsible for the training and education of the ruling class's heirs—who achieved the most intimacy with the continent. The Greeks' actual acquaintance with Africa in large measure had been confined to the upper (southern) and lower (northern) Nile regions. The Romans, however, achieved familiarity with peoples along the Nile but also assumed relations with African peoples of northwestern Africa (that is Libya and west of Libya) and as far south as Cameroon and the Sudan.[69] As the Greeks had in Egypt, the Romans found in north Africa peoples such as the Garamantes who were Black or mixed. (Evidence found in Cyprus of an earlier period, the sixth century B.C. tends to confirm the role of Blacks in even late Egyptian history.)[70] The Romans had as well encountered Black soldiers in the army of Hannibal the Carthaginian, which invaded Europe in 218 B.C. The Romans are also known to have sent military expeditions and to have established military posts and diplomatic relations among peoples south of Egypt. These efforts were in keeping with the attempt to secure the southern boundaries of their Egyptian colony and to preserve trade routes to Meroe, the eastern desert, and central Africa.[71] Peace, however, was elusive, as evidenced by the successive wars fought against the armies of the Ethiopian queen Candace during the last third of the first century B.C. In addition, an Ethiopian people, the Blemmyes, fought continuous wars with Roman armies from 250 A.D. to 545 A.D.[72] West of the Egyptian delta, Roman military expeditions in 86 A.D. and a few years later may have penetrated as far as Lake Chad.[73] The purpose seems to have been primarily the defense of trade routes and caravans, though joint efforts with the Garamantes may have related directly to the state interests of Rome's African allies. Yet despite their less than cordial relations with Africans, the Romans, like their Greek predecessors, did not evolve prejudices of color and race:

> [S]ocial intercourse did not give rise among the Greeks and Romans to the color prejudice of certain later western societies. The Greeks and Romans developed no doctrines of white superiority unsupported by facts or theoretical justifications for a color bar.
>
> The presence of large numbers of Negroes in a white society, according to some modern views, gives rise to anti-Negro feeling. Ethiopians were far from rare sights in the Greco-Roman, particularly the Roman, world. Yet the intense color prejudice of the modern world was lacking. Although it is impossible to estimate the Negro element in the classical world in terms of precise statistics, it is obvious that the Black population in Greece and Italy was larger than has been generally realized.[74]

The Dark Ages: Europe and Africa

After the dissolution of Roman administration, in the fifth century A.D., knowledge of either the ancient African period or of more contemporary periods, began to dissipate dramatically among European peoples. For Europeans beyond the Mediterranean it had never been extensive in any case, restricted largely to those privy to state affairs and those few engaged in the quite sparse literary traditions. In western Europe, its peoples isolated from the centers of civilization by geography, the rigors of transhumance and resettlement, the absence of urban centers, and the lateness of their development, the subsequent dominance of the Mediterranean area by Muslim peoples proved to be catastrophic for their knowledge of peoples beyond the eastern fringes of the European peninsula. As one example, in the mid-thirteenth century, Bartholomew Anglicus observed with unjustifiable certainty:

> Ethiopia, blue men's land, had first that name of color of men. For the sun is nigh and roasteth and toasteth them. And so the color of men showeth the strength of the star, for there is considerable heat. . . . In this land be many nations with divers faces wonderly and horribly shaper. There be two Ethiopias, one in the East and the other is Mauretania in the West, and that is more near Spain. And then is Numidia and the Province of Carthage. Then is Getula, and at last against the course of the sun is the land that is hight Ethiopia Adusta, burnt, and fables tell that there beyond the Antipodes men that have their feet against our feet.[75]

The ancient civilizations of the Old World, in Asia as well as Africa, became legends, preserved most constantly in the obscure and recondite histories of biblical narrative. As knowledge became more and more a monastic preserve, secular reconstructions assumed a certain rarity due to the church's commitment to the interpretation of history in accord with its perceptions of divine will.[76] Ethnocentrism, legitimated by the authorities of church and ignorance, the two fountains of medieval knowledge, became the basis for world knowledge. Ultimately, with the evolution of Christian ideology into a worldview, it was enough to know that mankind was divisible into two collectivities: the army of Light and the army of Darkness:

> Whether men wrote of an *imperium christianum*, a *regnum Europae*, or later of a *societal christiana*, there was the same impulse to separate the known securities of the "inside" from the dark and threatening forces of paganism, heresy, and schism which lay beyond the perimeter.[77]

Europe was God's world, the focus of divine attention; the rest of mankind belonged for the moment to Satan. For perhaps a thousand years or more, western European world historical consciousness was transformed into theosophy, demonology, and mythology.[78] And, indeed, in a most profound sense European notions of history, both theological and pseudo-theological, negated the possibility of the true existence of earlier civilizations. The perfectability of mankind, the eschatological vision, precluded the possibility of pre-Christian civilization having achieved any remarkable development in moral law, social organization, or natural history (science). For 600 years more, Cassiodorus' sixth-century prescription for putting "the devil and his work to flight" held sway over medieval education and knowledge:

> Let us who sincerely long to enter heaven through intellectual exertions believe that God disposes all things in accordance with his will, and let us . . . reject and condemn the vanities of the present life and carefully investigate the books of the Divine Scriptures in their normal order, so that by referring all things to the glory of the Creator we may profitably assign to the celestial mysteries that which those men have seemed to seek vainly for the sake of mortal praise. And, therefore, as the

blessed Augustine and other very learned Fathers say, secular writings should not be spurned. It is proper, however, as the Scripture states, to "meditate in the (divine) law day and night," for, though a worthy knowledge of some matters is occasionally obtained from secular writings, this law is the source of eternal life.[79]

Islam, Africa, and Europe

Ironically, south of the Pyrenees, encircling the Mediterranean extending beyond the Indus, the scholars among the figurative descendants of the prophet Abraham's first son, Ishmael, were becoming the direct heirs of ancient learning and thought. Lerner and Mahdi argue that this was made possible by the fact that in Islam the absorption of "new and alien sciences" was a juridical rather than a theological question and was thus resolved by the dispute of advocates before a jurist. The issue was whether or not these sciences interfered with beliefs prescribed by Law as defined by jurists. There was too, they note, an absence of ecclesiastical authority in Islam; an authority that might well have paralleled the medieval Christian Church in its preoccupation with competing "heresies."[80] Rodinson believes that perhaps even more significant was the ethos of Arab culture:

> Arab customs accepted and encouraged the adoption, by every clan, of people of all kinds and every nationality, who then became wholly Arab. . . . Persians, Syrians, Egyptians, Berbers, Goths, Greeks and a host of others joined the Arabs, considered themselves as Arabs and really became Arabs. But still greater numbers became Muslims.[81]

While the spiritual and most often the temporal authorities of Christendom shunned much of the learning amassed by pre-Christian civilizations, the Arabic-speaking scholars took to this knowledge as a legitimate booty of the wars won by Muslim armies. Arabic culture now began the absorption of the more developed scientific and philosophic thought of the defeated, just as earlier, the Persian and Syriac cultures had absorbed like elements of Greek culture once it was finally proscribed officially in the Christian Rome of the sixth century, and the Greeks before them took to the intellectual produce of Egyptian and Babylonian cultures.

Protected and facilitated by the expansion of Islamic states, Arabic scholars between the seventh and tenth centuries achieved access to the works of their Mediterranean predecessors. The most intensive period of translation into the Arabic from Greek, Sanskrit, Persian, and Syriac took place between 750 and 900 A.D.[82] Translations, however, appear to have been selective, since historical works were generally neglected during the earliest period of absorption. Translators, tending toward a predominance of physicians, demonstrated interests that generally attended to works in the fields of medicine, mathematics, and astronomy.

In the Islamic east, the artistic and intellectual center would gravitate from Damascus and Baghdad to Cairo, as the toll from incursions by Seljuq Turks, Christian Crusaders, Berbers, Arab nomads, and Mongol armies mounted. In the west, the al-

Maghrib, the most glorious centers of Islamic culture were to be found on the Iberian peninsula. It was in Spain and particularly Toledo (reacquired by "Christendom" in 1085 after more than 300 years of Muslim rule) that the work of translation was concentrated. In the twelfth century, following closely the eleventh-century translations, from Arabic to Latin, of Constantine the African (d. 1087) of medical writings, European scholars came face to face with the knowledge of the ancient world's philosophy, physics, mathematics, medicine, alchemy, and astronomy for the first time in almost 1,000 years:

> At the beginning of the twelfth century, Greek knowledge was available in Greek and in Arabic, but more accessible in the latter form. Moreover, many Greek works were lost in the original but available in Arabic translations. When the West became sufficiently mature to feel the need for deeper knowledge, when it wanted to renew its contacts with ancient thought, it turned to Arabic sources.
>
> Thus the main intellectual task of the twelfth and thirteenth centuries was one of translation. Much of the intellectual energy of medieval times was spent not in the creation of new intellectual values but in the transmission of older ones. Knowledge was won not by fresh and independent investigation but by translation, chiefly from Arabic.[83]

By the end of the twelfth century, the universities of Salerno and Bologna in Italy, Paris and Montpellier in France, and Oxford (and in the thirteenth century, Cambridge) in England had been founded on this quite extraordinary event.[84]

Islamic civilization, however, did more than simply function as a belated conduit in the development of Western civilization. Northern Africa as the end point to the gold trade with West Africa was systematically proscribed to European merchants. The purpose, apparently, was to maintain the secret of the sources of the mines and the trans-Saharan routes of trade. In the tenth century, however, the Arab traders began the extraction of a more variable wealth: slaves. Utilizing ports on the Red Sea coast, over the next 900 years, Arab slave traders plundered African societies for perhaps as many as 17 million people.[85]

That, however, is another story, perhaps another history. More to the point is the drawing of the following historical schemata that traduces some of the more consequential effects of Islamic civilization on European peoples, their histories, and their institutions. What is compelling, of course, is that the impact of Islam on Europeans goes far beyond the accepted lore of Muslim civilization as a "treasury for ancient knowledge." This was but an important petard. A much greater force confronted European destiny.

It was not as the descendants of legendary Hebrews or as the vessels of ancient knowledge that Muslims came to be most frequently represented among European peoples. Islam, a faith that embraced a multiracial civilization incorporating peoples from Arabia, Africa, the Near East, the East, and southern Europe, would be known by its armies. And Africans were prominent in its armies from the very beginning. Africans had fought in the pre-Islamic Arabian wars, and within the first century of the Islamic era (the Christian seventh century), their presence had already been noted in the empires of Europe.[86] Four hundred years later, when Christendom launched a furious counterassault against the enemy whose very being mocked the beliefs of Europe and materially diminished its daily life, Islam, and "blackamoors," was a familiar identity. The Christian encounter with Islam would have then both racial and economic resonances.

On account of their logistical appetites, the Christian Crusades, beginning in the eleventh century against the Saracens in Jerusalem, brought to fruition the mercantile Italian city-states of the Middle Age. These entrepôts dominated southern and western European commerce with the non-European world until the middle of the fourteenth century.[87] By the beginnings of that century, though Papal and regal levies for crusades increased in number and frequency, actual crusades had almost entirely ended. Once the religious enthusiasm and fanaticism that clothed the carnage of the crusades had abated, and the ambitions of Norman and Frankish feudal lords and their clerical allies had been satiated or overwhelmed by the weight of bureaucratic administrations and the seductions of corruption, the sea trade of the Italian coastal states turned from the merchandising of war, the conveyance of armies, and the financing of invasion, to the conventions of commercial trade and of course piracy.[88] Europe—whose population had been stimulated by a higher food productivity associated with new tillage technology, the clearing of cultivable lands for fuel, and as a concomitant to the preparation and transportation of its armies of invasion, and perhaps by benign climatic changes—had expanded.[89] Europe extended itself both horizontally into the establishment of new towns and the resettlement of old ones, and geopolitically—eastward into the lands of the Prussians, Slavs, and Christian Byzantium, westward into England, and south into the calves of the Iberian and Italian peninsulas.[90] The Christian and Jewish merchant lords and bankers of Venice, Florence, and Genoa, already implicated by the opportunities, associations, and investments of the previous period, successfully resisted their abhorrences of the Muslim infidel and his nefarious trades.[91] Following the much more frequent practice among clerics of purchasing dispensations to legitimize their bastard offspring, merchants bought dispensations for their commercial trafficking with the infidels. (Pope John XXII (1316–34) may have also used one if he had not had the fortune of being infallible, for he bought forty pieces of gold cloth from Damascus.) Meanwhile, the gold of Africa, the silks, spices, and sugar of the East and Asia Minor were measured by the Italians and their Islamic correspondents against European slaves (Slav, Turkish, Bulgar, and Circassian) and goods.[92]

Europe and the Eastern Trade

In Europe, however, the feudal system had exceeded its limits, politically, economically, and socially. The European crisis that followed manifested itself in the late thirteenth century and came to full maturity in the fourteenth and fifteenth centuries. Whatever its root causes—and Wallerstein reminds us of just how subtle the scholars'

debate has become by recalling that Edouard Perroy's thesis was that it was "a satura-
tion of population" and the limits of agrarian technology, while R. H. Hilton believed
that the primary cause was the overbearing expense of feudal superstructures inflated
by war and leached by peasant insurrections and famines[93]—Europe's population
declined, and its markets, trade, towns, villages, and cultivated areas contracted. It
was not, however, a purely internal affair, nor one entirely dependent upon events or
elements encompassed by human society. It remains for one such force to be noted
for the devastating role it played in the crisis of fourteenth-century Europe.

Along with quite a few other historians, Trevor-Roper has added to his list of
suspects behind the collapse of Europe the Mongol Empire and its dissolution in the
mid-fourteenth century. His reasons include the ideological importance that the
Mongol movement immediately assumed in the minds of European Christian rulers.

> Here was a powerful second front against Mamelukes and Turks; here also was a
> huge free-trade area from Budapest to Canton; and both could be exploited. . . .
>
> Thus, when the crusaders' way of imperialist colonization had failed, the alter-
> native way of "pure and friendly correspondence" succeeded, and in the century
> after the failure of the Crusades, Europe was still living, successfully, on the East. . . .
> The great, orderly, tolerant Mongol Empire.[94]

At first, that is in the 1220s, the Franks had mistaken the intent of the Mongols, basing
their expectations on the fragmentary reports on the Mongols by eastern Christians:

> These eastern Christians made a Christian "King David" out of the Mongol con-
> queror, who would have destroyed the Moslem empires, in order to head for the
> Holy Land and liberate Jerusalem.[95]

By the 1240s, after a series of exchanges between Mongol capitals and armies and
Frankish lords and popes, Christendom had been disabused of its error. It learned
that: "The program of the Mongols was wholly and entirely based on a rule given by
Chingis-khan: 'There is only one God in heaven, and on earth there is only one
sovereign, Chingis-khan.' "[96] The Mongol Empire ordered the Pope and the Christian
kings to submit. Still, by the 1260s Mongol and Franks were formally agreeing to joint
crusades against the Muslim Mamelukes, and by the first decades of the fourteenth
century the Italian "merchant republics" and the Mongols had established treaties of
commerce. This meant that whatever other significances Mongol stability, trade, and
technological exchange (e.g., China's gunpowder and printing techniques) would
have for a Europe still compelled by Christian dogma to abhor and shun the southern
infidels, the gold, which was largely brought out of Africa,[97] found its way to central
and eastern Asia only to pave the route to Europe of the Black Death. William McNeill
describes the plague's itinerary in its less nefarious terms:

> Not only did large numbers of persons travel very long distances across cultural and
> epidemiological frontiers; they also traversed a more northerly route than had ever

been intensively traveled before. The ancient Silk Road between China and Syria crossed the deserts of central Asia, passing from oasis to oasis. Now, in addition to this old route, caravans, soldiers and postal riders rode across the open grasslands. They created a territorially vast human web that linked the Mongol headquarters at Karakorum with Kazan and Astrakhan on the Volga, with Caffa in the Crimea, with Khanbaliq in China and with innumerable other caravanserais in between.[98]

Ostensibly, it was the revolt in the eastern end of the Mongol Empire, a revolt that would culminate in the establishment of the Ming Dynasty, which provided the chaotic conditions for the vermin to multiply. The account of the plague left by Ibn al-Ward (who died of plague at Aleppo in 1349) has been generally accepted: it began somewhere in what al-Ward termed "The Land of Darkness" (Yunnan-Burma) before 1331; it then spread to China and northern Asia, and then to central Asia and eastern Europe—all the time following the Mongol trade route between the Mediterranean and China; by the end of 1347, it crossed from Caffa on the Black Sea to the Sicilian port of Messina; within three years, it is estimated, more than 20 million Europeans (one-third to one-half the population of Europe) had joined the more than 60 million Chinese dead.[99]

Islam and the Making of Portugal

Keeping in mind that our interest in the effects of Muslim civilization on Europe is related to the attempt to reconstruct the processes by which the African past was extracted from European consciousness, perhaps the greatest irony of this history concerns the founding of the Portuguese state and the ruling class that ran it. The Portuguese state's expansion into Africa marks, of course, the beginnings of the modern era in European development: the "Age of Discovery." It also marks the beginnings of those encounters between the peoples of the European peninsula and the African continent that would produce the Negro.

The appearance and the development of the Portuguese state were also the results of processes both directly and indirectly related to Muslim civilization. Though Anglo-Saxonist shrouds persist in many English-language treatments of Portuguese history (no doubt in part attributable to Portugal's client relation to Britain since the eighteenth century), these stories bear some relationship to the past. For instance, in the mid-twelfth century, as Trevor-Roper recalls,

> a party of English and Flemish crusaders, sailing towards the Mediterranean to join the second crusade, arrived at the mouth of the river Souro. They were easily persuaded that there was no need to sail further. There were infidels in Portugal, and lands as rich as any in Palestine: the crusaders agreed; they stayed. Instead of Edessa they captured Lisbon; and having massacred the Muslim inhabitants and installed themselves on their lands, they forgot about the Christian kingdom of Jerusalem and founded that of Portugal.[100]

As a British historian, Trevor-Roper gives due weight to the English intervention but ignores their Iberian and French allies (e.g., Henry of Burgundy). Nevertheless, it is true that erstwhile crusaders played an important part in the establishment of Portugal during the colonial wars against the Muslims. As Americo Castro declares:

> The fleet engaged in the conquest of Lisbon had weighed anchor in England with 169 ships provided and manned by Englishmen, Germans, Flemings, Frenchmen, and Gascons. The towers raised for the conquest of the city were the work of Flemings, Englishmen, and an engineer from Pisa. All the booty was for the foreigners, who, through a pact with the Moors, took for themselves the gold, the silver, clothing, the horses, and the mules, and gave the city to the king.[101]

Three hundred years later, as the dominant legend goes on, unexercised by the wars and internal conflicts besetting the leading powers of western Europe; geographically proximate to the West African Atlantic coast;[102] with both a direct experience of long distance sea trade and one borrowed from the Italian merchants (who had begun their own commercial colonization of Portugal by the thirteenth century);[103] and with a powerful residue of Christian anti-Islamic adventurism, the Portuguese state launched the first of the great discoveries that would mature into the modern world systems of Europe and European colonies. By the fifteenth century, Portugal and her Italian (and English) partners had transformed sugar production, the plantation system, and, of course, the system of slavery from the islands of the eastern Mediterranean to those of the eastern Atlantic. By the sixteenth century, Spain had inherited the Italian capitalists and all that went with them—and so had the New World.[104]

Still, as Castro had warned: "It is impossible to understand the formation of the immense Portuguese Empire solely in terms of economic or statistical analysis."[105] It might be added that this is particularly the case when such analysis is based on indifferent historical reconstruction. The "peacefulness" of Portugal's fifteenth century, which C. R. Boxer asserts (and Wallerstein repeats)[106] for example, is to be doubted when one learns elsewhere that the century was punctuated by a martial and diplomatic war with Castile, and that the century ended with the homicidal suppression of a dynastic struggle.[107] Castro, himself, came to the conclusion that much more attention had to be paid to Portuguese nationalism:

> Portugal wanted and believed a history of her own, and she did this with such intensity that she was successful little by little incorporating both an imagined history and the practice of imagining it into the process of her authentic existence. The imperial enterprises; the enduring imprint of Portugal in Brazil, in the East Indies, and in Africa; the imposing figures of Vasco da Gama, Affonso de Albuquerque, Ferdinand Magellan, and others; the works of Gil Vicente and Camoems—all this and more have motivated the recreation of the origins of Portugal.[108]

This, however, was not a simple "nationalism": a mass ethos bound to a national destiny. The Portuguese of the twelfth, thirteenth, and fourteenth centuries were an extraordinary mix of western European and Mediterranean peoples. More important, the new nation's ruling classes, the nobility and the bourgeoisie who wove the ideological tapestry of nationalism and constructed those ideographs that framed their families and deeds, were drawn from the landed and titled aristocracies of Spain (Castile, Aragon, and Catalonia), France (Flanders and Burgundy), and England.[109] The threads of Portuguese nationalist identity were spun from a European source. Portugal inherited, consequently, not merely its royal houses—and their Italian capitalist creditors, but as well the mercantile and scientific migration that was the social and intellectual efflux of Venice, Genoa, Pisa, Majorca, Florence, Flanders, Catalonia, and England. With these disparate elements came, too, a certain malaise and the resolve to construct a state whose character would be distinct from the corrupt, chaotic, and mean societies from which they had fled or been driven:

> Those Europeans found Europe morally distasteful, with constant internecine wars between so-called Christian princes; with heresy rife, and schism a fact for almost forty years; with confused relations ever apparent between ecclesiastical and secular authority; with charity often non-existent; with marriage made a mockery, and adultery widespread; with lying and unvarnished thievery apparent on every side.[110]

It was again, this "nationalism," and particularly the element of Muslim antagonism, that played such a critical role in Portuguese expansionism in the fifteenth century. Robert Silverberg, in chronicling Portugal's and Europe's fascination with Prester John, has recorded:

> In 1411, when Portugal had arrived at an unaccustomed state of complete peace, Joao of Avis adopted a suggestion of his English-born queen, Philippa: to maintain the momentum of the national economy, he would send an armed expedition to North Africa. Joao and Philippa envisioned a conquest of the Moorish kingdom of Fez, thus opening the way for a Portuguese penetration, by land, of Prester John's kingdom, somewhere in the heart of Africa. With Prester John's cooperation, perhaps, a new spice route could be established, with caravans crossing Africa from Morocco to the Red Sea and bringing pepper and cloves to Lisbon.[111]

Dom Henrique (the Navigator), who is credited with marshalling the energies of Portugal, the resources of the Order of Christ, the skills and instruments of Europe's most developed seamanship, and the navigational wisdom of Muslim and Italian mathematicians, cartographers, astronomers, and geographers for the purpose of exploring Africa and its coastline for a route to the Indies and to Prester John, was of course the ascetic, celibate, and reclusive son of the newly royal Joao and Philippa. Following the Portuguese capture of Ceuta in 1415, for more than forty years, Dom Henrique dedicated himself to the achievement of his parents' dream. Henrique, however, was not distinctive in this regard. He was in reality simply a more psychologically severe version of his family and the class with whose destiny it was intimately linked.[112] Francis Rogers quite effectively argued:

The Lusitanian translation of the European dreams concerning the East into action was precipitated, not by Ceuta, but by the simultaneous Council of Constance. It gained further impetus with brother Pedro's travels . . . and final direction by Portuguese relations with Pope Eugenius IV and the Council of Ferrara-Florence-Rome. . . .

I am convinced that various manifestations of Western Europe's great Oriental dream came to bear on Pedro as he wandered, and that by, let us say, 1433 or 1434 (the beginning of Duarte's reign), the royal brothers, including and most especially Henry, had talked over at length the exciting reports related by Pedro upon his return.[113]

Gomes Eannes de Azurara, his historian contemporary, recorded Dom Henrique's motives:

1. [Henrique] desired to know what lands there were beyond the Canary Islands and a cape called Bojador. . . .
2. If in these territories there should be any population of Christians, or any harbours where men could enter without peril, they could bring back to the realm many merchandises at little cost. . . .
3. It was said that the power of the Moors of this land of Africa was very much greater than was generally thought, and that there were among them neither Christians nor other races. And because every wise man is moved by desire to know the strength of his enemy . . .
4. During one and thirty years of battles with the Moors, the Infante had never found Christian King or Seigneur outside this kingdom, who for the love of Our Lord Jesus Christ was willing to aid him in this war. He desired to know whether in those regions there might be any Christian princes in whom the charity and love of Christ were strong enough to cause them to aid him against these enemies of the faith.
5. . . . [L]ost souls should be saved.
6. [The astrological reason, from which all the others proceed, that as Henrique was born on 4 March 1394, he was under the influence of] the Ram, which is in the House of Mars, with the Sun in the ascendant. . . . [T]his indicated that this prince was bound to engage in great and noble conquests, and above all he was bound to attempt the discovery of things which were hidden from other men, and secret.[114]

Silverberg added, in order to underscore his own interest, that Henrique had "told one of his companions in 1442, he desired to have knowledge not only of Africa and the Indies but 'of the land of Prester John as well, if he could.' "[115] One hundred years later, at the beginning of the sixteenth century, the quest that had so obsessed the House of Avis from its own beginnings (and before it Europe for 300 years) was finally completed. Pero da Covilha, the Portuguese king (1495–1521) Manuel I's emissary to Prester John's kingdom, was discovered by his ambassadorial successors to have become an honored but unwilling captive for life of the court of Ethiopia.[116] Islam had provided for the emerging Europe a powerful ideological, economic, and political impulse.

There was, however, one element in Islamic civilization that had little or no effect on medieval Europe as the latter was being transformed into the center of a dominant world system. This was the Muslim concept of the slave. Great differences persisted between slavery in Western and Christian societies and slavery in Islam.

The Prophet had said:

Fear God concerning your slaves. Feed them with what you eat and clothe them with what you wear and do not give them work beyond their capacity. Those whom you like, keep, and those whom you dislike, sell. Do not cause pain to God's creation. He caused you to own them, and had He so wished he would have made them own you.[117]

The Islamic ideal concerning slavery was without parallel in Christian law and dogma. Islamic jurists had codified both the liabilities and the rights of slaves; customs among the Sunni, Shia, and Maliki schools had limited the rights of masters and extended the legal, religious, and social capacities of the slave. The Koran encouraged manumission as an act of piety, in many instances the punishment for criminal acts was less harsh for the slave than the freeman, slaves might purchase their freedom and might assume second-rank offices in state administration and the religious hierarchy. Since Muslim slavery was characteristically associated with unlimited potential for social mobility and much less racialism, it is not surprising to find whole dynasties in Muslim history founded by slaves (e.g., the Egyptian Mamelukes) or the emergence to prominence of Africans as soldiers, poets, philosophers, writers, and statesmen. As early as the eighth century,

Ibrahim, the son of a Black concubine of the caliph al-Mahdi (775–85) came very close to being caliph in 817–19 when a faction in Baghdad supported his candidature against the nominated successor of the caliph al-Ma'mun. In spite of being "excessively black and shiny" he was preferred by some 'Abbasid loyalists to the 'Alid candidate of Persian descent.[118]

Al-Mustansir, another such son, Hunwick reports, reigned in Egypt between 1036 and 1094. In the seventeenth century, Mulay Isma'il, sharing the same condition, ruled in Morocco. Even Black eunuchs such as Kafur who ruled Egypt for 22 years could achieve enormous power.

That Christendom failed to be impressed by Islamic law and customs on this matter is hardly surprising since the traditions of European slavery were already quite ancient and quite elaborately rationalized by the time of the appearance of Islam in the seventh century. Moreover, it was highly improbable that the Christian establishment of the medieval era would countenance the adaptation of customs from what they considered the ultimate Christian heresy—Islam, many believed, was based on sexual license and forced conversion;[119] and finally, Western xenophobia—so critical to the character of European identity and so fundamental to Christian slave systems—

expressed a revulsion toward Muslim ideals. "A fund of xenophobia was latent in the homogeneous culture of Europe,"[120] is how Norman Daniel has put it. Further:

[X]enophobia and hysteria were compounded at the inception of the Crusades and it is a mistake to view them as an isolable phenomenon They were just one European activity. Fighting, robbing, killing, trading, making profits, taking rents or tributes, all these were closely linked to philosophical and theological analysis, to the composition of history and propaganda, and even to love of one's neighbor. The Crusades renewed the idea that we need not do as we would be done by. They were also an expression of a much older history of suspicion. . . . The expectation of difference goes back to the cultural intolerance of "barbarians" which is one of the less useful legacies of Greece.[121]

This is not to deny that there were no differences among Christians respecting slavery. There were, in medieval Christendom, as later. Debates between Christian masters, notwithstanding, David Brion Davis observed that "the distinctive characteristic of medieval theology [was] to justify the existing world while providing the means for escaping from it."[122]

In the late Medieval Age, the defenders of slavery, whether the issue was the enslavement of Europeans, infidels, "Indians," or Blacks, frequently turned to the pages of Aristotle to justify slavery as a natural condition of some parts of mankind.[123] In the early sixteenth century, when Fray Bartolome de las Casas converted from colonialist to anticolonialist pamphleteer, it was Aristotle whom he was forced to confront and use for his own purposes:

He described Aristotle as "a gentile burning in Hell whose doctrine we do not need to follow, except in so far as it conforms with Christian truth." . . .

But . . . Las Casas equally applied the Aristotelian model to "prove" that the Indians were rational beings, not one whit inferior to the Spaniards or any European, ancient or modern for that matter, but in some respects even superior to Europeans.[124]

Las Casas's ploy met, however, with only quite limited success in either his own time or later. His *Very Brief Account of the Destruction of the Indies* was roundly denounced by his contemporaries and their successors. Aristotle's "aristocracy of race" was proved to be much closer to the core of Western civilization than the complaints of Las Casas, his fellow priests Motolinia and de Landa, or such co-sympathizers as governor de Castaneda of Nicaragua and the anonymous bureaucrat who reported on the brutal excesses of Viceroy de Mendoza of New Spain. As Mavis Campbell has suggested with polemical force:

It should not be too out of place to remind ourselves here that this concept of race has never since been too far from the European psyche, peering out sporadically, with blue eyes and lily white skin, whether through that grotesque Sepulveda [one of Las Casas' most persistent opponents] who spoke of the "Superior" Spaniards, and applied the very Greek word "barbarian" to the Indians, or through Count Gobineau or Richard Wagner and his son-in-law, Houston Stewart Chamberlain, or Thomas Carlyle who had much influence on New World slavery, culminating in the megalomaniac excesses of Hitler and the racist regimes in Southern Africa.[125]

Aristotle was thus sustained into the late nineteenth and early twentieth centuries until a more scientistic rationale could overtake the ideological needs of the New Imperialism. Still, through Aristotle the convergence of moral resolution and practical necessity between Christian societies of the medieval and modern periods and the slave societies of the pre-Christian eras was striking:

> [F]rom the Homeric period onward the passionate adherence of the Greeks to the desire for political and personal liberty made it difficult for them to find a satisfactory explanation of their own slave organization. . . . Plato's reaction took the form of a mild protest that Greeks should not enslave their fellow Greeks while, as a matter of fact, the Hellenes of his day were using their fellow Hellenes as slaves, and without much compunction about it. Aristotle's explanation of the origin of slavery was rationally based upon the then accepted theory of congenital and heritable differences in human capacities, as displayed both individually and in national totalities. . . . His definition of a slave in the *Politics* is not so admirable . . .: a slave is a tool with a soul. Only in the most superficial and materialistic sense is this true. The slave, as a human being, is not a tool; and a tool has not a soul.[126]

In Islamic societies, however, the nature and the thrust of religious authority left little leeway for the use of Aristotle or any other non-Muslim apologists of slavery in this fashion.

Islam and Eurocentrism

The history of Europe for the millennium following the fifth century of the Christian era had not been markedly unilinear. That immense span of time had contained little if any basis for teleological certainty. Indeed, there had been eras such as the eighth century when the very presence of Western high culture had been faint, preserved in scattered outposts whose own fate was made doubly uncertain by barbarian invasion and the pathetic social and material conditions of the pagan societies that surrounded them.

> By the year 700, European learning had fled to the bogs of Ireland or the wild coast of Northumbria. It was in the monasteries of Ireland that fugitive scholars preserved a knowledge of the Latin and even of the Greek classics. It was in a monastery in Northumbria that the greatest scholar of his time, the greatest historian of the whole Middle Ages, the Venerable Bede, lived and wrote. And it was from the monasteries of Ireland and England, in the eighth and ninth centuries, that English and Irish fugitives would return to a devastated Europe.[127]

Christendom slowly recovered. During what would be called the Dark Age, allied with barbarian chiefs and kings, converted or otherwise, the church gradually grew into the most mature base for the feudal organization that characterized the early Middle Ages. It acquired land, and the peasants and slaves who made that land productive and valuable. Without the slightest sense of its moral bankruptcy, moreover, the leaders of the Christian Church unmercifully exploited its human base, legitimating the brutality of the nobility, their secular kin, and sharing the profits from the labor of bound workers and a foreign trade more than eight centuries long that delivered European slaves (among other goods) to Muslim merchants. Feudal Europe, for a time, however, proved to be capable of expansion while rotting from within—but it was only for a time.

By the thirteenth century, that phase of European development was at a close; the system collapsed. The ruling classes of feudal Europe were succeeded by their Mediterranean factors: merchants, traders, and bankers. They in turn spawned or defined the roles for those actors who supplied capital, technical, and scientific expertise, and administrative skills to the states that would lead the emergence of capitalist Europe. By then, however, European culture and consciousness had been profoundly affected. Legend, as we have seen, acquired the authority of history. Moral authority continued to dissipate. The mystifying veil, which the feudal ruling classes had created to hide, or at least soften the crushing oppression that they had put in place, was in tatters. Prester John's first appearance in the European imagination of the twelfth century was consequently understandable.

The legend, if it indeed originated from within the ruling class, accomplished two very disparate ends: for one it presented Europe's intelligentsia with a powerful counterpoint, inspired by Christian idealism, biblical imagery and splendor, Roman law, and Greco-Egyptian civil craftsmanship. Here was the ideal Christian society, secure in its political body and spiritual soul. It was the measure by which the failures and insidious corruptions of actual Christendom could be calibrated in detail. A model Christian Empire, which, when compared to Europe, displayed those faults that had contributed to the inability to defeat Islam either spiritually or militarily. This was the legend's internal function.

Its other significance, however, was even more critical. The legend transmuted the world beyond Europe, "the Indies," into Eurocentric terms.[128] Whatever was the reality of those lands and their peoples, came to be less and less important. For the next 300 years, between the twelfth and the fifteenth centuries, the legend of Prester John provided Europe's scholars and their less learned coreligionists with a structured and obfuse prism through which the authenticity of every datum, every traveler's report, every intelligence of its foreign trade, every fable of its poets, and every phatic foible of its soldiery would be screened and strained. Even direct evidence was not immune, for in the next century, G. K. Hunter tells us, this "frame of reference" was sustained:

The new information which the English voyages of the sixteenth century brought to the national culture had to be fitted, as best it could, into a received image of what was important. This means that the facts were not received in quite the same way as they would have been in the nineteenth century. Historians of the last century were much taken with the idea of the Elizabethan imagination liberated by the voyagers. But there is little evidence of this outside the unhistorical supposition, "that's how I would have reacted." The voyages certainly did expand the physical horizon, but it is not clear that they expanded the cultural horizon at the same time. . . . The image of man in his theological, political and social aspects could not be much affected by the discovery of empty or primitive lands.[129]

The architects of European consciousness had begun the construction of that worldview that presumed the basic structure of other than European societies was at its foundation a European structure, that the moral, ideological, and spiritual scaffold of these societies was the same bottom structure discernible in European culture, that the measure of mankind was indeed the European. The legend of Prester John and his wondrous realm, the formidability of this purely Christian king who waited in patience for his Christian allies at the other end of the world, all this was the form of the impulse in its appropriate medieval costume. Thus, when the miraculous kingdom could not be located in the deserts and steppes of central Asia or even Cathay, it did not cease its fascination but was transferred to the south beyond the upper Nile. The fantasy and its attendant resolve to bend the very existence and being of other peoples into convenient shapes were important beginnings for the destruction of the African past. While the vitality of Islam had seemed to mock the pathetic feebleness of Christ's chosen, humiliating them in defeat and with the persistent threat of further occupations and invasions, the legend was compelling. And a basic lesson of propaganda was learned: Europe's destiny was incompatible with the autochthonous meaning of the non-European worlds. An increasingly prominent concomitant of the European millennium (roughly from the tenth to the present century) would be the refutation of those terms.

In freeing itself from Muslim colonization, Europe once again had a vigorous bourgeoisie and the state institutions to begin the construction of its own extra-European colonialism. From the fifteenth century on, that colonialism would encompass the lands of Asian, African, and New World peoples and engulf a substantial fraction of those peoples into the European traditions of slave labor and exploitation. Capitalists were, from this point on, no longer dependent upon the material restraints Europe presented for the primitive accumulation of capital. What Genoese, Pisantine, and Jewish capitalists accomplished for Portugal and Spain in the fourteenth, fifteenth, and sixteenth centuries, on their expulsions from Iberia they transferred to northwestern Europe. Soon after, an English bourgeoisie succeeded those of Belgium and the Netherlands in the domination of the now-extensive world system. We have, however, gone far beyond our immediate interests in the Muslim part in Europe's development. Here we must conclude, still somewhat arbitrarily and abruptly, the survey of the significance of Islam in European history. For the moment it will have to be sufficient to remind ourselves that Islam once represented a more powerful civilization, and, again, one closely identified in the European mind with African and Black peoples.

In retrospect the Western potential for creating the Negro had moved closer in a way to its realization. The cultural and ideological inventory was at hand. A native racialism had already displayed its usefulness for rationalizing social order, and with the advent of the Islamic intrusion into European history it had further proved its value by its transformation into an instrument of collective resistance and a negation of an unacceptable past. For the Negro to come into being all what was now required was an immediate cause, a specific purpose. The trade in African slaves, coming as it did as an extension of capitalism and racial arrogance, supplied both a powerful motive and a readily received object.

CHAPTER 5

THE ATLANTIC SLAVE TRADE AND AFRICAN LABOR

Fifteenth-century "Portugal," the singularly ambitious historical agent one encounters in countless scholarly studies, is a metaphor. It is, as we have already seen, largely a convenience, an appropriately deceptive categorical referent to what in actuality was a mixture of political and economic forces, both national and supranational in origins. The term "Portugal," while symbolizing a nation, has as well obscured these forces and their significance for what was a little nation of less than one million people. Moreover, Portugal was to play a critical role in exploiting the transfer of African labor to the New World. Consequently, for those concerned with the slave trade and its ultimate significance for Black people, a better understanding of the Portuguese nation is imperative. This is so, as I shall argue, because the same but not identical interests and dynamics that slowly formed Portugal into "an important pawn on the chessboard of European history,"[1] were also implicated in the transformation of African labor into capital. For this reason, it is worth our time to review and identify these elements as they appeared in Portugal's history.

There were several very real agencies whose interests and activities have been glorified as Portugal's national concerns in the general histories of the modern Western academy. Too often, however, the nature and identities of those agencies have been inadvertently disguised by the rather grander levels of generalization that have accompanied the search to capture their ethos. For some students of the era, the motives for European expansion were material and physical: "What western Europe needed in the fourteenth and fifteenth centuries," Wallerstein writes, "was food . . .

and fuel."[2] Braudel, on the other hand, has suggested that western Mediterranean overpopulation was the key to expansion.[3] There are also those who have argued, like Livermore, that the motivation was organizationally systemic, that the militaristic machinery of the *Reconquista* required new "targets of opportunity" if it were not to be turned inward.[4] Others, as we have noted earlier, with more attention to ideology, have supposed the real issue was the defeat of the Muslims and the revitalization of Christendom.[5] No single such explanation seems entirely correct or sufficiently specific, though all have been persuasively presented. The result is that at the grand level of reconstruction, the analysis of fifteenth-century Portugal and its historical role would appear to have no satisfactory measure for distilling this multiplicity of needs, actors, and historical forces. Still, though their number might be confusing, reconstruction of the actual power relations between these actors may simplify the task of their identification and assessment.

One generally unrecognized but crucial relationship, when we speak in strictly political terms, involved a relatively weak but native feudal ruling class and its more powerful extra-national ruling-class allies. Specifically, this amounted to an alliance between Portugal's House of Avis, with its neodynastic nobility and bourgeoisie,[6] and a strain of capitalistic aristocracy that had been bred in England by war and civil war, political chaos, and economic recession, and a close connection to an emerging British bourgeoisie. In fifteenth-century England, Postan has surmised:

> The great breeding season of English capitalism was in the early phases of the Hundred Years War, the time when the exigencies of Royal finance, new experiments in taxation, speculative ventures with wool, the collapse of Italian finance and the beginning of the new cloth industry, all combined to bring into existence a new race of war financiers and commercial speculators, army purveyors and wool-monopolists.[7]

Historically, the relationship between the maturing ruling classes of Portugal and England had been sealed at the end of the fourteenth century with the Treaty of Windsor (1386), which secured the Portuguese throne from the ambitions of Castile's monarchy, and was itself closed by the marriage between Joao of Avis and Philippa of Lancaster, the daughter of John of Gaunt. This alliance was one that the English had believed would ultimately lead to the acquisition of the throne of Castile.[8] The designs of the English on Castile were never fulfilled. The conclusion of the Hundred Years War, with its disastrous results on English territorial interests on the continent, a civil war in England and Spain's own national vigor at the end of the century, extinguished those interests. But the relationship with Portugal would prove to be one so valuable that it is still celebrated by English historians. In our own century, for example, Carus Wilson has written:

> Portugal's relations with England were consistently friendly. These two states were naturally disposed to be allies, since neither of them was on good terms with Castile. There was also kinship between their dynasties, and the men of both

countries were born seamen and adventurers. . . . The friendship . . . lasted on in spite of temporary ruptures through acts of violence and changes of dynasty in England; and throughout the fifteenth century the provisions made in this charter of commerce [the Treaty of Windsor] were confirmed, and the kings of both countries were pledged to punish infractions of it.[9]

As C. R. Boxer would have it, these Portuguese "kings" were, of course, "half-English princes." War had brought these two nobilities together. War had indeed been the very basis of their existence. War, finally, had so enlarged their political alliance until it achieved what could pass for historical proportions, surviving several centuries despite "temporary ruptures." Regardless, in the fifteenth century—when the necessary conditions for the Atlantic slave trade were being laid down—the link between the emerging bourgeoisies resident in (but not always native to) the two countries provided the basis for a North Atlantic commerce and the mercantilisms that would dominate their economies for the next three hundred years. This would prove no small matter for the directions in which the slave trade would develop.

The Genoese Bourgeoisie and the Age of Discovery

Even more important than these political relations, however, and certainly more directly germane to our interests in the Portuguese as the historical force that laid the basis for the Atlantic slave trade, were the merchants and bankers of Italian origins who colonized Portugal (and the Spanish kingdoms) during this period. Though Verlinden's use of the term "nation" is more figurative than political, his characterization of the historical significance of these capitalists is helpful:

> Italy was the only really colonizing nation during the middle ages. From the beginning of the crusades onwards, Venice, Pisa, Genoa, later Florence, and southern Italy under the Angevins as well as under the Aragonese, were interested in the Levant and in the economic and colonial possibilities offered there by the gradual waning of the Byzantine Empire. It is also at about the same time that Italian merchants appear in the Iberian peninsula, and obtain an influence that will persist until far into the modern period, both in European and colonial economy.[10]

Virginia Rau notes that "[t]he earliest documental references we have concerning the activities of Italian merchants in Portugal date from the XIIIth century. When they come to our notice, they had already boldly found their way into the Portuguese money market.")[11] These "Italian merchants" were in fact (in order of importance) Genoese and the sons of Piacenza, Milan, Florence, and Venice.[12] Further, we learn from Rau that by the fourteenth century, whose beginnings were appropriately marked by the appointment by King Diniz of a Genoese (Manuel Pezagno)[13] to the Portuguese admiralty in 1317, Lisbon had become "the great centre of Genoese trade."[14] With Lisbon and Oporto as bases of operation, the Genoese merchant-capitalists ensconced themselves into the entire structure of Portuguese power: serving as creditors to the monarchy, financiers for the state's ambitions and adventures, monopolists under royal charters of security, and ultimately Portuguese nobles by a series of events including royal decrees, marriage into the native nobility, and participation in military projects organized by the state.[15] Precisely as Rau's example of the Lomellini family would suggest—beginning with the appearance of Bartholomeu Lomellini, the merchant, in Portugal in 1424 and ending with integration of his heirs and relatives into the landed aristocracy of Madeira and the peninsular nobility by the end of the century—the Genoese merchant princes proved to be far more successfully adaptable than their countrymen (i.e., Italian) competitors. Unlike the arrogant Venetians, the Genoese made themselves available to their hosts financially, intellectually and fraternally. As Wallerstein has observed:

> To the extent that [the Portuguese bourgeoisie] lacked the capital, they found it readily available from the Genoese who, for reasons of their own having to do with their rivalry with Venice, were ready to finance the Portuguese. And the potential conflict of the indigenous and foreign bourgeoisie was muted by the willingness of the Genoese to assimilate into Portuguese culture over time.[16]

While the Venetians continued to concentrate on the domination of the Mediterranean, and the Florentines on their banking and wool trade in continental and north Atlantic commerce, the Genoese positioned themselves to take advantage of the trade that eventually would progress from the Maghreb, to the mid-Atlantic and finally to the trans-Atlantic.[17] By the middle of the fifteenth century, it was their capital that determined the direction and pace of "discovery." Verlinden remarks:

> Lagos [Portugal] became, from about 1310, an important harbor on the route of the Italian convoys to northwestern Europe. If one remembers that Lagos, much more than Sagres, was the starting point of the first Portuguese discoveries, the importance of the bonds, established there with Italian seamen and businessmen, grows evident.[18]

Moreover, it was the favored status of these Italians in Portugal that facilitated Portuguese claims at Rome resulting in Papal Bulls sympathetic to Portuguese commerce and state imperialism,[19] and it was Genoese capitalists who sustained the links between the English and Portuguese ruling classes by assuming a relationship to English trade and the state directly complementary to their presence in Portugal.[20]

In England, as in Portugal, Genoese made up the bulk of the Italian merchants who in turn composed the majority of alien merchants in that kingdom during the fifteenth century.[21] There, too, they won royal exemptions from commercial taxes and restrictions, and managed to monopolize imported goods as diverse as the foreign medicines (like medicated treacle) and other drugs in vogue during that century,[22] and Portuguese cork and sugar at whose points of origin they had already contracted exclusive monopolies.[23] Finally, in England, too, as creditors for its kings, as factors and merchants for royal monopolies, they came to occupy special positions in English trade:

> In vain the English petitioned against the lavish privileges obtained with a great sum by these merchants from needy kings whose financiers they had become, begging that they might be restricted to bringing goods of their own manufacture; unable to vie with the mighty Italian cities in wealth, the little English towns received scant attention.[24]

In an England rent by civil war, court intrigues, and a fractious aristocratic class, the financial support of the Italians along with their trade and concomitant sources of intelligence could be decisive. The English monarchy, with its Italian and other foreign commercial and financial collaborators, for the time being secured an independence from its native aristocratic and bourgeois classes.

It was in this way that Italian capitalists situated themselves to play a critical role in determining the pace, the character, and the structure of the early trans-Atlantic slave trade of the next century. Without them and the complicity of part of the English aristocracy and of the Portuguese and English merchant classes, and, of course, the clerical nobility of Rome, it is doubtful that a Portuguese Empire would ever have come into existence. Without that empire, nothing would be as it is.

The Portuguese Empire did come into being, however, and from the middle of the fifteenth century and for the next one hundred years—to the good fortunes of both its national and expatriate sponsors—its mixture of greed, piety, savagery, militarism, cultural arrogance, and statescraft swept across the world. Not surprisingly, given the long-standing preoccupations of medieval long-distance merchants, the winds of commercial interests blew the empire first to the south and east: Senegambia, Elmina, and Luanda along the west coast of Africa; Safala, Mozambique and Mombasa on the African east coast; Hormuz in the Persian Gulf; Goa on the Malabar coast of India; Malacca in Malay; and Ternate in the Moluccas. And if their several motives still perplex us, at least to some of them the issue was clear:

> When the Portuguese finally came ashore at Calicut, some astonished Tunisian traders in the crowd asked them what the devil had brought them so far. "Christians and spices," was the answer allegedly given by da Gama's men. . . . This close association between God and Mammon formed the hallmark of the empire founded by the Portuguese in the East, and, for that matter, in Africa and in Brazil as well.[25]

Once the Portuguese had rounded what was for them the Cape of Good Hope (and perhaps even before they reached that point), these voyagers had become actually an analogue of the Chinese who preceded them: we refer, of course, to the "seven massive" imperial expeditionary fleets commanded by the Muslim admiral Cheng Ho between 1405 and 1434 (Cheng Ho died that year) that had already confidently assayed these waters for trade and plunder.[26] The Chinese ventures that with their fleets of junks carrying sometimes as many as 40,000 people, amounted to convoys of "impressive intercontinental missiles" according to William Appleman Williams.[27] With its fleets the Chinese Empire successfully challenged the Arab and Muslim traders who had already grown accustomed to their own domination of the East African and Indian Ocean commercial trades. This did not please the former masters of the trade of these seas, but it did not seem to matter. Whatever the weight of their resistance it never amounted to enough to be included among the reasons speculated to underlie the apparently sudden imperial decision to forego further adventures in the area.[28] The withdrawal would seem to have been an affair internal to the Chinese Empire.

The Portuguese, less audaciously but necessarily more cunning,[29] accomplished the displacement of the area's "resident" tradesmen at the end of the century and the beginnings of the next. Momentarily, the maritime markets most coveted by Europeans were in the hands of the Portuguese/Italians—the African and south Atlantic trades with their gold, salt, malagueta pepper, gum, cork, cereals, sugar, and slaves; and the trade with the East with its spices, wools, and dyes.[30] This Portuguese monopoly was, however, not entirely uncontested in Europe.[31] In the Atlantic region, Castile's commercial strata had shadowed its rival's ventures along the Guinea coast from at least as early as 1453–54, laying claims through the Castilian crown to both Guinea and the Canary Islands.[32] The controversy between the "two Catholic kings" continued even beyond its formal resolution by the Treaty of Toledo (1480) and into the following century. It was punctuated by raids by each of the other's merchant shipping and trading posts, and by claims and counterclaims to ancient or papal privileges.[33] Though their defeat would prove to be only a temporary setback, the point is that the monarchal claimants of Spain lost. With the south Atlantic closed to them for legitimate merchant exploitation, the Spanish Crown and its native and Italian partners began to explore the possibilities of an entirely different route to the East.[34]

Genoese Capital, the Atlantic, and a Legend

For Spain, the key to its achievement of a western route to the "East" was, as it had been for the Portuguese Empire of the Indies, the Genoese. In particular, in Seville in 1492, the experience, energies, and ambitions of the Genoese became concentrated in the figure of Cristofolo Colombo (Christopher Columbus). Still it was not a simple or straightforward event, there were some elements of even this relationship between the Spanish and the Italians that in retrospect seem almost entirely fortuitous.

Although much of his background before his journey to Seville in 1485 will probably always remain obscure, Columbus was in many ways a natural if not typical bourgeois creation of Genoese capital, trade, and manufacturing. Born around 1451 of parents whose origins appear to have been in the Ligurian Republic, Columbus, at fourteen years of age, first took up his father's trade: wool weaving.[35] Notwithstanding the fictional constructions of his past that Columbus, his son Ferdinand, and Las

Casas would perpetrate, it appears he remained a weaver into his early twenties, taking part in occasional voyages in that capacity to Genoese possessions in the Mediterranean.[36] Around 1476, the documents of his contemporaries place him on a voyage to England undertaken by the bankers Giovanni Antonio di Negro and Nicolas Spinola. This trip was intercepted by French pirates, and the survivors, Columbus among them, found refuge in Lisbon.[37] Columbus settled in Lisbon and like some other notable Genoese bourgeoisie, he eventually married into Portuguese nobility. In his case, Felipa Moniz Perestrello, whose family had property on the island of Porto Santo near Madeira, became his wife and his entree into the stream of Portuguese overseas expansion.[38]

By all rights, the credit for Columbus's rediscovery of the "new world" beyond the ocean should have attached to the Portuguese throne. Columbus had taken up residence in Lisbon in 1477 and five years later had made his first attempt at petitioning for state sponsorship (and the grant of feudal privileges) at the royal court of Portugal. Interestingly enough, it is still not clear what Columbus had in mind at this stage for what he would persist in describing as his divinely appointed mission. It is very possible that Columbus's initial petition (1482) concerned islands in the Atlantic rather than the search for a mainland, but by 1484, a second submission spoke of Cipango (Japan) and Cathay (China).[39] Apparently, Columbus's application was clumsily constructed (Davies believed that Columbus had no command of written Latin until 1489 and never mastered the writing of Italian or Portuguese), his calculations unpersuasive, and his use of cosmographies authority suspect.[40] The court's Mathematical Junta, after a year of study of Columbus's proposal and consultation with Martin Behain,[41] the Nuremberg cartographer, convinced King Joao II to reject Columbus's project on the grounds that Joao had "information regarding the western lands more positive than the visions of Columbus."[42] If Joao's technical commission now appears to have been a bit dismissive of Columbus's scheme, the same could be said of Castile, the more enthused but still cautious Andalusian dukes of Medina-Sidonia and Medina-Celi, and the English Crown (in England, Columbus had been represented by his brother, Bartolomeo)—all of whom rejected the Genoese's petitions for support between 1485–89.

The Portuguese, however, seemed to have been on fairly firm ground, for at least by 1486 there is some indication that some of their seamen had sighted land west of the Azores. Verlinden is confident enough of this to conclude: "What is certain is that in 1486 the talk was no longer of one Island of the Seven Cities, but of the possibility of an archipelago or even a continent. Clearly, then, the period of the hypothetical or legendary island had passed."[43] For some at court, the western route across the seas to Cipango and Cathay—a distance calculated by the Florentine mathematician and cosmographer Toscanelli to be 5,000 miles and by Columbus as 3,500 miles— appeared to be a distinct possibility.[44] Thus, in 1487, the same year that (Verlinden points out) saw Pero da Covilhao and Afonso da Paiva pursuing Portuguese interests in India, Arabia, and Ethiopia, and Bartolomeu Dias round the Cape of Good Hope (all three contributions to the Portuguese commitment to the African route to the East), the Portuguese Crown had authorized its own exploration of a western route.[45] Since the bourgeoisie dominating the Genoese colony of Lisbon were unwilling to show any tangible interest in a western route, the Portuguese Crown's participation in the project mounted (and paid for) by the Flemish Azoresian Ferdinand van Olmen (Bartolome de las Cases would refer to him as Hernan de Olmos)[46] and the Portuguese Madeiran, Joham Afomso do Estreito, was limited to the ceding of jurisdictional powers and territorial rights in the new land. The Crown was apparently incapable of much more than that when it sought to act independently of its major commercial partners. Unfortunately for the Portuguese monarch, neither van Olmen nor Estreito ever returned from their winter excursion.

Columbus was a bit luckier than either of his predecessors in the Atlantic, for at least he had their example to profit from. Verlinden is convinced that "Columbus must have learned of the voyage in Seville, for there was active communication between the Italian colony of Lisbon and that of the great Andalusian port."[47] This would, of course, imply that the Genoese families, their joint-stock companies, and their banks were in the habit of exchanging or sharing information that might be of value to their commercial interests. Whatever the case might be, Columbus did find something of value in Seville:

> Italian bankers, much of whose activities were blocked by the Turks, were the financiers for a big part of ocean-borne trade. There was a Genoese commercial colony in Seville and local links with the Italian banking house of Spinola and Di Negri, Columbus's old employer. Francesco Pinelli, a Genoese banker of Seville and co-director of the Santa Hermandad, the Spanish state police, guaranteed a loan for the Columbus plan. Pinelli's fellow police director was none other than Luis de Santangel, the royal treasurer.[48]

With the support, at least, of these two highly placed Genoese, and several forms of assistance from the powerful Pinzon family, which dominated the port of Palos de la Frontera,[49] Columbus now had a project worthy of the Spanish Crown's official support. And if we recall that Columbus's appearance before Ferdinand and Isabella coincided historically with that moment when the Spanish Crown was intent upon its self-appointed mission to unify Spain, centralize state authority, vanquish its rivals among its own aristocracy, and acquire an independent source of capital for itself, Columbus and his Genoese collaborators and countrymen were an almost perfect instrument.

> Italian support was unquestionably well received, at least by the rulers. Ferdinand the Catholic, in particular, understood admirably the contribution Italian capital and techniques could make at that crucial time to his kingdom. Coming from the east of the peninsula, he was accustomed to look to the Mediterranean and Italy and considered economic relations with that country as obvious and natural. This

attitude of mind dictated a similar policy in Andalusia, in the Canary Islands, and in America, when destiny put control of these areas into his hands.[50]

Here was a resourceful community whose very existence rested on the persistence of its interdependence with the state. The colonial trade that the Genoese (and Italian) community dominated, the capital that it commanded, the inventory of science and culture that it possessed, all were Spanish at the pleasure of the state—no matter how independently powerful and significant they might appear to be. And for the moment it was the state's pleasure to balance the Italians (and also—but not for long—the Jews) against its own bourgeoisie and its still militaristic aristocracy.[51] Columbus's luck was holding.

With only the barest of exaggeration, then, it might be said that Columbus's achievements of 1492—beginning with the extraordinary concessions he acquired from his royal partners in April of that year at Santa Fe, and ending with the arrival of the ships under his command in the West Indian islands in October—amounted to one more level on the extraordinary financial scaffold that Genoese and other Italian capitalist families had been constructing in the Iberian peninsula for nearly 300 years. When Columbus came to terms with Ferdinand and Isabella, the road had been paved for him by Genoese admirals who had served Portuguese and Spanish kings for centuries; by Genoese, Piacentine, and Florentine merchants who had assumed the primary financial risks in colonizing the Portuguese Azores and Madeiran islands, and Spain's Canary Island group; by Italian factors and money lenders who had strung their capital from Algiers and Ceuta in north Africa, to Elmina and Luanda on the west coast of that continent, and east to the Moluccas and Nagasaki; and by an Italian bourgeoisie whose financial and technical character and business affairs had become totally assimilated to the interests of the Spanish and Portuguese states and their most adventurous aristocracies.[52] Whether Columbus was the extraordinary seaman that Samuel Eliot Morison has persisted in making him,[53] whether his obsessive personality and religious zeal were so compelling as to have cast a spell over Isabella and her religious advisers,[54] are all of secondary significance to the single fact of his origins and the legacy to which he was heir as a Genoese. This was the structural means of his accomplishment: the two-centuries-long apogee of Genoese influence in Spain and Portugal.[55] Thus, when Columbus and the others with him (and those who followed) came face to face with the Arawaks, the Tainos, the Aztecs, the Mayans, the Quechuas, and all the other inhabitants of the western hemisphere, it was this complex mixture of feudal authority and privilege, comingled with the appetites of emergent merchant capitalism, national ambitions, and missionary compulsions that stood at their backs.

African Labor as Capital

The use of slave labor in the New World of the sixteenth century by the Spanish Crown (and soon after the Portuguese) and its merchant concessionaires was consequently a most natural step. Slave labor had been a basis for colonial trade in the Mediterranean,[56] Africa, and the Indies; it was already the foundation of colonization in the Canaries, the Azores, and the Madeiran islands. At first, the relationship between capitalism, colonization, and slave labor had appeared almost coincidental. To some it still does. Philip Curtin, for example, has written:

> The choice between freedom and slavery . . . depended on European institutions and *habits of mind.* . . . One was the Mediterranean tradition of filling the gaps between the demand and supply of people by importing alien slaves. The Venetians used that device in their east Mediterranean colonies, where imported slave labor played an important role in agricultural development in Crete, Cyprus, and Chios. This *institutional habit* was no doubt reinforced by the fact that Venice was a city-state, not a large territorial unit with abundant population resources to be mobilized and sent overseas as colonists.[57]

Notwithstanding Philip Curtin's rather casual language in describing the process, we should remember that it was in Venice's affairs of trade that Oliver Cox situated "the first capitalistically organized commerce in human beings."[58] Still, at first as we have noted before, the slave trade had been more significant to Venetian commerce than slave labor.

As Italian capitalism matured, however, this emphasis on trade was to change for three reasons. Briefly, they were the expansion of the power of the Ottoman Turks in the eastern Mediterranean in the fifteenth century, the extension of sugar-cane cultivation from Asia Minor to Cyprus, Sicily, and the Atlantic islands (Madeira, Cape Verde, and the Azores) at the end of that century, and the collaboration of Genoese capitalists with the ruling classes of Iberia. These events transformed the incidental relationship between capitalism and slave labor into the very foundation of New World enterprise.[59]

Madeira, as it turned out, was the physical and historical juncture where these processes congealed. Sidney Greenfield observes:

> [W]ith the introduction of sugar cane and its commercial success . . . Canary Islanders and Moors—followed by Africans—as slaves, performed the necessary physical labor that enabled the upwardly mobile settlers of Madeira to develop a life style, derived from the tradition of the continental nobility but based upon the physical efforts of slaves producing commercial crops for sale on the markets of the continent, that characterized the emerging social institution of the slave plantation.[60]

The "Admiral of the Ocean Sea" was the embodied connective. Columbus, a son of Genoa, an agent of the Spanish Crown, an ambitious merchant who had married into one of the families of lesser Portuguese nobility which had acquired its new wealth from the early colonization of Madeira and the cultivation of sugar there, and the founder of Spain's Caribbean colonies had also brought sugar to the New World.[61] In England, where envy of Spain's monopoly was tempered by the Spanish Empire's seapower for at least the next century and a half, it was all said quite simple. Columbus's "West Indies" became known by English merchants as the "Sugar Islands."[62]

However, for the time being—that is the better part of the sixteenth century—Italo-Portuguese enterprise dominated the European trade with the Atlantic coast of Africa. This meant that African labor for the colonial plantations of Sao Tome, Cape Verde, the Azores, Madeira, and the West Indies, and the mines of New Spain and Peru was supplied by these merchants. "Until 1570," Leslie Rout Jr. maintains in an almost absolute consensus with other students of the trade, "the Portuguese had the lucrative slave trade entirely to themselves."[63] And as the colonies grew, so did their appetites for *piezas de Indias*,[64] "captives of just war." For Angola, as early as 1530, Jan Vansina calculates, "the annual export figures were from four to five thousand slaves a year—and if there were no more, this was due only to the lack of ships to carry them."[65] No wonder Affonso, the Catholic king of the Kongo and collaborator in the trade with the Portuguese Crown, had been shaken enough to write to his "partners" in 1526: "There are many traders in all corners of the country. Every day people are enslaved and kidnapped, even nobles, even members of the king's own family."[66] It seems the trade was already exceeding the boundaries of its commercial origins. Even the conquest of Portugal by Spain in 1580 did not retard the acceleration of the trade. Indeed, the Spanish left the trade to their Portuguese underlings to administer.[67] That relationship persisted until the Portuguese regained national independence in 1640. By 1650, it is estimated that 500,000 Blacks were living in Spanish America. More than 220,000 Africans had been transported to the ports of Cartagena and Veracruz by Portuguese merchants during the first 45 years (1595–1640) of their Spanish trade. Enriqueta Vila writes:

> It is undoubtedly the Portuguese era that marks the African ethnic influence in the new continent. It was the Portuguese who, by creating a vast network of traders, factors, and middlemen, and by profiting from the drop in the Indian population, achieved a market capable of absorbing such enormous quantities. . . . I believe that the Portuguese period was a special era for the slave trade, which was never repeated.[68]

"For Brazil," Inikori writes, "the first reliable census . . . in 1798 . . . showed that there were 1,988,000 negroes in that country by this time."[69] (By the eighteenth century, of course, Portugal's monopoly in the Atlantic slave trade had been superseded first by the Netherlands, and was now the business of the merchants and ruling classes of England and France.)

The Ledgers of a World System

The historiography of the Atlantic slave trade is immense and is still growing. Consequently, at least the outlines of the trade and the characteristics of those economies and societies that required slave labor are fairly well known. In any case, even the barest review of the literature would entail volumes in its own right and perhaps deflect us from our primary purpose here, to ascertain the material, social, and ideological foundations for the emergence of a Black radical tradition. Our attention, then, will be centered on the work that most directly bears on this problem.

The significance of African labor for the development and formation of the commercial and industrial capitalist systems can be only partially measured by numbers. This is the case because, first, the numbers we have are questionable, but more disconcerting, the relationship between the growth of capitalism and slave labor has persistently been in dispute. At least one influential "school" of historiography has denied this relationship, challenging the volume of the slave trade, its profitability, and in some instances even arguing for the benevolence of the trade and slavery. As Roderick McDonald puts it, "The shadows of Adam Smith and Ulrich B. Phillips loom large and dark over the profitability question, and their perspectives continue profoundly to influence the debate."[70] Still it is not quite the case, as McDonald terms it, that "you pays your money and you takes your pick."

With respect to the volume of the *piezas de Indias* transported to the New World, Philip Curtin's work is at the center of the storm. In 1969, Curtin authoritatively calculated that between 1451 and 1870, 9,566,000 African workers were brought to the Western Hemisphere. He further concluded that "it is extremely unlikely that the ultimate total will turn out to be less than 8,000,000 or more than 10,500,000."[71] This significantly lowered the figure most commonly used, 50,000,000. In 1976, however, I. E. Inikori published a critique of Curtin that took him to task for the casualness of his methodological and statistical computations, his shallow historicity and, in a subsequent debate, for the peculiarities of his logic and ideology.[72] Inikori's argument

> related to slave population and slave import figures in the Americas; slave smuggling and the inaccuracy of official slave export data in Portuguese African territories (Angola and Mozambique); understatement by the customs records of the volume and value of commodities employed by English merchants in the purchase of slaves on the African coast, as well as the number or tonnage of shipping employed.[73]

Inikori's treatment of customs records, contemporary censuses of slave populations, descriptions of population fluctuations due to epidemic and the varying conditions of work, and the studies of Eltis, Anstey, Daget, Peytraud, and Davis, would appear to support an upward revision of Curtin's figures by at least one-third.[74] A preliminary summation of Inikori's figures for only the major periods of the slave trade comes to 15,399,572.[75] Still, whatever the actual number was, the volume of the trade was enormous. The work of Inikori, McDonald, D. R. Murray, and others, however, serves to underscore dramatically Curtin's remark that before the nineteenth century the number of Africans crossing the Atlantic each year exceeded that of Europeans.[76] Moreover, as we shall see momentarily, the relative decline of European colonists to African populations from the end of the seventeenth century—and in some instances the decline of the Europeans was absolute—may have helped to confuse the issue of the profitability of the slave system.

With respect to the significance of African labor for the development of European-directed economies on both sides of the Atlantic, the literature again is substantial. We have already noted Marx's assessment in his letter to Annenkov in 1846, and his later treatment of the same issue in the first volume of *Capital*. For Marx, slavery had been "the chief momenta of primitive accumulation," "an economic category of the highest importance."[77] First, African workers had been transmuted by the perverted canons of mercantile capitalism into property. Then, African labor power as slave labor was integrated into the organic composition of nineteenth-century manufacturing and industrial capitalism, thus sustaining the emergence of an extra-European world market within which the accumulation of capital was garnered for the further development of industrial production.

Marx, however, was not the first to recognize the existence of a relationship between Britain's economic growth and the business in slaves. Williams reminded us that in eighteenth-century Liverpool, "the red brick Customs House was blazoned with Negro heads."[78] In 1788, to Bristol, which had preceded Liverpool in the slave trade, "The West Indian trade was worth . . . twice as much as all her other overseas commerce combined."[79] Even contemporary English writers were prescient enough to match the signs and lexicon of the streets. In 1839 at Oxford, Herman Merivale had anticipated Marx when he lectured:

We speak of the blood-cemented fabric of the prosperity of New Orleans or the Havanna: let us look at home. What raised Liverpool and Manchester from provincial towns to gigantic cities? What maintains now their ever active industry and their rapid accumulation of wealth? The exchange of their produce with that raised by the American slaves; and their present opulence is as really owing to the toil and suffering of the negro, as if his hands had excavated their docks and fabricated their steam-engines. Every trader who carries on commerce with those countries, from the great house which lends its name and funds to support the credit of the American Bank, down to the Birmingham merchant who makes a shipment of shackles to Cuba or the coast of Africa, is in his own way an upholder of slavery: and I do not see how any consumer who drinks coffee or wears cotton can escape from the same sweeping charge.[80]

A century later, Eric Williams, as we have noted, made the point again. So, too, has McDonald more recently:

Labour was the key to the development of the Americas; initially land was plentiful, capital was available to "prime the pump," and labour was provided by African and Afro-American slaves. The source of all value is labour; the value of the New World, the fabulous wealth of St. Domingue, Brazil, Jamaica and Cuba, created by slaves, was enjoyed not only by planters and in the colonies, but by the mother country. It was reinvested, purchased power and position, and stimulated development in commercial and industrial spheres.[81]

These assertions of Merivale, Marx, and McDonald, and the political economy of Williams's analysis can be buttressed in a myriad of ways. One writer indicates that quite early "England's colonies had begun to pay off, and by the middle of the seventeenth century, of a population about five and a half million it is estimated that about fifty thousand were at sea."[82] Moreover, the wealth of the plantations drew together the commercial bourgeoisie and the state, implicating them in behaviors and institutions entirely dependent on the existence of slavery and long-distance trade. In Spain, Portugal, the Netherlands, France, and England, the immensity of the profits to be made spawned extensive corruption as its tell-tale mark. The English and French colonists and planters were slower than their Spanish, Portuguese, and Dutch contemporaries to come to sugar but when they did—that is when tobacco ended its reign of wealth[83]—they, too, displayed their venality. For one, the colonies had helped to transform England into a bourgeois democracy with a capitalist and commercial trading economy. At the end of the seventeenth century, mercantile elements of the Christian nation had circumvented the religious prohibitions against usury, institutionalizing their financial freedom with the official establishment of the Bank of England in 1694. The rise of the English bourgeoisie of course occasioned the beginnings of the overturning of English society. The leading members of this mercantile clique had been associated with "republicanism, treason and Dutch connections" in the previous decade. "This was exactly the background," P. G. M. Dickson suggests, "that contemporaries expected plans for a national bank to have."[84] In France, the maritime bourgeoisie were forced into a much more dangerous game:

> The slave-trade and slavery were the economic basis of the French Revolution. "Sad irony of human history," comments Jaures. "The fortunes created at Bordeaux, at Nantes, by the slave-trade, gave to the bourgeoisie that pride which needed liberty and contributed to human emancipation." Nantes was the center of the slave-trade. . . . Nearly all the industries which developed in France during the eighteenth century had their origin in goods or commodities destined either for the coast of Guinea or for America . . . upon the success or failure of the traffic everything else depended.[85]

The demonstration of the relationship between slavery and the development of Western Europe, however, need not end here.

One other sort of direct evidence respecting the profitability of slave labor can be found in the later work of Richard Pares, a scholar who earlier on, McDonald reminds us, had questioned the relationship between capitalism and slavery.[86] Discussing the wealth of the planters themselves, Pares wrote in 1960:

> The absentee sugar planters were, with the East India Nabobs, the most conspicuous rich men of their time. Other absentee planters were nothing to them. There were some coffee and indigo absentees in France, but the tobacco planters of Virginia and even the rice planters of Carolina could not afford to behave in England like the sugar planters. They might go to England for their education but, unlike the sugar planters, they returned home when it was over; for in Virginia and Maryland, unlike the islands, life was tolerable and a real local patriotism came

more easily to the planters; besides, their estates were mostly too small to support an absentee owner for the whole of his life. Yet they lived a luxurious life at home.[87]

Another clue, also drawn from Pares, was the source of the capital that edged planters into the indebtedness for which they were notorious:

> The money came, in the last resort, from the planters themselves. . . . The money which was received from one planter was lent again, either to him or to another planter. . . . Thus it was the planter who was paying, so to speak, for his own enslavement. The profits of the plantations were the source which fed the indebtedness charged upon the plantations themselves. In this sense Adam Smith was wrong: the wealth of the British West Indies did not all proceed from the mother country; after some initial loans in the earliest period which merely primed the pump, the wealth of the West Indies was created out of the profits of the West Indies themselves, and, with some assistance from the British tax-payer, much of it found a permanent home in Great Britain.[88]

Even the fabled decline of European merchants in the New World in the eighteenth century provides little support to the thesis that the slave system was of marginal economic significance to metropolitan development. Here again the later Pares intervenes. He maintains that the explanation of this phenomenon lies both in K. G. B. Davies's assertion that the merchants had been displaced by planters engaged in entrepreneurship and the fact that Europeans were being displaced by Africans. "As the white populations diminished in most of the British islands, and were replaced by slaves who were hardly allowed to consume anything, the market for European goods must have fallen off quite considerably. (Incidentally, this reduction in the number of their customers helps to account for the decline of the class of resident merchants.)"[89] Finally, one might add the testimony of contemporaries. The comments come from widely different moments in the business of slavery but their sources, their specifics, and their timing all describe the enthusiasm with which the system of slavery was undertaken. From the archives of the first "large-scale introduction of Africans" into the New World, Vila discovers:

> In a report about the asientos taken to the Junta in 1612 it was affirmed that, should the trade be lost, not only would the income produced by it be lost, but also the sales tax (*alcabala*) and the export-import tax (*averia*) on the money that arrived from the Indies. . . . Moreover the buying and selling of slaves was one of the most important and lucrative sources of the Alcabalas.[90]

Almost 200 years later, on 20 February 1793 to be exact, Bryan Edwards wrote to Henry Dundas from Jamaica:

> Our harbours are full of Guineymen [African slave ships], yet the price keeps up enormously. Mr. Shirley gave £100 a head for a pick of 20 Koromantees out of a ship of Mr. Lindo's, and so long as the notion continues that the trade will be abolished, people will buy at any price, even to their own ruin, and the destruction

of half the negroes, for want of provisions. (Meaning that the planters are not in general provided with sufficient means to support so great an influx of newly imported negroes on a sudden.)[91]

From whatever vantage point one chooses, the relationship between slave labor, the slave trade, and the weaving of the early capitalist economies is apparent. Whatever were the alternatives, the point remains: historically, slavery was a critical foundation for capitalism.

The Column Marked "British Capitalism"

We may now have sufficient grounds for saying that in the New World, the British (and French) entrepreneurs—following the models provided by the Portuguese, Spanish, and the Dutch—substantially substituted human capital for commodities in the seventeenth and eighteenth centuries. We will follow this British trade for the moment because it seems the best documented, because it so firmly seats slavery in the movement from mercantile to industrial capitalism, and because many of the clearest tracings of a Black radical tradition lead back to it.

To be sure, the leaders of the colonizing efforts of Britain had begun by exporting those colonized peoples to whom they had immediate access, that is the Irish. We have already made mention of that fact as well as the collateral uses of labor from Germany and Great Britain itself. It appears that the earliest investors in the colonies—lord proprietors, politicians, and merchants according to Pares—had economic designs that at first could be met by a modest labor pool. As independent venturers, the landed rich seemed most frequently to anticipate that their colonies would produce an income resembling in form the manorial dues to which they were accustomed in England.[92] The joint companies, in which some lords along with merchant and public representatives of the bourgeoisie also took an interest, were typically more trade oriented. These companies were promoted for the colonial cultivation of cotton, tobacco, indigo, ginger, and the production of extractive industries such as timber, glass, iron, and precious metals.[93] Thus, until the arrival of sugar in the early 1640s, and the development of large plantations, labor was adequately supplied by Europeans: indentured peasants, political outcasts produced at varying times by national and civil wars, and poor or orphaned females (only some of whom possessed "bad reputations").[94] As Richard B. Moore reiterates, their lots were oppressive:

> Somewhat less onerous [than African slavery], but still quite oppressive, was the system of indentured slavery of Europeans, forced in one way or another into the colonies whether on the mainland or in the islands. Writing of this, the Jesuit priest, Joseph J. Williams, relates how Irish peasants were "hunted down as men hunt down game, and were forcibly put on board ship, and sold to the planters of Barbados."[95]

Between 1624 and 1634, tobacco became the main staple of the colonies, earning in that period profits that attracted more and more English and French planters to it. By the end of this period, a glut of tobacco had hit the market and prices declined. The resultant long depression of the late 1630s and early 1640s compelled the search for a new staple, despite the lingering expectations that tobacco would recover.[96] In England, an additional strain was being generated: "harried by depression and the ever growing threat of civil war, Englishmen left their homeland in such numbers during the 1630s that their exodus was called the 'Great Migration,' "[97] Batie tells us. Many of these newcomers settled in the West Indies, and particularly Barbados, which only made the attempt to locate a substitute for tobacco more desperate. The cunning of history then intervened, cutting off Europe's supply of New World sugar as one result of the wars for the possession of Brazil between the Spanish, the Portuguese, the Dutch and the Luso-Brazilians.[98]

The cultivation of sugar in the English colonies began consequently in the late 1630s. Once the techniques of sugar cultivation and refining were mastered, it rapidly displaced the less profitable crops of tobacco, indigo, and ginger in the islands. With the massive demands for labor that sugar production engendered, the appetite of colonial production for labor increasingly outpaced supply. Having already decimated those aboriginal populations they had encountered in the West Indies, the English mercantile and planter bourgeoisie found it necessary and expedient to expand their Irish (and homeland) strategy to West Africa. As they did so, the scale of their enterprise grew beyond anything seen in English history.

During the seventeenth century as a whole, Curtin claims, 60 percent of the slave trade in the New World "went to the Hispanic colonies."[99] This may, or may not have been the case, since Curtin's figures have been shown to have a rather erratic authority and accuracy. Here, at least, he has consistently maintained some caution (in the wrong direction)[100] and even, on occasion, admitted to error (again toward lessening the numbers of Africans impressed into slavery).[101] The more immediate concern, however, is that by the last quarter of that century, English merchants supplying slaves primarily to the British Caribbean had surpassed the Portuguese and the Dutch, their predecessors in the trade. Curtin's approximations reveal that while imports by the Portuguese and Dutch merchants during the first half of the century exceeded the English trade by a substantial margin (a combined 327,000 for the Dutch and Portuguese as compared to 20,700 for English traders), by the third quarter, the English territories had overtaken the Spanish colonies in labor imports. By the last 25 years of the seventeenth century, English merchants had more than doubled their performance in human trading for the previous quarter (69,000 for the earlier period versus 174,000) thereby besting their commercial contemporaries.[102] This achievement, again, was largely due to the demands of sugar production.

By the end of the eighteenth century and the abolition of the legal British slave trade in 1807, British factors, merchants, and traders alone were to account for the transportation of 3,699,572 more Africans to the New World.[103] If we were to accept

Curtin's argument concerning the levels of death in transit during this period, then perhaps as many as 400,000 or more of these people never saw the western end of the Atlantic.[104] They died "in transit," and thereby produced one profoundly tragic measure of the extent to which the development of the capitalist world system depended on labor its metropolis could not produce.

The Africans were, however, not the only ones to be so unfortunately used in the slave trade. The greed of the English and European merchants easily overran their racial and national sympathies. Thus it was that the crews of their slaving ships died at rates perhaps even higher than their human cargoes. In time, English seamen sang about their fate in graphic terms:

Beware and take care
Of the Bight of Benin:
For one that comes out,
There are forty go in.[105]

After the 1680s, Jamaica consistently began to exceed Barbados and the Leeward Islands in sugar exports. By the early 1700s, Jamaica's slave population followed suit, reflecting the island's preeminent role in British colonial commerce. By the end of the English trade in slaves, something like 38 percent of the slave labor force transported by English shippers had been relocated to Jamaica.[106]

In almost equal parts, the origins of these Africans had been along the routes that fed into the slave ports at the Bight of Biafra, the Gold Coast, Central Africa, the Bight of Benin, and Sierra Leone. This ethnic distribution, however, was not the result of consistent or regular patterns of recruitment. Initially, Orlando Patterson concludes, the predominant groups were the "Coromantees" (Kormantin was a port about 70 miles west of Accra), the Akan, and Ga-Andangme peoples. After 1675, and for the rest of the century, the British trade for Jamaica shifted to Angola and the Ewe-speaking peoples of Dahomey. Between 1700 and 1730, the Slave Coast and Ghana became the favorite sources only to be succeeded themselves in the years between 1730 and 1760 by the Niger and Cross deltas. At the end of the eighteenth century, the Congo once again became the dominant region, followed successively by the Niger and Cross deltas, the Gold Coast and (by a much smaller order) the Windward Coast.[107]

In many ways the Jamaican trade followed a pattern established by the European mercantile predecessors of the English. They, too, had deposited the majority of their African labor in the islands of the Greater and Lesser Antilles. Both tobacco and sugar had something to do with this since the islands possessed the ideal climate for the production of these crops. The Portuguese, with the lush tropical fertility of their Brazilian territories, had been the exception—an exception that Curtin maintains accounted for approximately 38 percent of the total number of African peoples brought to the New World.[108]

To the North American colonies it can be estimated that the British merchants sent approximately 20 percent of their slave cargoes in the eighteenth century. Surprisingly, perhaps, to many present-day North Americans, this amounted to less than 5 percent of the total number of Africans brought to the New World by European merchants. Curtin's best estimate is that 399,000 Africans were brought to the English colonies during the entirety of the slave trading period (another 28,000, he suggests, came to the continent by way of French traders supplying the Louisiana region).[109] Inikori, however, warns us that "meaningful import estimates for the United States are yet to be made."[110] This African population, however, differed from that distributed in Jamaica in that at least a quarter of these peoples had originated from Angolan ports. Nearly as many came from the Bight of Biafra, half as many from the Gold Coast and Senegambia, followed by ever decreasing proportions from the ports of Sierra Leone, the Bight of Benin, and Central Africa.[111]

In South Carolina, Blacks made up 60 percent of the colony's population in the eighteenth century. In Virginia, the comparable figure was 40 percent. They were used as laborers on the tobacco farms, and, later, on the cotton plantations, but they also worked "in mines, salt- and rope-works; and they trained as shipwrights, blacksmiths, and as various kinds of woodworkers, including carpenters, coopers, wheelwrights, and sawyers."[112] Those who were imported directly from Africa were termed "outlandish" to distinguish them from what their masters called the "new negroes" of the fields and the supposed deracinated, acculturated artisan slaves with whom they were more "comfortable." As Gerald Mullin has demonstrated, these distinctions were for the colonists practical considerations:

> In sample runs of the South Carolina *Gazette* in the early 1750s and 1771 there was clear evidence of tribal cooperation in advertisements for the return of four "new Gambia men"; three Angolans, "all short fellows"; six other Angolans . . . and four men from the "Fullah Country."[113]

The invention of the Negro was proceeding apace with the growth of slave labor. Somewhat paradoxically, the more that Africans and their descendants assimilated cultural materials from colonial society, the less human they became in the minds of the colonists. Just as instructive, the rebels among these Africans and "negroes" were described as "runaways," a term that has endured in the historiography of the period. It should be remembered, however, that it was from the efforts of men and women such as these that the Black settlements of Virginia's piedmont and the Afro-Creek "Exiles of Florida" (the Seminoles) would consist.[114] In similar fashion, the maroon peoples of the Caribbean and South America would be formed. They were as well, at the end of the eighteenth century, among the estimated 55,000 who fled to the British forces and the loyalist settlements when the colonists pursued the logic of the fear of their own enslavement to the point of revolution.[115]

Still, enough of the African laborers remained in the colonies of North America and the Indies to play a significant role in the development of the English imperial economy. The "triangular trade" in slaves, as Eric Williams asserted, broadened the "home market" by stimulating the production of British manufactures that English merchants exchanged in Africa for Black workers. Once in place, these workers formed the labor for British tropical production, craft work, and extractive industries. The end result was capital accumulation for the advance of productive forces in England and Europe (the Industrial Revolution), for the growth of staple industries in northern America (fisheries, food crops, etc.), for timber, ship-building, and textiles, and for the expansion of colonization and settlement. The concomitant, however, was the degradation of these African peoples and their social institutions when touched by that trade, and, as Walter Rodney has argued, the underdevelopment of Africa's economies.[116]

This trade, this movement of Black workers, though, did not end with slavery's legal termination in the nineteenth century. Leopold's Congo, Harry Johnston's Central Africa, Cecil Rhodes's southern Africa, Lugard's West Africa, Portuguese Africa, and French Africa as well as the New World's slave descendants all contributed to the further development of the capitalist world system. As peasants, as tenant farmers, as migrant laborers, as day laborers, as domestic servants, and as wage labor, their expropriation extended into the present century. Even in the destruction of the means of production, the wars that Marx and Engels had stipulated as inevitable in capitalism, Black labor was pressed into service.[117] They were exempt from no aspect of exploitation.

CHAPTER

6

THE HISTORICAL ARCHAEOLOGY OF THE BLACK RADICAL TRADITION

The role of Black labor in the expansion and preservation of capitalism was not, however, the whole of it. The deposition of Black peoples in the New World had still another consequence—a consequence entirely unintended and unanticipated by the tradesmen and ideologists of slavery. Still, the naivete of the Europeans was substantially of their own making: slavery, as a system and way of life, was hardly a propitious setting for much else. The "structured" ignorance that was an almost inevitable concomitant of the use of enslaved labor weighed heavily on European thought in general, irrespective of social ideology.

Marx had once assigned slavery to that stage of capitalism's development that he characterized as "primitive accumulation." He had not meant the term in any invidious sense but had intended simply to—in part—emphasize that the dominant capitalist mode of production bore little responsibility for the production and reproduction of the human materials it commanded in this aspect. Marx had meant by primitive accumulation that the *piezas de Indias* had been produced, materially and intellectually, by the societies from which they were taken and not by those by which they were exploited. The cargoes of the slave ships were real human beings, notwithstanding their manner of transport, the bills of *ladino*, the captains' logs and trade account books that designated them otherwise.

However, Marx had not realized fully that the cargoes of laborers also contained African cultures, critical mixes and admixtures of language and thought, of cosmology and metaphysics, of habits, beliefs, and morality. These were the actual terms of their humanity. These cargoes, then, did not consist of intellectual isolates or decultu-rated Blacks—men, women, and children separated from their previous universe. African labor brought the past with it, a past that had produced it and settled on it the first elements of consciousness and comprehension.

This was the embryo of the demon that would be visited on the whole enterprise of primitive accumulation. It would be through the historical and social consciousness of these Africans that the trade in slaves and the system of slave labor was infected with its contradiction. Much later, in the midst of the struggle against Portuguese imperialism in Guinea-Bissau in this century, Amilcar Cabral would reveal the nature of that contradiction:

> [I]mperialist domination, by denying the historical development of the dominated people, necessarily also denies their cultural development. It is . . . understood why imperialist domination, like all other foreign domination, for its own security, requires cultural oppression and the attempt at direct or indirect liquidation of the essential elements of the culture of the dominated people. . . . [I]t is generally within the culture that we find the seed of opposition.[1]

The transport of African labor to the mines and plantations of the Caribbean and subsequently to what would be known as the Americas meant also the transfer of African ontological and cosmological systems; African presumptions of the orga-nization and significance of social structure; African codes embodying historical consciousness and social experience; and African ideological and behavioral con-structions for the resolution of the inevitable conflict between the actual and the normative. Michael Craton grasps this when he recounts that:

> their African peasant roots clearly predisposed all slaves to regard plantation agri-culture as being as unnatural as the institution which sustained it. From the ear-liest days, runaway slaves settled around provision grounds (called "polinks" in the English colonies, "palenques" in the Spanish), worked in a manner owing something to African farming, something to the *conuco* agriculture of the Amer-indians. . . .
>
> More deeply, the slaves retained and developed concepts of family and kin quite beyond the comprehension and control of the master class, and a concept of land tenure that was in contradiction to that of the dominant European culture. . . . They wanted to live in family units, to have ready access to land of their own, and be free to develop their own culture, particularly their own, syncretized religion. These were the basic aspirations, which varied according to the different condi-tions in each of the colonies affected [by rebellion].[2]

These were the terms upon which the response of the enslaved to the slave system would be grounded.

History and the Mere Slave

But even to those unfamiliar with the histories of enslaved Africans, it should come as no surprise that these African peoples responded to slavery in several ways. In the North American slave experience, particularly with respect to the nineteenth century, the attempts to portray the "slave personality type," to identify a "plantation type"—a notion already firmly in place by the time the system produced its most celebrated post hoc apologist, Ulrich Bonnell Phillips—had as their results a veritable stock company of characters. John Blassingame, a recent contributor to a literature that has ranged from the observations of eighteenth and nineteenth centuries travelers and sometimes equally peripatetic abolitionists, plantation records, and memorabilia, "slave testimony," contemporary novels, and conventional historiography, has made a good effort to organize its depictions of the slave laborers.[3] He enumerated the masks, the posturings, and the more naked affects the African workers and their descendants displayed: the vain house servant, frequently wearing the airs and the clothes of those who owned the "house" and who made similar claims on the slave workers. The "Sambo," the docile, submissive, terrorized individual, broken by the omniscience of psychological and physical pain—often such men and women grew increasingly indifferent to the specter of punishment and suffering, both that of others and themselves. Separation, the trauma of realization that one had neither the right nor the power to resist what must have seemed so often to be the arbitrary or cruel removal from those who really mattered, too, registered its own particular marks:

> Angry, despondent, and overcome by grief, the slaves frequently never recovered from the shock of separation. Many became morose and indifferent to their work. Others went insane, talked to themselves, and had hallucinations about their loved ones. A few slaves developed suicidal tendencies.[4]

Others, still further along the path of "distraction," came to accept the assertion of the sanctity of whiteness and the shame of blackness. But Blassingame was convinced by contemporary testimony and observation that for the majority of the enslaved (the "fieldhands") the oppressiveness of the system compelled *social* rather than *psychological* fetters. For the most part, the slave laborers were "sullenly obedient and hostilely submissive," according to Blassingame. He contends:

> Having a variety of relationships, besides that with his master, the slave was able to preserve his self-esteem in spite of the cruel punishment he received. The docility of the slave was a sham, a mask to hide his true feelings and personality traits.[5]

Blassingame would conclude—too casually we will suggest—that "[t]he same range of personality types existed in the quarters as in the mansion."[6]

Leslie Howard Owens, another Black historian, exhibited even fewer reservations than Blassingame on the *naturalness* of rebelliousness within the domination of the American slave structure. Where Blassingame hedges, apparently conceding to the dichotomies frequently encountered in the literature on American slavery between "house slaves," and "field slaves,"[7] between the "cruel master" (redundancy) and the "benevolent master"[8] (contradiction), Owens asserted simply: "That slaves were discontented with their bondage is overwhelmingly documented by manuscript and narrative materials."[9] For Owens, then, rebelliousness was situational, its context the slave system.[10] Tracing what he termed the "logic of resistance," Owens noted among the slave workers the multiplicity of their responses to domination: the broken and misplaced tools, the burning of crops, the work slowdowns, the assistance and protection afforded to "runaways," stealing, flight, the forming of short-lived maroon communities, even self-mutilation and suicide.[11] Ultimately, of course, there was insurrection. The existential constancy of the slave system with its inevitable demonstrations and exercises of the collective and individual wills of the master class had as their result the persistence of attacks upon the system. "Suppression of minor and serious slave disturbances by the slave regime did not erase slave disobedience for long,"[12] Owens remarks. The slave system generated its own maelstrom. Aside from this dialectic, it seems, nothing else was fixed or static, certainly not the personalities in which the enslaved "publicly" dressed themselves: "some recognition of the slave's shifting rather than static identity is important to understanding why sometimes very little separated his minor acts of disobedience from his serious acts or threats of rebellion."[13] Most disturbing of all, perhaps, to the master class was the monstrous deception lying behind the Black docility it so desperately desired: "That there was some docility among slaves need not be denied. But it was not the norm. Masters and authorities repeatedly linked seemingly docile slaves to acts of resistance."[14] The psychological dividends for those who commanded the system were drawn from necessary vigilance: fear and paranoia, moral degeneration, and finally, according to some historians, a failure of will.[15]

Still, it is useful to pause here for a moment to consider what revisionists such as Blassingame and Owens and a score of other historians, Black and non-Black, in the past twenty years or so, have taken to be the issue.[16] Clearly, they have addressed themselves to one overriding claim: that the enslaved in time came to accept the terms of slavery. The practice of submission, so went the conventional wisdom embodied in the American disciplines of history, sociology, and psychology, became for the slaves the habits of inferiority; for their descendants, the psychological "marks of oppression," the culture of the dominated, the perverted, twisted familial structures of matriarchy and matrilocality (notice, if you will, how often the violation of the slave is referred to as "emasculation," "castration," etc.). The American revisionists in the main have sought to refute the tradition deposited in their national record and consciousness that *Blacks became slaves*, finally. They have chosen to come to terms with the reiterated public fantasy that the subsequent generations of "native sons" were fatally marked culturally and emotionally by the accommodations effected by their forebears. The American revisionists have attempted to supply academic substance to the insistence of their own generations that the material, political, and social circumstances of Blacks in the twentieth century are not the consequences of private or even collective psychopathologies among Blacks. They have transformed this African people into *human beings* capable of judgment, injury, accommodation and heroism. In short, a people possessing, as Blassingame put it, "the same range."

To this point, their project has been successfully executed. The scholarship, the narratives, the documents speak for themselves in a stridently eloquent way. Still this "political" triumph is but a partial one, for the defense of the slaves addresses its antagonists in their terms. Expectedly, in a post-slave society where the historical victory of the enslaved stratum was incomplete, the question of the humanity of the enslaved people would linger. It would, it follows, have to be spoken to. We now "know" what the master class certainly knew but for so long publicly denied only to be confronted with the truth in its nightmares, its sexual fantasies, and rotting social consciousness: the enslaved were human beings.[17] But the more authentic question was not whether the slaves (and the ex-slaves and their descendants) were human. It was, rather, just what *sort* of people they were . . . and could be. Slavery altered the conditions of their being, but it could not negate their being. Long before the troubled American republic of the nineteenth century even became a possibility, a part of the answer began its unfolding. As we shall soon see, its historical imprint is still clear.

Reds, Whites, and Blacks

African labor in the Western hemisphere became necessary only when native labor was exhausted and European labor became evidently inadequate.

Apparently, it took no longer than the period between Columbus's first and third voyages (1497) for the Spanish government to recognize and respond to the special problems it faced in depending upon its nationals for supplemental colonial labor. In June 1497, "a general order was issued to all justices in Spain authorizing the transportation to Hispaniola of criminals—with the exception of heretics, traitors, counterfeiters, and sodomites—in commutation of death or prison sentences."[18] This supply proving inadequate, the crown successively and contemporaneously resorted to white slavery (1504, 1512, 1521), foreign immigrants (1526), and inducing non-Castilian Spanish emigration (1511) as the shortage of Indian labor became more acute in the West Indies.[19] Nevertheless, by the mid-sixteenth century, Iberian capitalists had come to understand something that their English successors would only need to take to heart a hundred years later: the production of sugar required a labor force that was larger and more politically and morally unencumbering than Europe could supply.[20] At least in the beginning, the alternative had been the "Indian."

"It has been said of the Spanish conquistadors," Eric Williams was to write, "that first they fell on their knees, and then they fell on the aborigines."[21] From the first, it would seem, Columbus had little else in mind for these "wild people." The *repartimiento de Indios* (the division of Indians for tasks necessary to the colonial settlements) of Columbus and his immediate successor, Francisco de Bobadilla, became the *encomienda* in the hands of the third governor of the Indies, Nicolas de Ovando. C. H. Haring details:

The Indians were assigned in lots of fifty, a hundred, or more, by written deed or patent, to individual Spaniards to work on their farms and ranches or in the placer mines for gold dust. Sometimes they were given to officials or to parish priests in lieu of part of their annual salary. The effect was simply to parcel out the natives among the settlers to do with as they pleased.[22]

The consequences of their exploitation were dramatic:

The results are to be seen in the best estimates that have been prepared of the trend of population in Hispaniola. These place the population in 1492 at between 200,000 and 300,000. By 1508 the number was reduced to 60,000; in 1510 Oviedo doubted whether five hundred Indians of pure stock remained. In 1570 only two villages survived of those about whom Columbus had assured his sovereigns, less than eighty years before, that "there is no better nor gentler people in the world."[23]

Still the West Indies was only the beginning.

In Mexico, or New Spain (*Nueva Espana*) as it was then called, the native popula- tion has been estimated by Sherburne Cook and Woodrow Borah to have been 25 million or more at the beginning of the sixteenth century.[24] Whatever the true figure, this aboriginal population would become the object of a most intensive exploitation by its Spanish conquerors. Chilam Balam, a native of the Yucatan, recalling the days of the pre-Conquest, would write:

There was then no sickness; they had no aching bones; they had then no high fever; they had then no smallpox; they had then no burning chest; they had then no abdominal pain; they had then no consumption; they had then no headache. At that time the course of humanity was orderly. The foreigners made it otherwise when they arrived here.[25]

The world for which Chilam displayed such poetic nostalgia ended quickly. Within nine decades "diseases, wars, relocations, and the ecological changes wrought by Spanish settlement and control"[26] and (it should be added) slave labor had reduced the number of indigenous inhabitants to an estimated 1,075,000.[27] The Conquest had an even more insidious effect. As early as the 1514 census, according to C. O. Sauer, the *repartimiento* records of natives on Santo Domingo, working land seized for the crown, indicated an average of less than one child per family. Las Casas had indicated that in the period immediately prior to the Conquest, Indian women had averaged between three and five children each. Elsewhere, "Jaramillo Uribe remarks that at the beginning of the seventeenth century it was common in New Granada to find that half the Indian couples had no children. On the average they had only two children, and the family with four offspring was exceptional." Sanchez-Albornoz concludes: "It is evident that the Indians decreased not only on account of deaths, but also partially because they did not ensure the normal replacement of the generations."[28] This decimation of the "Indian" population, rather than the controversial royal decrees of 1542 (the Nuevas Leyes) that "prohibited the further enslavement of Indians except as punishment for rebellion against Spanish rule," resulted in a significant demand for additional labor toward the second half of the sixteenth century.[29] Ultimately, the source of that labor was to be the west coast of Africa.

Not unexpectedly, Las Casas, whose bitter charges against the conquistadors and whose calculations of the terrifying numbers of Indian deaths had done much toward obtaining the New Laws from Charles V, assumed full responsibility. He wrote of himself in his *Historia general de las Indias*: "The priest Las Casas was the first to suggest that one should introduce Africans to the West Indies. He did not know what he was doing."[30] It was, however, he would continue to maintain, a somewhat understandable error:

> In the old days, before there were any *ingenios*, we used to think in this island that, if a Negro were not hanged, he would never die, because we had never seen one die of illness, and we were sure that, like oranges, they had found their habitat, this island being more natural to them than Guinea. But after they were put to work in the *ingenios*, on account of the excessive labor they had to endure, and the drinks they take made from cane syrup, death and pestilence were the result, and many of them died.[31]

Las Casas, of course, had miscast himself in the drama and tragedy of Indian and African enslavement. It was an old tactic of his. Though not entirely innocent of guilt in this matter, he was only a link in the chains fastened around the necks of the enslaved. But as the son of an Andalusian aristocratic family, he was better placed than most to understand that his appeal to the Emperor on behalf of the Indian had to flatter the imperial ego as well as shock the imperial morality. Charles V of Spain was much more implicated in "the devastation of the Indies" than Las Casas thought it prudent to review. Hans Magnus Enzensberger captures the situation exactly:

> Of course Las Casas was completely aware that the Spanish crown was totally dependent on the income from the colonies. One year before the audience [1519] the Augsburg business firm Welser had financed the election of Charles V, and his dependency on the banks was notorious everywhere in Europe. Las Casas . . . charged that the conquistadors' violent behavior had cost the King many hundred thousand crowns year after year. . . . This line of argument . . . certainly must have made more of an impression on Charles V than all the theological and legal reasons that Las Casas brought to bear.[32]

It would still take Las Casas twenty more years to win this victory for his charges. Altogether, it is written, he would make 14 trips between the Old and New Worlds during this time pursuing his mission (several of these trips were command performances since he was forced to return to Spain to answer accusations of treason). In the end, his victory would be short and meaningless. Charles V revoked the New Laws three years after their appearance.[33] The natives of the conquered lands were already a vanishing presence. The survival of New Spain's economy was already being transferred to new hands.[34]

David Davidson argues that: "It is now fairly certain that in the period 1519–1650 the area [New Spain] received at least 120,000 slaves, or two-thirds of all the Africans imported into the Spanish possessions in America."[35] Enriqueta Vila's more recent studies, as we have already seen, confirm Davidson's impressions while substantially expanding the total number of transported Africans.[36] The colonial industries of sugar and cloth production, and later of the silver mines, were the primary sites to which African labor was assigned. As Indian labor atrophied during the second half of the century in consequence of its unnatural declines or legal restrictions[37] and the settlers "stumbled upon the richest silver mines in the world,"[38] African workers began their domination of the labor of the plantations and the mines. By 1570, Mexico contained over 20,000 Africans; by 1650, their numbers were believed to be closer to 35,000—by then, what amounted to a supplement to the more than 100,000 Afromestizoes of Black-Indian parentage. Again, by this latter period, Davidson states, 8,000–10,000 Africans could be found working the sugar plantations and cattle ranches in the eastern region around the coastal lowlands between Veracruz and Panuco and the slopes of the Sierra Madre Oriental; another 15,000 were absorbed by the silver mines and ranches of the regions north and west of Mexico City; 3,000–5,000 were bound to similar industries located between Puebla and the Pacific coast; and 20,000 to 50,000 employed in urban occupations in Mexico City and the valley of Mexico.[39] By the beginnings of the nineteenth century, Gonzalo Aguirre Beltran states, the descendants of these workers, who by then were classified in rough terms as Blacks, mulattos, and *zambos* (Afro-Indians), were reported by the 1810 census at 634,461, a little more than a tenth of the Mexican population.[40]

There is, however, much more to be understood of their presence in Mexico and the Spanish colonies of the Indies and South America than their mere numbers. The systematic transportation of Black labor to the New World had not always been an obvious or requisite step. For a few decades, as we have seen, it had not seemed necessary at all. When it did begin, it almost completely overturned the more casual application of Iberian racial structures that had already been transferred to the colonies.

In the beginning, that is, most probably in the decade that ended the fifteenth century but most certainly in the one that began the sixteenth, small groups of enslaved Africans had come to the New World as "companions" of the conquistadors.[41] When Nicolas de Ovando took up his governorship of Hispaniola in 1502, his company included "an unknown number of black and mulatto servitors."[42] They were *ladinos*, Hispanicized Blacks, but within the year Ovando requested of his queen that she prevent all future arrivals of such people.

He reported that those already on the island had been a source of scandal to the Indians, and some had fled their owners and established, independent settlements in the mountains. Concerned that the Indians might be led from the path of Christian righteousness, Isabella immediately barred the shipment of *ladinos*.[43]

The Queen of Castile, however, had provided only a short relief for *ladino* workers. She died in 1504 and the colonies that had previously been exclusively administered by Castile now came under the direction of her husband, Ferdinand of Aragon. Ferdinand, who at some point became convinced that "one black could do the work of four Indians," informed Ovando that the threat of Black rebellion was offset by the need of Black labor in the mines and plantations.[44] From 1505 until 1522, *ladino* slaves increasingly replaced the native work force as the latter was decimated by the discipline of the *encomienda*, disease, and demoralization. In the latter year, the policy prohibiting the import of *ladinos* was reinstituted. That policy was reiterated in 1530, 1532, 1543, 1550, and in the various *assientos* granted between 1595 and 1609. Henceforth, only *bozales*—Africans obtained in Africa—were to be eligible for transport to the New World.[45] We shall investigate the reasons behind this turn of fortune shortly.

A few *ladinos*, however, played less anonymous parts in the conquest of the New World. Leslie Rout characterizes them as "compatriots." One, Nuflo de Olano, accompanied Balboa in 1513.[46] Another, Juan Garrido (Handsome John),

> apparently crossed the atlantic as a freeman, participated in the siege of Tenochtitlan [1521] and, in subsequent conquests and explorations, tried his hand as an entrepreneur (with both Negro and Indian slaves of his own) in the early search for gold, and took his place as a citizen in the Spanish quarter of Mexico City.[47]

Garrido, whose fortunes were entirely linked with those of his patron, Hernan Cortes, died in poverty, a victim it is believed of the great plague that struck Mexico City in 1547.[48] Esteban (Estebanico) was with the less hardy Narvaez in Florida in 1528. Having survived his master, he completed an eight-year trek from Florida to Mexico City with three other conquistadors, only to perish at the hands of Zuni in 1538 while acting as a guide for another master, Friar Marcos de Niza.[49] Juan Valiente accompanied Alvarado's army in its march from Guatemala to Peru in 1534. In 1536 and 1540, Valiente fought with Valdivia's army against the Araucanian Indians in Chile. In 1546, when Valdivia granted him an estate, and in 1548, Valiente became the first *ladino* to receive an *encomienda*. Significantly enough, when he died in 1553 (killed in action against the Arauca), his old master, Alonso Valiente had begun legal action to reclaim him and any property he had amassed.[50] Other *ladinos* were to be found in the entourages of Avila (1514), Narvaez (during his initial appearance in the New World in 1520), Alvarado (in his expeditionary force into Guatemala in 1523), Montejo (in Yucatan in 1532), and Pizarro as well. Jose Franco reminds us, "the Spaniards frequently used Negroes and Indians as shock troops in their own internal wars."[51] Still, it seems they were as historically inconspicuous as the white slaves[52] who shared their condition in the New World of the early sixteenth century. In economic terms, however, theirs was the first phase that would lead ultimately to the placement of

Africans in the Indies, Nueva Espana, Peru, Columbia, Chile, Venezuela, Argentina, and Uruguay as domestics; growers of sugar, wheat, grapes, olives, cacao; miners of gold and silver; craft workers (blacksmiths, cobblers, brick masons, carpenters, tailors); teamsters; cowboys; pearl divers; and prostitutes.[53]

Their consequences, though, were not simply economic. Slave labor required the elaboration of systems of control and discipline. Moreover, the intercourse of the several races extant in Spain's new possessions precipitated the formation of rather complex racial codes and codifications. The results were practical while being barbaric and absurd:

> In Spanish America the lash, the stock, detention, and deprivation were standard means by which unruly and defiant slaves were kept in line. Some masters were known to have whipped their bondmen to death, while others continued to mutilate their dusky properties with hot branding irons even after the crown had prohibited this act. Worst of all were the vengeful sadists who made their slaves eat excrement and drink urine.[54]

Castration and the severing of other limbs were common and legal. Aguirre Beltran reports that some slave mulattos who were no longer phenotypically distinct from the ruling class had to be branded

> with hot irons in places where the insignia of servitude could not for a moment be hidden. The faces of many of them were completely covered with branded legends saying: "I am the slave of Senor Marque del Valle," "I am the slave of Dona Francisca Carrillo de Peralta."[55]

Such treatment and the almost inevitably foul conditions in which most of them labored reduced the active working lives of slaves to between ten and twenty years.[56]

Black Resistance: The Sixteenth Century

At first, as a rule, resistance among the enslaved Africans took the form of flight to native or "Indian" settlements. The notarial archive of the Mexican city of Puebla de los Angeles, for example, which is "virtually complete from 1540 on" is filled with the official reaction to mid-sixteenth-century "runaways."[57] Fugitives drew the attention of Hernan Cortes as early as 1523 and the first general uprising in Nueva Espana is thought to have occurred in 1537.[58] Some of these Africans, however, did not completely sever their contacts with the Spanish. Once freed by their own wits, they returned to plague the Spanish colonists, appropriating food, clothes, arms, tools, and even religious artifacts from the colonists' towns, their villages, and ranch homes, and from travelers along the roads connecting the ports and settlements. Once they armed themselves, the Spanish would refer to these "fugitives" as *cimarrones*.[59] (The English would incorporate the term into their own language as "maroons.") In 1503, we recall, Ovando had observed subversive activities among Hispaniola's *ladinos*. In the last month of 1522, Ovando's prevision was realized. Fittingly enough, slaves on the plantation of Diego Columbus (a son of the Admiral) revolted, killing some 15 colonists before they were themselves captured and executed.[60] This had been the occasion for the prohibition of future employ of *ladinos* as slave labor in the colonies. Similar revolts had occurred in Puerto Rico (1527), Santa Marta, Colombia (1529), and Panama (1531). Back in Hispaniola, Blacks had joined the native uprising of 1533. Resistance had continued for ten years.[61] Decades later, Spanish authorities continued to be concerned about such events. Viceroy Martin Enriquez had written Philip II:

> [I]t appears, Our Majesty, that the time is coming when these people will have become masters of the Indians, inasmuch as they were born among them and their maidens, and are men who dare to die as well as any Spaniard in the world. But if the Indians become corrupt and join with them, I do not know who will be in the position to resist them. It is evident that this mischief will take place in several years.[62]

Soon, however, the fugitive slaves grew numerous enough to begin the formation of their own settlements, communities that came to be known in Mexico as *palenques*.

Edgar Love recalls Aquirre Beltran's estimate that by 1579 some 2,000 Blacks had escaped from their masters. Love goes on to indicate that "[f]or more than a century, the escaped slave was a serious problem in many parts of Mexico."[63] David Davidson, writing of the third quarter of the century, declares:

> By the 1560s fugitive slaves from the mines of the north were terrorizing the regions from Guadalajara to Zacatecas, allying with the Indians and raiding ranches. In one case maroons from the mines of Guanajuato joined with unpacified Chichimec Indians in a brutal war with the settlers. The viceroy was informed that they were attacking travelers, burning ranches, and committing similar "misdeeds." To the east, slaves from the Pachuca mines took refuge in an inaccessible cave from which they sallied forth periodically to harass the countryside. Negroes from the Atotonilco and Tonavista mines joined them with arms, and created an impregnable *palenque*.[64]

The response of the representatives of the Spanish state was unequivocal. Between 1571 and 1574, royal decrees detailed new systems of control and surveillance, stipulating progressively harsher treatment of fugitives: 50 lashes for four days absence; 100 lashes and iron fetters for more than eight days absence; death for those missing for six months, commuted in some cases to castration.

> Yet neither the code of 1571–1574 nor the issuance of restrictive legislation in the 1570s and 1580s was of any avail. A viceregal order of 1579 revealed that the contagion of revolt nearly covered the entire settled area of the colony outside of Mexico City, in particular the provinces of Veracruz and Panuco, the area between Oaxaca and Gualtuco on the Pacific coast, and almost the whole of the *Gran Chichimeca*. Only emergency repressive measures and the continued importation of Africans maintained Mexico's slave labour supply.[65]

Nevertheless, African resistance in Mexico continued to mature in form and character. The struggle against slavery was being transferred into the battle to preserve the collective identity of African peoples. By the early seventeenth century, according to official colonial documents, at least one Black community, San Lorenzo de los Negros, had acquired its right to existence by war and treaty.

> The terms of the truce, as preserved in the archives, included eleven conditions stipulated by Yanga upon which he and his people would cease their raiding. The African demanded that all of his people who had fled before September of the past year (1608) be freed and promised that those who had escaped slavery after that date would be returned to their masters. He further stipulated that the palenque be given the status of a free town and that it have its own cabildo and a justicia mayor who was to be a Spanish layman. No other Spaniards were to live in the town, although they could visit on market days. . . . In return Yanga promised that for a fee the town would aid the viceroy in capturing fugitive slaves. The Negroes, he said, would aid the crown in case of an external attack on Mexico.[66]

In the mountains near Mt. Orizaba, led by this man called Yanga, "reputedly a Congolese chief from an African kingdom bordered by the Nyonga River,"[67] the "Yanguicos" had won the formal status as a free Black settlement. The mountains, however, seemed to promise much more security to some Yanguicos and other *cimarrones* than the words and treaties of their Spanish oppressors. Throughout New Spain *palenques* continued to multiply and, with a still undetermined frequency, to give occasion for the establishment of officially recognized free communities.[68] In a period between 1630 and 1635, for example, an agreement was reached with *cimarrones* whose redoubts had been established in the mountains of Totula, Palmilla, Tumbacarretas, and Totolinga near Veracruz. The town of San Lorenzo Cerralvo became their free settlement. In 1769, a similar history preceded the establishment of Nuestra Senora de Guadalupe de los Morenos de Amapa, near the southern tip of the modern state of Veracruz.[69] We have learned of their existence through quite recent research into the early colonial history of New Spain. In Colombia, their revolts are detailed in 1530, 1548, and again in the 1550s.[70] In 1552, Venezuela had its first major slave revolt. This rebellion of slaves who had worked in the mines of Buria was defeated in 1555. Nevertheless, by the beginning of the seventeenth century, independent Black communities with legal standing in the eyes of state agents had begun to appear.[71]

Palmares and Seventeenth-Century Marronage

In Brazil, which we have seen dominated the Portuguese slave trade, the maroon settlements (*quilombos*) that began in the sixteenth century would extend into the next. Ernesto Ennes, a scholar who was far from being in sympathy with the fugitives,[72] nevertheless recorded in 1948 from his review of the documents in the Arquivo Historico Colonial in Lisbon that he found "traces in every corner of Brazil" of *quilombos*.[73] Arthur Ramos, summarizing his own studies of Blacks in Brazil, declared:

From the beginnings of slavery, escapes were frequent. The escaped slaves, called locally, *quilombolas*, often gathered together in organized groups, known in Brazil as *quilombos*. . . . From the beginning, the owners complained of the frequent escapes of the slaves, demanding protection and security from the public authorities. Later the situation was met by the employment of the bush captain and by notices in the press, publicizing the loss of the slaves and urging collective action for their recapture.[74]

That the slaves had good reason to be concerned for their liberty, despite bland suggestions from scholars like A. J. R. Russell-Wood that the only thing at issue was their "adapting to a new diet, new environment, and new working conditions,"[75] is suggested by Stuart Schwartz's consideration of the sugar industry in colonial Bahia:

Added to the rigors inherent in the system of sugar production and to occasional acts of individual cruelty, slaves also suffered from a planned policy of punishment and terror as a means of control. Plantation owners believed that only by severity could work be accomplished and discipline maintained, especially when the ratio in the fields was often forty slaves to one white sharecropper or overseer. This sort of institutionalized brutality, when coupled with arduous labor, poor working conditions, and simple cruelty, contributed to the motivations for escape.[76]

The work of Ramos, R. K. Kent, Irene Diggs, Donald Pierson, Edison Carneiro, Schwartz, and Raymundo Nina Rodriques indicates that for Brazil as a whole, from the sixteenth century into the late nineteenth century, slave resistance, rebellions, and conspiracies were constants in that land.[77] In the seventeenth and eighteenth centuries, though, it was the maroon settlements that dominated the reaction to slavery.

In the Pernambuco region, the greatest settlement of all, the extraordinary state of Palmares would endure from 1605 to 1695. Palmares was a plural, designating the several settlements (palmars) that made up a community, which, though necessarily agrarian, was even more preoccupied with its defense. Diggs gives us this description:

The site of the quilombo of Os Palmares was a mountainous region, steep and precipitous—a natural defense of the inhabitants—but at the same time a virgin land whose exuberance was considered the best in the state of Pernambuco. The many fruit trees gave easy sustenance to those who knew where they were. Timber-yielding trees served various industrial uses. Most important of all trees was the *palmera pindoba*, the cocoanut palm, which . . . provided excellent food . . . and a delicious drink.[78]

In 1645, Bartholomeus Lintz, acting as a scout for the expeditions that the Dutch were to mount against Palmares, was the first hostile European to discover that the state consisted of several settlements (two major palmers of 5,000 inhabitants, and several small units totalling 6,000). By 1677, there were ten major palmars, one of which was the capital (*Macoco*) where the "king" (*Ganga-Zumba* from the Zanda signifying consensus ruler) resided, the whole state spanning over sixty leagues.[79] It was then estimated that the population numbered between 15,000 and 20,000, a mixture of Creoles and Africans largely drawn from the Angola-Congo regions. For almost a century, neither the Portuguese nor the interloper Dutch, nor the Creole *moradores* could destroy it, though they tried for more than seventy years. Even in the end, "[b]etween 1672–94," R. K. Kent tells us, "[i]t withstood on the average one Portuguese expedition every fifteen months."[80] There was, however, one important political development during this period. In 1678, "[a]s he had done earlier, whenever a new governor came to Pernambuco, Ganga-Zumba sued for peace." The treaty that was eventually signed, Kent quotes Nina Rodriques, "gave a real importance to the Negro State which now the Colony treated as one nation would another." The treaty, however, had little import for the *moradores*, who proceeded to claim and distribute among themselves a substantial portion of the "Negro State."[81] Ganga-Zumba's authority was breached:

> By 1679, a *palmarista* "captain named Zambi (whose uncle is Gana-Zona) was in revolt (with) Joao mulato, Canhonga, Gaspar (and) Amaro, having done the person of Ganga-Zumba to death." By March 1680, Zambi was being called upon to surrender, without success. The war was on once more.[82]

Zambi (Zumbi), according to Ramos, "was already a well-known chief, whose deeds amazed even the white soldiery."[83] He would apparently reign as king in New Palmares until its end almost two decades later. But in his accession to authority, it is possible to recognize what Ramos and others have described as "the Bantu origins" of Palmares.[84] The perception of authentic authority as identical with secured social integrity was characteristically Central African.[85]

Palmares did fall, eventually, in 1694, the result of campaigns launched by successive Portuguese governors of Pernambuco (Joao da Cunha Sotto-Mayor, Marques de Montebello, and Melo de Castro). The last expedition sent against it consisted of nearly 3,000 men and was in the field for several months. The final siege was established on 10 November 1693 and lasted until early February of the following year. The total cost of the adventure was estimated by Melo de Castro at somewhere near 1,400,000 cruzados.[86]

On the night of 5 February 1694, "Zumby," organizer of the defense of Palmares, having discovered that his position on Barriga mountain had been nearly encircled, sought a last desperate chance to escape. The result was described by Colonel Domingos Jorge Velho, the leader of the Portuguese forces:

> During the second watch of that night, between the fifth and sixth of February, suddenly and tumultuously [Zumby] with all his people and the equipment which could follow him through that space, made an exit. The sentinels of that post did not perceive them almost until the end. In the rear-guard Zumby himself was leaving, and at that point he was shot twice. As it was dark, and all this was taking place at the edge of the cliff, many—a matter of about two hundred—fell down the

cliff. As many others were killed. Of both sexes and all ages, five hundred and nineteen were taken prisoner.[87]

In Pernambuco, again according to Governor Melo de Castro, "This happy victory was regarded as no less important than the expulsion of the Dutch. It was, accordingly, celebrated by the whole population with displays of lights for six days and many other demonstrations of joy, without any command being given to them." Keeping in character, Ennes attributed this excitement to the "moral influence which it conferred on the authorities."[88] "Palmares," Ramos reminds us, "was not, however, the only outstanding case. In 1650 the slaves in Rio de Janeiro organized a number of quilombos which caused the police authorities of that region untold difficulties until suppressed by Captain Manoel Jordao da Silva."[89]

In this same century, the seventeenth century, the slaves of Jamaica joined the tradition of those in Brazil and Mexico. Barbara Kopytoff has summarized the conditions:

During the era of slavery, communities of maroons, or escaped slaves, sprang up throughout the New World. Wherever there were slave plantations, there was resistance in the form of runaways and slave revolts; and wherever mountains, swamps, or forests permitted the escaped slaves to gather, they formed communities. These ranged in size from Palmarres, in Brazil, with over ten thousand people, to the handfulls of runaways who hid on the fringes of plantations in the American South. While most . . . were destroyed . . . a few could not be reduced or even contained.[90]

The mid-century exploded with revolts on that island in 1669, 1672 (twice), 1678, 1682, 1685, and 1690. In Jamaica, marronage had begun during the period of Spanish colonization (1509–1655).[91] And in the very last years of Spanish resistance (1655–60) to British occupation of the island, at least three maroon camps played decisive roles in supporting the guerrilla campaign led by Christobal de Yassi against the British.[92] In the first month of 1660, however, the English made peace with one of the maroon chiefs, Juan Lubolo (Juan de Bola), who promptly went to aid them in the destruction of, first, the remaining major maroon camps, and, finally, Yassi's guerrillas. A little more than three years later, Juan de Bola met his appropriate fate. What reads like an official entry observed: "On the first day of November the outlying Negroes met with Juan de Bola and cut him to pieces; else all things were quiet in the country."[93] Three hundred years later, with an equal amount of sympathy David Buisseret and S. A. G. Taylor unhesitantly estimated: "His death seems to us an act of justice . . . he was 'the great traitor.' "[94]

During the next eighty years, two major maroon societies were formed in the highlands of Jamaica. One, the Windward Maroons, settling in the eastern mountains, had as its nucleus the Spanish maroons and those who subsequently joined them from the English plantations and towns. The other, the Leeward Maroons of the west-central interior, came into being in 1673 after the first of the slave rebellions during the

English period.[95] In 1690, another major rebellion, beginning on the Sutton estate, added more than 200 refugees to the Leeward settlements complex. Such was the primary fashion in which the settlements grew and maintained themselves:

> The maroon societies were formed, and their numbers increased, largely by slave rebellions and by individual and group escapes from the plantations. In addition, slaves were captured by maroons during raids, and slave or free Negroes, sent to fight the maroons, occasionally defected.
>
> Rebellions furnished the largest numbers, as many as several hundred at a time, but rebellions were only one of a number of occasions for escape. . . . There was a steady trickle of runaways, and the trickle became a stream whenever English punitive expeditions failed of their purpose.[96]

Apparently, too, because of the low ratio of women to men, the maroon communities were not yet self-reproducing.

Though Akan-speakers seemed to have been dominant among these Jamaican maroons, the political structure of the Leeward Maroons closely followed that found among the more central African *palmaristas* in Brazil. Cudjoe, who became a dominant Leeward maroon chieftain in the 1730s, employed a paramilitary organization that combined central authority with decentralized settlement. On the other hand, Kopytoff notes, "by the 1730s, the maroons in the east had coalesced into a kind of cooperative federation in contrast."[97] One clear distinction, though, between the Jamaican and Brazilian Blacks was the presence of "obeah men and women, magical practitioners" among the Windward and Leeward maroons.

> To the masters *Obeah* was simply witchcraft, detested both for its secrecy and its alleged skills in the poisoning of enemies. Even to blacks once assimilated, *Obeah* assumed a sinister aura because of its association with the casting of spells to cause harm as well as good. To the unassimilated, on the other hand, *Obeah* was both a genuine religion and a potent source of medicine. Obeah (like the Haitian *Voodoo*, or the Jamaican variant, *Myalism*, or Trinidadian *Shango*) sought ritualistic links with the spirit world beyond the shadows and the sacred trees, providing a mystical sense of continuity between the living, the dead, and those yet to be born.[98]

In Palmares, in keeping with the cosmologies of Congolese and Angolan societies, magicians had been banned as inimical to the king's authority.[99] Among those peoples it was most often the case that legitimacy of authority and the very existence of social order were concomitants to the eradication of sorcery and witchcraft.[100] In the British West Indies, the elimination of *obeah* had become an official preoccupation.[101] And for good reason. *Obeah* men and women were frequently the source of ideology for the slave rebellions:

> [O]beah functioned largely in the numerous rebellions of the slaves. This was particularly the case with the obeah-men from the Gold Coast. . . . In the plotting of these rebellions the obeah-man was essential in administering oaths of secrecy,

and, in cases, distributing fetishes which were supposed to immunize the insurgents from the arms of the whites.[102]

As it happened, *obeah* proved to be more resilient than its opponents. Indeed, it was never extinguished. It continued its mutational adaptation and development in Jamaica (and elsewhere) over the centuries, successively manifesting itself in the societies of Myalism in the eighteenth and nineteenth centuries, the Pocomania movement of the late nineteenth, and the Rastafarians of the present.[103] As we shall see, as it was with *obeah*, it was also the case with marronage.

Returning to the seventeenth century, the *palenques, mocambos, quilombos,* and maroon settlements that found sometimes tenuous, sometimes permanent existences in Mexico, Brazil, and Jamaica were replicated throughout the Spanish territories and the newer colonial possessions marking the expansions of British, French, and Dutch merchant, agrarian, and bureaucratic interests. In Colombia, near the city of Cartagena, a *palenque* known as San Basilio was founded at the beginning of the century. Earlier, in 1529 and 1550, revolts had occurred on the coast of this largely gold-, sugar-, and cacao-producing colony. But as the extractive industries moved further into the interior and Colombia's demand for labor had made it a major importer of Africans (200,000), revolts and the establishment of refugee settlements became more frequent. Nevertheless, Aguiles Escalante tells us:

> The most vigorous insurrectionist movement on the Caribbean coast of Colombia occurred in Cartagena de Indias at the beginning of the seventeenth century during the administration of Jeronimo de Sanzo Casarola. . . . The fiery and daring Domingo Bioho was the first slave to revolt publicly. Claiming to have been king of an African state, he plunged himself with thirty Negro men and women into the forests and the marshy areas of Matuna (south of the town of Tolu). . . . Domingo, now known as "King Benkos" . . . put an end to the period of colonial tranquility in Cartagena, Tolu, Mompós, Tenerife, and so forth, by assaulting and robbing plantations, cattle ranches, cultivated farms . . . even canoes carrying fellow Negroes who had been sent to fell large trees for lumber.[104]

Numerous expeditions against San Basilio failed and in 1612 and 1613, a treaty that included amnesty was offered by the governor, Diego Fernandez de Valesco. Many of the *palenqueros* accepted the terms, which included the abandonment of the settlement. But in 1619, when another major slave revolt occurred in Cartegena, Rout maintains the occasion was seized by a subsequent governor to mete out what he took to be a too-long deferred revenge on the ex-rebels.[105] Escalante, however, insists: "Governor Garcia Giron . . . uncovered a new plot by Benkos and captured him, and finally had him hanged."[106] Still, descendants of the San Basilio *palenque* were to be encountered in the hinterlands as late as 1790.[107] Not until the very last years of the seventeenth century (1696) did the last of the period's major slave rebellions in Colombia take place.

In Venezuela, the settlement of Nirgua, which Baron de Humboldt apparently with some cynicism referred to as the "Republic of *Zambos* and Mulattoes," was founded in similar circumstances in 1601.[108] As such, it was in a direct line of descent from the rebellions that began in the colony in 1532 and again in 1555 with the establishment of the Buria *palenque* associated with "King Miguel."[109] Venezuela, whose economy was a close replica of that of Colombia, would historically absorb a little more than half the number of slaves (121,000). However, for almost 300 years, Venezuela's Spanish settlements would have visited upon them the combined vengeance of Blacks, mulattos, Indians, and *zambos*. In its highlands and valleys, which became the sites for rebellious *cumbes*, the social bases of liberation movements became increasingly miscegenous after the seventeenth century. The same could be said of the towns that developed in close approximation to its ports and inland markets. In the countryside, the forming peasantry became anarchic. As far as is known, no vision of an African state was ever associated with the flights or rebellions recorded in Venezuela. In the towns, something more akin to class wars became the rule, pitting free Blacks, slaves, poor whites, mulattos, *zambos,* and sometimes *ladino* Indians against the Spanish ruling class. Perhaps another consequence of the deracination of Blacks and Indians was that in the eighteenth and nineteenth centuries Venezuela obtained a level of violence in its rebellions and reactions that was barely matched elsewhere in the slave societies.

Finally, in the British and French Guianas and Dutch Suriname, there occurred the most extraordinary instances of marronage, the formation of what in the literature is rightly referred to as the "Bush Negro tribes." These people—the Saramaka, Matawai, Kwinti, and the Djuka, Aluku, and Paramaka—constitute the most enduring and oldest examples of continuous marronage.[110] They are a people who, in the instance of Suriname, could be until quite recently in this century described as constituting "a state within a state." Their history, too, begins in the seventeenth century, somewhere near its second quarter. Richard Price, one of the best informed students of these communities, has observed:

> For some 300 years, the Guianas have been the classic setting for maroon communities. Though local maroons in French and British Guiana were wiped out by the end of the eighteenth century, the maroons of Suriname, known as "Bush Negroes," have long been the Hemisphere's largest maroon population. Except perhaps for Haiti, these have been the most highly developed independent societies and cultures in the history of Afro-America.[111]

Though the ancestries of these peoples are to be traced to the Windward, Gold, and Slave Coasts and to Loango/Angola, they fought and achieved a new identity: Bush Negro. That past demands attention.

The conditions that produced the maroon communities and ultimately the genesis of new peoples in the Guianas and Suriname were a product of a slave system in extremis. Its most important characteristic was that for African labor Suriname became the most lethal colony in the New World. As Price remarks: "The most striking feature of Suriname's demographic history is the extraordinary cost of its slave system in human lives." And R. D. Simons exclaimed: "[W]e have seen some plantations swallow as many as *four slave complements* in a period of twenty-five years."[112] The Dutch West Indies Companies and their successors were hard pressed to supply and resupply the colony's need for fresh African workers. Suriname's laboring population, then, was constantly being revitalized biologically and, as it turns out, culturally. In a colony where the ratio of Blacks to whites became as high as 25:1 (in the eighteenth century), and whose population maintained fewer than 10 percent Creoles for the first century, where labor was concentrated on large sugar, coffee, cacao, and then cotton plantations, Price seems entirely justified in asserting that "inter-*African* 'syncretism' . . . was almost everywhere the central process."[113]

> We can assert with some confidence, then, that within the earliest decades of the African presence in Suriname, the core of a new language and a new religion had been developed; and the subsequent century of massive new importations from Africa apparently had the effect merely of leading to secondary elaborations.[114]

It was not long before the rain forests that boldly defined the limits of cultivable land became the bounds for a resistance of an entirely different sort.

Marronage, of course, was a concomitant of slavery. Brutality was as much a raison d'être of the former as it was a condition of the latter. The English colonization of Suriname was of short duration (1651–67), but even before the Dutch invasion of the colony and the Treaty of Breda (1667), which formally ceded it to them, maroons had appeared.[115]

> By the beginning of the eighteenth century, the maroon population was estimated to have reached 5000 to 6000 . . . clearly an inflated figure, but indicative of the fear in which the colonists held the rebels.[116]

Extraordinary rewards were posted for the hunters of the liberationists, but even more remarkable are the "rewards" that became customary for maroons. Price cites an early (1718) contemporary report:

> If a slave runs away into the forest in order to evade work for a few weeks, upon his being captured his Achilles tendon is removed for the first offense, while for a second offense, if he wishes to increase the punishment, his right leg is amputated in order to stop him from running away; I myself was a witness to slaves being punished thus.[117]

Others were whipped to death with what was called the *Spaanse bok* (Spanish whip), or quartered alive, burned alive, decapitated, impaled with a meathook, or broken on scaffolds. Price argues that the multiplicity of travelers' accounts and local reports attesting to the "unusual brutality" of the Suriname planters of both Dutch and Portuguese Jewish origins fully substantiate that such practices were neither isolated nor unofficial: "the colony's judiciary was often as brutal as the individual plant-ers."[118] The report of the English mercenary, Captain J. G. Stedman, *Narrative, of a Five-Years' Expedition, Against the Revolted Negroes of Surinam, in Guiana, on the Wild*

[handwritten marginal note: Harsh Punishment]

Coast of South America; from the Year 1772, to 1777 (1796), is a classic and authentic account of a starkly brutal slave society. Price concludes:

> All in all, the excesses of colonial Suriname—in terms of both the brutality and the luxury amid which the planters lived—must be constantly kept in mind in building toward some understanding of the slaves' response.[119]

Thus were the beginnings of the Bush Negroes of that land, the oldest being the Saramaka people. And at the end of the eighteenth century, after more than five decades of intensive warfare, they achieved a formal peace.[120] But perhaps the last word should be from one of their own. In 1885, Johannes King recalled from the oral traditions of his people:

> The story of how our forefathers honored God and their early ancestors when they came to receive the presents [presented by the government to the Bush Negroes as confirmation of peace treaties] and then returned to their villages:
> When they got back safely to their villages, they fired many salutes for the people who had waited at home. These people came to the bank of the river singing, to escort them to shore. They played drums, danced, blew African trumpets, and sang, danced and celebrated the whole afternoon until nighttime and the whole night until morning. . . . And they played drums so! When they were finished, they would bring a bush drink that they made from sugar cane juice, and which is called bush rum. They would pour a libation on the ground. That was in order to give thanks to God and the ancestors. After that they would play for the obeahs and for the other gods who had helped them fight.[121]

The struggle that had begun in the seventeenth century had met its fruition among these African peoples far from the land of their ancestors.[122]

Black Resistance in North America

And so the litany of rebellions and marronage continued into the eighteenth century; in the Guianas of Berbice, Essequibo, and Demerara in the 1730s and 1760s; in Jamaica in the 1780s; in Cuba in the 1780s; in Venezuela in the 1730s and 1780s.[123] As the capitalist strata of western Europe achieved political, social, and ideological maturity, their jockeying for hegemony over the world system reduced African labor in its homelands and in the New World peripheries to pawns of power.[124] State banditry, as E. P. Thompson named it, became the modus operandi that weeded out the landed nobilities and integrated their survivors with the rising bourgeoisies.[125] Intensive exploitation of labor became the basis for purchasing new sortings of intra-European domination.[126] In the overseas territories, in the slave societies of Cuba, Brazil, North America, Jamaica, and Haiti, restive colonial elites amassed wealth but envisioned how much greater and diverse that wealth could become without the parasitism and restraints of state and trade imposed by the dominant orders in the mother countries. For these "ruling" elites, too, enslaved African labor, that is its super-exploitation, became the key to their liberation.[127] All—whether landed nobility, landed colonists, or the masters of long distance trade—believed the brutality of the slave system to be a practical necessity. Maroon settlements like those of Jamaica, Cuba, and North America had to be destroyed, or failing that, quarantined. They could not be allowed to contaminate a labor upon which so much depended. Frequently—too frequently for the masters, however, it did not seem to matter.

> Who, then, resisted slavery in the eighteenth century? The records concerning armed revolt indicate that it was mainly the African-born, including male and female, young and old, plantation slave and urban slave. This emphasis on the African-born may have been for the simple reason that Africans outnumbered the Creoles owing to the low birthrate on the plantations and the heavy importation of Africans.[128]

Wars of repression, then, still had to be undertaken, severe discipline maintained. Even then, the masters' nightmares kept recurring and their hysterias periodically assumed epidemic proportions.[129] As Christians, it might be added, they were possessed by a mythology of apocalypse too easily converted into frightening visions.[130] At every opportunity, as Joshua Giddings's tale of Florida reminds us, the logic of marronage was manifest.

> The efforts of the Carolinians to enslave the Indians, brought with them the natural and appropriate penalties. The Indians soon began to make their escape from service to the Indian country. This example was soon followed by the African slaves, who also fled to the Indian country, and, in order to secure themselves from pursuit, continued their journey into Florida.
>
> We are unable to fix the precise time when the persons thus exiled constituted a separate community. Their numbers had become so great in 1736, that they were formed into companies, and relied on by the Floridians as allies to aid in the defense of that territory. They were also permitted to occupy lands upon the same terms that were granted to the citizens of Spain; indeed, they in all respects became free subjects of the Spanish crown.[131]

In North America, the maroon communities of the mid-century in Florida, Virginia, and the Carolinas were anticipated by the slave revolt in New York City in 1712 and that of Stono, South Carolina, in 1739.[132] In the final seventy years of the century, Gerald Mullin found in Virginia newspapers alone advertisements for nearly 1,500 fugitives from slavery.[133]

Colonial North America was particularly vulnerable to slave liberation movements in those regions where Blacks made up a majority. At the century's beginning, South Carolina and the eastern counties of Virginia were two such areas. And in the early eighteenth century when South Carolina's African population was being hastily enlarged—at a rate in the 1730s of more than 1,000 per year, according to Peter Wood[134]—as a concomitant to the colony's growing domination by rice production, Harvey Wish writes that "the plantation-system had yielded bumper crops of slave uprisings and revolts."[135] In 1713, 1720, the 1730s, and the 1740s, conspiracies and actual rebellions were routinely reported to London. From the early 1780s the Black liberationists were further encouraged by the action of the Spanish king, Philip V, who authorized granting them liberty once they reached Florida.[136] In 1738, when sixty-nine slaves escaped to St. Augustine, they were settled at Pueblo de Gracia Real de Santa Terese de Mose, or "Moose," two and one-half miles north of the city.[137] Ten months later,

> In September 1739 South Carolina was shaken by an incident which became known as the Stono Uprising. A group of slaves struck a violent but abortive blow for liberation which resulted in the deaths of more than sixty people. Fewer than twenty-five white lives were taken, and property damage was localized, but the episode represented a new dimension in overt resistance. Free colonists, whose anxieties about controlling slaves had been growing for some time, saw their fears of open violence realized, and this in turn generated new fears.[138]

It was several months before the officials of the colony were satisfied that the Stono rebellion was over. By then, however, a second conspiracy, in June 1740, demanded their attention.[139] Reports of and official reactions to maroons continued into the 1740s but with the formation of Georgia as a colony free of Black slavery (until 1750), the southern route to liberty became more hazardous (both for the slaves and the Georgian colonists who sought to impede them). Still, Henry Laurens, "distinguished native," had cause to note in a letter dated 21 March 1748,[140] "a most horrid insurrection" in the colony.

In colonial Virginia, trials of "Negro rebels" began to dot the counties' records as early as the late seventeenth century.[141] Seldom very expansive, the records of the period most often reflected official fastidiousness. In James City county on 30 May 1688, for example, the disposition of a case remanded from Westmoreland County earlier (26 April) was concluded by the General Court: "It apeard that Sam a Negro Servt to Richard Metcalfe hath several times endeavoured to promote a Negro Insurreccon in this Colony." We shall never know what this man said to his accusers, his reasons or his achievements. We do know that Sam was ordered to be whipped around the town and fitted with an iron collar with four spriggs that he was to wear until his death. It was hoped that this would "deter him & others from the like evil practice for time to come."[142] Just how effective the General Court's punishment was can perhaps be judged by the fact that in the counties of Surrey, Isle of Wight, James City, Middlesex, and Gloucester, several plots involving first Indian and Blacks, and then Blacks separately were reported discovered in 1709, 1722, and 1723.[143] And in 1727, a maroon community of Indians and Blacks, which its inhabitants called des Natanapalle, was betrayed by a former resident.[144] Further marronage in Virginia and neighboring Maryland has been reported by Allan Kulikoff:

> A few Africans formed communities in the wilderness in the 1720s, when Black immigration was high and the frontier close to tidewater. . . .

At least two outlying runaway communities were established during the 1720s. Fifteen slaves began a settlement in 1729 on the frontier near present-day Lexington, Virginia. They ran from "a new Plantation on the head of the James River," taking tools, arms, clothing, and food with them. When captured, "they had already begun to clear the ground." Another small community evidently developed on the Maryland frontier in 1728 and 1729. Harry, one of the runaways, returned to southern Prince George's County to report on the place to his former shipmates. He told them that "there were many Negroes among the Indians at Monocosy" and tried to entice them to join the group by claiming that Indians were soon going to attack the whites.[145]

But the history of marronage in colonial Virginia is still far from complete. In a period (1718–69) during which Philip Curtin calculates the proportion of Africans brought directly to the colony increased, the absence of the mention of marronage in the 1750–80 years seems odd.[146] This is particularly the case when Gerald Mullin informs us advertised "runaways" were prominent, 12 percent of them being described as African-born or "outlandish," and a third of the fugitives were thought by their masters to be headed for inland North Carolina.[147] Nevertheless there is evidence of such communities in the late eighteenth century (1781) in what was by then a commonwealth, as well as references to maroon communities having been established in areas of South Carolina (1765) and Georgia (1771, 1772, 1780s) in the colonial and post-colonial periods.[148] Again, it was precisely in those places where Blacks constituted a substantial proportion of the population—North Carolina, where the 1790 census[149] put the slave population at 26.8 percent; Maryland, 34.7 percent; Georgia, 35.9 percent; Virginia, 40.9 percent; South Carolina, 43.7 percent—that the available records indicate rebellions and maroon activity was most likely to occur.

Moreover, it was precisely these Black populations that demonstrated, in the century's eighth decade, the capacity to respond to British overtures during the American rebellion and to the presence of British troops and propaganda. Jack Foner writes:

At the very time that the American Army ended the practice of recruiting blacks, the British adopted it, hoping in this way to overcome their acute manpower shortage, to cripple the rebellious colonies economically by inducing slaves to desert their rebel masters and seek refuge within the British lines, and to convince the blacks, by offering them liberty in exchange for military service, that their freedom depended on the success of British arms.[150]

Nonetheless, as Jeffrey Crow cautions, the slaves' response to the machinations of the British General Thomas Gage, and Lord Dunmore, governor of colonial Virginia, had its independent context:

But the slave unrest that accompanied the opening stages of the war was too widespread to have been the work of a single British conspiracy, though royal governors and military observers had often commented on the potential for a massive slave insurrection in the southern colonies. From the Chesapeake to the

Georgia coast, black insurgents sprang into action even before the British tendered their help.[151]

Rebellious slaves had always been attentive to the crises among their exploiters, and any momentary advantage, whether it be a master's absence for a few days, the French-Indian War, or a nationalist rebellion, was likely to be seized.[152] And on those rare occasions when the slaves perceived the appearance of a powerful ally, as with the British during the 1770s,[153] the consequences could be dramatic: "Contemporaries estimated that the South lost as many as 55,000 bondsmen," Crow suggests. Many evacuated with the British or were emancipated. Others simply attempted to pass as free Blacks.[154] By 1775, the leaders of the Continental Army had been compelled to compete with the British authorities for Blacks both for their efforts on land and sea.[155] And though some fractions of the ruling class continued to resist the enlargement of the slave soldiery—notably the state legislatures of Georgia and South Carolina—in the end more Blacks were enlisted as combatants by the nationalists than by their British opponents.[156] After the war, however, the British military proved to be the more faithful ally of the slave soldiers.[157] Not surprisingly, then, in the Carolinas, Georgia, and Virginia, the 1780s and the 1790s were times of rebellion in the young "republic."

> Black assertiveness in postwar North Carolina revealed a greater collective consciousness among slaves and an increasing willingness to use violence to liberate not only individuals but groups of slaves. In 1783 the Chowan County court tried the slave Grainge for the "atrocious Crime of endeavouring to Stir up Slaves for the Diabolical purpose of Murdering their Masters and Mistresses." . . .
>
> In the summer of 1795 Wilmington suffered sporadic attacks by a "number of runaway Negroes, who in the daytime secrete themselves in the swamps and woods" and at night commit "various depredations on the neighbouring plantations." . . In Bertie County in 1798 three black men were accused of heading a conspiracy of 150 slaves, armed with "Guns, clubs, Swords, and Knives."[158]

And it was not only the slaves who were dissatisfied with the political issue of the Rebellion. During the waning months of the war, whites joined them in attacks on plantations in Virginia's Goochland and City (formerly King George) counties.[159]

The Haitian Revolution

The eighteenth century ended with a movement of slaves to match the drama of Brazil's Palmares and the significance of the maroon settlements in Jamaica and Suriname during the preceding century. In Haiti, between 1791 and 1804, slave armies managed to defeat the French, Spanish, and English militaries—the most sophisticated armies of the day. Haiti thus became the second New World colony to achieve political independence from its European master and the first slave society to achieve the permanent destruction of a slave system. Modern Haiti constituted the western third of the island that sixteenth-century Spaniards had known as Hispaniola. Its early history during this Spanish occupation has already been rehearsed here. Having largely eliminated its native inhabitants and leached its sources of precious metals, the conquistadors quickly moved on. With the depopulation of Hispaniola and the complete domination of Spain's New World economy by the mines and plantations of Nueva Espana and Colombia after the mid-sixteenth century, the island retreated to the more remote pages of history. Only the eastern regions retained any substantial remnant of its colonial population while, as T. O. Ott, in slight imitation of the poetic form lilts, "the only inhabitants on the western part of the island were the roving herds of cattle and swine, which had escaped the Spanish."[160] In the seventeenth century, the western regions of what the French called Saint-Domingue acquired some settlements based on the activities of renegade seamen and pirates from Tortue (Tortuga). Attracted initially by the supply of meat in that region, and then subsequently encouraged by French colonial authorities (one of which, Bertrand d'Ogeron, imported women from Paris in the 1660s), the *boucaniers* (named for their diet of almost-burnt meat) gradually transformed into planters. Just as gradually, their French settlements in western Hispaniola reintroduced a slave system.[161] The census of 1681 recorded a slave population of 2,000 and that of 1687, one of 3,400. But after the Treaty of Ryswick (1697) in which Spain officially recognized French Saint-Domingue, and Louis XIV restricted the *boucaniers* plunder to slaves, the Black population increased rather rapidly. By 1701, an official memoir destined for the Ministers of Marine estimated the slave population at 20,000, and in 1754 a similar document put the figure then at 230,000.[162] On the eve of the Revolution, the slave population was estimated to be between 450,000 and 509,000, the white population, 30,000 and the mulatto population ("French colonies being what they are,"[163] as Norman Stone has observed) roughly equalling the whites. It was all quite understandable.

By 1790, Haiti was perhaps the most productive colony the modern world had known. Its sugar, coffee, indigo, and tobacco production was said to be greater than the total for British North America. And what the British West Indies had done for the economies of Bristol, Manchester, and the like, Saint-Domingue did for Nantes, Bordeaux, Marseilles, Orleans, Dieppe, Bercy-Paris, and another "dozen great towns." C. L. R. James commented:

> It received in its ports 1,587 ships, a greater number than Marseilles, and France used for the San Domingo trade alone 750 great vessels employing 24,000 sailors. In 1789 Britain's export trade would be 27 million pounds, that of France 17 million pounds, of which the trade of San Domingo would account for nearly 11 million pounds. The whole of Britain's colonial trade in that year amounted to only five million pounds.[164]

And all of it rested on slavery. "Negroes, and food for the negroes; that is the one rule for the Colonies," a French economist of the late eighteenth century declared.[165]

Haiti's slave population, however, was not self-reproducing. And even so severe a "Negrophobe" as Lothrop Stoddard had to admit to the reason why. Sandwiched between his evocation of the official rationalizations for the persistent destruction of the Black population—explanations that ranged from the truths of improper food, the exploitation of pregnant women, high infant morality, and venereal disease, to the absurdities of proposing the "nervous strain" on savages suddenly introduced to continuous labor, and the supposition of an analogy to the impact of captivity on the reproductive capacities of wild animals—Stoddard was compelled to acknowledge: "The general opinion seems to have been that the negroes were worked too hard, and . . . that this was often deliberately done, as many masters considered it cheaper to buy slaves than to breed them."[166] As a consequence, the colony was forced to import Africans at a rate, which, by the time of the revolution, had grown to at least 40,000 each year. In turn, Stoddard recognized, "One of the most important considerations for the history of the Revolution in San Domingo is the fact that a majority of the negro population was African-born."[167]

In its second slave era, then, Haiti had ultimately recapitulated some of the phenomenology of its first. Its slave system was cruel and genocidal; its master class made up of destitute aristocrats and others just as desperate to achieve the wealth and titles of noble status; its laboring class increasingly African; and its whites differentiated between the few who succeeded and then absented themselves and the many whose only achievement was as minor functionaries. One other such reoccurrence was marronage. Stoddard in typical fashion commented:

> there was always a minority of untamable spirits who burst their bonds and sought an outlaw's freedom. In a mountainous country like San Domingo this was easy, and soon every tract of forest and jungle came to have its wild denizens.
>
> . . . [A]s time went on, the numbers of the maroons steadily increased. During the year 1720 alone, over one thousand negroes took to the woods, while in 1751 a high official estimated the refugees in the mountains of the Spanish border at over three thousand.[168]

"Wild" outlawry was the most respect that scholars in the tradition joined by Stoddard could accord to the maroons. Despite repeated efforts to destroy the communities, they persisted, however, "devastating the countryside and inspiring fear in the Saint-Domingue settlers at the end of the eighteenth century."[169] Others, like the famed *Le Maniel*, made their peace with the colonial authorities only on the very eve of the revolution that would eventually make them redundant. Yet their importance, the significance they bore for the ideologists of the colonial regime, went far beyond their objective achievement. Like the revolution their existence foretold, they were demeaned and devalued by those who saw in them a contradiction to the myths of European superiority.

The precise, that is historical, relationship of the maroons to the Haitian revolution is still a matter of debate—particularly so among Haitian historians.[170] Some traditions hold that the maroons played no role in the revolution at all. Others declare that the maroons were "the principal origin of the rising of 1791."[171] If it were not Haiti about which the controversy revolved, the debate might have very well been settled by the available evidence. After all, voodoo, which James termed "the medium of the conspiracy" (of 1791), had also inspired earlier maroon revolts, the most important of which had occurred barely thirty years before under the guide of Mackandel; two of the Revolution's first leaders were maroons: Boukman "a fugitive slave from Jamaica," and Jean François "who had spent the last few years prior to 1791 as a maroon"; and, as well, when in late August, mulattos of the Western Province too rose up against the French, we know that they enlisted maroons whom they termed "the Swiss," (and whom they would eventually betray).[172] The maroons, it would seem, were an integral part of the disparate elements that crystallized into the Haitian Revolution. But they had been party to the genesis of a pariah nation, a Black republic that, in the first years of the nineteenth century, threatened the slave societies that were its neighbors and confounded the heirs to the more recent racial ideology. Haiti's maroons were part of an unacceptable entity. Their history and their historical character had become pawns; objects of contest between Haitian ideologues representing what David Nicholls calls "the black and mulatto legends of the past"; and related to the diminution of the revolution itself by European and American historians and scholars:[173]

> Divisions among the whites, the population structure, the international situation: these are all factors which must be taken in account when attempting to explain the course of events leading up to Haitian independence. To conclude from this that the black slave population played a merely passive role in the revolution would be seriously to misperceive the situation. Perhaps we may excuse the anthropologist Leyburn for a somewhat naive approach to the past, when he suggests that "it was not the resentment of slaves against their masters which caused the final explosion; the slaves were tinder used by others to keep the conflagration burning." Less innocent, however, is T. O. Ott in his explicitly historical work, *The Haitian Revolution*. The author clearly sees that "there was no monolithic cause of the slave rebellion," yet he commits himself to the extraordinary view that the whites and mulattos "handed them [the slaves] the colony by default," and "forced them into a course of action which they would not otherwise have adopted."[174]

Less comfortable with the dialectic that James employed so effectively in his study of the revolution (and which we will explore in Part III), Nicholls concluded: "the movement succeeded because of its structural relationship to the global situation. But this is not to say that the slaves were merely passive."[175] We should know, though, that Nicholls's tempered criticisms are of the milder and more recent expressions of an academic tradition some of whose elements appeared as early as October 1791.[176] And among its contributors were those of whom James declared in 1938 constituted a venal race of scholars, profiteering panders to national vanity, [who] have conspired to obscure the truth.[177]

The truth of the Haitian Revolution, however, was not long in doubt in the slave societies of the other West Indies and the Americas of the late eighteenth and early nineteenth centuries. For 13 years they were all—the masters fearfully, the slaves expectantly—witnesses to the struggles between slave armies and the forces of France, Britain, Spain, and then France again. They heard some version of the gigantic Boukman, the *Papaloi*, whose plan for a massive revolt had been constructed in the early months of 1791 and revealed to the authorities by the abortive uprising of the slaves in Limbe in early August. They understood how the racial arrogance of the colonials had deceived them into delay, deflecting their attention to the *petite blancs* rabble of Le Cap François whose greed masked as revolutionary ideals had to be behind any slave insurrection with this reported scale. They were fascinated by the details of the night of lightning, wind, and rain, 22 August, when Boukman called together the slaves of the Turpin, Flaville, Clement, Tremes, and Noe plantations of the northern plain and they began the mass destruction of the objects of their oppression. They heard how quickly the rebellion had spread. Suddenly, it seemed, 100,000 angry Blacks in the North Province alone had swept the plain clean of its century-old vestiges of slavery. In the Western Province, mulatto forces had joined the revolution and when it was propitious for them, betrayed it. Their treason to the insurgents was short-lived and their promised reward not forthcoming. They would rejoin the revolution—and betray it again. By late September, Boukman was dead and so were his comrades Gilles and John Baptiste. But the slaves were now transformed into Black armies, marching into battle "to African martial music and with unfurled banners inscribed with 'death to all whites.' "[178] From that moment on, the grand historical parade of the Haitian Revolution proceeded. The witnesses learned the names of Toussaint L'Ouverture, the ex-slave who had acquired slaves of his own before joining and then becoming the first overall commander of the Black revolution; Dessalines, the slave whose military genius and hatred of the whites would knit the movement back together again when it was wounded by Napoleon's treacherous betrayal of Toussaint, and propel it toward new revolutionary heights; Henri Christophe, the slave whose old intimacy with Cap François society would seduce him into becoming Emperor of Haiti, matching his station with the much grander presences of Napoleon. And perhaps if they were very attentive, they came to know other leaders like Moise, Jeannot, Jean François, and the French Republic's Sonthonax, and heard, no doubt with due anonymity, of the mysterious achievements of men like Hyacinth.[179]

The slaves of Haiti were in no way passive recipients. Haiti burned the ears of the slave owners in the New World at the beginning of the nineteenth century. They whispered its name, futilely conspiring to deny its legend and its very existence to their properties. But it was their ideologues, their intellectuals, their academies that succeeded in the larger suppression of the fact. Their weaponry was ridicule while those of their bourgeois masters were economic and diplomatic strangulation. And in this century, in due course, when the memory of the revolt had faded among most of the descendants of the master and slave classes of the Old and New Worlds, the still classic and unsurpassed study of the revolution by James appeared. Thus, for the moment, it is appropriate that he should have the last word. Of that revolution of slaves, James summed up his reconstruction of what had happened in Haiti:

> No one could have guessed the power that was born in them when Boukman gave the signal for revolt on that stormy August night in 1791. Rebellion, war, peace, economic organization, international diplomacy, administration, they had shown their capacity. . . . The national struggle against Bonaparte in Spain, the burning of Moscow by the Russians that fills the histories of the period, were anticipated and excelled by the blacks and Mulattoes of the island of San Domingo. The records are there. For self-sacrifice and heroism, the men, women and children who drove out the French stand second to no fighters for independence in any place or time. And the reason was simple. They had seen at last that without independence they could not maintain their liberty.[180]

But even before this Black rebellion was resolved, its impact was being felt elsewhere. From Haiti, the revolution extended to Louisiana in 1795, Virginia in 1800, and Louisiana again in 1811.[181] Quite recently, Eugene Genovese has remarked:

> Gabriel Prosser in 1800 and Denmark Vesey in 1822 consciously looked to Haiti for inspiration and support, and as late as 1840 slaves in South Carolina were interpreting news from Haiti as a harbinger of their own liberation. . . . The slaveholders . . . understood the potential of what they saw. References to the example and inspiration of Haiti reverberated across black America. The impact on David Walker may be readily see from his great *Appeal*. . . . And the slaveholders were not amused by celebrations of Haitian independence such as that staged in 1859 by free Negro masons in St. Louis, Missouri—a slave state. . . . The revolution in Saint-Domingue propelled a revolution in black consciousness throughout the New World.[182]

From Haiti and the "one great militia," which Du Bois[183] and Genovese claim the white South constituted, the revolutionary tradition lit up the horizon of Brazil's Bahia region. From 1807 to 1835, the chroniclers of Bahia recorded revolt after revolt: 1807, 1809, 1813, 1816, 1826, 1827, 1830, and the great "Hausa Revolt" in 1835. Again, it is the works of Nina Rodrigues, Artur Ramos, and more recently R. K. Kent and Stuart Schwartz—not always in agreement—that form the integument for both the recovery and the reconstruction of these events.

Black Brazil and Resistance

Brazil, by the second decade of the nineteenth century, had amassed a population, half free, half slave, of more or less 3,817,000.[184] It was then in the midst of the process of importing the almost two million Africans whose arrivals its records give evidence for between the years 1800 and 1850.[185] In a way all this activity with respect to the slave trade was quite in character for a society whose economy, social structure, and mores had become dominated by African labor. Brazil had become a slave society that obtained a scale of dependence unmatched by any other. Indeed, slave labor was so omnipresent in Brazil by these years that its uses far exceeded the elementary functions of material production. The presence of slaves had begun to invade the more subtle regions of "vanity" and "vice," providing to the master class "a certain pleasure of command and authority" as one mid-nineteenth-century Brazilian observer, Luiz Lacerda, put it.[186] Robert Conrad has made the same point more graphically:

A Bahian, writing in 1887, revealed that before 1850 wagons or carts were almost never used in his city to carry loads. Weights were carried on the heads of slaves or "by means of the most barbaric and antieconomic instrument imaginable—the pole and line," with which eight or even twelve men were sometimes employed in carrying a single burden. Wealthy persons were transported about Brazilian cities or even through the countryside in sedan chairs, palanquins, or hammocks with a similar lavish use of personnel.[187]

Now the slave was more than an object of luxury, as Lacerda had believed. The slave in nineteenth-century Brazil had become a costume, an item of social dress and self-presentation as well as the source of the energy that produced the real wealth of the economy.

With respect to that economy, Leslie Bethell has reconstructed its character:

[S]ugar remained the colony's major cash crop and large concentrations of slaves were still to be found on the sugar plantations of the Reconcavo (the fertile coastal area of Bahia), in Pernambuco, in the *baixada fluminense* (the coastal strip of what is now the state of Rio de Janeiro) and, a more recent development, in Sao Paulo. Slaves also worked both the cotton plantations of Pernambuco and southwest Maranhao (cotton represented 20 percent of the value of Brazil's exports at the beginning of the nineteenth century) and the tobacco and cacao plantations of Bahia and Alaboas. In the far south—Rio Grande de Sao Pedro . . . and Santa Catarina—negro slaves were employed in stockraising . . . in cereal production and in subsistence agriculture. There were also large numbers of slaves engaged in subsistence agriculture in Minas Gerais where the gold and diamond mines, which had flourished during the first half of the eighteenth century but which were now in decline, had served to attract slave labour to the area. In Rio de Janeiro, the viceregal capital since 1763, in Bahia, the former capital, and, indeed, in every other major town, slaves were widely employed as domestic servants, and *negros de ganho*—individual slaves who were hired out by their masters and paid wages—were to be found working as stevedores and porters in the docks, water and refuse carriers, and even as masons and carpenters. The Church—monasteries, convents and hospitals—owned slaves. The State owned and hired slaves for the building and maintenance of public works.[188]

Slavery, it appears, occupied most Brazilians and preoccupied all. And, finally, to the consternation of few Brazilians it seems, the etiquette of domination was extended far beyond the boundaries of race and color:

[T]he existence of white slaves in Brazil [w]as attested to in 1827 by a member of the national Chamber of Deputies. "It is a taint in the blood," as [Robert] Walsh put it with Anglo-Saxon incredulity, "which no length of time, no change in relationship, no alteration of colour can obliterate."[189]

Conrad, himself, observes: "If whites or near whites were sometimes kept in a state of slavery, mulattoes or blacks (sometimes slaves themselves) also owned slaves."[190]

Typically of the Caribbean and South America, however, the Africans of Brazil were what Philip Curtin unfortunately described as "a naturally decreasing slave population."[191] "Natural" in such instances may be the historical demographers way of indicating the unfavorable ratio of births to deaths in a population, but its use here is both unfortunate and unacceptable for two reasons: first, because it appears to draw our attention too narrowly to the slave as a biological organism presuming a normal environment; and second because such a phrase as "naturally decreasing" diminishes the painful reality and the tragic experience of Brazil's slave population. Bethell, on the other hand, puts this decrease in its historical context:

> The slave population of Brazil required regular replenishment through the transatlantic slave trade. One reason for this was the very high slave mortality rate. Many slaves never survived their initial acclimatization and training; others died as a result of poor diet, insanitary living conditions and disease. . . . More important, since it was considered most economic to "work out" slaves . . . and then to replace them with others, a great many Africans died from ill-treatment and sheer exhaustion. At the same time, the rate of natural reproduction amongst slaves was extremely low.[192]

In addition, he remarks, "there were, on the average, eight men to every two female slaves," and infant mortality was high. The end result, as Bethell has already been seen to conclude: "The slave population of Brazil required regular replenishment."

A second cause for the increase of slaves in early nineteenth-century Brazil was the rapid growth of the region's economy during this period. In this respect, Brazil was responding to political, economic, and financial forces in the world market. At its base, the spurt in the Brazilian economy was a consequence of the market demand for sugar and cotton: "[T]he American Revolutionary Wars, the French Revolutionary Wars, the Napoleonic Wars and, not least, the bloody uprising in the Caribbean sugar island of St. Domingue had crippled many of Brazil's economic rivals and raised world prices for tropical produce."[193] Parallel interests in the early part of the century also encouraged the extension of coffee cultivation in Brazil: "Planted in Maranhao in the Brazilian north during the first half of the eighteenth century, coffee was brought to Rio de Janeiro in the 1770s, and in the years immediately following the establishment of the Portuguese royal government in Rio (1808), coffee became the most important crop of the nearby mountainous hinterland."[194] Brazil was now this hemisphere's single most important site for slave production outside North America. The world economy was settling once again.

Of course, it was new sources of capital invested directly and indirectly in Brazil's trade and production that lay behind the massive slave imports of the period. And it was primarily an English merchant class (with support from Portuguese trade, American shipping, and other interests),[195] anxious to dominate or monopolize a world market whose tropical commodities had been expropriated from their French competitors by the Haitian Revolution, which subsidized both the effort at political independence for Brazil from Portugal and the accelerating Africanization of Brazil's economy.[196] Eric Williams reported: "It was said that seven-tenths of the goods used by Brazil for slave purchases were British manufactures, and it was whispered that the British were reluctant to destroy the barracoons on the coast because they would thereby destroy British Calicoes. In 1845, Peel refused to deny the fact that British subjects were engaged in the slave trade."[197] Notwithstanding the British government's persistent and public opposition to slavery and its efforts to compel Brazil to abolish the trade—to all of which historians have paid great attention—Williams observed:

> The British capitalists, however, remained unimpressed. In 1857 [30 January] an editorial in the London *Times* declared: "We know that for all mercantile purposes England is one of the States, and that, in effect, we are partners with the Southern planter; we hold a bill of sale over his goods and chattels, his live and dead stock, and take a lion's share in the profits of slavery; . . . we are clothing not only ourselves, but all the world besides, with the very cotton picked and cleaned by 'Uncle Tom' and his fellow-sufferers. It is our trade. . . ." British capitalism had destroyed West Indian slavery, but it continued to thrive on Brazilian, Cuban and American slavery.[198]

It was for this reason, Alan Manchester reports, the suppression of the Brazilian trade was unpopular in northern England, and that John Bright called attention to the four or five millions of capital and three millions of export to Brazil and demonstrated the damage done to British interests by the slave trade controversy."[199] And it was this relationship that was the basis of the charge of hypocrisy leveled at Britain by certain "Yankee" and Brazilian critics.[200]

Such, then, were the grounds for the scale of African importation into Brazil that occurred in the first half of the nineteenth century. In social terms, it meant, if we follow Ramos's calculations, two-thirds (2,414,000) of the Brazilian population would become Black (*preto*) or mulatto (*pardo*), and 1,930,000 of them slaves.[201]

Inevitably, in response to this vastly augmented slave population, by the early nineteenth century Brazilian planters and settlers had achieved an appropriate "sociology" of slave control. And though it appeared to develop in an almost total ignorance of the country's maroon history of the seventeenth and eighteenth centuries, and of the political exigencies that molded the particularities of the slave trade to the world economy (that is, the varying accesses to reservoirs of African labor), at some level we must presume it took them into account if only in a mystified fashion. Kent, describing this new and presumably comforting mythology of slave control, reconstructed it as succinctly as is possible:

For a long time the Portuguese morador or "settler" in Brazil had himself assumed that all slaves from Africa were "Angolas" or "Bantus" and since Brazilian agriculture was developed by the "Bantu" farmer his reputation continued to hold even long after it became apparent that "all Africans" were not "alike." For the "Angolas," sought at the *engenhos* (sugar mill and plantation complexes in the immediate hinterland of Bahia called *Reconcavo*), a composite belief in their "docility" and willingness to assimilate and in their greater "mechanical inclination" was grafted onto the earlier reputation of agricultural excellence. The "Minas" on the other hand encountered an entirely different demand: regarded as more enterprising and intelligent than "Angolas" and as poor plantation hands at the same time, they were valued as household slaves and in the trades and skills.[202]

In other words, those peoples who had in the most early era of the colony's development as a plantation and mining economy served as the source of labor were seen as pliable and naturally agrarian; those whose recruitment coincided with the region's beginning of urbanization and secondary manufacturing were also naturally inclined to those niches to which they were disposed. And, as we have already suggested, the collective myth denied the possibility of African resistance to slavery through its reliance on manageable characteristics: "docility" and "enterprising." This was made possible, perhaps, by the fact that "the basic form of slave resistance"[203] up to this moment had been *quilombos*, a habit that physically removed recalcitrant Africans from the society of whites. But though the legend is still maintained in some circles of Brazilian intelligentsia,[204] in the first third of the nineteenth century it was shattered. By the mid-nineteenth century, Joao Pandia Calogeras comments, "The Negroes came to be regarded as a dangerous element in the population, a menace to the lives and safety of their masters."[205] Rollie Poppino concurs, noting: "[T]he sharp rise in the number of slaves raised the specter of Negro rebellions," and moreover, "the steady increase in the Negro sector of the population was [seen to be] undermining the basically European culture of Brazil."[206] Though the details of the historical events that account for this change of attitude are still not entirely agreed upon or mastered, the broader character of those events is known. They were, as suggested, the rebellions of the 1808–35 period.

By the 1820s, Bahian and other Brazilian factors had become the dominant agents in the newly independent nation's slave trade. Now, with direct control of the slave market in the hands of collaborators close to the planters, it would be expected that the disposition of Africans would more faithfully adhere to the rules implied by the society's code of slave control: "Minas" to the urban areas, "Angolas" to the mills and their associated plantations. For the most part and for some time that is how it went. Inevitably, however, new exigencies compelled adaptation. This break, one historian surmises, was important both to the construction of the slave rebellions that followed as well as to their subsequent reconstruction.

Kent argues that in West Africa, the breakdown of the Old Oyo Empire of the Yorubas and the long succession of Yoruba Wars that followed in the early nineteenth century gave Bahia ready access to Yoruba craftsmen, and Kent reasons that this may have also been the cause for "a greater number of Hausa slaves [going] to the engenhos in the Reconcavo."[207] Two consequences, Kent believes, of the more complex slave demography that resulted were that first, contemporary local authorities and subsequently such scholars as Nina Rodrigues and Ramos had difficulty reconstructing the character that could be ascribed to the particular slave movements that emerged during the period.

The "Hausa revolts" between 1808 and 1835, Kent maintains, were a construct of part fact, part attempted manipulation by local planters and merchants of state authorities, and part prejudicial renderings of evidence of Muslim involvement. Hausa slaves were, no doubt, quite active as insurrectionists. Jose Rodrigues has written quite recently: "The least submissive Negroes in Brazil were the Hausas; they headed all uprisings in Bahia and in Brazil, being especially prominent in those of 1720, 1806, 1809, 1813, 1814, 1822, 1826, 1835, and 1838."[208] In Reconcavo, for instance, where Hausa had been sent to augment the slave labor of the *engenhos*, "quilombos were growing at an alarming rate all over the province by the turn of the nineteenth century. The fugitive slaves moreover were no longer avoiding even the towns, sometimes hiding within them and at other times 'descending to loot them.' "[209] Hausa were also implicated in the urban revolts of September 1808 and January 1809 that occurred in the Jaguaripe township and Bahia, respectively. A plantation revolt in the Bahian suburb of Itapoan, which broke out in late February 1814, also involved Hausa slaves. In December 1826, though, it was Yoruba (Nagos) refugees who abandoned Bahia to establish a *quilombo* at Urubu. Ramos writes:

> The leading figure in this conflict was a black woman, Zeferina, who was ultimately subdued and her arms taken from her. The confession of some of those captured made it clear that the Negroes had planned a much more elaborate uprising, repercussions of which were to be felt in the future.[210]

Again, it was Yoruba who were the basis for the urban revolt that broke out in Bahia in April 1830:

> A number of Yorubas broke into the hardware stores, from which they took arms and ammunition, proceeded then to the arming of some hundred more Negroes, and with this considerable band, attacked the police station of Soledade in one of the city's suburbs. Taken completely by surprise, the authorities were helpless. Before aid could be secured and a force organized, the Negroes wrought destruction in the city. The insurrectionists were finally put down with a large loss of life, some fifty perishing and as many more taken prisoners. The rest fled into the fastnesses of the wilderness.[211]

However, the great revolt of 1835 in Bahia, Ramos continues, was primarily a Hausa revolt and consequently Islamic in inspiration. "Their aggressiveness was a direct social heritage from the century old wars of religion which had assured the spread of

Islam in Africa. . . . The preponderant cause, let it be repeated, was religious."[212] Kent argues in contrast to Ramos (and Nina Rodrigues) that this revolt involved Hausa and Yoruba, primarily, but was led by Islamic leaders, the *Males*. Neither this revolt nor those that preceded it were holy wars (*querra santos*).

> There was . . . no doubt that "nearly all" of the insurgents knew how to read and write in unknown script, probably Arabic and used among the *Ussas* (Hausa) who appeared "to have now united with the Nagos." . . . A total of 234 reached the trial stage, but under the conditions of arrest it is not really possible to ascertain how many of these had been actually involved. . . . Nonetheless the Nagos, Hausa, Nupe (*Tapas*), Geges, and "Bornus" (Kanuri) accounted for 213 alone. The total included 14 women.[213]

Ramos and Nina Rodrigues, Kent suggests, erred in relying too much on the trial records of the defeated slaves and the personal papers and reports of Bahia's police chief, Goncalves Martins. Both sources were biased by the presumption that "every Muslim was a rebel and every rebel a Muslim."[214] "The Male-led revolt of 1835," Kent concludes, "will be understood in all of its aspects only through a most minute study of data relating to the *intra-African relations* within Bahia itself."[215]

Irrespective of the scholars' "debate" it is quite clear that the revolts were grounded on the syncretics of African cultural and ideological materials. Ramos, Nina Rodrigues, and Kent mention the Yoruba's secret society, *Obgoni*, as a source of that group's militancies, and everyone seems agreed that Islam played a tactical and strategic role in those movements for which the Hausa were directly responsible.[216] In the 1835 rebellion particularly, the warning issued by the Count of Arcos, one-time governor of Bahia (1810–18), appears to have been fully realized:

> The mightiest guarantee for the security of large Brazilian towns is the incompatibility of various African nations for if they ever overlook the enmity which naturally disunites them, those of Agomes will become brothers with the Nagos, the Geges with the Aussas, the Tapas with Sentys, and in this way the great and inevitable peril will darken and devastate Brazil. And, there is no doubt that misfortune can bring about the brotherhood of the unfortunate.[217]

As it happened, the "misfortune" was the Industrial Revolution and the further development of the capitalist world system. Together their need for primitive accumulation translated into slavery on a massive scale. In Bahia in 1835, the inevitable result was "the brotherhood of the unfortunate."

Resistance in the British West Indies

In the same decades of the nineteenth century, the world system showed a very different and apparently contradictory face to the British West Indies. In Jamaica, and the older colonies, no combination of the events that were proving so fortunate for

Brazil, Cuba, and other sugar-producing areas seemed to favor the colonial sugar producers. Having lost domination of the sugar market in the latter half of the previous century, their fortunes continued to plummet, buffeted by such diverse occurrences as market glut, drought, soil depletion, overproduction, and the re-routing of capital. Even the power of the West Indian planters was seen to turn against its possessors: the mercantilist trade restrictions that had preserved the English "home market" for them now became the limit to which they were bound. Technology even railed against them with the development by French interests of beet sugar to challenge the cane.[218] Eric Williams reported:

> Bankruptcies were the order of the day. Between 1799 and 1807, 65 plantations in Jamaica were abandoned, 32 were sold for debts, and in 1807 suits were pending against 115 others. Debt, disease and death were the only topics of conversation in the island. A parliamentary committee set up in 1807 discovered that the British West Indian planter was producing at a loss. . . . The committee attributed the main evil to the unfavorable state of the foreign market. In 1806 the surplus of sugar in England amounted to six thousand tons. Production had to be curtailed.[219]

More specifically, as Williams continued, it became clear that with the exception of Barbados, the older colonies were in decline. The newer colonies seemed to be replacing them in sugar production.

> Between 1813 and 1833 Jamaica's production declined by nearly one-sixth; the exports of Antigua, Nevis and Tobago by more than one-quarter, St. Kitts by nearly one-half, St. Lucia's by two-thirds, St. Vincent's by one-sixth, Grenada's by almost one-eighth. Dominica's exports showed a slight increase, while Barbados almost doubled in its exports. On the other hand, the output of the newer colonies increased, British Guiana's by two and a half times, Trinidad's by one-third.[220]

Trinidad's increase in productivity was less an indication of the new targets of opportunity for British capital than of the problems being encountered in the older colonies. Curacao, St. Eustatius, Saba, St. Martin, Tortola, Tobago, Grenada, and St. Vincent, Williams notes, were or were becoming "barren islands," their soils devastated by careless sugar cultivation.[221] Their planters found the transfer of slaves and other forms of capital to Trinidad both necessary and convenient.[222] Trinidad's shortage of labor, a problem acute enough to arrest the full utilization of its fertile soil, could only be addressed in this fashion after the abolition of the slave trade.

British Guiana, on the other hand, represented an occasion for the massive reproduction of new capital.

> Guyana had already progressed far while under Dutch control, containing twice as many slaves and producing twice the tonnage of sugar of Trinidad and Mauritius combined. But Guyana also contained large areas suitable for cultivation by those who did not wish to work on the estates.[223]

Jamaica, however, was the key. With half the total population of the British West Indies, Jamaica's sugar planters claimed one-third of the sugar produced in British colonies.[224] It was Jamaica's deteriorating role in the world economy that would set the forces of industrial capital against slave economics.

In 1807, according to Higman, the Jamaican slave population was around 350,000, the white population one-tenth as large, the freedmen even less numerous.[225] In 1832, both the slave populations and the whites had decreased to 312,876 and 25,000, respectively, while the freedman population had increased to 35,000.[226] The resident whites, however, were hardly the "white ruling class" that Mary Reckord supposes.[227] Craton writes: "[A]bsenteeism had become the rule for West Indian estates by the middle of the eighteenth century."[228] The most successful planters: the Beckfords, the Hibberts, the Longs, the Gladstones, the Codringtons, the Warners, the Pinneys, the Marryats, returned to England once their accumulations allowed it.[229] "Thereafter," Craton suggests, "the plantations were in the hands of overseers and attorneys, the most mediocre members of the imperial middle class." They

> had nothing but their color and a rudimentary ability to write accounts to distinguish them from the most assimilated of the creole blacks. They were an embattled, embittered class with few inner resources to resist the temptations of petty tyranny or the trauma of alienation. . . .
>
> Many plantation whites sank into a hopeless moral torpor, eating, drinking, and fornicating themselves into an early grave. Some of those kept on estates "to save the deficiency" were so base that even Edward Long had to record that they were heartily despised by what he called the "better sort" of slaves.[230]

A few planters remained, living in towns "or in a Great House," but "[a]t best, the politest society in the West Indies was a pale and philistine imitation of life in the metropolis."[231]

In England, the decline of the profitability of British West Indian sugar in the second half of the eighteenth century was countered by an effort to end the slave trade. Without the trade, Williams recounts, it was believed that France's colonial economy would collapse. English capital, that is its emerging industrial faction, was no longer obligated to a colonial empire. "Colonial independence was cheaper." Free trade and capital accumulation had become the means of further capitalist development, relegating primitive accumulation to a secondary role. Industrial capitalists and their humanitarian ideologues, initially costumed in nationalist Francophobia, were by the end of the eighteenth century prepared to meet West Indian interest on the field:

> The attack falls into three phases: the attack on the slave trade, the attack on slavery, the attack on the preferential sugar duties. The slave trade was abolished in 1807, slavery in 1833, the sugar preference in 1846. The three events are inseparable. The very vested interests which had been built up by the slave system now turned and

destroyed the system. The humanitarians, in attacking the system in its weakest and most indefensible spot, spoke a language that the masses could understand. They could never have succeeded a hundred years before when every important capitalist interest was on the side of the colonial system.[232]

This struggle, however, was not confined to Parliamentary acts, or limited to public discussion in the British Isles. As it proceeded toward the capture of the English public and the domination of state policy, its heat radiated out to the peripheries of the British mercantilist Empire. In the West Indies, colonial papers rehearsed the controversy, colonial assemblies hysterically and vehemently denounced their opponents, and public debate anticipated what could only be understood as the end of the colonial order. The African slaves in the British West Indies, of course, were also listening, a quieter party whose interest in these questions was as profound as any other. Having been given little occasion or opportunity to articulate their position, some secured for themselves an older form of expression: rebellion.

The immediate catalyst for slave rebellions in the British West Indies was the Slave Registry. Initially, the Registry had been promulgated to the Colonial Office as an instrument of slave reforms. In 1812, James Stephens, the Colonial Office lawyer, acting on behalf of "the inner circle of emancipists," had argued that:

> This moderate reform . . . would serve four purposes: to ascertain whether illegal slave importations were still occurring despite the abolition acts, to provide accurate statistics concerning slave mortality and fertility (by so doing further to publicize slave conditions), and thus to provoke further reforms.[233]

In 1815, a parliamentary campaign resulted in the first Order-in-Council for the Registry. The registration of slaves could now proceed in the Crown colonies (those without assemblies), and colonial governors would encourage colonial assemblies to enact their own registration procedures. The planters, however, recognized the Registry for what it was: an initiative to destroy the slave system. "Resisted by the planters even in Trinidad, implementation was delayed in the Guyanas, and in Jamaica it was categorically rejected."[234] Four months into 1816, in Barbados, it became clear that the Africans also recognized the import of the Registry:

> The rebellion broke out with shocking suddenness on Easter Sunday night, 14 April 1816, at a time when the slaves were free from work and had ample opportunities for organization under cover of the permitted festivities. Cane-field and cane-trash houses were fired as beacons in the south-eastern parishes, particularly St. Philip, one of the driest areas, with the highest ratio of slaves to whites. Up to seventy estates were affected. . . . Only 2 whites were killed in the fighting but probably about 100 slaves, with a further 144 executed, 170 deported, and innumerable floggings. Roaming slaves were shot on sight and Negro houses burned. . . . Captives were commonly tortured. . . . Convicted rebels were publicly executed in different parts of the island and their bodies—sometimes just their heads—in many cases exposed on their home estates.[235]

In the minds of some Barbadian planters, there was little doubt of the cause. Letters published in the London *Times* soon after the rebellion were furious:

> We have to thank the projectors of the registry bill for this. It seems, the poor deluded negroes took it into their heads, that they were so far emancipated by the British parliament, as to be allowed three days each week to themselves; and when their owners refused to comply with the demand, they almost immediately commenced burning the estates.

Another writer anticipated:

> This is the first instance of perhaps many yet to come of the fatal tendency to peace and security of those islands of the projected registry bill brought into the House of Commons last year. Such a result was naturally to be expected from any such measure of impolitic interference on the part of government at home between our legislatures and the slave population; but no one expected to taste its bitter fruit at so early a period. . . . [T]he principal instigators of this insurrection, who are negroes of the worst dispositions, but superior understandings, and some of whom can read and write, availed themselves of this parliamentary interference, and the public anxiety it occasioned, to instil into the minds of the slaves generally a belief that they were already freed by the king and parliament.

And Sir James Leith, governor of the island, in a lengthy and extraordinary "Address to the Slave Population of the Island of Barbados" warned:

> I have learned that a general belief had been mischievously propagated among you, that I was in possession of your manumissions, and that my return to Barbadoes would have put you in possession of your freedom. I can solemnly assure you, that my arrival has been one of the most painful periods of my life; when, in performing my duty, I have not only had to inform you of the cruel deception which the enemies of the state, and still more your own bitter foes, have practiced on both, but to feel myself called on by the offended laws to seek out and still to punish the guilty.[236]

The governor, though he did "not mean to enter into the origin and nature of slavery," assured his audience that "Slavery is not the institution of any particular colour, age or country," and that "Great Britain alone exerts her power to prevent an increase of slavery, and to render those who are now unavoidably in that state every practicable service which benevolence suggests." The Africans who participated in what they called the Bussa Rebellion knew the situation differently from the governor. They had the "Mingo" revolution (Haiti) as their model, their source of aid, and they knew their benefactor, Great Britain, required their active assistance in the struggle against slavery. Craton reports:

> Robert, of Simmon's estate . . . said that Nanny Grigg, "a negro woman at Simmon's who said she could read," had put round a rumour late in 1815 that all the slaves were to be freed on New Year's Day, and that:

"she said she had read it in the Newspapers, and that her Master was very uneasy at it: that she was always talking about it to the negroes, and told them that they were all damn fools to work, for that she would not, as freedom they were sure to get. That about a fortnight after New-year's Day, she said the negroes were to be freed on Easter Monday, and the only way to get it was to fight for it, otherwise they would not get it; and the way they were to do, was to set fire, as that was the way they did in Saint Domingo."[237]

The Registry, though, was only the immediate cause, slavery the more enduring one. Recall, almost one hundred years earlier, in Jamaica, another Nanny, the leader of the Windward Maroons, had similarly distinguished herself.[238] The first Nanny had left her name on the map of Jamaica, Nanny Town, but her other "possessions" she shared. Among them were the ethos of the Black radical tradition. Of course, it had not really belonged to her. Indeed, if possession were ever at issue, it would be the other way around. The tradition had produced her as it did the Nanny of Barbados.

It was the Registry again that served as a catalyst in the next large slave rebellion in the British West Indies. Its implementation delayed for a number of years, the reforms with which it was associated did not come into play until the early 1820s in some of the colonies. For Guiana, the sting of slave reform was felt in 1823. The reaction of the planters was, as usual, vocal, unrestrained, and public. In a population that consisted of 77,000 slaves, 3,500 whites and 2,500 freedmen, the debate was socially disastrous.[239]

Guiana's rich soil had been the basis for the intensive application of sugar cultivation.[240] For the slaves, this had the result of appreciably subverting the conditions under which they labored.[241] Discipline, prosecuted by an ever-vigilant white minority, was harsh and often arbitrary. The cruelty that the planters found necessary inevitably exceeded the latitudes indulged by the more humanitarian fractions of the plantocratic society. Some, it seems, found it impossible to restrain from criticizing the planters' open hostility toward the British Parliament and the Colonial Office, and their disregard for the minimal interests of the enslaved population. One of their numbers, the London Missionary Society's pastor, John Smith, was particularly vocal in the characterization of planter greed, what he perceived to be their treasonous claims, and their unchristian attitudes toward their human property.[242] A slave rebellion broke out in August, 1823. Fifty estates and perhaps as many as 30,000 Africans were involved. In two weeks, it was over: two whites killed, 100 slaves killed with the executions of many others to follow. In the next five months, rebels were tracked down, executed, and in some instances tried. Among its victims, the reaction claimed John Smith. Smith died in prison of consumption. Quamina, a rebel leader whose association with Smith was as chief deacon, "was tracked down with Indians and dogs, shot on 10th September, and gibbeted at the roadside in front of [Gladstone's] Success estate."[243] The planters and the British Parliament blamed the missionary and the Registry for the rebellion, but not slavery. Following that logic, Craton notes: "The overall effect was to slow the pace of emancipationism."[244]

Finally, among those rebellions that had their immediate inspirations in the abolitionist controversies and the slave registry, there is Jamaica. Three large and immediately imposing volumes, originally amassed by the Colonial Office concerning this event, rest in Britain's Public Records Office at Kew Gardens. They contain the official records from Jamaica of the trials of 626 men and women who took part in the "Slave Rebellion of 1831."[245] In the varied pens of the colonial recorders of the several counties and court martials of the island, they announce charge, testimony, disposition, and the occupational and bonded particularities of those Blacks who survived a more immediate expression of justice (officially there had been 207 slaves killed during the suppression of the rebellion).[246] Since the overriding concern was with identifiable culpability they tell us more about the networks constructed among the slaves than the reasons they had for engineering these lattices of exchanges. They also tell us more about the configuration of the slaves in the eyes of that "mediocrity" of the colonial middle class than the vision of the slaves themselves, and of themselves. Lastly, since these documents are the primary sources for such historians of the rebellion as Craton, Reckord, and Patterson, and even played a part in contemporary reports such as those of Henry Bleby, they have had another significance: the construction of the events is that bequeathed by the interrogators.[247] "[O]verseers and attorneys-turned-militiamen," Mary Reckord characterized them, intent on "not only restoring order, but vengeance for their losses and humiliation."[248] Not to be outdone, Craton has written of "the plantocratic psyche" as the source of their reactions to the rebellion, "their emphasis on rape," as a motive among the slaves, "a deep sexual insecurity."[249] Patterson has asserted that they were "selfish and incompetent," their "attitude toward slave revolts oscillated between extreme hysteria and unbelievable smugness."[250] Why, then, would its historians leave the identity of the slaves' activities in Jamaica in 1831 in such hands?

Perhaps the answer lies in the seductiveness of the account that emerges. In toto, the trials' records, which resulted in the executions of 312 slaves, assert the existence of a "Christmas Rebellion" in 1831, so named because the rebellion broke out on Monday evening, 27 December. Popularly known as the "Baptist War," the victors' inquiries indicated its leaders were Samuel ("Daddy Ruler") Sharpe, George Taylor, George Guthrie, and Johnson, Thomas Dove, Robert Gardner, Dehaney, and Tharp of the Black Regiment.[251] Planning for the rebellion had begun in August and had almost been betrayed by a series of incidents at the Salt Spring estate near Montego Bay and three estates in Trelawny parish several days prior to the planned outbreak. In its postmortem, the Jamaican assembly's commission of inquiry attributed the rebellion to several causes: the debate on the abolition of slavery that opened in the House of Commons in April; the Baptist, Wesleyan, and Moravian missionaries active especially in St. James's parish and Montego Bay, the centers of the rebellion; and rumors of a "free paper" issued by King William, manumitting the slaves, that was believed by slaves either to have been withheld by local whites or arriving with the returning Baptist missionary, Thomas Burchell.[252] In all a very neatly drawn scenario. Augmented later by the attribution of Christian millenarian elements, the emergence of a "clever," "relatively privileged elite" of slaves to lead such a rebellion, and situational factors ("slave density," geography, absenteeism, for instances), the actions of the slaves became entirely familiar and understandable.[253]

It does appear, though, that what has been constructed as a single rebellion was at least two such actions and maybe even several. For one, the rebellion with which Sharpe and his Baptist associates were identified was centered around the environs of Montego Bay and was pursued by its planners as a form of sit-down strike:

> Sharpe, according to the account he gave the Wesleyan missionary, Henry Bleby, who had several conversations with him when he was in jail, did not plan armed rebellion, but mass passive resistance. After the Christmas holidays when the cane harvest was due to begin, the slaves were to sit down and refuse to work until their masters acknowledged that they were free men and agreed to pay them wages. Sharpe expected that the whites would try to intimidate the strikers by shooting hostages as examples; but the slaves were not expected to fight back, simply to continue passive resistance.[254]

Sharpe, credited with a near-charismatic presence in the colonial inquiries—Bleby said Sharpe had "the feelings and passions of his hearers completely at his command,"[255] was apparently incapable of securing complete adherence to what W. L. Burn appropriately characterized as "a skeleton plot for a strike after Christmas."[256] In part, this seems to have been a consequence of his having to work through mission networks to which only some slaves were culturally and ideologically identified. Since his ideological material, according to Reckord, "was no doubt the language of radical Methodists in England," there were many slaves in the five parishes of concern who were not sympathetic to that tradition.[257] Seen from the perspective of the Christian missions:

> The religious groups among the slaves fell into three categories: groups consisting chiefly of mission members meeting on the estates and modelling themselves primarily on the mission churches; groups formed by mission converts, often church leaders, among slaves who did not attend mission churches; and thirdly, groups run by leaders who were independent of the missions, or repudiated them outright, while associating themselves with christianity—these latter tending to call themselves Baptists, "native" or "spirit" Baptists.[258]

The influence of Sharpe and his Baptist co-conspirators, then, was largely confined to those slaves whose conversion to Christianity had prepared them for passive resistance and sacrifice. Some slaves within that tradition, however, found such a position unacceptable. They chose instead armed revolt. John Fray was obviously one of those:

> The day before the Works were burnt John Fray said to John Gardiner [the Head Man], I see some of these people looking sulky, but if they do not join in the Freedom, and the Fire, we will cut off their Heads and make them we Negroes.[259]

Still others relied on the older tradition among them, the one that had sustained rebellion and marronage.

In the interior of western Jamaica, inspired by Sharpe's initiative, facilitated by the agitation and networks drawn by Sharpe and his colleagues, Johnson operating from the Retrieve estate, Gardner from the Greenwich, Dehany and Tharp organized an armed revolt. They chose to forego passive resistance and banded together to form the Black Regiment. Their model it would appear was drawn from the British West India Regiments organized between 1808 and 1815 but by now largely disbanded. Though most of the Blacks recruited for the nine regiments had come from Sierra Leone, a few had come from the West Indies, some had even been rebels held in the slave jail in Kingston. The West India Regiments had fought against the Napoleonic armies in the West Indies (in some instances Blacks had commanded white troops) and Black troops were still present in the Jamaican garrison at the time of the rebellion.[260] In any case, some slaves had taken to the field of battle quite comfortable with a military tradition:

> The rebels' military core was the Black regiment, about one hundred and fifty strong with fifty guns among them. The Black Regiment, under the command of Colonel Johnson of Retrieve estate, fought a successful action on the 28th of December 1831 against the Western Interior militia, which had retreated from its barracks in the interior to Old Montpelier estate, near Montego Bay. From there, the Black Regiment forced a further retreat to Montego Bay and put the country between Montego Bay, Lucea and Savannah-la-Mar in rebel hands. The Black Regiment then carried rebellion into the hills, invading estates and inviting recruits, burning properties on the border of St. James and setting off a trail of fires through the Great River Valley in Westmoreland and St. Elizabeth.[261]

Of course, Johnson, Gardner, Dove, Dehany, and Tharp—all Baptists—were among the Black Regiment's commanders. "Their work was supplemented by the activity of self-appointed leaders who took the opportunity to roam the country collecting recruits, looting and destroying and intimidating other slaves, enjoying a little brief authority," Reckord has written.[262] One such man was John Linton. And according to Angus McCail's testimony, Linton's appeal was simple and direct: "Angus McCail, I am surprised at you, to go and join the White people, don't you want freedom as well as me[?]"[263] Some slaves, though as Reckord correctly contends, "were intimidated and returned to work." For thousands of others this was not the case. Within two weeks, however, short of arms and experience, the armed rebellion "was virtually at an end."

Nevertheless, depending on the authority consulted, 20,000 to 60,000 slaves were taken up in the rebellion.[264] Moreover, Reckord, who has written about the rebellion in most detail, asserts,

> Most of the estates involved in the rebellion were neither part of the rebels' rudimentary military organization, nor organized for passive resistance. Their rebel-

lion consisted chiefly in the destruction of white property, and a brief heady disregard for routine combined with assertions of freedom.[265]

From among them, maroon units were formed and for two months, long after the suppression of the Black Regiment, they continued to resist the military, and the now emboldened colonial militia.[266] Given the framework of the trial records we know too little of these slaves' activities beyond the fact that many of them ended up like David Atkinson, "the Shell Blower," whose trial disposition read: "Hanged by the Neck, til he is dead, dead, dead."[267] Just how many can never be known. But the official parish returns were horrible enough: 626 tried, 312 executed, 300 flogged, imprisoned for life or transported. In this tragic record, however, the slave societies of the West Indies had also written their own end. In their brutal repression, their flirtations with treason against the Empire, and their ruthless campaigns against the missionaries, they had overplayed their hand, lending their own resources to the cause of the slaves.[268] By 1838, slavery in the British Empire had been officially abolished by a Parliament now "reformed" to enhance the power of industrial capital.[269] "The slaves," Mary Reckord reports, "had demonstrated to some at least of those in authority that it could prove more dangerous and expensive to maintain the old system than to abolish it."[270] And similar moments were to occur in the United States in 1863 and 25 years later in Brazil.[271] Still, Michael Craton has a point when he concludes:

> Slave rebellions were heroic, but heroic failure. Antonio Gramsci would doubtless have pointed out the ways in which the plantocracy re-formed its ranks, and metropolitan capital simply changed its tune, so that they continued to rule for at least a hundred years after 1838. Formal Emancipation was little more than a hegemonic trick. New forms of slavery were instituted by importing Asiatic "coolies" or simply wage slavery.[272]

The list, of course, should not have ended with wage slavery. It properly should also include peonage, sharecropping, tenant-farming, forced labor, penal labor, and modern peasantry. Nevertheless, we must also remind ourselves that whatever the forms primitive accumulation assumed, its social harvest would also include acts of resistance, rebellion, and, ultimately, revolution. In the peripheral and semi-peripheral regions of the modern world system, at least, Gramsci's hegemonic class rule was never to be more than a momentary presence.[273]

Africa: Revolt at the Source

In Africa itself, the same historical tradition was no less apparent in the nineteenth century. But we must also keep in mind the warning issued by C. L. R. James and George Padmore that it was the colonial habit not to maintain a very close record of these events:

> The difficulty . . . is to get accounts written in any detail. The British send out their punitive expeditions against revolting tribes and do not necessarily mention them

in the annual colonial reports. But if the revolt awakens public interest, a commission will investigate and make a report. This report will frequently clash violently with the accounts of participants, eye-witnesses, correspondents of newspapers, native and European, and persons living in the colony at the time. The French and Belgians, however, publish little of this kind.[274]

One of the several consequences of this habit and the intent behind it was to produce a companion academic literature that acted, as B. Magubane asserts, "as a powerful mystification of the real social forces at work."[275] No "image of the colonial social structure" emerged in the literature, Magubane maintains. Lucy Mair, speaking in behalf of her anthropologist colleagues who mined the British colonial fields, thought the reason quite obvious: "I think one has to answer the comment that we concentrated on 'the village' or 'the people' and took for granted the external sources of the changes that we documented. I think the reason is simply that one cannot do both at once."[276] However, she also admitted: "None of us, it is true, held that colonial rule ought to come to an immediate end. Who did in those days?"[277] For Mair, the hub of the District Commissioner's job was "securing an adequate labour supply" for European employers and preservation of the peace: "Lest it be thought that 'the preservation of peace' means the suppression of rebellion, it was much more concerned with the assaults of Africans on one another."[278] Such scholars as Mair, to generalize Magubane's observation, were hardly possessed with the mind-set to "see colonialism as a force and a social process, [rather than] as given, as an existential reality like a landscape."[279]

The European presence in Africa at the beginning of the century had been largely confined to a few settlements in southern Africa and to trading posts and factors on the northern, western, and eastern coasts. Even by mid-century, James and Padmore assert: "it is unlikely that more than one tenth of Africa was in European hands."[280] Nevertheless, the century had opened with resistance. In southern Africa, the Xhosas' Hundred Years War (1779–1880) with the white colonists was already into its third decade. Before its obviously impermanent conclusion, it would take this people as deeply into the historical tradition as any Black people, even the Haitians, had dared. The "Nongquase" or Cattle-Killing of 1856–57, which resulted in the deaths of tens of thousands of Xhosas by self-inflicted starvation, continues to evade Western comprehension.[281] The Zulu, too, came to the point of military resistance. From the emergence of the Zulu state in the early decades of the century to the wars of the 1870s and 1900s, the Zulu fought the disruption of their material and spiritual being. Eight thousand Zulu fell in battle in 1879 alone, the same year that the Assegais defeated the gun in the terrible encounter at Isandhlwana. Thirty years later, as the new century opened, the Zulu rose up once again.[282] As the century progressed, the European intrusion became more marked and resistances more numerous.

In Angola, the Portuguese fought wars of pacification in the 1850s and the 1880s.[283] In present-day Tanzania, the Yao and Hehe in the 1890s confronted the Germans who transgressed the bounds of good manners. Machemba, the Yao general, had written to them in Swahili: "If it should be friendship that you desire, then I am ready for it, today and always; but to be your subject, that I cannot be."[284] In the 1870s in West Africa, the Ashanti began their wars with the British; in the 1890s the Mendi of Sierra Leone did the same. And in 1896, as a complement to the achievement of the Haitian slaves one hundred years earlier, Manelik II of Ethiopia mounted an army of 100,000 in order to defeat the Italian invader. There were, of course, many others: the Yoruba of West Africa, the Baganda of East Africa, the peoples of the Atlas Mountains in the North, the Shona, Ndebele, Ndlambe, and Ngqika of the South.[285] Many of them had to wait a long time for their celebration, many are still waiting.

It was, though, the pattern, the construction, the evolving form that was and is most interesting. The historical integration that the slave trade had accomplished almost instantaneously in the New World was now occurring on the African continent. Discrete societies were slowly achieving the social organization that the attack on colonialism required. Terence Ranger, though not entirely comfortable with the "supra-rational" elements to which we have attended, thought such movements "eminently utilitarian":

> The resistances were a defiance of a power which enjoyed great technological superiority and began with a superiority of morale based upon it and upon confidence in its ability to shape the world. The religious leaders were able to oppose to this a morale which for the moment was as confident, if not more so, based upon *their* supposed ability to shape the world; and they were able to oppose to modern weapons the one great advantage that the Africans possessed, that of numbers. In no other way could the African peoples of the late nineteenth and early twentieth centuries . . . have offered a challenge to the Europeans. Moreover the so-called "superstitious" injunctions of the religious leaders not only served the purpose of creating a sense of the new society but also ensured the minimum of discipline essential in movements such as these.[286]

This achievement as a structural phenomenon was a concomitant of the world system and the imperialist expansion that it demanded. Its coherence, however, was based on the African identities of its peoples. As a structural process, its dynamics were seated in the very expansion of imperialism. This was the dialectic of imperialism and liberation, the contradiction that compelled the appearance of resistance and revolution out of the condition of oppression—even from its ideology. As Michael Taussig has written with early colonial Colombia in mind:

> The scanty accounts of Christianization suggest that conversion and consolidation of belief remained little more than a formality throughout the entire epoch of slavery. Indeed . . . the slaveowners regarded Christianized slaves as more rebellious and as poorer workers than those not indoctrinated, and would pay less for them. . . . Black popular religion could hardly endorse slavery and all it implied, nor could the slaves remain content with equality in God's eyes but not in their own.[287]

The peoples of Africa and the African diaspora had endured an integrating experience that left them not only with a common task but a shared vision.

CHAPTER

THE NATURE OF THE BLACK RADICAL TRADITION

7

This brings us finally to the character, or more accurately to the ideological, philosophical, and epistemological natures of the Black movement whose dialectical matrix we believe was capitalist slavery and imperialism. What events have been most consistently present in its phenomenology? Which social processes has it persistently reiterated? From which social processes is it demonstrably, that is, historically alienated? How does it relate to the political order? Which ideographic constructs and semantic codes has it most often exhibited? Where have its metaphysical boundaries been most certainly fixed? What are its epistemological systems? These are the questions that we now must address, relieved from paradigmatic and categorical imperatives that have so long plagued Western scholarship and whose insistence stemmed largely from their uncritical application and the unquestioned presumption that regardless of their historical origins they were universal. Having arrived at a historical moment, at a conjuncture, at an auspicious time where the verities of intellectual and analytical imitation are no longer as significant to the Black ideologue as they once were, where the now current but dominant traditions of Western thought have once again been revealed to have a casual rather than systemic or organic relationship to the myriad transformations of human development and history, when—and this is the central issue—the most formidable apparatus of physical domination and control have disintegrated in the face of the most unlikely oppositions (India, Algeria, Angola, Vietnam, Guinea-Bissau, Iran, Mozambique), the total configuration of human experience requires other forms.

Our first step is relatively easy because it was always there, always indicated, in the histories of the radical tradition. Again and again, in the reports, casual memoirs, official accounts, eye-witness observations, and histories of each of the tradition's episodes, from the sixteenth century to the events recounted in last week's or last month's journals, one note has occurred and recurred: the absence of mass violence.[1] Western observers, often candid in their amazement, have repeatedly remarked that in the vast series of encounters between Blacks and their oppressors, only some of which have been recounted above, Blacks have seldom employed the level of violence that they (the Westerners) understood the situation required.[2] When we recall that in the New World of the nineteenth century the approximately 60 whites killed in the Nat Turner insurrection was one of the largest totals for that century; when we recall that in the massive uprisings of slaves in 1831 in Jamaica—where 300,000 slaves lived under the domination of 30,000 whites—only 14 white casualties were reported, when in revolt after revolt we compare the massive and often indiscriminate reprisals of the civilized master class (the employment of terror) to the scale of violence of the slaves (and at present their descendants), at least one impression is that a very different and shared order of things existed among these brutally violated people.[3] Why did Nat Turner, admittedly a violent man, spare poor whites? Why did Toussaint escort his absent "master's" family to safety before joining the slave revolution? Why was "no white person killed in a slave rebellion in colonial Virginia"?[4] Why would Edmund Morgan or Gerald Mullin argue that slave brutality was directly related to acculturation, "that the more slaves came to resemble the indigent freemen whom they displaced, the more dangerous they became"?[5] Every century it was the same. The people with Chilembwe in 1915 force-marched European women and children to the safety of colonist settlement.[6] And in that tradition, in the 1930s, James ambivalently found Dessalines wanting for his transgressions of the tradition. Dessalines was a military genius, yes. He was shrewd, cunning, but he was also a man whose hatred had to be kept "in check."[7]

There was violence of course, but in this tradition it most often was turned inward: the active against the passive, or as was the case of the Nongquase of 1856, the community against its material aspect. This was not "savagery" as the gentlemen-soldiers of nineteenth- and twentieth-century European armies arrogantly reported to their beloved publics at home. Neither was it the "fratricide" of Fanon's extended Freudianism.[8] And only seldom was it the devouring "revolutionary terror" of the "international bourgeois democratic revolution" that Genovese's neo-Marxism has led him to acknowledge.[9] This violence was not inspired by an external object, it was not understood as a part of an attack on a system, or an engagement with an abstraction of oppressive structures and relations. Rather it was their "Jonestown," our Nongquase: The renunciation of actual being for historical being; the preservation of the ontological totality granted by a metaphysical system that had never allowed for property in either the physical, philosophical, temporal, legal, social, or psychic senses. For them defeat or victory was an internal affair. Like those in the 1950s who took to the mountains and forests of Kenya to become the Land and Freedom Army, the material or "objective" power of the enemy was irrelevant to their destinies. His machines, which flung metal missiles, his vessels of smoke, gas, fire, disease, all were of lesser relevance than the integral totality of the people themselves. This was what Chilembwe meant when he entreated his people to "strike a blow and die." This is what all the Jakobos in all the thousands of Chishawashas and at all the tens of thousands of beer-parties that dot the Black world have been saying for tens of generations: "we had only ourselves to blame for defeat."[10] This was a revolutionary consciousness that proceeded from the whole historical experience of Black people and not merely from the social formations of capitalist slavery or the relations of production of colonialism.

It becomes clear, then, that for the period between the mid-sixteenth and mid-nineteenth centuries, it was an African tradition that grounded collective resistance by Blacks to slavery and colonial imperialism. This is precisely what Gerald Mullin discovered and wrote about in his study of Blacks in eighteenth-century Virginia. There he concluded:

> Whatever the precise meaning of procurement for the African as a person, his fellowship or affectivity, a core area of human behavior, remained intact as a slave. Africans, assuming that resistance was a group activity, ran off with their own countrymen, and American-born slaves including mulattoes.[11]

Further on, he would make the point again, only differently and more to our immediate point: " 'Outlandish' Africans often reacted to their new condition by attempting to escape, either to return to Africa or to form settlements of fugitives to recreate their old life in the new land. These activities were not predicated upon the Africans' experience of plantation life, but on a total rejection of their lot."[12] Such was the stuff from which legends were made among the Africans. Where to deny to one's self the eating of salt (the "ocean-sea"?) was a guarantee of the retention of the power to fly, really fly, home.[13] All of it was a part of a tradition that was considerably different from what was made of the individualistic and often spontaneous motives that energized the runaway, the arsonist, the poisoner. It more easily sustained suicide than assault, and its ideological, psycho-social, cultural, and historical currencies were more charismatic than political. When its actualization was frustrated, it became *obeah, voodoo, myalism, pocomania*—the religions of the oppressed as Vittorio Lanternari put it.[14] When it was realized, it could become the Palmares, the Bush Negro settlements, and, at its heights, Haiti. But always, its focus was on the structures of the mind. Its epistemology granted supremacy to metaphysics not the material.

It was the mind, metaphysics, ideology, consciousness that was Mackandel's tool in mid-eighteenth-century Haiti. He persuaded the Blacks and their masters to sense the hatred of the slaves in palpable terms. Ordinary precautions were irrelevant, what the slaves could be physically obstructed from accomplishing was unimportant. Their hatred was a material force, capable of snuffing the lives from masters who had gone so far as to import their foods from France and had unloaded the precious cargo with their own hands. It was the same with Hyacinth. His army could rush the cannon of the French forces "without fear or care for the volleys," shoving their arms into the cannons' mouths. They knew, they believed that "if they were killed they would wake again in Africa." On that final day of March 1792, 2,000 of them "died," to a mere 100 of their opponents, but they were doubly blessed: they won the battle and even their dead were free.[15] Boukman possessed the same truth. And so did Romaine. Nanny, who had preceded her Haitian sister by sixty years, was warmed in her mountainous retreat in Jamaica by that very same consciousness. They lived on their terms, they died on their terms, they obtained their freedom on their terms. Thus it was with *obeah*men and *obeah*women, and *papaloi*. These were the terms that these African peasants and farmers had brought with them to their captivity. They were also the only terms in which their freedom could be acquired. At Richmond, Virginia, in the summer of 1800, Gabriel had not quite realized this vision, but his George Smith did. Smith believed in Africa and knew of the "outlandish people," that they dealt with "Witches and Wizards, and thus [would be] useful in Armies to tell when any calamity was to befall them."[16] In 1822 in Charleston, South Carolina, Denmark Vesey realized it, but his Gullah Jack knew it too little. And in 1830, old Nat brought it to fruition.

> Only Nat Turner, who charged his plan with supernatural signs, and sacred, poetic language that inspired action, was able to transcend the world of the plantation and the city. Only Turner led a "sustained" insurrection.[17]

It could not be otherwise. This is what the Black radical tradition made manifest. It was a consciousness implicated in what Amos Tutuola so many generations later would name "the bush of the ghosts."[18] In the twentieth century, when Black radical thinkers had acquired new habits of thought in keeping, some of them supposed, with the new conditions of their people, their task eventually became the revelation of the older tradition. Not surprisingly, they would discover it first in their history, and finally all around them.

The Black radical tradition that they were to rediscover from a Black historical experience nearly grounded under the intellectual weight and authority of the official European version of the past, was to be the foundation upon which they stood. From this vantage point they could survey the theoretical, ideological, and political instrumentation with which Western radicalism approached the problem of revolutionary social change. The Black radical tradition cast doubt on the extent to which capitalism penetrated and re-formed social life and on its ability to create entirely new categories of human experience stripped bare of the historical consciousness embedded in culture. It gave them cause to question the authority of a radical intelligentsia drawn by its own analyses from marginal and ambiguous social strata to construct an adequate manifestation of proletarian power. And it drew them more and more toward the actual discourse of revolutionary masses, the impulse to make history in their own terms. And finally, the Black radical tradition forced them to reevaluate the nature and historical roles of ideology and consciousness. After all it had been as an emergent African people and not as slaves that Black men and women had opposed enslavement. And long before the advent of the "madmen and specialists" (as Wole Soyinka phrased it), the military dictators and neocolonial petit bourgeoisies who in our own time have come to dominate Black societies in Africa and the Caribbean, the Black radical tradition had defined the terms of their destruction: the continuing development of a collective consciousness informed by the historical struggles for liberation and motivated by the shared sense of obligation to preserve the collective being, the ontological totality.

PART 3

BLACK RADICALISM AND MARXIST THEORY

CHAPTER 8

THE FORMATION OF AN INTELLIGENTSIA

It is not surprising that the appearance of a world revolutionary Black intelligentsia in the twentieth century, rather than the issue of a longer process, might be presumed by most observers to be a phenomenon unique and specific to this century. Several quite easily identified reasons have contributed to this presumption. For one, as we have seen, the history of Black peoples has been recast consistently in both naive and perverse ways. Most particularly the memory of Black rebelliousness to slavery and other forms of oppression was systematically distorted and suppressed in the service of racialist, Eurocentric, and ruling-class historiographies. The sum total was the dehumanizing of Blacks. The native responsiveness of the species was denied to African peoples. This distortion might have been a simpler matter if it had been merely a question of a gap occurring in the record, but the space had been filled with nonsense that was made credible by the conventions of racist thinking. For the unaware, nothing was amiss. It was this tangle to which the preceding chapters were addressed, and an attempt made toward the achievement of a greater consciousness of the past of African peoples.

A second basis for the misapprehension of the grounds upon which Black revolutionists had developed, however, was a different set of conventions in Western historiography. Certain habits respecting the framing of events, especially among scholars and ideologues accustomed to assuming the existence of qualitatively distinct stages of human development, tended to trivialize or diminish the significance of precedents of too longstanding account. Enmeshed as they were in historical traditions boasting of, say, Elizabethan and Edwardian eras, Jeffersonian or Jacksonian structures, and so on, rather singular and often superficial benchmarks had become the rule for establishing the setting of human activity. Divisions of historical time seemed particularly easy things to recognize, attribute, distribute, and declare. To such intellects, then, the twentieth century would seem a text in its own right. In a moment, we shall investigate how poor a preparation this would be for the proper placement of Black revolutionary thinkers.

Finally, of course, there was the overpowering spectacle of European radicalism and revolution apparently launched by the First World War. No matter their ideological or theoretical legacy, liberal or otherwise, it seemed to some that these events were bound to the immediate forces that overtook the older capitalist order in the twentieth century. Moreover, the names of twentieth-century revolutionists—Zapata, Lenin, Trotsky, Gandhi, Mao, Fidel, Lumumba, Ho Chi Minh, Cabral (and many others)—represented at the same time, more than Marx and Engels had anticipated in the nineteenth century, and much less. In any case, it was eminently obvious to them that Black revolutionary thought found its beginnings here. There was little cause to look elsewhere. In 1966, Eugene Genovese, the radical historian, neatly asserted all three propositions in an attack on the idea of a Black radical tradition in America:

> American radicals have long been imprisoned by the pernicious notion that the masses are necessarily both good and revolutionary. . . . This viewpoint now dominates the black liberation movement, which has been fed for decades by white radical historians who in this one respect have set the ideological pace for their liberal colleagues. It has become virtually sacrilege—or at least white chauvinism— to suggest that slavery was a social system within which whites and blacks lived in harmony as well as antagonism, that there is little evidence of massive, organized opposition to the regime, that the blacks did not establish a revolutionary tradition of much significance, and that our main problem is to discover the reasons for the widespread accommodation and, perhaps more important, the long-term effects both of the accommodation and of that resistance which did occur.[1]

Thus opposition to slavery was minimal; in "the absence or extreme weakness of such a tradition," Black nationalism *as a movement* was a twentieth-century phenomenon; and the regard accorded to the revolutionary politics of the Black masses has its source in "white" radicalism. In the present chapter we will explore in detail this final thesis: the presumed relationship between Black radicalism and the European radical movement. It is by far the more important of the three propositions associated with the misconception of Black radicalism. Nevertheless, some attention to the habits of historical construction is warranted. It will prove a useful preliminary step, I believe, in our effort to recognize the continuity that exists between the Black rebellions of the previous centuries and the first articulations of a world revolutionary Black theory in the present century.

Capitalism, Imperialism, and
the Black Middle Classes

In chapter 6, because we were rehearsing events that assumed their shapes not less than one hundred years or so ago, our historical narrative worked, with the Western convention of centuries as terms of periodization, as a convenient scaffold. However, social processes, that is historical developments, are neither the products of nor meaningfully framed by such evenly measured periodicities. The French historian Fernand Braudel, for one important instance, made this point by extending the sixteenth century—the historical moment of the dawning of the modern capitalist world in the West—much beyond its formal claim of one hundred years.[2] In a different manner, the Russian revolutionary Leon Trotsky, just as apposite a figure for our subject here, had earlier confronted such facile assumptions by calling them out as forms of foreshortened chiliasm or millenarianism.[3] Braudel understood that one hundred years was sometimes too short a period to encompass historical processes; Trotsky was amused by the suggestion that human activity might end or begin with the endings and beginnings of centuries. The point is that the construction of periods of time is only a sort of catchment for events. Their limited utility, though, is often abused when we turn from the *ordering* of things, that is chronological sequencings, to the *order* of things, that is the arrangement of their significances, meanings, and relations. Increments of time contoured to abstract measure rarely match the rhythms of human action. It is important to bear this in mind as we seek to come to terms with the Black theorists whose writings and thoughts have appeared primarily in the twentieth century. Their era began with the endings of slavery. They were, it might be said, the children of the slaves. The phenomenology of slavery formed and informed them. And in the vortex of its ending, more particularly in the wake of the social forces that compelled new and different situatings of Blacks and others destined to serve as labor forces, these theorists discovered their shared social and intellectual location. The twentieth century was for the most part their biographical station, but merely one site in the zone of their interrogation.

Still, in the post-slavery world order that was their setting, the Black ideologues who were to work in the twentieth century could not be other than strangers. This was to be their lot in whatever part of the Black world they were formed. C. L. R. James might have spoken for all of them when he wrote of the end of his school days: "There was no world for which I was fitted least of all the one I was now to enter."[4] In Africa and the West Indies, European empires and colonies were either being dramatically reshaped by the dictates of state and commerce or spawned at points formerly less accessible to capitalist expansion.[5] In the United States and the Caribbean again, Black peoples were no longer conveniently lodged in or organized by slave systems. The Blacks of the New World could no longer be casually pinioned by the curious as slaves or—at the margins of such systems—as freemen. And, inevitably, their societies and subcultures upon which the intelligentsia drew were steadily becoming less autochthonous. The social patterns, the habits of thought, language, and custom that had congealed in the laborers' communities of the Western hemisphere's slave systems, though in many senses fundamentally conservative, were no longer as impervious to the penetrations of Western cultures as they had been in their "native" circumstance. The masses of Black peoples in the New World and in their ancestral homelands—as peasants, farmers, peons, agrarian workers, migrant and immigrant workers, domestics, skilled, semi-skilled and unskilled industrial laborers, and as labor reserves—now assumed more diverse and diffuse positions in the economic order. Black labor's new mobility, organization, and adaptability also meant that the subcultures within which it had been historically enveloped were subject more often to the intrusions of material and ideographic elements from the agents of the economically determinative social order. Though it might be correctly argued that much of this penetration was at first incidental, some of it clearly was not. Language, that is the languages and consciousness of rule and the ruling classes, was an instance of the latter. These accretions would have profound effects on the ideologues of the Black world.

Marx and Engels, if we recall, had once conceived the notion that the bourgeoisie of Western Europe would succeed in transforming the whole of the world's nations into bourgeois societies—loci reduced to social orders of ruling and proletarian classes, as Marx declared in one of his prefaces to the first volume of *Capital*. Historically, however, capitalist expansion had had as its result only the most approximate relation to Marx's projected social divisions. In those parts of the world where resourceful indigenous ruling classes were encountered by the empire builders, collisions were inevitable. Not as inevitable were the results: some native elites were vanquished and destroyed, others not. Some, having led formidable anti-imperialist defenses, preserved much of their independent cultures, whittling down foreign influences to the mundane exchanges required by colonial administration. Many, however (and it is within the British Empire that one finds the best examples), became part of the apparatus of "indirect rule," a system whose rationale could be so concisely put forth by one of its mechanics, the British anthropologist, Margery Perham:

> The basic difficulty [in carrying out "indirect rule"] is one that will appear in its different aspects—education, land-tenure, economic production, law—in all our coming discussions. It is (and here I speak especially of Africa) the great gap between the culture of rulers and ruled. In administration, reduced to its simplest terms, it means that for the most part the people do not understand what we want them to do, or, if they understand, do not want to do it. . . . [W]e endeavor to instruct the leaders of the people in the objects of our policy, in the hope that they will, by their natural authority, at once diffuse the instruction and exact the necessary obedience.[6]

For a time the collaboration of native elites was sufficient for the imperialist and colonial authorities. At the peripheries of the world system where forms of coerced labor had obtained, peasantries existed in proximity to agrarian workers, unskilled workers to semi-skilled workers; labor reserves were directly and indirectly connected with those absorbed by the political instruments of authority: armies, militias, native police. By the last decades of the nineteenth century, however, social forces set loose by imperialist invasions, wars, occupations, administrations, and co-optations, were maturing.

In the middle tier of these societies rested the native petit bourgeoisie, wedged between the laboring classes beneath them and the foreign and native operatives of capital and the officials of the state above. Their social origins were complex and intertwined. One of their bases was the "mulatto" populations of the former slave societies and the colonies. This "brown" stratum was frequently the natural issue of racial systems where privilege of position and education was sometimes bestowed by white fathers (or mothers). In other instances it was the result of deliberate political policy. In his massive study, *Caste, Class and Race*, Oliver Cox stated the general rule:

> Where whites are mainly sojourning rulers, their numbers are usually relatively small. Ordinarily "home" is in Europe or America, and they seldom set their roots in the area. Here there is little hope of developing a significant white population. The white man's principal need is not a home but a satisfied and exploitable people to develop the resources of the country. This ruling class adopts a policy of "co-operation"; and, other things being equal, favors are distributed to the mixed bloods on the basis of their apparent degrees of whiteness among the people of color. Degrees of color tend to become a determinant of status in a continuous social-class gradient, with whites at its upper reaches . . . the lighter the complexion, the greater the economic and social opportunities.[7]

Another basis of the petit bourgeoisie was property. Some Blacks, but certainly with less frequency than occurred with what French colonialists termed the *petit blancs*, had translated particular skills, traditional positions and knowledge into property (including slaves during the slave era). With slavery abolished, some of this Black-controlled capital was reconverted into professional skills in succeeding generations.[8] Frequently, however, the native middle classes had been directly formed as functionaries of the state—civil servants, minor as well as middling—and as agents of landed, mercantile, or manufacturing capital (often absentee).[9] And for sure, there were other paths leading to the privileges of this stratum, some less "legitimate" or conventional.[10]

For colonial administrators, however, the most problematic origins for the native petit bourgeoisie were the mission schools. From the fifteenth century and before, the missions had all along served as a part of the rationale for European colonialist and imperialist aspirations. Still, the correspondence between the ends of missionary work and the goals of imperialism had never been entirely true. For one, the missionaries themselves, in the case of English imperialism, were often recruited from colonized peoples: that is, Scots, Irish, and Welsh.[11] Such soldiers for Christ could be often quite ambivalent about the colonial power. Just as troubling were the potential conflicts between faith and imperial interests. During the construction of slave systems and afterward, the teaching of the tenets of Christian beliefs had taken as one of its presumptions the fact of the savage and the savage's or pagan's need. It was thus axiomatic that the proof of the missionary's success was the creation of civilized Christians—natives whose familiarity with European (or Euro-American) cultures and habits were as intimate as their experience with Christ.[12] This meant, though, that Christian missionaries in some instances felt some ambivalence toward such colonial policies as "indirect rule," especially "when it [was] held to involve the strengthening of animism or Islam," as A. Victor Murray put it.[13] Most significant, however, were the attitudes colonial administrators developed toward the activities of the missions. The construction of Black Europeans was overly ambitious in their eyes. In 1938, Arthur Mayhew would advise an Oxford University summer session for colonial administrators that "Before the Great War education was undoubtedly too 'literary.'" And he then reported, with satisfaction, that "[f]rom 1925 onwards great emphasis was laid on vocational training."[14] Forty years later, Penelope Hetherington would penetrate Mayhew's objections:

> In the past missionaries had counted themselves successful if their work in the field of education had produced black Englishmen, Africans who seemed to have assimilated Western culture. But these missionary-educated Africans were anathema to many administrators and others. They were "cheeky" and demanded social equality and political rights.[15]

It had become necessary to rationalize colonial policy and mission education. The formation of native elites was to be more deliberate. In the beginning there would be an appropriate contingent of clerks and a limited number of professionals, not nationalistic intellectuals; in the West Indies, such was the educational policy laid down generally at the end of the nineteenth century. In Africa, where populations were large and mission schools relatively few, the same policy was inaugurated in the years following World War I,[16] and a common place by the 1930s. In 1933, the *Report on African Affairs* read in part:

> Two especially important objects have been kept in view in framing the educational policy of Nigeria. The first to spread a sound education as widely as possible among the masses in order to produce, in course of time, a literate population able to participate intelligently in the economic, social and political development of the country. The second ideal is to train up as soon as may be a body of men and women who can perform some of the tasks in Government work and private enterprise for which at the first impact of western civilization it is necessary to import Europeans.[17]

It soon became clear, however, that the colonial governments had moved too late. "Elite nationalism," one of the first political expressions of the Black petit bourgeoisie, was already propelling complements of the class into the older, more profound tradition of radicalism. Elliot Skinner would recall:

By the 1920s and 1930s, conflict and incoherence had spread into almost all aspects of life in colonial Africa. There appeared a group of Africans who had acquired the cultures of the colonizers and considered themselves to be British, French, and Portuguese. They had learned to consider Europe as home and had adopted European clothing, speech, and mannerisms.[18]

Such was also the case in the Caribbean and in America (where the emergence of a middle class among Blacks could easily be traced back to the eighteenth century).[19] Even in independent Haiti, where the Black and mulatto revolutionary armies had, by the beginnings of the nineteenth century, broken down into racial and class factions, a petit bourgeois nationalism found expression. The sugar-export sector of the Haitian economy had been destroyed during the revolutionary wars and subsequently was unable to compete with Cuban and Indian exports in the world system. And though a series of political eruptions from below had divided the land between large landowners (Black and mulatto) and peasants, the majority of the peasants were landless and frequently rebellious. Commercial pursuits and control of the administration of the state had increasingly become the arenas contended for by the Black and mulatto groups within the ruling class. But in this conflict, Alex Dupuy asserts, "the largely landowning black faction and its allies, frustrated by the mulattoes in their attempt to control the state, had recourse to a *noiriste* or black nationalist ideology, claiming to be the sole representatives of the people because of their common skin colour."[20] Inevitably, during the second half of the century, a radical Black ideology was articulated by renegades among the Black petit bourgeois intelligentsia. Eventually it was to mature in the work of Jean Price-Mars, Georges Sylvain, and Carlos Deambrosis Martins.[21] In every sector of the Black world, the dialectic of exploitation would shake an increasing number to their very roots. And in time, as the fractures and contradictions of Western domination became more compelling, their presence and their purpose would become electrifyingly clear.

Western Civilization and the Renegade Black Intelligentsia

In the Anglophone, Francophone, and Latin territories of both hemispheres, the Black "middle classes" had become broadly identified by culture and language, that is, their abilities to absorb the cultures of their ruling classes and the reading and speaking of European tongues. Deracination, social, and cultural alienation had become the measures of their "civility," loyalty, and usefulness. And of course they shared with the mass of Blacks the knowledge that these veneers were the historical artifices of the structuring of authority, caste, race, and class, and that their particular adaptiveness was the mark of privilege and status. As intermediaries between Black labor and the world system in Africa, the Caribbean and North America, as mediators between Black workers and the social tapestry woven by capitalist-determined forms of production, their skills were functional and the naturalness with which they obtained them only apparently so. In the West Indies as well as Africa, systems of colonial education tutored these complements of imperialism.[22] In North America in the decades following the Civil War, similar apparatuses were to be found in the southern states. Of his sector of the African diaspora, James has said: *C.L.R.*

> In every West Indian island, in those days from nineteen hundred for the first twenty or thirty years, there was always a secondary school. Always one. . . . In the school I went to there were nine masters, eight of them were either from Oxford or Cambridge, and the one who wasn't was a drawing master. Well, you needn't go to Oxford or Cambridge to be a drawing master.[23]

Still, for these Black middle strata just as it was the case for the vast majority of Blacks, the dominant class and whites in general were not intimates of any immediate sort. In the Caribbean and Africa for the most part, whites were of a relatively small number. In Latin and North America, where European populations were statistically dominant, for most Blacks the whites were existentially a distant, fearful, and oppressive presence. Whites marked the landscape, and in a way, the boundaries of Black life, their lives, their habits, their very appearance the testament and detail of a cruel and unyielding order of social and spiritual regulation. For the radical Black ideologues— almost entirely circumscribed by native petit bourgeoisies—it was not only inevitable but also imperative that they would first acquire the stance of internal aliens. Those of special interest to us here bear this out.

Black Intelligentsia From Trinidad came George Padmore, C. L. R. James, Eric Williams, and Oliver C. Cox. Padmore (born Malcolm Ivan Meredith Nurse) and James were the sons of school headmasters.[24] Eric Williams, one of their most illustrious if prodigal students, was a product of the same Black petit bourgeoisie—at a somewhat lesser rank.[25] Oliver Cromwell Cox, as his name suggests, was the son of middle strata parents who it appears had taken the authority of their colonial "betters" at its word.[26] In North America, W. E. B. Du Bois was reared by the "black Burghardts" amidst the more affluent white children of Great Barrington, Massachusetts. As he recalled his childhood in one of his autobiographies, *Darkwater*, it was some time before he discovered that he was "colored," and by then he had already absorbed the rather disdainful attitudes of his peers toward the few southern European immigrant families that made their appearance in Great Barrington.[27] Only Richard Wright, among the radical Black thinkers upon whom we shall lay emphasis, came from the Black substratum. But even here, the son of a sometime itinerant Mississippi farmer and general laborer was also, on his mother's side, the heir of a family with middle strata pretensions.[28] Again, with the exception of Wright, they had all begun their adult lives destined for professional careers. Their childhoods had born the marks peculiar to the Black middle strata—the presumption that being Black was incidental to their expected social stations. They were launched into maturity, as Wright would declare for himself during one of his moments of acute alienation, as representatives of "the

West."[29] Eventually this would prove to be the source of their contradictory compulsions, their strengths, and their weaknesses.

Among the vitalizing tools of the radical intelligentsia, of course the most crucial was words. Words were their means of placement and signification, the implements for discovery and revelation. With words they might and did construct new meanings, new alternatives, new realities for themselves and others. But language, that is Western culture, was more than some recumbent artifact to be used or not as the intelligentsia saw fit. Its place in their lives had been established long before they found the means of mastering it. Indeed, they were themselves in part defined by those languages of rule and commerce. In Frantz Fanon's poetic description, they were Black skins under white masks. James has quite effectively captured this contradiction:

> [Aime] Cesaire and I were talking one day, and I asked him: "Where do you come from?" He said, "Well I grew up in Martinique [and went to] the Victor Schoelscher school." . . . So I said: "What did you do there?" He told me: "Latin and Greek and French literature." And I said: "What next?" He said, "I went to France, and I went to the Ecole Normale Superiore." I said, "Yes I know that school. It is famous for producing scholars and Communists." (Cesaire was one of the first in each department: he was one of the finest scholars and he was a notable Communist.) And I said: "What did you do there?" And he said: "Latin and Greek and French literature." And then I said: "Where did you go from there?" And he said: "I went to the Sorbonne." And I said, "I suppose you did there Latin and Greek and French Literature?" And he said: "Exactly." He said, "But there is one thing more." And I asked: "What is that?" He said, "I went back to teach in Martinique, and I went to the Victor Schoelscher school, and there I taught Latin and Greek and French literature." So when Cesaire wrote his tremendous attack upon Western civilization, *In Return to My Native Land*, and said that Negritude was a statement for some concepts of civilization which the Black people had and which would be important in any development of civilization away from capitalist society, he was able to make this ferocious attack upon Western civilization because he knew it inside out. . . . He had spent some twenty years studying it.[30]

As it had been for Cesaire, so it was for all of them. They would all pass through the prepossessing claims of bourgeois ideology for Western cultural superiority with their only modestly disguised racialism. But eventually they would emerge convinced that a larger and different achievement was required. At first they would believe that the answer lay in the vision of class struggle, the war between brothers, as Julius Nyerere would later characterize Marxist socialist theory.[31] That conception, too, would prove to be insufficient. As Cox would write in his own summary considerations of Marx and Engels, their conceptualization of capitalism was only a partial realization of the historical forces that had created the Black ideologues and that they sought to comprehend and defeat.[32] Ineluctably, as we shall see, the events that did most to shape their era—the crises of world capitalism, the destructive dialectic of imperialism, and the historical and ideological revelations of the naivety of Western socialism—drove them into a deeper consciousness. Appropriately, what Padmore found it necessary to do in the mid-1930s, Wright in the early 1940s, and James at the end of that decade, was later echoed by Cesaire's declaration in 1956:

> What I demand of Marxism and Communism is that they serve the black peoples, not that the black peoples serve Marxism and Communism. Philosophies and movements must serve the people, not the people the doctrine and the movement. . . . A doctrine is of value only if it is conceived by us and for us, and revised through us. . . . We consider it our duty to make common cause with all who cherish truth and justice, in order to form organizations able to support effectively the black peoples in their present and future struggle—their struggle for justice, for culture, for dignity, for liberty. . . . Because of this, please accept my resignation from the Party.[33]

From such moments as these, each in his own time, turned his face to the historical tradition of Black liberation and became Black radicals. They began the realization of their history and their theoretical task. We shall now consider how this came about and what were its several theoretical and ideological significations. We shall proceed historically, adhering as closely as it is possible to the processes that encompassed scholarship, practice, and consciousness, and eventually spanned historiography and the development of a theory of Black struggle. As we shall discover, the contributions of these intellects are enormous, their productivity massive. For these reasons, necessarily we shall explore only a portion of their work. Hopefully our review will touch on the more important parts. Much, however, will remain still to be said, understood, and discussed. Theirs is a living legacy. But always we must keep in mind that their brilliance was also derivative. The truer genius was in the midst of the people of whom they wrote. There the struggle was more than words or ideas but life itself.

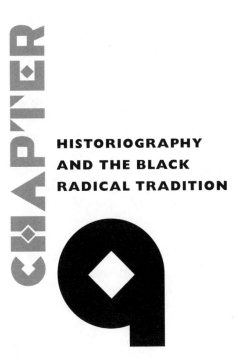

HISTORIOGRAPHY AND THE BLACK RADICAL TRADITION

Any discussion that attempts to assay the beginnings of radical Black historiography and intends to assess the significance of that tradition must take into account two figures: W. E. B. Du Bois and C. L. R. James. Du Bois, being the older (he was born in 1868), will be accorded pride of place.

Du Bois and the Myths of National History

William Edward Burghardt Du Bois was one of the finest historians ever developed in the United States. The writing of history, though, was but one of his achievements. Though excruciatingly shy, he combined statesmanship and political activism with scholarship. In this way he managed to influence the lives and thoughts of legions. And notwithstanding the rigors of research he found the time to inaugurate the systematic development of Black Studies; to found and edit for more than twenty years, *The Crisis*, the most influential Black political journal of its time; to command the intellectual leadership of the American Black movement; to catalyze the development of Pan-Africanism; and at the end of his days, to assume a role of leadership in the post–World War II peace movement. These, however, were merely the outlines of a complex life that extended over more than ninety years.[1] He was not, though, an entirely benign figure nor was his work consistently accorded the respect it was due. One might conclude that it was the multitude of Du Bois's activities that obscured his significance as a historian. But, as we shall see, it was not his range that was at issue with his detractors. The opposition to Du Bois was grounded on deeper reservations: the recognition that his work had origins independent of the impulses of Western liberal and radical thought. Thus, when his contribution to the American historical tradition should have been celebrated by its historians and scholars, the reaction of the academy was often vilification and neglect. And when he should have been recognized as one of the deans of radical historiography—in his seventh decade he became one of the two most sophisticated Marxist theorists in America[2]—the orthodox and "authorized" intellectuals accused him of Marxian heresies, racial chauvinism, and flawed conceptualization. There were, however, much more historic reasons for the intolerance found toward Du Bois's works. These reasons can only be identified and understood by a review and analysis of the historical, intellectual, and ideological contexts from which they arose.

It is by now generally understood that the formation of nation-states and political reigns precipitate the development of founding myths—myths of origin, in the language of anthropologists.[3] Though the process may have been obscured by time in more distant eras, the emergences of the bourgeoisies of the eighteenth and nineteenth centuries made it explicit. Their use of print and press, their appeals to and seductions of the classes they wished to dominate, made the fabrication of national myths quite evident. These myths were to be recognized in the official instruments of class hegemony: national creeds, social ideologies, philosophical tenets, constitutions, and the like, their function was to legitimate the social orders that had come into being. These myths made the new order a necessary one, an inevitable and benevolent event. They indicated to the national populace that the strains of historical novelty, the insecurities and anxieties accompanying the break with established forms were temporary, that change was natural, organic, and right. Founding myths were substituted for history, providing the appearance of historical narrative to what was in actuality part fact and part class-serving rationales. Endlessly elaborated, these myths were produced by ideologues who identified with the dominant creed and depended upon those classes in the society that possessed power and the capacities to extend social privilege.[4]

The formation of the American state provided no exception. The American Constitution, the Declaration of Independence, the considerations raised in the Federalist Papers were all expressions of the interests and creed of the American bourgeoisie.[5] Soon they were to be augmented by the myths of Frontier, the paternal Plantation, the competitive capitalism of the Yankee, the courage of the Plainsman, and later supplemented by the tragedy of the War between the States, the Rugged Individual, the excitement of the American Industrial Revolution, the generosity of the Melting Pot. Such were the romantic fictions that came to constitute the social ideology of the nation's bourgeoisie.[6] There was, though, an even older mythology, one that preceded the development of an American bourgeoisie with its nationalist sentiments and war of independence. Colonialism in America had required a different rationale: the Savage. Conveniently, as we have seen in the previous chapter, English colonialism had had available to it the savagery of the Irish to draw upon. The notion had traveled

Placed w/in other national myths

Colonialism needed savagery

well. When the need was for labor, the Irish, the poor of the metropole's cities, the African and the native American were comfortably herded together under the notion of savagery. When the issue had been the expropriation of the lands of the natives, there was little cause to respect the claims of savages or to comprehend their resistance as anything more than savagery.[7] Indeed, colonial thought expected quite the opposite. The colonists were the "advanced civilization." Such societies proved their historical significance by the destruction or domination of savage and backward peoples. *Colonists as advanced*

Eventually, of course, the ideologies of the pre-bourgeoisie and the bourgeoisie had fused. As the systems of manufacturing, plantation slavery, and farming had closed together into an integrated national economy sharing the exploitation of land, labor, and natural resources, the social ideology and historical consciousness of the ruling classes acquired two domestic enemies, the Indian and the Negro. In the early nineteenth century, the destruction of the native savage and the domination of the imported one became dual proofs of the superiority of the new nation. And once the native American peoples became incapable of resistance, they were further transformed and trivialized, becoming the romantic residue of an archaic past, living museum pieces.[8] For the Negro, however, it was a different story.

Throughout much of the nineteenth century, the African remained a substantial labor force for the further development of the country. As a consequence, the political, social, and cultural significance of the African was more enduring. This meant, as Craven suggests in the following example from seventeenth-century Virginia, that the efforts taken to resolve the opposition of the Black in American thought were so often deliberate and constant that they remained obvious and conscious:

> The crude humor with which shipmasters or purchasers drew upon ancient history or mythology for the names of Caesar, Hannibal, Nero, Jupiter, Pluto, or Minerva; the Primus and Secundus who headed one list; and the use more than once of Ape or Monkey for a name records principally an all-too-prevalent attitude of the white toward the black.[9]

During the era that followed, when manufacturing became the most advanced form of production and democratic institutions the most significant political creed, the African was represented as chattel in their economic image, as slaves in their political and social image, as brutish and therefore inaccessible to further development, and finally as Negro, that is without history. And later, during the industrialization of the country's economy, when individuality and manipulative acumen were at a premium, the Black was a pathetic sharecropper, unskilled and unambitious—the "happy darkies" for whom the society possessed a paternalistic obligation. Finally, in our own time, with the development of corporate structures and the myth of the intensively rationalized and rational society, Blacks became the irrational, the violent, criminal, caged beast. The cage was civilization and Western culture, obviously available to Blacks but inexplicably beyond their grasp.[10] *Blks as uncivilized*

Black historiography developed in opposition to this cloned thought and sensibility in American consciousness. This was not the intention. Nor, in its beginnings, did it seem likely, since the first efforts at writing the history of the race had occurred some decades after the ending of the ennobling literature that had accompanied the abolition movement. With the Emancipation signed, there was no longer a demand for historical excursions into the Negro's African past to substantiate their humanity and its irresistible degradation by slavery. The noble savage had ceased to have a function. But reconstruction had rekindled the ideological attack on Black people. Sixty years after the assault had been renewed, Du Bois would unhesitantly designate its source:

> The real frontal attack on Reconstruction, as interpreted by the leaders of national thought in 1870 and for some time thereafter, came from the universities and particularly from Columbia and Johns Hopkins.
>
> The movement began with Columbia University and with the advent of John W. Burgess of Tennessee and William A. Dunning of New Jersey as professors of political science and history.[11]

Their collective judgment of Black people, their "silence and contempt" as Du Bois characterized it, became American history. And since men such as these were also intimately involved in the construction of the nation's agenda for the academic study of its political processes and structures, their shared assessment of Blacks was also a prescription:

> In order to paint the South as a martyr to inescapable fate, to make the North the magnanimous emancipator, and to ridicule the Negro as the impossible joke in the whole development, we have in fifty years, by libel, innuendo and silence, so completely misstated and obliterated the history of the Negro in America and his relation to its work and government that today it is almost unknown. . . . It is not only part foundation of our present lawlessness and loss of democratic ideals it has, more than that, led the world to embrace and worship the color bar as social salvation and it is helping to range mankind in ranks of mutual hatred and contempt, at the summons of a cheap and false myth.[12]

The stakes had been high during the decades of the post bellum. As Thomas Rainboro had seen it in England's convulsive seventeenth century, the question posed in the years following the American Civil War was "Either poverty must use democracy to destroy the power of property, or property in fear of poverty will destroy democracy."[13] As ideologues for both victorious northern industrial capital and a now chastened southern agrarian capital, the white intelligentsia—academician and otherwise—rewove social and historical legends that accommodated the exploitative projects of those ruling classes. The political consciousness of Black labor, white labor, and immigrant labor were to be smothered by the social discipline implicit in the legends. Complemented by the terror of state militias, company police, and security agents, the persistent threats of immigration controls, the swelling ranks of reserve labor, racialism was reattired so that it might once again take its place among the inventory of labor disciplines. Driven by the necessity to respond quickly to the rush of working-class mobilizations following the war, capital and its ideologues had not dallied:

X In the year 1877, the signals were given for the rest of the century: the black would be put back; the strikes of white workers would not be tolerated; the industrial and political elites of North and South would take hold of the country and organize the greatest march of economic growth in human history. They would do it with the aid of, and at the expense of, black labor, white labor, Chinese labor, European immigrant labor, female labor, rewarding them differently by race, sex, national origin, and social class, in such a way as to create separate levels of oppression—a skillfull terracing to stabilize the pyramid of wealth.[14]

This new repression of Black labor was the immediate cause and the circumstance of the profusion of protest materials produced by the Black intelligentsia in the last decades of the nineteenth century. And Black history was their desperate invention.

Stunned by the suddenness of the reversal of both their own fortunes and those of the Black masses, the most representative spokesmen of the Black petit bourgeoisie responded with the journalistic and literary eloquence that they believed had so well served them and the slaves in previous eras. While the Black masses organized— sometimes secretly but increasingly openly, to protect their political rights, and then when they were lost, in order to emigrate to the American hinterlands or to Liberia— the Black intelligentsia remained wedded to the tactics of supplication. These representative colored men, as Painter has characterized them,[15] insisted on the identity they presumed to share with their white, class counterparts. As the editor of a Black newspaper in San Francisco had declared in 1862, as far as he could see Black Americans were "moved by the same impulses, guided by the same motives, and [had] the same Yankee-like go-aheadativeness of the white Americans."[16] Like many others of his station, he begged his audience's indulgence for being Black and thus obscuring his truer colors. Still it was a most disheartening period for many of them. They worked hard in their newspapers, pamphlets, their public lectures and Congressional appearances at establishing their Americanism, only to be rebuffed out of hand by the nation's dominant ideologues.[17]

Inevitably, it had occurred to some members of the Black petit bourgeoisie that their disadvantage in the ideological fray lay in part with their failure to engage the American legend. In the midst of a country whose ideationists were desperately attempting to forge a historically grounded national identity, their lot was reduced to an identification with the horror with which slavery had been concluded. In an America that was now being reconstituted by its ideologues on the mantle of a Manifest Destiny presumably inherited from its European origins,[18] the Black intelligentsia had a historical basis that was too shallow to support their demand to be included in the nation's destinies. Legend as history denied to them that right and, as well, their capabilities.[19] The aspirations of the Black middle class required a history that would, at once, absolve their guilt by association with the catastrophic ending of slavery; lend historical weight to the dignity they claimed as a class; and suggest their potential as participants in the country's future. They required a Black historiography that would challenge their exclusion from the nation's racial parochialisms while settling for those very values. When their historiography did begin, it was not so much a bold initiative against the certainties of nationalist and racialist histories as a plea for sympathy.

Black history thus began in the shadow of the national myths and as their dialectical negation. Consequently, it contained its own contradictions (e.g., the trivialization of social action) while enveloping those that occurred within the dominant American history. Generations later it would give rise to a more critical and truer opposition, but for the time being, it was to match American history in the coin of the realm; monument for monument, civilization for civilization, great man for great man. George Washington Williams, the first of the major Afro-American historians, left no doubt about these concerns.[20] In 1882, Williams had published his mammoth classic, A History of the Negro Race in America from 1619 to 1880; it consisted of two volumes totalling almost 1,100 pages. One may have already surmised that despite his titular boundaries, Williams had not confined himself to the events that began in the seventeenth century. Indeed, like many of his contemporary spokesmen,[21] he had found it appropriate to begin his search into the past by reviewing the role of Africans in the pre-Christian eras when "Western civilization," owing its immediate stimulus to Egyptian culture, had been centered around the Mediterranean. The contrast between these eras, the apogee in Williams's mind of African development, and the centuries of Negro enslavement that followed two millennia later, provided him with the opportunity to enunciate his beliefs:

His [the Negro's] position, it is true, in all history up to the present day, has been accidental, incidental and collateral. . . . His brightest days were when history was an infant; and since he early turned from God, he has found the cold face of hate and the hurtful hand of the Caucasian against him. The Negro type is the result of degradation. It is nothing more than the lowest strata of the African race. . . . His blood infected with the poison of his low habitation, his body shrivelled by disease, his intellect veiled in pagan superstitions, the noblest yearnings of his soul strangled at birth by the savage passions of a nature abandoned to sensuality,—the poor Negro of Africa deserves more our pity than our contempt.[22]

The confusion in Williams's thought was real. He wrote from both a Puritanical perspective with its echoes of God's election, but was, as well, mindful of the racialist nature of his people's degradation and oppression. But in the latter, he was again perversely diverted since his resolve to write a "true history of the Black man" stemmed from his wish to "incite the latter to greater effort in the struggle of citizenship and manhood." While attacking the most extreme ideological forms that hatred of Blacks had assumed ("sons of Ham," the "curse of Canaan") and while denouncing the institution of slavery, he still demonstrated a certain ambivalence. Tacit but unspoken, of course, was the notion that only a Black elite could realize the task of Negro resurrection.[23]

By the last decades of the nineteenth century, the ideological construction of the Black petit bourgeoisie had achieved its maturity. The tendency of the Black intelligentsia toward an elitist consciousness of race—a synthesis of Eurocentric racism and the preoccupation with imperial political forms—had achieved its broadest and most articulate expression. The social, and concomitant psychological and intellectual processes of the formation of a Black middle class begun in the eighteenth century had, by then, obtained an extensive and objective configuration.[24] No longer retarded by the political and economic structure of slavery and its hegemonic envelopments, freed from the moral compulsion of social identification with the Black peasantry and peons by the slaves' counterfeit freedom,[25] the ambitions of the Black *petit bourgeoisie* found realization in institutions consciously designed by themselves and sponsors for class's maintenance and augmentation.[26] With their position as a broker stratum seemingly secured from above by a ruling class that proffered them increments of privilege while ruthlessly repressing mass Black mobilization,[27] the ideological restraint that had been so much a part of the character of the class's earlier generations became less evident. The Black petit bourgeoisie could now indulge in the delusion of being capable of challenging the capitalist world system on what they took to be its own terms: race power.[28] The political ideology that emerged from their "Negro" universities and colleges, the pulpits above their denominationally stratified congregations, their professional associations, their creative literature, and their historiography was persistently mystically chauvinist,[29] authoritarian, and paternalistic. From the post-Reconstruction on into the next century, the logic of the formation of the Black petit bourgeoisie and its intelligentsia was building to these conclusions. As Jeremiah Moses argues:

> It was becoming apparent to the post-bellum generation of black leaders that individual accomplishments offered little protection from the threats and abuses of the caste-like American system. The middle class Negroes would remain victims of prejudice, so long as the masses remained untutored, impoverished, and demoralized. The goal of uplifting the freedmen was similar to the goal of uplifting Africa, and was to be carried on for the same purposes as the old antebellum African civilizationism. The building of an Afro-American culture would demonstrate to all the world that blacks were able and willing to make a contribution to American life, and were, therefore, fit to be United States citizens. As the masses were elevated, the bourgeoisie would rise correspondingly.[30]

These were the purposes that inspired Bishop David A. Payne of the African Methodist Episcopal Church (AME) to form the Bethel Literary and Historical Association in 1881,[31] which in 1897 was incorporated into the American Negro Academy by its founder, the Black Presbyterian Cambridge-trained missionary, Alexander Crummell;[32] which complemented the studied feminism of the National Association of

Colored Women (formerly the National Federation of Afro-American Women) cata- lyzed into being by Josephine St. Pierre Ruffin, Mary Church Terrell, Ida B. Wells, Margaret Murray Washington and others in 1895;[33] and provided a specific martial character to some Negro colleges.[34] Inevitably, spokesmen were driven to cosmetic excess: William Ferris declared that he preferred "Negrosaxon" to Negro, while Bos- ton's mulatto elite appropriated "Afro-American" to itself, and earlier, William C. Nell had employed "Black Saxons,"[35] but Crummell saw no need for equivocation. For him, the identity, function, and nature of their class were obvious:

> *Who* are to be the agents to raise and elevate this people to a higher plane of beings? The answer will at once flash upon your intelligence. It is to be affected (*sic*) by the scholars and philanthropists which come forth in these days from the schools. *They* are to be the scholars; for to transform, stimulate and uplift a people is a work of intelligence. It is a work which demands the clear induction of historic facts and their application to new circumstances,—a work which will require the most skill- ful resources and the wise practicality of superior men.[36]

According to W. J. Moses, it was Crummell who initiated the synthesis of his class's interests into a coherent ideology.[37] But it was others, I would suggest, like George W. Williams and Carter G. Woodson who codified it into a historiographic expression negating the national legend.[38] Still, what they achieved was but a fragile construc- tion, its integrity subject to challenge whenever capitalist indulgence, the foundation upon which it rested, might dissipate or be withdrawn. Mercifully, perhaps, it was also true that the possibility of this occurring was beyond the comprehension of most of them. Neither Social Darwinism nor their comfortable gospels suggested anything but the most temporary diversions as possible. When the crisis did come and Black people mobilized to struggle against it, the Black petit bourgeoisie was again largely unprepared to abandon their illusory partnership with power. Du Bois, like his predecessors and contemporaries, William Brown, Carter Woodson, Bishop Henry Turner, George Williams, and the West Indian–born Edward Wilmot Blyden,[39] had been deeply implicated in the "race uplift" historiographic tradition.

Du Bois was among the forty black intellectuals enlisted in the American Negro Academy of which Crummell was the first president. In the Academy's *Occasional Papers*, Du Bois published his Crummellian essay, "The Conservation of Races," showing that he was hardly out of step with the conservative Crummell during his years with the American Negro Academy. . . . The classical black nationalist traits of mysticism, authoritarianism, civilizationism and collectivism were strong elements in "The Conservation of Races." Du Bois called upon the Academy to exercise a firm leadership and to become "the epitome and expression of the intellect of the black-blooded people of America." The black leaders were not to organize for such mundane purposes as the stealing of political spoils, nor "merely to protest and pass resolutions." Black leadership should be united in its efforts to improve the black masses, to fight against loafing, gambling, crime, and prostitution . . . to

[margin, handwritten: Blks didnt want to give up power.]

strive for "the rearing of a race ideal in America and Africa, to the glory of God and the uplifting of the Negro people."[40]

In the earliest phase of his career, under the direct influence of Crummell, the Academy, and the omnipresent organizational politics of Booker T. Washington, Du Bois had found the notion of an elite, a Talented Tenth, appealing:

> The Negro race, like all races, is going to be saved by its exceptional men. The problem of education, then, among Negroes must first of all deal with the Talented Tenth; it is the problem of developing the Best of this race that they may guide the Mass away from the contamination and death of the Worst, in their own and other races.[41]

At the time he saw the difference between his design and that of Washington as quite significant. In time, he knew better. In his last autobiography, written in the "last decades of his 95 years," he made it clear that in the intervening years he had come to recognize that the differences between them were insignificant when compared to what they did not comprehend. Their dispute was not over ideology but power:

> I believed in the higher education of a Talented Tenth who through their knowledge of modern culture could guide the American Negro into a higher civilization. I knew that without this the Negro would have to accept white leadership, and that such leadership could not always be trusted. . . . Mr. Washington, on the other hand, believed that the Negro as an efficient worker could gain wealth and that eventually through his ownership of capital he would be able to achieve a recognized place in American culture. . . . [H]e proposed to put the emphasis at present upon training in the skilled trades and encouragement in industry and common labor.
> These two theories of Negro progress were not absolutely contradictory. Neither I nor Booker Washington understood the nature of capitalistic exploitation of labor, and the necessity of a direct attack on the principle of exploitation as the beginning of labor uplift.[42]

What Du Bois did resent, more and more, was the power that enveloped Washington and circulated through his fingers:

> Not only did presidents of the United States consult Booker T. Washington, but governors and congressmen; philanthropists conferred with him, scholars wrote to him. Tuskegee became a vast information bureau and center of advice. . . . After a time almost no Negro institution could collect funds without the recommendation or acquiescence of Mr. Washington. Few political appointments of Negroes were made anywhere in the United States without his consent. Even the careers of rising young colored men were very often determined by his advice and certainly his opposition was fatal. . . .
> Moreover, it must not be forgotten that his Tuskegee Machine was not solely the idea and activity of black folk at Tuskegee. It was largely encouraged and given

financial aid through certain white groups and individuals in the North. This Northern group had clear objectives. They were capitalists and employers of labor. . . . These Negroes were not to be encouraged as voters in the new democracy, nor were they to be left at the mercy of the reactionary South. They were good laborers and they could be made of tremendous profit to the North. They could become a strong labor force and properly guided they would restrain the unbridled demands of white labor, born of the Northern labor unions and now spreading to the South and encouraged by European socialism.[43]

It was not entirely the case, as Lawrence Reddick suggested in 1937,[44] that the "uplift" tradition from which Du Bois would eventually emerge possessed a deeply ingrained naivete. It would appear that the major part of its obtuseness resulted from the masks of deception behind which the struggle over power within the Black petit bourgeoisie was taking place. It was not merely an etiquette of intra-class divisions that made deception necessary.[45] The material stakes were high: in 1903, for example, Andrew Carnegie had extended a gift of $600,000 to Tuskegee.[46] Most significantly, however, the Black petit bourgeoisie was bound by a class strategy that narrowed their political range: the protests of the masses of Blacks could not be allowed to move beyond a diffuse state but at the same time must give the appearance of racial solidarity. The premium for which Du Bois challenged Washington was power not leadership. It was, however, the nature and setting of this struggle that propelled Du Bois beyond the accepted parameters of intra-class conflict.

The radicalization of Du Bois took place during a historical period characterized by a reintensification of the suppression of Blacks in the United States and the subsequent massive Black response. In the South and the Midwest, the Populist movement of the 1880s and 1890s, spurred by the conversion crisis of world capitalism and with its third-party aspirations built around an alliance between white and Black farmers/peasants and organized labor, had once again mobilized the Black masses.[47] Legal and illegal violence, election corruption, and a renewed emphasis on white supremacy were the combined responses of the ruling classes, industrial and planter, which orchestrated state and federal power and the instruments of propaganda.[48] Electoral restrictions stripping poor Blacks and whites from the vote were enacted in several states; lynchings accelerated (with the number of Black victims surpassing that of whites in 1889); and the Populist movement was transformed into a shambles by the unleashing of racial maneuvers.[49] The most dramatic response of the Black masses was migration. And when the cycle of drought, then heavy rains and the boll weevil vermin decimated cotton production in the years of 1915 and 1916 was combined with war industry and the cessation of European immigration, the migration of the Black masses became the Great Migration:

[E]arly migrations were dwarfed by the surge of black people northward after 1900, and especially after 1910. According to various contemporaneous estimates, between 1890 and 1910 around 200,000 black Southerners fled to the North; and between 1910 and 1920 another 300,000 to 1,000,000 followed. The Department of

Labor reported that in eighteen months of 1916–17 the migration was variously estimated at 200,000 to 700,000.[50]

A Black presence in the northern industrial sectors of the country became a new fact of the American experience.[51]

The most important consequence of these mass mobilizations, that is both the short-lived alliance with the agrarian rebellion of Populism and the urban migration, was that they amounted to a visible renunciation of the Black petit bourgeoisie's "leadership" by the Black peasantry. Hundreds of thousands of Blacks demonstrated that they were no longer willing to tolerate the social and economic insecurities of living in the rural South, to work in semi-slavery as the nation's cheapest labor, and to perish under the dual oppressions of the racist patronage of the white southern ruling class and the class opportunism of an ambitious and presumptuous Black petit bourgeoisie. It is not surprising, then, that in these circumstances some members of the Black middle class should discover in this an occasion for renouncing those among them who dominated their class's political and historical vision. In the same act, these renegades were drawn into the orbit of the masses of Blacks and the radical tradition. William Monroe Trotter, Du Bois's Harvard classmate, preceded him in this realization, and within the nexus of the Niagara Movement, begun in 1905, certainly disciplined Du Bois in this new militancy. Trotter, more than any other single individual, was responsible for transforming Du Bois from a cautious critic to a militant activist.[52] It was Du Bois, however, who by temperament, training, and experience would be capable of bringing this revolt to fruition; as his work certifies, it was to build in his intellect slowly, ineluctably. The evidence of his development was to be apparent from his evocation of the militancy of *John Browns*[53] published in 1909; through his short assay with the socialist movement,[54] his analysis of the imperialist basis of the Great War;[55] his reactions to Bolshevik Russia;[56] and the frustrations and compromises suffered as a race advocate operating in the national and international arenas of "bourgeois democratic politics" responsive to only one racial consciousness: white superiority.[57] By the time the most profound crisis in the history of world capitalism occurred, Du Bois was consciously divorced from the legend as well as its permutations.

[handwritten margin note: Recon. as pt. of American failures — blks as larger solution to democracy in American]

Du Bois and the Reconstruction of History and American Political Thought

In 1935, Du Bois published his third historical work on the economic forces and ideological dynamics that gave nineteenth-century America its character. Unlike the two previous studies, *The Suppression of the African Slave-Trade* and *John Brown*, which were more conventional in narrative and analysis, *Black Reconstruction in America* possessed a theory of history—a theory based on a foundation of economic analysis and class struggle.[58] It was not simply a historical work, but history subjected to theory. The emphasis was on the relations of things.

Du Bois, however, had not neglected the play of history, its scenario. He had intended to—and did—trace the critical phenomenology of the American Civil War and its aftermath, the Reconstruction. From his research there emerged a fundamentally revised construction of those periods that stood as a critique of American historiography with its racial biases, domineering regionalisms, and distorting philosophical commitments. Methodologically, moreover, *Black Reconstruction* possessed a rigor consciously designed to match and supersede Ulrich B. Phillips's earlier "classic" work on slavery, *American Negro Slavery*. Du Bois, in his attempt to authoritatively identify what he took to be the truer character of the Reconstruction era, seems to have realized the necessity of returning to the experience and training in historical research and writing he had gathered at Harvard University and the University of Berlin in the late nineteenth century but had eschewed in *John Brown*. His radical, and radically different interpretation of the war and its aftermath would conform formally to the methodological canons of historiography so that he might subvert the substance of that tradition.

Black Reconstruction, however, was more the result of another purpose, a concern that was quite different from the task of historical revision. Du Bois committed himself to the development of a theory of history, which by its emphasis on mass action was both a critique of the ideologies of American socialist movements and a revision of Marx's theory of revolution and class struggle. From the integument of America's Civil War and the Reconstruction, Du Bois attempted to identify the unique character of mass praxis, class consciousness, ideology, and contradiction as they had occurred in the dialectics of American social and historical developments. In so doing, he was going beyond the argument of American "exceptionalism" that had persisted in the ideology of the American Marxist Left.[59] He was seeking to identify historically and analytically the processes that during the Depression years had given American social dynamics their character and potentialities.

Ultimately, *Black Reconstruction* was a political work. In the confrontation with the nationalist and reactionary American intelligentsia at the level of historiography, in the confrontation with the political Left in terms of the theory of capitalism and the ideology of emergent socialism, Du Bois presumed to alert and instruct revolutionary Black leadership.

With regard to these several concerns, he had made his position quite clear in 1933—a period coincident with the writing of *Black Reconstruction*—in a remarkable lecture delivered before the participants of a Rosenwald Fund–sponsored conference at Howard University. Addressing himself to the role played by the American intellectual elite, Du Bois had argued:

> If we give Mr. Roosevelt the right to meddle with the dollar, if we give Herr Hitler the right to expel the Jew, if we give to Mussolini the right to think for Italians, we do this because we know nothing ourselves. We are as a nation ignorant of the function and meaning of money, and we are looking around helplessly to see if anybody else knows.

This is not, as some assume, the failure of democracy—it is the failure of education, of justice and of truth. We have lied so long about money and business, we do not know now where truth is.[60]

Unequivocally, Du Bois was associating the failure of the American nation to achieve an effective policy in the midst of the Depression with "the fact that it has no intelligent democracy. . . ." This, he believed, was a consequence of the ideological deceptions and misconceptions that characterized liberal American thought. Turning to the American Left, Du Bois was no less critical. Of the American Communist Party (CPUSA), Du Bois declared:

The task that I have recently been setting myself is to blunt the wedge the Communist party is driving into our group . . . and I do this, not because of any enmity or fear or essential disagreement with the Communists. If I were in Russia, I should be an enthusiastic Communist. If the Communist party in the United States had the leadership and knowledge which our situation calls for, I certainly should join it; but it is today ignorant of fact and history and the American scene and is trying to over-emphasize the truth that the natural leaders of the colored people, the educated and trained classes have had goals and interests different from the mass of Negroes.

There is a partial truth in this, and a partial falsehood. . . . American race prejudice has so pounded the mass of Negroes together that they have not separated into such economic classes; but on the other hand they undoubtedly have had the ideology and if they had been free we would have had within our race the same exploiting set-up that we see around about us.[61]

Immersed in research into post–Civil War "labor history," Du Bois was conscious of the problems that had beset mass movements bringing together whites and Blacks—problems that he felt spokesmen for Communism ignored.[62] Though now clearly ambivalent toward the Black petit bourgeoisie, he was still relying on the notion of racial solidarity (imposed from without) to defend his class from attacks from the Left. But by now Du Bois had begun to temper his own "Talented Tenth" program of social mobilization. At the conference he seemed mildly distressed with the "vanguardism" with which he had been earlier identified. In point of fact he had appeared to reverse his position. The Black elite of which he had been so optimistic in its "natural" function of leadership of the Black masses was now understood to be ideologically reactionary, a lesson he was learning within the National Association for the Advancement of Colored People.[63] This question of ideology and its impact on human motives and social relations would become a dominant theme of *Black Reconstruction*. But here, its immediate significance was its toll on Du Bois's thinking. It had forced him to reassess the Black masses and their revolutionary significance. He had at last begun to form a committed response to the indictment of the Black middle class and its intelligentsia, which the recent events of the late 1920s and early 1930s represented: the emergence of the mass movement, the Universal Negro Improvement

Association; the formation of the militant nationalists into the African Blood Brotherhood; and the Scottsboro debacle, which pitted the conservative NAACP against the Communist Party's International Labor Defense.[64] In accord with his criticisms of the American Communist Party, Du Bois was addressing himself directly to the problem of the alienation of the Black elite from the Black masses. He did this in part by reminding that elite, subtly, of its dependence upon the masses.[65] Yet he still had not himself reached the level of historical comprehension that he would demonstrate in *Black Reconstruction*. There he would come to a realization of the historical forces emergent from the people, specifically the capacities of the Black masses to take steps decisive to their own liberation.

Finally, in the Rosenwald Conference lecture, we find that Du Bois's analysis of the Depression, which international capitalism was experiencing in the 1930s, parallels his analysis of the crisis brought on by slavery in the earlier stage of American capitalist development. Both economically and politically, the Depression and the crisis of slavery would fundamentally transform the mode of capitalist relations. Furthermore, both had precipitated revolutionary movements and revolutionary social change.[66]

> [T]he matter of greatest import is that instead of our facing today a stable world, moving at a uniform rate of progress toward well-defined goals, we are facing revolution. I trust you will not be as scared by this word as you were Thursday [Du Bois was referring to the audience's reaction to a speech by Dr. Broadus Mitchell of Johns Hopkins University]. I am not discussing a coming revolution, I am trying to impress the fact upon you that you are already in the midst of a revolution; you are already in the midst of war; that there has been no war of modern times that has taken so great a sacrifice of human life and human spirit as the extraordinary period through which we are passing today.
>
> Some people envisage revolution chiefly as a matter of blood and guns and the more visible methods of force. But that, after all, is merely the temporary and outward manifestation. Real revolution is within. That comes before or after the explosion—is a matter of long suffering and deprivation, the death of courage and the bitter triumph of despair. This is the inevitable prelude to decisive and enormous change, and that is the thing that is on us now.
>
> We are not called upon then to discuss whether we want revolution or not. We have got it. Our problem is how we are coming out of it.[67]

On review, then, Du Bois had remarked on the weakness of American culture and its political institutions in the face of a deep crisis in its economic structure. He was concerned about the inability of the American Left as represented by the CPUSA—recall he had already tried the American Socialist Party and found it wanting 21 years before this lecture was given—to clearly identify the material force of racism as it related to the Left's struggle to destroy capitalism and replace it with socialism. He had exposed the ahistorical and materialistic ideology that dominated the Black elite and Black leadership. And, finally, he had indicated the failure of American revolutionists to recognize that one of the objective conditions for revolution, one which goes beyond the onslaught of economic crisis and emiseration, is a consciousness of the social processes of revolution.

Du Bois, however, was concerned for why these things had become true for American society in the 1930s. He was interested in determining how it was possible that American culture and its institutions had become so estranged from the democratic ideal with which they had so long been structurally and ideologically identified. Moreover, how was it possible that American socialists could be so ill-equipped to deal with the Black worker, the Black community, and the social relations of Black people? How had the Black elite become wedded ideologically to capitalism and grown alienated and contemptuous of the Black masses? Why was twentieth-century American revolutionary theory so ill-conceived, the revolutionary movement unrecognizable, and revolutionary change and transformation a matter of contingency rather than praxis? He believed the answers to these questions resided in the history of the Republic. More specifically, he pursued them in the contradictions of that history.

Slavery and Capitalism

In the beginning of *Black Reconstruction*, Du Bois identified the fundamental contradiction in American history; the contradiction that would subvert America's founding ideology, distort its institutions, traumatize its social relations and class formations, and, in the twentieth century, confuse its rebels and revolutionists:

> From the day of its birth, the anomaly of slavery plagued a nation which asserted the equality of all men, and sought to derive powers of government from the consent of the governed. Within sound of the voices of those who said this lived more than half a million black slaves, forming nearly one-fifth of the population of a new nation. (p. 3)[68]

> It was thus the black worker, as founding stone of a new economic system in the nineteenth century and for the modern world, who brought civil war in America. He was its underlying cause, in spite of every effort to base the strife upon union and national power. (p. 15)

Now let us pay close attention to what Du Bois was saying: slavery was the specific historical institution through which the Black *worker* had been introduced into the modern world system. However, it was not as *slaves* that one could come to an understanding of the significance that these Black men, women, and children had for American development. It was as *labor*. He had entitled the first chapter to *Black Reconstruction*, "The Black Worker."

The terms of his analysis were quite important to Du Bois. They were a part of his beginning of the transformation of the historiography of American civilization—the naming of things. In the changing of the names of things, he sought to provide the basis for a new conceptualization of their relationship. In the first three chapters of his work, Du Bois established the rules of his analysis. The institution of American slave labor could not be effectively conceptualized as a thing in and of itself. Rather, it was a particular historical development for world capitalism that expropriated the labor of African workers as primitive accumulation. American slavery was a *subsystem* of world capitalism.

Black labor became the foundation stone not only of the Southern social structure, but of Northern manufacture and commerce, of the English factory system, of European commerce, of buying and selling on a world-wide scale; new cities were built on the results of black labor, and a new labor problem involving all white labor, arose both in Europe and America. (p. 5)

And American slavery would also consist of social relations given their character by the ideology of white racial superiority.

[T]here was in 1863 a real meaning to slavery different from that we may apply to the laborer today. It was in part psychological, the enforced personal feeling of inferiority, the calling of another Master; the standing with hat in hand. It was the helplessness. It was the defenselessness of family life. It was the submergence below the arbitrary will of any sort of individual. (p. 9)

[The South's] subservient religious leaders reverted to the "curse of Canaan"; [its] pseudo-scientists gathered and supplemented all available doctrines of racial inferiority; [its] scattered schools and pedantic periodicals repeated these legends . . . a basis in reason, philanthropy and science was built up for Negro slavery. (p. 39)

All of this was necessary for the persistence of slavery through the seventeenth and eighteenth centuries, and for its meteoric development in the early nineteenth century. The tissue of the nation would develop, coded by its slave past.

Labor, Capitalism, and Slavery

Du Bois was arguing that once slavery was addressed in comprehensive terms, in world-historical terms, its true nature was revealed. Beneath its appearance as a "feudal agrarianism" lay the real relation of slavery to the emergence of modern capitalism. As America was a critical subsector of this developing system, the conflicts between American creed and reality, the contradictions of American society, the distortions of its social structures and political institutions ensued from its dependence on slavery and would resound throughout the system into the twentieth century.[69] Slavery, then, was not a historical aberration, it was not a "mistake" in an otherwise bourgeois democratic age. It was, and its imprints continued to be, *systemic*.

Here is the real modern labor problem. Here is the kernel of the problem of Religion and Democracy, of Humanity. Words and futile gestures avail nothing. Out of the exploitation of the dark proletariat comes the Surplus Value filched from human breasts which, in cultured lands, the Machine and harnessed Power

emancipation :
man & work

veil and conceal. The emancipation of man is the emancipation of labor and the emancipation of labor is the freeing of that basic majority of workers who are yellow, brown and black. (p. 16)[70]

In America, "free labor"—the vast majority of it supplied by immigrant Europeans from Ireland, England, Italy, and Germany—was also profoundly affected:

> The new labor that came to the United States, while it was poor, used to oppression and accustomed to a low standard of living, was not willing, after it reached America, to regard itself as a permanent laboring class and it is in the light of this fact that the labor movement among white Americans must be studied. The successful, well-paid American laboring class formed, because of its property and ideals, a petty bourgeoisie ready always to join capital in exploiting common labour, white and black, foreign and native. (p. 17)   *White workers*

Eschewing the traditions forming in the European labor movements that would mature into the nineteenth century's socialisms of the First and Second Internationals, syndicalism and anarchism, the transplanted European workers became preoccupied with the possibility of accumulating wealth and power, of becoming capitalists.

Thus it was that American liberalism in the nineteenth century, with its ideals of individualism and its antagonisms to socialism, became manifest in a particular way. Its character was molded by an economic order that severely delimited material well-being and a racial consciousness that at one and the same time removed an entire section of the working classes, the Blacks, from the possibility of access to that well-being while also supplying a fictive measure of status to non-Black workers.

> The wisest of the leaders could not clearly envisage just how slave labor in conjunction and competition with free labor tended to reduce all labor toward slavery. (p. 19)

It was only a minority of these non-Black workers that would join with liberal intellectuals and freedmen to form the abolitionist movement.[71] Du Bois had stated as early as 1915 that the "labor aristocracy" that was the result of the trade unionism of a materialistic labor movement—in Germany, England, and France as well as in the United States—was a crucial support to the imperialism and colonialism of the late nineteenth century.[72] In the United States, Black and non-Black labor became politically opposed "instead of becoming one great party." The northern non-Black working-class movement effectively excluded the freedmen, the slaves *and* the five million poor whites of the South. (It was even more specifically exclusionist after 1850 as it concentrated on a base of skilled industrial workers and craftsmen.) But it was a more generalized antagonism that would envelop Black and non-Black workers. During the Civil War itself, this conflict would erupt into race wars against Blacks. With the enactment of the Draft Laws in 1863, and with the encouragement of "pro slavery and pro-Southern" Copperheads from the North, the frustration of the non-Black workers, with their living and working conditions and the war, were turned against Blacks. In the summer of 1863, hundreds of Blacks were killed by mobs of workers in New York City.

> The report of the Merchants' Committee on the Draft Riot says of the Negroes: "Driven by fear of death at the hands of the mob, who the week previous had, as you remember, brutally murdered by hanging on trees and lamp posts, several of their number, and cruelly beaten and robbed many others, burning and sacking their houses, and driving nearly all from the streets, alleys and docks upon which they had previously obtained an honest though humble living—these people had been forced to take refuge on Blackwell's Island, at police stations, on the outskirts of the city, in the swamps and woods back of Bergen, New Jersey, at Weeksville, and in the barns and out-houses of the farmers of Long Island and Morrisania."(p. 103)

More than once, in *Black Reconstruction*, in his editorials in *The Crisis*, and other works, Du Bois would return to this period in order to identify the roots of racial violence in the labor movement of the twentieth century. It also provided, he believed, an explanation for the tradition of skepticism found among Blacks for organized labor.

What was true for the mainstream of the American labor movement was also a factor in the radical traditions in the country. Though mid-nineteenth-century socialism had been largely transferred from areas of Europe where antipathies toward Blacks were inconsequential, its adherents, too, had not been capable, generally, of resisting the corrosive influences of slavery. This had been the case for both Marxist and non-Marxist socialists. The precedents established during this period would be of no substantial help to twentieth-century socialists whether their programs directly or indirectly addressed themselves to "the Negro Problem."

> Even when the Marxian ideas arrived, there was a split; the earlier representatives of the Marxian philosophy in America agreed with the older Union movement in deprecating any entanglement with the abolition controversy. After all, abolition represented capital. The whole movement was based on mawkish sentimentality, and not on the demands of the workers, at least of the white workers. And so the early American Marxists simply gave up the idea of intruding the black worker into the socialist commonwealth at that time. (pp. 24–25)

Though there had been exceptions,[73] the lack of an identity between the interests of Black and non-Black workers was fairly consistent in the labor movement. Wherever one looked—among those who saw the movement in political-electoral terms, or those who advocated revolutionary violence, or those who were committed to economic trade unionism—the labor movement was most often at best ambivalent toward Black liberation and progress. The ideology of racism in combination with self-interest functioned to pit immigrant and poor white workers against the Black worker and the slave. And after the Civil War, the same social consciousness divided the working classes—immigrant and white—from the ex-slave. More than twenty

— contradictions in labor

years before the appearance of *Black Reconstruction*, and while his experience with the Socialist Party was still fresh in his mind, Du Bois had recognized this as a contradiction in the labor movement.[74] And during the intervening years, his anger had not dissipated. When it reappeared in *Black Reconstruction*, it was no longer simply a warning to a negligent labor movement, but an indictment. By then, the labor movement and capitalism were older and in deep crisis. By then, Du Bois spoke as a Black radical:

Slavery threatened free labor

> Indeed, the plight of the white working class throughout the world today is directly traceable to Negro slavery in America, on which modern commerce and industry was founded, and which persisted to threaten free labor until it was partially overthrown in 1863. The resulting color caste founded and retained by capitalism was adopted, forwarded and approved by white labor, and resulted in subordination of colored labor to white profits the world over. Thus the majority of the world's laborers, by the insistence of white labor, became the basis of a system of industry which ruined democracy and showed its perfect fruit in World War and Depression. And this book seeks to tell that story. (p. 30)

Slavery and Democracy

We have already noted how the idea of slavery, to Du Bois's mind, was opposed to the ideals of democracy. The ideology necessary to rationalize slavery disallowed the further development of liberal democracy except as a myth. But Du Bois understood that the relationship between slavery and democracy was not a question of the clash of ideas. His approach to history was similar in this respect to that which Marx and Engels had presented in *The German Ideology*:

> This conception of history . . . comes to the conclusion that all forms and products of consciousness cannot be dissolved by mental criticism, by resolution into "self-consciousness" or transformation into "apparitions," "spectres," "fancies," etc., but only by the practical overthrow of the actual social relations which give rise to this idealistic humbug.[75]

polit. institutions a result of slave system

For Du Bois, the creation of those political institutions and structures identified with American democracy involved congruence with the country's economic character, that is, with the slave system and capitalism. And so, though the American Constitution reflected the power of the plantocracy only in its devices for electoral representation, that had been sufficient advantage for the domination of the federal government by that class during the Republic's first several decades. This had meant a domination by a class that consisted of 7 percent of the South's population:

> It had in American history chosen eleven out of sixteen Presidents, seventeen out of twenty-eight Judges of the Supreme Court, fourteen out of nineteen Attorneys-General, twenty-one out of thirty-three Speakers of the House, eighty out of one hundred thirty-four Foreign Ministers. (p. 47)

Consequent to this power, the plantocracy had established a legal structure that effectively eliminated the civil rights of the nine million Black and poor white workers to be found in the South in the mid-nineteenth century. This perversion of the apparatus of representative democracy had survived the Civil War and the Reconstruction, and had persisted into the next century despite the challenges of Populism, organized labor, political radicalism, the Depression, and the mass Black movement of the UNIA.[76] Federalism had evolved into states' rights, the ideological dressing for first, slavery, and then the Black Codes, Jim Crow, and more contemporary forms of repression. Each shift in the apparatus of repression had been associated with the changing forms of exploitation as Blacks moved from being slaves to being sharecroppers and peons, and finally, to being proletariats or a labor reserve.

In the North, "the dictatorship of property" had been manifest in capital and investment. Not as rich or as powerful as the plantocrats in the beginning, the northern merchants, manufacturers, and industrialists had developed on the backs of southern agriculture and European labor. The North exploited its labor more efficiently, not having to absorb the costs of developing it during its nonproductive years. Those costs were incurred by the socioeconomic sectors of Ireland, Germany, Italy, and England. The North supplied the middlemen between the South and its European and domestic markets; it supplied the shipping and transportation for the South's produce. It was also in the process of developing a national economy of total integration before the Civil War, while the South was becoming increasingly dependent.

> In the world market, the merchants and manufacturers had all the advantages of unity, knowledge, and purpose, and could hammer down the price of raw material. The slaveholder, therefore, saw Northern merchants and manufacturers enrich themselves from the results of Southern agriculture (p. 41). His capitalistic rivals of the North were hard-working, simple-living zealots devoting their whole energy and intelligence to building up an industrial system. They quickly monopolized transport and mines and factories and they were more than willing to include the big plantations. . . . The result was that Northern and European industry set prices for Southern cotton, tobacco and sugar which left a narrow margin of profit for the planter. (p. 37)

Capital, both industrial and financial, continued to grow until the northern industrialists could challenge the political power of the plantocrats. And while it grew, it too undermined the structures of democracy:

> The North had yielded to democracy, but only because democracy was curbed by a dictatorship of property and investment which left in the hands of the leaders of industry such economic power as insured their mastery and their profits. Less than this they knew perfectly well they could not yield, and more than this they would not. (p. 46)

Once the industrial class emerged as dominant in the nation, it possessed not only its own basis of power and the social relations historically related to that power, but it also had available to it the instruments of repression created by the now subordinate southern ruling class. In its struggle with labor, it could activate racism to divide the labor movement into antagonistic forces. Moreover, the permutations of the instrument appeared endless: Black against white; Anglo-Saxon against southern and eastern European; domestic against immigrant; proletariat against share-cropper; white American against Asian, Black, Latin American, and so on.

Reconstruction and the Black Elite

One of the most revealing aspects of *Black Reconstruction* was Du Bois's assessment of the Black petit bourgeoisie, that element of Black society with which he had been most closely associated for most of his then 67 years. For the first time in his public pronouncements, he was resolved to expose the extent to which his beloved elite, through the logic of its own development, had moved apart from the Black masses. As he reckoned it, the process of bourgeoisification and alienation that had begun during slavery had not revealed its contradiction until the Reconstruction. Suddenly, the petit bourgeoisie were confronted with the political expression of Black labor:

> The difference that now came was that an indefinitely larger number of Negroes than ever before was enfranchised suddenly, and 99 percent of them belonged to the laboring class, whereas by law the Negroes who voted in the early history of the country were for the most part property holders, and prospective if not actual constituents of a petty bourgeoisie. (p. 350)

Still, during these first heady days following the Emancipation and the ending of the Civil War, the Black petit bourgeoisie had presumed to lead. Quite soon, however, its ideological and political vacuity had begun to be apparent, its leadership nominal and at its best mere mediation between the demands of the Black masses and the power of the ruling classes:

> When freedom came, this mass of Negro labor was not without intelligent leadership, and a leadership which because of former race prejudice and the present Color Line, could not be divorced from the laboring mass, as had been the case with the poor whites. . . . Free Negroes from the North, most of whom had been born in the South and knew conditions, came back in considerable numbers during Reconstruction, and took their place as leaders. The result was that the Negroes were not, as they are sometimes painted, simply a mass of densely ignorant toilers. . . .
>
> It was, however, a leadership which was not at all clear in its economic thought. On the whole, it believed in the accumulation of wealth and the exploitation of labor as the normal method of economic development. But it also believed in the right to vote as the basis and defense of economic life, and gradually but surely it was forced by the demand of the mass of Negro laborers to face the problem of land. Thus the Negro leaders gradually but certainly turned toward emphasis on economic emancipation. (pp. 350–51)

Inevitably, however, even these tenuous links between the elite strata and Black labor had disintegrated. Du Bois now believed he understood the forces that had made a mockery of the racial solidarity that had been the elite's evangelism.

First there was the ambivalence of the Black petit bourgeoisie:

> The Negro's own black leadership was naturally of many sorts. Some, like the whites, were petty bourgeois, seeking to climb to wealth; others were educated men, helping to develop a new nation without regard to mere race lines, while a third group were idealists, trying to uplift the Negro race and put them on a par with the whites. . . . In the minds of very few of them was there any clear and distinct plan for the development of a laboring class into a position of power and mastery over the modern industrial state. (p. 612)

They were to pay, sometimes with their lives, when the changing order of privilege concomitant to the continuing development of northern industrial wealth left them vulnerable:

> The bargain of 1876 . . . left capital as represented by the old planter class, the new Northern capitalist, and the capitalist that began to rise out of the poor whites, with a control of labor greater than in any modern industrial state in civilized hands (p. 630). A lawlessness which, in 1865–1868, was still spasmodic and episodic, now became organized, and its real underlying industrial causes obscured by political excuses and race hatred. Using a technique of mass and midnight murder, the South began widely organized aggression upon the Negroes. . . . Armed guerrilla warfare killed thousands of Negroes; political riots were staged; their causes or occasions were always obscure, their results always certain: ten to one hundred times as many Negroes were killed as whites. (p. 674)

The violence and terror that descended upon Blacks during the fifty years that followed Reconstruction, left the Black elite shaken and pared down to its opportunists:

> Negroes did not surrender the ballot easily or immediately. . . . But it was a losing battle, with public opinion, industry, wealth, and religion against them. Their own leaders decried "politics" and preached submission. All their efforts toward manly self-assertion were distracted by defeatism and counsels of despair, backed by the powerful propaganda of a religion which taught meekness, sacrifice and humility (pp. 692–93). This brings us to the situation when Booker T. Washington became the leader of the Negro race and advised them to depend upon industrial education and work rather than politics. The better class of Southern Negroes stopped voting for a generation. (p. 694)

Through its wealth and educational institutions the Black elite survived, growing more remote from the masses of Blacks as its ability to reproduce itself developed:

> They avoided the mistake of trying to meet force by force. They bent to the storm of beating, lynching and murder, and kept their souls in spite of public and private

insult of every description; they built an inner culture which the world recognizes in spite of the fact that it is still half-strangled and inarticulate. (p. 667)

In this relative social isolation, its culture continued to adopt forms from the class peers from which it was estranged by race. But by the constant terror, the entire Black community had been turned in on itself; and by the persistence of poverty, its social stratifications had been stabilized. However, the resources of the Black community were too few to support a mobility of more than incremental significance. With the Black migration to the North and West, which occurred at the turn of the century, this situation would change but only slightly.[77] Meanwhile, though Du Bois still could not admit it, the idealism of the Black petit bourgeoisie had been transformed into an ideology that served to hold the Black community as a semi-preserve for the more effective exploitation by its elite. As he had made clear at the Rosenwald Conference, racial solidarity still overrode a radical critique of his class:

> We must rid ourselves of the persistent idea that the advance of mankind consists of the scaling off of layers who become incorporated with the world's upper and ruling classes, leaving always dead and inert below the ignorant and unenlightened mass of men. Our professional classes are not aristocrats and our masters—they are and must be the most efficient of our servants and thinkers whose legitimate reward is the advancement of the great mass of American Negroes and with them the uplift of all men.[78]

— critical analytical to how society works

Du Bois, Marx, and Marxism

There is, however, a final aspect of significance in *Black Reconstruction* that demands close attention. From the vantage point of a Black radical historiography, Du Bois was one of the first American theorists to sympathetically confront Marxist thought in critical and independent terms. Undaunted by the political and personal concerns of Blacks in the American Communist Party, which frequently manifested themselves as a search for ideological orthodoxy in their work and writings, Du Bois had little reason or awareness for cautiously threading an ideological position between Ruthenberg, Lovestone, and Foster in the CPUSA or Trotsky, Bukharin, and Stalin in the Communist International.[79] As such, he could attempt to come to terms with Marx himself unmediated by Lenin or the emerging doctrines to be known as Marxist-Leninism.[80] And in so doing, he was articulating in theoretical terms the intersections between the Black radical tradition and historical materialism only vaguely hinted at in the formal organizations of the time. It was in those then irreconcilable roles—as a Black radical thinker and as a sympathetic critic of Marx—that Du Bois was to make some of his most important contributions concerning Black social movements. However, unless we continue to evoke a consciousness of the historical moment in which Du Bois was working, we have little chance of recognizing the nature of the thought to which he addressed himself in *Black Reconstruction*.

Since its inception, Marxism has meant to some a critical scientific system, a way of understanding, comprehending, and affecting history.[81] The way in which Trotsky expressed his own excitement about Marxism underscores this point: "The important thing . . . is to see clearly. One can say of communism, above all, that it gives more clarity. We must liberate man from all that prevents his seeing."[82] The history of Marxist thought and Marxist organizations, however, has been more ambiguous. Concomitant with this presumed clarity, this way of seeing, was the emergence of its corrosives, its oppositions. The nature of change argued in Marxism, the dialectic, would lead one to anticipate just such oppositions to occur in Marxism. Specifically with the appearances of political dogma, historical certainty, and epistemological variations on empiricism, the history of Marxist thinkers has confirmed this expectation. This is not merely a question of distinguishing the true Marxists—that is, the "founders," Marx and Engels—from their less gifted epigoni.[83] It is not an intellectual or theoretical problem.

Dogma, certainty, and facticity are social and political phenomena. In Marxism they have emerged out of a context of specific organizational demands and definite collective and individual needs framed by particular historical and political dynamics. And it was with respect to these phenomena as they had manifested themselves in the American Communist Party organization in the late 1920s and early 1930s that Du Bois focused his work on revolutionary theory. To understand the significance to Marxist thought of what Du Bois was doing it is only necessary to recall that the American Communist Party in the 1930s was situated in the most advanced capitalist society in the world. Consequently it was soon to be the second most important communist party in the world, displacing the German movement but behind the Bolsheviks. To Marxist-Communists, the historical role of the CPUSA had been determined by the principles of Leninism: it was the vanguard of the most advanced proletarian movement.[84] It was this party's ideological dogma, its existential creed and theoretical orthodoxy as they related to Blacks that compelled Du Bois to a reassessment of Marx.

The first war of the world in the twentieth century is a watershed for those events that directly influenced the special character of the American Communist movement and the party's policies toward Blacks. It was during the war, or because of the war, or in the aftermath of the war that these events occurred. First, there was the transformation of international socialism: the Comintern succeeded the Second International as the leading force of the socialist movement. Second, in the United States, a Black emigration from the South resulted in the formation of northern, urban Black communities and subsequently, a new form of racial consciousness: Black nationalism. Third, beginning almost simultaneously with the formation of the American party, there was the intercession of the Comintern: Lenin and then Stalin on the "Negro Question." These were the critical events. It is necessary now to look at them in more detail.

Bolshevism and American Communism

The Second International succumbed to two forces: nationalism and revolutionary failure. With regard to nationalism, World War I found the majority of the workers of

England, Germany, France, and Austro-Hungary willing to go to the battlefields under national leadership in order to fight against each other. International worker solidarity upon which socialism was based disintegrated. The socialist movement had failed to maintain the dichotomy between the interests of workers and the interests of capitalist ruling classes. State nationalism had triumphed as the dominant ideology of the working classes. The pacifist tactics of the socialists had proved to be effective only in those countries that were either noncombatants or those, like the United States, which had been slow to enter the fray.[85]

Moreover, the revolutionary movements led by socialists failed—all, that is, but one. The Bolshevik Party had gained control over the revolutions in Russia, but in Germany, England, France, Hungary, and elsewhere, socialist revolutions either failed to materialize or when they did were aborted.[86] Thus, in the most advanced industrialized societies—the presumed site of revolution—no revolutions were brought about, no workers movements came to power. In point of fact, the only two successful revolutions of the period had occurred in societies whose populations were predominantly peasants: Mexico and Russia. Not only were they predominantly peasant societies but peasant movements had played critical roles in the triumphs of their revolutions, throwing into question the presumption that industrial workers were to be the "instruments of philosophy."[87] It is not surprising, then, that the organization of the international socialist movement atrophied.

The Second International had also come increasingly to represent or signify that revolution would come through the instruments and structures of bourgeois society: political reform through the institutions of bourgeois democracy.[88] When the International collapsed, so did its tactical and ideological resolutions. What appeared to replace them was the Third International dominated by Lenin and the policies of his Bolshevik cadre. Tactically, a renewed commitment to violent struggle became evident in the movement. Moreover, with the formation of the Third International, it became necessary for member national parties to pledge their loyalties to the Comintern, the Soviet Union and, in practical terms, to the Bolshevik Party. The defense of the Soviet Union was to be the highest priority. Party discipline was to conform to the dictates of the Executive Committee of the Comintern—a Committee chaired by Zinoviev, the second leading Bolshevik:[89]

> Each party desirous of affiliating with the Communist International should be obliged to render every possible assistance to the Soviet Republics in their struggle against all counter-revolutionary forces. The Communist parties should carry on a precise and definite propaganda to induce the workers to refuse to transport any kind of military equipment intended for fighting against the Soviet Republics, and should also by legal or illegal means carry on a propaganda amongst the troops sent against the workers' republics, etc.
>
> . . . All the resolutions of the congresses of the Communist International, as well as the resolutions of the Executive Committee are binding for all parties joining the Communist International.[90]

Still, the vigor with which the Comintern pursued and institutionalized its hegemony had no immediate effect on the American communist movement. The history and organizations of revolutionary socialists and workers movements in the United States had been too disparate for any authority, domestic or otherwise, to impose cohesion and/or subordination.

The crucial social basis for radical workers' movements in the United States was provided by the forces of labor recruited to American industrial production. Commenting on the first decade and a half of the twentieth century, Nathan Glazer argued:

> One central fact about the American working class in this period, and during subsequent decades, too, must be remembered: it was largely composed of immigrants. The working force in the steel mills, the coal mines, the textile factories, the clothing shop was overwhelmingly foreign-born, and that part of it that was not was concentrated in supervisory jobs and in the more highly paid skilled occupations.[91]

Earlier, as we have seen, the African and Afro-American agrarian workers had supplied the critical surplus value that supported the transformation of the economy into an industrialized and ultimately capital-intensive one. In turn, late nineteenth-century European immigrants—expropriated, trained, reproduced, and disciplined by European sectors of the world economy (in Germany, England, Ireland, and Italy primarily)—constituted the labor forces uniquely developed and historically necessary for the American industrial transformation. But most of these European immigrant workers had come from societies in which labor movements were already developed. In fact most of these movements had by the mid-nineteenth century developed unique and particular complexes of tactics, strategy, and ideology. Whole traditions in these labor movements and oppositions in those traditions had been achieved. These were a part of the political, organizational, and ideological cultures that accompanied the foreign workers to America. Theodore Draper observes:

> From the very outset, the American Socialist movement was peculiarly indebted to the immigrants for both its progress and its problems. The first convention of the Socialist Labor Party in 1877 was composed of representatives of seventeen German sections, seven English, three Bohemian, one French, and a general women's Section. Immigrants naturally assumed the role of teachers and organizers, but they were mainly concerned with teaching and organizing themselves.
>
> The Socialist Labor party was never more than an American head on an immigrant body.[92]

As these peoples dispersed and/or concentrated in the United States according to various social and economic determinants, their traditions were either conserved, adapted, or dissipated. Two ways in which they were conserved were through ethnic-specific and industrial-specific communities. The labor movement—whether it was trade unionist, electoral-party, or revolutionary—was largely organized on the basis of national, ethnic, and industrial groups:

In the Socialist Party of 1914, the membership in the Northeastern and Midwestern states was largely . . . Jews, Germans, Poles, Czechs and Slovaks, Hungarians, South Slavs, and many others. . . .

Later immigrant groups, however, formed parties or groupings that were still related to the Socialist parties of their respective countries, of which so many had been members. These federations of immigrant workers played a special role in American socialism.[93]

This, then, was one critical contradiction in early American socialist development. The organizing principle was ethnicity while at the same time nationalism—a logical conclusion of ethnicity—endangered and frustrated socialist unity. Ethnicity dominated the movement organizationally, ideologically, conceptually, and theoretically. This objective contradiction was a persistent character of the socialist and labor movements and would reach critical proportions in response to both European and American events (i.e., the Franco-Prussian War in the 1870s; World War I; and ethnic competition for jobs and its subsequent violence).[94] Even among the minority sections of the socialist movement—the English-language federations—there was a basic conflict between nationalism and socialism. Much of the membership of these federations was in fact made up from second-generation immigrant clusters. Among the factors involved in the decision to become socialists and communists, Gabriel Almond argued, was the assimilative motive. Almond maintained that the English-language federations were influenced by both the organizational priority of Americanization so as to influence the development of a "native" American working class, and their members' own sociopsychological needs.[95]

The American Communist Party was formed, then, during a time of some theoretical and ideological confusion. In point of fact, the movement in the United States had broken down into so many competing ideological factions in the early 1920s that it became necessary for the Comintern to impose order, uniting them into a single party.[96] The party that resulted was dominated by foreign-language federations, the most powerful being the Russian and Finnish federations. The federations, though, were still often more concerned with the fortunes of the movement in their homelands than in America. Nationalism and nationalist rivalries were, consequently, a part of the party's historical character.[97] When one adds to this situation the disputes inherited from the Second International concerning the nature of capitalism and the form the socialist revolution would assume, the appearance of Bolshevik hegemony can be understood to have been both a further force for chaos and order. The success of the Bolshevik party gave the Russian-language association an advantage—for a time—in influencing party policy, but it also intensified ideological disputes and theoretical quarrels, since the Bolsheviks were a historical anomaly in classical Marxist terms. But a form of Russian nationalism had assumed dominance in the American movement as it had throughout the Comintern. Though this idea was acceptable to many in the American movement, it could also be expected to encounter opposition especially among those peoples who had been historically subject to Tsarist Russia's imperialism.[98] In a movement dominated by national parties and subparties, the character of the Comintern and the consequent inflation of the political influence of Russian nationals in the United States was bound to produce or revitalize counter-nationalisms. The growing power of specifically Russian Jews in the movement created or exasperated cleavages within the Communist movement that were not resolved even by the late 1920s.[99] Regardless, the direct influence of the Bolsheviks on the American movement that had begun as early as late 1916—months before its own spectacular successes and nearly three years before the first World Congress of the Communist International—would seldom be seriously challenged in the next forty or fifty years.

Black Nationalism

For Blacks, in sociological and political terms, one of the most important events in American history at the time of the First World War was the migration to the sites of urban and particularly northern industry. With the outbreak of the war, the European immigration of laborers had been severely restricted by both the exigencies of war and Congressionally imposed controls. In addition, war-time conscription had removed thousands of white workers from their jobs while at the same time war was opening markets to U.S. goods and increasing the demand for labor. The war, then, produced a labor scarcity in American industry. In such a labor market, workers had an advantage in their demands for wage increases; and as the term of the war lengthened, job action as a labor tactic became more diffused among workers, including the semi-skilled. Northeastern industrialists and their counterparts in the Midwest attempted to resolve the problem of increasing labor costs and labor militancy by recruiting southern and Caribbean Blacks.

As we had noted, at this time the overwhelming majority of American Blacks lived in the rural South. Despite the campaigns of terror and violence directed against them, and which had been a constant undercurrent in their lives since the Reconstruction, most of them were still reluctant to break historical, social, and cultural ties by migrating to confrontations with northern antipathies. To meet this problem, corporate managers had developed a sophisticated propaganda campaign to excite the interests of southern Black workers. Labor recruiters were sent South with instructions to fill the empty freight cars often accompanying them; Black newspapers (some subsidized by northern industrialists), led by the *Chicago Defender*, ran articles on the opportunities for employment in the North juxtaposed with accounts of the anti-Black activities of southern whites. Robert Abbott, editor of the *Defender*, was relentless:

> Abbott put out a "national edition" of his weekly, aimed at southern blacks. It carried in red ink such headlines as: 100 NEGROES MURDERED WEEKLY IN UNITED STATES BY WHITE AMERICANS; LYNCHING—A NATIONAL DISGRACE; and WHITE GEN-

TLEMAN RAPES COLORED GIRL. Accompanying a lynching story was a picture of the lynch victim's severed head, with the caption: NOT BELGIUM—AMERICA. Poems entitled *Land of Hope* and *Bound for the Promised Land* urged blacks to go North, and editorials boosted Chicago as the best place for them to go. Want ads offered jobs at attractive wages in and around Chicago. In news items, anecdotes, cartoons, and photos, the *Defender* crystallized the underlying economic and social causes of black suffering into immediate motives for flight.[100]

The promise of economic integration into some of the most advanced sectors of American production had its impact. As noted, an estimated quarter of a million to a million Black workers and their families migrated during the war years, substantially increasing the populations of the Black communities situated in the critical industrial areas east of the Mississippi.

This migratory flood coincided with one emanating from the English-speaking West Indies. The poverty and deteriorating well-being of Caribbean Blacks were the direct legacies of colonialism. Tens of thousands of West Indians came to the United States during the first decades of the twentieth century. It was work, too, that attracted them, and so they located in precisely the same Black communities that received the internal migration:

> One unusual and complicating feature of the New York ghetto in Harlem was the presence of two quite different nonwhite populations. By far the larger was the group of southern migrants, but a minority not to be ignored had originated in the Caribbean islands, chiefly the British West Indies, with some from the Dutch West Indies, Cuba, and Puerto Rico. To the 5000 foreign-born blacks who lived in New York in 1900 were added 28,000 more during the war decade. In 1917 the New York *Times* estimated that they formed one quarter of the population of Harlem.[101]

The congregating of these peoples, the deep disruptions that accompanied their translocations, and the persistent hostility with which they were confronted forced them on to each other, politically and socially. As such it became necessary for them to develop social and political forms that would transcend the particularistic identities due to specific historical differences. It was within this particular milieu that both the UNIA and the African Blood Brotherhood (ABB) emerged; and both would have enormous consequence for the American Communist Party's efforts at organizing Blacks.

It has never been possible to characterize the United Negro Improvement Association in precise terms. Its dominant ideology was eclectic: incorporating elements of Christianity, socialism, revolutionary nationalism, and race solidarity. As an organization; it exhibited a range of structures responsive to circumstance and personality. Responsibility for policy- and decision-making varied as well. They were formed in accordance with ideological factors: the circumstance of situationally crucial individuals; the nature of the issues; and the momentary fortunes of the organization. Too, the organization did change over time, responding to the political and social significances of the interactions between itself and its social and political environment. Nevertheless, observers have most frequently typified the organization as ideologically a "back to Africa" movement; or for very different reasons, and with implicit organizational characterizations, as "the Garvey movement." It was never quite so obviously simple.[102]

The UNIA's main thrust appears to have been toward the development of a powerful Black nation economically organized by a modified form of capitalism.[103] This powerful entity was to become the guardian of the interests of Blacks in Africa (where it was to be located) and those dispersed in the African diaspora. The nation was to be founded on a technocratic elite recruited from the Black peoples of the world. This elite, in turn, would create the structures necessary for the nation's survival and its development until it was strong enough to play its historical role and absorb and generate subsequent generations of trained, disciplined nationalists. As a number of historians have noted, in many ways both directly and indirectly, the UNIA had incorporated elements of the self-help movement identified with Booker T. Washington; but without the restrictions imposed upon that movement, the UNIA had pushed the concept to its logical conclusion.[104] In pursuit of this ideal, the organization had developed structures that anticipated a national formation. The UNIA had possessed a protonational bureaucracy; security forces with women auxiliaries; a national church; an international network of chapters (or consulates); and the beginnings of an economic base consisting of a series of small businesses and service industries. Hundreds of thousands—perhaps millions—of Blacks were enrolled in the organization. Though recruitment went on primarily in the United States and the West Indies, the UNIA possessed dues-paying members in Africa and Latin America. The scale of the organization made the UNIA by far and away the largest nationalist organization to emerge among Blacks in America. In these terms, the organization's significance still remains unrivalled in U.S. history.[105]

Since most histories of the organization were written by its critics, distortions of the UNIA abound in the literature. They are especially marked with regard to its founder and principal organizer, Marcus Garvey.[106] Even Du Bois, while participating in the opposition to the UNIA, had contributed exposes of its financial practices and bitter characterizations of Garvey.[107] But the one predominant tactic of the UNIA's critics was to identify the organization with Garvey, thus tending to reduce their criticisms to studies of aberrant personality or political opportunism. Robert Bagnall, one such critic, writing in A. Philip Randolph's and Chandler Owen's paper, *The Messenger*, described Garvey as

a Jamaican Negro of unmixed stock, squat, stocky, fat, and sleek, with protruding jaws, and heavy jowls, small bright pig-like eyes and rather bull-dog-like face. Boastful, egotistic, tyrannical, intolerant, cunning, shifty, smooth and suave, avaricious; . . . as adept as a cuttle-fish in beclouding an issue he cannot meet, prolix in the nth degree in devising new schemes to gain the money of poor ignorant Negroes; gifted at self-advertisement, without shame in self-laudation, promising ever, but never fulfilling, without regard for veracity, a lover of pomp and tawdry finery and garish display, a bully with his own folk but servile in the presence of the Klan, a sheer opportunist and demagogic charlatan.[108]

Others with more charity came to the same point. Claude McKay would write in his *Harlem: Negro Metropolis*:

> The movement of Marcus Garvey in Harlem was glorious with romance and riotous, clashing emotions. Like the wise men of the ancient world, this peacock-parading Negro of the New World, hoodooed by the "Negromancy" of Africa, followed a star—a Black Star. A weaver of dreams, he translated into a fantastic pattern of reality the gaudy strands of the vicarious desires of the submerged members of the Negro race.
>
> There has never been a Negro leader like Garvey. None ever enjoyed a fraction of his universal popularity. He winged his way into the firmament of the white world holding aloft a black star and exhorting the Negro people to gaze upon and follow it.[109]

In this way the UNIA became known as "the Garvey movement." This has always implied or bespoken the presence of autocratic authority and demagoguery. As principal spokesman and symbol of the UNIA, Garvey became the object of study rather than the masses of people involved in making the organization. Robert Hill, Tony Martin, and Theodore Vincent are three historians who have recently begun to correct that fault.

> The UNIA's official demands, set down in a Declaration of Rights of the Negro Peoples of the World, included the right to vote, a fair share of political patronage, representation on juries and on the judge's bench, and full freedom of press, speech, and assembly for all. The UNIA sought these basic freedoms primarily to create and strengthen a separate black world, while groups like the NAACP would utilize these freedoms primarily to create an integrated world.
>
> Socially, the UNIA was a huge club and fraternal order. . . . For Garveyites, there was the fraternal camaraderie of all the black people of the world. UNIA parades, Saturday night parties, women's group luncheons, etc., had a significance far beyond that of providing social diversion. Their affairs were designed to build a pride and confidence in blackness.[110]

Clearly, the UNIA possessed a substantial cadre and several tiers of secondary leadership. It was a complex organization functioning on a number of levels simultaneously. And its popular appeals and attractive political style were combined with pragmatic programs of racial achievement. For the five years of its peak development, from 1918 to 1923, it became the most formidable movement in the history of American Blacks.

Like the UNIA, the organizational cadre of the African Blood Brotherhood consisted largely of West Indians and Afro-Americans who had developed professionally as social agitators and journalist-propagandists. Its founding organizers in 1919 were

Cyril Briggs (Nevis Island), Richard B. Moore (Barbados), and W. A. Domingo (Jamaica).[111] Later, in the period between 1920 and 1922, Otto Huiswoud (Surinam) and a number of important Afro-American radicals joined the movement, including Otto Hall, Haywood Hall (Harry Haywood), Edward Doty, Grace Campbell, H. V. Phillips, Gordon Owens, Alonzo Isabel, and Lovett Fort-Whiteman.[112]

> The largest membership was in the New York home office, but there were sizable contingents in Chicago, Baltimore, Omaha and West Virginia. . . . The ABB also established groups in the Caribbean area; in Trinidad, Surinam, British Guiana, Santo Domingo and the Windward Islands. At its height, the ABB had only three to five thousand members, most of them ex-servicemen. . . . The number was kept small, in part by design, but the possibilities of danger, and the Brotherhood's militantly nationalistic and left-wing ideology, undoubtedly alienated and confused many people. The ABB saw itself as a tight-knit, semi-clandestine, paramilitary group which hoped to act for a "worldwide federation" of black organizations. The Brotherhood's official program stated, in part: "In order to build a strong and effective movement on the platform of liberation for the Negro people, protection of their rights to Life, Liberty and the Pursuit of Happiness, etc., all Negro organizations should get together on a Federation basis, thus creating a united centralized movement.[113]

For the bulk of its dozen-odd years of existence, the ABB was a secret, paramilitary organization dedicated to the "immediate protection and ultimate liberation of Negroes everywhere."[114] This aspect of its ideology, however, was not a true reflection of its origins or future.

When the Brotherhood was first proposed in Briggs's monthly magazine, *The Crusader*, it was designated The African Blood Brotherhood "for African Liberation and Redemption." Even earlier, though, *The Crusader* had

> advertised itself as the "Publicity Organ of the Hamitic League of the World" (June 1919, p. 1). This so-called Hamitic League, with headquarters in Omaha, Nebraska, set itself the task of uniting the so-called Hamitic peoples, the chief ethnic group of North Africa. One of its leaders, George Wells Parker, made contact with Briggs and they agreed to support each other. . . . The reference to the Hamitic League was removed from The Crusader in the issue of January 1921.[115]

The Brotherhood's beginnings inadvertently exposed a degree of identity-confusion among its founders. A similar confusion would mark its appeals and the designation of the audience the organization presumed to address.[116] In the next decade, that audience would be transformed from Hamitics to Africans, then Negroes and, finally, Black workers. Behind the fluctuations, however, was the premise enunciated by Briggs in 1917:

> Departing from Garvey's plan for a Negro state in Africa, he advanced the idea that the "race problem" could be solved by setting up an independent Negro nation on

American territory. "Considering that the more we are outnumbered, the weaker we will get, and the weaker we get the less respect, justice or opportunity we will obtain, is it not time to consider a separate political existence, with a government that will represent, consider, and advance us?" he argued.[117]

Briggs, for one, had spun away from the paternalistic projects of African colonization and African missionizing that had concerned "race-men" like Crummell, Turner, and Du Bois, and his fellow West Indians, Blyden, Garvey, and J. Albert Thorne.[118]

It seems fair to say that the African Blood Brotherhood had begun as a revolutionary nationalist organization.[119] It soon, however, came to be influenced by the socialism of Lenin, Trotsky, Stalin, and state Bolshevism. And once several of its cadre were absorbed into the American Communist Party, it came to be accepted that in both the United States and Africa, the Brotherhood would act as an ideological, organizational, and military vanguard. In its closest rapprochement with the CPUSA, it was conceived as the core of a liberating force developed in the hinterlands of Africa and the shock troops of a Black and white revolutionary movement in the United States.[120] Finally, the Brotherhood, or at least prominent members of that organization—Briggs, Moore, and especially Harry Haywood—appears to have provided to the Party the immediate ideological stimulus for the development of the Comintern's position after 1928 that Blacks constituted a "national question" in America.[121]

Within a year or two of its founding in 1919, the Brotherhood's leadership in New York and Chicago was acting in concert with officials of the Communist movement in attempting infiltration and/or subversion of the UNIA. The leaders of the UNIA, having found difficulty in respecting Black nationalists who had conceded the principles of autonomous leadership and "race first" action, were now the subjects of intrigues, public charges and recriminations, and betrayals. Though several historians have traced the antagonism between the Brotherhood and the UNIA to supposed differences on the issues of the roles of socialism and white workers in the Black movement, they do not appear to be the crux of the matter. Much of the rancor between the organizations was a result of the Brotherhood's insidious tactics, its growing dependence and domination by the CPUSA, and its persistent attempts—by Briggs, Domingo, Moore, and others—to unseat Garvey and the rest of the UNIA's "Negro Zionist" leaders. According to Tony Martin, Briggs's several cycles of position-reversals toward the UNIA were begun in 1921. In anticipation of the UNIA's First International Convention, Briggs

offered Garvey a proposition—that Garvey (with his international mass movement, perhaps millions strong) should enter into a program of joint action with the ABB (an obscure organization of a thousand or two) for African liberation. . . . Briggs then took the opportunity provided by Garvey's assembled multitude to do a little recruiting for himself and passed around copies of the ABB program.

The next ploy in Briggs' attempt to impose a communist united front on Garvey was to have his white communist friend Rose Pastor Stokes address the convention. She expatiated on Russia's desire to free Africa and on the need for black-white working class unity. She then called on Garvey to take a stand in relation to her communist overtures. Garvey was polite but noncommittal. The final stroke in Briggs' strategy was to have ABB delegates to the convention introduce a motion for endorsement of the communist program. The motion was debated and tabled. The ABB, piqued at this setback, them immediately published a *Negro Congress Bulletin* on August 24, almost entirely devoted to a scurrilous misrepresentation of the UNIA convention.[122]

Whatever motives Briggs and his associates might have had, this pattern of contradictory approaches to the UNIA would characterize the relations of the two organizations until the demise of the Brotherhood in the 1930s. In the Party, Briggs, Moore, Haywood, Otto Hall, Fort-Whiteman, and others found a complementary radical element and a potential international ally for the struggle against colonialism and world capital. Within the UNIA, Garvey for one, felt much more sympathy for the Russian Communists than for the Brotherhood and its American Communist colleagues.[123]

Blacks and Communism

In its beginnings, the American Communist movement required no special policy with regard to Blacks. Having been constituted from the rebellious Left Wing of the socialist movement did not signify for these communists a departure from the presumption that Blacks were simply a segment of the unskilled working classes.[124] Moreover, with the American socialist movement drawn predominantly from immigrant ethnic and national minorities, the notion of class solidarity was of substantial importance to the movement, theoretically and practically. It provided a category of political activity through which the diverse social elements of the revolutionary movement—ethnics and nationalities, workers and intellectuals—could be reconciled, transcending their several particular interests. The absence of such a class consciousness among Blacks, and in its stead the presence of a racial consciousness, was seen by early American Communists as both an ideological backwardness and a potential threat to the integrity of the socialist movement itself.[125] To the degree that the early movement became aware of Black nationalism, that, too, would be unacceptable. Black nationalism was intolerable to a movement so constantly close to foundering on national and ethnic divisions. This concern was made manifest by the frequency with which "Back to Africa" ideologies were described as "Zionist" and compared to "Back to Palestine" movements among the Jews—a substantial and influential minority in the early socialist movement.[126] The party consistently opposed Black nationalism until its own variant: self-determination, emerged in the Soviet Union in 1928. The UNIA, as the strongest organization among Blacks with a nationalist ideology, was characterized as a bourgeois reactionary group and made a focus of the attack on Black nationalism. American racism did not justify the program of Black nationalism. European immigrants with other than Anglo-Saxon origins were also targets of racist abuses and discriminations. Racism, then, was merely an element of ruling-class ideology and white "chauvinism" its political position. Thus the social context of Blacks was adapted by ideologues in the socialist movement to the social experience of European immigrant workers.[127]

The Communist parties did not actively recruit Blacks until 1921. This change in policy seems to be largely the responsibility of Lenin, and is even more remarkable when we recall that Lenin's name was barely known to any of the national elements in the American movement four years earlier.[128] Nevertheless, it was Lenin who raised the "Negro Question" at the Second Congress of the Communist International in 1920. And it was Lenin who wrote to the party in America, "some time in 1921 expressing surprise that their reports to Moscow made no mention of party work among Negroes and urging that they should be recognized as a strategically important element in Communist activity.[129] The American Communist Party then began its recruitment of Blacks, primarily, though, radical Black intellectuals and nationalist organizers. The nucleus, as we have pointed out, was those who made up the majority of the Supreme Council of the African Blood Brotherhood. Still, the historical and theoretical antecedents of the American Communist Party's work among American Blacks and its eventual positions on Black nationalism were substantially drawn from the experiences of Russian revolutionists.

In the same year that Lenin had addressed the Second Congress of the Comintern, he had written in *"Left-Wing" Communism—An Infantile Disorder*:

> [T]o reject compromises "on principle," to reject the permissibility of compromises in general, no matter of what kind, is childishness, which it is difficult even to consider seriously. . . . There are different kinds of compromises.[130]

Here Lenin was mounting an attack on what he termed "left opportunism," that is, political action and judgment that used the texts of Marx and Engels to criticize and oppose Lenin and the Bolshevik Party's leadership. The setting was 1920. In Russia, the civil war was still undecided; and in Europe, the revolutionary movement had been "temporarily" defeated. Lenin was urging a tactical retreat. This document was meant to stem criticism that emerged from other Russian revolutionists who insisted that the revolution must maintain an international arena and scope, and could not be secured in one national territory. Through the document and other activities, Lenin hoped to defuse the "left deviationists" before they became an unmanageable and disruptive force at the Second Congress, and broke the Bolshevik Party's control and direction of the Third International. Despite its logical inconsistencies, historical omissions, and distortions, and its contradictions of Marxist theory, his document became one of the most significant works of the first decade of the Third International. Much of this was to be attributed to Lenin's authority in the movement as the world's most powerful Communist; but as important was the work's legitimation of accommodation to world capitalism and imperialism. It provided a pragmatic modus vivendi for Communist parties elsewhere to survive while maintaining the illusion of being revolutionary rather than reformist.[131]

The thread of Lenin's argument and his political declarations could be traced stylistically to his critique of the "Left Communists" in 1918, when in writing *"Left-Wing" Childishness and the Petty-Bourgeois Mentality*, Lenin had been forced to defend the development of state-capitalist bureaucracy and the Brest Treaty with the Ukrainian government. Substantively, the thread could be found in his characterization of the revolutionary party as the vanguard of the revolutionary masses:

> By educating the workers' party, Marxism educates the vanguard of the proletariat, capable of assuming power and *leading the whole people* to socialism, of directing and organizing the new system, of being teacher, the guide, the leader of all the working and exploited people in organizing their social life without the bourgeoisie and against the bourgeoisie.[132]

To Lenin, the party was the possessor of true historical consciousness, and was the true instrument of history. The party was Marxist theory in practice. It did what it did because the proletariat had demonstrated that it was insufficiently class-conscious.[133] It followed, then, for Lenin, that opposition to the tasks defined for itself by the party could only come from two sources: the reactionary bourgeoisie on the right, and the pseudo-Marxist, petit bourgeoisie "intellectual" opportunists on the left. If, in order to survive, the party acting as the state compromised with Germany, Austro-Hungary, Bulgaria, and Turkey (the Quadruple Alliance) at Brest-Litovsk, it could not be accused of compromising *in general*. The alternative had been continued war and defeat. One must distinguish, Lenin argued, between "obligatory" compromises (preservation) and those compromises that transformed one into "accomplices in banditry." The Bolshevik Party made only obligatory compromises . . . except when it made "minor and easily remediable" errors. With a bit of sophistry, Lenin declared:

> What applies to individuals also applies—with necessary modifications—to politics and parties. It is not he who makes no mistakes that is intelligent. There are no such men, nor can there be. It is he whose errors are not very grave and who is able to rectify them easily and quickly that is intelligent.[134]

Programmatically and tactically, Lenin was laying the grounds for member parties of the Comintern in Europe and elsewhere to assume nonrevolutionary positions for the moment. Party members were instructed to join parties, movements, and organizations and to attempt to influence policy toward reformist demands necessarily intolerable to capitalism. "Communists should not rest content with teaching the proletariat its ultimate aims, but should lend impetus to every practical move leading the proletariat into the struggle for these ultimate aims."[135]

In 1920, and again in 1921, Lenin had indicated disappointment in the direction and organizational priorities established by the American Communist Party. He suggested further that Blacks should play a critical role in the party and in the vanguard of the workers' movement since Blacks occupied the most oppressive sector of the American society, and were clearly to be expected to be the most angry element in the United States. All of this was somewhat characteristic of Lenin as he rationalized the basic opportunism that had dominated the history of the Bolshevik movement.[136]

However, Lenin had found no basis of support for his declarations within the American delegation to the Second Congress. Indeed, in the person of the Harvard-trained revolutionary writer, John Reed, the American delegation, preoccupied with the image of the UNIA, repudiated Lenin's position:

> Reed defined the American Negro problem as "that of a strong racial and social movement, and of a proletarian labor movement advancing very fast in class-consciousness." He alluded to the Garvey movement in terms that ruled out all Negro nationalism and separatism: "The Negroes have no demands for national independence. All movements aiming at a separate national existence for Negroes fail, as did the 'Back to Africa Movement' of a few years ago. They consider themselves first of all Americans at home in the United States. This makes it very much simpler for the Communists."[137]

For the time being, the Comintern was satisfied by a vague plan to invite Black revolutionists to a future congress.

Two such figures attended the Fourth Congress of the Communist International in 1922: Otto Huiswoud, as an official delegate, and Claude McKay, as an unofficial and non-Communist observer. McKay and Huiswoud ("the mulatto delegate," as McKay would refer to him in his autobiography, *A Long Way From Home*) tended to complement each other in both official and informal discussions of the "Negro Question."

> When the American Negro delegate was invited to attend meetings and my mulatto colleague went, the people asked: "But where is the *chorny* (the black)?" The mulatto delegate said: "Say, fellow, you're all right for propaganda. It's a pity you'll never make a disciplined party member."[138]

And with the aid of the Japanese revolutionary, Sen Katayama, who had spent some time in the United States working as a cook and other things on the west and east coasts, had been a founder of the unified and Bolshevized American Party, and now sat on the commission for national and colonial questions,[139] McKay and Huiswoud successfully presented to the Comintern sessions a more realistic basis for discussion. And it was at the Fourth Congress that the Comintern made its first formal declaration of policy toward American Blacks: Early the following year, Rose Pastor Stokes, the radical wife of J. C. Phelps Stokes one of the NAACP's millionaire-sponsors, returned to the United States and reported to her fellow party members:

> One of the most significant developments in the Fourth Congress of the Communist International was the creation of a Negro Commission and the adoption of the Commission's Thesis on the Negro Question which concludes with the declaration that "the Fourth Congress recognizes the necessity of supporting every form of Negro Movement which tends to undermine capitalism and Imperialism or to impede their further progress," pledges the Communist International to fight "for race equality of the Negro with the White people, for equal wages and political and social rights," to "exert every effort to admit Negroes into Trade Unions"

and to "take immediate steps to hold a general Negro Conference or Congress in Moscow."

Two American Negroes were guests of the Congress. One, a poet, the other a speaker and organizer, both young and energetic, devoted to the cause of Negro liberation and responsive to the ideals of the revolutionary proletariat. They charmed the delegates with their fine personalities.[140]

According to Mrs. Stokes, the Negro Commission itself was international in its membership, made up of delegates from the United States, Belgium, France, England, Java, British South Africa, Japan, Holland, and Russia. The perspective of the Commission was thus international, reflecting the internationalism of Marxist organization, the theory of capitalism, and its membership. As the chairman of the Commission, Comrade Sasha [Stokes] had announced:

> [T]he world Negro movement must be organized: in America, as the center of Negro culture and the crystallization of Negro protest; in Africa, the reservoir of human labor for the further development of Capitalism; in Central America (Costa Rica, Guatemala, Colombia, Nicaragua, and other "Independent" Republics), where American Imperialism dominates; in Puerto Rico, Haiti, Santo Domingo and other islands washed by the waters of the Caribbean . . . in South Africa and the Congo . . . in East Africa.[141]

The work among Blacks in America, then, was to be one sector in a world movement against colonialism and imperialism as the contemporary stages of world capitalism. The Communist International was to be the vehicle through which the enslaved white workers of Europe and America and the "revolutionary workers and peasants of the whole world" would converge on the common enemy:

> It is the task of the Communist International to point out to the Negro people that they are not the only people suffering from the oppression of Capitalism and Imperialism; that the workers and peasants of Europe and Asia and of the Americas are also the victims of Imperialism; that the struggle against Imperialism is not the struggle of any one people but of all the peoples of the world; that in China and India, in Persia and Turkey, in Egypt and Morocco the oppressed colored colonial peoples are rising against the same evils that the Negroes are rising against—racial oppression and discrimination, and intensified industrial exploitation; that these peoples are striving for the same ends that the Negroes are striving for—political, industrial and social liberation and equality.[142]

Notwithstanding its contradictions and ideological formulations, this *Theses on the Negro Question* was a quite remarkable document. Certainly its New World–centric view limited it (for example, the proposition that the "center of Negro culture and . . . protest" was in America). Certainly the presumption that a proletarianized Black people in America was the most advanced sector of the Black world was more a vulgarization of Marx than a product of analysis. But just as certain, this statement was a more sophisticated presentation of the world system than had been developed in the earlier internationalism of the UNIA. The Commission had successfully urged the Fourth Congress to recognize the relationship between the "Negro Question" and the "Colonial Question."

The intention behind the Negro Commission of the Fourth Congress was to substitute system- and class-consciousness for race-consciousness among American Blacks. Yet one enduring lesson learned from the UNIA was that Blacks were capable of organizing on an international scale. The Negro Commission suggested that the UNIA's was only a particular form of race-consciousness and that it was possible for race-consciousness to be transformed into a progressive force. A world-historical race-consciousness, recognizing the exploitation of Blacks as Blacks, but as part of and related to the exploitation of other workers could develop from the earlier form. The historical problem posed before the Comintern and its member parties—and especially for American Communism—was whether the Communist movement had the capabilities to perform this transformation. Starting with the efforts of Huiswoud, McKay, and Katayama, it had become increasingly clear to the leadership of the Comintern—Radek, Zinoviev, Trotsky, Lenin, and later, Stalin—that only a special program could attract large numbers of Black workers to the movement. After 1922, the tutelage and training of Black cadres in the Soviet Union was taken quite seriously. The most critical of the results was the formulation of the "nation within a nation" thesis announced by the Sixth Congress in 1928.

Haywood Hall (Harry Haywood) was one of the American Blacks brought to the Soviet Union to study at the University of Toilers of the East (KUTVA). When he arrived in April 1926, he joined a small colony of Black students that included his brother Otto Hall (John Jones) O. J. and Jane Golden, Harold Williams (Dessalines), Roy Mahoney (Jim Farmer), Maude White (who arrived in December 1927), and Bankole (a Gold Coast inhabitant).[143] Of the seven Black students at KUTVA[144] and the Blacks who arrived in the Soviet Union as delegates to the Sixth Congress in 1928, Haywood alone advocated the position of "self-determination" for American Blacks. Haywood's own conversion had come in the Winter of 1928 when in preparation for the Congress, he had responded to a dismissive report on the UNIA authored by his brother, Otto:

> In the discussion, I pointed out that Otto's position was not merely a rejection of Garveyism but also a denial of nationalism as a legitimate trend in the Black freedom movement. I felt that it amounted to throwing out the baby with the bathwater. With my insight sharpened by previous discussions, I argued further that the nationalism reflected in the Garvey movement was not a foreign transplant, nor did it spring full-blown from the brow of Jove. On the contrary, it was an indigenous product, arising from the soil of Black super-exploitation and oppression in the United States. It expressed the yearnings of millions of Blacks for a nation of their own.
>
> As I pursued this logic, a totally new thought occurred to me, and for me it was

the clincher. The Garvey movement is dead, I reasoned, but not Black nationalism. Nationalism, which Garvey diverted under the slogan of Back to Africa, was an authentic trend, likely to flare up again in periods of crisis and stress. Such a movement might again fall under the leadership of utopian visionaries who would seek to divert it from the struggle against the main enemy, U.S. imperialism, and on to a reactionary separatist path. The only way such a diversion of the struggle could be forestalled was by presenting a revolutionary alternative to Blacks.

... I was the first American communist (with perhaps the exception of Briggs) to support the thesis that U.S. Blacks constituted an oppressed nation.[145]

N. Nasanov (Bob Katz), a Russian representative of the Young Communist League, having spent some time in the United States, was already convinced that American Blacks constituted a national question. Katayama was as well, and suggested to Haywood that Lenin had supported the idea. But they, and similarly minded Soviet Communists, had found difficulty in locating any American Blacks to support their position.[146] Nasanov heard Haywood's arguments and promptly requested his collaboration. From the moment Haywood voiced his commitment to Black nationalism, the momentum was established for the self-determination line that would become the Comintern's official policy after the Congress. The resolutions and discussion papers drafted by Haywood and Nasanov eventually culminated in the language on the "American Negro Question" included in the Congress report, "Theses on the Revolutionary Movement in the Colonies and Semi-Colonies," 12 December 1928:

> In those regions of the South in which compact Negro masses are living, it is essential to put forward the slogan of the Right of Self-determination for Negroes. A radical transformation of the agrarian structure of the Southern States is one of the basic tasks of the revolution. Negro Communists must explain to non-Negro workers and peasants that only their close union with the white proletariat and joint struggle with them against the American bourgeoisie can lead to their liberation from barbarous exploitation, and that only the victorious proletarian revolution will completely and permanently solve the agrarian and national questions of the Southern United States in the interests of the overwhelming majority of the Negro population of the country.[147]

Black self-determination was presented to the American Communist Party as a fait accompli. And for years the true origins of the line would be a mystery to members of the American Communist movement as well as to its historians.[148] Its meaning, however, was clear: as Josef Pogany (John Pepper) characterized it (or as Haywood argues, caricatured it) in the line's first American exposure, the logic of self-determination would conclude in a "Negro Soviet Republic."[149]

As a strategy, Black self-determination addressed itself to several concerns within the Comintern and the American movement. First of all, by the procedure through which it was established, it underlined the leadership of the Comintern over its national parties. Moreover, legitimated by the existence of other national liberation movements as well as the earlier history of American Blacks, it also relieved somewhat the disappointments of some Third Internationalists caused by the failure of an immediate world revolution to develop—national liberation struggles were by their nature protracted ones. As a political model, it was also useful as a means of expression for those nationalisms and chauvinisms of longer duration in the American Communist Party: many ideologues in the American movement identified their own nationalist sensibilities with Black nationalism.[150] Finally, it was believed it was the most effective means of approaching one of the oldest American peoples, the "Negro," first through its radical nationalist intelligentsia, and then its masses. Not only should self-determination attract Blacks, it was argued, but it could also be the litmus for determining the degree of progressiveness among non-Black party militants while weakening the ruling class by jarring the Bourbon pseudo-aristocracy from its industrial and finance-capitalist sponsors.

Still the theoretical basis for the party's identification of Blacks as a nation was quite unorthodox in terms of Marxist theory. Marx and Engels had both distinguished between "nations" and "nationalities," recognizing in the former the capacity for independent economic existence and in the latter an incapacity. Engels had expressed himself quite clearly:

> There is no country in Europe where there are not different nationalities under the same government. . . . Here, then, we perceive the difference between the "principles of *nationalities*" and the old democratic and working-class tenet as to the right of the great European *nations* to separate and independent existence. The "principle of nationalities" leaves entirely untouched the great question of the right of national existence for the historic peoples of Europe; nay if it touches it is merely to disturb it. The principle of nationalities raises two sorts of questions: first of all, questions of boundary between these great historic peoples; and secondly, questions as to the right to independent national existence of those numerous small relics of peoples which, after having figured for a longer or shorter period on the stage of history, were finally absorbed as integral portions into one or the other of those more powerful nations whose greater vitality enabled them to overcome greater obstacles.[151]

The logical extension from Marx or Engels would have been to identify the Blacks of America as a national minority or as a nationality, but not as a nation. For Marx and Engels, the nation was a quite particular historical phenomenon:

> Since the end of the Middle Ages, history has been moving towards a Europe made up of large national states. Only such national states constitute the normal political framework for the dominant European bourgeois class and, in addition, they are the indispensable prerequisites . . . without which the rule of the proletariat cannot exist.[152]

Engels's historicism branded the nation as an instrument of the bourgeoisie; its emergence was concomitant to the development of a bourgeois society, a capitalist society. And once nation and then the transnational became realized, it was possible for an international revolutionary movement to command the society that had produced it. For Marx, both language and culture appeared to be secondary phenomena, the first to be associated with nationality, the second, with the dominant class. Unfortunately, throughout the nineteenth century and into the next, much of the theoretical grammar brought by Marx, Engels, Lenin, and other Marxists to the analysis of American phenomena and processes was similarly naive. It was naive because of its ahistoricity and its tendency toward the use of aggregative concepts to the point of superfluousness. Ultimately, its naivete was contradictory: at the historical point of massive immigration, the application of race and class, the grammar's two most fundamental categories, presumed the existence among the majority of American workers of a white working class; thus the eventual appearance of a Black nation suggested an opposite historical momentum.[153] Lenin proved to be the theoretical and ideological midwife, but it was Stalin, it came to be believed in the American Communist Party and by its historians, who had provided the theoretical basis for the party's position that Blacks were a nation within a nation. "If there was a 'genius' in this scheme," Theodore Draper would declare, "it was undoubtedly Stalin."[154] However, the contrast between Stalin and Engels and Marx was dramatic. In what was to be one of the most frequently cited justifications for the Comintern's "Negro program," Stalin had entirely forsaken analytical sophistication:

> A nation is a historically established, stable community of people, coming into existence on the basis of a community of language, territory, economic life, and psychological constitution, which manifest themselves in a community of culture.[155]

This extraordinary passage is perhaps characteristic of Stalin's theoretical contributions to Marxist thought and to world knowledge. First, it too is ahistoric, since no contemporary nation has emerged in this way; second, it is abstract and vague, utilizing such phrases as "psychological constitution"; third, it is tautological: community manifests itself as community; and finally, it is not Marxian, tending as it does toward an evolutionary paradigm as opposed to that of historical materialism. Its one apposite feature was that it was in keeping with the ideological and programmatic opportunism that characterized Stalin's immediate predecessor. The policy implications of this passage fit quite well into the rationalizations found in *"Left-Wing" Communism.* This is, perhaps, another sort of proof that the policy was a gloss on the history of Black movements and not the independent product of the Soviet Union's political elite. Like formulations on other national liberation struggles one discovers in Comintern declarations, it was political opportunism searching for theoretical justifications. It thus represented the critical importance to the Soviet Party of forming alliances with movements that were emerging from theoretically "precapitalist" societies. Given historical necessity, Marxist-Leninism compromised itself theoretically with nationalism, and as such institutionalized the force that had brought the Second International to its submission. It might be said in the most simple-minded reading of the dialectic, that the Third International was a synthesis of the thesis (socialism) and anti-thesis (national chauvinism) of the Second.

As the official policy of the American Communist Party, self-determination—the Black Belt Thesis—would survive Stalin, but only barely. And even while Stalin was a dominant figure in the world Communist movement, it would have its ups and downs, responding to the national and international dynamics of the revolutionary movement.

> The policy of Negro self-determination has lived twice and died twice. After over-throwing Lovestone's "revisionism," Browder made self-determination one of the cardinal articles of faith of his leadership. In November 1943, long after it had ceased to show any signs of life, he delivered a funeral oration over the corpse of self-determination; he explained that the Negro people had already exercised the historical right of self-determination—by rejecting it. After overthrowing Brow-der's "revisionism," Foster made self-determination one of the cardinal articles of faith of his leadership. In 1946 self-determination was reincarnated in a slightly watered-down version—as a programmatic demand and not as an immediate slogan of action.
>
> In 1958, the Communist leadership again buried the corpse of the right of self-determination. It decided that the American Negro people were no longer a "stable community"; that the Negro national question was no longer "essentially a peasant question"; that the Negroes did not possess any distinctively "common psychologi-cal make-up"; that the main currents of Negro thought and leadership "histori-cally, and universally at the present time" flowed toward equality with other Ameri-cans; that the American Negro people did not constitute a nation; and therefore that the right of self-determination did not apply to them.[156]

Lenin had compelled the American Communist Party to take the Black American as a critical element in its policy and organization. Stalin, himself a member of a Russian national minority, had been the authority through which the Comintern and the American Communist Party had come to recognize Blacks as an oppressed nation.[157] And for a while the policies directly influenced by these two Bolsheviks had been successful: thousands of Blacks came into the CPUSA during the 1930s in response to the party's attentions and expressed intentions.[158] However, in the background were the UNIA and the Brotherhood. They had established the political and ideological preconditions for the party's policies and its successes. It was the UNIA that had embodied the Black radical tradition and primed the Black masses with a sense of nationhood. It was the UNIA and the ABB through which many of the early Black activists in the party had passed. And it was the UNIA and the Brotherhood that had demonstrated the capacities of Blacks to organize politically and respond ideo-logically. It remains a telling point on the nature of the early American Commu-nist movement that the significance of these examples had to depend upon Soviet-directed policy to be revealed.

In the light of this account of Russian and Comintern intervention into the affairs of the American Communist Party, it would appear to be a historical irony that it was through Du Bois's work that a first reassessment of Marxian revolutionary theory was attempted. It was Du Bois who introduced into American Marxism a critical interpretation of the nature and significance of revolution—based in large measure on the developments of the Russian Revolution and the American Reconstruction period.

Du Bois and Radical Theory

As a Black, Du Bois was sensitive to the contradictions in American society, in particular to the material force of racism. He was even more *conscious* of racism since in his early years he had been cocooned from it. He was a young man by the time he was forced to openly confront the culture of racism. Later, as a Black scholar, he had had an immediate and profound experience with the false histories produced in that culture. Both his training at Harvard with its history department largely influenced by German historiography, and his studies in Berlin had left him with an acute sensitivity for myth and propaganda in history. And as we have suggested earlier, as a critic of Marx, Du Bois had possessed no obligations to Marxist or Leninist dogma, nor to the vagaries of historical analysis and interpretation that characterized American Communist thought. Given these attributes, enveloped by the events of the post–World War I period, Du Bois obtained the skills to seize the advantage created by this crisis of capitalism:

> [S]omebody in each era must make clear the facts with utter disregard to his own wish and desire and belief. What we have got to know, so far as possible, are the things that actually happened in the world. . . . [T]he historian has no right, posing as scientist, to conceal or distort facts; and until we distinguish between these two functions of the chronicler of human action, we are going to render it easy for a muddled world out of sheer ignorance to make the same mistake ten times over. (p. 722)

He had written these words with American historiography in mind. But we may also assume he had an additional application at hand.

Among the several truths that Du Bois set out to establish in *Black Reconstruction*, there were a number that related directly to Marxist and Leninist theory. Specifically, his ideas concerned the emergence of capitalism; the nature of revolutionary consciousness; and the nature of revolutionary organization. As we recall, first Du Bois would insist on the world-historical significance of American slavery in the emergence of modern capitalism and imperialism. In this, he went no further than Marx, but this is merely where he began. Next, he would demonstrate, historically, the revolutionary force of slave and peasant laborers—this in opposition to a reactionary industrial working class. Finally, with Lenin in mind, Du Bois would question the presumed roles of a vanguard and the masses in the development of revolutionary consciousness and effective revolutionary action.

With regard to the first issue—the relationship between the destruction of slavery and the emergence of modern capitalism and imperialism—Du Bois argued that the American Reconstruction period was *the* historical moment in the developing world system. This was the moment when world capitalism assumed the character that would persist into the twentieth century:

> The abolition of American slavery started the transportation of capital from white to black countries where slavery prevailed, with the same tremendous and awful consequences upon the laboring classes of the world which we see about us today. When raw material could not be raised in a country like the United States, it could be raised in the tropics and semi-tropics under a dictatorship of industry, commerce and manufacture and with no free farming class.
>
> The competition of a slave-directed agriculture in the West Indies and South America, in Africa and Asia, eventually ruined the economic efficiency of agriculture in the United States and in Europe and precipitated the modern economic degradation of the white farmer, while it put into the hands of the owners of the machine such a monopoly of raw material that their domination of white labor was more and more complete. (p. 48)

According to Du Bois, this was not a necessary development but the one that followed upon the dismantling and destruction of the "dictatorship of labor" established in the southern United States during the Reconstruction:

> [T]here began to rise in America in 1876 a new capitalism and a new enslavement of labor. . . .
>
> The world wept because the exploiting group of New World masters, greed and jealousy became so fierce that they fought for trade and markets and materials and slaves all over the world until at last in 1914 the world flamed in war. The fantastic structure fell, leaving grotesque Profits and Poverty, Plenty and Starvation, Empire and Democracy, staring at each other across World Depression. (p. 634)

But rather than seeing this process as inevitable due to the contradiction between the modes of production and the relations of production, Du Bois argued that it was made possible by the ideologies of racism, and, to a lesser extent, individualism. It was these ideologies as historical forces that had precluded the emergence of a powerful labor movement in the United States—a movement whose nucleus would have consisted of the nine million ex-slave and white peasant workers of the South. The force of these ideologies manifested itself after the war when these workers did not move to the next logical step: the institutionalization of their historical convergence in order to dominate the Reconstruction's "dictatorship of labor." Without this movement, the revolution begun in 1855 with John Brown's Kansas raids could not continue.[159] The failure to achieve a consciousness of themselves as a class was not a consequence of the absence of the concentration of production in agriculture, as some Marxists might presume, for in the North workers had had this experience, yet their labor movement was predominantly trade-unionist.[160] On the other hand, in the South, where the character of production with regard to the concentration of labor was more ambiguous, it was these workers, Black and white, who had produced the "General Strike" decisive in ending the Civil War.

The General Strike had not been planned or consciously organized. Instead, what Du Bois termed a "General Strike" was the total impact on the secessionist South of a series of actions circumstantially related to each other: some 200,000 Black workers, most of them slaves, had become part of the Union's military forces. These, and an even larger number of Blacks, had withdrawn their productive labor and paramilitary services from the Confederacy, transferring a substantial portion of them to the Union. In addition, tens of thousands of slaves and poor whites had emigrated from the South. The former were escaping slavery, the latter their poverty and the demands and ravages of a war in which they had no vested interest. The result was to critically weaken the secessionists. The ordering of these diverse actions was then a consequence of the social order to which they were reactions. The contradictions within southern society rather than a revolutionary vanguard knit these phenomena into a historical force. After the war, a different ordering would be required to integrate these phenomena into a political movement. This could be accomplished if only the ruling ideologies of the society were transcended. This was not done.

> [T]he power of the Negro vote in the South was certain to go gradually toward reform.
>
> It was this contingency that the poor whites of all grades feared. It meant to them a reestablishment of that subordination under Negro labor which they had suffered during slavery. They, therefore, interposed by violence to increase the natural antagonism between Southerners of the planter class and Northerners who represented the military dictatorship as well as capital. . . .
>
> The efforts at reform, therefore, at first widely applauded, one by one began to go down before a new philosophy which represented understanding between the planters and poor whites. . . . [I]t was accompanied by . . . eagerness on the part of the poor whites to check the demands of the Negroes by any means, and by willingness to do the dirty work of the revolution that was coming, with its blood and crass cruelties, its bitter words, upheaval and turmoil. This was the birth and being of the Ku Klux Klan. (p. 623)

But it was not merely a matter of the antagonisms of the poor whites against the Blacks being revitalized by the prominence assumed by the latter during the Reconstruction. The "deep economic foundation" for these antagonisms was in fact being challenged by proposals to radically alter land tenure put forward by Black legislators. Rather, it was the remnants of the southern ruling class that focused the attention of poor whites on to the Black workers. The ruling class had been so weakened by the war that for the first time it was forced to aggressively recruit poor whites as its allies. "The masters feared their former slaves. . . . They lied about the Negroes. . . . They forestalled the danger of a united Southern labor movement by appealing to the fear and hate of white labor. . . . They encouraged them to ridicule Negroes and beat them, kill and burn their bodies. The planters even gave the poor whites their daughters in marriage" (p. 633).

It was in this fashion that the bond between the two elements of the southern working class failed to materialize. By necessity, Du Bois felt, Blacks fixed class alliances with northern capitalists and petit bourgeois Radical Republicans. Both alliances were by nature short-lived. Once Northern capital had sufficiently penetrated the southern economic sector so as to dominate its future development, it ceased to depend on Black electorates and state legislatures responsive to Blacks and the radical petit bourgeoisie. The alliance ended with the withdrawal of Federal troops from the South and the destruction of the governments supported by the bureaucracy of occupation. By the 1880s, the under-capitalized character of southern agrarian production was established and the need for external sources of raw materials more than apparent. In Mexico, the Philippines, Haiti, the Caribbean and Pacific islands, and elsewhere, northern capitalists constructed their own forms of slavery: but ones for which they could not easily be held accountable or among which they would be compelled to live.

Turning now to the question of revolutionary consciousness and organization, it is again Du Bois's presentation of the General Strike that provides a critique of Marxist thought. But first we should recall just what constituted Marxist theory in America at the time.

At the time of Du Bois's writing of *Black Reconstruction*, Marxism came in several forms depending on which revolutionary or intellectual tradition one considered. Raphael Samuel has maintained that such "mutations of Marxism" were to be expected and, indeed, had been preceded by changes in Marx's own writings:[161]

> In Russia Marxism came into existence as a critical trend within populism, in Italy in the form of a syncretism with positivist sociology, in Austria—and Bulgaria—in tandem with the thought of Lassalle. Second International Marxism was a heterodox affair, with numerous tendencies competing for political attention, and nothing approaching a finished body of doctrine. Marxism was necessarily superimposed on preexisting modes of thought which it incorporated rather than displaced, and which were regarded as being intrinsic to the new outlook. . . .
>
> The contours change radically in the period of the Third International, but Marxism, despite its increasingly Party-minded character, was very far from being hermetically sealed. In the 1920s there was a vigorous, indeed furious, philosophical debate within the Soviet Union itself, with rival schools contending in the name of dialectical materialism.[162]

But generally, in the order of prestige in revolutionary socialism, first were the available works of Marx and Engels and their nearest contemporaries in Europe and Russia.[163] These constituted the classical texts of Marxism. Second, there were the works of the Soviet intelligentsia, Plekhanov, Lenin, Bukharin, Trotsky, and Stalin.[164]

From 1917 on, these writings became more significant to the socialist movement. With the bureaucratization of the Russian Revolution and the institutionalization of the Comintern, Stalin and his interpretations of Lenin's thought ultimately superseded all other Marxist writers in authority.

> All serious theoretical work ceased in the Soviet Union after collectivization. Trotsky was driven into exile in 1929, and assassinated in 1940; Ryazanov was stripped of his positions in 1931 and died in a labour camp in 1939; Bukharin was silenced in 1929 and shot in 1938; Preobrazhensky was broken by 1930 and perished in jail in 1938. Marxism was largely reduced to a memento in Russia, as Stalin's rule reached its apogee.[165]

In the United States, dichotomies reflecting the conflicts in Europe and Russia could be found. But in America, Party propagandists were much more prominent than independent theorists. The presence of theorists in the party had been substantially reduced by the events of the late 1920s and early 1930s. The expulsions of a "Trotskyite" left followed by the "Lovestone" right; the spectacle of the purges of veterans of the Russian Revolution from the Bolshevik Party; the compromises of the Popular Front period after 1933; and the protracted demise of capitalism, had all taken their toll, especially on revolutionary theory:

> Marx's emphasis upon the historic inevitability of revolution had diminishing importance for Party members and left intellectuals alike in the thirties. Communists may have claimed Marxism as their own, but it was merely a ceremonial claim after the Popular Front had been announced. There were, however, few times in CP history when Marxist theory was applied in a serious and sustained analysis of American society. And even the non-Communist intellectual . . . made only infrequent and incomplete stabs at such analyses.[166]

Revolution had been relegated to the background while more pressing needs—like support for the New Deal; the pursuit of "collective security" for the Soviet Union; the organization of the new unionism represented by the Congress of Industrial Organizations (CIO); and the fight for state assistance to the unemployed and elderly—assumed priority. Finally, though Marxism might continue to develop elsewhere within the nexus of Communist Parties, in Europe its further elaboration in the thirties seems to have been confined to Germany, France, and Italy. And even then, as Perry Anderson suggests, the tradition was strained:

> Astonishingly, within the entire corpus of Western Marxism, there is not one single serious appraisal or sustained critique of the work of one major theorist by another, revealing close textual knowledge or minimal analytic care in its treatment. At most, there are cursory aspersions or casual commendations, both equally ill-read and superficial. Typical examples of this mutual slovenliness are the few vague remarks directed by Sartre at Lukács; the scattered and anachronistic asides of Adorno on Sartre; the virulent invective of Colletti against Marcuse; the amateur

confusion of Althusser between Gramsci and Colletti; the peremptory dismissal by Della Volpe of Althusser.[167]

Still, much was in disarray.

Despite the shared premise that human emancipation was to be identical with the achievement of the socialist revolution, the writings produced by Marxian theorists contained serious disagreements and differences with respect to the historical processes and structural elements involved in the emergence of the revolution. Among the areas of contention were questions regarding the nature of class consciousness; the role of a revolutionary party; and the political nature of the peasantry and other "precapitalist" laboring classes. Since it is impossible to even summarize the volume of conflicting opinion to be found in Marxist literature, we will concern ourselves with only those aspects to which Du Bois addressed himself.[168]

Marx and Engels had argued that the alienation intrinsic to the capitalist mode of production, the contradictions arising between that mode and the social relations accompanying it, and the extension of expropriation could result in a socialist revolution led by the industrial working classes. Though the revolution itself was not inevitable (that would have amounted to economic determinism), the role of this specific kind of worker in such a revolution was certain.[169] The historical dialectic identified the industrial worker—the proletariat—as the negation of capitalist society; the force produced by capitalism that could finally destroy it. Capitalism pitted one class, the bourgeoisie, against another, the proletariat. This was the specific character of the class struggle in capitalist society. However, since there were more than two classes in all the nineteenth-century societies that Marx and Engels studied, it became necessary for them to identify and assign to these other classes particular historical roles. The petit bourgeoisie were both nominally and historically the middlemen of capitalism: its managers, technicians, small merchants, and shopkeepers. Unlike the bourgeoisie, the petit bourgeoisie did not own or control the means of production. Still, it was a class whose members recognized their dependence on the bourgeoisie for social privileges. Their political loyalties were to the bourgeoisie and as such they were understood to be reactionary by their class-nature.[170] A fourth class, the lumpen-proletariat, too, was reactionary. The class was characterized as one that fed off the proletariat in a parasitic manner. The lumpen-proletariat were the thieves, the thugs, the prostitutes, "people without a definite occupation and a stable domicile."[171] It was from this class that the society recruited many of those who would form its coercive instruments: the army, the state militias, the police. The fifth class was the peasantry. This was the class that came closest to the poor whites and Black workers of the antebellum period in terms of its systemic relationship to industrial capitalism, its social organization, and its historical origins.[172] For Marx and Engels, the peasantry was a remnant of the precapitalist society. But unlike other residues from feudalism, for example, the clergy, the aristocracy, and the artisan-craftsmen, the peasantry continued to be of importance in capitalist society. Both the peasantry and the bourgeoisie had been negations of feudalism, however the peasantry's "narrow-minded" self-interest had been intent on destroying feudalist relations by moving historically backward to small, individual land-holdings and away from the inclusive, nationally integrated economic structures for which the bourgeoisie aspired. In feudalism, the bourgeoisie had been a historically progressive contradiction, and the peasantry a historically reactionary negation. With the destruction of feudalism by capitalist forces, the peasantry became reactionary in a different way. The peasantry was now a potential ally of the bourgeoisie to be poised against the political force of industrial labor and the socialist revolution.

Lenin and Trotsky, coming from Tsarist Russia, a society dominated by a peasant-subsistence or "backward" economy, saw the peasantry differently from Marx or Engels.[173] In the central and western Russian countryside at the end of the nineteenth century, the remnants of Russian "feudalism" were to be found in the aristocracy and the poor peasantry. There were, too, the *kulaks* consisting of a rural bourgeoisie supported by capitalist agriculture, and a middle peasantry essentially locked into modified forms of subsistence agriculture. The roving peasantry, the rural proletariat, according to Lenin, emerged from the poor peasants who worked either for the *kulaks*, the landlords or some exceptional middle peasants. Both Lenin and Trotsky agreed that the rural relations of production were subject to "internal" antagonisms of class struggle (*kulaks* versus poor peasants) and, most importantly, that the peasantry could be an ally to the working-class movement. In 1901, for example, Lenin had observed:

> Our rural laborers are still too closely connected with the peasantry, they are still too heavily burdened with the misfortunes of the peasantry generally, to enable the movement of rural workers to assume national significance either now or in the immediate future . . . the whole essence of our agrarian programme is that the rural proletariat must fight together with the rich peasantry for the abolition of the remnants of serfdom, for the cut-off lands.[174]

But in 1905, after several years of recurring peasant uprisings, his view of the "rural proletariat" was more sanguine: "We must explain to it that its interests are antagonistic to those of the bourgeois peasantry; we must call upon it to fight for the socialist revolution.[175] Though Trotsky and Lenin were opposed to the "Black Partition" (Marx's term for the extra-legal seizure and breaking up of land into small, individual holdings), they saw it as a tactic for momentarily attracting the peasantry to the side of the revolution. Once the dictatorship of the proletariat was secured, other arrangements could be made for the peasants.[176]

Part of the reason for the judgments made by Marx or Engels of the peasantry had to do with the conditions of work that circumscribed peasant production and the social relations that fixed the peasants into prescribed links of exchange. Marx saw the peasantry as a "vast mass" consisting of functional clones: simple cultivators, proximate but without significant intercourse; lacking in all but the most rudimentary political organization or consciousness.[177] Engels, too, was impressed by the "great space" that peasants occupied, and ascribed to them a tradition of submissiveness and loyalty to particular masters.[178] Neither suggested that the peasantry was capable of independent political action. And if we compared the descriptions found in Marx and Engels of peasant life with those of Du Bois concerning the slaves and poor whites, we would discover striking and important similarities. Of the slave workers, Du Bois commented:

> [B]efore the war, the slave was curiously isolated; this was the policy, and the effective policy of the slave system, which made the plantation the center of a black group with a network of white folk around and about, who kept the slaves from contact with each other. Of course, clandestine contact there always was; the passing of Negroes to and fro on errands; particularly the semi-freedom and mingling in cities; and yet, the mass of slaves were curiously provincial and kept out of the currents of information. (pp. 121–22)

In the masters' domiciles, the complexities of the relationships between labor and the exploiters of labor many times included bonds of sentiment, but more importantly and persistently the house servants had realized "The masters had stood between them and a world in which they had no legal protection except the master." And that "The masters were their source of information"(p. 123). Earlier in the work, Du Bois had suggested, "Any mass movement under such circumstances must materialize slowly and painfully" (p. 57). And of the poor white workers, ignored as he believed by the American labor movement, the abolitionists, northern capitalists and southern planters, Du Bois reckoned similarly pessimistic judgments could be made. He reiterated Francis Simkins's and Robert Woody's bleak description of their conditions:

> A wretched log hut or two are the only habitations in sight. Here reside, or rather take shelter, the miserable cultivators of the ground, or a still more destitute class who make a precarious living by peddling "lightwood" in the city. . . .
>   These cabins . . . are dens of filth. . . . Their faces are bedaubed with the muddy accumulation of weeks. . . . The poor wretches seem startled when you address them, and answer your questions cowering like culprits. (p. 26)

Du Bois added that the poor whites were also bound to the master class: "Indeed, the natural leaders of the poor whites, the small farmer, the merchant, the professional man, the white mechanic and slave overseer, were bound to the planters and repelled from the slaves. . . . [T]he only heaven that attracted them was the life of the great Southern planter" (p. 27). Yet in the midst of the Civil War, it was these two peoples, the Black and the white workers, who had mounted the rebellions, the "General Strike," which had turned loose the revolutionary dynamics that Du Bois would describe as "the most extraordinary experiments of Marxism that the world, before the Russian revolution, had seen" (p. 358). One hundred thousand poor whites had deserted the Confederate armies and perhaps a half million Black workers had abandoned the plantations. It was the same pattern, indeed, that would come to fruition in Russia. Like the American slaves and the poor whites, in the midst of war the Russian peasantry would desert their armies in the field. Their rebellion, too, marked the beginnings of revolution.

Like most informed men and women of his time, Du Bois was deeply impressed by the Russian Revolution and he believed he could write and speak of it without having "to dogmatize with Marx or Lenin."[179] He had referred to what he considered a significant element of the revolution as early as 1917 when he criticized the American Socialist Party's ideologues for praising the successes of the Russian peasantry while ignoring the achievements of American Blacks:

> Revolution is discussed, but it is the successful revolution of white folk and not the unsuccessful revolution of black soldiers in Texas. You do not stop to consider whether the Russian peasant had any more to endure than the black soldiers of the 24th Infantry.[180]

The processes of the Russian Revolution were a framework for his interpretation of Reconstruction because it, too, had begun among an agrarian, peasant people. It was a characteristic shared by all the revolutions that Du Bois linked in significance to the American Civil War and its Reconstruction: that is, France, Spain, India, and China (p. 708). In addition, since before his visit to the Soviet Union in 1926, he had been cautious about the nature of class-consciousness among workers in Russia, the United States, and elsewhere. In 1927, when he had returned from the Soviet Union, he had written:

> Does this mean that Russia has "put over" her new psychology? Not by any means. She is trying and trying hard, but there are plenty of people in Russia who still hate and despise the workingman's blouses and the peasant's straw shoes; and plenty of workers who regret the passing of the free-handed Russian nobility, who miss the splendid pageantry of the Czars and who cling doggedly to religious dogma and superstition.[181]

And despite his note to the tenth chapter of *Black Reconstruction,* which explained why he was not using his original title for that chapter ("The Dictatorship of the Black Proletariat in South Carolina"),[182] Du Bois knew the Russian Revolution was a dictatorship of the proletariat that was less democratic and less dependent upon conscious action of the workers than was to be found in the post–Civil War period in America:

> As the [Russian] workingman is today neither skilled nor intelligent to any such extent as his responsibilities demand, there is within his ranks the Communist Party, directing the proletariat toward their future dictatorship. This is nothing new.[183]

And in 1938, Du Bois would declare:

> When now the realities of the situation were posed to men, two radical solutions were suddenly resorted to: Russian communism and fascism. They both did away

with democracy, and substituted oligarchic control of government and industry of thought and action. Communism aimed at eventual democracy and even elimination of the state, but sought this by a dogmatic program, laid down ninety years ago by a great thinker, but largely invalidated by nearly a century of extraordinary social change.[184]

Like Lenin, but for different reasons and in a different way, Du Bois had realized that Marx had not anticipated the historical transformations of capitalism, specifically, the complicating phenomena of imperialism. And caution, as well, was required in any application of Marx to the situation of American Blacks:

> It was a great loss to American Negroes that the great mind of Marx and his extraordinary insight into industrial conditions could not have been brought to bear at first hand upon the history of the American Negro between 1876 and the World War. Whatever he said and did concerning the uplift of the working class must, therefore, be modified so far as Negroes are concerned by the fact that he had not studied at first hand their peculiar race problem here in America.[185]

This left a monumental gap in the analysis of capitalism and its developments, assigning Marx's own work to a specific historical period. Du Bois would conclude, while working on *Black Reconstruction*, that "we can only say, as it seems to me, that the Marxian philosophy is a true diagnosis of the situation in Europe in the middle of the nineteenth century despite some of its logical difficulties."[186]

In American Marxism, Lenin had largely replaced Marx as the definitive revolutionary thinker by the early 1920s. Where Marx had anticipated and depended upon the rise of class consciousness, Lenin had posited the party in its stead. For Lenin, the party, a small group of trained, disciplined, and professional revolutionists, constituted a necessary first stage in the development of the dictatorship of the proletariat. The party would deliberately and scientifically create the conditions for the evolution of worker consciousness and for socialism. Where Marx had presumed that a bourgeois society established by a bourgeois revolution was a necessary condition for the evolution of a conscious socialist movement. Lenin, in April of 1917, would declare that the process had been completed in Russia in less than three months.[187]

Du Bois had been skeptical of Marx and Lenin on both scores. In *Black Reconstruction*, he reviewed the events of the American post bellum with a Hegelian sense of the "cunning of Reason." The slaves freed themselves, Du Bois thought, not by way of an objective consciousness of their condition but rather by the dictates of religious myth:

> The mass of slaves, even the more intelligent ones, and certainly the great group of field hands, were in religious and hysterical fervour. This was the coming of the Lord. This was the fulfillment of prophecy and legend. It was the Golden Dawn, after chains of a thousand years. It was everything miraculous and perfect and promising. (p. 122)

And the other figures in the drama of emancipation, from Lincoln down to the poor whites, were just as much overtaken by the unintended consequences of their actions:

Lincoln had never been an Abolitionist; he had never believed in full Negro citizenship; he had tried desperately to win the war without Negro soldiers, and he had emancipated the slaves only on account of military necessity. (p. 153)

Freedom for the slave was the logical result of a crazy attempt to wage war in the midst of four million black slaves, and trying the while sublimely to ignore the interests of those slaves in the outcome of the fighting. (p. 121)

Leaders, then, led in increments. The northern field officers who put the fugitive slaves to work did not intend to free them . . . but they did. The Confederacy moved to preserve slavery . . . it helped to end it. Groups moved to the logic of immediate self-interest and to historical paradox. Consciousness, when it did develop, had come later in the process of the events. The revolution had *caused* the formation of revolutionary consciousness and had not been caused by it. The revolution was spontaneous.

To the second point, the precondition of bourgeois society, Du Bois maintained that no bourgeois society was the setting of this revolution. The dominant ideology of the society was that of the plantocracy, a dictatorship of labor and land with no democratic pretensions. But of more significance, the ideology of the plantocracy had not been the ideology of the slaves. The slaves had produced their own culture and their own consciousness by adapting the forms of the non-Black society to the conceptualizations derived from their own historical roots and social conditions. In some instances, indeed, elements produced by the slave culture had become the dominant ones in white southern culture. The process had spanned generations: "[T]he rolling periods of Hebrew prophecy and biblical legend furnished inaccurate but splendid words. The subtle folk-lore of Africa, with whimsy and parable, veiled wish and wisdom; and above all fell the anointed chrism of the slave music, the only gift of pure art in America" (p. 14). This was the human experience from which the rebellion rose. Torn from it were the principles of "right and wrong, vengeance and love . . . sweet Beauty and Truth" that would serve as guideposts to the ex-slaves. It was the tradition critical to the framing of the survival of these new people.

Du Bois, despite all the diversions and distractions of intellect, social origins, and ambition that had marked his even then long life, had at last come to the Black radical tradition. In the midst of the most fearsome maelstrom his age had seen, and with the pitiable reaction of the declared revolutionary opposition in mind, his purposeful interrogation of the past had led him to the hidden specter of Black revolutionists. Their revolution had failed, of course. And with its failure had gone the second and truer possibility of an American democracy. But until the writing of *Black Reconstruction*, the only mark on American historical consciousness left by their movement had been a revised legend of their savagery. Du Bois had understood, finally, that this was insufficient. "Somebody in each era," he had written, "must make clear the facts." With that declaration, the first ledger of radical Black historiography had been filled."[188]

In *Black Reconstruction*, Du Bois had striven to enrich the critique of capitalism and bourgeois society that had merged into the dominant strains of Western radicalism. He had no choice if he was to comprehend the crises of war and depression that devastated the world system in his lifetime, and the rebellion and revolution in Asia, Europe, Africa, and the New World that were their concomitants. Du Bois came to believe that the preservation of the capitalist world system, its very expansion in the nineteenth and twentieth centuries, had involved the absorption of new sources of labor power, not by their conversion into wage labor but by coercion. Characteristically, capitalist imperialism had magnified the capacity for capital accumulation by force variously disguised as state nationalism, benevolent colonialism, race destiny, or the civilizing mission. Except in scattered instances, the peasantries of the Third World had become neither urban nor rural proletariats but near-slaves. For most, their social development had been effectively arrested. The result, relative to their own recent pasts and the situation of European workers, was retardation. Indeed, whole populations had been eliminated either during "pacification" or through forced labor. The belief that capitalism would advance African and Asian and other peasantries had for the most part proved to be misplaced. Beyond Western Europe, the capitalist world system had produced social and economic chaos. No theory of history that conceptualized capitalism as a progressive historical force, qualitatively increasing the mastery of human beings over the material bases of their existence, was adequate to the task of making the experiences of the modern world comprehensible. For Du Bois, America in the first half of the nineteenth century, a society in which manufacturing and industrial capitalism had been married to slave production, had been a microcosm of the world system. The advanced sectors of the world economy could expand just so long as they could dominate and rationalize by brute force the exploitation of essentially nonindustrial and agrarian labor. The expansion of American slavery in the nineteenth century was not an anachronism but a forewarning. But so too, he believed, was its defeat.

It was also true, as Marx, Engels, and others had anticipated, that there were contradictions to the world economy and the systems of coercion upon which it depended. However, Du Bois came to perceive that they were not limited to the contradictions discerned by the radical Western intelligentsia. In the long run, that is, by the beginnings of the twentieth century, the vision of the destruction of bourgeois society entertained by Western socialists had been shown to be of only partial relevance. The working classes of Europe and America had indeed mounted militant assaults on their ruling classes. But in defeat they had also displayed their vulnerabilities to bourgeois nationalism and racialist sentiment. Elsewhere other realities had too come to the fore. The shocks to Western imperialism, which in the previous century had appeared to European radicals to be at the margins of the world revolution, were by the 1930s occupying center stage. The Indian Mutiny, the Boxer Rebellion, the nationalist struggles that had erupted in the Sudan, Algeria, Morocco, Somalia, Abyssinia, West and southern Africa, and carried over into the twentieth century—the "people's wars"—had achieved major historical significance in the revolutions in Mexico, China, and Russia. And in every instance, peasants and agrarian workers had been the primary social bases of rebellion and revolution. Nowhere, not even in Russia, where a rebellious urban proletariat was a fraction of the mobilized working classes, had a bourgeois social order formed a precondition for revolutionary struggle. Revolutionary consciousness had formed in the process of anti-imperialist and nationalist struggles, and the beginnings of resistance had often been initiated by ideological constructions remote from the proletarian consciousness that was a presumption of Marx's theory of revolution. The idiom of revolutionary consciousness had been historical and cultural rather than the "mirror of production." The oppositions that had struck most deeply at capitalist domination and imperialism had been those formed outside the logic of bourgeois hegemony. In *Black Reconstruction*, Du Bois had tried to give these processes a concrete, historical appearance. Again he had had very little choice in the matter. The ideology of the Black struggle, the revolutionary consciousness of the slaves, had appeared to his Westernized eyes, part legend, part whimsy, part art. Yet he realized it had been sufficient to arouse them into mass resistance and had provided them with a vision of the world they preferred. Their collective action had achieved the force of a historical antilogic to racism, slavery, and capitalism.

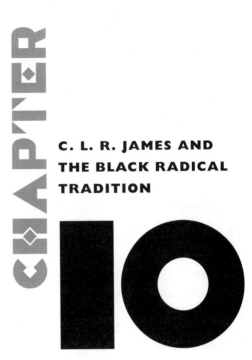

C. L. R. JAMES AND THE BLACK RADICAL TRADITION

10

Black Labor and the Black Middle Classes in Trinidad

In the warm Caribbean Sea, where colonies of African labor were compressed on to the Antilles—the tropic archipelago that serpentined its way from the open claw of the Yucatan and Floridian peninsulas of Central and North America to the northern crowns of Venezuela and Colombia in South America—the same Black antilogic extended itself into the twentieth century. In the earlier century, it had destroyed the plantation economy upon which the momentum of African slavery rested.[1] But the Africanization of the islands—their transformation from forced labor into peasant economies where daily life was mediated by the cultural syncretisms of the diaspora— had been incomplete. Political power had been transferred from the venal order of the plantocracies to an uneasy accommodation between the imperial bureaucracy at the metropoles and the highest strata among the entrenched white minorities. Even Haiti, to employ the language of Rainboro again, was witnessing the destruction of democracy by property in fear of poverty.[2] In the British possessions, racial arrogance assumed the posture of trusteeship over the islands' Black populations and determined its proper structure should be that of the system of crown colonies.

> The Colonial Office soon realized . . . that the West Indies were quite unsuited for self-government. How could assemblies so blatantly unrepresentative of the bulk of the population be granted responsibility, asked the veteran civil servant, Sir Henry Taylor? As the islands were fast becoming financial liabilities, the old representative

constitutions became a bar to good government. The new free populations could never by "represented" under existing conditions. Thus the idea took root that the West Indies should be persuaded to reconsider their constitutions and become crown colonies.

By 1875 all the Caribbean colonies except Barbados (to which might be added the Bahamas and Bermuda) agreed to give up their old constitutions and become Crown colonies. In 1868 the colonial secretary announced that the new legislative councils would all have a basic feature: "that the power of the Crown in the Legislature, if pressed to its extreme limit, would avail to overcome every resistance that could be made at it." In other words, the British government had stepped into the West Indies to protect the population from the power of the former slave-owning class.[3]

The alternative, as was demonstrated by the Black rebellion in Jamaica in 1865, was to suffer the colonial oligarchy's inadvertent but constant encouragement to violent Black militancy.[4] This, we may surmise, was an unacceptable political risk to the architects and guardians of the Empire whose over-extended charge had already absorbed the disastrous mutiny in the Indian sepoy army in 1857 (and the subsequent occupation of India by British troops),[5] and was as well a senior and chartered member in the European "scramble" for Africa and Asia. Neither the English people themselves nor the masses of imperial subjects could be expected to perpetually accede to the imperial myth of civilizing in the face of the overtly selfish and cata-strophic preoccupations of white settler colonists.

For the Black peasants and workers in the British West Indies, however, the "new imperialism" that displaced the Caribbean oligarchy was by far the more formidable enemy. While government power in the British home isles ricocheted between the Liberal and Conservative parties, as it had after the Reform Bills of 1867 and 1884, while state policy staggered between "free trade, free production, the freedom of nationalities" (that is, home rule for the Irish and Welsh), and anti-imperialism[6] and the alternative of aggressive, jingoistic imperialism, popular support for a global British presence was measurably inconstant. Even a Select Committee of the House of Commons, as early as 1865 had "recommended that most British colonies should be given up as soon as possible and that they should be prepared for independence."[7] An industrialized Britain was then more than a match for its European rivals and its domestic economy reflected its international domination of commerce. But in the last decades of the nineteenth century, "Britain was and knew herself to be threatened by 'empires.'"[8] Sandwiched between the diplomatic and mercantile momenta of Germany, France, Russia, and the United States, overdrawn by financial scandal and mismanagement, the weakened British economy and a restive public encouraged and compelled the imperialist faction that, until then, could only pursue its vision with restraint. Even the final liberal government of the nineteenth century (1892–95) was overwhelmed by the imperialist ethos.[9] By the fateful Conservative victory in 1895, imperialism had come to dominate the public mind. With its offer of new markets for a diminished trade, new lands for British settlement, with its new nationalistic "half-penny" press and its imperialist literati and intelligentsia,[10] the imperialism of the businessman's Parliament, masked as national interest and destiny, seemed to fulfill the wildest fancy:

No doubt [in 1891] the population of Great Britain barely exceeded 38,000,000, but there were nearly 2,000,000 British subjects in Cape Colony and Natal, over 600,000 in New Zealand, over 3,000,000 in Australia, and 5,000,000 in Canada. Add to these figures the Indian subjects of Great Britain, almost 300,000,000, and a further 46,000,000 in the remaining territories under some form of British rule or influence and the total amounted to 394,600,000. What other State could hope to rival such a figure. . . . The area of the Empire was also on the increase: in September 1896, a statesman calculated that in twelve years 2,600,000 square miles had been added to it—that is to say twenty-four times the area of Great Britain. In 1895, it was 11,335,000 square miles. A few more annexations and it would amount to a quarter of the entire land surface of the globe.

This was the object which the convinced imperialists deliberately pursued.[11]

For another two generations, the lives of the West Indian masses and those of other colonial subjects would be directly affected by representatives of a ruling class bathed by its self-manufactured glory and whose monumental conceit hid from it the source and scale of the horrors with which it would be associated. As if to satisfy Marx's contempt and add to Engels's class humiliation, the English bourgeoisie and its European confederates sank into the historical swamp of pretentious imperialism and counter-preening nationalisms from which the carnivore of global warfare disgorged. Reckless provocations, diplomatic inanition (followed by its military genus) and intoxications with empire inexorably led the ruling classes of Europe to that destruction of their means of production and their labor forces that they signified with the name "World War."

In Trinidad, during the seven-plus decades between the formal abolition of slavery in the British possessions and the slaughter of a generation in the early twentieth century, the massive withdrawal of labor from the plantations by the Africans and Creoles[12] had led to some dramatic countermoves on the part of the sugar estates companies and the planters.[13] With the moral pretensions of the abolitionists still resonating in public discourse, the former owners of Black labor resorted to pseudo-Calvinist rhetoric to elicit support from Parliament for their next exercise in the exploitation of labor. Their leading spokesman, William Burnley, lamented

the paucity of the labouring population, which prevents competition among them; and they are enabled to make more money than is good and advantageous for them which I consider to be the great cause why, instead of advancing in moral improvement, they are rather retrograding at the present period; for I hold that it is impossible for any moral improvement to take place in a community where the want of a good character and a good reputation interpose no serious obstacle to a man gaining a lucrative employment.[14]

New immigrants, they all agreed, would be necessary. The competition of immigrant labor would discipline Trinidad's Black workers to reasonable wages and regular hours of labor. This would, in turn, make it possible for British sugar producers to undermine the slave sugar of their foreign competitors in the European market. "Free Trade, after all, meant the free movement of men as well as of goods."[15]

There were three possible sources of immigrant labor that were immediately at hand: the other islands of the West Indies; the free Negroes of the United States; and the Africans liberated by the Royal Navy from "illegal" slave ships along the West African coast. None of these sources, however, proved sufficient. Although an estimated 10,278 West Indians immigrated to Trinidad between 1839 and 1849 (in the same period another 7,582 went to British Guiana), and between 1841 and 1861, 3,581 liberated Africans from Sierra Leone and St. Helena arrived, and an even smaller number of free Blacks made their way from Delaware, Maryland, New Jersey, Pennsylvania, and New York, the lure of Trinidad's sugar fields was shortlived, the sources of immigration too irregular.[16] Somewhat tardily, indeed, following the leads of Parliament, the East India Company and the planters of British Guiana, the Trinidadian ruling class and its metropole partners turned their attention to India.[17] For the next 70 years, from 1845 to 1917, Indian indentured labor became the basis for the sugar plantations of western Trinidad.[18] "Indians, both indentured and free, had become the backbone of Trinidad's plantation labor force by about 1860."[19]

> About 143,000 Indians came to Trinidad up to 1917. Immigration began in 1845; there was a break in 1848–51; then from 1851 right down to 1917 Indians arrived steadily each year. Between 1845 and 1892, 93,569 labourers came, channelled through two main Indian ports, Calcutta in the North, and Madras in the South. The great majority, however, came from Calcutta and after 1872 there were no more arrivals from Madras.[20]

They were, for the most part, peasants from the northeast of India, the United Provinces (now Uttar Pradesh), and Bihar, and amounted to a mere fraction of the hundreds of thousands of Indians who abandoned the region in the nineteenth century's last decades to find their ways to the West Indies, Fiji, Natal, and Nepal.

> This area, the seat of ancient cultures, was overpopulated and economically depressed in the later part of the nineteenth century. The extreme heat in the summer, the floods in the monsoon leading to whole-scale destruction of crops, and the recurrent famines made life difficult under the British rule. Rural indebtedness was appalling and agriculture was "by no means an easy business by which to make a living." Moreover, the Mutiny-cum-Revolt of 1857 had a disastrous socioeconomic effect on this region.[21]

Propelled by these circumstances into the far extremities of the British colonial system, they brought with them their culture: their languages, their castes, their music, and their religions.[22] And up to the First World War, it came to be accepted that they served in Trinidad as a "substantial counterpoise against troubles with the negroes and vice versa."[23] "Coolie" labor, to be sure, had provided momentary succor for sugar production. And Trinidad's economy, diversified by cocoa production and, in the last decades of the nineteenth century, oil and asphalt industries,[24] rode above the depression that visited the other West Indian monocultures in the last quarter of that century. But a deeper social process was occurring, one beneath the apparent antipathy between "coolie" and Creole. Where they were thrown together, the existential vice of labor was drawing East and West Indian into certain cultural approximations:

> In 1865 a fierce riot over precedence broke out between the Indians of Woodford Lodge and Endeavour Estate at Chaguanas. Creoles and Chinese went to the help of their workmates; loyalties to the estate transcended those of race in the fighting. . . .
>
> Rowdy elements among the Creoles were joining in the Hosein celebrations in the 1850s. For them it was like Donnybrook Fair where people went in the hope of a fight. But also Negroes began to take a more respectable part in the procession as drummers for which they were paid in rum or cash, and, as in Mauritius in the 1850s, the *taziyas* were sometimes borne by Negroes.[25]

The significance of these events should have been clear, but the whites were deceived by their discourse of domination.[26] That error was of strategic proportions in a society that by the opening decades of the next century was 4 percent white, 15 percent mulatto, 1 percent Chinese, and 80 percent of African and East Indian origins and descent.[27]

The dead season of collective resistance in Trinidad, the time up to the earliest years of the twentieth century, was both real and partially imagined. Because "the Creole population had nearly all withdrawn from the estates,"[28] it was certainly not until they were drawn as workers to the docks, the railways, and public works, and to the oil fields and asphalt works that they would obtain an effective cause and objective circumstance to openly challenge the crown and the white minority. Meanwhile, they claimed their liberation in other ways:

> Black labourers in Trinidad, during this period, reacted to the oppressive society they lived in by attempting to reduce their dependence on the plantation, by seeking to create an area of freedom for themselves, however limited. They tried to become peasants or artisans; if they failed, they drifted to the towns. In the towns, constant urban unrest reflected an awareness of oppression. The bands fought each other because they were unable to attack the real sources of their misery or powerlessness, not because they were unaware of them.[29]

Thus the ideologic and phatic ingredients of the radical tradition of the slaves was preserved by the African Creoles (who were augmented by the liberated Africans) in their culture: their language, the *patois* "not understood by most policeman, magistrates, and officials";[30] their profane festivals such as Canboulay and the jamet Carnival where thinly veiled disregard for Anglican and Catholic moralities abound; in their syncretistic religious sects and noisy wakes; in their music and dance.[31] These evoked hostility and disgust among the Anglicized colored classes, shocked the upper-class whites, and inspired discomfort in official Trinidad. In 1868, *obeah* was outlawed; in 1883, drum dances (Calenda, Belaire, Bongo) were prohibited as "immoral"; in 1884 and 1895, the festivals or aspects of them (band stick-fighting, the wearing of masks) were suppressed. In time, too, it was believed and expected, public primary education would eradicate "Creole." But the verse of Calypso suggested the spirit of liberation, the sense of dignity was unextinguishable. There one found a quiet but steeled expression of outrage.

> Can't beat me drum
> In my own, my native land.
> Can't have we Carnival
> In my own, my native land.
> Can't have we Bacchanal
> In my own, my native land.
> In my own, native land.
> In me own native land,
> Moen pasca dancer, common moen viel.[32]

Indian indentured workers, who had now assumed the economic role of the slaves (and in the eyes of many, white and Creole, their status as well),[33] were understandably somewhat distant from collective resistance. Within 20 years of the arrival of the first 225 Indians on the *Fatel Rozack* in 1845, according to Donald Wood, their semi-segregated communities and villages had quite successfully begun the replication of much of the social striation of the subcontinent: vast chasms had been opened between the prosperous who had obtained land, shops, or managed to become money-lenders, and the "coolie" masses.[34] Within 20 more years, in several hundred villages woven around sugar and their own industries of wet rice, maize, and peas,[35] the blanket of their transferred society muffled their response to being cheated, abused, extorted, and exploited by white and countryman alike. Periodically there were labor strikes on the estates (a series of them occurred in the 1880s), but the initial expression of Indian consciousness was liberal rather than resistant.[36] Chinese workers, their importation abortively curtailed to less than 2,500 in total, racially melted into one or other of the Black populations or acquired their independence through crafts, the cultivation and marketing of garden vegetables, or further migration.[37]

For the whites, particularly the more numerous and culturally dominant "French Creoles,"[38] the crown, its governor, its colonial administration, and its Legislative Council were an annoyance. Elective representation would have been preferable, but the provision of an abundant supply of cheap labor in Indian immigration had largely calmed their concerns about the crown colony system. Still, the "birds of passage," that is the colonial officials and their families, were extended status among the upper classes in deference to their positions. For the most part, neither their culture in the national sense and in its amount, nor their education or descent qualified them for acceptance otherwise.

> The governing power was, of course, "North European"; and the superstructure of government, law, and education derived from Britain. But there was an important elite group which cherished ideas and values which were Latin and French rather than Anglo-Saxon. White Creoles of French and Spanish descent outnumbered the English Creoles and British residents, and were almost certainly more influential in setting the tone of the society.[39]

And not until the aristocratic French Creoles were thoroughly Anglicized and substantially displaced by British capital and British upper-class families in the late nineteenth century was there any possibility of a whole-hearted reception in that quarter. The British faction (primarily English and Scottish), which during the decline of French Creole sugar fortunes in the mid-century had for a time sought to forcibly Anglicize and subordinate the "foreign" Creoles, had been subdued since Governor Gordon's regime in the late 1860s.[40] They were content to leave the settling in of the white hierarchy to time.[41] But despite their differences, the white elite held the line on two matters. The first involved representative government. The elite would raise this issue on those occasions when their more aggressive ambitions were thwarted by the crown's executive or by the British Parliament. The Water Riot of 1903 and the troubles simultaneous to the First World War were just such occasions.[42] The second was the colored and Black middle classes, a presence increasingly difficult to ignore. They "represented a greater threat to continued white control of the society [than the black and Indian masses], even though their numbers were relatively few; they held the key to the political and social future of Trinidad, and some far-seeing Trinidadians realised it."[43]

Only the colored and Black middle classes, whose development had been in a sense interrupted only to build up to a crescendo in the last quarter of the nineteenth century, were as a class unassuaged by Trinidad's prosperity and uncomfortable in the island's catacomb of class and racial relations.

> [T]he coloured and black middle class consisted of two distinct groups. There was a small group of families of mixed African and European descent who were the descendants of the French free people of colour settled in Trinidad since the 1780s. Secondly, there were the people, both black and coloured, who can be described as "self-made." They were the descendants of the Trinidad ex-slaves, or of "Liberated" African immigrants, or of immigrants from the eastern Caribbean. And they had acquired their middle-class status mainly through their command of British culture and their white-collar jobs.[44]

The second of the colored classes, having come into being while Trinidad was under a British colonial order, was never allowed to obtain the prominence of the Romains,

Philips, Angernons, Montrichards, Maresses, and the Beaubruns of the first (which P. G. L. Borde, the French Creole historian, had described as having "formed a second society parallel to the first; and no less distinguished than it").[45] In British Trinidad, the colored and Black middle classes had fallen from their previous heights, ceasing to be able to claim a share in the island's upper classes:

> Probably a majority of educated black and coloured men in this period were civil servants. With commerce virtually closed to them, teaching, the professions, and the service offered the only viable alternatives, except for the relatively small number of coloured planters. Only a small minority could hope to obtain the university education essential for law or medicine. This left employment in the service, including teaching in the government schools, as the only source of acceptable white-collar jobs.[46]

The distribution of privilege and advantage in a racially determinant society frustrated their larger vision: the achievement of equality with the white oligarchy, the acquisition of power. Like their counterparts among Black petit bourgeoisie elsewhere, they resented the arbitration to which the belief in Black inferiority assigned them.

> A correspondent to the *Telegraph* wrote that no amount of wealth or education enabled a man in Trinidad to enjoy social prestige, if he lacked "the correct tinge." Planters of wealth, merit, and character were "tabooed," being without the 'colonial passport' . . . more potent than education, habits, principles, behaviour, wealth, talent, or even genius itself. People outside the West Indies had no idea of the actual position of the educated man "of the *incorrect* tinge." It was especially galling when coloured men of "good" family were subjected to discrimination.[47]

And so, though it had not been necessary to respond to Anthony Trollope when in 1859 he published his anti-Black tome, *The West Indies and the Spanish Main*, by 1888 when Froude's *The English in the West Indies* appeared, a challenge from the newer elements of the middle class was imperative.[48] Interestingly enough it came from a Black and not a colored representative, and was fundamentally radical. Jacob Thomas,[49] in his *Froudacity: West Indian Fables Explained*, set before his readers a broader canvas than the "childish insults of the blacks" with which Froude had been intellectually satisfied:

> The intra-African negro is clearly powerless to struggle successfully against personal enslavement, annexation, or volunteer (or fight for) protection of his territory. What we ask, will in the coming ages be the opinion and attitudes of the extra-Africans: ten millions in the Western hemisphere, dispersed so widely over the surface of the globe, apt apprentices in every conceivable department of civilised culture. Will these men remain for ever too poor, too isolated from one another, for grand racial combination, or will the naturally opulent cradle of their people,

too long a place of violence and unholy greed, become at length the sacred watch-word of a generation willing and able to conquer or perish under its inspiration.[50]

Thomas, whose parents had been slaves only a few years before his birth, who had himself grown up and taught in the pathetically inadequate little country schools that had been distributed by the government among the rural Black masses, and whose command of the *patois* had resulted in his writing *Creole Grammar* in 1869, spoke not for the middle class. He rejected their ambition and the master from which it was copied. The middle classes, however, could not reject him. He was the most impor-tant Black intellectual in Trinidad during his lifetime. His "efforts were important to the coloured and black middle class, for they seemed to show that this group was more cultured than the dominant whites, who were dismissed as being crassly mate-rialistic. Thomas' literary activities indicated that non-whites were the cultural lead-ers."[51] And though the majority of the colored and Black middle classes were pained to lever their lives, their families and their reputations away from association with the Black masses, a few Black men of letters, like Samuel Carter and Joseph Lewis (the editors of *New Era*), William Herbert (editor of *Trinidad Press*, and then *Trini-dad Colonist*), H. A. Nurse (George Padmore's father), and the barrister Henry Syl-vester Williams, achieved, respectively, closer approximations to Thomas's compre-hension.[52] Williams, of course, the primary initiator of the Pan-African Conference that convened in London in July 1900, came closest.[53] He chose to realize Thomas's ideal. He and Thomas, along with other explicitly political figures in the colored and Black middle classes (Henry Alcazar, Edgar Maresse-Smith, and C. Prudhomme David) active in the official affairs of Trinidad, tentatively began the radicalization of the island's public discourse. It was, however, a second thrust of the middle classes that set the tone and lent that discourse a particular character.

The society arranged by these generations of the colored and Black middle classes of Trinidad was a chiaroscuro of the white upper classes. Its priorities had little to do with the elements of the radical tradition sounded in Thomas's *Froudacity*.[54] In their society, the shadings of privilege and status, acceptability and tolerance, the play etiquette of Brown upon Black were as subtle a social art as could be devised with the cultural, historical, political, educational, familial, and financial materials in their hands. One almost had to be a Trinidadian, one with a special intuition at that, to know what was required and expected, what indeed were the possibilities for any of their young launching into the orbit of adult intercourse. While the white elite seemed to possess the convenience of bold denominational distinctions, the more easily measured amassed acreage or fortune, and the property of names that could be located in the historical traditions frankly elaborated in Trinidadian literature and journalism, the standard deviations among the colored and Black middle classes were many times of such tiny gradation that an instinctive social subtlety was a sine qua non. Gross disparities, to be sure existed, but they occurred too infrequently for custom or habit to be unerring guides. In any case, the highly esteemed place of the light-complexioned elite was easily enough achieved over a generation or two. Though its value was not appreciably lessened by "mixed" marriages, simple color was considered a crude and rude measure at best. Any Black aspirant sufficiently talented, ambitious, or sponsored by professional training or family affluence could ensure his/her grandchildren would be phenotypically eligible for the pinnacle of intra-class recognition. There was though the ceiling beyond which the Black could not rise. Anticipating that closure, many of the Blacks, particularly the intelligentsia, sought to substitute education and literature as currency in the inter-class exchange. Where Thomas had succeeded, others naturally strove, hoping to draw the legitimizing attentions of white and colored alike and thereby rolling aside the stone of caste for themselves and hopefully for their children. The highest coin, as was the case among the Victorian English intelligentsia itself, was literature. It was the mark of the educated Black:

> Probably because education was so important in their rise in status, the members of this group attached great weight to cultural and intellectual life. They boasted of their command of British culture, their ability to speak and write "good" English, their interest in things of the mind. It was literacy, familiarity with books, the possession of "culture" which mattered, as well as an occupation which involved no manual labour. These things were more essential criteria for membership of the middle class than wealth or lightness of skin. . . . In one sense they formed an intelligentsia, in that they took pride in being the most cultured sector of the community, although they were not part of the ruling class.
>
> They attached so much importance to culture because they had no other valuable and valued possession to hold on to. . . .
>
> It is not surprising, therefore, that members of the coloured and black middle class often took the lead in literary or intellectual activities.[55]

In journalism and literary criticism they grew to be supreme, outdistancing the whites in their celebration and message of the most advanced social ideas, literary forms, and preoccupations available to an English-speaking public. Thus, when it was their turn to articulate a challenge to colonialism and racial domination, their superior education and intellect were both their rationale and their tool.[56] They were, indeed, the basis for the nationalism that C. L. R. James exhibited in his first political work, *The Case for West-Indian Self Government*:

> On his arrival in the West Indies [the colonial official] experiences a shock. Here is a thoroughly civilised community, wearing the same clothes that he does, speaking no other language but his own, with its best men as good as, and only too often, better than himself. What is the effect on the colonial Englishman when he recognises, as he has to recognise, the quality of those over whom he is placed in authority? Men have to justify themselves, and he falls heavily back on the "ability of the Anglo-Saxon to govern," "the trusteeship of the mother country until such

time" (always in the distant future) "as these colonies can stand by themselves," etc., etc.[57]

For a community such as ours, where, although there is race prejudice, there is no race antagonism, where the people have reached their present level in wealth, education, and general culture, the Crown Colony system of government has no place. It was useful in its day, but that day is now over. It is a fraud, because it is based on assumptions of superiority which have no foundation in fact. Admirable as are their gifts in this direction, yet administrative capacity is not the monopoly of the English; and even if it were, charity begins at home, especially in these difficult times.[58]

The Black Victorian
Becomes a Black Jacobin

Cyril Lionel Robert James was born in Trinidad in 1901, "the son of a Black Trinidadian school teacher, grandson just over half a century after the abolition of slavery of a sugar-estate pan boiler and an engine driver."[59] His earliest years were in Tunapuna, a village of 3,000 by his account, situated half way between the capital at Port of Spain to the west and Arima to the east. It had been along the road between Port of Spain and Arima that the ex-slaves had founded many of their new villages in the 1840s.[60] In the valleys around Tunapuna, "liberated" Africans had settled, planting their gardens in the hillsides, and 30 years later, in the 1870s, it was one of the sites where the dancing and fighting bands with their territorial and semisecret codes had proliferated. Tunapuna had "boasted gangs called Sweet Evening Bells, Tiepins, Greyhounds, Island Builders."[61] As a child in a slightly more respectable Tunapuna, James recalls that he had quite early begun to absorb much of the survival ethic that had attached itself to the Black middle class of which he was a part:

I was about six years of age when I got hold of my mother's copy of Shakespeare. There were 37 plays in it, or 36, and there was an illustration in the front of each play. The illustration had below it the Act and the Scene which it illustrated and I remember the illustration before *Julius Caesar* saying, "How ill this taper burns." Now I could not read a play of Shakespeare but I remember perfectly looking up the Act and Scenes stated at the foot of the illustration and reading that particular scene. I am quite sure that before I was seven I had read all those scenes.[62]

Notwithstanding the availability of adventure stories in his mother's library, the child's reading was hardly what Richard Small described as "the normal youth's interest." James was being trained in and was exhibiting the lessons of his class. In that prescribed inventory there was contained also the Puritan importance of class propriety:

I was fascinated by the calypso singers and the sometimes ribald ditties they sang in their tents during carnival time. But, like many of the black middle class, to my mother a calypso was a matter for ne'er-do-wells and at best the common people. I was made to understand that the road to the calypso tent was the road to hell, and there were always plenty of examples of hell's inhabitants to whom she could point.[63]

The sexual and moral customs of the Black lower classes, for all their vitality and attractiveness, amounted to a rejection of English bourgeois sensibility, they were an affront to the morality of the colonial model set before the natives. Unquestionably, in a Black family that knew the rules, this implicitly political statement had no place in the future of a properly instructed young Black man. "Good" society, white, Black, and colored, conspired against what it interpreted as Dionysian, Satanic humors. Cricket, however, was lionized in the culture of James's class. Indeed, from all indications, its presence pervaded every strata of Trinidadian society. Richard Small reported:

> The membership of the various clubs was determined by occupation and social class and at that time, even more sharply than now, that discrimination would be virtually the same as differentiation according to color. Queens Park Club, the controllers of cricket in the island, were white and wealthy; Shamrock, Catholic French Creole traders and cocoa planters; Maple, middle class of brown skin; Shannon, the Black middle class version, white collar office types, and teachers; and then Stingo, the tradesman, artisan, worker. . . . Add to that that almost everybody played or took an interest in cricket and that it was played for up to eight months of the year, and some estimate of its potential for social and sublimated social expression will be grasped.[64]

Cricket was James's father's game, his uncle Cuffie's and Aunt Judith's game, his cousin Cudjoe's game; an interest even to be found in his grandfather, the extraordinary Josh Rudder. It was a game of the English school boy. "Recreation meant cricket, for in those days, except for infrequent athletic sports meetings, cricket was the only game. Our house was superbly situated, exactly behind the wicket."[65] For James, then, it was a natural obsession; one to which he would turn as he sought to make his way in the adult world; and one to which he would return when he sought to make comprehensible his life and the colonial world in which he was raised.

The Trinidad of James's young life was already showing signs of popular agitation. In 1897, following the models of the English Workingmen's Association of the 1830s and the Leeds Workingmen's Parliamentary Reform Association organized in 1861, the Trinidad Workingmen's Association was founded. With a membership of 50 skilled and unskilled workers, which included Black carpenters, masons, tailors, and at least one pharmacist and one chemist, it was, according to Brinsley Samaroo, the first such organization in the British West Indies:

> [T]he Trinidad body emerged as one concerned with both trade union and political pressure group functions. It was founded just before the visit of the 1897 Royal Commission, sent to the British West Indies to examine the seriousness of the sugar depression and to recommend measures for bringing relief to the colonies. The

Association's first president, Walter Mills, a pharmacist, gave evidence before the Commission. . . . Mills complained against the insanitary conditions of the colony's towns, dwellings and estates . . . press[ed] for a reduction in taxes, especially on foodstuffs and agricultural implements used by the labouring people . . . better transport facilities, the setting up of minor industries, the introduction of Savings Banks and the further opening of Crown Lands. In addition, the Association was strongly opposed to state-aided Indian immigration which, Mills claimed, increased the competition for the "starvation wages paid on sugar estates." . . . Above all, Mills said, the colony should be granted elective government.[66]

The Association soon lapsed only to be reactivated, affiliating itself in 1906 with the new British Labour Party.[67] Now with hundreds of members, it began to function as a representative of the working classes, campaigning for labor reform and agitating for shorter working hours, sick leave, and against the "color bar," expanding its membership by attracting the "traditionally apolitical" East Indian worker. The colonial government was unsurprisingly hostile, advising the Colonial Office of the Association's dubious character:

> Its members, some of whom are of but doubtful reputation, are for the most part not workingmen, and have no stake in the colony. They have adopted their title simply with the object of securing recognition by the English Labour Party and thus obtaining for themselves an importance that they would not otherwise possess.[68]

But Europe and the colonial governments of the British and French empires were soon caught up in the First World War. It would prove to be a historical force from which the empires would never recover. The war itself, over and above the toll it exacted in Europe (but not entirely European), was a fundamental contradiction to the raison d'être of the British Empire: the assumption was that "the defence of the self-governing colonies from external attack and the maintenance of sea-power were British responsibilities."[69] During the war, India alone with 1½ million men and women in British uniforms of one sort or another supplied more troops than all the other dominions and colonies (Canada, Australia, New Zealand, South Africa were dominions) together.[70] And what India had done for Britain, Africa did for France: "Over 545,000 African native soldiers," wrote George Padmore, "were employed by France, chiefly as shock troops in stemming the tide of the German advance during the most critical periods of the war."[71] Tens of thousands of Africans also served with Germany, Belgium, and British forces in East Africa, while from the United States, of the 342,277 Black troops who served, 200,000 fought with the French army, uniformed as French soldiers.[72] From the West Indies, troops were also mobilized, most of them, some 20,000, serving in the British West India Regiment. However, there had been problems. For some, certain considerations overrode loyalty to Britain:

> In Trinidad the press used the term "better class" to describe the whites and the lighter-complexioned mulattos who constituted the merchant and planter class. In

Barbados the term used was "the best class." When enlistment of recruits started in 1915 the "better class" young men throughout the British West Indies refused to join, except as officers, in the same contingents as the black soldiers. Arthur Andrew Cipriani, a Corsican creole who was leading the campaign for recruits complained that "our better class young men are shirking" from joining the public contingents "because of the lamentable question of colour which lies at the bottom of everything in these parts." . . . Some "better class" soldiers came to London and joined British regiments, the majority joined with "better class" soldiers in the other colonies to form the Merchants' and Planters' Contingent.[73]

But the advent of the Great War had brought to the fore a more considerable and mean enemy of colonial interests:

> [N]ot everyone was prepared to make sacrifices for the general good. The colony's merchants saw the start of the war in Europe as a signal for an immediate increase in prices. On the very day of the government's announcement that the war had started in Europe, *The Port of Spain Gazette* reported that prices had risen steeply.[74]

This inflation of prices broke the backs of the Black working class in the island's cash economy, and was the primary cause of the strikes that followed: oil workers struck in 1917, railworkers, scavengers, stevedores, sweepers, sugar, and dock workers in 1919, asphalt and railworkers again in 1920.[75] And the Trinidad Workingmen's Association, joined after the war by returning ex-soldiers enraged over the racial discrimination they had experienced in military service,[76] was at the center of the agitation. This was the basis of the social force that Captain Cipriani, returning from the same war, would lead into the Trinidad Labour Party in 1932:

> Contact with Europe during the first World War gave West Indian radicals a first-hand opportunity to learn from Europe and so the postwar period was increasingly "Socialist" in the way that West Indians understood the term. Cipriani wore a red button on his lapel and many of his followers wore red shirts in imitation of the "Reds" of the Bolshevik revolution of 1917.[77]

In these years, Trinidad had become a part of the postwar Black movement that within twenty or so years would pull all the empires apart:

> [J]ust as the 1914–18 war saw the Indian nationalists make great strides, so there were important stirrings elsewhere. In 1915, riots in central Ceylon led an alarmist governor to proclaim martial law and to imprison many notable Sinhalese. They included Don Stephen Senanayake (later the first prime minister), who never quite forgave the British. In 1918 the Ceylon National Congress was formed following the Indian precedent. In the same year as the Ceylon riots an abortive rising in Nyasaland, led by the Rev. John Chilembwe, demonstrated the growing passion of African nationalism. . . .
>
>   In West Africa the Indian nationalists had eager admirers. When India was invited to the War Cabinet in 1917 they cried: "Why not West Africa as well?" As

India and the Dominions were invited to the peace conference in 1919, Dr. Nanka-Bruce of the Gold Coast sent resolutions to the western powers so that "the voice of West Africa" could also be heard at Versailles. The first [*sic*] Pan-African Congress met in Paris in 1919. . . .

At the same time in Kenya the Kikuyu began to organize political associations. Lives were lost in Nairobi riots in 1922. ·. . . Similarly, a few political movements were growing in the West Indies, such as the "Representative Government Association" of Grenada, founded in 1914, and Captain Cipriani's "Trinidad Workingmen's Association," which flourished at the end of the war. Marcus Garvey of Jamaica founded the Negro nationalist "Universal Negro Improvement Association," which had brief international fame at the end of the war.[78]

James, however, though he was aware of these events, kept his distance. "In politics I took little interest."[79] He had finished school in 1918 and was content to tend his two passions, his two disciplines: cricket and literature.

I had a circle of friends (most of them white) with whom I exchanged ideas, books, records and manuscripts. We published local magazines and gave lectures or wrote articles on Wordsworth, the English Drama, and Poetry as a Criticism of Life. We lived according to the tenets of Matthew Arnold, spreading sweetness and light and the best that has been thought and said in the world. . . . Never losing sight of my plan to go abroad and write, I studied and practiced assiduously the art of fiction.[80]

He had, to be sure, made choices, political choices, with which he would find it increasingly difficult to live as the forces of the world bore down on him and the Black radical tradition acquired its revolutionary form. Still, his earliest direction was in contrast to that of Malcolm Nurse, his childhood playmate.[81] Nurse, matriculating at the Roman Catholic College of Immaculate Conception and the private Pamphylian High School, also graduated in 1918. For a few years, he, as did James, would work as a reporter (for the *Weekly Guardian*). In 1925, he would emigrate to the United States, and within two years of his arrival he would join the American Communist Party. It was then that Nurse would become George Padmore. But even before leaving Trinidad, he had developed an open antagonism to imperialism. The *Guardian* had provided him with an object:

The job bored him, there was no scope for thoughtful writing and he detested his editor, Edward J. Partridge, an Englishman who demanded subservience from his black staff. When Partridge died, Nurse wrote that he had been "one of the most arrogant agents of British Imperialism I have ever encountered. I held him in utter contempt, and had hoped to use my pen in exposing his role before the colonial workers and peasants whom he oppressed through his dirty sheet the *Guardian*."[82]

James and Padmore would meet in London in 1932.[83] By then James would have just become a Trotskyist, and Padmore was barely a year from the end of his work with the Communist movement.[84] Their political collaboration would begin in 1935.

While still in Trinidad, James had taught in school, played cricket (for Maple), and worked as a part-time reporter. As a Black journalist on the island in the early 1920s, he witnessed the maturing of nationalist politics under Cipriani. Richard Small, however, suggests that: "It was not until 1924 that James started paying anything like close attention to [Cipriani's] speeches and not till 1931 that he became a follower of Cipriani."[85] It was his conversation in 1923 with Learie Constantine, the cricketer, that had unnerved him, and, perhaps begun the process:

> I was holding forth about some example of low West Indian cricket morals when Constantine grew grave with an almost aggressive expression on his face.
> "You have it all wrong, you know," he said coldly.
> "What did I have all wrong?"
> "You have it all wrong. You believe all that you read in those books. They are no better than we."
> I floundered around. I hadn't intended to say that they were better than we. Yet a great deal of what I had been saying was just that.
> Constantine reverted to an old theme.
> "I have told you that we *won* that match. We *won* it."
> The conversation broke up, leaving me somewhat bewildered.
> "They are no better than we." I knew we were man for man as good as anybody. I had known that since my schooldays. But if that were the truth, it was not the whole truth.[86]

James's politics like those of Cipriani, however, remained within the parameters of parliamentarianism. He would need Marxism, he maintained later, to break with that assumption.[87] By the late 1920s he was a nationalist, but though he had read Garvey's *Negro World*, had interviewed Garvey himself when the latter visited Trinidad after his expulsion from the United States, and was also familiar with some of Du Bois's early works, James's vision had still only partially progressed beyond the ideological tradition in which he had been reared: "I hadn't really the faintest idea about Black politics then, nor was there any talk about any African or Black revolt."[88] His commitment was to fiction writing, an intent that had born some fruit in the publication of some of his short stories, and the development of the manuscript for what would become *Minty Alley*.[89] Nevertheless, his political apprenticeship had begun and he was preparing to write a biography of Cipriani:

> I began to study the history of the islands. I collected *Hansards*, old White Papers, reports of Royal Commissions. There were plenty around which nobody wanted. It was all very simple and straightforward. For background I had the Whig interpretation of history and the declarations of the British Labour Party. For foreground there were the black masses, the brown professional and clerical middle classes, the Europeans and local whites, Stingo and Shannon, Maple and Queen's Park. My hitherto vague ideas of freedom crystallized around a political conviction: we should be free to govern ourselves.[90]

It was then that Constantine, the more disruptive political force in James's social milieu, intervened. Constantine wanted to write a book, one which from his experience of playing cricket in England since 1929 might express his insights into the game and English society. He invited James to England to collaborate with him on the project. In March of 1932, James left for England. He would not return to Trinidad for 26 years.[91]

British Socialism

The socialist traditions in the British metropole to which Anglophone Blacks of Africa and the Caribbean were exposed differed decidedly from those of their Francophone and American counterparts. For one, the history of the development of socialist movements and socialist thought in Britain had been marked by unique historical events: the formation of the first significant industrial working class; the defeat of the revolutionary and then the parliamentary reform (Charter) movements in the early nineteenth century; British domination of international capital and trade during most of the century; the ambiguous presence of Marx and Engels in Britain from the mid-nineteenth century until their deaths in 1883 and 1895, respectively; the founding of the First International in 1864; the appearance of the new British Empire, and the concomitant intensification of Anglo-Saxonism as a national ideology. One of the historical consequences of these several events was the persistence into the twentieth century of a working-class movement with strong trade unionist sympathies:

> [In 1895] the total membership of the unions of the United Kingdom, including those which were not represented at the Congress [of British Trade Unions that year], was estimated at one and a half million—that is, say, about a fifth of the entire number of adult male workers. There was nothing like it in any other great nation. Moreover, an estimate of the strength of the working class not confined to a general view of the country as a whole, but distinguishing between the different districts and branches of the national industry yielded even more striking results. . . . In Lancashire, Durham, and Northumberland the trade unions contained at least a tenth of the entire population, and half the adult male workers. It would be true to say that for the Lancashire cotton spinner or weaver, the miner in Durham or Northumberland, membership of a trade union was in practice compulsory.
>
> Indeed the size of this army of workmen was perhaps the best security that the unions would pursue a prudent policy. In a highly civilized country there are not a million or a million and a half revolutionaries; and of the British unions, about the year 1895, the most conservative and cautious were precisely those whose membership included the largest proportion of the men employed in the trade.[92]

This impulse was joined by the formation of specifically political and electoral arms of the socialist movement: the Independent Labour Party (founded in 1893) and the Labour Party (circa 1900). Together, the trade unions and the parliamentary parties had a decisive effect on worker militancy:

While there is evidence to suggest a degree of working-class mistrust of the state in its everyday forms, the British labour movement had tended to insert both its industrial and political activities within the existing national political structure; in Gramscian terms it lacked a sufficiently hegemonic perspective to challenge the central institutions of state power.[93]

Finally, English nationalism or Anglo-Saxonism, so powerful an ideological phenomenon during the last quarter of the nineteenth century, to some extent insulated British socialists from a ready acceptance or submission to socialist currents originating from the continent.[94] The political and ideological impacts of organizations like the Marxian Henry Hyndman's Social Democratic Federation (1883), which exhibited its founder's hostility to trade unionism,[95] William Morris's "patrician" Socialist League (1885), and the Socialist Labour Party (c.1900) inspired by the visionary American intellectual Daniel DeLeon, were of only indirect significance.

> Prior to 1917 there were only two Marxist organisations of any consequence. These were the British Socialist Party (B.S.P.) and the Socialist Labour Party (S.L.P.). The B.S.P. was the direct descendant of the Social Democratic Federation (S.D.F.) founded in 1883 under the leadership of Hyndman, having been formed in 1911 as a coalition of the S.D.F., sections of the non-Marxist I.L.P., the *Clarion* movement and various local socialist societies. The membership of the S.D.F. during the nineteenth century never exceeded 4,000; the B.S.P.'s initial nominal membership of 40,000 declined to no more than a third that number by the outbreak of war, and active membership was considerably less. The S.L.P. had split away from the S.D.F. at the turn of the century. It was purer in doctrine and correspondingly much smaller; the membership never exceeded a thousand, the majority concentrated in Scotland.[96]

More well-known (and affluent) was the Fabian Society (Sidney and Beatrice Webb, George Bernard Shaw, Annie Besant, Graham Wallas, Sydney Olivier, G. D. H. Cole, and Margaret Cole) whose tendencies were broad enough to encompass imperialism, state socialism, and anarchy.[97] Their mark would be more enduring in British thought, not the least for their establishment of the London School of Economics.[98] But it was "Labour Socialism," the anti-Marxist, reformist, ethical, and pragmatic resolution to the class war, that directed the policies of the British trade unions and the Labour Party, and to which British workers mostly attended:

> By their very nature the rank and file—the men and women who bought and sold literature rather than wrote it, and listened to speeches rather than gave them— produced very little material of their own. We need to know more of these anonymous men and women who swelled the ranks of the trades councils, constituency parties and I.L.P. branches up and down the country. But such testimony as we do have, supplemented by the local Labour press and other historical records, testifies to the pervasive influence of Labour Socialism. Particular phrases such as "a higher social consciousness," "the social organism," "the Socialist Commonwealth," "let us

call to the man with the muck-rake," "ballot boxes and not bullets," etc. are en-countered repeatedly.[99]

When eventually, after the Russian Revolution and the founding of the Communist Party of Great Britain (CPGB), an "uncompromisingly" revolutionary Marxist party appeared, it was still the case that very little success would accrue to Marxism among the working classes. As Neal Wood maintains: "British communism has to a great extent been shaped by its development in the shadow of what has become the largest and most powerful Social Democratic Party in the world." Much of the history of the CPGB and its differences from Communist parties elsewhere can perhaps be explained by the gargantuan strength and effectiveness of the Labour Party.[100] And neither the postwar economic decline of the 1920s nor even the Depression, coming on the heels of the party's fiasco in the General Strike of 1926,[101] could salvage the CPGB as a mass party.[102]

For the most part, then, following the Depression, English Marxism became a creature more of the sons and daughters of the middle and upper-middle classes than of English workers. Massive unemployment in their ranks, the emergence of fascist movements in Europe, a decade of the display of the corruption and incompetence of "bourgeois democracy," and the spectacular achievements of the Russian Revolution, had worked their magic:

> Changes in the intellectual life of a nation can often be perceived at an early date among university students. Prior to the nineteen-thirties British students had never exhibited the political fervor so characteristic on the continent. Consequently, it must have been with some satisfaction that Karl Radek was able to announce to the Congress of Soviet Writers in 1934 that "In the heart of bourgeois England, in Oxford, where the sons of the bourgeoisie receive their final polish, we observe the crystallization of a group which sees salvation only together with the proletariat." The beginning of an unprecedented political ferment took place in 1931, when embryonic communist organizations were established at London and Cambridge Universities by students returning from Germany. . . . A Marxist Society saw the light of day at the London School of Economics in 1931, and the radical Cosmopolitan Society replaced the old International Society. Oxford's notorious October Club, founded in January 1932, was banned in November of the following year, ostensibly for its criticism of the Officers' Training Corps.[103]

Nevertheless, class arrogance, bitter divisions between workers and the class of the intelligentsia,[104] the residues of xenophobia (so central in the earlier century to the role of Irish workers in the British working-class movement and later as a support for imperialism), all worked against the possibility of the British Communist movement becoming a dominant force among the country's proletariat. Indeed, counterforces to the CPGB and Bolshevism had already developed in the 1920s among British workers with the emergence of "the Plebs League, the National Guilds League, sections of the I.L.P., the Workers' Socialist Federation (W.S.F.) and the South Wales Socialist Society

(S.W.S.S.)."[105] By the 1930s, British Marxism—the intellectual and moral residue of British Communism—had achieved its most enduring influences among university intellectuals;[106] and British socialism had been transformed into an electoral phenomenon with the Labour Party and the ILP as its most significant manifestations.[107]

Black Radicals in the Metropole

During these same years, the British Empire's African and Caribbean subjects were not frequent visitors to the metropole. In actuality, they had much less access to Britain than their Francophone counterparts had to the European continent. Nevertheless, African merchants were frequent visitors to London, and in time Black students from the emerging middle classes or sponsored by missionary societies found their way to the British Isles.[108] Still, many of the figures who would emerge as important ideologues, theorists, and activists in the anti-imperialist movements in the British colonies after World War I and World War II, were forced to take rather circuitous routes before arriving in Britain. Padmore, like Azikiwe of Nigeria, Nkrumah of the Gold Coast, and P. K. I. Seme of South Africa, came to Britain from the United States. With its tradition of Black colleges and universities, America was a much more hospitable and accessible route to further education, but experience in the metropole was still important. T. Ras Makonnen (George T. N. Griffith) came to Britain via America and Denmark. A few others, like Johnstone (Jomo) Kenyatta of Kenya, spent a number of penurious years in the metropole and on the Continent caught between colonial officialdom, missionary networks of limited resources, and rather haphazard employment.[109] The administrators of British colonialism, as we have seen, particularly in those colonies where European settlement had occurred, were generally hostile to natives acquiring Western education outside the auspices of the missionary schools or much beyond an elementary level. Some Blacks in both the nineteenth and early twentieth centuries did make it to Britain for advanced training or to further pursue professional careers. Usually the sons of the fledgling colonial middle classes found all over the Empire, they remained within the margins of what was expected of them. Among them, however, were such figures as Henry Sylvester Williams (Trinidad), already discussed, Harold Moody (Jamaica), T. R. Makonnen (British Guiana), Mohamed Ali Duse (Egypt), and James—all of whom would play prominent roles in Black politics in Britain but who traveled to Britain with at least professional interests in mind. Once there, these experienced some changes of minds, augmenting their original intents or entirely devoting themselves to Black liberation. Among their achievements in Britain would be the establishment of newspapers like Mohamed Ali Duse's *African Times and Orient Review* (where Marcus Garvey received his first introduction to Pan-Africanism);[110] such publishing presses as Makonnen's Pan-African Publishing Company; and the founding of a series of social and political organizations: the Afro-West Indian Literary Society (1900), the Ethiopian Progressive Association (1906), the Union of Students of African Descent (1917), the West African Students Union (1925), and the League of Coloured Peoples (1931).[111]

During the interim between the world wars, a few members of the colonial Black intelligentsia working in Britain were closely associated with Marxist or Communist movements. Padmore, prominent in the Third International until 1933, was to head the Red International of Labour Unions' (the RILU or *Profintern*) International Trade Union Committee of Negro Workers (ITUC-NW); Rajani Palme Dutt, an English-born Eurasian who studied at Oxford, would become the leading theoretician of the CPGB for 40 years; Peter Blackman, a Barbadian who had worked in West Africa as a missionary, would become a prominent spokesman and journalist for the CPGB (he had been preceded by two other Barbadians, Chris Jones of the Colonial Seamen's Association, and Arnold Ward); Shapurji Saklatvala, a physician born in Bombay, was one of the first two Communists standing for Parliament to be elected, he represented North Battersea in 1922; and, of course, James was to be well-known as a writer and speaker for the Trotskyist movement.[112] Left politicians, such as Willie Gallacher, the Communist MP, Fenner Brockway and Rev. Reginald Sorenson among the left wing of the Labour Party (and in Brockway's instance, the Independent Labour Party), and the independent Reginald Reynolds, were all associates of the radical faction of this Black intelligentsia in Britain.[113] But just as some events, like the worldwide depression of the late 1920s and 1930s, would propel some members of this intelligentsia toward the left, others caused them to seriously question the commitment of European radicals, and particularly European Communists, to their causes. In the early and middle 1930s, two such events, the Third International's disbanding of the International Trade Union Committee of Negro Workers in 1933, and the press revelation of the Soviet Union's trade with Italy in war materials during the Italo-Ethiopian War (in contravention to League of Nations sanctions),[114] proved to be critical. In Britain, the most radical Black activists generally turned toward Pan-Africanism as the form of their political work while retaining aspects of Marxism for their critique of capitalism and imperialism.

In these early decades of the century, as had been the case for most of the previous century, the significance of the metropole for colonial Black intelligentsias was their interest in preparing for a role in, and for some a share of, the Empire. Others—for instance tribal authorities or missionaries—might appear in London seeking official relief from this or that manifestation of greed or injustice on the parts of colonial administrators or settlers. But for the ambitious, this was entirely a waste of the seat of Empire. For them, as James would testify of his own arrival in Britain, it was often a case of the "British intellectual going to Britain."[115] Many, of course, returned to their colonial homelands—particularly those from West Africa and the more populous islands of the Caribbean—but quite a few remained in England for the rest of their lives. And as the century proceeded, their numbers were substantially, if intermittently, augmented by the arrivals of Blacks with peasant and urban working-class backgrounds, propelled toward the metropole by the more chaotic forces that catalyzed or were the results of the crises in the world system: that is, wars and labor shortages.[116] Finally, a smaller number of these Blacks, but certainly the most prominent, came to the Western metropoles to pursue careers in sport and entertainment, careers that would be certainly delimited if not entirely proscribed in their native ground.[117] In some part, members of the Black intelligentsia resident in Britain acted as a mediation for Black labor in the metropole and the colonies. As doctors, like Peter Milliard (British Guiana), they tended to the needs of the Black and white working classes in the industrial ghettos; as barristers, like H. S. Williams and Learie Constantine, they often acted in the interests of colonial appellants, or were active in civil and welfare rights.[118] Others, such as Makonnen in Manchester, and Samuel Opoba ("Sam Okoh") and "Joka" in Liverpool, established restaurants and dance clubs for colonial students, seamen, and immigrant workers, Black and white. Still others, like Edward G. Sankey, later a Nigerian businessman, acted as scribes and personal counselors.[119] Britain was at "the centre of gravity."[120] It was the source of authority for the Empire, the highest seat of appeal from the sometimes arbitrary ravages of colonial policy and authority. It was the site so persistently and idyllicly envisioned in the literary and historical texts employed in the "colony of schools" that ringed the Empire, and where they could extend their intellectual and professional attainments and anticipate being permitted to come into their rightful heritage. England was, in short, the natural setting for this British, if Black, middle class, frustrated at home as so many of them were by their recognition of the "two Englands—the England of the colonies and that of the metropolis."[121] The first, they knew, was constricted by the castelike boundaries of racialist order; the second, they believed, was fair-minded and a virtual meritocracy.

Only a few among them came to Britain for explicitly political purposes. Makonnen and Padmore did, but such others as Williams their predecessor and James their contemporary, acquired those purposes while living in Britain. Together, they helped to constitute that generation of Black intellectuals that—at their historical juncture—presumed or perhaps understood that the project of anti-imperialism had to be centered in the metropole. After their time and because of their work, decolonization and Black liberation would return to their native lands.

Makonnen had first come to Britain in 1935. He returned two years later and took up residence for 20 years. He was a Pan-Africanist when he arrived and remained so, deserving to be ranked along with Du Bois, Kwame Nkrumah, and Padmore in that movement. Indeed, he was more responsible than anyone else for bringing the movement together at Manchester in 1945 for the Fifth Pan-African Congress—the last time many of them would meet as ideologues without power.[122] As a publisher, Makonnen had been the first to publish Eric Williams's work and had published some of the writings of Kenyatta and Padmore as well.[123] For Makonnen, who had lived for a time in the United States, the center of the British Empire was a most significant platform. He celebrated the contrast between its liberalism and that of his own society in British Guiana. It did not take him long to come to the belief that colonial radicals could depend upon British traditions of free speech and a free press in their attack on the Empire.

What was it like to be a black man in the Britain of the 1930s? Certainly we were not rich; far from it. But we were generally happy in our lot—just to know that we were challenging one of the greatest empires in the world. Imagine what it meant to us to go to Hyde Park to speak to a race of people who were considered our masters, and tell them right out what we felt about their empire and about them . . . write any tract we wanted to; make terrible speeches; all this when you knew very well that back in the colonies even to say "God is love" might get the authorities after you![124]

Persistently anti-Communist throughout his life, a man who could and did beseech his brothers: "If you are interested in communism, then buy the book. . . . Don't join the club!"[125] Makonnen could still appreciate the "leveling" in British political life that minimized national groups and negated "the Negro Problem" that he had experienced as so prevalent in America.

The few West Indians, West Africans or Somalis who worked in the ports or in London were certainly living under terrible conditions but these were not different from those of the Welsh miner, or the appalling area of the Glasgow slums. . . . [W]e were able to see the worker, the struggle of the proletariat much more clearly than across the Atlantic.[126]

More important to him, the same sort of solidarity was true of Blacks. Because Blacks were so few in Britain, he believed, kinship overrode class. Unlike America where a pretentious urban Black middle class had become alienated from the majority of working-class Blacks, those in pre–World War II Britain formed a responsive fraternity. When in England some of them became disoriented and went "*shenzi*," "instead of being disgraced we would provide money to pay for their passage [home]."[127] Harold Moody's League of Coloured People and various members of the radical Left were also a part of this services network. The most central characteristic of England for Makonnen, however, seemed a result of imperial inadvertence. While in Britain the ruling classes commanded the society by virtue of a certain hegemonic grace, in the colonies the more brutal machinery of domination persisted. Those Blacks who made the journey between these two polarities could never be the same:

[W]hen you look at the results of those Africans who had been to England, you wouldn't be far wrong in saying that England had been the executioner of its own colonial empire. In the sense that she had allowed these blacks to feel the contrast between freedom in the metropolis and slavery in the colonies.[128]

Padmore, it seems, despite his vigorous opposition to British imperialism, shared Makonnen's enthusiasm for the metropole. He was also impressed by the liberal traditions of what he had learned as a Marxist to identify as "bourgeois democracy." The same man, we are told, who in 1931 detailed the exploitation, "Bloody deeds," and "hypocripsy" of the Empire in Africa and the West Indies (in his *The Life and Struggles of Negro Toilers*), was also capable of exclaiming to Makonnen in near-reckless admiration:

[T]he security people, they know we are here; they come into our offices pretending to be buying books or magazines, and sometimes when we're returning from a trip to Russia, they hold us back after crossing the Channel. But you can joke with them and say, "We've just been across to get some Russian gold, and we're coming back to enrich the old country." Instead of giving you the American cattle-prod treatment, they laugh it off.[129]

Of course, it was all delusion. There was, in the 1930s, little that was quaint or liberal about British politics or generous about the British state. While it was true that in a small niche of British society the Popular Front and its Third International allies flourished, that radical writers and artists could produce political and literary journals such as *Storm*, *Cambridge Left*, *Left*, the *Left Review*, *New Verse*, and others, that such weeklies as *The Tribune* or Claud Cockburn's *The Week* could be published, that the Left Book Club could be organized, and drama groups like Unity Theatre and the Group Theatre could perform, that mass mobilizations like the unemployed of the Jarrow Crusade (1936) could demonstrate, and thousands volunteer for the Spanish Civil War's International Brigade (some 2,762 were thought to have gone to Spain, 1,762 wounded, 543 killed),[130] it was also true that power in British society was being employed for other things. In the streets, Sir Oswald Mosley's tens of thousands of British Union Fascists exacted a terrible physical toll on antifascists, and destroyed shops like those in London's Mile End Road owned by Jews.[131] Julian Symons recalled: "Certainly the police force, never notably sympathetic towards Left-wing movements, seemed always to assume very readily the task of protecting the Fascists from opposition."[132] But the official faces of British politics were no less venal. In 1936, at its Edinburgh conference, the Labour Party had "turned its back on the needs of republican Spain,"[133] and even earlier the National Government embarked on a "neutralist" course between fascist states and their victims.[134] Yet the same state had no pretensions toward neutrality where its Empire was concerned. Black activists in Britain in the 1930s were subject to the same "heavy manners"—as West Indians would say—as their predecessors. Just as in the 1920s, Mohamed Ali Duse had been "constantly trailed" by MI5, by Scotland Yard, and agents of the Colonial Office,[135] and Claude McKay, listed in the files of the British Secret Service, was prevented from returning to Jamaica decades after his single year (1919–21) of radical journalism in England,[136] British Intelligence and the Colonial Office had taken note of Padmore (as early as 1931) and proceeded to neutralize his work in Africa.[137] In the Caribbean, particularly during the workers' strikes of 1937–38, Black activism was ruthlessly suppressed. And when the Second World War followed, many of these "subversives" were duly interned.[138] But the delusion of liberalism of which Makonnen and Padmore spoke was also self-delusion, a piece of a larger misconception. To them and many of their fellows, England, the second England, the meritocratic England of romance novels and Whig histories, was the embodiment of fair play and deep moral regulation. It was an ideal, then, that even the most committed anti-imperialists among them found difficult to shake. Not even the gross imperfections and racism they confronted in the metropole dissuaded them. It was as though they had come to accept that as

Black Englishmen a part of their political mission was to correct the errant mother-land. Of all of them, it was James who would come closest to understanding why this was so. Doubtlessly it was his comprehension of English society that provided him with insight into British imperialism, British liberalism, and the British Left. On this score, he would proceed far beyond the economism of Engels, Marx, and many of the most recent British Marxists.[139]

Perhaps one reason for James's less euphoric reaction to English society was that his introduction to the country had differed in important ways from those of Makonnen and Padmore. Living in Lancashire with Learie and Norma Constantine, physically remote from the more typical sites of middle-class radicalism and organized politics, James was enveloped by a more contemplative work and a more mundane politics. Through Constantine, to be sure, he had gained access to the *Manchester Guardian* and was soon substituting for Neville Cardus, the paper's cricket correspondent. But his major preoccupations: the collaboration with Constantine on *Cricket and I*, the public lectures on the West Indies, the editing of *The Life of Captain Cipriani*, provided him the opportunity to read Lenin, Stalin, and Trotsky, to review the lie of labor politics in Britain, and to meet with British workers for discussions removed from super-heated circumstances. Indeed, he would later admit that the development of his critical stance regarding the Labour Party (with which he had identified as a "Ciprianian" nationalist) was due to discussions with Lancashire workers that brought discredit on the Party's leadership: "My Labour and Socialist ideas had been got from books and were rather abstract. These humorously cynical working men were a revelation and brought me down to earth."[140] Apparently sharing their disillusionment with the Labour Party, he soon found an alternative:

> I read the *History of the Russian Revolution* [Trotsky] because I was very much interested in history and the book seemed to offer some analysis of modern society. At the end of reading the book, Spring 1934, I became a Trotskyist—in my mind, and later joined. It was clear in my mind that I was not going to be a Stalinist.[141]

It was from this political base and ideology that he would write *World Revolution: 1917–1936. The Rise and Fall of the Communist International* in 1937, and translate Boris Souvarine's *Stalin* in 1938.[142] It was as a Trotskyist that James would author *The Black Jacobins*, the work for which he is best known. First published in 1938, this still formidable study of the Haitian and French revolutions and their signification for British abolitionism, was at one and the same time an analysis of the relationship between revolutionary masses and leadership, and an attempt to establish the historical legacy of African revolutionary struggles. Within the same volume it is not difficult to unearth a critique of Stalinism, an expression of Trotsky's concept of permanent revolution, and the elaboration of Lenin's theory of the dictatorship of the proletariat—all constructed upon Marx's extraordinary determination of the primitive, that is, the imperialist accumulation of capital. It was from the beginning recognized as an extraordinary work. We will return to it shortly.

However, it was a second turn of consciousness that provided James with a perspective on English society. That development is recounted in *Beyond a Boundary*, James's most exquisite statement on British imperialism and the development of English bourgeois society. Published in 1963, it was a sort of autobiographic study—Sylvia Wynter has called it an "autosociographical system[143]—ostensibly of the game of cricket. Here James excavated his entrance into English society as a proper member of the English middle class, steeped in the public school code. His memory of being a Black boy at Queen's Royal College in Trinidad characterized the bourgeois morality and rationalism to which he and his fellow colonials were introduced:

> [I]nside the classrooms the code had little success. Sneaking was taboo, but we lied and cheated without any sense of shame. I know I did. . . .
>
> But as soon as we stepped on to the cricket or football field, more particularly the cricket field, all was changed. . . . [W]e learned to obey the umpire's decision without question, however irrational it was. We learned to play with the team, which meant subordinating your personal inclinations, and even interests, to the good of the whole. We kept a stiff upper lip in that we did not complain about ill-fortune. We did not denounce failure, but "Well tried" or "Hard luck" came easily to our lips. We were generous to opponents and congratulated them on victories, even when we knew they did not deserve it. . . . On the playing field we did what ought to be done.[144]

Cricket, he writes, became one of his obsessions. He played it, he read about it, and in time as we have noted he came to write about it. In a way, his youth was dominated by the game; cricket was the means of his introduction to the island's Brown middle class; it selected his personal friends; it grounded his perceptions of manhood and the judgments he would make of other men; and eventually, through Constantine, it became the reason for his coming to England. His other obsession was literature. This, too, was an emanation of the English bourgeoisie. For James, it had begun with William Makepeace Thackeray: "I laughed without satiety at Thackeray's constant jokes and sneers and gibes at the aristocracy and at people in high places. Thackeray, not Marx, bears the heaviest responsibility for me."[145]

> After Thackeray there was Dickens, George Eliot and the whole bunch of English novelists. Followed the poets in Matthew Arnold's selections, Shelley, Keats and Byron; Milton and Spenser. . . . I discovered criticism: Hazlitt, Lamb and Coleridge, Saintsbury and Gosse. . . . Burke led me to the speeches: Canning, Lord Brougham, John Bright.[146]

But the two—cricket and English literature—were complements. Each of them, as he was to discover in England, were cultural and ideological expressions of the same social order, a bourgeois order grounded on capitalism, systematized in the nineteenth century by Thomas Arnold's philosophy of the public school, tutored by the moral persuasions of Thomas Hughes, and embodied in the play of W. G. Grace, the cricketer.[147] The game and its place in the social history of England told it all:

It was created by the yeoman farmer, the gamekeeper, the potter, the tinker, the Nottingham coal-miner, the Yorkshire factory hand. These artisans made it, men of hand and eye. Rich and idle young noblemen and some substantial city people contributed money, organization and prestige.

The class of the population that seems to have contributed least was the class destined to appropriate the game and convert it into a national institution. This was the solid Victorian middle class. It was accumulating wealth. It had won its first political victory in the Reform Bill of 1832 and it would win its second with the Repeal of the Corn Laws in 1846. It was on its way. More than most newcomers it was raw. . . . The Victorian middle classes read Dickens, loved Dickens, worshipped Dickens as few writers have been before or since. It is a very bold assumption that they did not understand what Dickens was saying. . . . Dickens saw Victorian England always with the eyes of a pre-Victorian. His ideal England was the England of Hazlitt and of Pickwick. Man of genius as he was, the Victorians were more perspicacious than he. They were not looking backwards. They wanted a culture, a way of life of their own. They found it symbolized for them in the work of the three men, first in Thomas Arnold, the famous headmaster of Rugby, secondly in Thomas Hughes, the author of *Tom Brown's Schooldays*, and lastly in W. G. Grace. These three men, more than all others, created Victorianism, and to leave out Grace is to misconceive the other two.[148]

Cricket and football as organized games had begun as expressions of the "artistic instincts" of the English rural and artisan classes. Had James had available to him what E. P. Thompson was concurrently formulating in *The Making of the English Working Class* (what might be mistaken for coincidence if one were not aware that both James and Thompson were Marxist historians; both were responding to a recent experience of profound political disillusionment; for James, his defeat at the hands of Eric Williams upon his return to Trinidad,[149] for Thompson, his resignation from a British Communist Party he reckoned morally and politically comatosed by Stalinism;[150] and both were, in Thompson's words, "attempting to defend, re-examine and extend the Marxist tradition at a time of political and theoretical disaster"),[151] he would have had no reason to hesitate in assigning this emergence of organized games to the process of working-class formation in England. These games, more particularly their organization and their preindustrial spirit "untainted by any serious corruption," were one aspect of the cultural mediation constructed by the working classes as a response to the historical processes of capitalist dislocation, expropriation, and a deepening alienation. James, however, could only hint a comprehension of that signification: "[W]hen the common people were not at work, one thing they wanted was organized sports and games."[152] The reflexive logic of his own development drew his attention elsewhere. He focused his analysis on what the games came to signify for the ruling classes, the classes whose capacities for literary and philosophical articulation had done so much to form his own consciousness.

For James, the starting point for understanding the English ruling classes and their hegemony over the laboring classes at home and abroad was in the historical parallel he discovered between ancient Greece and nineteenth- and twentieth-century Imperial Britain. It was a natural place for him to begin, he was British and "Greco-Roman we are."[153] In both societies, he recognized a relationship that fused power and organized games; an almost fanatical obsession with athletics, cemented (as he wrote of the Greeks) to the assertion of "the national unity of Greek civilization and the consciousness of themselves as separate from the barbarians who surrounded them."[154]

> The first recorded date in European history is 776 b.c., the date of the first Olympic Games. The Greek states made unceasing war against one another. But when the four-yearly games approached they declared a national truce, the various competitors assembled at Olympia, the games were held and when these were over the wars began again. . . . To every Greek city and every colony (as far away as Italy, Sicily, Africa, Egypt and Marseilles) the envoys went from Olympia with the invitations, and the communities sent their representatives and their official deputations. Forty thousand pilgrims would assemble, including the most distinguished members of Greek society.[155]

But, James insisted, the whole spectacle and its apparent but deceptive parallel in British society required closer analysis. Such an inspection would reveal the subtle dialectic between culture and the exercise of domination:

> The games were *not* introduced into Greece by the popular democracy. In fact, when the democracy came into power it lifted another type of celebration [the tragic drama] to a position of eminence to which the games soon took second place.
>
> The Olympic Games had been a festival of the feudal aristocracy and the bourgeoisie of Greece. Only the bourgeoisie had the money to stand the expense of the competitors. . . . Only the aristocratic families were in a position to take part in the chariot races.[156]

In England, organized sport had been a mass phenomenon, a spontaneous and public creation. And then, just as with land and labor, the rising bourgeoisie had expropriated it for their own purposes. Undisciplined, vulgar, and lacking self-confidence,[157] they had sensed that their reliance on naked force in their personae as expropriators, exploiters, and imperialists would ultimately destroy them if they could not establish to their own satisfaction their right to rule: "They wanted a culture, a way of life of their own."

> Arnold believed in religion and he believed in character. Scarcely less powerful in his conceptions was the role of the intellect. . . . The English ruling classes accepted Arnold's aims and accepted also his methods in general. But with an unerring instinct they separated from it the cultivation of the intellect and substituted for it organized games, with cricket at the heart of the curriculum.[158]

The public school and its regimen of organized games and athleticism provided them with a way of life. John Rae, himself a headmaster, concurs:

> Athleticism was a complex phenomenon at the heart of which was a belief that compulsory, competitive team games identified and developed qualities of character that were admirable in themselves and essential for "life's long earnest strife." . . . [F]or some sixty years from 1853 to 1914 this belief dominated not only the public-school system but also those areas of British and Imperial society where public-school men played the leading roles. . . .
>
> By 1900 the original rationale for organized games had been long forgotten and athleticism had developed its own ideological justification. Games not only postponed the mental torment of sex. They taught a morality. They developed manliness and toughness without which an expanding empire could not be run. They encouraged patriotism as the fierce loyalty to house and school was transferred to the regiment and the country.[159]

Though it might be said: "By it a ruling class disciplined and trained itself for the more supple and effective exercise of power,"[160] James believed such an interpretation was too mechanistic, too much the clever manipulation, too much the literal translation of what Arnold had intended. The psychological expression of the emergent English bourgeoisie had been drawn from the historical and cultural materials within which it had generated. James preferred to see the forms of their hegemony as extracted from a movement of the national culture; a renewal of English life drawing on the Puritan past but universal enough to affect other peoples far removed from its origins: "This signifies, as so often in any deeply national movement, that it contained elements of universality that went beyond the bounds of the originating nation."[161] It would be, he maintained, the only contribution that English education would make to the general educational ideas of Western civilization. He was not as sure (or as clear) as he might have been in the company of Thompson of the process he termed "modern civilization." But he did reveal one of its consequences. The English ruling bourgeoisie, at first, had required a discipline for themselves, for their own raison d'être and reproduction. They found their instrument among the cultural goods produced by the working classes. What they extracted or embedded in athleticism were rules of class, moral values, and a utilitarian rationalism. What they shared in the social spectacle of the games became part of the cement that bonded the several social orders into an identical imperial mission—one that would include even those natives at the peripheries whose claims to an English identity would amount to a tragic mistake. In the absence of more telling evidence, we must surmise that James discovered that mistake in England, 30 years before he sat down to write *Beyond a Boundary*.

When James and his contemporaries appeared in the metropole in the 1920s and 1930s, the England in which they had been immersed had already passed. Indeed, except in the airy fantasies manufactured by the ruling classes and their intelligentsia, it may never have existed. Among those elements that truly made a difference, the working classes were becoming detached from their identifications with the bourgeoisie and the nobility. English workers were militantly demonstrating that they were no longer persuaded that their future and that of the ruling classes were identical. Their betrayal by capitalism, manifested in the millions of unemployed, made many, for the moment, no longer willing to fight imperialist wars. By the mid-1930s, their declared interests could be found in demonstrations like the Hunger March of 1934 and the Jarrow Crusade of 1936; and they formed into militant grass-roots groups like the National Unemployed Workers' Movement, their numbers swelling even the membership figures of the CPGB (in one year, 1935–36, the Party went from 7,000 to 11,500).[162] The material crises of world capital and the political incompetence of the ruling classes, despite the repeated betrayals by the leaderships of the Labour Party and the trade union movement, provided a basis for a certain regeneration of the formal working-class movement and its electoral aspect. Membership in the trade unions expanded,[163] and the Labour Party, in disgrace in 1931, made substantial gains (as did the CPGB) in the municipal elections of 1932, 1933, and 1934, and the general election of 1935.[164] The organized Left, however, was not a major beneficiary.

For Padmore, Makonnen, and their African comrades, I. T. A. Wallace-Johnson and Kenyatta, in the anti-imperialist Left, there was another difference. Inevitably, even James realized that the illusion of the Empire as a global fraternity, benevolently orchestrated by advanced races for the interests of backward ones, was at best remote from the actualities they encountered. England, with its ever-broadening, grubby, dark poverty, its "low-life" fascists actively aligned and identified with factions of the ruling classes, its vulgar displays of racism (which "inexplicably" victimized those among the colonials who were proudest of being British), and its political mediocrity, inspired contempt, not confidence. The sheer pettiness of political discourse and bureaucratic cant betrayed what one expected from the "English heritage" or even from a respected enemy. These were not the actions of pretentious colonial administrators, they were manifestations in the home country itself. And while revolutionary movements of grandeur, scale, and vision could be seen emerging among "backward" peoples in India, Ceylon, China, and Africa, while even the Japanese ruling classes were mounting a massive territorial empire and the Soviets rationalizing one, the Left in Britain displayed characteristic factionalism, ideological "toadyism," and a politics dishonorably distant from the working classes and their struggles. Abandoned, as Padmore believed, by their most powerful ally, the world Communist movement, thoroughly disgusted with the duplicity of imperial policy, they turned toward the Black radical tradition.

The Theory of the Black Jacobin

The thirties were rich in political dramas that might ground Black radical intelligentsias in their own historical traditions. Their indulgence in the militant rhetoric of the Western European Left, evoking images of emergent revolutionary lower orders of its own would have logically brought them to it eventually. For in the older sense of the word, who was more proletarian than Blacks in the imperialist and capitalist order? But it was a different, though not unrelated, historical logic that was maturing. They read Du Bois's *Black Reconstruction* with its evocation of the brilliance of Black radicalism in nineteenth-century America, and they recognized its unmistakable debt to the Black masses of the early twentieth century who had produced the Chilembwes, the Garveys, the Lamine Senghors, and the Simon Kimbangus.[165] And then in 1934–35, when the Fascist Italian army invaded Ethiopia, the dam burst. Makonnen recalled:

> It's very important to put the response of the black world to the Ethiopian War into perspective, especially since it is easy to get the impression that pan-Africanism was just some type of petty protest activity—a few blacks occasionally meeting in conference and sending resolutions here and there. But the real dimensions can only be gathered by estimating the kind of vast support that Ethiopia enjoyed amongst blacks everywhere. We were only one centre, the International African Friends of Ethiopia, but that title was very accurate. Letters simply poured into our office from blacks on three continents asking where could they register. . . . And the same was true of Africa. When the Italians entered Addis Ababa, it was reported that school children wept in the Gold Coast. . . .
>
> It brought home to many black people the reality of colonialism, and exposed its true nature. They could then see that the stories of Lenin and Trotsky, or Sun Yat-sen, must have their African counterparts. . . . It was clear that imperialism was a force to be reckoned with because here it was attacking the black man's last citadel.[166]

Within the International African Friends of Ethiopia, however, there were disagreements as to what was to be done. Makonnen believed that the "collective security" of the League of Nations (to which Italy belonged and, paradoxically, through Italy, Ethiopia's membership had been accepted) should be invoked, arguing that it was a chimera unless Fascist Italy was stopped. James, who chaired the IAFE, was ambivalent, however. As an International Socialist, he accepted the Independent Labour Party's position that all the British and French capitalists were concerned with was using Ethiopia as a pretext for a war to destroy their rivals.[167] The "defense" of Ethiopia was a mask for an imperialist war. He opposed the League of Nations and the concessions (in return for sanctions against Italy) its "diplomats" had extorted from the Emperor, himself a feudal reactionary.[168] As a Black man, however, he had other imperatives. With Garvey in Hyde Park, denouncing Mussolini as "the arch barbarian of our times" and vigorously urging Blacks to support Abyssinia despite the Emperor's infamous reluctance at identifying himself as a Black man,[169] with the world-wide popular response among Blacks, James's ground was prescribed:

> I offered myself through the Abyssinian Embassy here to take service under the Emperor, military or otherwise.

My reasons for this were simple. International Socialists in Britain fight British Imperialism because obviously it is more convenient to do so than fight, for instance, German Imperialism. But Italian Capitalism is the same enemy, only a little further removed.

My hope was to get into the army. It would have given me an opportunity to make contact not only with the masses of the Abyssinians and other Africans, but in the ranks with them I would have had the best possible opportunity of putting across the International Socialist case. I believed also that I could have been useful in helping to organise anti-Fascist propaganda among the Italian troops.

And finally, I would have had an invaluable opportunity of gaining actual military experience on the African field where one of the most savage battles between Capitalism and its opponents is going to be fought before very many years. . . .

I did not intend to spend the rest of my life in Abyssinia, but, all things considered, I thought, and still think, that two or three years there, given the fact that I am a Negro and am especially interested in the African revolution, was well worth the attempt.[170]

Obviously, James was in conflict. But by early 1936, the situation had resolved itself for the moment: the occupation of Ethiopia was an accomplished fact, and the emperor was in exile in Britain.[171] By the end of the year, however, the Spanish Civil War had begun. Now the entire international Left was at war.[172] And Blacks from Africa, the Caribbean, and America joined the International Brigades to fight against the fascist forces of Spain, Germany, and Italy.[173] (And some Blacks fought for fascism: the Moroccan soldiers, General Franco's "storm-troopers.") But even before the International Brigades were withdrawn from Spain in 1938–39, the West Indies exploded into strikes and brutal repression.[174] The world seemed enveloped in struggle and Blacks and the Black struggle were a part of that world. For many radicals, an unavoidable lesson of the era was the necessity for armed resistance to oppression and exploitation. But for James, what the Italian army had done in Ethiopia: the killing of tens of thousands of peasants, and the complicity of the "bourgeois democracies" was instruction enough:

Africans and people of African descent, especially those who have been poisoned by British Imperialist education, needed a lesson. They have got it. Every succeeding day shows exactly the real motives which move imperialism in its contact with Africa, shows the incredible savagery and duplicity of European Imperialism in its quest for markets and raw materials. Let the lesson sink deep.[175]

The lesson sank deeper than he imagined. His tutorship under European radical thought had come to an end. From this point on his work would leap beyond the doctrinaire constructions of the anti-Stalinist Left and Engels and Marx themselves. The force of the Black radical tradition merged with the exigencies of Black masses in movement to form a new theory and ideology in James's writings.

In James's view, with only the most sporadic support to be expected from the

European working classes and the European Left, the radical Black intelligentsia was now compelled to seek the liberation of their peoples by their own means.[176] But some of the others with whom he was to be associated in the successor of the IAFE, the International African Service Bureau (1937), did not agree. When Padmore, for example, expressed his own reservations in *How Britain Rules Africa*, James leveled a withering criticism:

> It is on the future of Africa that the author, himself a man of African descent, is grievously disappointing. He heads one section, "Will Britain Betray Her Trust?" as if he were some missionary or Labour politician. In the true tradition of Lenin he insists on the right of the African people to choose their own development. But, astonishingly, he welcomes the appeal of "enlightened and far-sighted sections of the ruling classes of Europe with colonial interests in Africa" to co-operate with Africans. That is madness. How does the lion co-operate with the lamb?
>
> Africans must win their own freedom. Nobody will win it for them. They need co-operation, but that co-operation must be with the revolutionary movement in Europe and Asia. There is no other way out. Each movement will neglect the other at its peril, and there is not much time left.[177]

He had not forsaken the anticipation of an industrial proletarian revolution but he had become aware of the existence of a more vigorous Black opposition than that with which he was familiar in his own class.[178] In the crushing of the Ethiopian people he had seen the naked face of Western imperialism. More importantly, however, in Ethiopia, Spain, and the Caribbean, he had witnessed the capacities for resistance of ordinary Black people, the transformation of peasants and workers into liberation forces. Unlike Padmore, whose sojourn at the pinnacle of international Communism had left him uncertain, when he could no longer rely on that source, or Kenyatta and Williams, whose encounters with the imperial and capitalist metropoles so impressed them as to advise caution, James became convinced that successful armed rebellion among Black peoples was possible. The "colonial struggle and the metropolitan struggle" were identical on that score.[179] For a time, this view prevailed: armed rebellion among Blacks became the official position of the IASB. But after 1938, with James away in America on a lecture tour that would last for 15 years, that stand was modified by his associates:

> The work of the Bureau continued all through the war and in 1945 there came a sharp break with the theory. . . . The Bureau changed its position from the achievement of independence by armed rebellion to the achievement of independence by non-violent mass action. But to say that is one thing, to carry it out in practice is another. . . . To stake independence upon armed rebellion was therefore to have as a precondition the collapse or military paralysis of the metropolitan government. It was in other words to place the initiative for African struggle upon the European proletariat. . . .
>
> But by the end of the war the proletariat of Britain and France had not spoken.

Imperialism still held sway at home. Only a radical alteration in theory could form a basis for action. The perspective of armed rebellion was abandoned (though held in reserve) and non-violent mass action was substituted.[180]

While they pinned their hopes on the disintegrative force that war represented for the empires, on the resurrection of liberal ideology expressed by ruling classes made desperate by that war, and on the political consequences of the practical support given by colonials to the imperial countries during the war, James immersed himself in the American Trotskyist movement and the struggles of Black workers.[181] And he, too, became reconciled to nonviolent action:

> [A]s a result of the war, of revolutions and crises which had shaken contemporary society to its foundations for almost forty consecutive years, the bourgeoisie had lost its self-confidence in the face of a united mass movement. . . . [W]hen all is said and done the new political directive, breaking with the well-established ideas of the prewar period, is one of the great theoretical achievements of the present age, perhaps the first real break towards what the marxist movement requires today, the application of the traditional principles of marxism in complete independence of the stalinist perversion. It is to be noted that the theory did not reject armed rebellion, but held it in reserve in the event that the political and moral pressure envisaged failed to influence British imperialism.[182]

But "nonviolent mass action" threw the Black struggle back into the hands of the petit bourgeoisie, albeit a radical petit bourgeoisie. It was they who would mediate between the mass movement and the representatives of imperialism. And neither James nor any of the others ever came to terms with this theoretical error.[183] It was simply the case that the demand for the right of Black people to govern themselves (the position adopted at the Fifth Pan-African Congress in Manchester in 1945) articulated by a radical intelligentsia speaking on behalf of the dominated would have historical consequences quite different from those that resulted from the Black masses seizing their liberation.[184]

Nevertheless, James's intervention had been significant. He had made a singular contribution to radical Black historiography when he and his comrades in the IASB were mapping out their contending positions in the last years of the third, and during the fourth decade of the century. It was then that Padmore had written *How Britain Rules Africa*, Eric Williams his *The Negro in the Caribbean*, Kenyatta his *Kenya: Land of Conflict*, and James *The Black Jacobins*. The first three had proposed national independence for African peoples but were addressed to the colonial powers. The fourth had not appealed. Instead, it was a declaration of war for liberation. "[T]hose black Haitian labourers and the Mulattoes have given us an example to study. . . . The imperialists envisage an eternity of African exploitation: the African is backward, ignorant. . . . They dream dreams."[185]

The theoretical frame for *The Black Jacobins* was, of course, the theories of revolution developed by Marx, Engels, Lenin, and Trotsky. James asserted that fact rather frequently in the text. It was not, however, entirely the case. From Marx and Engels, he had taken the concept of a revolutionary class and the economic foundations for its historical emergence. But the slaves of Haiti were not a Marxian proletariat. No matter to James: the processes of social formation were the same:

> The slaves worked on the land, and, like revolutionary peasants everywhere, they aimed at the extermination of their oppressors. But working and living together in gangs of hundreds on the huge sugar-factories which covered North Plain, they were closer to a modern proletariat than any group of workers in existence at the time, and the rising was, therefore, a thoroughly prepared and organized mass movement. (pp. 85–86)

Moreover, James seemed willing to challenge Marx and Engels on the very grounds they had laid for the sociological and political significance of early capitalism. While they had been content to locate the formation of the modern revolutionary proletariat at the core of capitalist industrial production, James was insisting that the sphere be broadened. "At the same time as the French [masses], the half-savage slaves of San Domingo were showing themselves subject to the same historical laws as the advanced workers of revolutionary Paris" (p. 243). Capitalism had produced its social and historical negations in both poles of its expropriation: capitalist accumulation gave birth to the proletariat at the manufacturing core; "primitive accumulation" deposited the social base for the revolutionary masses in the peripheries. But what distinguished the formations of these revolutionary classes was the source of their ideological and cultural developments. While the European proletariat had been formed through and by the ideas of the bourgeoisie ("the ruling ideas," Marx and Engels had maintained, "were the ideas of the ruling class"), in Haiti and presumably elsewhere among slave populations, the Africans had constructed their own revolutionary culture:

> [O]ne does not need education or encouragement to cherish a dream of freedom. At their midnight celebrations of Voodoo, their African cult, they danced and sang, usually this favorite song:

> Eh! Eh! Bomba! Heu! Heu!
> Canga, bafio te!
> Canga, Moune de le!
> Canga, do ki la!
> Canga, li!

> "We swear to destroy the whites and all that they possess; let us die rather than fail to keep this vow." The colonists knew this song and tried to stamp it out, and the Voodoo cult with which it was linked. In vain. (p. 18)

> Voodoo was the medium of the conspiracy. In spite of all prohibitions, the slaves traveled miles to sing and dance and practice the rites and talk; and now, since the revolution, to hear the political news and make their plans. (p. 86)

This was a complete departure from the way in which Marx and Engels had conceptualized the transformative and rationalizing significance of the bourgeoisie. It *implied* (and James did not see this) that bourgeois culture and thought and ideology were irrelevant to the development of revolutionary consciousness among Black and other Third World peoples. It broke with the evolutionist chain in, the closed dialectic of, historical materialism. But where James was to hesitate, Cabral, as we have noted before, would stride boldly forward:

> [N]ational liberation is the phenomenon in which a given socio-economic whole rejects the negation of its historical process. In other words, the national liberation of a people is the regaining of the historical personality of that people, its return to history through the destruction of the imperialist domination to which it was subjected.[186]

But James's effort to level Marxist theory to the requirements of Black radical historiography was not finished. Though he bore a great respect for the work and thought of Lenin, there too he suggested a more imaginative treatment. With Lenin's notion of a cadre of professional revolutionists, the beginnings of the vanguard party in mind, James went so far as to designate an entire stratum, describing in precise terms how it was formed: "The leaders of a revolution are usually those who have been able to profit by the cultural advantages of the system they are attacking" (p. 19). This was an admission of class pride that neither Lenin nor Marx or Engels had been prepared to make.[187] Though surely it was an inadvertent admission, one that revealed James's own class origins, it also reflected a certain historical clarity.[188] The petit bourgeois intelligentsia had played dominant roles in Marxist thought as well as in the Bolshevik victory in Russia. The theory and the ideology of revolution was theirs, and unarguably too, the Russian state. They had brought to the working-class movement their "superior knowledge and the political vices which usually accompany it," as James would say of Toussaint (p. 95).

In San Domingo, the revolutionary masses had found a most propitious figure in Toussaint L'Ouverture. He knew the enemy better than they. That had been one of his rewards as a functionary in the slave system.

> His post as steward of the livestock had given him experience in administration, authority, and intercourse with those who ran the plantation. Men who, by sheer ability and character, find themselves occupying positions usually reserved for persons of a different upbringing, education and class, usually perform those duties with exceptional care and devoted labour. In addition . . . [he had] read Caesar's Commentaries . . . read and re-read the long volume by the Abbe Raynal. . . . [H]e had a thorough grounding in the economics and politics, not only of San Domingo, but of all the great empires of Europe. . . . His superb intellect had therefore had some opportunity of cultivating itself in general affairs at home and abroad. (p. 91)

But in the end, Toussaint had also failed the revolution. James more than sympathized with some of Toussaint's failures: "Toussaint knew the backwardness of the labourers; he made them work, but he wanted to see them civilised and advanced in culture. . . . He was anxious to see the blacks acquire the social deportment of the better class whites with their Versailles manners" (p. 246). And he also believed that Toussaint was correct in thinking that the propertied whites who remained or returned to San Domingo were needed to help the former slaves to construct a modern state: "His unrealistic attitude to the former masters, at home and abroad, sprang not from any abstract humanitarianism or loyalty, but from a recognition that they alone had what San Domingo society needed" (p. 290). This last in almost direct contradiction to his beliefs 30 years later: "Slaves ran the plantations; those tremendous plantations, the great source of wealth of so many English aristocrats and merchants, the merchant princes who cut such a figure in English society (and French too, but we are speaking of English society)."[189] Yet others, even more recently, have agreed with the earlier James.[190] In 1938, however, James knew that the former slaves, Toussaint's contemporaries, did not agree. When they acted on those beliefs and rebelled against Toussaint because they were no longer willing to accept his egoistic compromises with the colonial bourgeoisie and the Bonapartist regime in France, Toussaint had them hunted down and executed (p. 285). That tragedy, James argued, was because Toussaint "explained nothing, and allowed the masses to think that their old enemies were being favoured at their expense" (p. 284). But more importantly, James insisted, Toussaint's failure had been the result of events beyond his control: "If he failed, it is for the same reason that the Russian socialist revolution failed, even after all its achievements—the defeat of the revolution in Europe" (p. 283). But James was quite aware that there was much that had been within Toussaint's range and much that he had botched. He seemed to sense that for all the importance that might be rightly placed on the counterrevolution in Europe and for all the genius that could be ascribed to Toussaint in the early periods of the revolution, there was still something that was terribly wrong in the man's make-up. Indeed, James admitted, Haitian leaders of much narrower experience and education than Toussaint would overcome difficulties that his psychology could not confront. And in an extraordinary series of paragraphs he tried to reconcile his admiration for the man, for the revolutionary masses that had constructed him (as I would argue), and these figures to whom history attached the completion of the Haitian revolution. These passages better than most reveal the sources of James's contradictions in 1938:

> [B]etween Toussaint and his people there was no fundamental difference of outlook or of aim. Knowing the race question for the political and social question that it was, he tried to deal with it in a purely political and social way. It was a grave error. Lenin in his thesis to the Second Congress of the Communist International warned the white revolutionaries—a warning they badly need—that such has been the effect of the policy of imperialism on the relationship between advanced and

backward peoples that European Communists will have to make wide concessions to natives of colonial countries in order to overcome the justified prejudice which these feel toward all classes in the oppressing countries. Toussaint, as his power grew, forgot that. He ignored the black laborers, bewildered them at the very moment that he needed them most, and to bewilder the masses is to strike the deadliest of all blows at the revolution. . . . The whites were whites of the old regime. Dessalines did not care what they said or thought. The black labourers had to do the fighting—and it was they who needed reassurance. It was not that Toussaint had any illusions about the whites. He had none whatever. . . .

Yet Toussaint's error sprang from the very qualities that made him what he was. It is easy to see to-day, as his generals saw after he was dead, where he had erred. It does not mean that they or any of us would have done better in his place. If Dessalines could see so clearly and simply, it was because the ties that bound this uneducated soldier to French civilisation were of the slenderest. He saw what was under his nose so well because he saw no further. Toussaint's failure was the failure of enlightenment, not of darkness. (pp. 286, 287, 288)

Alas, from no less an authority than James himself, we know this last defense of Toussaint was not without its element of rationalization. As Toussaint wasted away in his prison in the Jura mountains, writing his letters of supplication to the little emperor, his vision gave him away: "Despite the treachery of France he still saw himself as a part of the French Republic 'one and indivisible.' He could not think otherwise . . . there was a limit beyond which he could not go" (p. 364). We, of course, recognize James (and perhaps even his impressions of Padmore) in these assertions. We can see the declared identification of a Black revolutionary intelligentsia with the masses; the willingness to continue the submission to "scientific socialism" by denying the material force of ideology while indicating a bitter disappointment with the Communist movement; the patronizing attitude toward the organic leaders of the masses; and the ambivalent pride of place presumed for the Westernized ideologue. Moreover, it is clear that James was looking critically at his own class. Unlike his confederates, he was compelled to face up to the boundaries beyond which the revolutionary petit bourgeoisie could not be trusted. For that reason he was to insist often that the revolutionary masses must preserve to themselves the direction of the revolutionary movement, never deferring to professional revolutionists, parties, or the intelligentsia. But we shall return to that in a moment.

Coming to Terms with the Marxist Tradition

The year following the printing of *Jacobins*, James published *A History of Negro Revolt*. This was to be his last sustained statement on Pan-Africanism until the appearance of *Nkrumah and the Ghana Revolution*. It was, though, a minor piece, summarizing in historical shorthand some of the occasions of Black rebellion in the diaspora and Africa in the eighteenth, nineteenth, and twentieth centuries.[191] It would prove to be of some use three decades later but it was casually written, more a public lecture than a study. James was now at the center of the Trotskyist international movement,[192] and soon he was to be just as immersed in the American theater, stirring things up in New York, disputing with Trotsky over the Negro Question,[193] organizing share-croppers and tenant farmers in southeast Missouri.[194]

Ten years after *Jacobins*, James wrote a second masterpiece amid a crisis in which he was deeply involved. And on this occasion he found it necessary to frontally assault some of the principal figures of the Marxist movement. *Notes on Dialectics* was written in the late 1940s[195] a moment when the preoccupations of the Second World War had faded, leaving American Marxists free to ponder the changed circumstances they faced: the significance of postwar arrangements between the Soviet Union and the "Western powers"; the reactions of their country's working classes to the domination of the world economies by American capital; the orchestrated expulsions of Communists from the American labor movement; the convergent pressures on the Communist movement from the American government and the Soviet Union, and— for Trotskyists—the future of the Fourth International shorn of Trotsky, its unifying symbol.[196] By now James had become a prominent intellectual and organizer in the Socialist Workers' Party (swp), the American representation of the Fourth International. In this restricted arena it is fair to say he was being recognized for what he was: one of the leading Marxist historian/philosophers in the country. With Max Shachtman, however, he and others had withdrawn from the swp. In the early 1940s they formed the Workers' Party with 600 or so members.[197] Then, in 1942, a further split had occurred, a group centering around James and Raya Dunayevskaya, the Johnson-Forest tendency, had left the "Shachtmanites."[198] Later, in 1949 or so, the Johnson-Forest tendency would rejoin the swp only to become resolutely independent again two years later.[199] They required more:

> We had broken with Trotsky's analysis of the nature of the Russian state since the death of Lenin. . . . We came to the conclusion that a fundamental investigation still remained to be done, on Hegel's *Science of Logic* (with that of course had to be associated the smaller *Logic*, a section of Hegel's *Encyclopedia*).[200]

Notes on Dialectics was James's contribution: it was his logical and philosophical consideration and reconstruction of the history of the labor movement in relation to the formation of revolutionary action, parties, and revolutionary thought in the European experience. The grammar of the work, its logical structure, was grounded on Hegel's construction of the dialectic. It was at once an exposition of Hegel's philosophical method and the historical movement of the working classes. And when it was written its immediate purpose was to provide a rationale and a historical object for the political activity of his small organization: To preserve for his comrades the claim for the Leninism of an authentic socialism.[201] It was they who were seeking to contain a catastrophe, to rescue Marxism from its self-inflicted wounds (Stalinism and Trotskyism) thus preserving its theoretical and political core (historical materialism and the revolutionary proletariat). Their task was not an easy one. It was not just the political battle to be waged: a small organization in opposition to former (Trotskyist) colleagues, in opposition to Stalinism, the trade union bureaucracies, the apparatuses of the American state, and world capitalism. Those forces were more than balanced, they believed, since they were in the company of the proletarian masses. History and numbers were on their side. More decisive were the contradictions they hoped to rationalize. As Marxists they were compelled to juggle contending impulses. They were a radical intelligentsia contemptuous of the revolutionary petit bourgeoisie, in some sense themselves. They were revolutionary ideologues charged by their tradition to "criticize everything" while conserving the figures of Marx and Lenin. They were committed to the abolition of parties but their entire political history had been in association and contention with revolutionary parties. They were renegade bourgeois ideologists, trained in the ruling ideas of their time yet they believed in the imperative of penetrating the consciousness of the working classes in order to comprehend the proletariat's historical activity. And despite their sometimes feverish energies they were essentially contemplative didactics coupled with revolutionary action. James could not escape these contradictions any more than Grace Lee (Boggs) or Dunayevskaya. Neither could *Notes on Dialectics*. It contained an ideate from which James had no intention of departing but was compelled to leave behind. He supposed Hegel's dialectic would resolve the dilemma.

The delinquent premise was restated by James in the 1980 edition of the work: "What is then the beginning of the labour movement? We find the historical beginning in the French revolution *as Marx saw it*" (p. 10; my emphasis). This was the unchallengeable presupposition: Marxists had to begin where Marx had begun and as Marx had begun. It meant that the assumption made in Marx's vision of modern history had to persist in James's consideration of social revolution: the notion that implied that the proletariat constituted a class like the bourgeoisie. Like most Marxists, James was quite unwilling to contemplate that, as Cornelius Castoriadis has made clearer than anyone, since the appearance of the bourgeoisie was historically the origin of the category class it would be philosophically and historically impossible for the proletariat to recapitulate the social and ideological experience of the bourgeoisie. It could not become a class in those terms.[202] But there had to be limits within which the Johnson-Forest tendency was to remain. They had realized almost too late that as Trotskyists, without knowing it, they had flirted with the disintegration of Marxism: "[T]rotskyist thinking, persisted in, led the posing of the question of the disintegration of marxist theory, questioning whether we might not have to ask ourselves if it were valid" (p. 56). Their need to do things differently was to be a disciplined need. And in his consideration of Lenin, Trotsky, Stalin, and Marx, James made good use of his predecessors, holding strictly to the lights of the tradition. His critique, notwithstanding his fundamental deference, was true to form: internally consistent, devastatingly powerful, erudite, and logically near-flawless. Within its own terms James would take the philosophic discourse of the Marxian tradition to its most complete realization in the postwar years.

He began by assuring his comrades that their appearance, their work, and their politics, based on the evolution of state-capitalism and the proletarian impulse for an organizational form that transcended the revolutionary party, were anticipated in Hegel's *Science of Logic*: their's were the "new ideas" Hegel had anticipated. The opposition to them among Stalinists, Trotskyists, and Shachtmanites was corrupted by formalism and opportunism. Paraphrasing Hegel, James asserted:

> Imperceptibly the new ideas became familiar even to their opposers, who appropriated them and—though persistently slighting and gainsaying the sources and principles of those ideas—yet had to accept their results.
>
> We can see this is our whole development. The chief, or one of the most striking examples is our application of the law of value to the Russian economy. Today these God-damned scoundrels all turn up and say "of course"! But you could look through the literature of the Fourth International for pages and pages. I do not remember any statements to that effect. (p. 13)

He reminded them that Hegel had distinguished between vulgar empiricism, understanding, and Reason (dialectical thought), charging each with a certain value, a certain threshold of thought. The Dialectic was the ultimate realization of the Mind, of the Subject. Clearly, he suggested, Lenin had been capable of dialectical thought, capable of transcending through his thought the old categories (Second International) that he had inherited: "The Russian revolution of February caused violent changes in Lenin's categories. World War I set him revising the categories of the Second International" (p. 17). On the other hand, however, Trotsky had been limited to Understanding, a necessary and useful stage of thought but one that could end in its reduction to absolute categories: "He would have been able to lecture you on changing categories most profoundly. He talked about it all the time. But fixed and finite determinations held him by the throat to the end" (p. 18). Trotsky had been unwilling to recognize the true significance of Stalinism: "stalinism as a necessary, an inevitable, form of development of the labour movement. The workers are not mistaken. They are not deceived. Not in any serious sense of these words. They are making an experience that is necessary to their own development" (p. 30). Trotsky had been convinced that a labor bureaucracy (as had occurred with the old category: the Second International) would protect private property; Trotsky had been committed to the end to winning the debate with Stalin over the permanent revolution versus socialism in one country. While the Stalinists were practical and went about seizing and then preserving their power (and, incidentally, state property), Trotsky continued to defend himself in the most fixed terms: contending with his ghosts over who was closer to Lenin.

> Thus the debate, beginning with socialism in a single country, remained for ever and ever within the categories of leninism. Stalin said: whatever I do is leninism. Trotsky said no: it is not leninism. I am the genuine leninist. That was the setting. Stalin was not very serious about it. His actions were pure empiricism. Trotsky was

serious about this leninism and was caught in it and strangled in it. He was entirely wrong in every theoretical and practical conclusion that was drawn from the debate. . . . The debate was that socialism *could* not be built in a single country. Does anyone believe that Stalin or any of his people believe that what is in Russia is socialism? Only an utter fool can think so. What the debate was about was whether the state-property system would be maintained without a revolution sooner or later in the West. (p. 350)

And of course while Trotsky was preoccupied, fixed at the level of Understanding, he never possessed the energy nor the insight to realize that Stalinism . . . could only be understood by revealing its economic basis: "He did not see that the revolutionary Third International had succumbed to state capitalism aided by Russian imperialism. He never wrote about the economic changes, what he thought about it, if he did, he never thought of sufficient importance to set down. . . ." "Astonishing, isn't it?" (p. 37). Those who wished to continue with the struggles of the proletariat, to comprehend the emergence of Stalinism, could no longer afford to indulge Trotsky:

The new categories, the impulses, the instinctive actions, the strong knots formed, were observed, talked about, but always incorporated into the old shell; state capitalism or reformist international that would destroy private property and refuse to support the bourgeoisie in imperialist war, an anti-proletarian bureaucracy that throve on state property and would defend it to the last against private property, all the knots, impulses, etc. which drove these into the mind, were allowed in only in so far as they filled into the formed and finished categories which Lenin left. That is why what were the results of Reason in one generation become Understanding in another, and the negating, the transcending of the determinations into a higher unity cannot be done. (p. 34)

Trotsky had thus mistaken Stalinism for a workers' bureaucracy, he had been incapable of transcending the once powerful categories derived from the experience of the Second International (p. 59) in order to recognize the further maturation of the contradictions of a workers' movement in capitalist society. Hegel, of course, had anticipated Trotsky's error: consciousness discovering what "was truth only for the particular vision, criterion, standards with which it looked on the world" (p. 54).[203] Appearance had superseded Actuality:

But you and I are dialecticians. We know that stalinism today is the true state of the labour movement. It is revolutionary, repudiating parliamentarianism, private property, national defence, and national boundaries. It is however attached to an imperialism as patron and is bureaucratic and aims at totalitarian control of labour and then of capital. (p. 43)

. . . To know true reality, to understand the labour movement, is to know that at each stage it degenerates but splits to re-instate its self-identity, its unity, but that this unity comes from divisions within its own self. . . .

Stalinism is a bitter obstacle. But see it as part of a process. Through the process of its own development, the seriousness, the suffering, the patience, and the labour of the negative, the labour movement goes through all its experiences and reaches its completely realized self only by conquering them one after the other. And only at the end, when the labour movement finds itself fully realized will we see what it is in very truth. (p. 65)

Lenin had recognized the workers in Hegel's discussions of the Doctrines of Being and Essence. It could be seen that his note on the *Logic* contained his revolutionary program in formation (pp. 98–106). He had discerned the self-movement of the proletariat, the movement that was the working class's being. He comprehended that:

The essence of a thing is the fact that it must move, reflect itself, negate the reflection, which was nothing, become being, and then become nothing again, while the thing itself must move on because it is its nature to do so. . . . The essence of the proletariat is its movement to incorporate in itself experience of the evils of capitalism until it overcomes capitalism itself. (p. 78)

James insisted that Lenin would have understood that "The history of the Third International is the history of the supersession of leninism by stalinism," and that finally, "If the Fourth International is to supersede stalinism then it must 'contain' stalinism in its concept of itself. It begins from all the things that stalinism took over from leninism and kept. . . . The Other of stalinism is an international socialist economic order, embracing from the start whole continents" (p. 87). Because "this amazing, this incredible man" (p. 138) had understood the Soviets when they came in 1917[204] (but admittedly not in 1905), Lenin would know that in a movement dominated by the capitalist perversion of the revolutionary party he created:

There is nothing more to organize. You can organize workers as workers, You can create a special organization of revolutionary workers. But once you have those two you have reached an end. Organization as we have known it is at an end. The task is to abolish organization. The task today is to call for, to teach, to illustrate, to develop spontaneity—the free creative activity of the proletariat. The proletariat will find its method of proletarian organization. And, contradiction par excellence, at this stage the vanguard can only organize itself on the basis of the destruction of the stranglehold that the existing organizations have on the proletariat by means of which it is suffering such ghastly defeats. (p. 117)

Stalinism, the counterrevolution that had emerged from "arrested" Leninism (p. 150), would inevitably and spontaneously be opposed by the workers' movement because the "great masses or classes" only learned through "struggle against some concrete thing" (p. 93).

The proletariat itself will smash stalinism to pieces. This experience will teach it its final lesson, that the future lies in itself, and not in anything which claims to represent it or direct it. (p. 92)

James finished the work, harvesting all these materials. He culled them in order to present one of the most exciting historical constructions to be produced by a Marxist thinker. Patiently, deliberately, systematically, but always mediated by his lyrical and sometimes mischievous literary "voice," he distilled from 300 years of European history the processes and lineages of the contending forces within the proletarian movement: the revolutionary petit bourgeoisie and the working masses. The former, he maintained, made its first appearance in the English Civil War of the seventeenth century as radical democrats; the latter were the social basis for the revolutionary masses behind the French Revolution. However, each had undergone transformations through the long years between their appearances and the present (that is, 1948). These changes were the results not of years, but of capitalism. These two opposing historical forces had at last reached their final articulation in Stalinism and Fascism. In Stalinism, the petit bourgeoisie had organized the attempted destruction of the revolutionary proletariat. The petit bourgeoisie began by using the workers to destroy the bourgeoisie and then the suppression of the workers' movement had followed. In Fascism, the petit bourgeoisie had become the social instrument of the increasingly desperate bourgeoisie in the effort to destroy the same historical subject: the workers' movement. Together Fascism and Stalinism constituted the objective movement (centralization) of capitalist organization (p. 201). The continuing development of the organization of capitalist production and the bureaucratic administration of state capitalism had called forth a petit bourgeois class of enormous skill, responsibility, and ambitions. Within those same centuries, then, though it was possible to trace the maturation of the bourgeoisie and the working classes, *it was also necessary to recognize the transformation of the petit bourgeoisie. It was necessary because this strata had presumed the leadership of the proletarian movement and then betrayed it.* Now the radical intelligentsia at the service of the proletarian revolution—activists like those in the Johnson-Forest tendency—had to respond to these events. First it had to comprehend them, ceasing to identify the perversion of petit bourgeois leadership with the authentic forces of the revolution. Second, the "vanguard of the vanguard" had to assist the proletariat in the destruction of the "revolutionary proletarian" bureaucracy. The direction of the world was in the hands of the workers: "The proletariat will decide. The thing is to tell the proletariat to decide" (p. 181).

To the misfortune of *Notes on Dialectics*, it was an internal document. Thus for two decades its distribution was restricted, the more so since the movement to which it was addressed was small. It would not be widely read for 30 years. But, though James came to recognize it as his most extraordinary work, it did contain certain limitations. The most obvious problem stemmed from James's fascination for Hegel's mode of argumentation: the distillation of history into rich concentrates used solely for the grounding of abstract discourse. It was also the case that this history was exclusively European—an inadvertent but natural substantiation of Hegel's own assertion of where history could occur. James's style was also familiar in another way: the language was the combative one of Marxist exegeses (inherited from German philosophy)—a dismissive tongue used to humiliate opposition. Its results were predictable corollaries: the absolute deprecation of the Fallen (Stalin, Trotsky, Shachtman, etc.) in contrast to oratory for True Thinkers (Hegel, Marx, Engels, Lenin). James relished the form and employed it consistently until he was able to rescue the tenor of his argument in the historical flourish with which he ended. Still, *Notes on Dialectics* was a remarkable achievement. It was a too rare example of a living, active, grappling Marxism. Its conceits were small ones given the company it kept. Though its author had not hesitated to assume the role of headmaster to Western Marxists, his grounds were substantial: the questions then being raised in the Marxist movement were so misconceived as inevitably to suggest abolition of the tradition itself. He had in many ways succeeded in anchoring Marx's thought in the twentieth century when to many it seemed that Lenin had accomplished the very opposite: its annihilation as a reference. He had shown a new direction when it seemed all such possibilities were at an end.

Our treatment of James must end here. However, his writing and politics continued. Deported from the United States in 1952, he returned to Britain, spent a few years at home in Trinidad only to return to the United States then Britain. Following *Notes on Dialectics*, he wrote *State Capitalism and World Revolution* (1950). At Ellis Island, while awaiting action by the U.S. Department of Immigration and Naturalization, he composed *Mariners, Renegades and Castaways*, a politico-literary critique of Herman Melville's *Moby-Dick* and *Pierre* that included observations on detention and his personal, conflict-ridden encounter with "American" Communist prisoners. Within the next ten years he was to publish *Facing Reality* (with Grace Lee and Pierre Chaulieu, 1958), *Modern Politics* (his 1960 lectures in Trinidad), *Beyond a Boundary*, a significant appendix to the reissue of *The Black Jacobins* (1963), and a stream of reviews, introductions, articles, and position papers the range of which is suggested in the recently published collections: *The Future in the Present* and *Spheres of Existence*. Of his major works, it was the first that would draw James into the orbit of radical thought in the 1960s and afterward. It was the Black diaspora, particularly the militant Black petit bourgeoisie that had grown impatient with American apartheid, which would rediscover *Jacobins*. First the book and then the author would help them to confirm their ideological struggle with bourgeois culture. The mass Black movement provided the compulsion. James astounded this new Black intelligentsia with his brilliant thought, his provocative analyses, and his grasp of Black history. He became once again "Nello" to intimates two generations younger than his contemporaries, he became the teacher they could honor, a living, absorbing link between themselves and a past of which most had only a vague notion (or, just as frequently, a profound expectation). But he also sometimes saddened them, pitching divisive battles in fields peopled only with Marxian phantoms.[205] When they had recovered him, he had again become accustomed to presenting himself as a "Black European."[206] Some came to understand something of what he expected of them. But he also learned: "[A] great deal of my time has been spent in seeing how much I failed to understand when I was young and my whole life was toward European literature, European sociology. Now I'm beginning to see and it is helping me to write."[207] Perhaps his long-awaited autobiography will ultimately demonstrate just how permanently their reflective gift of the Black radical tradition has affected him. What he gave them is no mystery.

CHAPTER

RICHARD WRIGHT
AND THE CRITIQUE
OF CLASS THEORY

11

Marxist Theory and the
Black Radical Intellectual

In one sense the first systemization of Black radical historiography was constructed by figures such as G. W. Williams, J. J. Thomas, Du Bois, James, and Padmore for precisely the complex reasons suggested by James when he wrote on revolutionary leaders: they had directly profited from the "cultural advantages" of the system upon which they mounted their ideographic attack. As the heirs of Black petit bourgeoisies, they enjoyed in the order of things the intellectual beneficence of the ruling order from which they posited their critique. A less obvious process fueled their rebellion. Ambitious and accomplished in the very skills that were understood to qualify them for leading roles in bourgeois society—which "naturally" demarcated extraordinary individuals (dominators) from the ordinary populace—their loyalties to the existing order were contingent only on its consistency. Inevitably, when racial order subverted their experience of the "universals" of Western civilization, they were confronted with but two alternatives: to bitterly endure the cynically indulged illusion or to attempt its realization. Obviously when these figures chose the latter it was not a choice characteristic of their class. Still subject to what James had described as the inherent "political vices" associated with their social origins, their seduction by those aspects of Marxism that were owed to the sources of its genesis is understandable. Marxism's intellectual power and pedigree, its promise of a hidden truth, its open opposition to an insidious social order, its alternative mapping of the historical origins of the ruling classes, which they had come to despise, and its identification with the underclasses, made it an almost irresistible companion. Moreover, Marxists were under no obligation to minimize what the total thrust of bourgeois thought was orchestrated to deny: that the "natural" social order tended toward instability and chaos. On the contrary, Marxian logic composed a historical order from the anarchic, wrenching social forces within the capitalist world system. Marxism was (and remains) a superior grammar for synthesizing the degradation of labor with the growing destabilization of capitalist production and accelerating technological development; the increasing resort to state coercion mediated by bureaucratic rationalism; and the strangulation of whole regions (most of them formerly colonies) through pricing mechanisms, market manipulation, monopolization of advanced technology, the international organization of production, international banking, military assistance, and the stultifying dependencies of monocultural economics. Marxism, too, implied that it was the particular privilege of the revolutionary intellectual to comprehend this deeper, extra-existential order. And in the generation of these Black intellectuals, with apparent finality Marxism was confirmed in its historical authority by the Russian Revolution.

This last identification, though, was to prove to be an ambiguous one. In the minds of Black intellectuals, within a quarter of a century, the significance of the Third International had substantially degenerated. For some, like Padmore, and later Cox, international Communism (Stalinism) was simply another deceitful Western invention; for others like James it was its own perversion; finally, for those who were to share Du Bois's experience, it seemed merely a convenient means of protest. However, detached from the Communist movement, Marxist theory could retain important capacities. Notwithstanding its weaknesses, there was in Marxism a critical discourse to which no bourgeois ideology adequately responded. Capitalism's global regularities of war, expanding poverty and exploitation, the concentration of wealth, and the extension of repression persisted. Bourgeois thinkers displaced these endemic phenomena with the notion of termed, resolvable dysfunctions. Marxists correctly declared they were no such things.

There was, however, much more to these radical Black intellectuals than their class origins and the contradictions they experienced consequent to the racial castes of Western civilization. More profoundly than "scientific" Marxism could suggest, they were an element of a historically emergent social force, the Black radical movement. And though intellectually disciplined in such ways as to oppose its conscious realization, their ideological nurturing as Blacks prepared them for its eventual recognition. It is possible to see, even in such Westernized intellects as James and Du Bois, that the historical force of the Black movement was the more powerful influence. Even their discovery of Western radicalism proved to be insufficient. As we have seen, it became necessary to both of them to attempt to bring Marxist theory to bear on a historical phenomenon for which its analytical vocabulary was inadequate. From the moments of these efforts, neither Du Bois nor James, nor Padmore nor Cox could sustain a commitment to orthodox Marxism.

But there were also others in whose work a similar contestation could be discerned; others emergent from Black societies and in search of an articulated opposition to Western racism and bourgeois society. One of these, Richard Wright, is of particular interest. Unlike those upon whom we have already focused, Wright was not of the petit bourgeoisie. His roots were in the Black peasantry of the American South. His encounter with Marxism and the Communist movement was largely unmediated by the cultural misdirections that accompanied the intellectual awakenings of middle-class Black men and women. His childhood and adolescence in Mississippi, subject to the most direct exposure to racist brutality and brutalization, provided him little appreciation for or expectations of bourgeois society and its culture.[1] He came to Marxism for reasons that were fundamentally different from those of our previous subjects. And when he withdrew, he was different too. His insights into his experience of the Communist movement and into Marxist thought suggest an alternative penetration into the relationship between European radical thought and the historical configurations of the Black movement.

The ambiguity surrounding Wright is, in part, a consequence of his own intellectual odyssey. More precisely it is a consequence of his public honesty about the voyage. It was a journey that took him from Marxism, and through Existentialism, and finally to Black nationalism—a journey that could be retraced biographically from his membership in the American Communist Party in the early 1930s to his death in France in 1960.

But another and equally important source for the undefined character of Wright's legacy is the several and remarkably extensive campaigns of vilification launched against him by the American Left, the American liberal intelligentsia and American bureaucrats. These ranged from the literary attacks on Wright by writers such as James Baldwin,[2] to the political assaults of figures like James Ford,[3] Ben Burns,[4] then editor of *Ebony*, the deliberately distorted reports in *Time* magazine on Wright and others,[5] the machinations of the Central Intelligence Agency,[6] and threats from once-powerful, but now almost forgotten anti-Communists like David Schine.[7] It appears to be a fair statement that though these distinct and, in some instances, opposing political factions had rather different interests in the destruction of Wright's influence on American politics and literature, they did concur on the desirability of the suppression of his work and ideas.[8]

In any case, the result was the same: Wright's self-imposed geographical exile was transformed into an intellectual and political isolation. Moreover, some of these same forces sought further retribution from Wright by filling his life in Europe and Great Britain with harassments of both petty and terrifying dimensions.[9] It was intended that Wright realize the full consequence of criticizing American domestic racial policies and attacking American foreign policy in the Third World.

Yet despite his detractors and their sponsors, despite the established and powerful political and cultural authorities of American society, some of Wright's work and ideas survived. The re-emergence of Wright's importance in American thought may appear at first ironical. So many of his critics are now rather thin shadows in history.

But, more accurately, it is the result of the social and historical contradictions of American capitalism and its particular social order.

In the midst of the Black consciousness and nationalist movements of the 1960s, the seemingly irresistible dictates of the market compelled the republishing of the *Outsider* (1965), *Native Son* (1966), *Black Boy* (1966), *Eight Men* (1969), and later, *American Hunger* (1977).[10] They were works that spoke to a generation that Wright did not live to see but had anticipated. Significant, too, was the emergence of younger and equally militant Black writers and playwrights (among them John A. Williams, Leroi Jones, Ed Bullins, Melvin Van Peebles, and Ishmael Reed). Much of their work would have fallen quite easily into what one American critic, Robert Bone, had called "the Wright School" ("For the Wright School, literature is an emotional catharsis—a means of dispelling the inner tensions of race. Their novels often amount to a prolonged cry of anguish and despair. Too close to their material, feeling it too intensely, these novelists lack a sense of form and of thematic line."),[11] except for the fact that Bone had already announced the death of that school 20 years earlier: "By the late 1940s the vein of literary material unearthed by Richard Wright had been all but worked out. The market for protest had become saturated."[12] It does appear that Bone was a bit premature.

More remarkable, however, than the sheer survival of Wright's work, is the theoretical and analytical power of his ideas. This achievement of Wright's, with the stimulus of historical materialism and psychoanalysis, fell much closer to an emergent European literature (Sartre, Merleau-Ponty, Koestler, Lukács, Marcuse, Kolakowski) in the post–Second World War period than to any American fashion. Like many European Left intellectuals, Wright was moving beyond classical Marxism and the Marxism inspired by Lenin in order to come to terms with a world constituted of material and spiritual forces historically unique. Wright's reach, consequently, can be said to be much longer than that implied by the terms employed by many of his American critics. He was never merely a "racial novelist," a "protest writer," or a "literary rebel."[13] Indeed, much of his work was a direct confrontation with the leading ideas and ideational systems of contemporary Western political and social thought. His arena was the totality of Western civilization and its constitutive elements: industrialization, urbanization, alienation, class, racism, exploitation, and the hegemony of bourgeois ideology. His work thus constituted an inquiry.

Wright's persistence in his investigation of Western society was an important factor contributing to the achievement of a certain consistency in his work. As artist, as essayist, as critic, as political activist, it is clear that he arranged and rearranged many times the elements making up the phenomenological display of Western development. He knew the names of Western experience but was less certain of what he knew of their nature and their systemic and historical relationships. There were questions to which he still had to find answers: was the working class a social reality? Could class consciousness supersede racism as an ideology? Was the party the vanguard of the proletariat? Was Marxism more than a critique of capitalism? These were some of the issues to which Wright had not found satisfactory answers in organized and organizational politics. Ultimately, it would be because of his particular skill for transforming theoretical abstractions and constructs into recognizably human experience that it became possible for him to make those distinctions between dogma and reality so important to his development.

Theoretically and ideologically, Wright came to terms with Western thought and life through Black nationalism. However, the basis for his critique of Western society was his experience of the historical formation of Black peoples in Africa and the diaspora, from the Gold Coast to the Mississippi Delta.[14] Psychically and intellectually he was drawn to attend those same forces that produced the critical inspections of W. E. B. Du Bois, George Padmore, and C. L. R. James. As Michel Fabre puts it:

> Wright's originality, then, is that he completely understood and often reiterated . . . that the situation of the Black in the twentieth century, and in particular during the crucial period from the Depression to the advent of Black Power, was exceptional. These years saw the awakening of the Third World and with it the enormous mutation of our civilisation. "The liberation of the colored peoples of the world is the most important event of our century," is a refrain that runs throughout Wright's work. The same message, delivered half a century before by W. E. B. Du Bois, did not have the same existentialist dimension.[15]

Wright had not created these forces that were transforming Western society, but it was his intention to give these events a meaning independent of those interpretations bounded by the interests of Western civilization as articulated by its intellectuals and ideologues.

Still there are some who have argued that Wright fulfilled little of his promise. Harold Cruse, among them, has written that Wright "was so ideologically blinded by the smog of Jewish-Marxist nationalism that he was unable to see his *own* clearly"; that Wright had not understood "that the classics of Marx and Engels were written not for the proletariat but for the intelligentsia,"[16] and, finally, that "He could not gather into himself all the ingredients of nationalism; to create values and mould concepts by which his race was to 'struggle, live and die.' "[17]

Here, then, are two of the several interpretations that attach to Wright's significance. The first places him within a tradition of radical Black thinkers. The second expels him from that same legacy. In the following pages we shall examine which of these two summaries of Wright's work is more appropriate.

The Novel as Politics

Richard Wright was by his work primarily a novelist. But as a novelist involved in social action, his novels were more than a complaint against or an observation of the human condition. Wright intended that his writing engage and confront a political reality of movement. He was a novelist who recognized that a part of his task was to come to terms with the character of social change and the agencies that emerged as attempts to direct that change. His early development consciously reflected this concern, beginning with his 1937 essay, "Blueprint for Negro Writing." In this essay we see the first suggestions of a critical independence of thought in Wright.

> Perspective . . . is that fixed point in intellectual space where a writer stands to view the struggles, hopes, and sufferings of his people. . . . Of all the problems faced by writers who as a whole have never allied themselves with world movements, perspective *is* the most difficult of achievement.[18]

Wright was quite openly declaring that he meant his work to reflect a committed intellect, one informed by a political intention and the process of historical movement. He was also dedicating himself to the task that would occupy him for the remaining 23 years of his life: the location of his "perspective" in the complex of struggles for liberation in the Third World. As we shall see, what Wright ultimately discovered was a psychological and intellectual locus unlike anything his experience of Western radicalism and activism could encompass. Fortunately, a great part of his preparation for that discovery can be found in his novels.

When we consider Richard Wright's fictional and explicitly political work, three novels (*Native Son, The Outsider,* and "Island of Hallucination" this latter eventually published under the title *American Hunger*) and one collection of short stories (*Uncle Tom's Children*) stand out. Together, these works both chronicle and interpret Wright's experiences with American communism and political action. They also constitute studies of Marxism as a theory of history and social revolution, of the social and psychological development of the American working class, and of the historical and ideological development of American Blacks. Serious attention to these works should not be deflected by the form through which Wright sought to articulate his ideas. Indeed, it must be recognized that his works are uniquely suited to their tasks. Using this form, Wright could reconstruct and weight the extraordinary complexities and subtleties of radical politics as he and others had experienced it. His characters could live with and struggle through crises he had encountered. They could "test" the meanings and significances he had given to those experiences. His novels were consequently much more *authentic* documents than the conventional forms of history, biography, and political tract for they were constructed from lives with which he was intimate. In these novels, Wright could achieve his intention of weaving living consciousness into the impress of social theory and ideology.[19]

Wright had joined the American Communist movement in the early 1930s. This was a period that coincided with an intensification of the party's work among Blacks following the Sixth Congress of the Comintern's "resolution on the Negro Question" in 1928 and the beginnings of the Scottsboro trials in 1931. Wright left the party a decade later. During those years he worked in the movement in the various capacities of organizer, member of a Black party cell in Chicago, officer in the John Reed Clubs and writer for the Communist press. At first, his work for the party was to take place primarily in Chicago; later he was transferred to Harlem.[20] It was, of course, during this time that his writing was most directly influenced by the party. He proved to be very good at it. By 1937, the year he had published "Blueprint . . .," he had become, in Daniel Aaron's words, "the Party's most illustrious proletarian author."[21]

Wright took this responsibility as a proletarian writer quite seriously. He was committed to the task of expressing working-class thought, consciousness, and experience. One recollection of this period is his first impression of the party: "The Communists, I felt, had oversimplified the experience of those whom they sought to lead. . . . [T]hey had missed the meaning of the lives of the masses."[22] Wright meant to put this right, the proletariat had to be allowed its own voice. It was just as clear to him that he carried a particular, racial responsibility toward the Black working classes:

> The Negro writer who seeks to function within his race as a purposeful agent has a serious responsibility . . . a deep, informed, and complex consciousness is necessary; a consciousness which draws for its strength upon the fluid lore of a great people, and moulds this lore with the concepts that move and direct the forces of history today. . . . [T]he Negro writer . . . is being called upon to do no less than create values by which his race is to struggle, live and die . . . because his writing possesses the potential cunning to steal into the inmost recesses of the human heart, because he can create myths and symbols that inspire a faith in life.[23]

As a Black writer, Wright was presuming that the intelligentsia had the obligation to construct the ideological and symbolic means through which an emerging Black movement would be formed. Still, the work of this intelligentsia had to be grounded in the culture of their people.

Working with these conceptions, Wright was clearly reflecting an earlier Marxian tradition, one in which Lenin had transformed a "renegade" petit bourgeoisie into a revolutionary vanguard.[24] (Wright appears to have always opposed the Stalinist anti-intellectualism that marked the Communist movement domestically and internationally in the 1930s.) But Wright was also mindful of a second and separate tradition that had emerged among Blacks in the United States during the late eighteenth and mid-nineteenth centuries. At these historical moments from among the ranks of free Blacks, there had emerged an intellectually, economically, and politically elite class that had assumed leadership on behalf of the largely enslaved Black masses. This nucleus later contributed significantly to the formation of the Black middle class. The ethos of this class and its sociohistorical traditions had been given its most enduring name by W. E. B. Du Bois: the talented tenth.[25] Wright was thus suffusing two distinct and opposing traditions. But more important, even here, while he was ostensibly addressing Black intellectuals, he was also going about the work of re-creating his world in his own ideological terms.

Wright's Social Theory

Wright, in having constructed the character of Bigger Thomas in *Native Son*, has been attributed with a variety of achievements, intents, and concerns. Addison Gayle, echoing many of his critical predecessors, argues that Wright created the archetypal stereotype of the Black man, thus releasing American consciousness from that particular beast of burden.[26] Elsewhere one finds *Native Son* understood as "a complement of that monstrous legend it was written to destroy. Bigger is Uncle Tom's descendant, flesh of his flesh, exactly opposite a portrait";[27] as a study in the psychology of the outcast;[28] and as a statement of the human predicament.[29] In other words, Wright's early work has been characterized by a variety of critics along a continuum ranging between a racially specific protest to a universal declaration. It might be useful, however, to add another and quite different dimension to *Native Son*—a dimension found in Wright's own consciousness of the work.

In 1944, upon his formal declaration of leave from the American Communist Party (the break occurred in 1942), Wright made a number of his other concerns quite clear. Some of them had to do with the reasons he first became a part of American radicalism.

> It was not the economics of Communism, nor the great power of trade unions, nor the excitement of underground politics that claimed me; my attention was caught by the similarity of the experience of workers in other lands, by the possibility of uniting scattered but kindred people into a whole. . . . [H]ere at last, in the realm of revolutionary expression, Negro experience could find a home, a functioning value and role.[30]

Marxist propaganda suggested to him that Blacks need not be alone in their struggle for liberation and dignity. The specter of a world proletariat, united and strong, Black and white fascinated Wright.

Before that evening of his intellectual conversion he had looked upon the party as a white man's organization and therefore something to be distrusted, especially in its pretensions concerning Blacks. More important, until that moment he had dismissed as a personal fantasy, as a painful, frustrating dream, the organization of the poor and oppressed. Again, on that same evening—his first visit to a John Reed Club—Wright commented, "I was meeting men and women whom I should know for decades to come, who were to form the first sustained friendships in my life."[31] He had discovered not merely an important, historical vista but someone with whom to share it.

Still, beyond the social vision of Marxism and the fraternity of American communism, Wright's decision to become a part of this movement was motivated by one other element: the opportunity to transform himself from "passive" victim to active advocate.

> Here, then, was something that I could do, reveal, say. The Communists, I felt, had oversimplified the experience of those whom they sought to lead. In their efforts to recruit masses, they had missed the meaning of the lives of the masses, had conceived of people in too abstract a manner. I would try to put some of that meaning back, I would tell Communists how common people felt, and I would tell common people of the self-sacrifice of the Communists who strove for unity among them.[32]

Wright perceived his task as providing to the movement a language and images that would give meaning to the abstracted proletariat of party ideology. This complex of motives—vision, fraternity, and task—might seem sufficient to explain to the readers of *Uncle Tom's Children, Lawd Today,* and *Native Son,* Wright's sociological and political preoccupations in his early works. Yet Wright, as we shall see, was to have a very different experience, which provided other and very different themes for the last of these three works.

Wright had entered the party naive of its history, its factionalism, and its purgative vocabulary.[33] As we have seen, he had not been convinced earlier of the sincerity of American Communists. This is somewhat surprising given the enormous vitality of the party's "Negro work" at the time, work that included the defense of the Scottsboro boys; the confrontation with conservative Black organizations; the organizing of Unemployed Councils and Tenant Leagues; the development of the Black Belt Thesis on self-determination and the organizing of the League of Struggle for Negro Rights and, on the international level, the International Trade Union Committee of Negro Workers.[34] Though he was then a hospital worker, he had identified himself as a writer, and as a writer, he was categorized by those in the party's ranks as an "intellectual." This meant that Wright was to be subjected to the diffidence shown to intellectuals, but, more significantly among his Black comrades, that he was also to be held in suspicion for "petit-bourgeois tendencies"—that is, selfish interests—and worse: Trotskyism. The result was inevitable:

> Successive disillusionments had transformed his original enthusiastic and total dedication into wariness. His individualism was against him; he was at the mercy of leaders like Oliver Law and Harry Haywood, ostracized from unit 205 by certain black comrades and even denigrated.[35]

Invited to the party trial of another Black party member (one upon whose early experience in the South Wright had based his short story, "Big Boy Leaves Home"), Wright realized that the trial was also meant for someone else:

> The blindness of their limited lives—lives truncated and impoverished by the oppression they had suffered long before they had ever heard of Communism— made them think that I was with their enemies. American life had so corrupted their consciousness that they were unable to recognize their friends when they saw them. I know that if they had held state power I should have been declared guilty of treason.[36]

He recognized among his Black co-workers an anger dammed up to the level of destruction of self. It was not an ideology that lay at the base of their need to physically violate errant comrades. Their dogmatism was an enveloping shield against egocide. Their conformity was a symptom of their desperate and collective need for each other. Wright would write later: "They're blind. . . . Their enemies have blinded them with too much oppression."[37]

This, then, is the crisis that informed the development of Bigger Thomas. *Native*

Son was the result of Wright's resolve to have his say, his revision of American Marxism as it emerged from the lives and practices of American Communists:

> I would hurl words into this darkness and wait for an echo; and if an echo sounded, no matter how faintly, I would send other words to tell, to march, to fight, to create a sense of the hunger for life that gnaws in us all, to keep alive in our hearts a sense of the inexpressibly human.[38]

In *Native Son*, Wright sought to display a more authentic, more historical, more precise image of the proletariat to which the party had committed itself. He had begun this task in *Lawd Today* and it came to fruition in the form of Bigger Thomas. Wright, hesitant at wrestling with Marxism on theoretical terms, pursued his critique of American Left ideology in his own terms: the novel. Bigger Thomas's lack of class consciousness—more precisely the odyssey of his development of consciousness—is deliberate and purposive. This was not simply a literary device, but a means of coming to grips with the abstraction and romanticization of the proletariat that had infected Western Communist ideology.

At the time of Wright's sojourn in the party (1934–42), the primary focus of the movement in Western Europe and the United States was the defeat of fascism. It was a fundamental tenet of party work that fascism was an instrument of the ruling class designed to meet the crisis of world capitalism embodied in the Depression. As such, fascism as an ideology was presumed to be alien to the working class. Earl Browder, as general secretary of the American Communist Party, had made this position abundantly clear in reports, speeches, and articles during the late 1930s.[39] As the official voice of the American Communist Party Browder had argued that the struggle of the movement was preeminently a political one:

> What is the message that this powerful voice of the Communist Party is giving to America? First of all, it is the message of the need for the great mass of the people, the workers and farmers, to organize for their own protection.[40]

Browder's strategy was a simple one: "The growth of the Communist Party is the greatest guarantee against reaction and fascism."[41]

Browder's leadership had positioned the party in support of the New Deal and Roosevelt's administration under the presumption that American workers were not ready to confront the issue of socialism.[42] In effect, the party pursued the contradictory aims of reform and revolution. This was in part a consequence, as Wilhelm Reich had pointed out with respect to the German Communist movement during the Weimar Republic, of failing to distinguish between the abstraction of class consciousness and its specific, historical form.[43] Just as critically, however, the party was committed by the instructions of the Comintern to a united front with its class enemies.

For Wright the question of the consciousness of workers and consequently that of political organization was more complex. It involved—as he was to write in defense of *Native Son*—"the dark and hidden places of the human personality."[44] In the essay, "How 'Bigger' Was Born," Wright had been more explicit:

the civilization which had given birth to Bigger contained no spiritual sustenance, had created no culture which could hold and claim his allegiance and faith, had sensitized him and had left him stranded, a free agent to roam the streets of our cities, a hot and whirling vortex of undisciplined and unchannelized impulses.

. . . I was fascinated by the similarity of the emotional tensions of Bigger in America and Bigger in Nazi Germany and Bigger in Old Russia. All Bigger Thomases, white and black, felt tense, afraid, nervous, hysterical, and restless. . . . [C]ertain modern experiences were creating types of personalities whose existence ignored racial and national lines of demarcation.[45]

Wright was attempting to come to terms with the psychological consequence of a historical condition of which the leadership in the Communist movement was only vaguely aware. Wright was insisting on the necessity for understanding the working class in their own terms. He was concerned with the ability of proletarian masses to reproduce themselves spiritually and culturally. If they could no longer re-create the social ideologies that had sustained them, it would not be possible for them to fulfill the historical role that Marxian theory assigned them. Moreover, the fragmentation of personality, social relations, and ideology that Wright observed and re-created was so total that its political and historical implications seriously challenged the presumptions of the Communist movement:

I felt that Bigger, an American product, a native son of this land, carried within him the potentialities of either Communism or Fascism. . . . Whether he'll follow some gaudy, hysterical leader who'll promise rashly to fill the void in him, or whether he'll come to an understanding with the millions of his kindred fellow workers under trade-unions or revolutionary guidance depends upon the future drift of events in America. But . . . Bigger Thomas, conditioned as his organism is, will not become an ardent, or even a Luke-warm, supporter of the *status quo*.[46]

He realized that no political movement that, for ideological reasons, presumed the progressive character of the working class would succeed.

Wright's novel, subsequently, was a refutation of radical dogma from the vantage point of Black experience. He sought first to re-create that experience, and in so doing to force a confrontation between it and socialist ideology. Bigger Thomas's character was specific to the historical experience of Blacks in the United States, but his nature was proletarian, that is world-historical. When Wright gave the consciousness of Bigger Thomas a nationalist character, he was addressing himself to both those aspects of his creation. He wrote that he was "confronted with that part of him that was dual in aspect . . . a part of *all* Negroes and *all* whites."[47] If the American revolutionary movement could not come to terms with the *appeals* of fascism, then it could not begin to understand the immediate *nature* of the working class.[48] He agreed with Marx that capitalism as a form of organization led to the destruction of social consciousness founded on noncapitalist social orders. He did not accept, however, the notion that this process led to a new ideological synthesis. The truer result, the observed result, was "a world that existed on a plane of animal sensation alone."[49] The Nazi movement succeeded because it offered in the stead of an existential terror, a new, unambiguous social order, "the implicit, almost unconscious, or preconscious assumptions and ideals upon which whole nations and races act and live."[50]

Yet Wright's analysis did not end there. He had something more to say about the nature of revolutionary action. His analysis both underscored the absolute character of revolutionary commitment and also spoke to Marxian class analysis.

> I remember reading a passage in a book dealing with old Russia which said: "We must be ready to make endless sacrifices if we are to be able to overthrow the Czar." . . . Actions and feelings of men ten thousand miles from home helped me to understand the moods and impulses of those walking the streets of Chicago and Dixie.[51]

Wright recognized in his Bigger Thomases the desperation that was the precondition for the making of total and violent revolutionary commitments. He understood those commitments to be less ones of choice than of compulsion. The more total the degradation of the human being, the more total the reaction—"the *need* for a whole life and *acted* out of that need."[52]

He also refused to dismiss the Bigger Thomases as lumpen-proletariat or to distinguish them from the proletariat. In *Native Son* he actually anticipated a thesis on violence and the lumper-proletariat that would become better known later through the work of Frantz Fanon. For Wright, the violence of the lumper-proletariat was not only an objective force of revolution; violence could not be separated out from the formation of consciousness.

> "I didn't want to kill" Bigger shouted. "But what I killed for, I *am*."[53]

What, precisely, the Bigger Thomases would kill for, Wright could not answer. He had stated his thesis and it was now left to the "future drift of events" to make that determination, that is, the capacity of the American radical movement to develop a critical political theory. This, of course, was not to be the case.[54]

Wright had emerged from the Depression with a clear and powerful image of American society and world history. With the writing of *Uncle Tom's Children* and *Native Son* he had extracted from the misery of poverty and imminent social collapse an understanding of a systemic integration in which racism was a secondary, residual phenomenon. He had no reason to doubt that the disintegration of the capitalist world was really a promise of liberation—a promise that enveloped the whole of humanity. Yet he possessed few illusions about this process of disintegration. He knew, in social terms, even in human terms, that the immediate costs would be unparalleled violence, brutality, and vengeance. At first he hoped that this historical transformation would be surgical in its order. He believed in a conscious, deliberate, and magnanimous workers' movement. By the time he was writing *Native Son*, however, this ordered revolution had been replaced by a chaos consisting of the collective action of a brutalized human force. The destruction of capitalism would come at the hands of the brute social force it had itself created. Still, Wright saw this brutalized mass as the *promise* of the future. Unlike Marx, Wright anticipated barbarism *and* socialism.

Blacks as the Negation of Capitalism

For Wright, it was not sufficient for Black liberation that his people come to terms with the critique of capitalist society. He had observed: "Marxism is but the starting point. No theory of life can take the place of life."[55] As a critique of capitalist society, Marxism was necessary, of course, but it was ultimately an *internal* critique. The epistemological nature of historical materialism took bourgeois society on its own terms, that is, presuming the primacy of economic forces and structures.[56] As such, the historical development from feudalism of the bourgeoisie as a class served as a logical model for the emergence of the proletariat as a negation of capitalist society.[57] Wright appeared quite early to have understood this thesis as a fundamental error in Marxist thought. Even as early as 1937, he had begun to argue that it was necessary that Blacks transform the Marxist critique into an expression of their own emergence as a negation of Western capitalism.

Though immersed in the American radical movement with its Eurocentric ideology, it had not taken Wright very long to reach the conclusion that the historic development of Black people in the United States constituted the most total contradiction to Western capitalist society:[58]

> The workers of a minority people, chafing under exploitation, forge organisational forms of struggle. . . . Lacking the handicaps of false ambition and property, they have access to a wide social vision and a deep social consciousness. . . . Their organizations show greater strength, adaptability, and efficiency than any other group or class in society.

Wright assumed that the alienation of Black workers from American society was more total than that experienced by the "white" working classes formed in Europe and America. This, indeed, was the more profound significance of Black nationalism, and one with which the Black intellectual had to come to terms:

> [T]he emotional expression of group-feeling which puzzles so many whites and leads them to deplore what they call "black chauvinism" is not a morbidly inherent trait of the Negro, but rather the reflex expression of a life whose roots are imbedded deeply in Southern soil. Negro writers must accept the nationalist implications of their lives. . . . [T]hey must accept the concept of nationalism because, in order to transcend it, they must *possess* and *understand* it. And a nationalist spirit in Negro writing means a nationalism carrying the highest possible pitch of social consciousness. It means a nationalism that knows its origins, its limitations, that is aware of the dangers of its position, that knows its ultimate aims are unrealisable within the framework of capitalist America; a nationalism whose reason for being

lies in the simple fact of self-possession and in the consciousness of the interdependence of people in modern society.[59]

Wright's argument and its language strongly suggest the elements within the party with which he was in ideological conflict. In using the phrase "black chauvinism"—its second element being a term used most frequently within the party as a more objective interpretation for what was commonly referred to as nationalism—Wright designated his first target: white Marxian ideologues. His second target, deracinated Black intellectuals, were addressed as the recipients of a new history. They had to be made to realize that Black nationalism was an initial and historically logical stage of a more profoundly universal consciousness.

Wright was arguing that American Blacks had been re-created from their African origins by an oppressive system of capitalist exploitation that had at one and the same time integrated them into the emergent organization of industrial production while suspending them from the full impact of bourgeois ideology. Perhaps Wright put this most succinctly several years later in *The Outsider* when Ely Houston, one of Wright's two spokesmen in the novel, observed:

> The way Negroes were transported to this country and sold into slavery, then stripped of their tribal culture and held in bondage; and then allowed so teasingly and over so long a period of time, to be sucked into our way of life is something which resembles the rise of all men. . . .
>
> They are outsiders and . . . [t]hey are going to be self-conscious; they are going to be gifted with a double vision, for, being Negroes, they are going to be both *inside* and *outside* of our culture at the same time. . . . Negroes will develop unique and specially defined psychological types. They will become psychological men, like the Jews. . . . They will not only be Americans or Negroes; they will be centers of knowing, so to speak. . . . The political, social, and psychological consequences of this will be enormous.[60]

Wright believed that racism, the very character of the system by which Black workers had been exploited, had mediated their internalization of the ruling ideas of American society. He went on to assert that, unlike the dominant sectors of European and Euro-American proletariats, the Black proletariat—historically from the legal and political disciplines of slavery to its peculiar condition as free wage labor—had developed a psychic and cultural identity independent from bourgeois ideology. This construction of Wright's pushed the insights of Du Bois[61] and others far beyond the critique of Black-white labor solidarity. What Wright was suggesting went even beyond the most extreme position in the 1930s of American radicals that Blacks were the vanguard of the American working class.[62]

Wright was asserting that the Black revolutionary movement, in the process of transcending a chauvinistic nationalism, was emerging as a historical force that would challenge the very foundation of Western civilization:

Reduced to its simplest terms, theme for Negro writers will rise from understanding the meaning of their being transplanted from a "savage" to a "civilized" culture in implications. It means that Negro writers must have in their consciousness the fore-shortened picture of the *whole*, nourishing culture from which they were torn in Africa, and of the long, complex (and for the most part, unconscious) struggle to regain in some form and under alien conditions of life a *whole* culture again.[63]

For Wright, it was at precisely this point, in the culture's ideational, conceptual, and ideological extension, that the writer and other intellectuals are required. In the construction of myths and symbols emergent from the experience of Black people, the responsibility of the intellectuals was "to create values by which [their] race is to struggle, live and die." This is precisely the task Wright was assuming sixteen years later in *The Outsider*.

The Outsider as a Critique of Christianity and Marxism

The Outsider was completed several years after Wright had left the American Communist movement. It was received, however, as a further elaboration of Wright's reason for his action.[64] Yet the novel's treatment of the party was less in the tradition of Chester Himes's vitriolic *Lonely Crusade* or Ralph Ellison's satiric *The Invisible Man* than in that of Arthur Koestler's *Darkness at Noon*.[65] Though Wright did develop in *The Outsider* a critique of the American Left's race politics and of Stalinism, his intent was much broader, his object much more far ranging.

The novel is a parable. It is a moral, philosophic, and political exercise. Like the myth in phatic groups, the purpose is to demonstrate the terrible consequence to the human spirit as well as to social organization of a total exorcizing of social ideology. In *White Man Listen*, Wright would declare:

I maintain that the ultimate effect of white Europe upon Asia and Africa was to cast millions into a kind of spiritual void; I maintain that it suffused their lives with a sense of meaninglessness. I argue that it was not merely physical suffering or economic deprivation that has set over a billion and a half colored people in violent political motion. . . . The dynamic concept of the void that must be filled, a void created by a thoughtless and brutal impact of the West upon a billion and a half people, is more powerful than the concept of class conflict, and more universal.[66]

Without myths, that is, without meaning, consciousness is set adrift into terror. The desperation that is the condition of this degree of alienation (or Max Scheler's *ressentiment*, or Husserl's "crisis")[67] inevitably requires violence. Violence is the final, the last possible form that social action may assume.

Moreover, Wright was demonstrating both the necessity and inevitability of ideology *and* its arbitrariness. No matter what meanings ideologies systematize, they are always subject to the abuses of power. When ideology is used for the purpose of domination, it must be opposed, not by a counterideology but by the negation of ideology: theory. In short, he was making the case for the necessity for a critical commitment, the sort of commitment that achieves its purpose by extraction from the historical legacy: the culture of a people. Such a commitment is made possible only through a consciousness capable of re-creating meaning.

In *The Outsider*, Wright sought to subvert the two ideological and philosophic traditions at the heart of modern Western culture. First, he ridiculed the Judeo-Christian tradition by creating a protagonist whose very name is contradiction: Cross Damon—the demon Christ. Cross Damon has escaped Judeo-Christian morality through the recognition of its operative psychic force: a destructive, debilitating dread-guilt. Just as Marx earlier had recognized that religion (that is Judaism) "is the sigh of the oppressed creature, the sentiment of a heartless world, and the soul of soulless conditions,"[68] Wright had perceived the truer historical significance of Christianity among Blacks as not an instrument of domination but as a philosophic adaptation to oppression.

Moreover, he understood the resignation of Black Christianity as only one element in the culture of Blacks. In Black music, another more strident voice existed opposing that guilt:

> [T]his music was the rhythmic flauntings of guilty feelings, the syncopated out-pourings of frightened joy existing in guises forbidden and despised by others. . . . Negroes had been made to live in but not of the land of their birth. . . . [T]he injunctions of an alien Christianity and the strictures of white laws had evoked in them the very longings and desires that that religion and law had been designed to stifle. . . . [B]lue-jazz was a rebel art blooming seditiously under the condemnations of a Protestant ethic. . . . Blue-jazz was the scornful gesture of men turned ecstatic in their state of rejection . . . the recreations of the innocently criminal.[69]

The forces of science and technology and the processes of the proletarianization of Black workers were orchestrating the supercession of Black Christian resignation by this second, derisively angry, consciousness.

Yet Wright was also critical of Marxism, the second and more modern radical Western tradition. It, too, was profoundly limited theoretically, and subject to the abuses of narrow political interests. Marxism had ultimately failed to come to terms with nationalism, with consciousness, with racism, with Western civilization, with industrialization, and with the history of Blacks. Wright had already demonstrated some of its limitations in *Native Son*. Daniel Aaron, commenting on Bigger Thomas's Communist lawyer, had observed, "Even Boris Max never really understands Bigger, and is frightened by Bigger's vision of himself."[70] Wright made this same point even more tellingly in *The Outsider*. Wright maintained that the purposes of Marxism as employed in American Communism were less analytical than political. The result was neither theory nor praxis but the achievement of power. Ironically, in the second novel, it was the character of Hilton, also a party functionary, who spoke for Wright. Hilton, driven to candor by desperation, betrays the crude agreement upon which party support of Black liberation depended: manipulation. Wright (Cross) then reflects to himself:

> Did the average white American suspect that men like Hilton existed, men who could easily rise above the racial hatred of the mob and cynically make use of the defensive attitudes instilled in Negroes as weapons in their own bitter struggle for power?[71]

But Wright would instruct us never to expect to hear such revelations as Hilton's. He had heard them as a part of his experience, an experience that he would subject to the Marxian critique that was now also a part of his way of grappling with reality.

Marxism as an ideology and theory of history, Wright argued, was a product of a petit bourgeoisie, in particular, the intellectuals:

> You must assume that I know what this is all about. Don't tell me about the nobility of labor, the glorious future. You don't believe in that. That's for others, and you damn well know it. . . . You Jealous Rebels are intellectuals who know your history and you are anxious not to make the mistakes of your predecessors in rebellious undertakings.[72]

He was no longer convinced that Marxism as a theory, as a theory of history or social revolution, was correct but he did understand its seductiveness. He would write in 1960: "Marxist ideology in particular is but a transitory make-shift pending a more accurate diagnosis. . . . Communism may be but a painful compromise containing a definition of man by sheer default."[73] He suspected that Marxism, alike with Christianity as an ideology, masked "complexities of history and social experience." Its truer function was the social and intellectual cohesion of the petit bourgeoisie—a class very different from the proletariat:

> [O]ne minority section of the white society in or under which he lives will offer the educated elite of Asia and Africa or black America an interpretation of the world which impels to action, thereby assuaging his feelings of inferiority. Nine times out of ten it can be easily pointed out that the ideology offered has no relation to the plight of the educated black, brown, or yellow elite. . . . But that ideology does solve something. . . . [I]t enabled the Negro or Asian or African to meet revolutionary fragments of the hostile race on a plane of equality.[74]

Still, in this his most devastating criticism of Communism, Wright was relying on a notion of class struggle:

> These men who rise to challenge the rulers are jealous men. They feel that they are just as good as the men who rule; indeed, they suspect that they are better. They see the countless mistakes that are being made by the men who rule and they think that they could do a more honest, a much cleaner job, a more efficient job.[75]

Such was Wright's thesis on the development of Marxism as a class-specific ideology. And in some ways, he was echoing Marx's own but more mystical explanation of Marxism:

> Finally, in times when the class struggle nears the decisive hour, the process of dissolution going on within the ruling class, in fact within the whole range of society, assumes such a violent, glaring character, that a small section of the ruling class cuts itself adrift, and joins the revolutionary class, the class that holds the future in its hand . . . so now a portion of the bourgeoisie goes over to the proletariat, and in particular, a portion of the bourgeois ideologists, who have raised themselves to the level of comprehending theoretically the historical movement as a whole.[76]

By the early 1950s, Wright had come to his similar conclusion—one that we have seen he retained for the rest of his life—but with a different meaning: Marxist theory was an expression of petit bourgeois consciousness and its critique of bourgeois society and capitalism was most fundamentally addressed to that class's suffocation by the authority of the bourgeois ruling class.

Yet the opposition of Marxist theory to capitalist society was useful to Wright, *theoretically*. Indeed, the historical and revolutionary role that Wright assigned to Blacks had at its base a materialist dialectic. As previously indicated, Wright recognized Black nationalism as a product, in part, of both the objective necessities of capitalist development and accumulation, and its system of exploitation. As he turned toward the ideology of Black nationalism, he sought to comprehend its emergence in the contradictions of day-to-day experience:

> [E]very day in this land some white man is cussing out some defenseless Negro. But that white bastard is too stupid to realise that his actions are being duplicated a million times in a million other spots by other whites who feel hatred for Negroes just like he does. He's too blind to see that this daily wave of a million tiny assaults builds up a vast reservoir of resentment in Negroes.[77]

Thus Wright echoed another powerful contribution to the development of Marxism: Hegel's the Cunning of Reason.

But where Wright differed most with others who could employ a Marxist approach was in his characterization of the historical forces of ideology. Ideology was the special political instrument of the petit bourgeoisie. Wright was arguing that the renegades of this class that had served historically to produce the dominant ideas of the bourgeoisie, had themselves become contemptuous of the ruling class. The Jealous Rebels had declared, as Marx himself had written: "the bourgeoisie is unfit any longer to be the ruling class in society, and to impose its conditions of existence upon society as an overriding law. It is unfit to rule because it is incompetent."[78]

In his criticisms of Marxism, then, Wright was not entirely rejecting it but was attempting to locate it, to provide a sense of the boundaries of its authority. As a *theory* of society, he found it dissatisfying, indeed, reductionist. By itself it was insufficiently prescient of the several levels of collective consciousness. As an *ideology*, he recognized that it had never transcended its origins. It remained an ideology *for* the working classes rather than an ideology *of* the working classes. However, as a *method* of social analysis he found it compelling. He had not abandoned the conception of the relations of production as a basis for the critique of capitalist society nor the importance of the class relations of production. Still, the critique of capitalism was only the beginning of the struggle for liberation.

It is from this critical perspective that Wright joins with one of the few Black women he has sympathetically drawn, Sarah Hunter. When she cajoles her husband, Bob, the frightened and party-subservient Black organizer, she is speaking for Wright: "everywhere I've looked . . . I've seen nothing but white folks kicking niggers who are kneeling down." "I want to be one of them who tells the *others* to obey, see? Read your Marx and organize."[79]

From his experience in the American Communist Party, and from *his* reading of Marx, Wright had come to the conclusion that no people's liberation is the result of their abject surrender of critical judgment. Certainly it was not the prerogative of Black intellectuals to surrender the cultural heritage of their people: the emergent revolutionary consciousness of Black nationalism.

Very little remains then of the Wright that Harold Cruse presents to us. Perhaps, like Baldwin, Cruse had also felt the need "to kill the father." Doubtless, too, the explanation for Cruse's error is much more complex. But irrespective of the origins of Cruse's portrait of Wright, a closer reading of the central works written by Wright over a span of more than two decades reveals a most powerful and self-possessed Black thinker. Wright struggled toward a synthesis of Marxism and Black nationalist thought to match those of his colleagues, George Padmore and C. L. R. James. And together, their several works—along with those of Du Bois—are an extraordinary legacy to Blacks in the Western hemisphere and elsewhere. In them, one can discover an independent and richly suggestive critique of the modern world—a critique whose voice is the most authentic sounding of the brutal depths of Western civilization and its history. There lies, in those works, the beginnings of Black revolutionary theory. "[A]t the moment when a people begin to realize a *meaning* in their suffering, the civilization that engenders that suffering is doomed."[80]

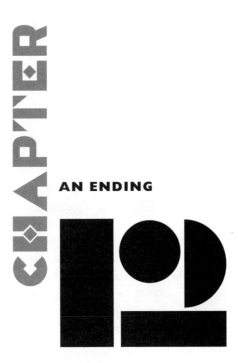

CHAPTER

AN ENDING

12

The persevering reader perhaps even in spite of my efforts will by now have fathomed the concerns that have shaped the present study. But it is an important convention of the storyteller and the scholar to summarize the tale, to have the last word. It is a final opportunity for the narrator to get things right, to draw the moral or expose the hidden ironies. There is, indeed, something more to be said about what may be the significance of the argument and why it assumed the specific form that it did. As is my habit, I will now take up those subjects back to front.

The work was conceived as primarily a theoretical discourse. This may come as a bit of a surprise to some readers because for the most part I purposely eschewed theoretical language. Instead, I believed it necessary to refer the exposition of the argument to historical materials. Certainly this minimized the risk of reductionist abstraction. Most importantly though, it served the purpose of resurrecting events that have systematically been made to vanish from our intellectual consciousness. The work required a certain destructuring of American and Western historiography. For the realization of new theory we require new history. As has been pointed out in most of the West's intellectual traditions, the practice of theory is informed by struggle. Here the points of combat were threefold: an opposition to the ideas purporting to situate African peoples that have dominated European literature; a critique of a socialist intellectual tradition that, too infrequently, or casually, has interrogated its own bases for being; and a consideration of the import of the ambivalences with which Westernized Black radical intelligentsia first began the formulation of Black radical theory. The terrain was not made by choice but dictated by historical inheritance.

When the investigation into the conflicts extant between Western radicalism and the struggle for Black liberation was initiated, it was with the gnawing intuition that something known to be fundamental to the Western experience was being trivialized by the American radical tradition. Among my colleagues there was the sense that something so important as to challenge the very foundations of progressive politics and thought lay beyond the conceptualizations that admittedly had inspired formidable displays of progressive work and activity. Some knowledge, some aspect of Black consciousness was unaccounted for in the Marxist explication of the historical processes and source of the motives to which were attributed the social formations of the modern world. In its conceptually formidable reaction against irresponsible power, calculated social destruction, and the systematic exploitation of human beings, there seemed to us to be a discernible reluctance in Western radicalism, or to put it more strongly, a flight from the recognition that something more than objective material forces were responsible for "the nastiness" as Peter Blackman puts it. There was the sense that something of a more profound nature than the obsession with property was askew in a civilization that could organize and celebrate—on a scale beyond previous human experience—the brutal degradations of life and the most acute violations of human destiny. It seemed a certainty that the system of capitalism was part of it, but as well symptomatic of it. It needed a name as the philosopher Hobbes might say. It was not simply a question of outrage or concern for Black survival. It was a matter of comprehension.

The outrage, I believe, was most certainly informed by the Africanity of our consciousness—some epistemological measure culturally embedded in our minds that deemed that the racial capitalism we have been witness to was an unacceptable standard of human conduct. It was also the case that the source of our outrage characterized that conduct as inexplicable. The depths to which racialist behavior has fouled Western agencies transgressed against a world-consciousness rooted in our African past. Nevertheless, the sense of deep sadness at the spectacle of Western racial oppression is shared with other non-Western peoples. In these circumstances and in a certain sense only, Black survival must of course be taken as problematical. But its truer significance has been determined by received tradition.

I have said that the inquiry into what lay behind the sense of the inadequacies of the Marxian critique was compelled by the question of understanding. The encounter between African and European had been abrupt, not so much in historical terms as in philosophical ones. The Western civilization that burst forth from its medieval quarantine prosecuted its racial sense of social order, its feudal habits of domination, with a vengeance. By the ending of the Middle Ages, racialism was a routine manifestation, finding expression even in the more exotic mental recesses of the maniac and hysterical. For 400 years, from the fifteenth to the nineteenth century, while the capitalist mode of production in Europe engulfed agrarian and artisanal workers, transforming them over the generations into expropriated, dependent fodder for concentration in factories, disciplined to the rhythms and turbulences of the manufacturing process, the organizers of the capitalist world system appropriated Black labor power as *constant* capital. Blacks were extracted from their social formations through mechanisms that, by design and historical coincidence, minimized the disruption of the production of labor. While vast reserves of labor were amassed in the Poor Houses and slums of Europe's cities and manufacturing towns and villages, in the African hinterland some semblance of traditional life continued to reproduce itself, sharing its social product—human beings—with the Atlantic slave system. For those African men and women whose lives were interrupted by enslavement and transportation, it was reasonable to expect that they would attempt, and in some ways realize, the re-creation of their lives. It was not, however, an understanding of the Europeans that preserved those Africans in the grasp of slavers, planters, merchants, and colonizers. Rather, it was the ability to conserve their native consciousness of the world from alien intrusion, the ability to imaginatively re-create a precedent metaphysic while being subjected to enslavement, racial domination, and repression. This was the raw material of the Black radical tradition, the values, ideas, conceptions, and constructions of reality from which resistance was manufactured. And in each instance of resistance, the social and psychological dynamics that are shared by human communities in long-term crises resolved for the rebels the particular moment, the collective and personal chemistries that congealed into social movement. But it was the materials constructed from a shared philosophy developed in the African past and transmitted as culture, from which revolutionary consciousness was realized and the ideology of struggle formed.

As we have commented, though rebellion might appear warranted to the Europeans who witnessed the uprisings of African peoples, the forms that Black resistance assumed were incomprehensible. Ultimately many such witnesses fell easily into whatever language was on hand to evoke mystery: the participants in Black resistance were seen as having reverted to savagery; were under the influence of satanic madmen; had passed beyond the threshold of sanity. To the Europeans charged with the responsibilities of preserving the sources of Black labor or control over that labor, the only effective response to Black rebellion was massive, indiscriminate violence and afterward the routine of brutality. More frequently than not, the logic of racial domination that had already endured for centuries invoked no alternatives. On this score it had always to be an unequal contest, not because of the superiority of weapons or the preponderance of numbers but because such violence did not come naturally to African peoples. The civilizations of Europe and Africa in those terms had also been very different. For far longer than a millennium, the history of Europe had amounted to an almost uninterrupted chronology of fratricidal warfare and its celebration. The museums of the civilization are the current testament to that preoccupation, its histories chilling accounts. In Africa, where the incident of state and imperial formations and total warfare were rarer, conflict could and was more frequently resolved by migration and resettlement. Eventually the penetration of Islam into Africa and the organization of the Red Sea and Mediterranean slave systems had made some real difference but it was the scale of the Atlantic slave trade and the racial cacophony of European colonialism that would dictate the more profound adjustment to violence. And this too was misunderstood by the Europeans, translated as might be expected into the discourse of superior and inferior races. While the European ruling classes humbled their own workers by force and cultural hegemony, the points of contact between Europeans and Blacks were enveloped by violence.

The first forms of struggle in the Black radical tradition, however, were not structured by a critique of Western society but from a rejection of European slavery and a revulsion of racism in its totality. Even then, the more fundamental impulse of Black resistance was the preservation of a particular social and historical consciousness rather than the revolutionary transformation of feudal or merchant capitalist Europe. Why the pathology of race was so dominant a part of Western consciousness or what might be done to change that character was of less concern than how Black peoples might survive the encounter. This perhaps is part of the explanation of why, so often, Black slave resistance naturally evolved to marronage as the manifestation of the African's determination to disengage, to retreat from contact. To reconstitute the community, Black radicals took to the bush, to the mountains, to the interior.

Just as in Africa until the last quarter of the nineteenth century retreat had been a possible response of African peoples, it was similarly the case at the sites of slave labor. In the Caribbean islands as well as in Latin America and North America, Black peoples found means of disengagement. Away from the plantations, in the security of mountain retreats, on the continent toward the up-country sources of the great rivers that emptied into the ocean at the coasts, Black communities could be reestablished. And the very existence of such settlements enhanced the morale of those who remained in captivity. Over the generations, the successive depositions of new labor, the maroon settlements, and the legends of such communities further enriched the radical tradition. And each generation among the slaves contributed to the further broadening of Black consciousness and the ideology of the tradition. And while the trade itself expanded in response to the interactions of exchange, commodity-demands and surplus production in the world system, within the slave communities a Black people evolved. Manifest expressions of Black radicalism such as marronage, arson, the destruction of work tools, and even open rebellion were complemented by less overt forms. When separation was not possible, open revolts might fester; where rebellion was immediately impractical, the people prepared themselves through *obeah*, voodoo, Islam, and Black Christianity. Through these they induced charismatic expectations, socializing and hardening themselves and their young with beliefs, myths, and messianic visions that would allow them, someday, to attempt the impossible. Their history confirmed these processes; their fruition could be seen in the *papaloi* of the Haitian Revolution; the *obeah* men and women who crowd the trial records of slave rebellions in the Caribbean and elsewhere; the Muslim revolts in Brazil; the rebel preachers who appear at the center of resistance in Jamaica, Suriname, and North America. Through it all, of course, the perturbations of the world system constituted the parameters, the conditions of being of Black resistance.

In seventeenth-century colonial North America, marronage appeared first. But as the eighteenth century succeeded the seventeenth, marronage as the prevalent form of Black resistance became increasingly difficult, as merchant and manufacturing capitalists expanded plantation slavery, rationalized the structures of domination between the colonies, and defeated the native Americans. As slave communities formed, marronage was eventually superseded. By the middle of the eighteenth century, for the mass of Blacks the steady transfusion, via the Atlantic, of new Africans, the genius of Black Christianity, the construction of Creole dialects, the founding of Black and Seminole-like maroon communities, the flight to the Black quarters of southern cities, the plotting and actualizing of rebellions, and the construction of familial and communal relations in the slave quarters, were all a part of their preservation as an African people and the nurture of the Black radical tradition. On the other hand, the drift toward assimilation to the Europeans by a fraction of the Black population was of little importance. The crude racialism that walled American culture exacted a toll that only the most desperately alienated at the racial and psychological margins of the Black and white societies could be expected to pay. By the end of the century, new possibilities for Black radicalism arose with first the colonial rebellion and then the Haitian Revolution. Blacks fought with the English against the rebels and witnessed the more relevant resistance in Haiti. And well into the nineteenth century, the experience absorbed by Black participants in the rebellion of the colonial ruling class against its English superiors and the example (and the indirect if not direct assistance) of the Haitian revolutionists facilitated mass resistance as the dominant expression of Black radicalism. Like the Haitian slaves, disengagement was the ideological currency of the rebel American Blacks; the absolute rejection of American society and the persistent denunciation of racialism as a basis of civilized conduct. Before the Civil War, with slave production now more important economically than it had ever been as a direct result of the industrial revolutionizing of English manufacturing, the Black radical commitment was echoed by the ideologists of the slave rebellions and the Black refugees from slavery. It was given expression among the militant Black "abolitionists," in the assemblies of the emigration movement, and among Blacks such as the Chatham conventioneers who, with John Brown, planned the overthrow of the slave system. The evidence of the tradition's persistence and ideological vitality among the Black slave masses was to be found not only in the rebellions and the underground but as well in the shouts, the spirituals, the sermons, and the very textual body of Black Christianity. After the Civil War, in the wake of the years of fighting and the subsequent years of being victimized by terror and the manipulations of the industrial, financial, and plantocratic classes, streams of Black emigrationists sought again the safety of distance. In the late nineteenth century, like their migrating counterparts in South Africa, Brazil, and Cuba who desperately sought for distance from European settlements, American Blacks were convinced anew that their preservation as a people was at stake. The possibilities of that option, however, were already receding. New conditions, new resolves, and new stratagems were overtaking them.

The formal endings of slave systems of production in the nineteenth century marked the beginnings of a profound reorganization of the capitalist world system. In Europe, Africa, Asia, and the Americas, through the deepening penetrations of monopoly capitalism and the impositions of hegemonic colonialisms, slaves were displaced as a source of cheap labor power by peasants and migrant laborers. In Africa, whereas the slave trade had dislocated the reproductive cycles of certain social formations along the coasts of West and southern Africa, the "new imperialism" of monopoly capitalism demanded a more destructive form of appropriation and exploitation. The colonial state parasitized the peasants of the continent's agrarian hinterlands, transforming traditional economic sectors from the project of reproduction into the source and support of forcibly recruited labor and the sites of cash-crop monoculture and the extraction of minerals and raw materials. To the extent that wage labor expanded in Africa, its level of support was limited to maintenance and not reproduction of labor. In the New World there were also changes. The systems of reconstitution of Black communities were, as well, assaulted by forms of forced labor: peonage, share-cropping, and less than subsistence farming. Moreover, Black workers were subject to displacement from productive land and to publicly and privately organized campaigns of terror and intimidation. Ineluctably, resistance was propelled toward new forms, new consciousness, and new ideologies.

The anticolonial struggles that were increasingly mounted from the mid-nineteenth century on were the beginnings of the transformation of Black radicalism into an engaged confrontation with European domination. Indeed, it was as a response to the mass resistances to colonialism that the other human contradictions to which colonial domination was inherently vulnerable were catalyzed. The very nature of colonial dominance required the adaptation or creation of privileged strata among the dominated people. And from the conflict, which was inevitable between the native "bourgeoisie" and their colonial masters, a renegade intelligentsia was induced, one to which the idea of a total opposition, a nationalist confrontation and critique of Western society was necessary and natural. The experience of the Black petit bourgeoisies, their intimacy with European power, culture, society, and racism, and their contradictory relations to them, in time drew from their number nationalists and radical nationalists. While the nationalists generally confined their attentions to the struggles at home where their ambitions could most immediately be realized, the radical nationalists were really internationalists, settling into variants of Pan-Africanism or socialism. Invariably, some of the radicals would be ideologically attracted to the opposition movements gestated within Western society itself. Their ambivalence toward the Black masses, their social and psychological identifications with European culture made the analytical and theoretical authority of European socialism an almost irresistible political ideology. For some that proved sufficient. For others, however, the continuing formation of militant nationalist and workers' movements in the colonial world raised questions about the breadth and acuity of European socialists. And as mass Black radicalism adapted to the instrument of people's wars as the form of the anti-imperialist struggle, its revolutionary intelligentsia began the critique or relocation of socialist theory. For them, the struggles of the European working classes were linked with the anti-imperialist movements of the nonindustrial world. The gulf between class struggle and anti-imperialist and nationalist activity began to be closed.

In the Caribbean and North America (where a racial politics analogous to that of colonialism had produced a complementary Black radical intelligentsia), when for much of the first half of the twentieth century the crises of monopoly capitalism struck the world system, a generation of these ideologues was already formed and ready to respond to the social upheavals in Europe, America, and the colonial world. Others affixed themselves to socialist movements after the rebellions of European workers had subsided and bourgeois democracy, the liberal representation of monopoly capitalism from its infancy, gave way in Italy, Germany, and Spain to the more openly repressive face of the fascist state. To the colonial and American Black radicals, the objections raised to fascism by liberal and socialist ideologues brought to the fore the parallels between colonialism and fascism and the ambivalence, hypocrisies, and impotence of the intellectuals in the metropoles of the European empires. Many of the leading activists among the Black intelligentsia, having previously committed themselves to drawing their nationalist struggles within the orbit of the socialist movement, found it necessary to move past their European comrades. It was both natural and historically logical that some would resurrect Pan-Africanism as a radical ideology and recognize further its potential as a radical theory of struggle and history. From the early 1930s on, a radical Pan-Africanism emerged. And in the work of Du Bois, James, and Wright, of Oliver Cox, Eric Williams, and George Padmore, the elements of its first phase were discernible.

When Du Bois and James set about the recovery of the history of the revolutionary Black struggle, they were driven from an implied to an explicit critique of Marxism. As Black men grown sensitive to the day-to-day heroism demanded for Black survival, they were particularly troubled by the casual application of preformed categories to Black social movements. It appeared to them that Western Marxists, unconsciously bound by a Eurocentric perspective, could not account for nor correctly assess the revolutionary forces emerging from the Third World. The racial metaphysics of Western consciousness—the legacy of a civilization—shielded their fellow socialists from the recognition of racialism's influence on the development and structures of the capitalist system, and conceptually pardoned them from a more acute inquiry into the categories of their own thought. Without some form of intervention, the socialist movement would be doomed to disaster.

The first initiative of Du Bois, who himself had been matured by his encounter with American Black nationalism, was to reassess the historical role of the industrial working classes. In the beginning he had intended a modest proposal: without the aid of the Black masses, no American working-class movement could succeed in overturning the capitalist ruling class. However, his investigation of the Black radical tradition of the mid-nineteenth century pushed his analysis further and deeper, beyond the presumptions of the revolutionary theory and politics of his time. Anticipating the more sustained expositions of Eric Williams and Oliver Cox, Du Bois became convinced that capitalism and slavery were related systemically; that monopoly capitalism had extended rather than arrested that relationship; and that the forces implicated in the dissolution of capitalism could emerge from the contradictions of that relationship. History provided his evidence. In the turbulence of the American Civil War and a social revolution carried through by the mobilized slaves and the white agrarian workers, it had been the manufacturing and industrial working classes that had hesitated, drawn to counterrevolution by racism and a short-sighted perception of their class interest. The class struggle had been distorted and a proletarian revolutionary consciousness among nineteenth-century American workers had been effectively interdicted by the ideological power of racism and the seductiveness of the bourgeois myth of social mobility. It was the slaves (in truth an enslaved peasantry) and other agrarian workers who had mounted the attack on capitalism. It was, Du Bois observed, from the periphery and not the center that the most sustained threat to the American capitalist system had materialized. The rebellious slaves, vitalized by a world-consciousness drawn from African lore and composing their American experience into a rebellious art, had constituted one of the crucial social bases in contradiction to bourgeois society. For Du Bois, the recovery of this last fact became as elementary to revolutionary theory as a recognition of the peasant masses whose revolts in Russia, Mexico, and China had rocked the ruling classes of the twentieth century. Just as important for him, however, was the realization that the racism of the American "white" working classes and their general ideological immaturity had abnegated the extent to which the conditions of capitalist production and relations alone could be held responsible for the social development of the American proletariat. The collective and individual identities of American workers had responded as much to race as they had to class. The relations of production were not determinant. Du Bois would pursue this issue politically but not theoretically. Nevertheless, it had become clear to him that in Marxist theory much uncertainty remained with respect to the significance that could be made of the historical appearance of the proletarian class under capitalism and the evolution of working-class consciousness.

In the reconstruction of the Haitian Revolution, James in his way reached even deeper into the Black radical tradition and into the issue of its resolution within Marxism. More an internationalist than even Du Bois, notwithstanding the latter's broad experience and wide concerns, James had intellectually absorbed the conflicting traditions associated with the cultural raison d'être of Victorian imperialism, the doctrines of Marxist-Leninism, and the nascent radical nationalism of colonial Trinidad. But as an ideologue of the Fourth International movement he had been led to a rigorous critique of them all and a rejection of any easy accommodation. Concurring with Du Bois's intuition that Western radicalism had indulged a tendency to peripheralize the antiracist and anti-imperialist struggles, James attempted a theoretical reconciliation of the Black and Western radical traditions. With the Russian Revolution in mind, he framed the Haitian Revolution against the Bolshevik model. But his attempt to lend Marxian authority to the slave revolutionists forced to the surface an unintended consideration. While he might suspend the disquieting realization that the revolution had occurred in the absence of those conditions and the particular consciousness that Marxian theory determined necessary for a modern social revolution, he could not avoid a kindred problem: the reevaluation of the nature and the historical role of the revolutionary petit bourgeois intelligentsia and its presumptions. For a decade after the appearance of *The Black Jacobins*, James would wrestle with the social and ideological ambivalence of this "renegade" strata, eventually articulating a critique of it as the source of leadership of the revolutionary masses. In Haiti as well as in Russia, Lenin's theory of "the dictatorship of the proletariat" had been shown to be insufficient. No revolutionary cadre, divorced from the masses, ensconced in state bureaucracy, and abrogating to itself the determination of the best interests of the masses, could sustain the revolution or itself. James would come to the theoretical position that "in the decisive hour" (as Marx and Engels were wont to say) it was only the consciousness and activity of the revolutionary masses that could preserve the revolution from compromise, betrayal, or the ill-considered usurpation of revolutionary authority. It was his study of the revolutionary masses of Haiti, France, Russia and Africa, and his work in England, America and Trinidad rather than the Bolshevik state that would persuade him of the actual fact of Lenin's dictum: "every cook can govern."

But it was Richard Wright who was better placed than either Du Bois, James, Padmore, Williams, or Cox to articulate the revolutionary consciousness of the Black masses and to assess the cultural debilitation of Marxian politics. Wright had as his vantage points his origins in the rural and urban Black working classes and his experience of the American Communist movement. Unlike Du Bois who came to Black cultural life from its margins and would stand at a distance to describe the revolutionary ideas of the American slaves as a mixture of legend, whimsy, and art, and unlike James whose appreciation of Black culture was often cerebral ("the medium" is how James would describe the voodoo ideology of the Haitian revolutionists, and the calypso of the West Indian masses) when not single-minded (about cricket and the novels of his age-mates and peers), Wright evoked in his writings the language and experience of "ordinary" Black men and women. In this way he pressed home the recognition that whatever the objective forces propelling a people toward struggle, resistance, and revolution, they would come to that struggle in their own cultural terms. Among Blacks, a culture of a mass conscious of itself had evolved from African civilization, the centuries of resistance to slavery, and the opposition to a racial social order. In the syncopations and the phrases, the scamp and the beat, the lyric and melody of Black language, Black beliefs, Black music, sexual and social relations and encounters, Wright's work reconstructed the resonances of Black American consciousness in its contests with reality. The quests pursued in his novels and essays were set to the improvisational possibilities obtained in that Black culture's collisions with its own parameters and those prescribed by the market forces and labor demands of capitalism and by a racialist culture. From the measured discourse of a Black culture he illustrated the limits of a socialist movement that persisted in too many abstractions, too far removed, and was prey to the arrogance of racial paternalism. Wright made it clear that the objections raised by Du Bois, Padmore, James,

Williams, Cox, and other Black radicals were grounded from below in the historical consciousness of the Black masses. In Wright's time, in part because of the various native and immigrant national and ethnic constituents making it up, the "white" working class had not yet obtained a collective historical and cultural integration of its own. As a class brought into being at the end of the nineteenth and the beginning of the twentieth century by racial capitalism, to the extent that it existed, the workers' collective consciousness remained a racial one subject to the disciplining ideologies of the bourgeois class and responsive to what they had been led to believe was "American culture." While that was true, only a small fraction of the class was capable of an alliance with the Black liberation struggle. In the meanwhile, it became increasingly clear to Wright and his colleagues that the project of revolutionary change required reassessment and reconceptualization.

It is now a generation later. In the intervening years the Black radical tradition has matured, assuming new forms in revolutionary movements in Africa, the Caribbean, and North America. In the ideas of revolutionaries, among them Patrice Lumumba, Kwame Nkrumah, Amilcar Cabral, Julius Nyerere, Robert Mugabe, Augustinho Neto, Eduardo Mondlane, Marcelino dos Santos, Frantz Fanon, Aime Cesaire, Walter Rodney, and Angela Davis, Black radicalism has remained a currency of resistance and revolt. However, the evolution of Black radicalism has occurred while it has not been conscious of itself as a tradition. Doubtlessly there have been advantages to this. There have been no sacred texts to be preserved from the ravages of history. There have been no intellects or leaders whose authority secured ideological and theoretical conformity and protected their ideas from criticism. There has been no theory to inoculate the movements of resistance from change. But it, too, is certain that there have been disadvantages; partial comprehensions that it has now become imperative to transcend. The fractioning of African peoples is dysfunctional.

Meanwhile the clock of "modern times" is running down. Within Western culture, that is the very civilization that in recent centuries has dominated a quarter of the world and acquired so little consciousness in its experience with the rest, what once were but faint signs of breakdown are now in bold evidence. Not even the brilliant wizardry of high technological achievement can mute the rumblings from the degenerating mechanism. It is the occasion of opposition and contradiction and the moment of opportunity. That is because the times that mark the dissolutions of civilizations compound the maturations of both internal and external processes.

Physically and ideologically, and for rather unique historical reasons, African peoples bridge the decline of one world order and the eruption (we may surmise) of another. It is a frightful and uncertain space of being. If we are to survive, we must take nothing that is dead and choose wisely from among the dying.

The industrial nations are self-destructing. Others, too, of course, will be affected. But the racial mythology that accompanied capitalist industrial formation and provided its social structures engendered no truly profound alternatives. The social, ideological, and political oppositions generated within Western societies have proven unequal to the task. They have acquired historical significance only when they received comfort in the consciousness of Third World peoples. There they mingled with other cultures, taking their place among social priorities and historical visions largely alien from their sites of origin. Such instances were the agrarian socialist revolutions among the Indian peasants of Mexico early in this century; the coterminous social revolutions and nationalist upheavals within the Russian Empire; the revolutionary peasant movements of China and India; and in the period following the Second World War, the national liberation movements of Madagascar and Cuba and on the continents of Africa and Central and South America. The critique of the capitalist world system acquired determinant force not from movements of industrial workers in the metropoles but from those of the "backward" peoples of the world. Only an inherited but rationalized racial arrogance and a romanticism stiffened by pseudo-science could manage to legitimate a denial of these occurrences. Western Marxism, in either of its two variants—critical-humanist or scientific—has proven insufficiently radical to expose and root out the racialist order that contaminates its analytic and philosophic applications or to come to effective terms with the implications of its own class origins. As a result, it has been mistaken for something it is not: a *total* theory of liberation. The ensuing errors have sometimes been horrendous, inducing in their wake dogmas of certainty characterized by desperation.

The Black radical tradition suggests a more complete contradiction. In social and political practice, it has acquired its immediate momentum from the necessity to respond to the persisting threats to African peoples characteristic of the modern world system. Over the many generations, the specificity of resistance—at best securing only a momentary respite—has given way to the imperatives of broader collectivities. Particular languages, cultures, and social sensibilities have evolved into world-historical consciousness. The distinctions of political space and historical time have fallen away so that the making of one Black collective identity suffuses nationalisms. Harbored in the African diaspora there is a single historical identity that is in opposition to the systemic privations of racial capitalism. Ideologically, it cements pain to purpose, experience to expectation, consciousness to collective action. It deepens with each disappointment at false mediation and reconciliation, and is crystallized into ever-increasing cores by betrayal and repression. The resoluteness of the Black radical tradition advances as each generation assembles the data of its experience to an ideology of liberation. The experimentation with Western political inventories of change, specifically nationalism and class struggle, is coming to a close. Black radicalism is transcending those traditions in order to adhere to its own authority. It will arrive as points of resistance here, rebellion there, and mass revolutionary movements still elsewhere. But each instance will be formed by the Black radical tradition in an awareness of the others and the consciousness that there remains nothing to which it may return. Molded by a long and brutal experience and rooted in a specifically African development, the tradition will provide for no compromise between liberation and annihilation.

The radical nationalist movements of our time in Africa and the African diaspora have come at a historical moment when substantial numbers of the world's Black peoples are under the threat of physical annihilation or the promise of prolonged and frightening debilitation. The famines that have always accompanied the capitalist world system's penetration of societies have increased in intensity and frequency. The appearance of literally millions of Black refugees, drifting helplessly beyond the threshold of human sensibility, their emaciated bodies feeding on their own tissues, have become commonplace. The systematic attack on radical Black polities, and the manipulation of venal political puppets are now routine occurrences. Where Blacks were once assured of some sort of minimal existence as a source of cheap labor, mass unemployment and conditions of housing and health that are of near-genocidal proportions obtain. The charades of neocolonialism and race relations have worn thin. In the metropoles, imprisonment, the stupor of drugs, the use of lethal force by public authorities and private citizens, and the more petty humiliations of racial discrimination have become epidemic. And over the heads of all, but most particularly those of the Third World, hangs the discipline of massive nuclear force. Not one day passes without confirmation of the availability and the willingness to use force in the Third World. It is not the province of one people to be the solution or the problem. But a civilization maddened by its own perverse assumptions and contradictions is loose in the world. A Black radical tradition formed in opposition to that civilization and conscious of itself is one part of the solution. Whether the other oppositions generated from within Western society and without will mature remains problematical. But for now we must be as one.

NOTES

Chapter One

1. One of the most extraordinary expressions of the expectations associated with the appearance of capitalism was Marx's caustic appraisal of the bourgeoisie's world-historical significance:

> The bourgeoisie, wherever it has got the upper hand, has put an end to all feudal, patriarchal, idyllic relations. It has pitilessly torn asunder the motley feudal ties that bound man to his "natural superiors," and has left remaining no other nexus between man and man than naked self-interest, than callous "cash payment." . . .

> The bourgeoisie has stripped of its halo every occupation hitherto honoured. . . .

> The bourgeoisie has torn away from the family its sentimental veil. . . .

> The bourgeoisie cannot exist without constantly revolutionizing the instruments of production, and thereby the relations of production, and with them the whole relations of society. . . .

> The bourgeoisie has, through its exploitation of the world-market, given cosmopolitan character to production and consumption in every country. (Karl Marx and Friedrich Engels, *The Communist Manifesto*, in Robert Tucker [ed.], *The Marx-Engels Reader*, W. W. Norton, New York, 1972, pp. 337–38)

A more recent version of this vision of capitalism—reflecting both its authors' views and those of directors of multinational (or global) corporations—is much less poetic but still as certain. "The power of the global corporation derives from its unique capacity to use finance, technology, and advanced marketing skills to integrate production on a worldwide scale and thus to realize the ancient capitalist dream of One Great Market." Richard Barnet and Ronald Muller, *Global Reach*, Simon and Schuster, New York, 1974, p. 18.

2. Paul Sweezy et al., *The Transition from Feudalism to Capitalism*, New Left Books, London, 1976; and Karl Marx, *Pre-Capitalist Economic Formations*, International Publishers, New York, 1965.

3. Fernand Braudel, *Capitalism and Material Life, 1400–1800*, Harper and Row, New York, 1973, pp. xiii–xv.

4. Karl Marx, *The German Ideology*, in Robert Tucker, op. cit., pp. 158–61.

5. Robert Latouche, *The Birth of Western Economy*, Barnes and Noble Inc., New York, 1961, p. 309.

6. Petr Kropotkin, *Mutual Aid*, Extending Horizon Books, Boston, n.d., pp. 117–18; Henri Pirenne, *Mohammed and Charlemagne*, Unwin University Books, London, 1968, pp. 17–19, pp. 184–85; and William C. Bark, *Origins of the Medieval World*, Stanford University Press, Stanford, 1958, pp. 26–27. Denys Hay reminds us: "for neither Greeks nor Romans did Europe mean much. Fear of Persia lent colour to the Greek attitude to the continents, but the empire of Alexander the Great was in Asia, not Europe, while the remnants of this were conquered by a Rome which made its greatest advances in the north and west of Europe. What cemented together the Greek world, and after it the world of Rome, was the inland sea, which linked all but the most remote provinces, which was literally the cradle of Greek civilization and which even the Romans, averse as they were to maritime adventure, annexed as '*Mare nostrum*.' Beyond the serenity of the Mediterranean (as later ages were to call it) and the outposts of order carried outwards by the Mediterranean conquerors, Greek or Roman, lay barbarism. Barbarians, as the Romans knew well enough, were confined to no particular continent, and were particularly troublesome in Europe itself." Hay, *Europe: The Emergence of an Idea*, Edinburgh University Press, Edinburgh, 1968, p. 4.

7. Oscar Halecki, *The Millennium of Europe*, Notre Dame University Press, South Bend, Indiana, 1963, p. 50.

8. Denis de Rougemont, *The Idea of Europe*, Macmillan Co., New York, 1966, pp. 47–49, 53; and Duncan McMillan, "Charlemagne Legends," *Encyclopaedia Britannica*, William Benton, Chicago, 1965, 5:291–92.

9. H. Munro Chadwick, *The Nationalities of Europe and the Growth of National Ideologies*, Cambridge University Press, Cambridge, 1945, pp. 50–75.

10. Along with the Italic, the Hellenic, the Indian, the Iranian and Armenian, these are said sometimes to constitute the Indo-European languages; see G. L. Brook, *A History of the English Language*, W. W. Norton and Co. Inc., New York, 1958, pp. 30–60.

11. Chadwick, op. cit., pp. 14–49.

12. According to Chadwick, Basque presumably "represents the language, or one of the languages, of the ancient Iberians," ibid., p. 49. Brook argues that there is evidence going back to the sixth century, B.C. of Etruscan, Oscan, and Umbrian being spoken in Italy; Brook, op. cit., pp. 36–37.

13. Henri Pirenne, op. cit., pp. 17–71.

14. Ibid., pp. 36–37.

15. Ibid., pp. 28, 32.

16. Ibid., p. 37. Pirenne reports that Gautier put the number of Roman Africans at seven to eight million in the fifth century, and that Doren, for the same century, estimates that Italy's population ranged between five and six million.

17. Latouche, op. cit., p. 70.

18. Ibid., pp. 59–60, 71; Pirenne, op. cit., pp. 75–79.

19. Frank Snowden, *Blacks in Antiquity*, Harvard University Press, Cambridge, 1970, pp. 170–71.

20. Both Pirenne and Latouche argue that long before the mounting of political pressures on the Germanic tribes by subsequent "barbarian" peoples—the Iranians, Mongols, Slavs, and Hungarians—the Goths were motivated by essentially economic reasons to integrate with the more productive peoples of the Empire. Pirenne, op. cit., pp. 37–39; Latouche, op. cit., pp. 42–45.

21. David Brion Davis, *The Problems of Slavery in Western Civilization*, Cornell University Press, Ithaca, 1966, pp. 29–61. The break in historical and cultural continuity that took place between the disintegration of Greco-Roman civilization and the rise of Germanic civilization had at one time immense significance to western European intelligentsias. Following *Germania*, written by the first-century Roman historian Tacitus, which contrasted the decadence of Rome to the martial virility of the Germanic tribes, they constructed myths of origin that distinguished superior cultures and races from inferior ones. At the latest, from the sixteenth century and well into the twentieth century, English, German, and French scholars generally distinguished "their" own Germanic cultural, racial, and philological roots from earlier (e.g., Celtic, Greco-Roman) and putatively later (the Normans) peoples. See Reginald Horsman, *Race and Manifest Destiny*, Harvard University Press, Cambridge, 1981, pp. 9–42. George Mosse reminds us that excerpts from *Germania* were a part of the standard curriculum "for the teaching of English constitutional history until well after the Second World War." Mosse, *Toward the Final Solution*, J. M. Dent and Sons, London, 1978, p. 48.

22. For Greek and Roman slavery, see William L. Westermann, *The Slave Systems of Greek and Roman Antiquity*, American Philosophical Society, Philadelphia, 1955, and Snowden, op. cit.; for the feudal period, see R. Welldon Finn, *An Introduction to Domesday Book*, Longmans, London, 1963, pp. 118–21, as cited by Davis, op. cit., pp. 38–39, and Iris Origo, "The Domestic Enemy: The Eastern Slaves in Tuscany in the Fourteenth and Fifteenth Centuries," *Speculum* 30, no. 3 (July 1955): 321–66, and Latouche, op. cit., pp. 123–25; for Genoese and Venetian trades, see Henri Pirenne, *Economic and Social History of Medieval Europe*, Harcourt, Brace and World, New York, 1937, pp. 16–20; Davis, op. cit., pp. 43, 52; and Fernand Braudel, *The Mediterranean and the Mediterranean World in the Age of Philip II*, Harper and Row, New York, 1976, 1:290–93 and 2:754–55—both Davis and Braudel are largely based upon the work of Charles Verlinden, *L'esclavage dans l'Europe medievale*, vol. 1, Peninsule Iberique, Brugge, France, 1955; and for the modern era see Eric Williams, *Capitalism and Slavery*, Capricorn Books, New York, 1966.

23. Davis, op. cit., pp. 33, 37.

24. Immanuel Wallerstein, *The Modern World System*, Academic Press, New York, 1974, pp. 86–90. Wallerstein wishes to distinguish between the economic and legal-political conditions of New World slavery and a capitalist "serfdom" ("coerced cash crop labour") in eastern Europe and among "natives" of the New World (the *encomienda*) of the sixteenth century. His definition of "coerced cash-crop labour" ("a system of agricultural labour control wherein peasants are required by some legal process enforced by the state to labour at least part of the time on a large domain producing some product for sale on the world market" p. 91) would appear to serve as well as a description of slavery. The point is that alone it does not distinguish the presumably distinct forms of forced labor. David Brion Davis observes that for at least the medieval era, the distinctions were not as clear-cut in daily life as modern scholars would suggest. Davis, op. cit., p. 33.

25. Pirenne, *Mohammed and Charlemagne*, op. cit., p. 140. In a note to the text, Pirenne observes: "These things were retained: the language, the currency, writing (papyrus) weights and measures, the kinds of foodstuffs in common use, the social classes, the religion—the role of Arianism has been exaggerated—art, the law, the administration, the taxes, the economic organization." Ibid.

26. Latouche, op. cit., pp. 97–116; Pirenne, *Economic and Social History of Medieval Europe*, op. cit., pp. 39–40.

27. Dirk Jellema, "Frisian Trade in the Dark Ages," *Speculum* 30, no. 1 (January 1955): 15–36; and

Latouche, op. cit., pp. 120–23. The decline of trade in Merovingian Europe is an important aspect of the attempt to challenge Henri Pirenne's "thesis" that the Muslim invasion of Europe by ending the European Mediterranean trade with its social and cultural concomitants precipitated the beginnings of a "new" European civilization inaugurated by Charlemagne's empire. See Pirenne, *Mohammed and Charlemagne*, op. cit., pp. 162–85, Latouche, op. cit., pp. 117–88; Bark, op. cit., pp. 6–28; and Alfred Havighurst (ed.), *The Pirenne Thesis*, D. C. Heath and Co., Boston, 1958.

28. Latouche, op. cit., p. 139.

29. Pirenne, *Mohammed and Charlemagne*, op. cit., pp. 184–85; Braudel, op. cit., p. 222.

30. Latouche, op. cit., pp. 173–74.

31. Ibid., pp. 297–98. Even by the late sixteenth century, the contrast in urban life was still great between the European hinterland and the Mediterranean, Braudel writes: "[T]he Mediterranean region in the sixteenth century (and it must be extended to its maximum when we are talking of towns) was unique in its immensity. In the sixteenth century no other region in the world had such a developed urban network. Paris and London were just on the threshold of their modern careers. The towns of the Low Countries and southern Germany (the latter bathing in the reflected glory of the Mediterranean, the former stimulated economically by merchants and sailors from the South), further north the industrious but small towns of the Hanseatic League, all of these towns, thriving and beautiful though they might be, did not make up a network as closely knit and complex as that of the Mediterranean, where town followed town in endless strings, punctuated by great cities: Venice, Genoa, Florence, Milan, Barcelona, Seville, Algiers, Naples, Constantinople, Cairo." Braudel, *The Mediterranean*, op. cit., pp. 277–78.

32. "Raoul Glaber has described with an insistence verging on sadism the appalling famine which preceded the year 1033. He notes for instance that at the fair at Tournus in Burgundy, a man was offering human flesh for sale, ready cooked on a butcher's stall." Latouche, op. cit., p. 298.

33. Bark, op. cit., pp. 70–82.

34. Pirenne, *The Economic and Social History of Medieval Europe*, op. cit., pp. 44–49; and Lopez and Raymond, *Medieval Trade in the Mediterranean World*, Oxford University Press, Oxford, 1955, pp. 87–104.

35. Pirenne, *Medieval Cities, Their Origins and the Revival of Trade*, Princeton University Press, Princeton, 1948, p. 140.

36. Pirenne, *Economic and Social History of Medieval Europe*, op. cit., p. 44.

37. Pirenne, *Medieval Cities*, op. cit., p. 6.

38. Pirenne, *Economic and Social History of Medieval Europe*, op. cit., p. 40.

39. Pirenne, *Medieval Cities*, op. cit., pp. 114–15. Denys Hay, though in disagreement with Pirenne's interpretation of the origins of these merchants, does not specifically cite the evidentiary basis of his view. *Europe in the Fourteenth and Fifteenth Centuries*, Longman, London, 1966, p. 71.

40. Ibid., p. 126. Elsewhere Pirenne has explained: "[I]t is incontestable that commerce and industry were originally recruited from among landless men, who lived, so to speak, on the margin of a society where land alone was the basis of existence." *Economic and Social History of Medieval Europe*, op. cit., p. 45.

41. Pirenne, *Medieval Cities*, op. cit., pp. 143–44. In eastern Europe, it was a quite different story since the political and economic powers of the towns were quixotic and short lived: "[T]he towns were compelled to surrender their ancient rights of harbouring serfs; they were compelled to abandon leagues with other towns; and the lords were even able to avoid using the towns as markets for their grain by selling it direct to exporters."; Hay, op. cit., p. 41.

42. Pirenne, op. cit., p. 81.

43. Ibid., pp. 100–101.

44. Ibid., p. 155, and Pirenne, *Economic and Social History of Medieval Europe*, op. cit., pp. 35–36.

45. Karl Polanyi, *The Great Transformation*, Beacon Press, Boston, 1957, p. 64.

46. Ibid.; and Pirenne, *The Economic and Social History of Medieval Europe*, op. cit., pp. 160–66.

47. Pirenne, *Medieval Cities*, op. cit., pp. 154–56.

48. Pirenne, *The Economic and Social History of Medieval Europe*, op. cit., pp. 57–58 ; and Hay, op. cit., p. 77.

49. Pirenne, *Medieval Cities*, op. cit., p. 193. See also Michael Tigar and Madeleine Levy, *Law and the Rise of Capitalism*, Monthly Review Press, 1977, pp. 80–96; elsewhere, Tigar and Levy summarize their review of the earliest thrusts of the bourgeoisie against the feudal order: "The great achievement of the bourgeoisie in this period [1000 to 1200] was to wrest from seigneurs in hundreds of separate localities the recognition of an independent status within the feudal hierarchy. The urban movement . . . demanded one major concession from the seigneur: a charter . . . the status of *bourgeois, burgher*, or burgess" (p. 111).

50. Hay, op. cit., pp. 39, 370.

51. Ibid., pp. 373–74.

52. Origo, op. cit., p. 326.

53. Origo, op. cit., pp. 328, 336; Davis, op. cit., p. 43; and Hay, op. cit., pp. 75–76.

54. Origo, op. cit., p. 336.

55. Hay, op. cit., p. 76. Hay observes that: "In these slave-owning communities of the Christian Mediter-

ranean there is not much evidence that slaves were used in agriculture" (ibid.). Charles Verlinden does not agree: "In Spain female slaves were generally cheaper than males, although the opposite was true in most of Italy. This was because much of the slave manpower in Spain was used in agriculture and in industry, whereas in Italy the domestic slave predominated in the cities and therefore more female workers were required." Charles Verlinden, "The Transfer of Colonial Techniques from the Mediterranean to the Atlantic," in *The Beginnings of Modern Colonization*, Cornell University Press, Ithaca, 1970, p. 29.

56. Charles Verlinden notes: "The Latin word *sclavus*, the common source of the words *esclave, esclavo, escravo, schiavo, Sklave,* and *slave,* did not take root during that initial period [pre-Middle Ages] when slavery was common to the whole of Europe. . . . It was only when slaves were recruited from entirely new sources that other terms appeared to indicate the nonfree, and among these were *sclavus,* derived from the ethnic name of the Slav people and popularized. It appeared first in its Latin form in tenth century Germany." "Medieval Slavery in Europe and Colonial Slavery in America," Verlinden, op. cit., pp. 35–36.

57. Charles Verlinden, "The Transfer of Colonial Techniques," op. cit., pp. 31–32.

58. Giuliano Procacci, *The History of the Italian People*, Weidenfeld and Nicolson, London, 1970, pp. 44–45.

59. R. H. Tawney has commented on the several forms of capitalism in European history. The occasion for his remarks was the review of Maurice Dobb's *Studies in the Development of Capitalism* (Routledge, London, 1946): "Mr. Dobb's limitation of the term 'capitalism' to a particular system of production, under which labour is employed on the basis of a wage contract to produce surplus value for the owner of capital, might seem, at first sight, to escape some of the ambiguities inherent in less restricted interpretations; but it raises problems of its own. It is not merely that, as he would agree, financial and commercial capitalism have been highly developed in circumstances when the institution, as interpreted by him, has been a feeble plant, and that to exclude these varieties on the ground that they do not fall within the four corners of the nineteenth-century definition is to beg the question. It is that, as his work shows, the origins and growth of the industrial species require for their elucidation to be considered in relation to the history of other members of the family, some of which have been among its progenitors. Obviously the capitalism of our day rests predominantly on a wage-system, and the latter is so familiar that it is tempting to treat it as historically a constant." Tawney, "A History of Capitalism," *Economic History Review*, 2d ser., vol. 2, no.3 (1950): 310–11.

60. Marian Malowist, "The Economic and Social Development of the Baltic Countries from the Fifteenth to the Seventeenth Centuries," *Economic History Review*, 2d ser., vol. 12, no. 2 (1959): 177–78, and Wallerstein, op. cit., pp. 21–26.

61. Hay, op. cit., p. 34.

62. Ibid., pp. 34–35.

63. Norman Cohn, *The Pursuit of the Millennium*, Oxford University Press, New York, 1970, pp. 198–99; and Hay, op. cit., pp. 35–37; and Procacci, op. cit., p. 46.

64. E. M. Carus-Wilson and Olive Coleman, *England's Export Trade, 1275–1547*, Oxford University Press, Oxford, 1963, pp. 201–7.

65. Hay, op. cit., p. 387.

66. Ibid., p. 389.

67. P. Ramsey, "The European Economy in the Sixteenth Century," *Economic History Review*, 2d ser., vol. 12, no. 3 (April 1960): 458.

68. Hay, op. cit., p. 389.

69. Ibid.; and Wallerstein, op. cit., p. 148.

70. Halil Inalcik, *The Ottoman Empire*, Weidenfeld and Nicolson, London, 1966, pp. 133–39.

71. K. G. Davies, "The Mess of the Middle Class," *Past and Present*, no. 22 (July 1962): 82.

72. As quoted by Immanuel Wallerstein, op. cit., p. 124 note.

73. Davies, op. cit., p. 79.

74. In his important but flawed study of mercantilism, Eli Heckscher made a point on the conceptualization of capitalism related to that of Davies quoted above in the text. Heckscher commented "that the method of treating all sorts of disconnected tendencies, paving the way to modern economic conditions, under the common name of 'modern capitalism' appears to me confusing and a thing to be shunned." *Mercantilism*, George Allen and Unwin, London, 1955, 1:14.

75. The phrase is Immanuel Wallerstein's, op. cit., p. 133; see also Perry Anderson, *Lineages of the Absolute State*, New Left Books, London, 1974, pp. 40–41.

76. V. G. Kiernan, "State and Nation in Western Europe," *Past and Present*, no. 31 (July 1965): 34.

77. Ibid., pp. 25–26.

78. "War for [the monarchy] was not an optional policy, but an organic need. . . . The whole State apparatus that rulers were putting together piecemeal was largely a by-product of war. During its adolescence, the sixteenth and seventeenth Centuries, fighting was almost continuous; later on it grew rather more intermittent." Ibid., p. 31.

79. Wallerstein, op. cit., pp. 136–39. For an extensive discussion of the state-merchant associations see Heckscher, op. cit., vol. 1, pp. 340–455.

80. Braudel, *The Mediterranean*, op. cit., vol. 1, p. 344, and vol. 2, p. 695.

81. See D. C. Coleman, "Eli Heckscher and the Idea of Mercantilism," *Scandinavian Economic History Review* 5, no. 1 (1957): 3–4.

82. Wallerstein, op. cit., pp. 146–47.

83. Coleman, op. cit., pp. 18–19; see also Carl Bucher, *Industrial Evolution*, August Kelley, New York, 1968 (Orio 1901), pp. 136–39.

84. Heckscher, op. cit., vol. 2, pp. 14–15. Wallerstein apparently has some problems with this particular attribution to sixteenth-century bourgeoisie. While relying on Kiernan for his own characterization—rather loosely—Wallerstein presents an interpretation that is inconsistent with respect to the distinctions to be made between statism and nationalism: "It was only in the late seventeenth and eighteenth Centuries within the framework of mercantilism that nationalism would find its first real advocates amongst the bourgeoisie. But in the sixteenth century, the interests of the bourgeoisie were not yet surely fixed on the state. Too large a number were more interested in open than in closed economies. And for state builders, premature nationalism risked its crystallization around too small an ethno-territorial entity. At an early point, statism could almost be said to be anti-nationalist, since the boundaries of 'nationalist' sentiment were often narrower than the bounds of the monarch's state." Wallerstein, op. cit., p. 146; see also Kiernan, op. cit., pp. 29–30.

85. See Coleman, op. cit., p. 21.

86. Heckscher, op. cit., vol. 2, p. 18.

87. Ibid., pp. 18–23; see also Wallerstein, op. cit., pp. 196–97.

88. Fernand Braudel: "Beginning in the sixteenth century and with more eclat in this century of renewal, the States—at least those who would live, prosper and especially resist the exhausting expenses of land and sea warfare—the States dominate, deform economic life, subject it to a network of constraints; they capture it in their net . . . the part of economic life that was at that point most modern, that which we would readily designate as operating within the framework of largescale merchant capitalism was linked to these financial ups and downs of the State." Quoted by Wallerstein, op. cit., p. 138 note.

89. Friedrich Hertz, *Race and Civilization*, KTAV (no place), 1970, p. 4; see also Hannah Arendt, *The Origins of Totalitarianism*, Meridian Books, Cleveland, 1958, pp. 161–65, and Henri Peyre, *Historical and Political Essays*, University of Nebraska, (no place), 1968, pp. 29–30. (Peyre acknowledges his debt to Jacques Barzun, see *The French Race*, Kennirat, New York, 1966 Oris.1432, and Race, Harcourt Brace, New York, 1932.) One should also mention that with respect to the Ham legend and its origins as a rationalization for African slavery in North America, Winthrop Jordan in his highly regarded study *White Over Black* (University of North Carolina Press, Chapel Hill, 1968), in company with most American scholars, has virtually ignored the phenomenon of racist attitudes among Europeans toward other Europeans—this despite his claim to be familiar with the relevant literature (see his appendix, "Essay on Sources").

90. Hertz, op. cit., p. 6.

91. Heckscher, op. cit., vol. 2, p. 18.

92. V. B. Kiernan, "Foreign Mercenaries and Absolute Monarchy," *Past and Present*, no. 2 (April 1957): 76–77.

93. Ibid., p. 68; see also Braudel, *The Mediterranean*, op. cit., 2:739–43.

94. Kiernan, op. cit., p. 74.

95. Ibid., p. 78.

96. Ibid., p. 69.

97. Ibid., p. 72.

98. That there were several other sides to the relation of the state to mercenaries is attested to by Braudel (*The Mediterranean*, op. cit., vol. 2): "Sea-pirates were aided and abetted by powerful towns and cities. Pirates on land, bandits, received regular backing from nobles. Robber bands were often led, or more or less closely directed, by some genuine noblemen" (p. 749); "banditry had other origins besides the crisis in noble fortunes: it issued from peasantry and populace alike. This was a groundswell—'a flood tide' as an eighteenth-century historian called it, which stirred up a variety of waters. As a political and social (though not religious) reaction, it had both aristocratic and popular components (the 'mountain kings' in the Roman Campagna and around Naples were more often than not peasants and humble folk)" (p. 751).

99. The nineteenth-century armies of imperialist Europe continued the tradition of relying on substantial recruitment among ethnic minorities, "riff-raff," outcasts, aliens and the peasantry: to the million serfs of the Russian army were added the Asiatic Bashkirs and Kalmucks, Ingush and Ossietin; the Corsicans and Bretons of the French army were augmented by the Legion founded on Kabyle swordsmen, Swiss and other European mercenaries, but by mid-century the army itself had come to be dominated by West Africans; in the Philippines, the Spanish army was native, as was the Dutch army of the East Indies. In India, the East India Company and the Bengal army (1842) employed between them upward of 70,000 natives in their

sepoy regiments. In Britain itself, in 1832, the Irish accounted for 42 percent of the army. See V. G. Kiernan, *European Empires from Conquest to Collapse*, Leicester University Press, Leicester, 1982, pp. 17–32.

100. Bucher, op. cit., p. 346; Wallerstein, op. cit., p. 117; see also Stephen Castles and Godula Kosack, *Immigrant Workers and Class Structure in Western Europe*, Oxford University Press, London, 1973, pp. 15–25; Braudel says it best: "These indispensable immigrants were not always unskilled labourers or men of little aptitude. They often brought with them new techniques that were as indispensable as their persons to urban life. The Jews, driven out by their religious beliefs not their poverty, played an exceptional role in these transfers of technology. . . . There were other valuable immigrants, itinerant artists for instance attracted by expanding towns which were extending their public buildings; or merchants, particularly the Italian merchants and bankers, who activated and indeed created such cities as Lisbon, Seville, Medina del Campo, Lyons and Antwerp. An urban community needs all sorts and conditions of men, not least rich men. Towns attracted the wealthy just as they attracted the proletariat, though for very different reasons." *The Mediterranean*, op. cit., 1:336–37.

101. Wallerstein, op. cit., pp. 118–19; Bucher makes a similar comment, op. cit., p. 353.

102. Chaim Bermant, *London's East End*, Macmillan Publishing, New York, 1975, pp. 30–31.

103. Ibid., p. 43; see also E. P. Thompson, op. cit., pp. 469–85; and Stephen Castles and Godula Kosack, op. cit., pp. 16–17.

104. See Paul Lazarsfeld and Anthony Oberschall, "Max Weber and Empirical Social Research," *American Sociological Review* 30, no. 2 (April 1965): 185–88.

105. See Stephen Castles and Godula Kosack, "The Function of Labour Immigration in Western European Capitalism," *New Left Review*, no. 73 (May–June 1972): 6; and Bucher, op. cit., pp. 367–68.

106. See David Brody, *Steelworkers in America*, Harper Torchbooks, New York, 1969, pp. 96–99.

107. See Howard Brett Melendy, *The Oriental Americans*, Twayne Publishers, New York, 1972; Mary R. Coolidge, *Chinese Immigration*, Arno Press, New York, 1969 (orig. 1909); and Stuart Miller, *The Unwelcome Immigrant*, University of California Press, Berkeley, 1969.

108. "A 'nation' is etymologically a 'birth,' or a 'being born,' and hence a race, a kin or kind having a common origin or, more loosely, a common language and other institutions. . . . There is not only an original and individual birth for each system but a continual birth of new institutions within it, a continual transformation of old institutions, and even a rebirth of the nation after death." Max Fisch's introduction to *The New Science of Giambattista Vico*, Cornell University Press, Ithaca, 1970, p. xxiii; see also Friedrich Hertz for an example of the length to which the monarchy was willing to go to produce the appropriate illusion: "The theory already put forward by Bodin that the Franks were a people of Gallic stock who had wandered into Germany, and from there had returned later as deliverers of their brothers from the Roman yoke, came into favour under Louis XIV. Within the French people there was, therefore, no racial difference, but national unity of the kind so much desired by the absolute monarchy. This theory very conveniently lent support to the desire for the annexation of the Rhine, the restoration of which, as old Frankish territory, he affected to demand," op. cit., p. 5.

109. Kiernan, op. cit., *Past and Present*, no. 31, p. 27.

110. Robert S. Lopez, *The Birth of Europe*, Phoenix House, London, 1966, pp. 103–4.

111. Robert S. Lopez and Irving Raymond (eds.), *Medieval Trade in the Mediterranean World*, Oxford University Press, Oxford, 1955, pp. 79–80 and 87–107.

112. Braudel, *The Mediterranean*, op. cit., 1:321.

113. Ibid., 2:695.

114. Halil Inalcik, *The Ottoman Empire*, Weidenfeld and Nicolson, London, 1966, pp. 133–39.

115. Braudel, *The Mediterranean*, op. cit., 1:336–37.

116. Ibid., p. 322.

117. Ibid., p. 344.

118. Ibid., p. 334.

119. Ibid., pp. 334–36.

120. See Charles Verlinden, op. cit.; Eric Williams, op. cit.; and David Brion Davis, op. cit.

121. See Karl Mannhein, *Ideology and Utopia*, Harcourt, Brace and World, New York, 1936, pp. 121–24; and Hertz, op. cit., pp. 6, 10.

122. T. K. Derry and M. G. Blakeway, *The Making of Pre-Industrial Britain*, John Murray, London, 1973, passim.

123. See Arendt, op. cit., pp. 165–67; Hertz, op. cit., pp. 1–19.

124. Reginald Horsman, 1981, pp. 14–15.

125. Ibid., chap. 2.

126. Louis Snyder, *The Idea of Racialism*, D. Van Nostrand, Princeton, 1962, pp. 39–40 (also see pp. 20–23 and 39–53); see also Snyder's *Race*, Longmans, Green and Co., New York, 1939, pp. 93–95; Magnus Hirschfield, *Racism*, Victor Gollancz, London, 1938. (Hirschfield, interestingly, traces the usage of the term "race" from its introduction in scientific literature by Comte de Buffon in 1749, to its appearance in the

prolegomena of Immanuel Kant's summer course in 1775 at Konigsberg in the form of White Race, Negro Race, Hunnish Race, Hindu Race, and mongrel races, pp. 51–54.)

127. See Eric Hobsbawm, "Some Reflections on Nationalism," in T. J. Nossiter, A. H. Hanson, and Stein Rokkan (eds.), *Imagination and Precision in the Social Sciences*, Faber and Faber, London, 1972, pp. 385–406.

128. See Karl Marx and Friedrich Engels, *The Communist Manifesto*, in Robert Tucker (ed.), *The Marx-Engels Reader*, op. cit., 1972, pp. 342–43.

129. See Louis Snyder, *The Idea of Racialism*, op. cit., pp. 155–65 for excerpts from various National Socialist thinkers in Germany including Adolf Hitler, Alfred Rosenberg, Ernst Hauer, Felix Fischer-Dodeleben, Wilhelm Klesserow, Ernst Krieck, Walter Darre, Herman Gauch, and, as well, appropriate selections from the Nuremberg Laws (1935); see also Mannheim, op. cit., pp. 134–46; M. N. Roy, *Fascism*, Best Books, Jijnasa, 1976, pp. 33–43; and Renzo De Felice, *Interpretations of Fascism*, Harvard University Press, Cambridge, 1977, pp. 176–78.

130. See William Styron, "Hell Reconsidered," *New York Review of Books*, 29 June 1978, pp. 10–12, 14.

Chapter Two

1. E. P. Thompson, *The Making of the English Working Class*, p. 9.

2. Thompson himself, if I recall correctly, mentions Blacks in his study of late eighteenth and early nineteenth century English working classes on only two occasions! One of these instances is his reference to a Black artisan; the other is the appearance of a Black man as a representation of Satan in a nightmare recalled by a dissident minister.

3. Excerpts from the introductions of two of the many studies of socialist history will suffice in demonstrating the persistence of the identification of socialism with the two "revolutions." George Lichtheim in his Preface writes: "The purpose of the present work is . . . to clarify the origins of socialism, both as a world-view and is the specific response of workers and intellectuals to the twofold upheaval of the French Revolution and the Industrial Revolution," *The Origins of Socialism*, Praeger, New York, 1969, p. vii. G. D. H. Cole, though somewhat uneasy about the periodization and definitiveness of the Industrial Revolution, nevertheless succumbs to the convenience of the phrase and its popular significations. He observes: "It is now commonplace to say that from 1789 onwards Europe was in the throes of three kinds of revolutionary change—*political* and *social*, symbolized by the events in France and their repercussions in other countries, *industrial*, marked by the advent of steam power and the extended application of scientific techniques in manufacture and in civil and mechanical engineering, and *agrarian*, involving vast changes in methods of land-cultivation and stock-breeding, and in the character of rural life." *A History of Socialist Thought*, vol. 1, *Socialist Thought, the Forerunners, 1789–1850*, St. Martin's Press, New York, 1953, p. 10.

4. Asa Briggs, "The Language of 'Class' in Early Nineteenth-Century England," in Asa Briggs and John Saville (eds.), *Essays in Labour History*, Macmillan, London, 1960, p. 43; see also Melvin Kranzberg's "Industrial Revolution," in *Encyclopaedia Britannica*, 1965, 12:210–15.

5. A. E. Musson, "Continental Influences on the Industrial Revolution in Great Britain," in Barrie Ratcliffe (ed.), *Great Britain and Her World, 1750–1914*, Manchester University Press, Manchester, 1975, p. 73. For industrialization in France in the early nineteenth century, see W. O. Henderson, *The Industrial Revolution in Europe*, Quadrangle, Chicago, 1961, pp. 86–88.

6. For example, Musson notes that: "In the smelting and refining of metallic ores . . . German skill and capital . . . were extremely important. Water-powered technology and mining operations were further developed . . . from Dutch and German experience. It was from the Continent, moreover, that the blast furnace and iron casting were introduced into England in the sixteenth century, followed by rolling and slitting mills for the products of the forge." Ibid.

7. E. J. Hobsbawm, "Economic Fluctuations and Some Social Movements Since 1800," in *Economic History Review*, 2d ser., vol. 5, no. 1 (1952): 17, 19.

8. Hobsbawm cautions, "Our best indices are mortality rates (average expectation of life, infantile, TB mortality, etc.), morbidity rates and anthropometric data. Unfortunately in Britain we lack any reliable anthropometric data such as the French, and any index of health such as the percentage of rejected recruits. Nor have we any useful morbidity figures." "The British Standard of Living 1790–1850," in Hobsbawm's *Labouring Men*, Weidenfeld and Nicolson, London, 1964, p. 71. Hobsbawm's comments take place in the context of a debate with the "optimists" interpretation of the social consequences of the appearance of industrial forms of production; Hobsbawm sides with the "pessimists." "It is today heterodox to believe that early industrialization was a catastrophe for the labouring poor . . . let alone that their standard of living declined. This article proposes to show that the currently accepted view is based on insufficient evidence. . . . It is dangerous to reject the consensus of informed and intelligent contemporaries of industrialization, a majority of whom, as even critics admit, took the dark view. . . . For the sake of convenience the classical (Ricardo-Malthus-Marx-Toynbee-Hammond) view will be called the *pessimistic*, the modern (Clapham-Ashton-Hayek) view the *optimistic* school." Ibid., p. 64.

9. Norman Longmate, *The Workhouse*, St. Martin's Press, New York, 1974, pp. 45ff; for further evidence of the hostility of the ruling classes toward the poor and the punitive use of workhouses, see E. P. Thompson, *The Making of the English Working Class*, op. cit., pp. 266–68.

10. Hobsbawm, "The British Standard," op. cit., p. 73.

11. See Longmate, op. cit., p. 44; and Thompson, op. cit., pp. 217–24.

12. See Hobsbawm's discussion of unemployment patterns and social eruptions and the manner in which these were affected by the convergences in the nineteenth century of agrarian-based depressions with the less seasonal patterns of industrial business cycles, "Economic Fluctuations," op. cit., pp. 4–9.

13. Ibid., pp. 10–11, and Thompson, op. cit., pp. 219–21.

14. Hobsbawm, "The British Standard," op. cit., p. 74.

15. Thompson, op. cit., p. 250.

16. As quoted by Thompson, ibid.

17. Hobsbawm, "The British Standard," op. cit., p. 73.

18. See Thompson, op. cit., pp. 247–48. Thompson comments that "the rewards of the 'march of progress' always seemed to be gathered by someone else . . . for these particular insecurities were only a facet of the general insecurity of all skills during this period" (p. 248).

19. See Brian Inglis, *Poverty and the Industrial Revolution*, Hodder and Stoughton, London, 1971, passim; and A. J. Taylor, "Progress and Poverty in Britain," *History* 45 (Feb. 1960): 16–31.

20. E. P. Thompson, op. cit., pp. 320–21.

21. Hobsbawm suggests, "The habit of industrial solidarity must be learned, like that of working a regular week; so must the common sense of demanding concessions when conditions are favourable, not when hunger suggests. There is thus a natural time-lag, before new workers become an 'effective' labour movement. . . . Various factors may precipitate such artificially retarded entrances of workers into organized labour activity. The news of labour unrest elsewhere, once it penetrates the new area, may set it off. So may political events and stresses, e.g. the French general election of 1936 or the setting up of Congress provincial governments in India in 1937." "Economic Fluctuations," op. cit., p. 21.

22. J. L. Hammond, "The Industrial Revolution and Discontent," *Economic History Review* 2, no. 2 (January 1930): 224–25.

23. Ibid., pp. 221, 223.

24. Asa Briggs, op. cit., p. 64. It is interesting that Mill's eldest son, John Stuart Mill, displayed a family resemblance in his own views toward the working classes. Nicholas Mansergh reports that "Having noted in his Representative Government that the Conservative Party was by the law of its composition the stupidest party, Mill observed in a pamphlet that the English working classes, though differing from those of some other countries in being ashamed of it, were yet generally liars." *The Irish Question, 1840–1921*, University of Toronto Press, Toronto, 1965, p. 117.

25. See Hobsbawm's "The Machine Breakers," in *Labouring Men*, op. cit., pp. 5–22; and George Rude's essay on "Luddism," in his *The Crowd in History*, John Wiley and Sons, New York, 1964, pp. 79–92.

26. Hobsbawm, ibid., pp. 10–11.

27. Ibid.; and Hobsbawm's "Economic Fluctuations," op. cit., pp. 5–9; and E. P. Thompson, op. cit., pp. 225–28.

28. Ibid., p. 13.

29. See the curious transition that Marx makes in *The Communist Manifesto* (op. cit.) from his discussion of the bourgeoisie to his account of the appearance of the proletariat in history. The point that class as determined by the history of bourgeoisies, and class with respect to the proletariat are concretely and philosophically different is made by Cornelius Castoriadis: "The history of the workers' movement is the history of the activity of human subjects belonging to a socioeconomic category created by capitalism. Through their activity and that of others who fought at their side, this category has transformed itself into a class of a type for which history offers no analogies." "On the History of the Workers' Movement," *Telos*, no. 30 (Winter 1976–77): 38.

30. Rude, op. cit., p. 230; see also L. P. Curtis, Jr., *Anglo-Saxons and Celts*, University of Bridgeport, Bridgeport, 1968, pp. 31–33.

31. See J. L. Hammond, op. cit., pp. 215–26; and Hobsbawm, "History and 'The Dark Satanic Mills' " and "The Standard of Living Debate: A Postscript," in *Labouring Men*, op. cit., for more on the vissicitudes of English labor historiography.

32. At least one implication of recognizing that the industrial working class of the early nineteenth century was a minority class is suggested in Hammond's concession to J. H. Clapham: "Dr. Clapham is . . . entitled to point out that in 1831 the building trades employed more heads of families than the cotton industry, and that the cotton workers were greatly outnumbered by the domestic servants. Certain of the calamities or losses that accompanied the Industrial Revolution fell only on part of the working class population, and that not the largest part." Hammond, op. cit., p. 216. As we have seen in the text, Hammond does not agree with Clapham but does acknowledge a warrant for the latter's assertions; in like

manner, one must note that Hobsbawm, Mayhew, and Thompson take on the optimists on the statistical turf of reliability and validity of data.

33. Thompson, op. cit., pp. 828–29.

34. Ibid., p. 831; and R. A. Huttenback, *Racism and Empire*, Cornell University Press, Ithaca, 1976, pp. 15–22.

35. See Royden Harrison, "The British Labour Movement and the International in 1864," in Ralph Miliband and John Saville (eds.), *The Socialist Register 1964*, Merlin Press, London, 1964, pp. 293–308.

36. Ibid., p. 306; and W. H. Fraser, "Trade Unionism," in J. T. Ward (ed), *Popular Movements c. 1830–1850*, Macmillan, London, 1970, p. 113. For the role of the Irish Question in the defection of English labor from class praxis, see Mansergh, op. cit., pp. 113–21.

37. Thompson, op. cit., pp. 828–29.

38. Eric Williams, *Capitalism and Slavery*, op. cit., Maurice Dobb, op. cit.; and R. H. Tawney, op. cit.

39. See Edward Norman, *A History of Modern Ireland*, Allen Lane the Penguin Press, London, 1971, pp. 33–44.

40. Thomas W. Heyck, *The Dimensions of British Radicalism: The Case of Ireland*, University of Illinois Press, Urbana, 1974, p. ix.

41. James A. Froude, *The English in Ireland*, Scribner, Armstrong, New York, 1874, 3:11–17.

42. Michael Hechter, *Internal Colonialism*, University of California Press, Berkeley, 1975, pp. 72–73.

43. For a rather succinct treatment of Anglo-Saxonism as an ideology, see L. P. Curtis, Jr., op. cit., pp. 10–14. Briefly Curtis identifies the ideology with "1. an identifiable and historically authenticated race or people known as the Anglo-Saxons who shared common ties of blood, language, geographical origin, and culture . . . traced right back to the Jutes, Angles, and Saxons . . . between the Baltic and the Black Forest. 2. Civil and religious liberties enjoyed . . . in predominantly Anglo-Saxon societies . . . attributable to the peculiar genius of the Anglo-Saxons in political affairs. 3. a combination of virtues and talents which made them superior in all important respects to any other comparable racial or cultural group in the world. 4. Such specifically Anglo-Saxon attributes as reason, restraint, self control, love of freedom and hatred of anarchy, respect for law and distrust of enthusiasm were actually transmissible from one generation . . . to the next in a kind of biologically determined entailed inheritance. 5. threats . . . of racial deterioration through the strains and pressures of a highly urbanized and industrialized society, or of 'race suicide' through a deliberate limitation of family size, or of the adulteration and contamination of Anglo-Saxon blood by mixture with 'foreign' blood, whether that of the Irish, Jews, Italians, French, and so on" (pp. 11–12).

44. James A. Froude, *The English in Ireland*, op. cit., 1873, 1:14.

45. Ibid. Froude's comments bear some resemblance to those of Karl Marx, see "Outline of a Report on the Irish Question to the Communist Educational Association of German Workers in London," in the Marx-Engels collection entitled *Ireland and the Irish Question*, International Publishers, New York, 1972, p. 127.

46. Ibid., p. 16.

47. Ibid., pp. 24–25.

48. Ibid, p. 35, see also Hechter, op. cit., p. 72.

49. Hechter, op. cit., p. 72. Hechter plays a little loose with dates (he puts the Act of Irish Union in 1801 when its official date is 1 August 1800) and periodization. The policy of the plantation of Ireland begins under Elizabeth I, not James I. See Froude, op. cit., 1:49–51; and Mansergh, op. cit., p. 40.

50. Froude, op. cit., 1:52–65. O'Neill is an Irish title of pre-Conquest authority that was used "as the symbol of the Irish independent sovereignty" (p. 59).

51. R. D. Edwards' contribution on "The Tudors," in the essay "Ireland," in *Encyclopaedia Britannica*, 1965, 12:556–57.

52. Mansergh, op. cit., p. 40.

53. Froude cites Petty's figures from the latter's *Political Arithmetick* (1699); Froude, op. cit., 1:133. Marx, somewhat earlier, identified Petty as "the father of English political economy" but characterized him as "just a frivolous, grasping, unprincipled adventurer"; see Marx, *A Contribution to the Critique of Political Economy*, International Publishers, New York, 1970 (orig. 1859), pp. 53 and 55 respectively. For Petty's interests in Ireland, see Eric Strauss, *Irish Nationalism and British Democracy*, Columbia University Press, New York, 1951, pp. 13–16.

54. Froude, ibid., pp. 219–85.

55. Hechter asserts: "It was not until the Cromwellian Settlement that religious differences came to be the dominant political cleavage in Irish society. Cromwell's policies toward the adherents of Catholicism were harsh. For a time Catholic clergy were killed whenever they could be found. Of more lasting import, Catholic landowners, of either Anglo-Norman or Irish descent, were very largely stripped of their land; this expropriated land was then used as payment for Cromwell's military lieutenants in the Irish campaign. By 1688 nearly 80 per cent of Irish land was in the hands of Englishmen and Scottish Protestants." Hechter, op.

cit., p. 103. Marx observes that another form of retribution during Cromwell's rule was "the sale of many Irish into slavery in the West Indies"; Marx, "Outline of a Report," op. cit., p. 128.

56. Hechter, ibid., pp. 84, 93–94.

57. Ibid., p. 92. Engels had occasion to take on "the Irish landowners and the English bourgeois" who saw the condition of Ireland in the nineteenth century as a natural phenomenon: "Compared with England, Ireland is more suited to cattle-rearing on the whole; but if England is compared with France, she too is more suited to cattle-rearing. Are we to conclude that the whole of England should be transformed into cattle pastures, and the whole agricultural population be sent into the factory towns or to America?" Engels, "History of Ireland," in Marx and Engels, *Ireland and the Irish Question*, op. cit., p. 190. For more on the effects of free trade on Irish industry, see Strauss, op. cit., p. 120.

58. Thompson, op. cit., p. 429.

59. Ibid., p. 432.

60. Ibid., pp. 432–33. For more on "labour-rhythms" and a much more satisfying treatment of the English workers" "Puritan temperament," see Thompson's essay, "Time, Work-Discipline, and Industrial Capitalism," in *Past and Present*, no. 38 (December 1967): 56–97.

61. Friedrich Engels, *The Condition of the Working Class in England in 1844*, George Allen and Unwin, London, 1950 (orig. 1845), p. 92. Strauss supports Thompson's views on "the crippling experience of work in mills and mines" on English workers as the reason for the superior strength of Irish workers; see Strauss, op. cit., p. 122. His final assessment, however, concurs with that of Engels (p. 124).

62. Thompson, *The Making of the English Working Class*, op. cit., pp. 424–25.

63. Eric Strauss, op. cit., pp. 126–27; and J. T. Ward, *Chartism*, Harper and Row, New York, 1974, pp. 64–65, 77.

64. Strauss, op. cit., pp. 72, 127–31; and Thompson, *The Making of the English Working Class*, op. cit., p. 443.

65. Engels, *Condition of the Working Class*, op. cit., p. 124. Like many other European writers in the nineteenth century, Engels tended to use the term "race" in both its biological sense, and in the sense of a class. The confusions that ensued both for Engels and his reader are evident in the passages that follow that quoted in the text: "The rough egotism of the English bourgeoisie would have kept its hold upon the working-class much more firmly if the Irish nature, generous to a fault, and ruled primarily by sentiment, had not intervened, and softened the cold, rational English character in part by a mixture of the races, and in part by the ordinary contact of life. In view of all this, it is not surprising that the working-class has gradually become a race wholly apart from the English bourgeoisie. . . . Thus they are two radically dissimilar nations, as unlike as difference of race could make them, of whom we on the Continent have known but one, the bourgeoisie" (ibid.).

66. Thompson, *Making of the English Working Class*, op. cit., p. 443.

67. Ward, *Chartism*, op. cit., pp. 239–43; Thompson, *Making of the English Working Class*, op. cit., p. 441; and Strauss, op. cit., pp. 126–27.

68. Thompson, *Making of the English Working Class*, op. cit., p. 226; "transportation" was, of course, to penal colonies such as New South Wales or Botany Bay in Australia, and necessarily entailed sentences of several years. See also, Engels, *Condition of the Working Class*, op. cit., pp. 212–27.

69. W. E. B. Du Bois, "The African Roots of the War," *Atlantic Monthly*, May 1915, pp. 707–14. Du Bois used the phrase "labor aristocracy" to refer to the material share of European industrial workers as contrasted to the degrading conditions of peasants and agrarian laborers in Africa, Asia and Latin America. His use of the term predates that of Lenin (*Imperialism, the Highest Stage of Capitalism*, which Lenin forwarded to his publisher in manuscript form in June 1916; see V. L. Lenin, *Selected Works*, International Publishers, New York, 1967, 1:859, n. 317) and is significantly different from Lenin's reference to the leaders of trade unions by the term.

70. Marx's comments on this emigration from Ireland are interesting: "One country—Ireland—has been saved from revolting almost to her last man, by the emigration to this country [the U.S.]; emigration, likewise, hither, says the *London Times*, 'has prevented cannon from being planted in the streets of London'; but the Indian Empire is too far off for our succour." "Parliamentary Debate on India," *New York Daily Tribune*, 25 June 1853, as reprinted in Shlomo Avineri (ed.), *Karl Marx on Colonialism and Modernization*, Anchor Books, Garden City, 1969, p. 87.

71. Strauss, op. cit., pp. 158–69. Another force that might have been expected to have played a major part in the "socialization" of the English working class, the mass schools, did not appear until almost mid-century. Indeed state support to schools did not begin until 1833 when matched grants were extended to the two societies most significantly involved in the "moral" tutoring of working-class children, the British and Foreign School Society, and the National Society. Still, it was not until the 1850s and 1860s that mass schooling by the state was established. The textbooks of this period testify to the preoccupation with Anglo-Saxonism in working-class education. See William Lazonick, "The Subjection of Labour to Capital: The Rise of the Capitalist System," *Review of Radical Political Economics* 10, no. 1 (Spring 1978): 10–14, and R. Webb, *The British Working Class Reader*, Kelley, New York, 1971, chaps. 2 and 3.

72. Letter from Marx to Engels, 10 December 1869, in *Ireland and the Irish Question*, op. cit., p. 284. The depth of the feeling between Irish and English workers clearly disappointed Marx: "Every industrial and commercial centre in England now possesses a working class *divided* into two *hostile* camps, English proletarians and Irish proletarians. The ordinary English worker hates the Irish worker as a competitor who lowers his standard of life. In relation to the Irish worker he feels himself a member of the *ruling nation* and so turns himself into a tool of the aristocrats and capitalists of his country against Ireland thus strengthening their domination *over himself.* He cherishes religious, social, and national prejudices against the Irish worker. His attitude towards him is much the same as that of the 'poor whites' to the 'niggers' in the former slave states of the U.S.A. The Irishman pays him back with interest in his own money. He sees in the English worker at once the accomplice and the stupid tool of the *English rule in Ireland.*" Marx to Sigfrid Meyer and August Vogt, 9 April 1870, ibid., pp. 293–94.

73. See Strauss, op. cit., pp. 142–69.

74. Ibid., pp. 119–21.

75. See Castles and Kosack, "The Function of Labour Immigration in Western European Capitalism," op. cit., pp. 5–10. A thesis that is complementary to the present one that stresses the importance of ethnic and national divisions in the English working class has been put forth by William Lazonick. Focusing on divisions of labor based upon sex, Lazonick records how this other "precapitalist" tradition affected working-class organization and consciousness: "The acceptance of the sex-based division of labour by the male-dominated unions created the possibility, and perhaps even the necessity, of patriarchal working-class polities" (p. 9). Further on he states, "[T]he integration of pre-capitalist patriarchal culture into the realm of capitalist production and the realm of working-class politics served to perpetuate economic inequality between the sexes, keeping the working-class woman materially dependent on the wage of the working-class man" (p. 10). Lazonick, op. cit.

76. See Avineri's discussion of Marx on the proletariat, in Avineri, *The Social and Political Thought of Karl Marx*, Cambridge University Press, Cambridge, 1968, pp. 52–64.

77. See the excerpt from the "Confidential Communication," which Marx sent to the Executive of the German Social-Democratic Workers' Party, 28 March 1870, as a response to Bakunin's criticisms of the use made of the Irish Question in factional fights in the I.W.M.A., in *Ireland and the Irish Question*, op. cit., pp. 160–63, and P. Berresford Ellis, *A History of the Irish Working Class*, George Braziller, New York, 1973, pp. 122–51.

78. Avineri, *The Social and Political Thought of Karl Marx*, op. cit., p. 61; see also Isaiah Berlin, "Historical Materialism," in Tom Bottomore (ed.), *Karl Marx*, Prentice-Hall, Englewood Cliffs, 1973, pp. 64–65.

79. Engels to Joseph Bloch, 21–22 September 1890, in Robert Tucker, op. cit., p. 642.

80. Engels once wrote that "history is . . . simply meant to comprise all the spheres—political, juridical, philosophical, theological—belonging to *society* and not only to nature." Engels to Franz Mehring, 14 July 1893, ibid., p. 649.

81. In a letter to Conrad Schmidt, in October 1890, Engels wrote: "[T]he philosophy of every epoch, since it is a definite sphere in the division of labour, has as its presupposition certain definite thought material handed down to it by its predecessors, from which it takes its start." Ibid., pp. 646–47.

82. Engels to Joseph Bloch, op. cit., p. 641. Engels is paraphrasing Marx's opening statement in *The Eighteenth Brumaire of Louis Bonaparte*: "Men make their own history, but they do not make it just as they please; they do not make it under circumstances chosen by themselves, but under circumstances directly found, given and transmitted from the past. The tradition of all the dead generations weighs like a nightmare on the brain of the living." Tucker, op. cit., p. 437. Georg Lukács, on the other hand, took a very different view of the possibilities of critical knowledge (a position identical with that of the two young men who had collaborated on *The Communist Manifesto*): "To the degree to which capitalism carried out the socialization of all relations it became possible to achieve self-knowledge, the true, concrete self-knowledge of man as a *social being.*" Lukács, *History and Class Consciousness*, MIT Press, Cambridge, 1968, p. 237.

83. Berlin, op. cit., p. 67.

Chapter Three

1. Norman MacKenzie, *Socialism: A Short History*, Harper Colophon, New York, 1969, p. 20; and Cole, *A History of Socialist Thought*, op. cit., 1:8–9. Lichtheim would have us begin (as he does) the history of socialism with the appearance of the word "around 1830," for one, because "in dealing with a major political and ideological current one cannot disregard the manner in which it has defined itself" (p. 3). But one must remember that he is of that school of scholars that can write of socialist history that "it is in part the story of a movement which had to emancipate itself from inherited illusions before it could attain a consciousness of its true nature" (p. vii). Certain habits of mind—presumably from the Hegelian legacy here—betray the best intentions. George Lichtheim, *The Origins of Socialism*, Praeger, New York, 1969.

2. Norman Cohn, *The Pursuit of the Millennium*, op. cit., p. 187.

3. Ibid., pp. 191–99.

4. Ibid., p. 195.

5. Ibid., pp. 198–280, and Friedrich Engels, *The Peasant War in Germany*, in Leonard Krieger (ed.), *The German Revolutions*, University of Chicago Press, Chicago, 1967, pp. 35–52.

6. See Cole, op. cit., pp. 14–16 for Rousseau as one instance, and *The German Ideology* (op. cit.) by Marx and Engels as another, for the appearance of the historical category "primitive communism."

7. Engels, "Socialism: Utopian and Scientific," in Robert Tucker (ed.), *The Marx-Engels Reader*, op. cit., p. 607; see also Karl Marx, "On the Jewish Question," ibid., p. 49. Engels declared that: "The revolutionary opposition to feudalism was alive throughout all the Middle Ages. According to conditions of the time, it appeared either in the form of mysticism, as open heresy, or of armed insurrection. As mysticism, it is well known how indispensable it was for the reformers of the Sixteenth Century. . . . In the other two forms of medieval heresy, we find as early as the Twelfth Century the precursors of the great division between the middle class and the peasant plebeian opposition which caused the collapse of the peasant war. This division is manifest throughout the later Middle Ages." *The Peasant War in Germany*, op. cit., p. 35.

8. See, for example, E. J. Hobsbawm, "Trends in the British Labour Movement since 1850," in *Labouring Men*, op. cit., esp. pp. 323–25; T. J. Nossiter, "Shopkeeper Radicalism in the 19th Century" in T. J. Nossiter, A. H. Hanson, and Stein Rokkan (eds.), *Imagination and Precision in the Social Sciences*, Faber and Faber, London, 1972, pp. 407–8; Albert Soboul, *The French Revolution: 1787–1799*, Random House, New York, 1974, pp. 3–31; and E. J. Hobsbawm, *The Age of Revolution: 1789–1848*, Mentor, New York, 1962, pp. 285–90, 357–58.

9. Albert Fried and Ronald Sanders (eds.), *Socialist Thought*, Edinburgh University Press, Edinburgh, 1964, pp. 15–16. Morelly, an eighteenth-century writer of obscure origins, greatly influenced Babeuf, the French radical discussed in the text below.

10. The last two phrases are those of G. D. H. Cole, op. cit., p. 14; see also Marx and Engels, *The Communist Manifesto*, op. cit., p. 346.

11. See Herbert Marcuse, *Reason and Revolution*, Beacon Press, Boston, 1968, pp. 323–28.

12. Karl Marx, "Theses on Feuerbach," in Tucker (ed.), *The Marx-Engels Reader*, op. cit., p. 109, and also John Passmore, *The Perfectibility of Man*, Duckworth, London, 1970, pp. 212–38.

13. J. A. Schumpeter, *Capitalism, Socialism and Democracy*, Unwin, London, 1965, pp. 12–13.

14. Lichtheim, op. cit., pp. 3, 9.

15. David McLellan, for example, indicates that "in general the membership of the International tended to be composed more of artisans than of the industrial proletariat." *Karl Marx: His Life and Thought*, Harper Colophon, New York, 1973, p. 387.

16. David McLellan, *Marx before Marxism*, Macmillan, London, 1970, p. 13.

17. Karl Marx, *The Holy Family*, as quoted by Georg Lukács, *History and Class Consciousness*, MIT Press, Cambridge, 1968, p. 46.

18. Lenin wrote in 1901/2: "We have said that *there could not have been* Social-Democratic consciousness among the workers. It would have to be brought to them from without. The history of all countries shows that the working class, exclusively by its own effort, is able to develop only trade union consciousness, i.e., the conviction that it is necessary to combine in unions, fight the employers, and strive to compel the government to pass necessary labour legislation, etc. The theory of socialism, however, grew out of the philosophical, historical, and economic theories elaborated by educated representatives of the propertied classes, by intellectuals. By their social status the founders of modern scientific socialism, Marx and Engels, themselves belonged to the bourgeois intelligentsia." Lenin, *What Is to Be Done?* in *Lenin, Selected Works*, International Publishers, New York, 1967, 1:122. Marx acknowledged his class origins in *The Communist Manifesto*: "Finally, in times when the class struggle nears the decisive hour . . . a portion of the bourgeoisie goes over to the proletariat, and in particular, a portion of the bourgeois ideologists, who have raised themselves to the level of comprehending theoretically the historical movement as a whole." Tucker (ed.), *The Marx-Engels Reader*, op. cit., p. 343. Sometime later, in 1867, Marx made perfectly clear his perception of his role in the workers' movement in a letter to Engels: "And in the next revolution, which is perhaps nearer than it appears, *we* (i.e., you and I) will have this powerful engine [the International] in our hands" (as opposed to being in the hands of "these fools of Proudhonists" or the "swine among the English Trade unionists"). Quoted by William Lazonick, "The Subjection of Labour to Capital: The Rise of the Capitalist System," *Review of Radical Political Economics* 10, no. 1 (Spring 1978): 23 (for a more complete version of the letter, see McLellan, *Karl Marx*, op. cit., p. 378).

19. Karl Marx, *The Eighteenth Brumaire of Louis Bonaparte*, in Tucker (ed.), *The Marx-Engel Reader*, op. cit., pp. 462, 464.

20. Karl Marx, *The Communist Manifesto*, ibid., p. 345.

21. For England, see Thompson, *The Making of the English Working Class*, op. cit., p. 213, and Rude, op. cit., p. 84; for France, see Marx, *The Eighteenth Brumaire of Louis Bonaparte*, op. cit., p. 515; Rude, op. cit., pp. 164, 176; and G. D. H. Cole, *A History of Socialist Thought*, op. cit., 1:18.

22. Albert Soboul, op. cit., pp. 46–47, 52.

23. Rude, op. cit., pp. 240–41.

24. Soboul, op. cit., pp. 18, 488–92.

25. G. D. H. Cole, op. cit., p. 20. Lichtheim states that "[t]he extreme wing of the French Revolution may thus be said to have given birth to a set of notions which, while never successfully pursued in France, were destined to become politically effective in Russia. The crucial factor is the belief that the abolition of poverty demands a temporary dictatorship which will dispossess the rich, who are also the effective holders of power. The dictatorship will be exercised in the name of the people (or the proletariat), and it will come to an end when its enemies have been forcibly removed or otherwise rendered harmless," op. cit., p. 22. See also David Caute, *Communism and the French Intellectuals, 1914–1960*, Macmillan, New York, 1964, pp. 13, 286, 290.

26. Lichtheim, op. cit., p. 21.

27. Soboul, op. cit., pp. 14–18.

28. See Caute, op. cit., p. 292; and Soboul, op. cit., pp. 410–38.

29. Soboul, op. cit., p. 438.

30. Ibid., p. 491.

31. Cole, *A History of Socialist Thought*, op. cit., 1:20–21.

32. Ibid., p. 18. Soboul comments: "The political organization of the Conspiracy marked a break with the methods used till that time by the popular movement. At the centre of the organization stood the leading group, backed by a small number of hardened militants; then there came the fringe of sympathizers, comprising patriots and democrats (in the Year II sense of the word), who were not involved in the secrecy, and who seem not to have shared the new revolutionary ideal; finally, there were the masses themselves, who were to be coaxed into participation. In sum, Babeurs was an organizational conspiracy par excellence, but one in which the problem of the necessary links with the masses seems to have been largely unresolved." Soboul, op. cit., pp. 490–91.

33. David Caute, op. cit., p. 290.

34. Robert Tucker, *Philosophy and Myth in Karl Marx*, Cambridge University Press, Cambridge, 1971, pp. 73–105; Franz Mehring, *Karl Marx, The Story of His Life*, University of Michigan Press, Ann Arbor, 1969, pp. 15–57; and David McLellan, *Karl Marx*, op. cit., pp. 16–77.

35. Karl Marx (Maurice Dobb, ed.), *A Contribution to the Critique of Political Economy*, International Publishers, New York, 1970, p. 20.

36. See Karl Marx and Friedrich Engels, *The German Ideology*, in R. Tucker (ed.), *The Marx-Engels Reader*, op. cit., pp. 113–57.

37. See Marx's letters to Kugelmann, 12 and 16 April 1871, in *Karl Marx and Frederick Engels, Selected Works*, International Publishers, New York, 1972, 1:679–81; and Engels's "Introduction to Karl Marx's Work *The Class Struggles in France 1848 to 1850*," ibid., p. 651; and Mehring, op. cit., pp. 156–59, 215, 447–54.

38. McLellan Karl Marx, op. cit., pp. 290–359; and Mehring, op. cit., pp. 208–24.

39. For the quarrel with Vogt, see McLellan, ibid., pp. 310–15; and Mehring, op. cit. pp. 280–97; for Lassalle, McLellan, ibid., pp. 315–25; and Mehring, ibid., pp. 265–78; for Mazzini, McLellan, ibid., pp. 258–61; and Mehring, ibid., pp. 241–42; for Engels see McLellan, ibid., pp. 278–80, 331–32; and Mehring, ibid., pp. 303–5.

40. In a letter to Ferdinand Freiligrath, Marx wrote: "After the 'League' was dissolved in November 1852 on my proposition, I no longer belonged to any Society whether secret or public, nor do I; thus the party in this completely ephemeral sense ceased to exist for me eight years ago . . . thus I know nothing of the party, in the sense of your letter, since 1852." Quoted by McLellan, ibid., pp. 313–14.

41. Mehring, op. cit., p. 276.

42. See G. O. Griffith, *Mazzini, Prophet of Modern Europe*, Hodder and Stoughton, London, 1932, pp. 64, 235–36; and Stringfellow Barr, *Mazzini, Portrait of an Exile*, Holt, New York, 1935, pp. 238–40.

43. R. R. Palmer, with Joel Colton, *A History of the Modern World*, Knopf, New York, 1959, p. 514.

44. Lynn Case, *Franco-Italian Relations, 1860–1865*, AMS Press, New York, 1970 (orig. 1932), pp. 3–31.

45. Franz Mehring, op. cit., pp. 268–69; see also Sir Adolphus W. Ward, *Germany, 1815–1890*, Cambridge University Press, Cambridge, 1917, 2:33–47, for the development of the *Nationalverein* movement and German participation in the Italian war.

46. Geoffrey Barraclough, *The Origins of Modern Germany*, Capricorn, New York 1963, p. 414; and James Joll, "The German Confederation, 1815–1866," *Encyclopaedia Britannica*, 1965, 10:310–16.

47. Barraclough, op. cit., p. 412.

48. George Lichtheim, *Marxism: An Historical and Critical Survey*, Praeger, New York, 1973, pp. 69–70.

49. W. O. Henderson, *The Industrial Revolution in Europe*, op. cit., pp. 21–22; and Friedrich Engels, *Germany: Revolution and Counter-Revolution*, in Leonard Krieger (ed.), *The German Revolutions*, op. cit., pp. 126–29.

50. Barraclough, op. cit., p. 414. Though Barraclough finds some of Engels's remarks on the ultimate failure of the middle classes to prosecute a democratic revolution a bit rash, he does endorse (apparently) observations like the following written by Engels: "[I]t is quite as evident, and equally borne out by the history of all modern countries, that the agricultural population, in consequences of its dispersion over a

great space, and of the difficulty of bringing about an agreement among any considerable portion of it, never can attempt a successful independent movement; they require the initiatory impulse of the more concentrated, more enlightened, more easily moved people of the towns." *Germany: Revolution and Counter-Revolution*, op. cit., p. 131.

51. Barraclough, op. cit., pp. 414–16.

52. Barraclough, ibid.; and Engels, *Germany: Revolution and Counter-Revolution*, op. cit., pp. 168–77.

53. Lichtheim, *Marxism*, op. cit., p. 78. Elsewhere Lichtheim asserts: "[I]t is pertinent to recall that in 1848 both men could publicly and privately associate themselves with the cause of German national unification, while remaining true to the principles laid down in the publications of the Communist League. Under German conditions, nationalism was an integral part of the democratic programme, to which the Communist group was committed since it represented the extreme left wing of the democratic movement." Ibid., p. 72.

54. Barraclough, op. cit., pp. 417–18.

55. Ibid., p. 421.

56. McLellan, *Karl Marx*, op. cit., pp. 316–17; and Mehring, op. cit., pp. 270–71.

57. W. O. Henderson notes that "In 1861, when Marx was visiting Lassalle in Berlin, he wrote to Engels that it was believed in the most exalted military circles that Po und Rhein had been written by a Prussian general." Henderson, *The Life of Friedrich Engels*, vol. 1, Frank Cass, London, 1976, p. 209.

58. Mehring, op. cit., pp. 274–75.

59. As quoted by Anthony Smith, *Theories of Nationalism*, Harper and Row, New York, 1971, p. 73.

60. Mehring, op. cit., p. 272.

61. Arno Schirokauer, Lassalle, *The Power of Illusion and the Illusion of Power*, George Allen and Unwin, London, 1931, pp. 202–3. It is ironic that Lassalle's sensitivity to the crowd mentality of nationalism brought him close to demagoguery in the eyes of some of his contemporaries and colleagues. In this particular instance his analytical instincts were correct, German nationalism was in opposition to revolutionary consciousness. See George Brandes, *Ferdinand Lassalle*, Bergman, New York, 1968 (orig. 1874 and 1875), p. 190; and Mehring, op. cit., p. 276.

62. McLellan, *Karl Marx*, op. cit., p. 317.

63. Mehring, op. cit., p. 271.

64. McLellan, Karl Marx, op. cit., p. 317.

65. G. D. H. Cole partially accounts for the differences between Marx/Engels and Lassalle in programmatic terms: "No doubt there was much, in theory, that they had in common; and the issues which divided them seemed unimportant to most of their followers. But in practical politics they were poles apart, because Marx was for the bourgeoisie against the Prussian State, whereas Lassalle was fully prepared to side with the Prussian State against the bourgeoisie." Cole, *A History of Socialist Thought: Socialist Thought, Marxism and Anarchism, 1850–1890*, vol. 2, Macmillan, London, 1954, p. 72.

66. Mehring, op. cit., pp. 271–72.

67. See Horace Davis, "Nations, Colonies and Social Classes: The Position of Marx and Engels," *Science and Society* 29, no. 1 (Winter 1965): 42; Anthony Smith, op. cit., p. 301; and Solomon Bloom, *The World of Nations*, Columbia University Press, New York, 1941, p. 194. (Bloom would prefer to see Marx as a "jealous" personality in his differences with Lassalle than attribute them to Marx's nationalism though Bloom's evidence—as Davis suggests—supports the latter interpretation.)

68. For more on Marx's political ambitions, see McLellan, *Karl Marx*, op. cit., p. 378; and Cole, *A History of Socialist Thought*, op. cit., 2:74.

69. Karl Marx, *Capital*, International Publishers, New York, 1977, 1:737.

70. Ibid., pp. 747–48.

71. Ibid., p. 754.

72. Ibid., p. 757.

73. In 1887/88, Engels would write: "Since the end of the Middle Ages, history had been moving towards a Europe made up of large, national states. Only such national states constitute the normal political framework for the dominant European bourgeois class . . ., and, in addition, they are the indispensable prerequisite for the establishment of the harmonious international collaboration of nations without which the rule of the proletariat cannot exist." Engels, *The Role of Force in History*, International Publishers, New York, 1972, pp. 29–30.

74. In May 1875, Marx wrote to the Esenach faction of the German Social Democratic Movement: "The German workers' party . . . shows that its socialist ideas are not even skin-deep; in that, instead of treating existing society . . . as the basis of the existing state . . . , it treats the state rather as [an] independent entity that possesses its own intellectual, ethical and libertarian bases. . . . 'Present-day society' is capitalist society, which exists in all civilized countries, more or less free from medieval admixture, more or less modified by the special historical development of each country, more or less developed." Marx, "Critique of the Gotha Program," in Robert Tucker (ed.), *The Marx-Engels Reader*, op. cit., p. 394.

75. "The bourgeois period of history has to create the material basis of the new world—on the one hand

the universal intercourse founded upon the mutual dependency of mankind, and the means of that intercourse; on the other hand the development of the productive powers of man and the transformation of material production into a scientific domination of natural agencies." Marx, "The Future Results of British Rule in India," in Shlomo Avineri, *Karl Marx on Colonialism and Modernization*, Doubleday, Garden City, 1968, p. 138.

76. Karl Marx, *The Class Struggles in France, 1848–50*, in Saul Padover (ed.), *Karl Marx: On Revolution*, McGraw-Hill, New York, 1971, p. 162.

77. Karl Marx, *The Communist Manifesto*, op. cit., p. 339. For Lichtheim, see his *Marxism: An Historical and Political Study*, op. cit., p. 86.

78. "The bourgeoisie, by the rapid improvement of all instruments of production, by the immensely facilitated means of communication, draws all, even the most barbarian, nations into civilization." Marx, *The Communist Manifesto*, op. cit., p. 339.

79. "The bourgeoisie finds itself involved in a constant battle. At first with the aristocracy; later on, with those portions of the bourgeoisie itself, whose interests have become antagonistic to the progress of industry; at all times, with the bourgeoisie of foreign countries." Ibid., p. 343.

80. Ibid., p. 339.

81. Lichtheim surmises that: "Unlike the majority of German political theorists of his age, notably the liberals, Marx regarded England rather than France as the exception from the general European rule. France was the 'classical' case: just as in medieval times it had been the centre of feudalism, so now its national life provided the clearest possible view of the class conflicts which were splitting society apart, even though economically Britain was further advanced along the same road. But France was also the 'model' in that its political institutions had been refashioned by the greatest and most successful of 'bourgeois revolutions.'" Lichtheim, *Marxism: An Historical and Critical Study*, op. cit., pp. 86–87.

82. Shlomo Aveneri, *Karl Marx on Colonialism and Modernization*, op. cit., p. 469; see also Karl Marx and Friedrich Engels, *The Russian Menace to Europe*, Paul Blackstock and Bert Hoselitz (eds.), Free Press, Glencoe, 1952, pp. 216–18, 274–75.

83. Marx and Engels, *The Russian Menace*, op. cit., p. 278; see ibid., p. 280 for the English translation of the German editions of 1867 and 1872.

84. Lichtheim makes the interesting observation that: "Having with some reluctance adopted the view that national emancipation in Ireland must precede democratic revolution in England, and not vice versa, Marx continued to advocate a federal relationship between the two countries rather than complete separation. This later became the standard Social-Democratic approach to nationality questions and even found a dim echo in Leninism." Lichtheim, *Marxism: An Historical and Critical Study*, op. cit., p. 84.

85. Engels, *The Role of Force in History*, op. cit., pp. 34–35. For a discussion of Marx and Engels as German nationalists (and particularly Engels's transformation from young nationalist to internationalist), see Horace Davis, op. cit., pp. 44–51.

86. See Lichtheim, *Marxism: An Historical and Critical Study*, op. cit., p. 85; Horace Davis, *Nationalism and Socialism*, Monthly Review, New York, 1967, pp. 3, 22–23, 218; and Mihailo Makovic, "Stalinism and Marxism," in Robert Tucker, *Stalinism*, W. W. Norton, New York, 1977, pp. 315–17. (Makovic suggests that Engels's attitude was formed during the 1848/1849 revolutions when counter-revolutionary armies were organized among the Slavs to repress social movements in central and eastern Europe.)

87. See Marx and Engels, *Ireland and the Irish Question*, op. cit.

88. See Michael Lowy, "Marxists and the National Question," *New Left Review*, no. 96 (March/April 1976): 82–83.

89. See Horace Davis, "Nations, Colonies and Social Classes: The Position of Marx and Engels," op. cit., pp. 28–31.

90. Engels, "The Magyar Struggle," in Marx and Engels, *The Revolutions of 1848*, International Publishers, New York, 1973, pp. 221–23.

91. "[T]here was a tendency towards economism in his idea that the 'standardization of industrial production and corresponding living conditions' helps to dissolve national barriers . . . and antagonisms, as though national differences could be equated simply with differences in the production process." Lowy, op. cit., p. 82.

92. "[S]uch an argument owed more to the conservative principles of the historical school of law (Savigny, etc.) than to the revolutionary ideas of historical materialism." Ibid., p. 84.

93. Horace Davis, *Nationalism and Socialism*, Monthly Review Press, New York, 1967, pp. 50–51.

94. Davis, ibid., p. 57.

95. See "The National Question," an appendix to Peter Nettl's *Rosa Luxemburg*, Oxford University Press, Oxford, 1969, pp. 500–519.

96. See Lowy, op. cit., p. 91; and George Haupt, Michael Lowy, Claudie Weill, *Les Marxistes et la Question Nationale*, François Maspero, Paris, 1974, pp. 50–52.

97. Lowy, op. cit., pp. 93–94; and Haupt, Lowy, Weill, op. cit., pp. 23, 30, 45–50; see also J. V. Stalin, "Marxism and the National Question," in *Works*, Foreign Languages, Moscow, 1953, 2:300–381.

98. Franz Borkenau, *World Communism*, University of Michigan Press, Ann Arbor, 1971 (orig. 1939), p. 94.

99. Lowy, op. cit., pp. 89–91.

100. Ibid., p. 90.

101. Ibid., p. 96; and Haupt, Lowy, Weill, op. cit., pp. 52–61.

102. Joseph Stalin, "Marxism and the National Question," op. cit., p. 307. Lowy erroneously (op. cit.) argues that Lenin had several occasions to refer to Stalin's work but was never terribly excited by it. Lenin's attitude may be illustrated by the remarks found in note 130, Stalin, ibid., pp. 417–18.

103. Ibid., p. 321.

104. Tom Nairn, "The Modern Janus," *New Left Review*, no. 94 (November–December 1975): 21.

105. Ibid., pp. 10, 12, 13.

106. Jean Baudrillard, *The Mirror of Production*, Telos, St. Louis, 1975, p. 33.

107. Alex Callinicos, *Althusser's Marxism*, NLB, London, 1976, p. 87.

108. Theodore Draper, *The Roots of American Communism*, Viking, New York, 1957, chap. 5.

109. Letter to Joseph Bloch, 21/22 September 1890, in Tucker (ed.), *The Marx-Engels Reader*, op. cit., p. 642.

110. Letter to Franz Mehring, 14 July 1893, ibid., p. 650.

111. Nairn, op. cit., p. 25.

112. Ibid., p. 17.

113. Raymond Williams has written: "[T]he reason for the . . . weakness in Marxism is not difficult to find: it lay in the received formula of base and superstructure, which in ordinary hands converted very quickly to an interpretation of superstructure a simple reflection, representation, ideological expression." Williams, "Literature and Sociology," *New Left Review*, no. 67 (May–June 1971): 9.

114. Georg Lukács, op. cit., pp. 110–49.

Chapter Four

1. For example, E. David Cronon remarks as late as 1972: "Garvey appeared fortuitously at a time when the Negro masses were awaiting a black Moses, and he became the instrument through which they could express their longings and deep discontent. The current of black nationalism which he helped to set in motion has not yet run its course, for, as one of his followers once boasted, Marcus Garvey opened windows in the minds of Negroes." ("Afterword: An Enduring Legacy," in E. David Cronon (ed.), *Marcus Garvey*, Prentice-Hall, Englewood Cliffs, 1972, p. 168). Cronon sustains this interpretation of Garvey's as a unique historical entity from his earlier study: *Black Moses: The Story of Marcus Garvey and the Universal Negro Improvement Association*, University of Wisconsin Press, Madison, 1955. By distinguishing Garvey in this way, Cronon constructed a personality and characterized a social ideology cut off from the historical roots suggested by one of his own contributors, George Shepperson ("Garvey as Pan-Africanist," in Cronon (ed.), *Marcus Garvey*, op. cit., pp. 144–47). More significantly, he ignored the broader historical vision articulated by C. L. R. James as early as 1938: "Though often retarded and sometimes diverted, the current of history, observed from an eminence, can be seen to unite strange and diverse tributaries in its own embracing logic. The San Domingo revolutionaries, the black arm in the Civil War, were unconscious but potent levers in two great propulsions forward of modern civilization. . . . This it is which lifts out of bleakness and invests with meaning a record of failure almost unrelieved. The African bruises and breaks himself against his bars in the interest of freedoms wider than his own." C. L. R. James, *A History of Pan-African Revolt*, Drum and Spear, Washington, D.C., 1969 (originally published in 1938), pp. 99–100.

2. Though Theodore Draper (*The Rediscovery of Black Nationalism*, Secker and Warburg, London, 1971) was one of the first post-war historians to "discover" a nationalist tradition—he traces the beginnings of Black nationalism to the "migrationism" or "emigrationism" (p. 4) of the late eighteenth and early nineteenth centuries—his work was a bit polemical. Positing the existence of two opposing manifestations of Black nationalism: "emigrationism" and "internal statism," Draper argues that Black nationalism was always of limited significance among Blacks. The care with which his investigation was conducted is perhaps best seen by reviewing his treatment of the nineteenth-century emigration movement. In general, his analysis suffers from a disorganized emphasis on the opinions and actions of Black freemen and rather questionable "samples" of mass opinion: "The great mass of American Negroes preferred to wage an uphill battle to become part of the nationalism where they were born rather than to take the risk of losing what they had without gaining what they were promised" (p. 12). The "great mass" that Draper refers to was of course the almost half million Free Blacks of the antebellum period. His "sampling" seems to have been confined to the limited successes of the American Society for Colonizing the Free People of Color in the United States (approximately 12,000 Black colonists in the first fifty years since its inception in 1817); a smattering of anticolonization declarations; the ambivalence of Martin Delaney (pp. 21–41); and the pragmatic reservations of procolonizationists such as Henry Turner, James T. Holly, and Henry H. Garnet (pp. 42–47). Though Draper acknowledges that at least 10,000 Blacks emigrated to Haiti in the early

nineteenth century and a similar number to Canada (p. 19); that opposition to colonization was sometimes tactical (to maintain pressure against slavery), sometimes based on distorted images of Africa (p. 18) or class-specific interests of an emerging Negro "middle class" (pp. 45–46), somehow a few dozen instances of anti-colonization declarations and a treatment of emigrationist movements that is dominated by a reconstruction of Delany's political activity (20 of 33 pages) are allowed more weight than the tens of thousands who emigrated in the early nineteenth century and the untold numbers who took their leaves of the United States (and sometimes the New World) both earlier (see Immanuel Geiss, *The Pan-African Movement*, Methuen, London, 1974, pp. 52–57; and Floyd Miller, *The Search for a Black Nationality*, University of Illinois Press, Urbana, 1975) and later (William Bittle and Gilbert Geis, *The Longest Way Home*, Wayne State University Press, Detroit, 1964; and Edwin Redkey, *Black Exodus*, Yale University Press, New Haven, 1969). Draper's emphasis on the opposition to the Colonization Society does not account for the proliferation of Black emigration societies and movements, nor the distinction then drawn between African colonization and interests in Haiti, Canada, Latin America, Ohio, and the Western Frontier as sites of future settlement. If Delaney was an ambivalent supporter of emigration, James Forten and Richard Allen were ambivalent opponents (see Miller, op. cit.). Draper relies on Louis Mehlinger's "The Attitudes of the Free Negro toward African Colonization" (*Journal of Negro History* 1, no. 3 [July 1916]: 176–301) for evidence of mass rejection of the Colonization Society. He might have pointed out that Mehlinger's basic source is William Lloyd Garrison's *Thoughts on African Colonization* (Garrison and Knapp, Boston, 1832), and *Thoughts on Colonization*, which recorded protests not entirely uninfluenced by Garrison: "William Lloyd Garrison orchestrated numerous black protest meetings announcing that blacks would not leave the United States" (Miller, op. cit., p. 55). (Garrison, in turn, had been convinced of the society's purportedly racist duplicity by the Black ex-colonizationists Forten and Allen; see William L. Katz, "Earliest Responses of American Negroes and Whites to African Colonization," introduction to Garrison's *Thoughts on African Colonization*, Arno, New York, 1968, pp. i–xi. Even so, Mehlinger cites numerous instances of southern and northern Black support for colonization, though he neglects to mention the (negative) effects of unsuccessful Haitian emigration in the 1820s (ibid., pp. 74–82) or their role in pushing abolitionists from gradualist positions on slavery to "immediatism" (ibid., p. 90; and John L. Thomas, *The Liberator: William Lloyd Garrison*, Little, Brown, Boston, 1963, p. 465, 26n). Draper seems to also have been convinced that the merits of emigration, colonization, and internal statism could be determined by identifying them as originally "white fantasies" (Draper, op. cit., pp. 13, 14, 48, 57). The example of Draper is apparently contagious: see, for example, Raymond Hall, *Black Separatism in the United States*, University Press of New England, Hanover, 1978, pp. 21, 33–37. Like Draper, Hall makes no larger effort to discover the sentiments of those Blacks (slave or freemen) who were beyond the strata of elites who consequently dominate the historical record. Redkey's study of the 1890–1910 period is one attempt to extend this question: "Whether he knew it or not, Garvey was part of a long tradition of black nationalism in the United States. Garvey's followers, moreover, were the same Southern black marginal farmers who had responded to the emigration appeals of Bishop Turner and his followers a generation earlier. . . . In the pattern of earlier African emigration movements, the lower-class blacks responded eagerly when flamboyant *Marcus Garvey* pointed the way. No longer isolated on scattered farms and restrained by southern conditions as Turner's followers had been, the black proletariat, crowded into urban ghettoes and disillusioned with their new homes, spread nationalism far and fast. Garvey himself may have been a foreigner but his millions of supporters manifested an old American response of black nationalism." Redkey, op. cit., p. 294.

3. In an otherwise remarkable work, E. U. Essien-Udom, in his study of the Black American Muslim movement tracing its Black nationalist roots to early nineteenth-century "Negro rationalism" (Paul Cuffe and the emigration movement), distinguished Negro nationalism as an exclusive concern for the welfare of American Blacks, *Black Nationalism*, University of Chicago Press, Chicago, 1962, pp. 17–19. Cuffe himself declared his interest differently: "Having been informed that there was a settlement of people of colour at Sierra Leone under the immediate guardianship of a civilized power, I have for these many years past felt a lively interest in their behalf, wishing that the inhabitants of the colony might become established in the truth, and thereby be instrumental in its promotion amongst our African brethren"; even making an effort during this visit (1810–11) to the colony to dissuade the "Mendingo Tribe" from further involvement in the slave trade: "As they themselves were not willing to submit to the bonds of slavery, I endeavoured to hold this out as a light to convince them of their error. But the prejudice of education had taken too firm hold of their minds to admit of much effect from reason on this subject." Paul Cuffe, "A Brief Account of the Settlement and Present Situation of the Colony of Sierra Leone in Africa," in Adelaide C. Hill and Martin Kilson (eds.), *Apropos of Africa*, Frank Cass, London, 1969, pp. 14, 17–

18. For the neglect of the historical tradition of Black radicalism, see the bibliographic essays of Redkey, op. cit., p. 312; and Miller, op. cit., p. 281.

4. Walter Rodney, "Upper Guinea and the Significance of the Origins of Africans Enslaved in the New World," *Journal of Negro History* 54, no. 4 (October 1969): 345.

5. G. W. F. Hegel, *The Philosophy of History* (ed.) C. J. Friedrich, Dover, New York, 1956, pp. 80, 93, 96, 99. Interestingly enough, Johann Gottfried von Herder, the eighteenth-century German thinker whose work

Hegel knew well (we are told that Hegel never acknowledged Herder's influence), was one of the rare European philosophers who attempted to come to terms with national traditions beyond that of Europe: "[H]ow seldom does an European hear from the native of any country the praise, 'he is a rational man like us!'" And further: "The European has no idea of the boiling passions and imaginations, that glow in the Negro's breast; and the Hindoo has no conception of the restless desires, that chase the European from one end of the World to the other." Herder, *Reflections on the Philosophy of the History of Mankind*, University of Chicago Press, Chicago, 1968 (orig. 1784– 91), pp. 32 and 75 respectively. For Hegel's relationship with Herder, see Frank Manuel's introduction, ibid., p. xvii.

6. Winthrop Jordan reminds us of the antiquity of these notions in his treatment of David Hume's "valuation of color": "Hume was convinced that the peoples near the poles and in the tropics were essentially inferior to those in the temperate zones, a conviction which can be traced historically back through European thought to the Greeks—who also lived in a temperate climate. What Hume did in 1748, though, was to go ancient philosophers one better by hitching superiority to complexion." Jordan then goes on to quote Hume directly: "I am apt to suspect the negroes, and in general all the other species of men (for there are four or five different kinds) to be naturally inferior to the whites. There never was a civilized nation of any other complexion than white, nor even any individual eminent either in action or speculation. No ingenious manufactures amongst them, no arts, no sciences." Jordan, *White Over Black*, Penguin, Baltimore, 1969, p. 253. (Neither M. L. Finley or Frank Snowden would agree with Jordan's interpretation of racial thought among the "ancients." Both argue that the racial awareness of the Greeks and Romans tended to be objective rather than irrational. For Finley, see "Between Slavery and Freedom," *Comparative Studies in Society and History* 6, no. 3 (April 1964): 246; and for Snowden, *Blacks in Antiquity*, Harvard University Press, Cambridge, 1970, pp. 176–95. (Jordan's view corresponds with that of Friedrich Hertz according to Louis Ruchames: *Racial Thought in America*, Grossett and Dunlap, New York, 1969, pp. 1–2.) Since a complete demonstration of the frequency with which European historians and social analysts have relied upon a Eurocentric worldview for the basis of their work would be tedious because of the very nature of its dimensions, a few instances drawn from the works of eminent scholars should suffice. Moving forward from Hegel and Hume, there is Edward H. Carr's widely praised collection of Cambridge lectures, *What Is History?* (Vintage, New York, 1961). In his final lecture, Carr observed: "It is only within the last two hundred years at most, even in a few advanced countries, that social, political, and historical consciousness has begun to spread to anything like a majority of the population. It is only today that it has become possible for the first time even to imagine a whole world consisting of peoples who have in the fullest sense entered into history and become the concern, no longer of the colonial administrator or of the anthropologist, but of the historian" (p. 199). In 1969, Boniface Obichere, a Nigerian professor of history, recalled that: "The present Regius Professor of Modern History at Oxford, Hugh Trevor-Roper, expressed the opinion that he didn't think Africa and Asia had any history, except that history which began with European enterprise in these places." And further, "that the whole of African history was, in the words of Professors R. Robinson and J. A. Gallagher in *Africa and the Victorians*, 'a gigantic footnote'; to something that Britain was doing in Asia or in England, and so on." Obichere, "African History and Western Civilization," in Armstead Robinson, Craig Foster, and Donald Ogilvie (eds.), *Black Studies in the University*, Bantam, New York, 1969, pp. 87, 88, respectively. An examination of Trevor-Roper's lecture indicates that Obichere's accusation was a bit on the generous side: "Perhaps, in the future, there will be some African history to teach. But at present there is none: there is only the history of the Europeans in Africa. The rest is darkness, like the history of pre-European, pre-Columbian America. And darkness is not a subject of history. Please do not misunderstand me. I do not deny that men existed even in dark countries and dark centuries, nor that they had political life and culture, interesting to sociologists and anthropologists; but history, I believe, is essentially a form of movement, and purposive movement too. It is not a mere phantasmagoria of changing shapes and costumes, of battles and conquests, dynasties and usurpations, social forms and social disintegration. . . . [W]e may neglect our own history and amuse ourselves with the unrewarding gyrations of barbarous tribes in picturesque but irrelevant corners of the globe: tribes whose chief function in history, in my opinion, is to show to the present an image of the past from which, by history, it has escaped; or shall I seek to avoid the indignation of the medievalists by saying, from which it has changed?" "The Rise of Christian Europe I: The Great Recovery," in *The Listener*, 28 November 1963, p. 871. For a summary of the development of European thought on non-Western peoples, see Philip Curtin's "Introduction: Imperialism as Intellectual History," in Curtin (ed.), *Imperialism*, Walker, New York, 1971, pp. xiii–xvii. For specific instances in the social sciences, see Bernard Magubanc, "A Critical Look at Indices Used in the Study of Social Change in Colonial Africa," *Current Anthropology* 12, nos. 4–5 (October–December 1971): 419–31.

7. In some sense, even the most careful scholars are still reluctant in their recognition of the European precedents for a slave system of African labor. Edmund Morgan, for example in his study of colonial Virginia, in summarizing the character of "private enterprise" in the colony conjectures: "We may also see Virginians beginning to move toward a system of labor that treated men as things." Though it sounds like Morgan is describing the initial *beginnings* of this system, this is difficult to square with the evidence he

himself has amassed, which led him (one paragraph earlier) to observe: "A servant, by going to Virginia, became for a number of years a thing, a commodity with a price." Further, Morgan had already encountered this system in the mother country: "In England itself, after labor became more valuable, the demand produced a certain amount of buying and selling of industrial apprentices." Edmund Morgan, *American Slavery, American Freedom*, W. W. Norton, New York, 1975, pp. 129 and 128, respectively. The imprimatur of the racial order that had developed for centuries within Europe was decidedly on the mind of Benjamin Franklin when he wrote: "The Number of purely white People in the World is proportionately very small. All Africa is black or tawny. Asia chiefly tawny. America (exclusive of the new Comers) wholly so. And in Europe, the Spaniards, Italians, French, Russians and Swedes, are generally of what we call a swarthy Complexion; as are the Germans also, the Saxons only excepted, who with the English, make the principal Body of White People on the Face of the Earth. I could wish their Numbers were increased." Quoted by Winthrop Jordan, op. cit., p. 254. As Jordan commented, "if Europeans were white, some were whiter than others" (ibid.).

8. "Uncle Tom at Home," anonymous contributor, *Putnam's Monthly* 8, no. 43 (July 1856): 4–5. The article is a classic example of wrong-headed erudition; its author leaning heavily on the accounts of scientific explorers (for example, Heinrich Barth's *Travels and Discoveries in North and Central Africa*, 5 vols, Longmans Green, London, 1857), and military adventurers (Major Denham, Captain Clapperton, and the late Dr. Oudney, *Travels and Discoveries in Northern and Central Africa*, 4 vols., John Murray, London, 1831). In the short career of *Putnam's Monthly* (1853–58 before being absorbed by Emerson's; and a second series, 1958–71 before being purchased by Scribner's), it effectively challenged the cream of literary magazines being produced in New York (its own base of operation) and Boston (see Algernon Tassin, *The Magazine in America*, Dodd, Mead, New York, 1916, pp. 205–31, 315). Ironically, despite its editorial sympathies with Negrophobia, and the frequency with which it published contributions from writers in the "slave states," it did not escape the scorn of southern literati. (See Frank L. Mott, *A History of American Magazines*, 1741–1850, vol. 1, Harvard University Press, Cambridge, 1939, p. 648; "A Special Editorial Note for the People South of Mason and Dixon's Line," *Putnam's Monthly* 3, no. 15 [March 1854]: 343–44; and Tassin, op. cit., p. 186.)

9. For the background and general character of reaction to the Fugitive Slave Act of 1850, see Mary F. Berry, *Black Resistance, White Law*, Appleton-Century-Croft, New York, 1971, pp. 72–77; and John Hope Franklin, *From Slavery to Freedom*, Knopf, New York, 1967, pp. 260–66, 367–70. For another interesting account see William Z. Foster, *The Negro People in American History*, International, New York, 1970, pp. 167–71. Foster particularly emphasizes the violence that accompanied the passage and implementation of the act; violence that was both resistant and compliant in cause. Relying on the first issue of the *New York Times* (18 September 1851), Foster unfortunately confuses the events at Christiana, Pennsylvania, involving William Parker. Foster identified Parker as a "free Negro" when the case was that Parker was a runaway slave from Maryland. Moreover, it was Parker who had helped form a vigilante organization against slave catching in the Christiana area. It was this group that organized the resistance to the Gorsuches' attempts to reclaim their slave properties, killing the Gorsuches (Edward and Dickinson, father and son were killed; a nephew, Joshua, was wounded) in the process. See William Parker's account "Fugitives Resist Kidnapping," in Charles Nichols (ed.), *Black Men in Chains*, Lawrence Hill, New York, 1972, pp. 281–315. For John Brown, see Stephen Oates, *To Purge This Land with Blood*, Harper Torchbooks, New York, 1970.

10. Milton Cantor, in his essay on seventeenth-century America concludes that "The Negro then was permanently bound by biological and anthropological chains. In order to guarantee the viability of his debasement, pro-slavery writers pulled out all stops. Slavery was justified by climate and economic necessity; by reliance upon history, the Bible, the Providential design. It was argued, in the colonial period, that English America could not be developed without the peculiar institution. White men were physiologically unable to labor in hot climates; Negroes alone had this power." Nor were these opinions limited to those sympathetic to slavery: "So widespread was this conviction of inequality that many anti-slavery writers acknowledged it." "The Image of the Negro in Colonial Literature," in Seymour Gross and John Edward Hardy (eds.), *Images of The Negro in American Literature*, University of Chicago Press, Chicago, 1966, pp. 43 and 31, respectively. See also Matthew Mellon, *Early American Views on Negro Slavery*, Bergman, New York, 1969; and Jordan, op. cit., pp. 253–55, 286, 305–7.

11. David Brion Davis, *The Problem of Slavery in Western Culture*, Cornell University Press, Ithaca, 1966, p. 453.

12. "[I]n order to maintain its income without sacrifice or exertion, the South fell back on a doctrine of racial differences which it asserted made higher intelligence and increased efficiency impossible for Negro labour. Wishing such an excuse for lazy indulgence, the planter easily found, invented and proved it. His subservient religious leaders reverted to the 'Curse of Canaan'; his pseudo-scientists gathered and supplemented all available doctrines of race inferiority; his scattered schools and pedantic periodicals repeated these legends, until for the average planter born after 1840 it was impossible not to believe that all valid laws in psychology, economics and politics stopped with the Negro race." W. E. B. Du Bois, *Black Reconstruction in America, 1860–1880*, World Publishing, Cleveland, 1969, pp. 30–39. Benita Parry has discovered that the

Anglo community in India and its British home intelligentsia produced similar "legends" concerning the Indian; see *Delusions and Discoveries*, University of California Press, Berkeley, 1972, pp. 1–70.

13. David Brion Davis, op. cit., pp. 464–82; Cantor, op. cit., p. 53; and Jordan, op. cit., ch. 13.

14. Davis comments that "one of the most comprehensive modern studies of a West African culture presents a picture strikingly similar to that of eighteenth-century accounts." Davis, op. cit., p. 465. Davis is referring, in the former, to the work of Melville and Frances Herskovitts (see ibid., note 47).

15. Ibid.

16. In his preface, Davis stated: "I hope to demonstrate that slavery has always been a source of social and psychological tension, but that in Western culture it was associated with certain religious and philosophical doctrines that gave it the highest sanction. The underlying contradiction of slavery became more manifest when the institution was closely linked with American colonization, which was also seen as affording mankind the opportunity to create a more perfect society." Ibid., p. ix.

17. "[T]he historian, rather like the modern student of race-awareness in very young children, must remain tentative and indeed baffled as to whether white men originally responded adversely to the Negro's color because of strictly accidental prior culture valuation of blackness *per se*, instinctual repulsion founded on physiological processes or perhaps fear of the night which may have had adaptive value in human evolution, the association of dirt and darkened complexion with the lower classes in Europe, or association of blackness with Negroes who were inferior in culture or status." Jordan, op. cit., p. 257.

18. Davis, op. cit., p. 447.

19. Ibid., pp. 455–59.

20. Brian Street, in his reconstruction of the history of the relationship between scientific thought and the racial theories that wove through English literature of the Victorian period, concludes: "The link between race and culture, physical and mental qualities, having been established, any subjective feelings with regard to the 'character' of other races can be given scientific backing. If the criteria for distinguishing between races of men depended upon such subjective considerations, Voltaire and Rousseau could claim that Negroes were naturally inferior to Europeans in mental ability, and Hume that 'there never was a civilised nation of any other complexion than white' . . . , with as much justification as Blumenbach could claim that the Caucasian was the most beautiful . . . chauvinism was rendered in 'scientific' terms in the late nineteenth century." *The Savage in Literature*, Routledge and Kegan Paul, London, 1975, pp. 54–55. In 1894, Sir Harry Johnston, the first Commissioner of British Central Africa, broke through a particular barrier of racial theory by posing one solution to the otherwise hopeless future of the inferior races: "On the whole I think the admixture of yellow that the negro requires should come from India, and that Eastern Africa and British Central Africa should become the America of the Hindu. The mixture of the two races would give the Indian the physical development which he lacks, and he in his turn would transmit to his half negro offspring the industry, ambition, and aspiration towards a civilized life which the negro so markedly lacks." Quoted by H. Alan Cairns, *Prelude to Imperialism*, Routledge and Kegan Paul, London, 1965, p. 207.

21. See Michael Banton and Jonathan Harwood, *The Race Concept*, Praeger, New York, 1975, pp. 13–42. Philip Curtin reminds us that "aboriginal mortality" was taken as one proof of the natural racial order by nineteenth-century British scientists: "The exterminated people were all of 'the colored races,' while the exterminators always appeared to be European. It seemed obvious that some natural law of race relations was at work, that the extinction of the non-Europeans was part of the natural evolution of the world." *The Image of Africa*, University of Wisconsin Press, Madison, 1964, p. 374.

22. See Wesley Frank Craven, *The Legend of the Founding Fathers*, New York University Press, New York, 1956, pp. 39–44, 56–85.

23. It is still possible to discover examples or variations of the legend of American foundations in contemporary textbooks. When Milton Cummings and David Wise, under the subtitle "The paradox of colonial democracy," state that "Colonial America was not a very democratic place by contemporary standards," their suggestion is that a defense exists of colonial society in its own terms (not to mention the implication that the more contemporary standards of democracy have been achieved). See Cummings and Wise, *Democracy Under Pressure*, Harcourt, Brace, Jovanovich, New York, 1977, p. 38. Whatever Cummings and Wise imagine the standards of the seventeenth century to be, they could hardly be described as democratic or the basis for paradox: "Virginians could be so heavily exploited, legally and illegally, partly because they were selected for that purpose: they were brought to the colony in order to be exploited. From the beginning Englishmen had thought of their New World possessions as a place in which to make use of people who were useless at home." Morgan, op. cit., p. 235. "Our first settlers brought with them across the ocean the class distinctions of the Old World. The American wilderness modified and complicated these distinctions, but it did not eliminate them. And the more the population grew—the greater the wealth, the more complex the society—the sharper became the differences between upper and lower classes. The white indentured servant supplied the basic lower-class labor force in the seventeenth century, the Negro slave in the eighteenth century, both supplemented by town laborers of various types." Howard Zinn, *The Politics of History*, Beacon Press, Boston, 1970, p. 60.

24. Roy Nichols tells us that in the 1850s "Thirty-one of these state parties, plus some more or less fluid

groups in the territories, acknowledged the name Democrat, and in national conventions styled themselves the 'American Democracy.' " These were, in spite of their informal pretensions, minority parties, representing specific interests and particular regions. The strains of sectional disputes over the organization of new territories tore through this fabric of compromise in the 1850s. "The opponents of the Democrats were beginning to make this appeal. Pleas were heard for the acceptance of the democratic principle as the means of substituting fair play for the fractious negativism of minorities; there was no more equitable rule than the will of the majority. Such sporting words, however, did not make southerners forget the warning of the census. If the voice of the majority became the will of the Republic, they might well be at the mercy of their free state neighbors. They feared the tyranny of numbers. Plainly the effort by northern spokesmen to make democracy a cohesive formula would have only slightly more chance of success than the labor of their southern antagonists to secure the acceptance of regionalism and the recognition of the right of minority veto." It appears that slight as it was, this "chance" was too large a risk for the southern ruling class. It became one factor that led to the Civil War. Nichols, *The Disruption of American Democracy*, Collier Books, New York, 1962, pp. 20 and 52, respectively.

25. Edmund Morgan, op. cit., p. 90. A little later, Morgan would put these attitudes in more political and racial terms: "The standard justification of slavery in the seventeenth century was that captives taken in war had forfeited their lives and might be enslaved. Yet Englishmen did not think of enslaving prisoners in European wars. . . . There was something different about the Indians. Whatever the particular nation or tribe or group they belonged to, they were not civil, not Christian; perhaps not quite human in the way that white Christian Europeans were. It was no good trying to give them a stake in society—they stood outside society." Ibid., p. 233.

26. Franklin, "Observations concerning the increase of Mankind, Peopling of Countries, &c," in *The Papers of Benjamin Franklin*, Leonard W. Labaree (ed.), Yale University Press, New Haven, 1961, p. 228. Franklin concluded this essay with: "And while we are, as I may call it, Scouring our Planet, by clearing America of Woods, and so making this Side of our Globe reflect a brighter Light to the Eyes of Inhabitants in Mars or Venus, why should we in the Sight of Superior Beings, darken its People? why increase the Sons of Africa, by Planting them in America, where we have so fair an Opportunity, by excluding all Blacks and Tawneys, of increasing the lovely White and Red? But perhaps I am partial to the Complexion of my Country, for such Kind of Partiality is natural to Mankind." Ibid., p. 234.

27. See Morgan, op. cit., pp. 327–37, 305–15. Reviewing the court records of Lancaster County, Virginia, Smith concludes: "In 1757 there were no servant cases, nor in 1764, from which it may be inferred that slaves had practically replaced white servants. . . . These figures are fairly typical, as far as I can discover, of any colonial county in those regions." A. E. Smith, op. cit., p. 278.

28. Hofstadter, *America at 1750*, Alfred Knopf, New York, 1971, p. 34.

29. See A. E. Smith, op. cit., chapters 11 and 12; Hofstadter, op. cit., pp. 49–58. In her attempt to assess the extent to which the ruling class was exclusionist during the heady period of the revolutionary era, Linda Grant De Pauw noted an extraordinary conservatism among her academic predecessors who had studied the period: "The most extreme estimate of unfreedom in colonial America I have found is that of Howard Zinn who estimates that the proportion of the population in 'physical or economic bondage' was 'about one-third of the total,' " Howard Zinn, *The Politics of History*, Beacon Press, Boston, 1970, p. 60. De Pauw, "Land of the Unfree: Legal Limitations on Liberty in Pre-revolutionary America," *Maryland Historical Magazine* 68, no. 4 (Winter 1973): 356, n. 9. As the quote that follows in the text above indicates, De Pauw was much less sanguine.

30. De Pauw, op. cit., p. 356. Ferdinand Lundberg, *Cracks in the Constitution*, Lyle Stuart, New York, 1980, p. 18.

31. "[I]f 'democracy' implies government by consent of the governed or at least by consent of a majority of those governed and not merely of an adult white male elite, then those historians from Bancroft to Brown who have described American society of the mid-eighteenth century as 'democratic' are simply wrong." Ibid., p. 368.

32. See Morgan, op. cit., pp. 250–70.

33. A. E. Smith, op. cit., p. 285; Hofstadter, op. cit., p. 34.

34. Smith, op. cit., pp. 286–88.

35. Hofstadter, op. cit., p. 34.

36. "The vast majority of them worked out their time without suffering excessive cruelty or want, received their freedom dues without suing for them, and left no evidences from which to tell the stories of their careers. These points need to be emphasized, for nearly all accounts of white servitude are principally based on the records of courts of justice." Smith, op. cit., p. 278.

37. Morgan is willing to argue that "In the eyes of unpoor Englishmen the poor bore many of the marks of an alien race." Morgan, op. cit., pp. 325–26. In the next breath, however, he declares: "To be sure, poverty was not genetically hereditary. . . . The poor were not born of another color than the rest of the population, but legislation could offer a substitute for color" (ibid.). He appears to link specifically racial prejudice to differences in color; that is without color, a prejudice may emerge that is only like racism: "The contempt

that lay behind these proposals [the enslavement of the poor] and behind many of the workhouse schemes is not easy to distinguish from the kind of contempt that today we call racism" (ibid., p. 325). The parallels he pursues between English domination of the Irish in the sixteenth century and native Americans from the seventeenth century on, however, would suggest otherwise, see ibid., p. 20. Here again, is an instance where the existence of European racism toward other Europeans is simply denied in both analytical and historical terms.

38. A. E. Smith, op. cit., pp. 288–89.

39. "Beginning in 1728, a vastly increased movement from Ireland began, and by far the greatest number of servants and redemptioners came from that country during the eighteenth century. . . . The German migration, second in volume only to the Irish, began also about 1720, reached its height in the middle of the century, and did not, like the English and Irish, increase during the 1770s." Ibid., p. 336. See also Hofstadter, op. cit., pp. 17–30.

40. Smith, op. cit., p. 134.

41. Ibid., p. 325.

42. Nicholas Canny, "The Ideology of English Colonization: From Ireland to America," *William and Mary Quarterly*, 3d ser., vol. 30, no. 4 (October 1972): 596–97.

43. Hofstadter, op. cit., pp. 19–24.

44. Quoted by Hofstadter, ibid., p. 32.

45. Samuel Krislov has recorded an interesting episode that confirms the growing concern for Black resistance in the late eighteenth and early nineteenth centuries: "In 1802 in a confidential letter to the chairman of a Senate committee, Postmaster General Gideon Granger urged [passage of a Post Office provision which forbade Black employment], suggesting there were objections to Negro mail carriers 'of a nature too delicate to engraft into a report which may become public, yet too important to be omitted or passed over without full consideration.' Such a role as distributing the mail might teach Negroes the pernicious doctrine 'that a man's rights do not depend on his color.' The Postmaster General cautioned against 'everything which tends to increase their knowledge of natural rights, of men and things, or that affords them an opportunity of associating, acquiring and commuting sentiments, and of establishing a chain or line of intelligence.' " Krislov, *The Negro in Federal Employment*, University of Minnesota Press, Minneapolis, 1967, p. 9. The provision was passed and remained in law (if not in practice) until 1865. See also Mary Frances Berry, op. cit., pp. 1–17.

46. Chief Justice Roger Taney of the U.S. Supreme Court, in the majority opinion made public in 1857 that settled *Dred Scott v. Sanford*, established this position as the law of the land until its effective repeal by the Civil War Amendments. Taney, in summarizing "the public history of every European nation," argued that the Constitution of the United States could not have encompassed rights for Blacks: "They had for more than a century before been regarded as beings of an inferior order, and altogether unfit to associate with the white race, either in social or political relations; and so far inferior, that they had no rights which the white man was bound to respect; and that the negro might justly and lawfully be reduced to slavery for his benefit." Further, "if the language, as understood in that day, would embrace them, the conduct of the distinguished men who framed the Declaration of Independence would have been utterly and flagrantly inconsistent with the principles they asserted; and instead of the sympathy of mankind, to which they so confidently appealed, they would have deserved and received universal rebuke and reprobation. Yet the men who framed this declaration were great men—high in literary acquirements—high in their sense of honor, and incapable of asserting principles inconsistent with those on which they were acting. They perfectly understood the meaning of the language they used, and how it would be understood by others; and they knew that it would not in any part of the civilized world be supposed to embrace the negro race, which, by common consent, had been excluded from civilized Governments and the family of nations, and doomed to slavery." Ruchames, op. cit., pp. 398–400. Given his predilection for "public history," had the subject of their social equality come before him, Taney could have come to similar conclusions about the majority of those who were becoming members of the "white race." Prior to the forging of racial consensus, in both Europe and the New World, the "racial" inferiorities of most of these proto-whites was well established by the literati and intelligentsia classes. Indeed, some of Taney's contemporaries did fear that his decision suggested "that there were federal or state constitutional inhibitions on the power of the northern states to preserve their free status, to protect their black and white populations within or outside their domicile." William Wiecek, "Slavery and Abolition Before the United States Supreme Court, 1820–1860," *Journal of American History* 65, no. 1 (June 1978): 55. In a quite informative if sometimes curiously written article on the legal history of slavery in the United States, A. E. Keir Nash reminds his readers that the courts of the nation did not consistently distinguish the rights of whites from those of Black slaves and Black free men. Nash, "Reason of Slavery: Understanding the Judicial Role in the Peculiar Institution," *Vanderbilt Law Review* 32, no. 1 (January 1979): 7–218. As such, it would appear appropriate to assume that the state systems of justice during the first half of the nineteenth century were not exclusively concerned with "white dominance" as one of Nash's critics, Michael Hindus, has suggested. See Hindus, "Black Justice Under White Law: Criminal Prosecutions of Blacks in Antebellum South Carolina," *Journal of American*

History 63, no. 3 (December 1976): 599. Nash, however, while recognizing that there is something to the notion that the history of criminal law in Western societies "reflects" the origins of that law in slave punishments (for presumably enslaved Europeans) and the extension of these penalties "from the lowest classes upwards through the social strata" (op. cit., p. 51, the suggestion originates with J. Thorsten Sellin in his *Slavery and the Penal System*, Elseiver, New York, 1976, p. viii), never quite comes to terms with Hindus' suggestion that another characteristic of the penal codes of the nineteenth century was class domination. See Hindus, op. cit., pp. 575–76, note 30. Nash's avoidance of this interpretative possibility is perhaps most dramatically displayed in one of the curiosities in his essay: the construction of a historically naive empiricist opponent (Nash terms this figure "the ameliorative Whig" and at other times a "silent southerner") for his critics and academic competitors (op. cit., pp. 30–70). Since Nash's alter ego is largely satisfied in confronting Nash's opponents with statistical sets of alternative "proofs," the structural forms and historical processes transferred from the Old World and emergent in the New that provided nineteenth-century America its political economy and the setting of its legal systems are largely ignored. Nash's "Whiggery," for example, in assigning statistical integrity to numbers of convictions, acquittals, indictments, lengths of sentence and the like, fails to take into account the peculiarities of the "crimes of speech"for which slaves and Black free men were held responsible (Hindus, op. cit., pp. 587–89); the fact that slaves were whipped on grounds of improper behavior *after* acquittals from criminal charges against them (ibid., p. 593); that the numbers of executions of slave offenders were probably depressed by the likelihood of claims for compensation from their owners (ibid., p. 596); and that trial evidence might be significantly distorted by restrictions placed on slave testimony (ibid., p. 578).

47. Marx to P. V. Annenkov, Brussels, 28 December 1846, reprinted in Karl Marx, *The Poverty of Philosophy*, International Publishers, New York, 1971, p. 188. A more frequently read treatment of slavery and industrial capitalism can be found in Chapter 31 of *Capital*, where Marx argues: "The discovery of gold and silver in America, the extirpation, enslavement and entombment in mines of the aboriginal population, the beginning of the conquest and looting of the East Indies the turning of Africa into a warren for the commercial hunting of black-skins, signalised the rosy dawn of the era of capitalist production. These idyllic proceedings are the chief momenta of primitive accumulation." Marx, *Capital*, vol. 1, International Publishers, New York, 1977, p. 751. There is much that is true here but also much that is not. A hundred years after Marx described primitive accumulation and set it between the stages of feudalism and capitalism, Oliver C. Cox, the Black theorist, tried to correct Marx's error: "[Marx] begins his analysis of the nature of capitalism almost where he might have ended it; and as is commonly the case in classical economics, he relegates as subsidiary the very things which should have been the center of his study. . . . His 'primitive accumulation' is none other than fundamentally capitalist accumulation; and, to assume that feudal society dissolved before capitalist society began is to over-emphasize the fragility of feudalism and to discount its uses to the development of capitalism." Cox, *Capitalism as a System*, Monthly Review Press, New York, 1964, pp. 213–14. Among many contemporary Marxists, however, there is still a tendency to misconstrue the importance and application of the concept of primitive accumulation. Charles Post, for instance, in a recent article on capitalism in nineteenth-century America seems content to conceptualize slave labor power in terms of primitive accumulation while entirely ignoring its application to "immigrant labour power." See Post, "The American Road to Capitalism," *New Left Review* 133 (May–June 1982): 31–35, 44–45.

48. Eugene Genovese and Elizabeth Fox-Genovese, as two of the more prominent of American historians who identify their work with the analytical categories and relationships associated with Marx, appear highly ambiguous on the relationship between slave production and industrialization. Their remarks consistently distinguish parts of an international or world economic system from other parts according to modes of production. Thus recently they have distinguished between "the slave economies of the New World," and "the free labor economies" of North America and Europe. The logical thrust of their argument transforms these distinctions into oppositions between slavery ("pre-capitalist" or "archaic relations of production") and industrialization within particular "economics" (e.g., the American South). The consequence, in the work of the Genoveses, is an aborted design of the eighteenth- and nineteenth-centuries' world system substantiated by a foreshortened sense of the system's historical development and the forms of its integrations. Compare, for example, the following two statements, which follow closely upon each other in a single essay: "[Modern colonial and plantation economies] have arisen from the world capitalist mode of production and have, from the beginning and virtually by definition, functioned within a world market. But they have simultaneously rested on slave or other dependent labor systems that have deprived them of the best social and ideological as well as economic advantages of a market in labor-power, in contradistinction to that market in labor itself which slavery's capitalization of labor made possible." And: "The colonial expansion of capitalism not only absorbed precapitalist economic systems; it created them. The enserfment of the Russian peasants during and after the sixteenth century, the second serfdom in eastern Europe, the economic exploitation of the highland Indian communities of Mexico and Peru, and the rise of plantation-based slave regimes in the American lowlands may, from this point of view, be seen as varying expressions of colonial capitalist expansion. They represent nothing so much as the power of

commercial capital to adjust unfree labour systems to the rising demand of West European mass markets, which themselves, however paradoxically, arose on free labor—represented a major advance over quasi-seigneurial alternatives, for it permitted greater economic rationalization and a more flexible labor market." "The Slave Economies in Political Perspective," *Journal of American History* 66, no. 1 (June 1979): 22. Paradox is hardly an analytical term, certainly not for Marxists, and here it is plainly inaccurate. It is also difficult to understand how capitalism might "create" precapitalist forms of labor.

49. See Eric Williams, *Capitalism and Slavery*, Capricorn, New York, 1966, pp. 98–107; and Walter Rodney, *How Europe Underdeveloped Africa*, Bogle-L'Ouverture, London, 1972, pp. 92–101.

50. Cox, op. cit., pp. 165–66.

51. Williams, op. cit., p. 52.

52. Philip Curtin, "The Atlantic Slave Trade, 1600–1800," in J. F. A. Ajayi and Michael Crowder (eds.), *History of West Africa*, Columbia University Press, New York, 1972, 1:240.

53. In this respect it is interesting to recall Count Constantin de Volney's impressions after his journey to Egypt in 1783–85: "But returning to Egypt, the lesson she teaches history contains many reflections for philosophy. What a subject for meditation, to see the present barbarism and ignorance of the Copts, descendants of the alliance between the profound genius of the Egyptians and the brilliant mind of the Greeks! Just think that this race of black men, today our slave and the object of our scorn, is the very race to which we owe our arts, sciences, and even the use of speech! Just imagine, finally, that it is in the midst of peoples who call themselves the greatest friends of liberty and humanity that one has approved the most barbarous slavery and questioned whether black men have the same kind of intelligence as Whites!" Quoted by Cheikh Anta Diop, *The African Origin of Civilization*, Lawrence Hill, New York, 1974, pp. 27–28.

54. Hermann Kees, *Ancient Egypt*, University of Chicago Press, Chicago, 1961, pp. 52–53, 100–101.

55. Margaret S. Drowser, "Egypt: Archaeology and History," in *Encyclopaedia Britannica*, University of Chicago Press, Chicago, 1965, 8:37.

56. Diop, op. cit., p. 110.

57. Frank Snowden, *Blacks in Antiquity*, Harvard University Press, Cambridge, 1970, pp. 103–4.

58. Ibid.; and Drowser, op. cit., p. 40; George Thomson, *The First Philosophers*, Lawrence and Wishart, London, 1977 (orig. 1955), pp. 191–93.

59. See Snowden, op. cit., pp. 286–87, note 55.

60. "The story of King Sesostris in Europe and of some of his soldiers who settled by the Phasis River has been related to Herodotus's report of black, woolly-haired Colchians and has been interpreted as evidence of a classical tradition that there were Ethiopians among the troops of the Egyptian Sesostris." Snowden, op. cit., p. 121.

61. Ibid., pp. 104–5.

62. See the extraordinary work of George James, *Stolen Legacy*, Philosophical Library, New York, 1954 (republished by Julian Richardson, San Francisco, 1976), chapters 1–111. Since James's work is sometimes difficult to obtain, the reader is advised that the sources (beyond primary works) James normally relies on are Henri Frankfort's *The Ancient Egyptian Religion*, Harper, New York, 1961, and Eva Sandford's *The Mediterranean World in Ancient Times* (publisher unlisted). Yosef ben-Jochannan has in turn relied on James for the treatment of this era in his own work, for example, *Africa: Mother of Civilization, Alkebu-Lan*, New York, 1971, pp. 375–440. See also Diop, op. cit., p. 45. One may also consult Eduard Zeller, *Outlines of the History of Greek Philosophy*, Routledge and Kegan Paul, London, 1948, pp. 8, 23, 26–93; Theodor Gomperz, *Greek Thinkers*, John Murray, London, 1906, 1:5–16, 43; Margaret Murray, *The Splendour That Was Egypt*, Sidgwick and Jackson, London, 1964 (orig. 1949); Henry Olela, 1979, and Lanciany Keita, 1979.

63. "Greek traditions place the installation of Egyptian colonies in Greece at approximately [the middle of the second millennium, B.C.]: Cecrops settled in Attica; Danaus, brother of Aegyptus, in Argolis; he taught the Greeks agriculture as well as metallurgy (iron)." Diop, op. cit., p. 110. See also Plato's *Timaeus* for the suggestion that Greek and African relations were already merely vague memories by the fourth century B.C. George James notes: "One of the military policies adopted by the Greek military authorities at Alexandria was the issue of commands to the leading Egyptian Priests for information concerning the Egyptian history, philosophy and religion. . . . Accordingly, we are told that Ptolemy I Soter, in order to elicit the secrets of Egyptian wisdom or mystery system, ordered Manetho, the High Priest of the temple of Isis at Sebennytus in Lower Egypt, to write the philosophy, and the history of the religion of the Egyptians. Accordingly, Manetho published several volumes concerning these respective fields, and Ptolemy issued an order prohibiting the translation of these books which had to be kept on reserve in the Library, for instruction of the Greeks by the Egyptian Priests." James, op. cit., pp. 49–50. Drowser informs us: "The priest Manetho had perhaps better sources [than Herodotus] when he wrote his *Aegyptiaca* about 240 B.C.; the surviving extracts from this work, ill-copied by later classical writers who quoted it for their own polemic ends, show how valuable a work has been lost. As it is, Manetho's list of the 30 dynasties of kings of pharaonic Egypt, in spite of the garbled forms of the names and miscopying of figures, has triumphantly survived the test of archaeology and is still retained by Egyptologists as the basis of the reconstructed history of Egypt." Drowser, op. cit., p. 31. Recall, Manetho was writing 200 years after Herodotus!

64. A. E. Taylor has disputed the historical character of *Timaeus*, but his interpretation of this section of the dialogue transforms it into purposeless nonsense; see A. E. Taylor, *Plato, The Man and His Work*, World Publishing, Cleveland, 1966, pp. 438–40, and Margaret Murray, op. cit., p. 53.

65. Drowser, op. cit., p. 31.

66. Diop, op. cit., p. 150.

67. Snowden, op. cit., p. 109. See also Snowden, ibid., pp. 289–90; and Diop, op. cit., pp. 85–98; and Boyce Rensberger, "Nubian Monarchy Called Oldest," *New York Times*, 1 March 1979, pp. A1 and A16, which begins: "Evidence of the oldest recognizable monarchy in human history, preceding the rise of the earliest Egyptian kings by several generations, has been discovered in artifacts from ancient Nubia in Africa. . . . The new findings suggest that the ancient Nubians may have reached this stage of political development as long ago as 3300 B.C., several generations before the earliest documented Egyptian kin." For the predominant view—one which presumed the relationship was the reverse, see Charles C. Seligman, *Egypt and Negro Africa*, Routledge and Sons, London, 1933.

68. See Kees, op. cit., pp. 334–35.

69. See Snowden, op. cit., pp. 112, 126; and Keith Irvine, *The Rise of the Colored Races*, W. W. Norton, New York, 1970, pp. 16–17.

70. "The most convincing explanation of Negroid stone figures found in Cyprus is that the sculptures were portraits of Ethiopians in the civil and military service of the Egyptians during Egyptian occupation of the island under Amasis (568–525 B.C.). The sculptures in question were discovered in Ayla Irini and, according to E. Gjerstad, on the basis of style cannot be dated later than 560 B.C." Snowden, op. cit. pp. 122–23.

71. Ibid., pp. 131–32.

72. Ibid., pp. 136–41.

73. Ibid., pp. 141–42.

74. Ibid., p. 183.

75. Irvine, op. cit., pp. 22–23. "In Western Europe, where the majority of the population lived in villages and hamlets and were preoccupied with the problems of survival. . . . In a world in which lived giants such as Gog and Magog, headless men with eyes in their stomachs, and the troglodytes of Libya—single-footed cave-dwellers who shielded themselves from the heat of the sun by lying on their backs and using their huge feet as umbrellas—the fact that some variations of skin color were also reported among foreigners must have appeared as a minor detail." Ibid.

76. See Walter Ullmann, *The Growth of Papal Government in the Middle Ages*, Methuen, London, 1965, p. 88.

77. Sheldon Wolin, *The Politics of Vision*, Little, Brown, Boston, 1960, p. 105.

78. Contemplating the significance for Western Europe of the sixteenth century, Herbert Butterfield wrote: "Until a period not long before the Renaissance, the intellectual leadership of such civilizations as existed in this quarter of the globe had remained with the lands in the eastern half of the Mediterranean or in empires that stretched farther still into what we call the Middle East. While our Anglo-Saxon forefathers were semi-barbarian, Constantinople and Baghdad were fabulously wealthy cities, contemptuous of the backwardness of the Christian West." He went on to write that: "For two thousand years the general appearance of the world and the activities of men had varied astonishingly little [for Western Europeans]—the sky-line for ever the same—so much so that men were not conscious of either progress or process in history, save as one city or state might rise by effort or good fortune while another fell. . . . Now [in the seventeenth century], however, change became so quick as to be perceptible with the naked eye, and the face of the earth and the activities of men were to alter more in a century than they had previously done in a thousand years." *The Origins of Modern Science*, Free Press, New York, 1957, pp. 187–88, 199. For seventeenth century, especially in England, see Marie Boas Hall, "Scientific Thought," in Allardyce Nicoll (ed.), *Shakespeare in His Own Age*, Shakespeare Survey 17, Cambridge University Press, Cambridge, 1964, pp. 138–51. Even international diplomacy was marked by medieval conceptions, see Franklin L. Baumer, "England, the Turk, and the Common Corps of Christendom," *American Historical Review* 50, no. 1 (October 1944): 26–48. William Carroll Bark, while reluctant to accept the more somber hues of the "Dark Age," admits that a significant "deflect[ion] from science-philosophy to theology-philosophy" took place during the Patristic Age and the following feudal period. See his *The Origins of the Medieval World*, Stanford University Press, Stanford, 1958, p. 72. See also Reginald Poole, *Illustrations of the History of Medieval Thought and Learning*, Dover, New York, 1960, pp. 198–245; and the excellent study by Frances A. Yates, *The Occult Philosophy in the Elizabethan Age*, Routledge and Kegan Paul, London, 1979.

79. Norman Cantor (ed.), *The Medieval World, 300–1300*, Macmillan Company, New York, 1963, p. 111. See also Hugh Trevor-Roper, "The Rise of Christian Europe: The Dark Ages," *The Listener*, 12 December 1963, pp. 975–79. Trevor-Roper, somewhat dramatically asserts: "[T]he old diehards believed that pagan literature was by definition suspect: at least it could only be made safe by prudent excisions: was not an Israelite forbidden to marry a heathen captive, however desirable, unless he first shaved her head and pared her nails? (Deut. xxi, 12). "The Rise of Christian Europe: The Medieval Renaissance," *The Listener*, 26 December 1963, p. 1062.

80. Ralph Lerner and Muhsin Mahdi (eds.), *Medieval Political Philosophy*, Free Press of Glencoe, New York, 1963, p. 13. For the preoccupation with heresy in medieval Europe, see Norman Cohn, *The Pursuit of the Millennium*, Oxford University Press, New York, 1970; and Trevor-Roper, "The Medieval Renaissance," op. cit., pp. 1064–65.

81. Maxime Rodinson, *Mohammed*, Vintage, New York, 1974, p. 297.

82. Eugene A. Myers, *Arabic Thought and the Western World in the Golden Age of Islam*, Frederick Ungar Publishing, New York, 1964, pp. 76–77.

83. Ibid., pp. 132–33. "The discovery that the Arabs, as also the Byzantines, possessed the key to this new learning, soon set Europe buzzing, and to every point of contact the new 'masters' sent out to bring it in." Hugh Trevor-Roper, "The Medieval Renaissance," op. cit., p. 1062.

84. Myers, ibid., p. 96; Trevor-Roper, ibid., pp. 1063–64.

85. Ralph Austen, "The Islamic Slave Trade Out of Africa (Red Sea and Indian Ocean)," in Henry Gemery and Jan Hogendorn (eds.), *The Uncommon Market: Quantitative Studies in the Atlantic Slave Trade*, Academic Press, New York, 1979.

86. Daniel Pipes, "Black Soldiers in Early Muslim Armies," *The International Journal of African Historical Studies* 13, no. 1 (1980): 87–94.

87. Michael Tigar and Madeleine Levy, *Law and the Rise of Capitalism*, Monthly Review Press, New York, 1977, pp. 55, 61; E. R. Chamberlin, *Everyday Life in Renaissance Times*, Capricorn Books, New York, 1967, pp. 64–65; Hugh Trevor-Roper, "The Rise of Christian Europe: The Crusades," *The Listener*, 19 December 1963, p. 1022.

88. See Fernand Braudel, *The Mediterranean and the Mediterranean World in the Age of Philip II*, Harper and Row, New York, 1973, 2:743–44.

89. Marc Bloch, *French Rural History*, University of California Press, Berkeley, 1966, pp. 7–8; Braudel, *The Mediterranean*, op. cit., pp. 142–43; Wallerstein, op. cit., pp. 44–45. William McNeill, following on the work of Emmanuel Le Roy Ladurie and H. H. Lamb, concludes that: "In Europe, a 'Little Ice Age' starting about 1300 climaxed between 1550 and 1850 and has been succeeded by warmer temperatures in the twentieth century." McNeill, *Plagues and People*, Anchor Books, Garden City, 1977, p. 297 n. 23. Wallerstein, referring to the work of Gustaf Utterstrom, makes a similar point: "Utterstrom reminds us that climatic change might have had special bearing on the earlier periods in the transformation of Europe. 'The primitive agriculture of the Middle Ages must have been much more dependent on favorable weather than is modern agriculture with its high technical standards.'" Wallerstein, op. cit., p. 34.

90. Hugh Trevor-Roper has put this most dramatically: "My point is that the Crusades were not just a religious movement. . . . They were not even, by themselves, the cause of the European break-through. They were part of a much larger, much wider process: a process which can be seen all over Europe and on all the frontiers of western Christendom: beyond the Pyrenees, beyond the Elbe, on the Scottish border, in Ireland. This process is essentially a north European process. It is based on a new population-growth and new techniques, agricultural, social, military. . . . Perhaps, as Gibbon wrote, the Crusades were a diversion of this great expansion into the sideline of unprofitable imperialism; perhaps the imperialism was inseparable from the expansion." *The Rise of Christian Europe*, Harcourt, Brace and World, New York, 1965, pp. 127–28.

91. "Merchants regularly paid fines for breaking every law that concerned their business, and went on as before. The wealth of Venice and Genoa was made in trade with the infidels of Syria and Egypt despite papal prohibition. Prior to the 14th century, it has been said, men 'could hardly imagine the merchant's strongbox without picturing the devil squatting on the lid.' Whether the merchant too saw the devil as he counted coins, whether he lived with a sense of guilt, is hard to assess." Barbara Tuchman, *A Distant Mirror*, Ballentine Books, New York, 1977, p. 38. See also Iris Origo, *The Merchant of Prato*, Alfred Knopf, New York, 1957, pp. 80, 123; Tigar and Levy, op. cit., pp. 74–75.

92. "In the early centuries central and eastern Europe was a fruitful source and the trade in these so-called 'Slavs' (*Saqaliba*) was in the hands of Christians and Jews until they were sold into the hands of Muslim merchants on the shores of the Mediterranean or the Caspian Sea. From the eleventh century, when more powerful polities began to emerge in Europe, this source began to dry up, but slaves of European origin were still obtained by raiding and piracy within the Mediterranean and along the Atlantic Coast. European Christian powers of the area had no scruples about paying the Muslims back in their own coin. Another major source of slaves was Central Asia, the home of diverse nomadic tribes speaking Turkic languages." J. O. Hunwick, "Black Africans in the Islamic World: An Understudied Dimension of the Black Diaspora," *Tarikh* 5, no. 4 (1978): 23. For the intra-European trade in slaves, see Iris Origo: "[I]t was the labour shortage after the Black Death of 1348 that suddenly caused a demand for domestic slaves to revive, and brought them to Italy not only from Spain and Africa, but from the Balkans, Constantinople, Cyprus and Crete, and, above all, from the shores of the Black Sea. . . . Many of them mere children of nine or ten, they belonged to a great variety of different races: yellow-skinned, slanting-eyed Tartars, handsome fair Circassians, Greeks, Russians, Georgians, Alans, and Lesghians. Sold by their parents for a crust of bread, or kidnapped by Tartar raiders and Italian sailors, they were brought from the slave-markets of Tana and

Caffa, of Constantinople, Cyprus, and Crete to the Venetian and Genoese quays, where they were bought by dealers and forwarded to customers inland." Origo, *The Merchant of Prato*, op. cit., p. 90. For Pope John XXII, see ibid., p. 8.

93. Wallerstein, op. cit., pp. 21–24. Tuchman prefers to reconcile demographic, climatic, technological, and sociopolitical bases for the crisis, op. cit., pp. 24–48.

94. Trevor-Roper, *Rise of Christian Europe*, op. cit., p. 177.

95. Jean Richard, "The Mongols and the Franks," *Journal of Asian History* 3, no. 1 (1969): 45. Peter Forbath tells us a bit more of the story: "In 1221, with the Fifth Crusade shattered in the defeat at Cairo, Jacques of Vitry, the Bishop of Acre last of the Crusader states to survive, wrote to Pope Honorius III that 'A new and mighty protector of Christianity has arisen. He is King David of India, who has taken the field of battle against the unbelievers at the head of an army of unparalleled size.' This King David, who according to Bishop Jacques was commonly called Prester John, was believed to be the son or grandson of the Prester John who had been awaited at the time of the Second Crusade. . . . This king, it was to turn out, was Genghis Khan." Forbath, *The River Congo*, D. P. Dutton, New York, 1979, p. 28.

96. Jean Richard, ibid., p. 48.

97. See R. S. Lopez, H. A. Miskimin, and Abraham Udovitch, "England to Egypt, 1350–1500: Long-term Trends and Long-distance Trade," in M. A. Cook (ed.), *Studies in the Economic History of the Middle East from the Rise of Islam to the Present Day*, Oxford University Press, London, 1970, as cited by Wallerstein, op. cit., p. 40 n. 85.

98. William McNeill, op. cit., pp. 133–34.

99. Ibid., chap. 4; Tuchman, op. cit., pp. 92–102.

100. Trevor-Roper, *Rise of Christian Europe*, op. cit., pp. 119–20.

101. Americo Castro, *The Structure of Spanish History*, Princeton University Press, Princeton, 1954, p. 670. For more detail of the English role–based on the Contemporary Accounts of an Englishman and Two Germans (ibid.)—see Violet Shillington, "The Beginnings of the Anglo-Portuguese Alliance," *Translations of the Royal Historical Society* 20 (1906): 109–32; and Edgar Prestage, "The Anglo-Portuguese Alliance," ibid., 4th ser., vol. 17 (1934): 69–100.

102. Wallerstein, op. cit., pp. 49ff.

103. See Charles Verlinden, "The Italian Colony of Lisbon and the Development of Portuguese Metropolitan and Colonial Economy," in Verlinden's collection of essays, *The Beginnings of Modern Colonization*, Cornell University Press, Ithaca, 1970, pp. 98–112. A glimpse of the importance of Italian traders in European and Mediterranean trade and the structures of their commercial houses and banks can be found in Origo's detailed study of Datini (*The Merchant of Prato*, op. cit.), pp. 70–73.

104. See Verlinden, "Some Aspects of Slavery in Medieval Italian Colonies," ibid., pp. 79–97.

105. Castro, op. cit., p. 668.

106. See C. R. Boxer, *Four Centuries of Portuguese Expansion, 1415–1825*, Witwatersrand University Press, Johannesburg, 1965, p. 6 (as cited by Wallerstein, op. cit., p. 50 n. 133).

107. See Harold V. Livermore, "Portugal," in *Encyclopaedia Britannica*, 1965, 18:276–77; and C. Raymond Beazley, "Prince Henry of Portugal and His Political, Commercial and Colonizing Work," *American Historical Review* 17, no. 2 (January 1923): 253–54. Also of interest is A. J. R. Russell-Wood, *Fidalgos and Philanthropists*, University of California Press, Berkeley, 1968, pp. 6–7.

108. Castro, op. cit., pp. 668–69. Castro here also takes time to acknowledge his differences with Portuguese scholars: "It is obvious . . . that the militant impetus and support for . . . Peninsular vivisection could not arise spontaneously. . . . The initial motivation of that rebellion does not lie in the proto-Portuguese character of that country. . . . That is why two apparently contradictory ways of understanding the origin of Portugal—my own and that of Portuguese historians who opposed it—can both be true." Ibid., p. 669.

109. See Livermore, op. cit., pp. 275–76.

110. Francis M. Rogers, "The Attraction of the East and Early Portuguese Discoveries," *Luso-Brazilian Review* 1, no. 1 (June 1964): 46. Rogers goes on to remind us of the rich utopianism contained in the letter presumably written by Prester John in 1165 and its great popular acceptance for the next 300 years or so. The letter whatever its origins (some scholars have argued that it was written by or on the authority of Frederick Barbarossa; others that its author was an anonymous Levantine Christian monk) described the realm of Prester John in terms that put contemporary Europe to shame, in material as well as social terms. The letter was consequently a critique of Europe, its decay, its chaos, its corruption, and its moral dissolution. See also Vsevolod Slessarev, *Prester John: The Letter and the Legend*, University of Minnesota Press, Minneapolis, 1959; and Robert Silverberg, *The Realm of Prester John*, Doubleday, Garden City, 1972, pp. 40–73.

111. Robert Silverberg, op. cit., p. 194.

112. That the Prince was a man of unusual personality can be surmised from the following lines extracted from his contemporary and court chronicler, Gomes Eannes de Azurara: "Neither luxury nor avarice ever found a home within his breast, for as to the former he was so temperate that all his life was passed in

purest chastity and as a virgin the earth received him at his death again to herself: . . . It would be hard to tell how many nights he passed in which his eyes knew no sleep; and his body was so transformed by the use of abstinence that it seemed as if Don Henry had made its nature to be different from that of other men. . . . The Infant drank wine only for a very small part of his life, and that in his youth, but afterwards he abstained entirely from it. . . . Well-nigh one-half of the year he spent in fasting, and the hands of the poor never went away empty from his presence." G. E. de Azurara, *The Chronicle of the Discovery and Conquest of Guinea*, C. R. Beazley and E. Prestage (eds.), Burt Franklin and E. Prestage (eds.), Burt Franklin Publisher, New York, 1896, vol. 1, chap. 4, pp. 12–15.

113. Francis Rogers, op. cit., p. 50.

114. Gomes Eannes de Azurara, op. cit., chap. 7, pp. 27–30.

115. Robert Silverberg, op. cit., p. 197.

116. Ibid., pp. 200–205. Covilha (Covilhao) was sent by King Joao II (1495–1521) in 1487 on a mission to "discover and learn about Prester John." Covilha and his companion, Alfonso de Paiva, traveled by way of Barcelona, Naples, Rhodes, Alexandria, and Cairo. From there they trekked to Tor, Suakin, and Aden with caravans of Muslims. At Aden they parted, Covilha pushing on east to Calicut, Goa and Ormuz Paiva reportedly to Ethiopia. Upon his return to Cairo, Covilha learned of Paiva's death (either in Cairo or Ethiopia, the reports vary). Disguising himself as a Muslim Covilha proceeded first to Jedda, Mecca, and Medina, and finally reached Abyssinia sometime in 1490 or thereabouts. Thirty years later, in 1590, he related his mission to Rodrigo de Lima and Francisco Alvarez. He remained in Abyssinia upon their departure, still the honored guest of his host, "Presser John." See also Francisco Alvares, *Narrative of the Portuguese Embassy to Abyssinia during the Years 1520–1527*, Lord Stanley of Alderley (ed.), Burt Franklin Publisher, New York, 1970, and Boxer, op. cit., p. 12.

117. J. O. Hunwick, op. cit., p. 22. William McKee Evans has made the unique claim that: "In view of the broad-minded ethnic and social attitudes of the Prophet as well as the noblest of his followers, it is ironic that the lands of Islam became the cradle of modern racial stratification and of many of the ideas that are still used to justify special privileges defined by skin color and other racial characteristics. Muslims aspired to a universal brotherhood of believers. But prominent among their actual achievements was the forging of new links between blackness and debasement. It was under the Muslims that slavery became largely a racial institution." ("From the Land of Canaan to the Land of Guinea: The Strange Odyssey of the 'Sons of Ham,'" *American Historical Review* 85, no. 1 [February 1980]: 28.) The logic of Evans's argument rests on several assumptions: 1. "[T]he rise of Islam eliminated from the Mediterranean slave trade an important source of light-skinned slaves . . . [because] . . . Islamic law . . . held that no freeborn Muslim could be sold into slavery" (ibid.); 2. "During the later Middle Ages a number of European states developed, with sophisticated military organizations that could answer the challenge of Islam blow for blow. . . . few European slaves were available for purchase during the later Middle Ages because of the more orderly political conditions in France, England, the German Empire, and other countries . . . the supply from Europe was reduced to a minimum, and those came mainly from the Slavic lands." (ibid., pp. 28–29); and 3. "[M]ost black Africans lived in ethnically fragmented, often mutually antagonistic, societies that could offer little resistance to raids from the Sudanese or other Muslim states." (ibid., p. 29). Ultimately, Evans argues, racial myths emerge to justify and rationalize existing power relationships. Just how the myths of racial stratification made their way into Christian European cosmology is not made very clear in Evans' account. The single instance cited by Evans comes from Azurara's recounting of a "noble Moor" successfully bargaining for his own release from his Christian captors in exchange for ten "black Moors." The justification for the exchange, however, is not that of the Moor—whatever it might have been—but of Azurara who referred to the Judeo Christian myth of Noah's sons (Azurara mistakenly identified Ham, the "father of Canaan," as Cain). Nevertheless, Evans is certain that: "As historical events redirected the slave trade, as European slavery entered what the leading authority [Charles Verlinden] on medieval slavery has called its 'Negro' period, Christians began to look at blacks in ways that had been characteristic of racially stratified Muslim countries for some seven centuries" (ibid., pp. 38–39).

Evans acknowledges that his "chief authority on Muslim race relations and racial altitudes" is Gernot Rotter's unpublished dissertation "Die Stellung des Negers in der islamisch-arabischen Geselschaft bis XVI Jahrhundert," 1967. Other important sources are Bernard Lewis, *Race and Color in Islam*, Harper and Row, New York, 1970; and Adam Mez, *The Renaissance of Islam*, Luzac and Co., London, 1937. Rotter's unpublished work made its initial appearance with equal significance in Bernard Lewis's work. See *Race and Color*, p. 2 n. 1. For a treatment of the ideological currents within which Lewis swims, see Edward Said, *Orientalism*, Pantheon, New York, 1978, pp. 315–21; and Maxine Rodinson, "The Western Image and Western Studies of Islam," in Joseph Schacht and C. E. Bosworth (eds.), *The Legacy of Islam*, Oxford University Press, London, 1974, pp. 9–62. Evans's use of his sources is, however, sometimes quite curious. For instance, he uses Iris Origo's work as one confirmation for his contention that Christian Europe and its rulers denied Christian slaves to the Muslim trade. On precisely the same page cited by Evans, Origo says something quite different: "Nevertheless, it is quite plain that many of the Genoese and Venetian traders in the Black Sea paid little heed as to whether the human wares they carried had, or had not, been sanctied by baptism. The deeds of sale in Caffa and Pera in 1289 show that many of the slaves who were sold there belonged to peoples professing either the Catholic or Orthodox faith, since they included Circassians, Greeks, Russians, Georgians, Alans, and Lesghians . . . this did not prevent their sale" ("The Domestic Enemy," op. cit., p. 328). Evans's citing of Mez is equally cavalier. He uses Mez to confirm: "That slaves were predominantly black in Egypt during the period ca. 950–1250" (Evans, op. cit., p. 26 n. 28); that Islamic racial stratification led to untrained white slaves being valued as high as 1,000 diners, while Black slaves "fetched no more than 25–30 diners" (ibid., p. 29 and n. 41); and that one expression of Muslim contempt for Blacks was the belief that "blacks were 'fickle and careless. Dancing and beating time are engrained in their nature. They say: were the negro to fall from heaven to the earth he would beat time falling' " (ibid., p. 32). What Mez actually wrote is interesting in comparison. Of slaves in Egypt, Mez wrote: "In the 4th/10th century, Egypt, South Arabia, and North Africa, were the *chief markets* for black slaves" (my emphasis). Mez, op. cit., p. 157. Of slave prices, Mez commented: "Like the negro-servant today the black house-slave was chiefly employed as door-keeper. In a society which, above everything else, valued good poetry and fine music, artistically talented and trained boys and girls would inevitably be in great demand . . . and for such girls so trained the price was from 10 to 20,000 marks. . . . As with us, famous singers and female artists had their fancy prices. About 300/912 a female singer was sold in an aristocratic circle for 13,000 diners (130,000 marks), the broker making 1,000 diners" (ibid., pp. 157–58). Mez also put a slightly different interpretation on Black dancing. Adding his own coloring to the remarks of the Christian physician Ibn Botlan (ca. early eleventh century) to whom Evans turns for a characterization of Muslim attitudes toward Blacks and dancing, Mez noted: "The negro must always dance. Like the German when he has shaken off the work-day mood he feels an unconquerable passion to sing" (ibid., p. 161 n. 2). Evans appears to be equally slick with historical reconstruction as he is with his scholarly references. Compare his comment: "Tens of thousands of black Africans, for example, labored on land reclamation projects in Iraq. Blacks were also used in the copper and salt mines of the Sahara. Wherever the work was demanding and the conditions harsh, black slaves were likely to be found" (p. 30). J. O. Hunwick provides a somewhat fuller description. "[I]n a limited number of instances African slave labour was used in large-scale agricultural works, as it was also used, on a lesser scale, in mining and industry. The best known and best documented instance of such 'plantation slavery' is the use made of large numbers of East African slaves— Zanj—in draining the salt marshes at the mouth of the Tigris and Euphrates rivers around Basra. . . . The Zanj enter history only in 868 when they began their fifteen-year revolt which shook the foundations of the 'Abbasid caliphate.' " Hunwick continues: "Once the movement gained success it was joined by some of the Black troops of the caliphal guard sent to fight it, and by some Bedouin and marsh Arabs. . . . The Zanj built their own capital, al-Mukhtara and another fortified town, al-Mani'a. In 870 they captured the flourishing seaport of Ubulla and in 871 they sacked Basra with enormous slaughter. . . . It was not until 880 that the caliph's brother, freed of other pressing military preoccupations, was able to take serious steps against the Zanj. Even then, it took three years of very hard campaigning to crush the movement and seize its towns. . . . The major experiment with 'plantation slavery' in the Islamic world had ended in disaster" (Hunwick, op. cit., pp. 33–34). Hunwick also mentions the enormous variety of occupations of Black slaves in Islamic society: household slaves, revenue officers, poets, musicians, professional soldiers, eunuchs, rulers and colonial administrators, scholars, and concubines, to suggest the range. (See also Ralph Austen, op. cit.)

The final contradiction in Evans's thesis is presented in its entirety in his own words. Sandwiching the discussion of a number of Islamic rulers who were Black and the racial complaints of a number of prominent Muslim poets who were also Black, Evans makes the following remarks: "Despite the general polarization of Muslim society into low-status blacks and high-status whites, no clearly defined color bar emerged" (Evans, op. cit., p. 31). It should also be noted that earlier Evans had written: "In certain contexts, especially when comparing themselves to more northerly peoples, Arabs of this period thought of themselves as 'black' " (p. 24 n. 23). Still, he insists that the terms "Mamluk" and "Abd" came to distinguish respectively European from other slaves while David Ayalon remarks on the variable use of the term "Mamluk" in his "Studies on the Structure of the Mamluk Army," pt. 2, *Bulletin of the School of Oriental and African Studies* 15 (1953): 466; and his "Studies in Al-Jabarti," in *Studies on the Mamluks in Egypt*, Variorum Press, London, 1977, pp. 316–17. And finally, "Muslim attitudes toward blacks were mixed, but amid their ambivalence one can detect here and there most of those notions making up that cluster of ideas were recognized as modern Western racial prejudice" (pp. 31–32). How a racially stratified "pigmentocracy" (Evans's terms) manages to avoid the formation of a color bar is not clarified by Evans. In short, Evans's thesis is analytically flawed, not supported by his own "evidence," and suspiciously convenient at this moment of renewed Western hostility toward Islamic peoples. Moreover, he never seems to get around to explaining why or how the ideologues of a society so ideologically hostile to Islamic beliefs and with a quite ancient and sophisticated racial consciousness of its own would bother or need bother to borrow such an ambivalently held social ideology.

118. Hunwick, op. cit., p. 28.

119. Norman Daniel has argued: "Of the points that I summarised, most had a long life. The 'fraudulent'

or 'hypocritical' character of Muhammad's claim to prophesy, while he was an ambitious schemer, a bandit and a lecher; the emphasis on Islam as a falling short of Christianity, a sum of heresy, particularly in connection with the Trinity; preoccupation with the Qur'anic teaching of Christ; the general lines, if not all the details, of the most unflattering biography of Muhammad, and particularly the weight given to the influence of Sergius and other guides upon him; the enormous Importance given to two moral questions, the public reliance on force and the supposed private laxity in sexual matters; the ridicule and contempt of the Qur'anic Paradise; the suspicion of determinist and predestinarian ethics; the interest in Islamic religious practices, the admission of some Islamic practice as a good example, but the treatment of the cult in general in vain; all these, with some differences in emphasis, but with great continuity in the attitude of intellectual contempt, long dominated Christian and European thought." *Islam and the West*, Edinburgh University Press, Edinburgh, 1960, p. 276. (See also pp. 144–46.)

120. Norman Daniel, *The Arabs and Medieval Europe*, Longman, London, 1979, p. 115.

121. Ibid., pp. 327–28.

122. Davis, *The Problem of Slavery in Western Culture*, op. cit., p. 94.

123. "The Philosophy of Aristotle had such an authority in sixteenth and seventeenth century Spain, that any attack on him 'was regarded as a dangerous heresy,' and the *Politics* enjoyed a *respecto casi supersticioso*." Mavis Campbell, "Aristotle and Black Slavery: A Study in Race Prejudice," *Race* 15, no. 3 (January 1974): 285–86.

124. Ibid., p. 286.

125. Ibid., pp. 290–91.

126. William Westermann, *The Slave Systems of Greek and Roman Antiquity*, American Philosophical Society, Philadelphia, 1955, p. 156.

127. Trevor-Roper, *Rise of Christian Europe*, op. cit., pp. 88–89.

128. Abbas Hamdani has recalled: " 'The word India in the middle Ages,' says Charles Nowell, 'had no exact geographical meaning to Europeans; it was a convenient expression denoting the East beyond the Mohammedan world.' " "Columbus and the Recovery of Jerusalem," *Journal of the American Oriental Society* 99, no. 1 (January–March 1979): 39. Later Hamdani observes, "George Kimble in his *Geography in the Middle Ages* (London, 1938, 128 n.), observes that the term 'Indies' is 'a vague term, for in the Middle Ages there were at least three Indias, viz., India Minor, India Major and India Tertia, i.e. Sind, Hind and Zinj of the Arabs. The first two were located in Asia, the last in Africa (Ethiopia).' " Ibid., p. 46 n. 11.

129. G. K. Hunter, "Elizabethans and Foreigners," in Awardyce Nicoll (ed.), *Shakespeare in His Own Age, Shakespeare Survey 17*, Cambridge University Press, Cambridge, 1964, p. 40.

Chapter Five

1. Alan Manchester, *British Preeminence in Brazil: Its Rise and Decline*, Octagon Books, New York, 1964, p. 1.

2. Immanuel Wallerstein, *The Modern World-System*, Academic Press, New York, 1974, p. 42; see also Boxer, *Four Centuries*, op. cit., p. 9.

3. Wallerstein, ibid., p. 47.

4. "According to the chroniclers, the idea of carrying on the Reconquest in North Africa was suggested by the need to find useful employment for those who had lived on frontier raids for almost a quarter of a century, and by the desire of John's sons to be armed knights in a real conflict such as the older generation had known." H. V. Livermore, "Portuguese History," in H. V. Livermore (ed.), *Portugal and Brazil*, Clarendon Press, Oxford, 1963, p. 59. Partially cited in Wallerstein, op. cit., p. 46.

5. See pp. 118ff, chapter 4; and especially Francis Rogers op. cit., pp. 54ff.

6. Livermore states: "With the passing of the old dynasty some of the older nobility had clung to Castile and disappeared from Portugal. Their places had been taken by a new nobility formed of John of Avis's supporters, almost all new men, recently enriched, ambitious, and loyal." Livermore, "Portuguese History," op. cit., p. 60. Wallerstein provides an interesting characterization of the Portuguese bourgeoisie: "The interests of the bourgeoisie for once did not conflict with those of the nobility. Prepared for modern capitalism by a long apprenticeship in long-distance trading and by the experience of living in one of the most highly monetized areas of Europe (because of the economic involvement with the Islamic Mediterranean world), the bourgeoisie too sought to escape the confines of the small Portuguese market." Wallerstein, op. cit., pp. 51–52. His interpretation of the relationship between this bourgeoisie and its Genoese colleagues differs from mine (see text below) and is uncharacteristically lacking in cited scholastic authority.

7. M. Postan, "The Fifteenth Century," *Economic History Review* 9, no. 2 (May 1939): 165. In this short essay, Postan recounts the deterioration of English domestic production—agricultural as well as manufacturing—and foreign trade in the fifteenth century.

8. Livermore, "Portuguese History," op. cit., pp. 58–59. Livermore is most likely referring to the Treaty of Windsor not Westminster. See Manchester, op. cit., p. 2, see also Carus Wilson, "The Overseas Trade of

Bristol," in Eileen Power and M. M. Postan (eds.), *Studies in English Trade in the Fifteenth Century*, Routledge and Kegan Paul, London, 1951, p. 220.

9. Carus Wilson, op. cit., p. 220. Alan Manchester notes that in the seventeenth century "British merchants in Lisbon [submitted] . . . a complaint against the non-execution of privileges justly theirs, with certain papers showing the nature of these privileges. Arranged chronologically, these documents were: a charter dated August 10, 1400, by which D. Joao I conceded to the English the same privileges as had been conceded to the Genoese; a charter dated October 29, 1450, by which D. Affonso V conceded to the English the right to a special judge in all commercial cases which should arise between them and the Portuguese; a charter dated March 28, 1451, by Affonso V, granting the right to Englishmen to live and move about at will within the Portuguese kingdom; and the letter patent, dated February 7, 1495, by which D. Manuel granted special privileges to merchants from certain German cities." Manchester, op. cit., p. 5. Unlike Manchester, Wilson makes no attempt to reconcile the fact of this linkage between the two "states" with his predilection for the nation as a unit of historical analysis. This serves him badly when, in a few pages on (ibid., pp. 222–24), he must deal with piracy between the "Portuguese and English." It should have occurred to him that he was dealing with different entrepreneurial factions, some quite reconciled to mutual collaborations and shared interests, others, unaffected by treaties of alliance and still quite comfortably mutually antagonistic and piratically competitive.

10. Charles Verlinden, "Italian Influence in Iberian Colonization," *Hispanic American Historical Review* 33, no. 2 (May 1953): 199; and Wallerstein, op. cit., pp. 49ff.

11. Virginia Rau, "A Family of Italian Merchants in Portugal in the XVth Century: The Lomellini," in *Studi in Onore di Armando Sapori*, Instituto Editoriale Cisalpino, Milano, 1957, 1:717.

12. Verlinden comments: "After the appearance of Florentines in the Portuguese records in 1338 . . . only Milanese, Piacentines, and Lombards are mentioned, and more often Genoese. But one must not think that the Venetians did not play an active role in Portugal. . . . Nevertheless, the position of the Genoese and Piacentine merchants seems to have been more important, especially in Lisbon itself." Verlinden, "The Italian Colony of Lisbon and the Development of Portuguese Metropolitan and Colonial Economy," in Verlinden, *The Beginnings of Modern Colonization*, op. cit., p. 101.

13. About the Pezagno (Pessagno) family, Verlinden writes: "The merchant Salveto Pessagno, a member of a Genoese family which played a large part in Atlantic trade—particularly with England—and which provided Portugal with a series of admirals from 1317 on, died in Famagusta toward the end of the century." Verlinden, "Some Aspects of Slavery in Medieval Italian Colonies," op. cit., p. 89; see also Verlinden, "The Italian Colony of Lisbon," ibid., pp. 98–99 n. 3.

14. Rau, op. cit., p. 718.

15. See H. V. Livermore, "Portuguese History," op. cit., pp. 60–61; Rau, op. cit., passim; and Verlinden, "The Italian Colony of Lisbon," op. cit., p. 110.

16. Wallerstein, op. cit., p. 52.

17. See Verlinden, "The most frequently mentioned of the Italian merchants in Portugal is Bartolomeo Marchionni. The one who appeared in 1511 among the outfitters of the ship "Bretoa" is another Bartolomeo Marchionni, presumably a relative of the man encountered around 1443 in connection with the coral agreement. No doubt it was the second of these namesakes who was given the task of supplying Pero da Covilhao and Afonso de Paiva with money during the course of their voyage in search of India and Prester John. "The Italian Colony in Lisbon," op. cit., p. 107.

18. Verlinden, "Italian influence in Iberian Colonization," op. cit., pp. 202–3.

19. Verlinden, "Navigateurs, marchands et colons italiens au service de la decouverte et de la colonisation portugaise sous Henri le Navigateur," *Le Moyen Age* 64, no. 4 (1958): 468–70.

20. See Montague Guiseppi, "Alien Merchants in England in the Fifteenth Century," *Transactions of the Royal Historical Society*, new ser., vol. 9 (1895): 88–90; W. I. Haward, The Financial Transactions between the Lancastrian Government and the Merchants of the Staple from 1449 to 1461," in Eileen Power and M. M. Postan, op. cit., p. 315; and Martin Holmes, "Evil May-Day, 1517," *History Today* 15, no. 9 (September 1965): 642–43.

21. Guiseppi, op. cit., p. 94.

22. Thrupp, "The Grocers of London, A Study of Distributive Trade," in Eileen Power and M. M. Postan, op. cit., pp. 250, 290.

23. Rau, op. cit., p. 723; Carus Wilson, op. cit., p. 221; and Verlinden, "The Italian Colony of Lisbon," op. cit., pp. 104–5.

24. Carus Wilson, op. cit., p. 225; see also Guiseppi, op. cit., pp. 90, 93; and Verlinden, "The Italian Colony of Lisbon," op. cit., p. 111.

25. Boxer, *Four Centuries of Portuguese Expansion*, op. cit., p. 14.

26. C. A. Curwen records: "In the third year of [Yung Lo's] reign (1405) began that remarkable series of seven maritime expeditions which rank among the great feats of seamanship of all time. They were commanded by a Chinese Muslim, a court eunuch called Cheng Ho. On the first voyage his fleet consisted of sixty-three ships, constructed with watertight compartments, the largest of which are said to have been

over 400 feet long and 180 feet wide, with four decks. The total complement was 27,560, including troops, officials, and officers, and 180 doctors. This expedition reached India. In subsequent voyages Cheng Ho's ships visited more than thirty countries in the Indian Ocean and archipelago, the Persian Gulf, Aden, and the east coast of Africa." Curwen, "China," in Douglas Johnson (ed.), *The Making of the Modern World: Europe Discovers the World*, Barnes and Noble, New York, 1971, 1:341–42. See also Wallerstein's discussion of the Chinese empire's long-distance trade in Wallerstein, op. cit., pp. 52ff.

27. William Appleman Williams, "Empire as a Way of Life," *The Nation*, 2–9 August 1980, p. 104.

28. It is interesting to contrast Williams's use of the Chinese example with Wallerstein's defense of what he terms "materialist arguments." Williams writes: "The Chinese came, they traded, they observed. They made no effort to create an empire or even an imperial sphere of influence. Upon returning home, their reports engendered a major debate. The decision was made to burn and otherwise destroy the great fleets. . . . The point is not to present the Chinese as immaculately disinterested, or whiter than white. It is simply to note that we now know that the capacity for empire does not lead irresistibly or inevitably to the reality of empire." Williams, op. cit., p. 104. Wallerstein, on the other hand, appears utterly convinced that the voluntaristic explanation is both sufficient *and* too indeterminate. His argument seems to be that the Chinese imperial structure acted as a political, technological, and ideological constraint on the development of a bourgeoisie—prematurely developed? he wonders aloud—identified with the further development of capitalism in China and colonial expansion. He concludes: "So China, if anything seemingly better placed prima facie to move forward to capitalism in terms of already having an extensive state bureaucracy, being further advanced in terms of the monetization of the economy and possibly of technology as well, was nonetheless less well placed after all. It was burdened by an imperial political structure. It was burdened by the 'rationality' of its value system which denied the state the leverage for change (had it wished to use it) that European monarchs found in the mysticality of European feudal loyalties." Wallerstein, op. cit., p. 63.

29. Boxer recounts that: "After rounding the Cape of Good Hope, and calling at various Arab-Swahili ports along the east coast of Africa, da Gama reached Malmdi, where he received the help of Ahmad-Ibn-Madjid, the most famous Arab pilot of his age, and one who knew the Indian Ocean better than any other man living. Thanks to his guidance, the Portuguese were enabled to reach Calicut, the major emporium of the pepper trade. . . . Not unnaturally, Ibn Madjid's memory is still execrated by the majority of his fellow countrymen and co-religionists; and he himself bitterly bewailed in his old age what he had done." Boxer, op. cit., pp. 13–14.

30. Of the sixteenth century, Fernand Braudel has written: "The commercial activity of the sea, concentrating more and more in the West, tipped the balance, spelling the inexorable decline of the eastern basin which had for so long been the source of wealth. The shift brought little joy to Milan, but brought Genoa and Florence to prominence. Genoa for her share, and a lion's share it was, acquired the Spanish and American trade. . . . In the second half of the century, Genoa took the lead. . . . Foreign catchment was the most important, and it was by this means that Florence and Genoa gained control of all the economically backward regions, whether in Eastern Europe or southern Italy, in the Balkans, France, or the Iberian peninsula." Braudel, *The Mediterranean*, op. cit., 1:393.

31. One should be aware, as Robert Knecht reminds us that in "the Indies . . . the superiority of the Europeans was confined to the sea." Knecht, "The Discoveries," in Douglas Johnson, op. cit., p. 27.

32. John William Blake in his documentary history of *Europeans in West Africa, 1450–1460*, vol. 1 (Kraus, Nendeln, 1967), asserts that the records he has gathered "show that between 1453 and 1480 Andalusian seamen and traders sent many ships to the West African coast, and that the government of Castile claimed exclusive possession of Guinea" (p. 186, see also p. 189).

33. Ibid., p. 191; see also Edgar Prestage, "Vasco da Gama and the Way to the Indies," in Arthur Percival Newton (ed.), the *Great Age of Discovery*, University of London, London, 1932, p. 49.

34. Hans Koning, *Columbus: His Enterprise*, Monthly Review Press, New York, 1976, pp. 13–14.

35. Arthur P. Newton, "Christopher Columbus and his First Voyage," in Newton (ed.), op. cit., pp. 76ff.

36. See Newton, op. cit., p. 77; and Koning, op. cit., p. 22.

37. Newton, op. cit., p. 78.

38. Koning believes that Felipa's family was of Italian origins, op. cit., p. 25. On the other hand, Newton's reconstruction of her family's history makes it very clear that her genealogy contained Italian elements as well as Portuguese lesser nobility, op. cit., p. 79.

39. Arthur Davies, "Origins of Colombian Cosmography," in *Studi Colombiana*, Stabilimento Arti Grafiche ed Affini, Genova, 1952, 2:59–62.

40. Ibid., p. 61.

41. Ibid., p. 62. Martin Behain (or Behaim) is described by Verlinden as a German knight, who, at least by 1486, was living on Fayal in the Azores. At this later time he is supposed to have been enlisted by the Portuguese court in an ill-fated attempt to cross the Atlantic (see text below). Behain, as it turned out, missed the boat. See Verlinden, "A Precursor of Columbus: The Fleming Ferdinand van Olmen (1487)," in Verlinden, *The Beginnings of Modern Colonization*, op. cit., pp. 190–91; also see Newton, op. cit., pp. 90–91.

42. Arthur Davies, op. cit., p. 63.

43. Verlinden, "A Precursor," op. cit., p. 189.

44. See Arthur Davies, op. cit., pp. 62–64; and Knecht, op. cit., pp. 29–30.

45. Verlinden,"A Precursor," op. cit., p. 194.

46. Ibid., p. 193.

47. Ibid.

48. Hans Koning, op. cit., pp. 39–40.

49. The brothers, Martin, Francisco, and Vincente Pinzon, were, according to Las Casas, the dominant force in Palos de la Frontera (See Newton, op. cit., pp. 87–88). Martin, after a business trip to Rome, which included a visit to the Papal Court in 1491, had returned to Palos with detailed information on an Atlantic route that he had gathered from the Papal library. He shared this material with Columbus and helped to arrange with Pinelli and Santangel for a police fine against Palos to be redirected for support of Columbus's project. Martin and Vincente sailed with Columbus as captains of the Pinta and Nina. Martin, however, died during this first voyage. The family subsequently entered into a prolonged legal attempt to secure from Columbus what they presumed was their share of the wealth he secured from the New World.

50. Charles Verlinden, "Italian Influence on Spanish Economy and Colonization during the Reign of Ferdinand of Castile," in Verlinden, *The Beginnings of Modern Colonization*, op. cit., p. 130.

51. Ibid., pp. 114–20. Americo Castro concluded: "The Italians" form of life had more points of contact with the Jews than with the Spanish Christians. In the Middle Ages there were dynasties of great Genoese traders . . . ; the Genoese continued to engage in banking negotiations between Spain and her American dominions when there were no Jews to do this." Castro, op. cit., p. 513 n. 98.

52. Verlinden, "Italian Influence in Iberian Colonization," op. cit., p. 210; Fernand Braudel, *The Mediterranean*, op. cit., 1:364–65.

53. Samuel Eliot Morison, "Columbus as a Navigator," in *Studi Colombiani*, op. cit., 2:39–48; and *Admiral of the Ocean Sea*, 2 vols., Little, Brown and Company, Boston, 1942.

54. Newton, op. cit., pp. 88–89.

55. "Genoa . . . operated the most sophisticated credit machinery of the Middle Ages. A detailed study has shown that the city was already modern, ahead of its time, in the fifteenth century, daily handling endorsements of bills of exchange and ricorsa agreements, an early form of kite-flying, to use modern barkers' jargon. Genoa's early role as intermediary between Seville and the New World, her official alliance with Spain in 1523 did the rest: she became the leading financial city of the world, in the period of rising inflation and prosperity that characterized the second half of the sixteenth century—the century of Genoa, the city where commerce was beginning to appear a rather inferior activity." Braudel, *The Mediterranean*, op. cit., 1:321.

56. Jacob Streider concluded: "The Italian city states developed a colonial system in the Mediterranean, a system which was a precursor and a prototype for Spain and Portugal in the fifteenth and sixteenth centuries, and even for Holland in the seventeenth." (Cited by Oliver C. Cox, *The Foundations of Capitalism*, Philosophical Library, New York, 1959, p. 85 n. 36.)

57. Philip Curtin, "Slavery and Empire," in Vera Rubin and Arthur Tuden (eds.), *Comparative Perspectives on Slavery in New World Plantation Societies*, Annals of the New York Academy of Sciences, vol. 292, 27 June 1977, p. 3.

58. Oliver C. Cox, *The Foundations of Capitalism*, op. cit., p. 70.

59. Sidney M. Greenfield, "Madeira and the Beginnings of New World Sugar Cane Cultivation and Plantation Slavery: A Study in Institution Building," in Rubin and Tuden (eds.), op. cit., p. 545.

60. Ibid., pp. 541–42.

61. Ibid., p. 548.

62. J. H. Parry, *The Establishment of the European Hegemony: 1415–1715*, Harper and Row, New York, 1966, p. 73.

63. Leslie R. Rout, Jr., *The African Experience in Spanish America*, Cambridge University Press, Cambridge, 1976, p. 28.

64. The term *"pieza de Indias"* (or *peca de Indias*)—piece of the Indies—became a common or standard measure of slaves in the late sixteenth century. Just how early it became standardized is unclear but its general meaning and use has been clarified by Enriqueta Vila and C. R. Boxer. Vila writes: "It can be seen from the account books of the royal treasury officials [of Spain] that at times, when counting small blacks of less than 12 years of age, known as *muleques*, it was customary to count two of them as one when it came to the payment of duties. Also suckling infants, known as *crias* or *bambos*, were considered free of duties and formed one 'piece' together with their mothers. All this was applied in an arbitrary manner, with no fixed standards. The oldest royal decree found so far, regulating the payment of duties on these blacks, is a *cedula* of 12 July 1624, addressed by Felipe IV to all the authorities of the Indies, in which are included some basic rules for general application: a *muleque* of seven years old should be counted as half a slave, and duty should not be charged on those of less than that age." Vila, "The Large-Scale Introduction of Africans into Veracruz and Cartagena," in Rubin and Tuden (eds.), op. cit., p. 270. On the other hand, Boxer asserts:

"[T]he peca de Indias . . . was defined in 1678 as being 'a Negro from fifteen to twenty-five years old; from eight to fifteen, and from twenty-five to thirty-five, three pass for two; beneath eight, and from thirty-five to forty-five, two pass for one' sucking infants follow their mothers without accompt; all above forty-five years, with the diseased, are valued by arbiters." Boxer, *The Golden Age of Brazil, 1695–1750*, University of California Press, Berkeley 1962, p. 5.

65. Jan Vansina, *Kingdoms of the Savanna*, University of Wisconsin Press, Madison, 1966, p. 53 (cited by J. E. Inikori, "Measuring the Atlantic Slave Trade: A Rejoinder by J. E. Inikori," *Journal of African History* 17, no. 4 [1976]: 613).

66. Ibid., p. 52.

67. K. G. Davies, *The Royal African Company*, Atheneum, New York, 1970, p. 13; Enriqueta Vila, op. cit., passim.

68. Vila, op. cit., p. 275; Walter Rodney reported that "Most of the slaves imported into Mexico and Central America during the sixteenth and early seventeenth centuries were from the upper Guinea coast." Rodney,"Portuguese Attempts at Monopoly on the Upper Guinea Coast, 1580–1650," *Journal of African History* 6, no. 3 (1965): 309.

69. J. E. Inikori, "Measuring the Atlantic Slave Trade: An Assessment of Curtin and Anstey," *Journal of African History*, 17, no. 2 (1976): 204–5.

70. Roderick MacDonald, "The Williams Thesis: A Comment on the State of Scholarship," *Caribbean Quarterly*, 25, no. 3 (September 1979): 63.

71. Curtin, *The Atlantic Slave Trade: A Census*, op. cit., p. 87.

72. Inikori's criticisms are important enough to warrant quotation. Of Curtin's statistics Inikori writes: "All the computations required by the formula employ only two slave population figures—the figure at the beginning and the figure at the end of the given period. While this poses no problme for compound interest calculations. . .the same is not true for a slave population that was subject to considerable hazards (which may have had no regular pattern) affecting the year-to-year movement of the total population and import figures." "Measuring the Atlantic Slave Trade: An Assessment," op. cit., p. 198. Respecting Curtin's historical sensitivities, Inikori states: "The amount of historical evidence supporting my argumentin this aspect of my original paper is really so substantial that only Curtin's ignorance of the historical data can make him write in the way he does. General statistical theory of random error does not take precedence over historical data. . . . Arguments about the inaccuracy of official records based on a large amount of historical data can only be countered with opposing historical data, not with vague theories of random error. . . . In fact, all the statements made by government officials which I quoted in my original paper were based on actual investigations." "Measuring the Atlantic Slave Trade: A Rejoinder," op. cit., p. 617. Finally, of Curtin's logic of defense, Inikori cautions: "The key to a proper understanding of Curtin's comments is his statement that what I said deliberately falsified the estimates so as to minimize the size of the trade. Ordinary error without a political or other bias would be more random; . . . With this misconception it apparently became an emotional issue for Curtin to defend his 'honor' at all cost. . . . The logic that runs through Curtin's paper is that only 'a political or other bias' can skew the frequency of error in a set of estimates in one direction. . . . The naivety of this logic is too obvious to warrant much comment. Suffice it to say that the frequency of error in a set of estimates can be skewed in any direction for several reasons that have nothing to do with 'a political or other bias.' And, for that matter, a man can have a political motive and yet produce an accurate estimate." Ibid., pp. 609–10.

73. Inikori, "Measuring the Atlantic Slave Trade: A Rejoinder," op. cit., p. 615.

74. D. Eltis, "The Direction and Fluctuation of the Trans-Atlantic Slave Trade, 1821–43: A Revision of the 1845 Parliamentary Paper," unpublished paper presented at the Mathematical Social Science Board Semi-nar on the Economics of the Slave Trade, Colby College, Waterville, Maine, 20–22 August 1975; Roger Anstey, *The Atlantic Slave Trade and British Abolition, 1760–1810*, Humanities Press, Atlantic Highlands, N.J.; and idem., "The Volume and Profitability of the British Slave Trade, 1761–1807," in Stanley Engerman and Eugene Genovese (eds.), *Race and Slavery in the Western Hemisphere*, Princeton University Press, Princeton, 1975, pp. 3–31; Serge Daget, "La Repression Britannique sur les Negriers Français du Traffic Illegal: Quelques conditions generales ou specifiques," unpublished paper presented at Maine, 20–22 August 1975; Lucien Peytraud, *L'Esclavage aux Antilles Français avant 1789 d'apres des documents inedits des Archives Coloniales, These Presentee a la Faculte des Lettres de Paris*, Paris, 1897; and Ralph Davis, *The Rise of the Atlantic Economies*, Weidenfeld and Nicolson, London, 1973.

75. Inikori does not present a total for the Atlantic slave trade. This figure was arrived at by totalling the amounts for the French West Indies, Brazil, and the English colonies which appear in Inikori's two essays, and interpolating an amount for Spanish America consistent with Inikori's treatment of pre-nineteenth-century Brazil's slave population. From Inikori's first essay ("Measuring the Atlantic Slave Trade: An Assessment," op. cit.), the numbers for the French West Indies are 3,000,000. For the English colonies in the eighteenth century and Brazil in the first half of the nineteenth century, the numbers are 3,699,572 and 3,700,000 respectively ("Measuring the Atlantic Slave Trade: A Rejoinder," op cit., pp. 623–24).

76. For Curtin's statement see note 52, chapter IV. I or D. R. Murray's critique of Curtin's figures, see

"Statistics of the Slave Trade in Cuba, 1790–1867," *Journal of Latin American Studies* 3, no. 2 (November 1971): 131–49. Richard Pares concurs with Curtin on this matter: "M. Debien has observed that the trickle of indentured peasants . . . dried up at various times in the second half of the seventeenth century: after 1666 few more such servants were sent to French St. Christopher; after 1685 few more to Guadeloupe. The same contrast can be seen between the older settled sugar colonies, like Barbados, which soon ceased to demand the services of any white men from Europe besides specialists, and the newer settlements, like Jamaica, which still, for a time, welcomed unskilled white labourers. Specialists—tradesmen, coachmen, refiners, private tutors—were still sent out to the plantations for another century; but the peasant, with his two hands and nothing much else, was no longer in demand. His place had been taken by an African." Pares, *Merchants and Planters*, Economic History Review Supplement, no.e, 1960, p. 19.

77. See note 47, previous chap.

78. Williams, *Capitalism and Slavery*, op. cit., p. 63.

79. Ibid., p. 61.

80. Herman Merivale, *Lectures on Colonization and Colonies*, Longman, Green, Longman, and Roberts, London, 1861 (repr. by Augustus Kelley, New York, 1967), p. 302.

81. Roderick McDonald, op. cit. pp. 65–66.

82. James Burke, *Connections*, Little, Brown, Boston, 1978, p. 192.

83. Robert Carlyle Batie, "Why Sugar, Economic Cycles and the Changing of Staples on the English and French Antilles, 1624–54," *Journal of Caribbean History* 8 (November 1976): 4–13.

84. P. G. M. Dickson, *The Financial Revolution in England*, Macmillan, London, 1967, pp. 55–56.

85. C. L. R. James, *The Black Jacobins*, op. cit., pp. 47–48.

86. Roderick McDonald, op. cit., pp. 63–64.

87. Richard Pares, op. cit., p. 38.

88. Ibid., p. 50.

89. Ibid., p. 33. The Davies piece to which Pares refers is K. G. B. Davies, "The Origin of the Commission System in the West India Trade," *Transactions of the Royal Historical Society*, 5th ser., vol. 2 (1952): 89–107.

90. Viva, op. cit., p. 277 n. 9.

91. Cited by Roderick McDonald in his "Measuring the British Slave Trade to Jamaica, 1789–1808: A Comment," *Economic History Review* 33, no. 2 (May 1980): 257–58.

92. Pares, op. cit., pp. 2–6.

93. Ibid., pp. 11, 63 n. 54; and Batie, op. cit., p. 1.

94. Pares, op. cit., p. 16.

95. Richard B. Moore, "On Barbadians and Minding Other People's Business," *New World Quarterly* 3, nos. 1 and 2, Dead Season and Croptime (1966/1967): 69.

96. Batie, op. cit., pp. 4–13; and Richard S. Dunn, *Sugar and Slaves: The Rise of the Planter Class in the English West Indies, 1624–1713*, University of North Carolina Press, Chapel Hill, 1972, p. 203.

97. Batie, op. cit., p. 16.

98. Ibid., pp. 15, 19.

99. Curtin, *The Atlantic Slave Trade*, op. cit., p. 126.

100. Ibid., pp. 118–26.

101. See Inikori, "Measuring the Atlantic Slave Trade: A Rejoinder," op. cit., p. 619.

102. Curtin's figures are used here not for their accuracy but for their relative weights. Curtin, *The Atlantic Slave Trade*, op. cit., p. 119.

103. Inikori, "Measuring the Atlantic Slave Trade: A Rejoinder," op. cit., pp. 612–15.

104. Curtin, *The Atlantic Slave Trade*, op. cit., chap. 10. This figure, it must be recalled, is only an "estimate" of the number of deaths associated with the British slave trade in the eighteenth century. For France, during the same century, Robert Stein, who (without attribution) puts the French slave trade at 1,150,000, also claims that "no fewer than 150,000 died before reaching the New World, and many more died within a year or two of arrival." Stein, "Mortality in the Eighteenth-Century French Slave Trade," *Journal of African History* 21, no. 1 (1980): 35.

105. Curtin, ibid., p. 282. For the period 1714–78, Stein puts the death "rate" of crews in the French slave trade at 13 percent and argues: "crew mortality was on the average higher than slave mortality at least along the coast and on the Middle Passage." Stein, "Mortality in the Eighteenth-Century French Slave Trade," op. cit., pp. 36–37.

106. Curtin, ibid, pp. 139–40.

107. Orlando Patterson, *The Sociology of Slavery*, Fairleigh Dickinson University Press, Rutherford, 1969, pp. 134–44.

108. Curtin, *The Atlantic Slave Trade*, op. cit., pp. 91–2.

109. Ibid., pp. 83, 268.

110. Inikori, "Measuring the Atlantic Slave Trade: An Assessment," op. cit., p. 222.

111. Curtin, *The Atlantic Slave Trade*, op. cit., pp. 144, 156–58.

112. Gerald Mullin, *Flight and Rebellion*, Oxford University Press, New York, 1972, p. 7.

113. Ibid., p. 43.

114. For the background of the Black maroon settlements of seventeenth-century Virginia and the Afro-Indian (Seminole) settlements of eighteenth-century Florida, see chapter 7. An early account of the Seminoles is given by Josh Giddings (1858).

115. See Nwabueze F. Okoye, "Chattel Slavery as the Nightmare of the American Revolutionaries," *William and Mary Quarterly*, 37 (January 1980): 3–5; Jeffrey Crow, "Slave Rebelliousness and Social Conflict in North Carolina 1775–1802," *William and Mary Quarterly*, ibid., p. 89; C. L. R. James, "The Atlantic Slave Trade," in James, *The Future in the Present*, Lawrence Hill, Westport, 1977, p. 246.

116. Walter Rodney, *How Europe Underdeveloped Africa*, Howard University Press, Washington D.C., 1972.

117. Karl Marx and Friedrich Engels, *The Communist Manifesto*, in Robert C. Tucker (ed.), *The Marx-Engels Reader*, W. W. Norton, New York, 1978, p. 478.

Chapter Six

1. Cabral, "National Liberation and Culture," in *Return to the Source*, Africa Information Service, 1973, pp. 42–43.

2. Michael Craton, "Proto-Peasant Revolts?: The Late Slave Rebellions in the British West Indies 1816–1832," *Past and Present* 85 (November 1979): 120–21. Robert Lacerte's work on the first four decades of Haitian independence, despite a tendency toward questionable assertions and presumptions (he persists in designating France as Haiti's "mother country" and declares that the presence of "whites" was indispensable for Haiti's post-revolutionary economic recovery), supports Craton's characterization of African peasant predispositions regarding plantation agriculture and land tenure. See Lacerte, "The First Land Reform in Latin America: The Reforms of Alexander Petion, 1809–1814," *Inter-American Economic Affairs* 28, no. 4 (Spring 1975): 77–85; and "Xenophobia and Economic Decline: The Haitian Case, 1820–1843," *The Americas* 37, no. 4 (April 1981): 499–515.

3. John Blassingame, *The Slave Community*, Oxford University Press, New York, 1972, pp. 189–216.

4. Ibid., p. 197.

5. Ibid., p. 201.

6. Ibid., p. 213.

7. On more than one occasion, Blassingame contends that: "It is no accident that the Sambo of Southern novels and plays was usually a house servant. Because the planters often had little contact with field hands, in white autobiographies it is almost always the house servant who is portrayed as the epitome of loyalty.... One reflection of the faithfulness of house servants and the low level of contact between field hands and whites is that, in an overwhelming majority of the cases where masters manumitted individual slaves, they were house servants." (Ibid., pp. 200–201.) On the other hand, Owens reminds us that: "Masters tortured and murdered some domestics, and house slaves killed slaveholders. Many acts against domestics went unpunished.... It is not easy to generalize about house slaves. They were a diverse class of bondsmen who helped to shape and reshape the character of their servitude in the Big House. In some respects theirs was a special kind of enslavement marked by privileges that most field hands never experienced, at least not in the same way. They did not, however, give in to it." Leslie Howard Owens, *This Species of Property*, Oxford University Press, New York, 1976, p. 120. Furthermore, Kenneth Stampp in *The Peculiar Institution*, Vintage Books, New York, 1956, states that at least a quarter of the American slave population in the nineteenth century were claimed by slaveholders "who had at their command as few as a half dozen fieldhands.... Lacking skilled craftsmen in their small slave forces, they still found it necessary to perform certain specialized tasks such as carpentering and repairing tools; and in an emergency (a crop rarely went from spring planting to fall harvesting without a crisis of some kind) they temporarily forgot their pride ... a master often had to choose between losing his crop and pitching in with his slaves" (p. 35).

8. Blassingame, op. cit., pp. 190ff.

9. Owens, op. cit., p. 78.

10. "At the core of such behavior was the slave's lack of accommodation to much that confronted him in bondage. Bondage continually worked against the bondsman, though he never left its functioning untempered with. The frustration was enormous." Ibid., p. 93.

11. Ibid., pp. 79–96.

12. Ibid., p. 103.

13. Ibid., p. 96.

14. Ibid., p. 103.

15. "The Southern planter suffered, not simply for his economic mistakes—the psychological effect of slavery upon him was fatal. The mere fact that a man could be, under the law, the actual master of the mind and body of human beings had to have disastrous effects. It tended to inflate the ego of most planters beyond all reason; they became arrogant, strutting, quarrelsome kinglets; they issued commands; they made laws; they shouted their order; they expected deference and self-abasement; they were choleric and

easily insulted. Their 'honor' became a vast and awful thing, requiring wide and insistent deference. Such of them as were inherently weak and inefficient were all the more easily angered, jealous and resentful; while the few who were superior, physically or mentally, conceived no bounds to their power and personal prestige. As the world had long learned, nothing is so calculated to ruin human nature as absolute power over human beings." W. E. B. Du Bois, *Black Reconstruction in America*, Harcourt, Brace and Company, New York, 1935, pp. 52–53. Earlier in the same work, Du Bois had noted: "[T]here is evidence that the necessities of their economic organization were continually changing and deteriorating their morale and pushing forward ruder, noisier, less cultivated elements than characterized the Southern gentleman of earlier days. Certainly, the cursing, brawling, whoring gamblers who largely represented the South in the late fifties, evidenced the inevitable deterioration that overtakes men when their desire for income and extravagance overwhelms their respect for human beings" (p. 43). James Roark, matching the desperation of the antebellum secessionist planter ideologues with the sentiments of such as Mary Ann Whittle, a plantation mistress ("we have an enemy in our bosoms who will shoot us in our beds"), and the Mississippian William Kirkland (who declared he had rather " 'be exterminated' than be forced to live in the same society 'with the slaves if freed' "), concluded: "Mixing reality with fantasy, planters feared that John Bull, Billy Yank, Johnny Poor White, and Nat Turner were all lurking in the shadows. That vision knotted the stomachs of more than just the cowardly." *Masters Without Slaves*, W. W. Norton, New York, 1977, pp. 4, 10, 16.

16. Among the revisionists might be included the names of Ira Berlin (*Slaves Without Masters*); Douglas Daniels (*Pioneer Urbanites*); Eric Foner (*Free Soil, Free Labor, Free Men*); George M. Frederickson (*The Black Image in the White Mind*); Eugene Genovese (*Roll, Jordan, Roll* and *From Rebellion to Revolution*); Herbert Gutman (*The Black Family in Slavery and Freedom*); Nathan Huggins (*John Brown*); Lawrence Levine (*Black Culture and Black Consciousness*); Leon Litwack (*Been in the Storm So Long*); Stephen Oates (*To Purge This Land with Blood*); Nell Irvin Painter (*The Exodusters*); Albert Raboteau (*The Slave Religion*); George Rawick (*From Sundown to Sunup*); Willie Lee Rose (*Rehearsal For Reconstruction*); and Robert Starobin (*Industrial Slavery in the Old South*).

17. Thomas Jefferson, a major slaveholder at the end of the eighteenth century and the beginning of the nineteenth and as president of the United States during its fledgling republicanism, bore an importance and significance to his own and subsequent American generations of literati that make of his life a prime illustration of the contradictory intuitions and social forces besetting the master class (and its subsequent apologists). Winthrop Jordan submits that for Jefferson, the humanity of the slaves was never in question: "Without question Negroes were members of that class. Hence Jefferson never for a moment considered the possibility that they might rightfully be enslaved." *White Over Black*, Penguin, Baltimore, 1969, p. 432. Still, Jefferson's racial sensibilities mixed his belief in the moral identity between Blacks and whites with his resistance to any consideration of equal passions, mental capacities, or sense of human beauty between Blacks and whites. Jordan exclaims: "Jefferson's confusion at times became monumental" (p. 453). Perhaps Jefferson's confusion was a product of his alleged relationship with his enslaved chambermaid, Sally Hemings. The alleged relationship has certainly taken its toll on some of his biographers. For example: John Chester Miller, *The Wolf by the Ears*, New American Library, New York, 1977. Miller begins his refutation of the accusations first leveled by Jefferson's contemporary, James Callender, by assuring his reader that Ms Hemings was not "black" as she was sometimes called, but actually a "quadroon." Miller then maintains that Sally Hemings was the last child of 14 ("of varying shades of color") born to this slave woman Betty Hemings and John Wayles, a wealthy Virginia planter. Wayles was, of course, also the father of Martha Skelton Wayles, Jefferson's bride in 1772. In 1773, Wayles died and his slave children and his mistress became the property of Jefferson at Monticello (p. 162), Miller suggests: "The special treatment meted out to Betty Hemings and her offspring by Jefferson may have assuaged but it hardly could have removed the harrowing sense of guilt Jefferson experienced by holding his late [she died in 1782] wife's half-brothers and half-sisters in servitude, particularly since he could see in these mulattoes the lineaments of his own wife. It is no wonder, therefore, that he conceived the overwhelming antipathy toward miscegenation which led him to favor putting all Afro-Americans beyond the possibility of admixture with whites. If, as the evidence indicates, his attitude toward mulattoes underwent a radical change in 1772–1773 it was probably owing to the astonishing discovery he made at that time of the sexual practices of his late father-in-law" (p. 163). Later, Miller argues that: "For Jefferson to have conducted a clandestine love affair with a slave woman and to have raised his children as slaves is completely at variance with his character, insofar as it can be determined by his acts and words" (p. 177). But then, "Jefferson asked to be judged by his acts rather than his words. But on the issue of slavery in America he emerges with greater luster if he is judged by his words rather than by his acts. For here he signally failed to live up to his own precepts." "Clearly, Jefferson shared the racial prejudice which compounded the problem of ridding the United States of what he called 'this great political and moral evil,' 'this blot on our country.' But he succeeded in concealing this prejudice from himself by imagining that he was acting in response to divine edicts" (pp. 277, 178). A final irony in Miller's defense of Jefferson's sexual morality is his argument that the proof that Jefferson had no special relationship with his chambermaid is that in his will he manumitted five slaves, all Hemingses. "But

Sally Hemings was not among those manumitted: her name appeared on the slave inventory of his estate and her value was set at fifty dollars" (p. 168). Hardly the act of a man wracked by guilt at the sight of his dead wife's "lineament." But the precedent of the Brazilian master, Pedro Domingues, "who consumed by jealousy at the thought of his concubine marrying . . . granted her her freedom, the ownership of his house and three slaves, on the condition that she should stay single for the rest of her life." C. R. Boxer, *Women in Iberian Expansion Overseas, 1415–1815*, Oxford University Press, New York, 1975, p. 59.

18. Eric Williams, *From Columbus to Castro*, Harper and Row, New York, 1970, pp. 37–38. One indication of the official attitude toward European labor was the apparent willingness of the authorities to suspend the racial hierarchies of Iberia in exchange for the generating of viable colonial settlements. C. R. Boxer recounts that despite the vigor of "race-prejudice" during this period of Iberian history ("concentrated against the 'Moors' (e.g. Muslims) and the Jews, mainly for religious reasons") and Africans (for their association with slavery), royal instructions and orders were sent out to the colonies in 1503 and 1514 encouraging inter-racial marriages between Europeans and Indians. *Women in Iberian Expansion*, op. cit., pp. 35–37.

19. Ibid., pp. 37–41.

20. Richard Hart cites the Spanish historian, Oviedo, who in 1546 wrote that the capitalization of a West Indian sugar plantation "often requires an investment of ten or twelve thousand gold ducats before it is complete and ready for operation. And if I should say fifteen thousand ducats I should not be exaggerating, for they require at least eighty or one hundred Negroes working all the time, and even one hundred and twenty or more to be well supplied; and close by a good herd or two of a thousand or two or three thousand head of cattle to feed the workers; aside from the expensive trained workers and foremen for making the sugar, and carts to haul the cane to the mill and bring wood." Hart, *Slaves Who Abolished Slavery*, vol.1, *Blacks in Bondage*, Institute of Social and Economic Research, University of the West Indies, Jamaica, 1980, p. 17.

21. Eric Williams, *From Columbus to Castro*, op. cit., p. 30.

22. C. H. Haring, *The Spanish Empire in America*, Harcourt, Brace and World, New York, 1963, p. 41.

23. Ibid., p. 33. Nicolas Sanchez-Albornoz disagrees with the figures but comes to the same conclusion. "The decline was undoubtedly of disastrous proportions. Even accepting conservative estimates, the pre-Columbian population of Hispaniola must have fallen from about one hundred thousand to only a few hundred in 1570. To make up for the lack of natives, Negro slaves and Indians from the Bahamas were introduced at an early date. That measure alone proves that depopulation there was worse than on the mainland." Sanchez-Albornoz, *The Population of Latin America: A History*, University of California Press, Berkeley, 1974, p. 42.

24. Sherburne Cook and Woodrow Borah, *The Aboriginal Population of Central Mexico on the Eve of the Spanish Conquest*, University of California Press, Berkeley, 1963, pp. 72–88.

25. Cited in Alfred W. Crosby, Jr., *The Columbian Exchange*, Greenwood Press, Westport, 1977, p. 36. See also Sanchez-Albornoz, op. cit., pp. 60–66.

26. David Davidson, "Negro Slave Control and Resistance in Colonial Mexico, 1519–1650," *Hispanic American Historical Review* 46, no. 3 (August 1966): 236. Alfred Crosby disputes the role of "brutality" in the destruction of native peoples. He argues: "The destruction of the Arawaks has been largely blamed on the Spanish cruelty, not only by the later Protestant historians of the 'Black Legend' school but also by such contemporary Spanish writers as Oviedo and Bartolome de Las Casas. Without doubt the early Spaniards brutally exploited the Indians. But it was obviously not in order to kill them off, for the early colonists had to deal with a chronic labor shortage and needed the Indians. Disease would seem to be a more logical explanation." Crosby, op. cit., p. 45. Both the impulses of greed and the dialectic of domination have claimed for their victim the logic of need.

27. David Davidson, op. cit., p. 236; and for a critical assessment of the figure originally developed by Cook, Borah and Lesley Byrd Simpson, see Rudolph A. Zambardino, "Mexico's Population in the Sixteenth Century: Demographic Anomaly or Mathematical Illusion?," *Journal of Interdisciplinary History* 11, no. 1 (Summer 1980): 1–27; and on the New World in general, see Sanchez-Albornoz, op. cit., pp. 32–36.

28. The works by Sauer (*The Early Spanish Main*, 1969) and Jaramillo Uribe ("La poblacion indigene de Colombia en el momento de la Conquista y sus transformaciones posteriores," *Anuario colombiano de historia social y de la cultura* 1, no. 2 [1964]: 239–93) are cited by Sanchez-Albornoz, op. cit., p. 54. Jaramillo Uribe is also cited for the following excerpt from Father Gumilla's *Orinoco ilustrado*: "[E]xperienced observers have noted that in areas where the Indian population has been noticeably reduced, many Indian women are childless and completely sterile . . . ; in those same places and areas, Indian women married to Europeans and to mestizas, *cuaterones*, malattoes, zambos, and Negroes are so fertile and produce so many children that they can rival Jewish women in this regard. . . . The difference is that the Indian woman with an Indian husband produces humble Indian children . . . Indian children are subject to depression, are spiritless and fearful and obliged to pay tribute, which though not excessive is regarded as a burden and a stigma . . . ; the majority of Indians have one child only, to satisfy their creative instincts and then take herbs to prevent the arrival of others." Sanchez-Albornoz, ibid., p. 56.

29. Peter Boyd-Bowman, "Negro Slaves in Early Colonial Mexico," *The Americas* 26, no. 2 (October 1969): 136.

30. Bartolome de Las Casas, *The Devastation of the Indies: A Brief Account*, Seabury Press, New York, 1974 (orig. 1542), p. 27.

31. Quoted by Eric Williams, *From Columbus to Castro*, op. cit., p. 43.

32. Introduction by Hans Magnus Enzensberger to Las Casas, op. cit., p. 26.

33. Ibid., pp. 29–30.

34. "But why Africans as the new slaves? Because of exhaustion of the supply of laborers indigenous to the region of the plantations, because Europe needed a source of labor from a reasonably well-populated region that was accessible and relatively near the region of usage. But it had to be from a region that was outside its world-economy so that Europe could feel unconcerned about the economic consequences for the breeding region of wide-scale removal of manpower as slaves. Western Africa filled the bill best." Wallerstein, *The Modern World-System*, op. cit., p. 89. See also Sanchez-Albornoz, op. cit., p. 72.

35. D. Davidson, op. cit., p. 236.

36. See chapter five, note 68 and text.

37. Antonio Vazquez de Espinosa recounts some of the measures used by Spanish colonists to delay the loss of Indian labor: "[A]lthough the Royal Council of the Indies . . . has tried to remedy this evil with warrants and the amelioration of this great hardship and enslavement of the Indians, and the Viceroy of New Spain appoints mill inspectors . . . since most of those who set out on such commissions, aim rather at their own enrichment . . . and since the mill owners pay them well, they leave the wretched Indians in the same slavery. . . . [T]he mill owners keep places provided in the mills in which they hide the wretched Indians against their will, so that they do not see or find them, and the poor fellows cannot complain about their wrongs." *Compendium and Description of the West Indies*, Smithsonian Institution Press, Washington, D.C., 1942 (orig. 1629), p. 134.

38. J. H. Parry, *Cambridge Economic History of Europe*, 4:199, cited by Wallerstein, op. cit., p. 187 n. 109.

39. D. Davidson, op. cit., p. 237.

40. Aguirre Beltran is cited by Rout, op. cit., p. 279. Edgar Love and Rout both call attention to the fact that Baron Alexander de Humboldt, the late eighteenth-century Prussian historical demographer, in his study of Mexico (*Political Essay on the Kingdom of New Spain*, 1793), had remarked "it appears that in all of New Spain there are not six thousand Negroes, and not more than nine or ten thousand slaves, of whom the greatest number belong to the ports of Acapulco and Veracruz." (See Love, "Negro Resistance to Spanish Rule in Colonial Mexico," *Journal of Negro History* 52, no. 2 (April 1967): 89.) Rout commented: "A contradictory picture is presented by Sherburne I. Cook, who was probably the first investigator to make a careful analysis of the 1793 royal census. Cook reveals that Spanish authorities estimated zambos, blacks, and mulattoes at 12 to 15 percent of the viceroyalty's 5,200,000 inhabitants." Rout, ibid.

41. Richard R. Wright, the Black historian, wrote at the beginning of this century: "It was during the year 1501 that Columbus was deposed from the government of the Indies, and he may probably himself have been cognizant of the fact that Negro slaves had been introduced into the new Spanish possessions." "The year 1501 is the date of the earliest reference in American history to Negroes coming from Spain to America. Sir Arthur Helps, in his Spanish Conquest in America, states that, in the year mentioned, instructions were given to the authorities that while Jews, Moors, or new converts were not to be permitted to go to the Indies or to remain there, 'Negroes born in the power of Christians were to be allowed to pass to the Indies.' " Wright, "Negro Companions of the Spanish Explorers," *American Anthropologist* 4, no. 2 (April/June 1902): 218. (Wright's piece bore this note from the editor of the journal: "The interest in this paper is enhanced by the fact that it is the result of research by a native of the race which took such a prominent part in the discovery and colonization of the New World." Ibid., p. 217.)

42. Rout, op. cit., p. 22.

43. Ibid., pp. 22–23.

44. See Rout, ibid.; and R. R. Wright, op. cit., pp. 218–19.

45. Rout, ibid., p. 24.

46. Ibid., p. 75.

47. Peter Gerhard, "A Black Conquistador in Mexico," *Hispanic American Historical Review* 58, no. 3 (August 1978): 452.

48. Ibid., p. 459. Gerhard notes: "Perhaps Garrido died in the great plague that was raging in 1547. On the other hand, someone called Juan Garrido was alive in Cuernavaca in March 1552." Ibid.

49. See R. R. Wright, op. cit., pp. 223–28.

50. Peter Boyd-Bowman in his "Negro Slaves in Early Colonial Mexico," op. cit., pp. 150–51, reproduces Alonso Valiente's formal claim on Juan Valiente from the Puebla archives.

51. Franco, "Maroons and Slave Rebellions in the Spanish Territories," in Richard Price (ed.), *Maroon Societies*, Anchor, Garden City, 1973, p. 36; also see R. R. Wright, op. cit., pp. 220–21; and Rout, op. cit., p. 75.

52. See Georges Scelle, "The Slave-Trade in the Spanish Colonies of America: The Assiento," *American Journal of International Law* 4, no. 3 (July 1910): 619.

53. See Rout, op. cit., pp. 77–79.

54. Ibid., p. 99. C. H. Haring commented: "In early days in the colonies, when fear of servile insurrection was widespread, some of the local legislation regarding Negro slaves was very barbarous." *The Spanish Empire in America*, op. cit., p. 202.

55. G. Aguirre Beltran, "Races in 17th Century Mexico," *Phylon* 6, no. 3 (1945): 215.

56. Colin Palmer, "Religion and Magic in Mexican Slave Society, 1570–1650," in Stanley L. Engerman and Eugene D. Genovese (eds.), *Race and Slavery in the Western Hemisphere: Quantitative Studies*, Princeton University Press, Princeton, 1975, p. 311.

57. Boyd-Bowman, op. cit., p. 134.

58. See Haring, op. cit., p. 206; Rout, op. cit., pp. 104–5; and R. R. Wright, op. cit., p. 222. David Davidson recalls: "[I]n 1523, the first slaves to revolt in the colony erected crosses to celebrate their freedom 'and to let it be known that they were Christians.' " Davidson, op. cit., p. 242.

59. Rout, op. cit., p. 101.

60. Ibid., pp. 104–5.

61. Scelle, *Histoire Politique de La Traite Negriere aux Indes de Castille*, 2 vols., Larose and Forcel, Paris, 1906, 1:167; and Jose L. Franco, op. cit., p. 35.

62. Quoted by Edgar Love, op. cit., p. 96.

63. Ibid., pp. 93, 95.

64. D. Davidson, op. cit., p. 244.

65. Ibid., pp. 145–46; see also Love, op. cit., p. 94.

66. D. Davidson, op. cit., pp. 249–50.

67. Love, op. cit., p. 97. Davidson follows the Jesuit Juan Laurencio in describing Yanga as a member of the "Bron" (i.e., Brong) nation, an Akan-speaking people of present-day Ghana. Laurencio was a member of the expedition led by Captain Pedro Gonzalo de Herrera that succeeded in bringing Yanga's settlement to a truce with Spanish authorities in the early months of 1609. D. Davidson, op. cit., p. 247. Rout asserts that Yanga "claimed to be a Congolese prince." Op. cit., p. 106. See Rout, ibid., pp. 30, 336 nn. 1 and 2 for a discussion of the confusion surrounding the use of the terms "Bron" and "Brarn" in Mexican historiography.

68. Love writes: "During the latter part of the sixteenth century the Spanish had to put down slave insurrections in Pachuca, Guanajuato, Juaspaltopic, Alvarado, Coatzacoalcos, Misantla, Jalapa, Huatulco, Tlalixcoyan, Zongolicia, Riconada, Huatusco, Orizaba, Rio Blanco, Anton Lizardo, Medellin, and Cuernavaca." Op. cit., p. 98. Love also describes the slave rebellion that took place in Mexico City in 1612, ibid., pp. 98–99. Rout observed: "Over a century later, the same general vicinity of Veracruz state, slave uprisings in sugar mills around the town of Cordoba (1725 and 1735) culminated in the mass flight of bondmen and a sudden burgeoning of *cimarron* activity. . . . Meanwhile, on the other coast, especially during the seventeenth and eighteenth centuries, slaves fleeing the Pacific Ocean ports of Guatulco and Acapulco set up *palenques* in the coastal highlands of the *costa chica*." Rout, op. cit., pp. 106–7.

69. See William B. Taylor, "The Foundation of Nuestra Senora de Guadalupe de los Morenos de Amapa," *The Americas* 26, no. 4 (April 1970): 439–46.

70. See Aquiles Escalante, "Palenques in Colombia," in Richard Price (ed.), *Maroon Societies*, op. cit., pp. 76–77; and Rout, op. cit., p. 109.

71. See Miguel Acosta Saignes, "Life in a Venezuelan Cumbe," in Richard Price, op. cit., pp. 64–73; and Rout, op. cit., p. 111.

72. Ennes accepts the rationalization that the enslavement of Blacks was necessary since "the European could not stand the sun. . . . Nor did the Indian submit to the intensive and continuous labor so essential for the progress of these industries." He continues his racialist constructions by praising "the Paulista strain which definitely took the lead, thanks to the heroic and adventurous spirit (*sic*) which they had inherited with their Portuguese background." Ennes, "The Palmares 'Republic' of Pernambuco: Its Final Destruction, 1697," *The Americas* 5, no. 2 (October 1948): 200.

73. Ibid., p. 201.

74. Arthur Ramos, *The Negro in Brazil*, Associated Publishers, Washington D.C., 1951 (orig. 1939), pp. 39–40. Stuart Schwartz maintains: "Through the first three centuries of Brazilian history runs a thread of slave resistance and colonist fear." "The *Mocambo*: Slave Resistance in Colonial Bahia," *Journal of Social History* 3, no. 4 (Summer 1970): 313.

75. A. J. R. Russell-Wood, "Black and Mulatto Brotherhoods in Colonial Brazil: A Study in Collective Behavior," *Hispanic American Historical Review* 54, no. 4 (November 1974): 571. On pp. 573–74 in the same article, Russell-Wood asserts: "The presence of groups of runaway slaves (*quilombos*) and uprisings by blacks and mulattoes (infinitely rarer than the 'running scared' correspondence of governors and town councils would suggest) might be advanced as evidence of psychosocial cohesion among such people. In fact, such alliances as there may have been proved temporary and too fragile to sustain challenge over a period of time." This, and similar comments, as well as reviews of the bibliographic and reference materials for this article and his previous study (*Fidalgos and Philanthropists*, University of California Press, Berkeley,

1968), suggest that Russell-Wood has chosen to ignore or dismiss most of the studies of Blacks in Brazil that have focused on the *quilombos*.

76. Schwartz, "The *Mocambo*," op. cit., p. 317.

77. Representative works of those not cited elsewhere are: Edison Carneiro, *Guerras de Los Palmares* (1944) and *Ladinos e crioulos* (1964); Donald Pierson, *Negroes in Brazil* (1942); and Raymundo Nina Rodrigues, *Os Africanos no Brasil* (1935).

78. Irene Diggs, "Zumbi and the Republic of Os Palmares," *Phylon* 14, no. 1 (1953): 62.

79. R. K. Kent, "Palmares: An African State in Brazil," *Journal of African History* 6, no. 2 (1965): 167–69.

80. Ibid., p. 162.

81. Ibid., p. 172.

82. Ibid., pp. 172–73.

83. Ramos, op. cit., p. 61; see also Diggs, op. cit., pp. 62–70.

84. Ramos writes: "The customs and usages of Palmares were modelled on those of Bantu origin with such changes and adaptations as the needs of a community in the new world required. On this, as well as many other points, our sources of information are inadequate." Ibid., p. 65. Kent, almost a quarter of a century later, concurs: "Assuming that Loanda was the main embarkation point for Pemambucan slaves, which is confirmed by the linguistic evidence, the model for Palmares could have come from nowhere else but central Africa. Can it be pinpointed? . . . The most likely answer is that the political system did not derive from a particular central African model, but from several. Only a far more detailed study of Palmares through additional sources in the archives of Angola and Torre do Tombo could refine the answer." Kent, op. cit., p. 175.

85. Georges Balandier has written: "The procedure of investiture involves the . . . attempt at reinforcement. Thus, in the ancient kingdom of Kongo, it establishes a symbolic return to origins, by means of a ceremonial that associates the new king, the elders and the people, and invokes the founding partners: the descendant of the founder and the representatives of the ancient occupants of the region that corresponds to the royal province, who have become the 'allies' of the Kongo kings. It invokes the spirits of the first kings. . . . It returns to the time of a history that has become myth and reveals the sovereign as the 'forger' and guardian of Kongo unity. The enthronement of the king assures not only the legitimacy of the power held, but also the rejuvenation of the kingship. It gives the people (for a time) the feeling of a new beginning." Balandier, *Political Anthropology*, Pantheon, New York, 1970, p. 114. See also Balandier's *Daily Life in the Kingdom of the Kongo*, Meridian, New York, 1969, chap. 1.

86. Ennes, op. cit., p. 213; see also Kent, op. cit., p. 173.

87. Ennes, ibid., pp. 209–10; see also Kent, op. cit., pp. 173–74.

88. Some indication of the morality to which Ennes refers with approval are the sentiments expressed by Colonel Domingos Jorge Velho while justifying his impressment of Indian natives into his army: "[W]e augment our troops, and with them we carry war to those obstinate ones who refuse to give up; and if afterwards we avail ourselves of them for our plowing, we do them no injustice, because it is that we may sustain them and also their children no less than ourselves and ours; and so far is this from enslaving them that it rather does them an inestimable favor in that it teaches them to plow, plant, reap and labor for their own support— a thing which, before the whites teach it to them, they do not know how to do." Ennes, op. cit., p. 207.

89. Ramos, op. cit., p. 40.

90. Barbara Klamon Kopytoff, "The Early Development of Jamaican Maroon Societies," *William and Mary Quarterly* 35, no. 2 (April 1978): 287.

91. See Irene Wright, "The Spanish Resistance to the English Occupation of Jamaica 1655–1660," *Royal Historical Society, Transactions*, 4th ser., vol. 12 (1930): 111–47 (cited by Kopytoff, op. cit., p. 289 n. 4).

92. See H. Orlando Patterson, "Slavery and Slave Revolts: A Sociohistorical Analysis of the First Maroon War, 1665–1740," in Richard Price (ed.), *Maroon Societies*, op. cit., pp. 253–55.

93. David Buisseret and S. A. G. Taylor, "Juan de Bolas and His Pelinco," *Caribbean Quarterly*, 24, nos. 1, 2 (March/June 1978): 5.

94. Ibid., p. 6.

95. Kopytoff, op. cit., pp. 288–92; and H. Orlando Patterson, *The Sociology of Slavery*, Fairleigh Dickinson University Press, Rutherford, 1969, pp. 267–69.

96. Kopytoff, op. cit., p. 293; and also Patterson, "Slavery and Slave Revolts," op. cit., p. 258.

97. Kopytoff, op. cit., p. 299.

98. Michael Craton, *Sinews of Empire*, Anchor, Garden City, 1974, p. 218; and also Patterson, *The Sociology of Slavery*, op. cit., pp. 185–95.

99. Ramos, recalling the mid-seventeenth-century reports of Palmares, writes: "The population included numerous artisans and a king governed with unostentatious justice, allowing no medicine men or witch doctors among his people." Ramos, op. cit., p. 57.

100. See Mary Douglas, *Purity and Danger*, Frederick Praeger, New York, 1966, pp. 94–108.

101. For an example, see *Return of Trials of Slaves: Jamaica, 1814–1818*, Colonial Office 137–147, Public Records Office, London.

102. Patterson, *Sociology of Slavery*, op. cit., p. 192.

103. See Monica Schuler, *"Alas, Alas, Kongo": A Social History of Indentured African Immigration into Jamaica, 1841–1865*, Johns Hopkins University Press, Baltimore, 1980, pp. 46, 136–37 n. 9; and Craton, *Sinews of Empire*, op. cit., p. 366 n. 67.

104. Escalante, op. cit., pp. 77–78. T. Lynn Smith suggests: "[M]aterials such as the letter dated July 24, 1545, which the Licenciado Miguel Diez Armendariz sent to the King indicate that not only were there already many Negroes in the colony but that not a few of them had got completely out of hand. This official raised grave accusations against the government of Cartagena, alleging that for more than nine years escaped Negroes had been out of control, forcing the Indians to work for them, sacking haciendas, and stealing women. When he wrote the escaped Negroes had just completed an assault upon the Pueblo of Tafeme where they killed over 20 persons, stole the gold and other valuables, destroyed the fields of corn, and carried away more than 250 Indians." Smith, "The Racial Composition of the Population of Colombia," *Journal of Inter-American Studies* 8, no. 2 (April 1966): 229. For the economy of the placer gold region, see William F. Sharp, "The Profitability of Slavery in the Colombian Choco, 1680–1810," *Hispanic American Historical Review* 55, no. 3 (August 1975): 468–95.

105. Rout argues that Benkos was "arbitrarily imprisoned and hanged." Rout, op. cit., p. 110.

106. Escalante, op. cit., p. 79.

107. "Around 1790 a Captain Latorre was trying to survey a road across the highlands from Cartagena into the interior when he came into contact with Negroids, many of whom were descendants of the *palenqueros* of San Basilio who had not accepted amnesty in 1612 or 1613. A number of bloody battles ensued before a settlement was reached. . . . All told, the *palenqueros* from the original settlement of San Basilio had remained completely independent for almost two centuries." Rout, op. cit., p. 110. William Sharp maintains a different historical sense from that of Rout and Smith. Sharp declares: "Cimarrones (runaways) presented a continual problem, and virtually every slave inventory listed one or more slaves as having fled. However, except in 1728, there were no mass escapes, and most of the slaves who ran away in 1728 were quickly recaptured." Sharp, op. cit., p. 480. Since Sharp is relying on official archives, he might have constructively used Licenciado Amendariz's skepticism of official sources (see note 104). As it is, Sharp has no way of explaining Smith's independent support of Amendariz's report: "[I]t is interesting to note that this part of what is now the Departamento of Bolivar is one of the few places in Colombia from which come reports of Negro communities in which the African language, dances, and customs, are still preserved. These small groups of Negroes are said to insist absolutely on endogamous marriage." Smith, op. cit., p. 229 n. 23.

108. Rout, op. cit., p. 112. The following account of Venezuela's slave rebellions follows Rout closely.

109. See Jose L. Franco, op. cit., p. 36.

110. "Today, there are Six Bush Negro tribes: the Djuka and Saramaka (each 15,000 to 20,000 people), the Matawai, Aluku and Paramaka (each closer to 2,000), and the Kwinti (fewer than 500)." Richard Price, *The Guiana Maroons: A Historical and Bibliographical Introduction*, Johns Hopkins University Press, Baltimore, 1976, pp. 3–4.

111. Ibid., p. 2.

112. Both quotes are taken from Price, ibid., p. 9.

113. Ibid., p. 21. Monica Schuler, writing of revolts that took place in Suriname as late as the late eighteenth century, insists on the persistence of ethnicity in the region but is ambiguous about the maroon communities: "In 1757 and again in 1772 large-scale slave rebellions broke out in Suriname. The Akan seem to have played an important role in these, and the Bush Negroes were indispensable to them. The latter revolt dragged on for a number of years with leadership eventually passing to a free-born Maroon." Schuler, "Ethnic Slave Rebellions in the Caribbean and the Guianas," *Journal of Social History* 3, no. 4 (Summer 1970): 379.

114. Price, op. cit., p. 21.

115. Ibid., pp. 22–23.

116. Ibid., p. 24. Price is referring to a report written in 1770 by Jan Jacob Hartsinck.

117. Ibid.; the quote is from L. D. Herlein, 1718.

118. Ibid., p. 26.

119. Ibid., p. 27.

120. Ibid., p. 3.

121. Johannes King, "Guerrilla Warfare: A Bush Negro View," in Richard Price (ed.), *Maroon Societies*, op. cit., pp. 302–4.

122. Quite recently, the history of the Bush Negroes had an interesting closure: "Several times, the Tribal [or Paramount] Chiefs (Granmans) of the Bush Negroes had expressed a wish to journey to West Africa, the land of their origin, in order to re-establish contact. . . . The journey [described here] was offered them by the Government of Surinam and made during three weeks in November 1970." Sylvia W. de Groot, "The Bush Negro Chiefs Visit Africa: Diary of an Historic Trip," in Richard Price (ed.), *Maroon Societies*, op. cit., p. 388. De Groot recorded the following observation by one of the chiefs upon his visit with a Ghanaian

king: "Granman Gazon, speaking in the form of a parable, was to remark: 'A dog is driven away from his yard. His master does not notice it or, at least, pays little attention to it and does not go looking for him to bring him back. When the dog finally gets hungry, he tries to find the way back home.' As he explained his meaning, 'Both the dog and his master (here the king) had fallen asleep for three hundred years. Now the dog is awake and has also awakened its master' " (p. 394).

123. See Rout, op. cit., pp. 119–20; Schuler, "Ethnic Slave Rebellions," op. cit., pp. 378–82; Francisco Perez de la Riva, "Cuban *Palenques*," in Richard Price (ed.), *Maroon Societies*, op. cit., pp. 49–59; and Jose L. Franco, op. cit., pp. 41–43.

124. "The period from 1600 to 1750 was dominated by the efforts of England and France first to destroy Dutch hegemony and then to succeed to the top position. In this long period of relative stagnation . . . the peripheral areas suffered greatly exacerbated exploitation of the direct producers and reduced advantage of the indigenous exploiting strata (reduced, that is, by comparison with similar strata in the core countries)." Immanuel Wallerstein, *The Modern World-System II*, Academic Press, New York, 1980, p. 241.

125. E. P. Thompson first used the term "brigandage" to describe this phenomenon. In 1965, while describing power in England as it assumed form in the second half of the eighteenth century, he wrote: "It should be seen less as government by an aristocracy . . . than as a parasitism—a racket, which the King himself could not break into except by becoming the croupier. It was not wholly a parasitism: the business of the nation had to be carried on, from time to time the 'independent' gentry—and their representatives in parliament—had to be appeased, there were even occasions (although one after another these are called into question as the disciples of Namier break into the archives of the last of the great mafiosi) when the interests of the nation or the class, rather than the family or faction, were consulted. Nor was it only a parasitism: being conducted upon so gigantic a scale, from bases in private and public wealth of such magnitude, and commanding influence which reached, by the most direct means, into the army, the navy, the chartered companies, the Church, the Law, it was bound to congeal into something that looks almost like an estate; to surround itself in a cocoon of ideological apologetics; and to nourish a style of life, of conspicuous—indeed, spectacular—consumption which is associated with a true aristocracy." Thompson, "The Peculiarities of the English," in Thompson's *The Poverty of Theory*, Monthly Review Press, New York, 1978 (orig. 1965), pp. 258–59. For state banditry, see Thompson's later work, *Whigs and Hunters*, Pantheon, New York, 1974, p. 294.

126. "In the westward trade in the first half of the eighteenth century was first of all sugar, and second of all the slaves who made the sugar possible. Britain clearly dominated world commerce in sugar as of 1700, but by 1750 primacy had passed to France." Wallerstein, *The Modern World-System II*, op. cit., pp. 269–70.

127. See F. Nwabueze Okoye, "Chattel Slavery as the Nightmare of the American Revolutionaries," *William and Mary Quarterly* 37, no. 1 (January 1980): 3–28, for a most acute discussion of the paradoxes that bemuddled American nationalists whose outrage "stemmed from their conviction that only black people in America were deserving of servile status" (p. 3).

128. Monica Schuler, "Ethnic Slave Rebellions," op. cit., p. 379.

129. See Forrest Wood's *Black Scare*, op. cit.

130. John Nelson, a late eighteenth-century English Methodist preacher, recalled one of his nightmares: "I dreamed I was in Yorkshire, going from Gomersal-Hill-Top to Cleckheaton; and about the middle of the lane, I thought I saw Satan coming to meet me in the shape of a tall, black man, and the hair of his head like snakes; . . . But I went on, ript open my clothes, and shewed him my naked breast, saying, 'See, here is the blood of Christ.' Then I thought he fled from me as fast as a hare could run." Quoted by E. P. Thompson in *The Making of the English Working Class*, Vintage, New York, 1966, p. 39.

131. Joshua Giddings, *The Exiles of Florida*, Follett, Foster and Co., Columbus, 1858, p. 2.

132. "Slave rebelliousness was a familiar reality in eighteenth-century America. This may explain why most historians who have studied blacks in the colonial and Revolutionary periods have never been drawn into the debate over the creation of docile Sambos that absorbed scholars of nineteenth-century slavery for so long." Jeffrey J. Crow, "Slave Rebelliousness and Social Conflict in North Carolina, 1775–1802," *William and Mary Quarterly* 37, no. 1 (January 1980): 80. See also Herbert Aptheker, *American Negro Slave Revolts*, International Publishers, New York, 1964 (orig. 1943), p. 172, and his "Negro Slave Revolts in the United States, 1526–1860," in Aptheker, *Essays in the History of the American Negro*, International Publishers, New York, 1945, p. 19, for the 1712 New York revolt; for the Stono uprising see Peter Wood, *Black Majority*, Norton, New York, 1975.

133. Gerald (Michael) Mullin, *Flight and Rebellion*, Oxford University Press, New York, 1972, pp. 89–103. Mullin's total is from study of the published advertisements of the period (1736–1801). As such, the figure of 1,500 cannot be taken as any true accounting of the numbers of fugitives during this period. Several historians of slavery, in quite different contexts, have indicated reasons for this: "Not all planters advertised in local newspapers for runaways. An advertisement might set ruthless slave kidnappers on the trail." Leslie Owens, op. cit., p. 87; "[U]prisings appear to have been attempted or planned repeatedly by slaves. For obvious reasons, published sources are irregular on these matters—the *South Carolina Gazette* refrained from mentioning the Stono incident, which occurred within twenty miles of Charlestown." Peter Wood,

op. cit., p. 298; and Herbert Aptheker noted, "The South Carolina *Gazette*, May 31, 1760 remarked: 'Good Reasons have been suggested to us, for not inserting in this Paper any Account of Insurrections, especially at this time.'" Aptheker, *American Negro Slave Revolts*, op. cit., p. 197 n. 98.

134. "[D]uring precisely those two decades *after* 1695 when rice production took permanent hold in South Carolina, the African portion of the population drew equal to, and then surpassed, the European portion. Black inhabitants probably did not actually outnumber whites until roughly 1708. But whatever the exact year in which a black majority was established, the development was unprecedented within England's North American colonies and was fully acknowledged long before the English crown took control of the proprietary settlement in 1720." Peter Wood, op. cit., p. 36. Elsewhere Wood commented: "The thought that newcomers from Africa were the slaves most likely to rebel does not appear to have been idle speculation, for the late 1730s, a time of conspicuous unrest, was also a time of massive importation. In fact, at no earlier or later date did recently arrived Africans (whom we might arbitrarily define as all those slave immigrants who had been in the colony less than a decade) comprise such a large proportion of South Carolina's Negro population. By 1740 the black inhabitants of the colony numbered roughly 39,000." Ibid., pp. 301–2. See also Mary Frances Berry, *Black Resistance/White Law*, Appleton-Century-Croft, New York, 1971, p. 3.

135. Harvey Wish, "American Slave Insurrections Before 1861," in William Chace and Peter Collier (eds.), *Justice Denied*, Harcourt, Brace and World, New York, 1970, p. 84.

136. For the earlier revolts, see Aptheker's *American Negro Slave Revolts*, op. cit., pp. 173–74, 182–91. For the Spanish initiative in the 1730s, see Wood, op. cit., pp. 306–7.

137. P. Wood, op. cit., p. 306.

138. Ibid., p. 308. See also Joshua Coffin, "An Account of Some of the Principal Slave Insurrections," in (no author), *Slave Insurrections, Selected Documents*, Negro Universities Press, Westport, 1970 (orig. 1860), p. 14.

139. Ibid., pp. 308–9, pp. 322–23.

140. Aptheker, *American Negro Slave Revolts*, op. cit., pp. 195–96. Laurens was a wealthy Charleston merchant.

141. See ibid., pp. 17–18. See also *The Negro in Virginia*, Virginia Writers' Project, Hastings House, New York, pp. 174–87.

142. See "Punishment for a Negro Rebel," Documents, *William and Mary Quarterly*, ser. 1, vol. 10, no. 3 (January 1902): 178.

143. Aptheker, *American Negro Slave Revolts*, op. cit., pp. 169–78; and *The Negro in Virginia*, op. cit., pp. 126–27, 140–41.

144. Ibid., p. 179.

145. Allan Kulikoff, "The Origins of Afro-American Society in Tidewater Maryland and Virginia, 1700–1790," *William and Mary Quarterly* 35, no. 2 (April 1978): 238–39.

146. Philip Curtin, *The Atlantic Slave Trade*, op. cit., p. 143.

147. See Mullin, op. cit., pp. 110–12, 129.

148. See Aptheker, *American Negro Slave Revolts*, op. cit., pp. 197, 199–200.

149. The 1790 census figures are cited by Ira Berlin, *Slaves Without Masters*, Vintage, New York, 1974, p. 23.

150. Jack D. Foner, *Blacks and the Military in American History*, Praeger, New York, 1974, p. 8. Michael Mullin writes: "George Washington warned that 'if the Virginians are wise, that arch traitor . . . Dunmore should be instantly crushed, if it takes the force of the whole army to do it; otherwise like a snowball rolling, his army will get size.'" Mullin, op. cit., p. 132.

151. Crow, op. cit., p. 83.

152. Aptheker, *American Negro Slave Revolts*, op. cit., pp. 19–20.

153. "British administrators and Virginia slaves had been well aware of one another throughout the eighteenth century. As the Revolution approached it became increasingly evident to the slaves that the British were white men with a significantly different view of slavery than their masters. Rumors of the Somerset Case, for example, encouraged slaves from even the most remote areas to run away and attempt to secure passage to England. (News of Lord Mansfield's decision, that in effect set free all Negroes brought to England as slaves, reached the colony by the summer 1772.)" Mullin, op. cit., pp. 130–31.

154. Crow, op. cit., p. 89.

155. See Benjamin Quarles, *The Negro in the American Revolution*, University of North Carolina Press, Chapel Hill, 1940, pp. 51–67; Winthrop Jordan, *White Over Black*, op. cit., pp. 302–3; Jack Foner, op. cit., pp. 3–19, 264; and Sidney Kaplan, *The Black Presence in the Era of the American Revolution, 1770–1800*, New York Graphic Society, Greenwich, 1973, pp. 31–71.

156. See Benjamin Quarles, "Lord Dunmore as Liberator," *William and Mary Quarterly* 15, no. 4 (October 1958): 494–507; and Jack Foner, op. cit., p. 15.

157. "The American Revolution brought some specific gains for blacks. Some slaves in fact obtained the freedom promised in return for military service. However, not all slaves who fought for the patriot cause were freed. In 1782 Virginia sold almost all the state-owned slaves in its navy. Blacks elsewhere had to resist

attempts by their masters to re-enslave them upon the expiration of their term enlistment. . . . Ironically, it appears that more blacks obtained their freedom by serving with the British than with the patriots." Foner, op. cit., pp. 17–18.

158. Crow, op. cit., pp. 93–94. See also, Herbert Aptheker, "Maroons Within the Present Limits of the United States," in Richard Price (ed.), *Maroon Societies*, op. cit., pp. 153–54.

159. See Aptheker, *American Negro Slave Revolts*, op. cit., pp. 106–7.

160. T. O. Ott, *The Haitian Revolution*, University of Tennessee Press, Knoxville, 1973, p. 4. "From about the end of the Sixteenth to the end of the Seventeenth Century (1697) when, at the signing of the Treaty of Ryswick, France acquired decisive control of the occidental part of Hispaniola, Haiti, the colony experienced what could be called a 'dark age.'" Alex Dupuy, "Spanish Colonialism and the Origin of Underdevelopment in Haiti," *Latin American Perspectives*, iss. 9, vol. 3, no. 2 (Spring 1976): 27.

161. Ibid., p. 5; and T. Lothrop Stoddard, *The French Revolution in San Domingo*, Houghton Mifflin, Boston, 1914, chapters 4 and 5.

162. Stoddard, op. cit., pp. 50–52; and David Nicholls, *From Dessalines to Duvalier*, Cambridge University Press, Cambridge, 1979, pp. 19–24.

163. Norman Stone, "The Many Tragedies of Haiti," *Times Literary Supplement*, 15 February 1980, p. 161.

164. James, *The Black Jacobins*, Vintage, New York, 1963 (orig. 1938), p. 50.

165. The quote is from Stoddard, op. cit., p. 50.

166. Ibid., p. 51.

167. Ibid., p. 53.

168. Ibid., pp. 62–63.

169. Yvan Debbasch, "Le Maniel: Further Notes," in Richard Price (ed.), *Maroon Societies*, op. cit., p. 145; for other contributions on the maroons in the French Caribbean, see Gabriel Debien, "Marronage in the French Caribbean," ibid., pp. 107–34; M. L. E. Moreau de Saint-Mery, "The Border Maroons of Saint-Domingue: Le Maniel," ibid., pp. 135–42; and Nicholls, op. cit., pp. 24, 31–32.

170. See David Nicholls, op. cit., pp. 24, 261–62; and Ott, op. cit., p. 18.

171. Nicholls, ibid.; James, op. cit., pp. 20–22.

172. For the "Swiss" see James, op. cit., pp. 98–100; and Ott, op. cit., pp. 51–52.

173. See David Nicholls, "A Work of Combat: Mulatto Historians and the Haitian Past, 1847–1867," *Journal of Interamerican Studies and World Affairs* 16, no. 1 (February 1974): 15–38.

174. Nicholls, *From Dessalines to Duvalier*, op. cit., p. 31. Nicholls refers to J. Leyburn's *The Haitian People* (1941), p. 15.

175. Ibid.

176. Stoddard writes: "[W]hen the first rumors reached France of the great negro insurrection of August, 1791, a retired officer of the *marechaussee* wrote an open letter to one of the daily papers, warning against exaggeration. He thinks that the reports then current may be based upon some acute access of the chronic marronage, and he gives a sketch of his own experiences which portrays a state of genuine guerrilla warfare." Stoddard, op. cit., p. 64.

177. James, op. cit., p. 51. James was referring directly to the British historians who concerned themselves especially with British abolition and whose work was specifically addressed by Eric Williams in his *Capitalism and Slavery*, op. cit.

178. This summary of the earliest days of the Haitian Revolution was culled from Ott, op. cit., pp. 47ff; and James, op. cit., pp. 85ff. The final quote is from Ott, op. cit., p. 51.

179. See James, passim.

180. Ibid., pp. 356–57.

181. See Jack D. L. Holmes, "The Abortive Slave Revolt at Pointe Coupee, Louisiana, 1795," *Louisiana History* 11, no. 4 (Fall 1970): 341–61.

182. Eugene Genovese, *From Rebellion to Revolution*, Louisiana State University Press, Baton Rouge, 1979, pp. 95–96.

183. W. E. B. Du Bois, *Black Reconstruction*, Atheneum, New York, 1962, p. 12.

184. See Robert Conrad, *The Destruction of Brazilian Slavery, 1850–1888*, University of California Press, Berkeley, 1972, pp. 281–83; the original source of the figure is Agostinho Marques Perdigao Malheiro, *A escravidao no Brasil*, 1944.

185. See R. K. Kent, "African Revolt in Bahia: 24–25 January 1835," *Journal of Social History* 3, no. 4 (Summer 1970): 335; and Conrad, op. cit., pp. 6–9.

186. Quoted by Conrad, op. cit., p. 13.

187. Ibid., p. 7.

188. Leslie Bethell, "The Independence of Brazil and the Abolition of the Brazilian Slave Trade: Anglo-Brazilian Relations, 1822–1826," *Latin American Studies* 1, no. 2 (November 1969): 117. Joao Pandia Calogeras commented: "For three centuries slaves had constituted the only form of labor and had been the basis of the material progress of Brazil. White labor . . . was almost non existent." *A History of Brazil*, University of North Carolina Press, Chapel Hill, 1959, p. 146.

189. Conrad, op. cit., p. 12.

190. Ibid., p. 13.

191. Curtin, *The Atlantic Slave Trade*, op. cit., p. 29.

192. Bethell, op. cit., pp. 117–18. For the eighteenth-century antecedents for the failure of Brazil's slave population to reproduce, see C. R. Boxer, *The Golden Age of Brazil*, op. cit., pp. 173–75.

193. Bethell, op. cit., p. 118; and Craton, *Sinews of Empire*, op. cit., p. 244.

194. Conrad, op. cit., p. 4.

195. "As repression [of the slave trade by the British government] became stronger, the Brazilian flag ceased to be used and was increasingly replaced by the Portuguese, Spanish, and finally the North American. The last instances of the trade were those of the schooner *Mary E. Smith*, apprehended in the port of Sao Mateus, Espirito Santo, and the *Vickery*, both in 1855." Jose Honorio Rodrigues, *Brazil and Africa*, University of California Press, Berkeley, 1965, p. 174. Rodrigues continues: "American capitalists, ship builders in New York, Providence, Boston, Salem, and Portland, or Philadelphia and Baltimore, profited greatly from the sale of their ships, built—and they knew it—for the trade and sold deliberately for voyages to the coast of Africa" (p. 176).

196. For Britain's role in Brazilian independence, see Bethell, op. cit., passim. For the role of English capital in the Brazilian slave trade, see Eric Williams, *Capitalism and Slavery*, op. cit., pp. 132, 172, 176; Rodrigues, op. cit., pp. 165, 168, 181; Bethell, op. cit., pp. 121, 136; Conrad, op. cit., p. 14; and Alan K. Manchester, *British Pre-eminence in Brazil*, Octagon Books, New York, 1964, p. 258 n. 23.

197. Eric Williams, *Capitalism and Slavery*, op. cit., p. 172. Williams reported: "Brazil took one-twentieth of total British exports in 1821, one-twelfth in 1832; the exports increased two and half times." Ibid., p. 132.

198. Ibid., p. 176.

199. Manchester, op. cit., p. 258 n. 23.

200. In 1827, the Brazilian legislator Cunha Matos had observed: "England aspires to dominate all of Asia, as by means of the settlements and wars that it is undertaking in Africa one must suppose it also aspires to complete dominion over that great region. The countries of both regions have the same commodities and products as Brazil, and as the British must prefer their own territories, they will seek by all means to set up obstacles for us; and to achieve this there is no better way than to deprive Brazil of additional labor: this is the true British policy. I believe with all my heart that Brazil will come to receive cotton and rice from Benguela, wax from China, and sugar from Tonkin: if this does not occur in my time, it will happen in my children's time, who will perhaps remember my prophecy." Quoted by Jose Rodrigues, op. cit., pp. 154–55. Lawrence F. Hill reported: "Some Yankee critics vowed that the British were more interested in securing for British merchants a monopoly of the African trade than in the welfare of the negroes. This was the explanation for the British refusal to destroy the factories along the African coast where all the supplies used in the purchase and transportation of the slaves were stored, for the goods; it was the explanation of the numerous treaties, which were largely of a commercial nature, negotiated by the London government with the African chiefs; it supported the allegation that the British cruisers more frequently made prizes of the slavers after the negroes had been taken on board than before. Other critics attacked the British practice which permitted the negroes liberated by the courts to be bound out to British planters in Guiana and the West Indies for periods of three to seven years. It was hard to see how this system of apprenticeship, which was occasionally extended to three consecutive terms, differed from outright slavery." Hill, "The Abolition of the African Slave Trade to Brazil," *Hispanic American Historical Review* 11, no. 2 (May 1931): 196–97.

201. Cited by Kent, "African Revolt in Bahia," op. cit., p. 335. See also Conrad, op. cit., p. 283; and J. V. D. Saunders, "The Brazilian Negro," *The Americas* 15, no. 3 (January 1959): 271.

202. Kent, ibid., p. 339. Recall, though, that the "Angolas," peoples recruited from an area bounded by the Zaire (Congo) river in the north, the Atlantic on the west, the Dande river on the south and the Kvango on the east, had been responsible for some of the major *quilombos* of the seventeenth and eighteenth centuries Boxer had identified: "The bulk of the slaves classified as 'Minas' were evidently of the Yoruba linguistic group, being Nagos and Geges; but the term also included the Twi-speaking Fanti-Ashanti from further west and the Calabar or Yefik from further east." The Golden Age of Brazil, op. cit., p. 176. Kent maintains that "Nago is known to have been the *lingua geral* of Bahian Africans from the turn of the century until the 1860s when it lost out to Brazilian Portuguese." Kent, "African Revolt in Bahia," op. cit., p. 339.

203. Stuart Schwartz "The *Mocambo*: Slave Resistance in Colonial Bahia," op. cit., p. 333.

204. Writing in the mid-1960s, Jose Rodrigues appears to have confused Brazilian lore and reality: "Despite the variety of tribes represented in Brazil, the Bantus were always preferred because they were less independent, more submissive, more reserved in behavior and loquacious in speech, and more adaptable. They accepted the religion, Christianity, and the social forms imposed upon them. The most characteristic Bantu type was the Angolan. Taller than other Negroes, less robust, they were communicative, talkative, and cordial. Less conformable were the Dahomeyan tribes (Jejes), the most important of which was the Nago, and the Mohammedans, who came mostly from northern Nigeria and were called Males. The least submissive Negroes in Brazil were the Hausas." Rodrigues, op. cit., pp. 44–45.

205. Calogeras, op. cit., p. 156.

206. Rollie Poppino, *Brazil, the Land and People*, Oxford University Press, New York, 1968, p. 167.

207. Kent, "African Revolt in Bahia," op. cit., p. 340.

208. Jose Rodrigues, op. cit., p. 45. Rodrigues, as we shall see shortly, was not entirely accurate. Hausas had participated in only some of these movements.

209. Kent, "African Revolt in Bahia," op. cit., p. 343.

210. Artur Ramos, op. cit., p. 47. For more on African women in Brazil, see Mary Karasch, "Black Worlds in the Tropics: Gilberto Freyre and the Women of Color in Brazil," *Proceedings of the Pacific Coast Council on Latin American Studies* 3 (1974): 19–29.

211. Ramos, op. cit., p. 48.

212. Ibid., p. 44.

213. Kent, "African Revolt in Bahia," op. cit., pp. 351–52.

214. Ibid., p. 355.

215. Ibid., p. 356.

216. Ramos seems to have mistakenly identified the Yoruba's Obgoni society with the Hausa: "It is important to recall that in the planning of the Negro revolts, the secret Hausa societies, called *Obgoni* or *Ohogobo*, played a most significant role." Ramos, op. cit., p. 46.

217. Quoted by Kent, "African Revolt in Bahia," op. cit., p. 344.

218. "In 1747, precisely the year when Beckford called sugar the wheat of the Caribbean, a Prussian chemist, Marggraf, in a communication to the Royal Academy of Science and Literature in Berlin, showed that various kinds of beetroot, the sweet taste of which was already known, contained sugar that could be extracted and crystallized in a fairly simple way. Where the Welsers and the Elector of Brandenburg-Prussia had failed in the attempt to gain for Germany a place in the Caribbean sun, beet sugar indicated that that place was after all unnecessary." Eric Williams, *From Columbus to Castro*, op. cit., p. 135. Williams also notes: "Thomas Jefferson, in his turn, in 1790, looked to maple sugar, produced by child labour, as a substitute for slave-grown cane." Ibid., pp. 134–35. In France, after the Revolutionary and Napoleonic wars, and the loss of her most important sugar colonies, the sugar-beet industry successfully substituted for cane. See W. O. Henderson, *The Industrial Revolution in Europe*, op. cit., pp. 91, 96–97; and Eric Williams, *Capitalism and Slavery*, op. cit., pp. 145–49.

219. Williams, *Capitalism and Slavery*, op. cit., p. 149.

220. Ibid., pp. 150–51.

221. Williams, *From Columbus to Castro*, op. cit., p. 305; and Craton, *Sinews of Empire*, op. cit., p. 244.

222. "In fact, no less than 22,000 slaves were shipped between British West Indian colonies more or less legally between 1808 and 1830." Craton, ibid., p. 271.

223. Ibid., p. 282.

224. Craton, "Proto-Peasant Revolts?," op. cit., p. 109; and Williams, *Capitalism and Slavery*, op. cit., p. 54.

225. B. W. Higman, "Slavery Remembered: The Celebration of Emancipation in Jamaica," *Journal of Caribbean History* 12 (1979): 55–56; and Curtin, *The Atlantic Slave Trade*, op. cit., pp. 52–59.

226. Craton, "Proto-Peasant Revolts?," op. cit., p. 109 n. 30.

227. Mary Reckord, "The Jamaican Slave Rebellion of 1831," *Past and Present*, 40, July 1968, p. 108.

228. Craton, *Sinews of Empire*, op. cit., p. 201; see also Williams, *Capitalism and Slavery*, op. cit., pp. 86–87.

229. Williams, ibid., pp. 87–91.

230. Craton, *Sinews of Empire*, op. cit., pp. 201–2 and pp. 205–6.

231. Ibid., p. 201.

232. Williams, *Capitalism and Slavery*, op. cit., pp. 1345–46, 142–43. C. L. R. James, much earlier, had recognized the same transfer of allegiance: "The British found that by the abolition of the mercantile system with America, they gained instead of losing. It was the first great lesson in the advantages of free trade. But if Britain gained, the British West Indies suffered. The rising industrial bourgeoisie, feeling its way to free trade and a greater exploitation of India, began to abuse the West Indies, called them 'sterile rocks,' and asked if the interest and independence of the nation should be sacrificed to 72,000 masters and 400,000 slaves." *The Black Jacobins*, op. cit., pp. 51–52.

233. Craton, *Sinews of Empire*, op. cit., p. 270.

234. Ibid., pp. 270–71.

235. Craton, "Proto-Peasant Revolts?," op. cit., pp. 101–2.

236. Private letters published under "Negro Insurrection," London *Times*, 5 June 1816.

237. Craton, "Proto-Peasant Revolts?," op. cit., p. 117.

238. Kopytoff, "The Early Political Development of Jamaican Maroon Societies," op. cit., p. 300.

239. Craton, "Proto-Peasant Revolts?," op. cit., p. 105 n. 23.

240. Williams, *From Columbus to Castro*, op. cit., pp. 304–6.

241. "In his speech in the House on 15 April 1831 [Thomas Fowell] Buxton made a telling comparison

between the continuing decline of the slave population as against the increase of the free blacks. He pointed out that in the past ten years the number of slaves in the West Indian colonies, excluding manumissions, had decreased by 45,800. The free Negroes of Haiti had, on the other hand, increased by about 500,000 or more than doubled in 20 years." Richard Hart, *Slaves Who Abolished Slavery*, op. cit., 1:221.

242. See Review, *Proceedings of a General Court Martial held at the Colony House in George Town on Monday the 13th Day of October 1823, Edinburgh Review*, xl, LXXXIX (March 1824): 244–45, 250–53. Also cited by Craton, "Proto-Peasant Revolts?," op. cit., p. 105, n. 23.

243. Craton, ibid., p. 106. For Smith's death see *Proceedings of Court Martial*, op. cit., pp. 268ff.

244. "[T]he general response in Parliament was shock at the rebellion of the Demerara slaves, which seemed to come in response to amelioration measures and to occur on what were regarded as the most benevolently ruled estates." Ibid., p. 109. Omissions in the official report on the rebellion played no small part in orchestrating public opinion; see *Proceedings of Court Martial*, op. cit., pp. 258–59.

245. *Slave Rebellion Trials: Jamaica, 1832*, Public Records Office, Colonial Office (C.O.) 137/185.

246. Mary Reckord believes a number of the instances in the evidence given during the trials "cast grave doubt on the official figure for slaves killed in the rebellion." Reckord, op. cit., p. 121. She is inclined, apparently, toward a higher figure. William Law Mathieson, earlier, had put the figure at "about 400," Mathieson, *British Slavery and Its Abolition*, Longmans, Green and Co., London, 1926, p. 214. Burn agreed with Mathieson's figure. W. L. Burn, *Emancipation and Apprenticeship in the British West Indies*, Jonathan Cape, London, 1937, p. 94.

247. For Henry Bleby, see his *Death Struggles of Slavery*, William Nichols, London, 1853.

248. Reckord, op. cit., p. 120.

249. Craton, "Proto-Peasant Revolts?," op. cit., p. 114. Mathieson observed: "Not many of the whites lost their lives in this conflict—ten killed, two murdered, and one or two burned in houses. When we consider that some fifty thousand slaves had broken loose, acts of cruelty or ill-usage were extremely rare; and there was no truth, or very little, in the stories of the violation of women." Mathieson, op. cit., p. 214. For Jamaica in an earlier period, Patterson had written: "The inflammatory thought of white women being raped by rebelling black slaves seeking racial vengeance rarely spurred men on to gallant deeds. Indeed, there is not one recorded case of rape during the revolts, though several white women were killed." Patterson, "Slavery and Slave Revolts: A Sociohistorical Analysis of the First Maroon War, 1665–1740," op. cit., p. 286. For Brazil, Kent and Schwartz made similar observations, see Kent, "Palmares: An African State in Brazil," op. cit., p. 170; and Schwartz, "The *Mocambo*: Slave Resistance in Colonial Bahia," op. cit., p. 328.

250. Patterson, *The Sociology of Slavery*, op. cit., pp. 282, 276.

251. Reckord, op. cit., pp. 113, 117ff.

252. Ibid., pp. 109–13, 124–25.

253. The elite thesis is Craton's reconsideration of his earlier argument in *Sinews of Empire*; Craton, "Proto-Peasant Revolts?," op. cit. pp. 116–25. The situational factors are among those named by Patterson in his *The Sociology of Slavery*, op. cit., pp. 274–79.

254. Reckord, op. cit., p. 113; and Bleby, op. cit., pp. 125–30. Mavis Campbell argues: "Many of the whites, it was later discovered, had actively encouraged the slaves to believe that they had received their freedom." Campbell, *The Dynamics of Change in a Slave Society*, Fairleigh Dickinson University Press, Rutherford, 1976, p. 171. James Stephen, the Colonial Office lawyer, had made similar remarks, declaring in a Memorandum of 22 March 1832, that "the charge of having fomented discontent among the slaves by a series of wilful, systematic and public misrepresentation of the designs of the English Government, by a course of agitation pursued in defiance of the most evident danger, and by the concealment from the authorities of the indications of the approaching calamity is preferred on grounds which it seems impossible to controvert." Quoted by W. L. Burn, op cit., p. 92.

255. Bleby, op. cit., p. 127.

256. W. L. Burn, op. cit., p. 93.

257. Reckord, op. cit., p. 114.

258. Ibid., p. 112.

259. C.O. 137/185, v.i., 467.

260. Roger Norman Buckley, *Slaves in Red Coats*, Yale University Press, New Haven, 1979, pp. 130–43; Bleby, op. cit., p. 10.

261. Reckord, op. cit., p. 117; Bleby, ibid., pp. 13–15.

262. Ibid., p. 118. After the rebellion's end, marronage appears to have increased, see Bleby, ibid., p. 102.

263. C.O. 137/185, v.i., 540.

264. Patterson uses the lower figure; *The Sociology of Slavery*, op. cit., p. 273. Craton employs the larger figure; "Proto-Peasant Revolts?," op. cit., p. 110.

265. Reckord, op. cit., p. 119. She also notes: "An independent conspiracy was formed among the head people on a small group of estates in Portland, and slaves from estates in St. Thomas in the East near Manchioneal planned to abscond to the bush where they built a hideout village." Ibid., p. 109 n. 3.

Mathieson also notes: "A sort of city of refuge was subsequently discovered in the deepest recesses of the woods, consisting of twenty-one houses, 'completely ready for occupation.'" Op. cit., p. 212 n. 1.

266. Craton, "Proto-Peasant Revolts?," op. cit., p. 110.

267. C.O. 137/185, v.i., 618.

268. "The event which made further postponement of the emancipation issue impossible was the rebellion raging in western Jamaica from the end of December 1831 which was finally suppressed at the beginning of April 1832. Destroying property worth well over a million pounds and coming as it did on the heels of numerous other revolts and conspiracies in other sugar colonies during the previous decade, the Jamaican rebellion was a sure indication that if slavery was not soon abolished from above it would be destroyed from below." Richard Hart, op. cit., p. 223. Reckord argues that the brutal repression laid slavery low: Reckord, op. cit., pp. 124–25.

269. Hart, ibid., and for the 1832 Reform Bill, see E. P. Thompson, *The Making of the English Working Class*, op. cit., pp. 807–12, 818–19; and Izhak Gross, "The Abolition of Negro Slavery and British Parliamentary Politics, 1832–33," *Historical Journal* 23, no. 1 (1980): 65–66, 79–85.

270. Reckord, op. cit., p. 125.

271. W. E. B. Du Bois, *Black Reconstruction in America, 1860–1880*, Meridian, New York 1962 (orig. 1935), ch. 4; and Robert Conrad, op. cit., pp. 184–86, 267–70.

272. Craton, "The Passion to Exist: Slave Rebellions in the British West Indies 1650–1832," *Journal of Caribbean History* 13 (1980): 19.

273. Perhaps the more familiar employment of Gramsci's notion of hegemony as applied to slavery is that of Eugene Genovese in his *Roll, Jordan, Roll*, op. cit. Genovese's treatment of North American plantation slavery as an instance where the master class achieved "command of the culture" (p. 658) has been effectively challenged by Herbert Gutman in *The Black Family in Slavery and Freedom, 1750–1925* Pantheon, New York, 1976, chap. 2, and Lawrence Levine, *Black Culture and Black Consciousness*, Oxford University Press, New York, 1977. Alan Dawley has observed: "If the idea of hegemony cannot be reduced to its ideological or cultural elements alone, might there also be something wrong in Genovese's attempt to appropriate it to explain the rule of slavemasters in terms of 'command of the culture?' During the long history of slavery in North America, the rule of the big planters was maintained through property: first in land, with ownership and inheritance confined to freemen, and second, in the bondsmen themselves, who were chattel, freely bought and sold. . . . Subjugated by race as well as relegated to economic dependency, they could scarcely reach out to ally with poor whites. On top of this they were subject to the lash, the patroller, the brace, the coffle. The masters had gotten along on these terms for 150 years before paternalism flowered on the plantation. Are we to believe that for the generation born after 1830 these severe authoritarian and economic modes of domination disappeared? On the contrary, plantation slavery is the last place to look for a North American example of a hegemonic culture as the basis for class rule." Dawley, "E. P. Thompson and the Peculiarities of the Americans," *Radical History Review* 19 (Winter 1978–79): 49–50.

274. C. L. R. James and George Padmore, "Revolts in Africa," in *The Future in the Present*, Lawrence Hill, Westport, 1977, p. 79. Much of this essay—as well as the quoted observations—first appeared in C. L. R. James, *A History of Negro Revolt* (1938), subsequently published as *A History of Pan-African Revolt*, Drum and Spear, Washington, D.C., 1969, pp. 58–59. Similar observations have been alluded to here: see *Proceedings of Court Martial*, op. cit., pp. 258–59; and Bleby, op. cit., passim.

275. Bernard Magubane, "A Critical Look at Indices Used in the Study of Social Change in Colonial Africa," *Current Anthropology* 12, nos. 4–5 (October–December 1971): 420. See also in the same issue the replies to Magubane and his own concluding comments.

276. Lucy Mair, "Anthropology and Colonial Policy," *African Affairs*, April 1975, p. 194. For more on British social anthropology and colonial administration, see David Goddard (ed.), *Ideology in Social Science*, Vintage, New York, 1973, pp. 61–75; and the articles by Evans-Pritchard, Mary Douglas, Edmund Leach, Lucy Mair, and Rodney Needham in the *Times Literary Supplement*, 6 July 1973; also see Wendy James, "The Anthropologist as Reluctant Imperialist," Stephen Feuchtwang, "The Discipline and Its Sponsors," and Abdel Ghaffar M. Ahmed, "Some Remarks from the Third World on Anthropology and Colonialism," all in Talal Asad (ed.), *Anthropology and the Colonial Encounter*, Humanities, New York, 1973, esp. Feuchtwang.

277. Mair, ibid., p. 192.

278. Ibid., p. 191.

279. Magubane, op. cit., p. 440.

280. James and Padmore, op. cit., p. 70; see also George Padmore, *Pan-Africanism or Communism*, Doubleday, New York, 1972.

281. See Bonnie Keller, "Millenarianism and Resistance: the Xhosa Cattle Killing," *Journal of Asian and African Studies* 13, nos. 1–2 (January/April 1978): 94–111. The narrative of the "evens" begins with the visions seen by a young Xhosa girl, Nongqause, her uncle, the diviner Mhlakaza, and others: "The means for ensuring the arrival of the golden age were surely among the most drastic that had ever been asked of

any people. Total herds of cattle, their most precious possession which symbolized to the Xhosa the continuity, vitality, and wealth of patrilineal kin groups, were to be completely destroyed. The reluctant were assured that destruction of the living herds mattered little since they, and all their ancestors, would return to repopulate the earth. Believers were told to consume all the corn in their storage pits, for on the morning of renewal they would find the pits refilled. The Xhosa were not to cultivate the fields and should sacrifice all poultry and other small stock" (p. 105). See also Edward Roux, *Time Longer Than Rope*, University of Wisconsin Press, Madison, 1964, pp. 32–44; Elias Canetti, *Crowds and Power*, Viking Press, New York, 1966, pp. 193–200; and also J. B. Peires, "Nxele, Ntsidana and the Origins of the Xhosa Religious Reaction," *Journal of African History* 20, no. 1 (1979): 51–61.

282. See David Clammer, *The Zulu War*, St. Martin's, New York, 1973. G. H. L. Le May, *Black and White in South Africa*, American Heritage Press, 1971; Roux, op. cit., pp. 45–53, 87–100; C. L. R. James, *A History of Pan-African Revolt*, op. cit., pp. 63ff; James Stuart, *A History of the Zulu Rebellion*, Macmillan, London, 1913; George Shopperson and Thomas Price, *Independent African*, Edinburgh University Press, Edinburgh, 1958, pp. 419ff; Shula Marks, "The Zulu Disturbances in Natal," in Robert Rotberg (ed.), *Rebellion in Black Africa*, Oxford University Press, London, 1971, pp. 24–59.

283. Gerald Bender, *Angola Under the Portuguese*, University of California Press, Berkeley, 1978, p. 138; Ronald Chilcote, *Emerging Nationalism in Portuguese Africa*, Hoover Institution, Stanford, 1969.

284. Basil Davidson, *The African Past*, Little, Brown, Boston, 1964, pp. 357–58.

285. See Ivor Wilks, *Asante in the Nineteenth Century*, Cambridge University Press, London, 1975; David Kimble, *A Political History of Ghana: The Rise of Gold Coast Nationalism, 1850–1928*, Oxford University Press, London, 1963; R. H. Kofi *Darkwah, Shewa, Menilek and the Ethiopian Empire, 1813–1889*, Heinemann, London, 1975; Harold Marcus, *The Life and Times of Menelik II*, Clarendon Press, Oxford, 1975; Obaro Ikime, "Colonial Conquest and African Resistance in the Niger Delta States," *Tarikh* 4, no. 3 (1973): 1–13; J. A. Atanda, "British Rule in Buganda," *Tarikh* 4, no. 4 (1974): 37–54; Elizabeth Hopkins, "The Nyabingi Cult of Southwestern Uganda," in R. Rotberg (ed.), *Rebellion in Black Africa*, op. cit., pp. 60–132; Ian Clegg, *Workers' Self-Management in Algeria*, Monthly Review Press, New York, 1971; T. O. Ranger, *Revolt in Southern Rhodesia, 1896–7*, Heinemann, London, 1967; D. N. Beach, " 'Chimurenga': The Shona Rising of 1896–97," *Journal of African History* 20, no. 3 (1979): 395–420; Michael Adas, *Prophets of Rebellion: Millenarian Protest Movements against the European Colonial Order*, University of North Carolina Press, Chapel Hill, 1979; and Terence Ranger, "The People in African Resistance: A Review," *Journal of Southern African Studies* 4, no. 1 (October 1977): 125–46, for a sample of the literature on African resistance.

286. T. O. Ranger, *Revolt in Southern Rhodesia*, op. cit., p. 352.

287. Michael Taussig, "Black Religion and Resistance in Colombia: Three Centuries of Social Struggle in the Cauca Valley," *Marxist Perspectives* 2, no. 2 (Summer 1979): 88–89.

Chapter Seven

1. "Atrocities by rebellious slaves in the United States did not occur often. Rebels killed whites but rarely tortured or mutilated them. They rarely, that is, committed against whites the outrages that whites regularly committed against them. Elsewhere in the hemisphere, where maroon wars and large-scale rebellions encouraged harsh actions, reactions, and reprisals, the level of violence and atrocity rose. But everywhere the overwhelming burden of evidence convicts the slaveholding regimes of countless crimes, including the most sadistic tortures, to every single act of barbarism by the slaves." Eugene Genovese, *From Rebellion to Revolution*, op. cit., p. 109.

2. Two observations by Henry Bleby during his investigation of the Jamaican rebellion in 1831 are quite typical: "The hired advocate of slavery, Mr. Bortwick, in his lectures of 1833, which were designed to defend and uphold the system, and cover or misrepresent its cruelties and oppressions, laid much stress on the murders, rapes, and other outrages, said to have been committed by the slaves in Jamaica during the insurrection; and the people of Great Britain were triumphantly referred to these as examples of what might be looked for from them in the event of their emancipation. But very few instances of such barbarities were ever brought before the public properly authenticated." And elsewhere: "I confess I have always regarded it as a singular feature in the history of that period, that so few instances occurred of cruelty practiced towards the whites, whether males or females, who at different times fell into the hands of the blacks. Fifty thousand slaves were, probably, more or less concerned in the insurrection; and amongst these, it may be, twenty—certainly not more—were directly accessory to such acts of atrocity as those which we have described." Bleby, op. cit., pp. 43 and 47, respectively.

3. Returning to the Jamaican rebellion of 1831 and the earlier (1816) Barbados revolt, we are reminded of Michael Craton's description of the repressions that followed. Of Barbados, he wrote: "Roaming slaves were shot on sight and Negro houses burned. . . . Captives were commonly tortured. . . . Convicted rebels were publicly executed in different parts of the island and their bodies—sometimes just their heads—in many cases exposed on their home estates" (p. 102). Things went similarly in Jamaica 15 years later: "Many slaves, including women and children were shot on sight, slave huts and provisions grounds were systemat-

ically burned, and there were numerous judicial murders by summary court martial" (p. 110). Craton, "Proto-Peasant Revolts?," op. cit. The literature of slave resistance and repression abounds in such cruelty. For the English public's reaction, see Bernard Semmel, *Jamaican Blood and Victorian Conscience*, Houghton Mifflin, Cambridge, 1963.

4. Edmund S. Morgan, *American Slavery, American Freedom*, op. cit., p. 309.

5. Ibid.

6. See George Shepperson and Thomas Price, *Independent African*, op. cit., pp. 272–73, 296–97.

7. C. L. R. James, *The Black Jacobins*, op. cit., p. 256; see also Genovese, *From Rebellion to Revolution*, op. cit., pp. 109–10.

8. Frantz Fanon, *The Wretched of the Earth*, Grove, New York, 1963.

9. Genovese, *From Rebellion to Revolution*, op. cit., pp. 9–11. Much of Genovese's argument (chap. 3) rests on the ideology of Toussaint L'Ouverture. Toussaint, however, was neither the initiator, the organizer, nor the ultimate and dominant ideologue of the slave revolutionaries or the colored revolutionists (see David Nicholls, *From Dessalines to Duvalier*, op. cit., pp. 11, 171). And if it is true that Toussaint had achieved the status of a slaveowner himself before the revolution (David Geggus, "Haitian Divorce": review, *Times Literary Supplement*, 5 December 1980), this provides a part of the basis for his attraction to French revolutionary bourgeois ideology (see James, *The Black Jacobins*, op. cit., pp. 91–93). In the present century, Amilcar Cabral has come closest to developing a comprehension of this phenomenon: see Cedric J. Robinson, "Amilcar Cabral and the Dialectic of Portuguese Colonialism," *Radical America* 15, no. 3 (May/June 1981): 39–57.

10. "Lawrence Vambe's two volumes of reminiscences [*From Rhodesia to Zimbabwe*, 1976], dedicated as they are 'To all of my fellow men who died in the cause of Freedom' . . . [draw] on his own memories of life in Chishawasha village when he was a child there in the 1920s to depict a society dominated by recollections of the resistances. . . . He describes how the men of the village would regularly discuss their memories of 1896 whenever a serious general problem confronted the village. . . . The risings of 1896, and the tragic readiness of all too many of the people to lose heart and go over to the enemy, form themes of Shona poetry." T. O. Ranger, "The People in African Resistance," op. cit., pp. 126–27.

11. Mullin, *Flight and Rebellion*, op. cit., p. 42.

12. Ibid., p. 18.

13. "The African [who] don't eat salt, they say they [be] come like a witch . . . those Africans who don't eat salt—and they interpret all things. And why you hear they say they fly away [it is because] they couldn't stand the work when the taskmaster then flog them; and they get up and they just sing their language, and they clapping their hands—so—and they just stretch out, and them gone—so—right back. And they never come back: Ishmael Webster. My grandmother had a grand aunt seventeen years old, and one day she in the kitchen, and she blew on her hand—toot, toot—and she disappear. She didn't eat salt and she went back to Africa: Elizabeth Spence." Monica Schuler, *"Alas, Alas, Kongo,"* op. cit., p. 93.

14. Vittorio Lanternari, *The Religions of the Oppressed*, New American Library, New York, 1965; for charisma, see Cedric J. Robinson, *The Terms of Order*, State University of New York, 1980, pp. 152–59.

15. C. L. R. James, *The Black Jacobins*, op. cit., pp. 20–21, 108–9.

16. Mullin, *Flight and Rebellion*, op. cit., p. 159.

17. Ibid., p. 160; see also the discussion of religion and resistance in Olli Alho, *The Religion of the Slaves*, Finnish Academy of Science and Letters, Helsinki, 1976, pp. 224–34.

18. Amos Tutuola, *My Life in the Bush of the Ghosts*, Faber and Faber, London, 1954.

Chapter Eight

1. Eugene Genovese, "The Legacy of Slavery and the Roots of Black Nationalism," in Edward Greer (ed.), *Black Liberation Politics: A Reader*, Allyn and Bacon, Boston, 1971, p. 43. According to George Rawick, Genovese was a member of the American Communist Party in his youth. Interview with Rawick, winter 1976. The original of Genovese's article appeared in *Studies on the Left* (6, no. 6 [November–December 1966]). In the same issue, Herbert Aptheker, one of the leading intellectuals in the American Communist Party and a major contributor to Black history, took Genovese to task, insisting that he recall that "the white radical historians followed and learned from Negro historians" and that: "There is no 'legend of armed black resistance to slavery.' It is not a legend—though the use of the word 'armed' is disarming. There is the fact of Negro resistance to enslavement—armed and unarmed, that is the great fact and it is not legendary at all." Greer, ibid., pp. 65–66. Genovese has subsequently rehabilitated himself in part (Genovese, 1974 and 1979) but his theoretical presumptions still remain suspect. See James D. Anderson, "Aunt Jemima in Dialectics: Genovese and Slave Culture," *Journal of Negro History* 61 (January 1976): 99–114; Edward Royce, "Genovese on Slave Revolts and Weiner on the Postbellum South," *Insurgent Sociologist* 10 (Fall 1980): 109–17; and David Gerber, "Can You Keep 'Em Down on the Plantation after They've Read Rousseau," *Radical America* 15, no. 6 (November–December 1981): 47–56.

2. See Fernand Braudel, *The Mediterranean and the Mediterranean World in the Age of Philip II*, Harper and Row, New York, 1976, 2 vols.

3. See Isaac Deutscher's comments on Leon Trotsky's "On Optimism and Pessimism, the Twentieth Century, and Other Things," in his *The Prophet Armed: Trotsky 1879–1921*, Oxford University Press, Oxford, 1979, pp. 53–54.

4. C. L. R. James, *Beyond a Boundary*, Hutchinson, London, 1963, p. 43.

5. For the global dimensions of the imperialist impulses of Europe's ruling classes, see E. J. Hobsbawm, *Industry and Empire*, Harmondsworth Penguin, 1968; and Michael Barrett Brown, *The Economics of Imperialism*, Harmondsworth Penguin, 1974. Hobsbawm observes: "[W]ith certain exceptions, capitalism was only beginning to seize hold of the underdeveloped world from the middle of the nineteenth century on, and to engage in intensive capitalist investment there. Very little of the world was actually colonized, occupied and ruled from abroad, the major exceptions being India and what today is Indonesia. . . . In world history this era, stretching from the defeat of Napoleon to the eighteen-seventies, perhaps to the end of the century if you like, may be described as the age of British power. . . . At all events, the moment when world capitalism was entirely successful, confident and secure, was comparatively brief, the mid-Victorian period, which may possibly be prolonged towards the end of the nineteenth century." "The Crisis of Capitalism in Historical Perspective," *Socialist Revolution* 30 (October–December 1976): 81. For the part of Africa in this process, see George Padmore, *Africa and World Peace*, Frank Cass, London, 1972 (original 1937); and R. E. Robinson and J. A. Gallagher (with Alice Denny), *Africa and the Victorians*, Macmillan, London, 1961.

6. M. Perham, "British Native Administration," in *Oxford University Summer School on Colonial Administration, Second Session, 27 June–8 July 1938*, Oxford University Press, Oxford, 1938, p. 50.

7. Oliver C. Cox, *Caste, Class and Race*, Modern Reader, New York, 1970 (original 1948), p. 360. See also George Beckford, *Persistent Poverty*, Oxford University Press, Oxford, 1972, pp. 39ff and 71ff.

8. For instances, see Wendell Bell, "Inequality in Independent Jamaica: A Preliminary Appraisal of Elite Performance," *Revista/Review Interamericana* (Summer 1977): 294–308; Carl Stone, *Class, Race and Political Behavior in Urban Jamaica*, University of the West Indies, Mona, 1973; C. L. R. James, "The West Indian Middle Classes," in *Spheres of Existence*, Allison and Busby, London, 1980, pp. 131–40, and his *The Black Jacobins*, Vintage, New York, 1963, pp. 36–44; Nell Painter, *Exodusters*, Alfred Knopf, New York, 1976, pp. 15ff, 40ff; and David Nicholls, *From Dessalines to Duvalier*, Cambridge University Press, Cambridge, 1979.

9. For examples, see J.-L. Miege, "The Colonial Past in the Present," and Rita Cruise-O'Brien, "Factors of Dependence," in W. H. Morris-Jones and George Fischer (eds.), *Decolonisation and After*, Frank Cass, London, 1980, pp. 43–44 and 283–309, respectively; Ian Scott, "Middle Class Politics in Zambia," *African Affairs* 77, no. 308 (July 1978): 321–34; Lillian Sanderson, "Education and Administrative Control in Colonial Sudan and Northern Nigeria," *African Affairs* 74, no. 297 (October 1975): 433; Cedric J. Robinson, "Amilcar Cabral and the Dialectic of Portuguese Colonialism," *Radical America*, May–June 1981, pp. 39–57; Ras Makonnen, *Pan-Africanism from Within*, Kenneth King (ed.), Oxford University Press, London, 1973, pp. 126–27; and C. L. R. James, "The West Indian Middle Classes," op. cit.

10. One inventory of the illegitimate or "shady" means by which Blacks have accumulated wealth is to be found in E. Franklin Frazier, *The Black Bourgeoisie*, Free Press, Glencoe, 1957; and his "Human, All Too Human: The Negro's Vested Interest in Segregation," *Survey Graphic*, January 1947, pp. 79–81.

11. See George Shepperson and Tom Price, *Independent African*, Edinburgh University Press, Edinburgh, 1958, pp. 242–55, 422–37.

12. This seems to have held true for even Black missionaries. Writing of Alexander Crummell, a prominent Afro-American missionary active in Liberia in the third quarter of the nineteenth century, Wilson Moses observes: "For Crummell, as for most people afflicted with Anglophilism, English speaking culture was a perfectly adequate synonym for civilization. The English language was self-evidently superior, he felt, to any of the indigenous tongues of West Africa. On at least two occasions Crummell was ready to point out that 'among the other providential events the fact that the exile of our fathers from their African homes to America, had given us, their children, at least this one item of compensation, namely, the possession of the Anglo-Saxon tongue . . . and that it was impossible to estimate too highly, the prerogatives and the elevation the Almighty has bestowed upon us, in our having as our own, the speech of Chaucer and Shakespeare, of Milton and Wordsworth, of Bacon and Burke, of Franklin and Webster.'" Moses, *The Golden Age of Black Nationalism, 1850–1925*, Archon, Hamden, 1978, p. 66.

13. A. Victor Murray, "Missions and Indirect Administration," in *Oxford University Summer School on Colonial Administration*, op. cit., p. 53.

14. Arthur Mayhew, "Education in the Colonies," ibid., pp. 84–85.

15. Penelope Hetherington, *British Paternalism and Africa, 1920–40*, Frank Cass, London, 1978, p. 111.

16. Lucy Mair, *Native Policies in Africa*, George Routledge, London, 1936, pp. 168–69.

17. Owen Clough (ed.), *Report on African Affairs for the Year 1933*, Empire Parliamentary Association, Billings and Sons, Guildford, 1933, p. 15. "During the period of colonialism, policies were implemented, particularly in the period between 1920 and 1950, drawing a small segment of the African population into

the non-African orbit. Efforts were particularly made to train a cadre of doctors, lawyers, journalists, religious leaders and intellectuals such as teachers and university staff." Peter Gutkind, "The Emergent African Urban Proletariat," Occasional Paper Series, no. 8, Center for Developing Area Studies, McGill University, Montreal, February 1974, p. 55.

18. Elliot Skinner, "The Persistence of Psychological and Structural Dependence After Colonialism," in Aguibou Yansane (ed.), *Decolonization and Dependence*, Greenwood Press, Westport, 1980, p. 74; see also Henri Grimal, *Decolonization: the British French, Dutch and Belgian Empires, 1919–1963*, Routledge and Kegan Paul, London, 1978, pp. 37–39. P. B. Harris suggested: "What colonial powers experienced (and for the large part did not like) was *elite* nationalism, that is a nationalism built around some powerful westernised African figure, an Nkrumah, a Kenyatta, a Leopold Senghor." *The Withdrawal of the Major European Powers from Africa*, Monographs on Political Science, no. 2, University College of Rhodesia, Salisbury, 1969, p. 4.

19. See Benjamin Quarles, *The Negro in the American Revolution*, University of North Carolina Press, Chapel Hill, 1961; Lerone Bennett, *Before the Mayflower*, Johnson Publications, Chicago, 1964; and Geiss, op. cit., pp. 32–35.

In Brazil and Cuba, the formation of Black petit bourgeoisies was retarded by a number of intervening factors. In Brazil, after the abolition of slavery and the organization of a republican government in the late nineteenth century, European workers were imported to provide the social base for industrialization, partly as a response to the failure of Blacks to appreciate the advantages of exchanging freedom for proletarianization. The liberal Brazilian sociologist, Florestan Fernandes, has lamented: "Seeing and feeling themselves free, the Negroes wanted to be treated like men or, as they saw it, like those who were masters of their own lives. A fatal lack of adaptation on the part of the Negroes and mulattos resulted. The attitude and behavior of the ex-slaves, who conceived of their freedom as being absolute, irritated white employers. The Negroes assumed that since they were 'free,' they could work when and where they pleased. They tended not to show up for work whenever they had money enough on hand to live for a while without working; they especially did not like to be remonstrated with, warned, or reprimanded." Fernandes, "The Weight of the Past," *Daedalus* 96 (Spring 1967): 563. Still, in cities like Bahia and Sao Paulo, a small Black petit bourgeoisie made an appearance at the turn of the century. However, since Black labor was already becoming incidental to Brazilian capitalists, that middle class was not encouraged or systematically nurtured. When they did produce reformist organizations like the *Frente Negra Brasileira* as happened between 1925 and 1935, those organizations were ruthlessly suppressed. It would not be until after the Second World War that a militant Black intelligentsia would re-emerge. See Florestan Fernandes, *The Negro in Brazilian Society*, Columbia University Press, New York, 1969, pp. 210–23; and Anani Dzidzienyo, "The Position of Blacks in Brazilian Society," *Minority Rights Group*, no. 7, London, 1979, pp. 2–11. In Cuba, the social and political bases for the Black petit bourgeois intelligentsia was undermined largely by the contradictions introduced by the revolutionary war against Spain at the end of the nineteenth century. The American military co-opted the revolution into the Spanish-American War. And during the American military occupation of Cuba, which began in 1898, the *Ejercito Libertador* (Liberation Army), three-quarters of which consisted of Black Cubans, was destroyed. See Lourdes Casal, "Race Relations in Contemporary Cuba," *Minority Rights Group*, no. 7, London, 1979, pp. 13–14, and Louis A. Perez, *Army Politics in Cuba, 1898–1958*, University of Pittsburgh Press, Pittsburgh, 1976, pp. 3–9. Reviewing the Cuban censuses of the nineteenth century and the decline of the Black and mulatto population between 1887 and 1899, Kenneth Kiple cannot help but wonder whether still another war was in progress: "Did the unhappy results of Spain's policy of reconcentration fall most heavily on the blacks? Was the war itself more of a racial war than has been portrayed, with black pitted, for the most part, against white? Did the blacks in fact bear the brunt of the fighting?" Kiple, *Blacks in Colonial Cuba, 1774–1899*, University of Florida Press, Gainesville, 1976, p. 81. Lourdes Casal has fewer doubts about a later event in Cuban history that has remained equally obscure. In 1912, the anti-Black movement in part inspired by American influence in Cuba reached a culmination. The suppression of an association of Black voters, the *Partido de los Independientes de Color*, led to armed revolt and "the ensuing racial war, still insufficiently studied, led to a nationwide extermination of blacks of quasi-genocidal proportions." Casal, op. cit., p. 14. This was "the little war of 1912." Casal recalls as a child listening to the stories in her family: "A grand-uncle of mine was assassinated, supposedly by orders of Monteagudo, the rural guard officer who terrorized blacks throughout the island. Chills went down my spine when I heard stories about blacks being hunted day and night; and black men being hung by their genitals from the lamp posts in the central plazas of small Cuban towns." Ibid., p. 12. See also Thomas T. Orum, "The Politics of Colour: The Racial Dimension of Cuban Politics during the Early Republican Years, 1900–1912," Ph.D. diss., Department of History, New York University, 1975 (cited by Casal).

20. Alex Dupuy, "Class Formation and Underdevelopment in Nineteenth-Century Haiti," *Race and Class* 24, no. 1 (Summer 1982): 24.

21. See David Nicholls, *From Dessalines to Duvalier*, Cambridge University Press, Cambridge, 1979, passim; and Imanuel Geis, op. cit., pp. 316ff.

22. For the founding and early years of these institutions, see Leslie Fishel, Jr. and Benjamin Quarles (eds.), *The Black American*, Scott, Foreshaw, Morrow, Glenview, 1970, pp. 160ff; and Arna Bontemps, *100 Years of Negro Freedom*, Dodd, Mead and Co., New York, 1961, passim. Some 75 years after the founding of the first "Negro College," Dean Kelly Miller of Howard University made the following assessment of their political relations: "Dean Miller divided Negro colleges into three types on the basis of the racial composition of their faculties. Lincoln (Pennsylvania) and Hampton were placed in the category of those under exclusive white control. Those with mixed directors and faculty included Fisk and Howard, and those wholly under Negro support and management were identified as Morehouse, Wilberforce, and Tuskegee." Cited by Robert Brisbane, *The Black Vanguard*, Judson Press, Valley Forge, 1970, p. 103. Dean Miller's analysis would shortly be proved a bit naive. The year prior to his complaint (1926), student strikes and demonstrations at Fisk and Howard Universities had led to the installation of Black administrations. Lincoln too underwent some administrative changes during that year as a response to Black student and faculty complaints, though at Hampton, in 1927, the results were less satisfactory. Brisbane, op. cit., pp. 101–11. Despite these concessions, it is clear that a few years later when a Congressional investigation into Communism at Howard University took place, the control of this institution (and probably its sister colleges and universities) was still firmly in the hands of its political and financial benefactors, i.e., representatives and officials of American capital. See Michael Wreszin, "The Dies Committee," in Arthur Schlesinger, Jr. and Roger Burns (eds.), *Congress Investigates*, Chelsea House, New York, 1975; and August Ogden, *The Dies Committee*, Catholic University Press of America, Washington, D.C., 1948, p. 87.

23. Interview with C. L. R. James, Binghamton, New York, Spring 1974.

24. See James R. Hooker, *Black Revolutionary: George Padmore's Path From Communism to Pan-Africanism*, Praeger, New York, 1970, pp. 2–3; and C. L. R. James, *Beyond a Boundary*, op. cit., pp. 17–18.

25. Eric Williams, *Inward Hunger*, Andre Deutsch, London, 1969, pp. 26–30.

26. See Gordon D. Morgan, "In Memoriam: Oliver C. Cox, 1901–1974," *Monthly Review*, May 1976, pp. 34–40.

27. "To me it was all in order and I took it philosophically. I cordially despised the poor Irish and South German, who slaved in the mills, and annexed the rich and well-to-do as my natural companions." W. E. B. Du Bois, *Darkwater*, Constable and Co., London, 1920, p. 10. See also Francis Broderick, *W. E. B. DuBois: Negro Leader in a Time of Crisis*, Stanford University Press, Stanford, 1959, pp. 2–6, for Du Bois's early racial ambivalence.

28. See Michel Fabre, *The Unfinished Quest of Richard Wright*, William Morrow, New York, 1973, pp. 4–30; and Addison Gayle, *Richard Wright: Ordeal of a Native Son*, Anchor/Doubleday, New York, 1980, pp. 2–5.

29. In the summer of 1953, Wright had traveled to the Gold Coast colony (now Ghana) to observe the beginnings of self-government scheduled for July of that year. His recollections of that journey were published as *Black Power* (Harper and Brothers, New York, 1954). In that record, he recalled a conversation with the *Efiduasihene*, Nana Kwame Dua Aware II where he had declared: "I'm black, Nana, but I'm Western; and you must never forget that we of the West brought you to this pass. We invaded your country and shattered your culture in the name of conquest and progress. And we didn't quite know what we were doing when we did it. If the West dared to have its way with you now, they'd harness your people again to solve their problems. . . . It's not of me, Nana, that you must ask advice" (p. 288). I have remarked on Wright's identity crisis in the Gold Coast in "A Case of Mistaken Identity," paper presented to the African Studies Association Conference, Los Angeles, November 1979. See also Gayle, op. cit., pp. 238–44, for the reactions of Wright to his first encounter with Africa.

30. Interview with C. L. R. James, Binghamton, New York, Spring 1974.

31. "European socialism was born of the Agrarian Revolution and the Industrial Revolution which followed it. . . . These two revolutions planted the seeds of conflict within society, and not only was European socialism born of that conflict, but its apostles sanctified the conflict itself into a philosophy. . . . The true African socialist does not look on one class of men as his brethren and another as his natural enemies. He does not form an alliance with the 'brethren' for the extermination of the 'non-brethren.'" Julius Nyerere, "Ujamaa—The Basis of African Socialism," in *Ujamaa: Essays on Socialism*, Oxford University Press, Dar es Salaam, 1979, p. 11.

32. "The working class in a leading nation, therefore, has sufficient reason to walk arm in arm with its oligarchy against the world. On imperialist questions, we should ordinarily expect this class to be nationalistic, because a threat to the imperial position of the nation tends to become a threat to its own welfare. The class struggle thus goes on at home, as I have indicated, for a larger share of the national income. But it is a struggle that tends to stop at the water's edge where antagonisms with rival imperialists and exploited backward peoples begin. The working people of a leading capitalist nation are likely to rise up in wrath against those of their fellows who disclaim the imperialist actions of the government, regarding them as traitors." Oliver C. Cox, *Capitalism as a System*, Monthly Review Press, New York, 1964, p. 194. Of Marxists, Cox declared: "Having accepted the fundamental Marxian postulates on the nature of capitalist society, Marxists cannot go back to Venetian, Hanseatic, Dutch or even early English imperialism for the

essential concepts of the components of that phenomenon. It thus becomes a crucially limiting position which entails procrustean operations in the handling of the facts of modern social change as they relentlessly impose themselves upon us. The rigid ideas concerning the role of industrial workers in modern revolutionary movements, and the earlier Marxian predictions giving precedence to the more advanced capitalist nations in the succession of socialist revolutions, are all derivatives of the theory." Ibid., p. 218.

33. Quoted by David Caute, *Communism and the French Intellectuals, 1914–1960*, Macmillan, New York, 1964, p. 211.

Chapter Nine

1. For a sense of Du Bois's range of interests and activities, see the tributes published by John Henrik Clarke, Esther Jackson, Ernest Kaiser, J. H. O'Dell (eds.), *Black Titan: W. E. B. Du Bois*, Beacon Press, Boston, 1970; the essays in Rayford Logan (ed.), *W. E. B. Du Bois: A Profile*, Hill and Wang, New York, 1971; Daniel Walden (ed.), *W. E. B. Du Bois: The Crisis Writings*, Fawcett, Greenwich, 1972; and, of course, Broderick, op. cit.

2. The second native American intellectual whose name should be included in any study of American Marxist theorists is Sidney Hook. Apparently under the influence of Georg Lukács in his earlier years, Hook published *From Hegel to Marx* in the 1930s. As well, he contributed some useful essays in the attempt to extend knowledge of Marxian thought in the United States. (Cf. "Materialism," *Encyclopedia of Social Sciences*, vol. 10, New York, 1933.) However, he is best know to later generations for his anti-Communism. See Cristiano Camporesi, "The Marxism of Sidney Hook," *Telos* (Summer 1972): 115–28; C. L. R. James, "The Philosophy of History and Necessity: A Few Words with Professor Hook," in *Spheres of Existence*, op. cit., pp. 49–58; and for some clues to Hook's political disaffection, Daniel Bell, *Marxian Socialism in the United States*, Princeton University Press, Princeton, 1967, pp. 139–40. Some 15 years earlier, Lenin had singled out Daniel De Leon for special mention; see *New York World*, 4 February 1919, p. 2; and Arthur Liebman, *Jews and the Left*, John Wiley, New York, 1979, pp. 449–51. Officially in the 1930s, the most prominent American Marxist thinker was Earl Browder, the General Secretary of the American Communist Party from 1930 to 1945: "During his leadership of the American C.I.," his closest friend in Moscow, Georgi Dimitrott, then General Secretary of the Communist International, described Browder as the leading Marxist in the English speaking world. From 1935 to 1945, Browder was praised and revered by the left in the United States almost as fervently as was Stalin in the Soviet Union. His published output would total perhaps two million words." Philip Jaffe, *The Rise and Fall of American Communism*, Horizon Press, New York, 1975, p. 17. For another insider's view of Browder, consult Joseph Starobin's *American Communism in Crisis, 1943–1957*, University of California Press, Berkeley, 1972, passim. Both Jaffe and Starobin were sympathetic to Browder (and wrote after his expulsion from leadership and his subsequent decanonization), and thus prove much more convincingly, though inadvertently, the case for his theoretical shallowness.

3. Since the phenomenon of the collective myth precedes by millennia the emergence of the modern state, and because Western thought has displayed this phenomenon as one of its enduring concerns, the relevant literature is massive. However, there are a number of works spanning a range of disciplines, intellectual traditions and even epistemologies to which one might refer, some are analytical while others are ideological. Each, though, is an attempt to provide proof or at least a demonstration of the thesis that social orders are accompanied by fabulous rationalizations. Among the analytical are Ernst Cassirer's *The Myth of the State*; Murray Edelman's *The Symbolic Uses of Politics*; Sigmund Freud's *Group Psychology and the Analysis of the Ego*; Petr Kropotkin's essay, "The State: Its Historic Role"; Marx and Engels, *The German Ideology*; Wilhelm Reich's *The Mass Psychology of Fascism*; Cedric J. Robinson, *The Terms of Order*; Max Weber, *Economy and Society*. Among those that are less analytical and more ideological are: Robert Dahl's *Pluralist Democracy in the United States*; Hegel's *Philosophy of Right*; Samuel Huntington's *Social Order in Changing Societies*, Seymour M. Lipset's *The First New Nation*; and Plato's *Republic*.

4. The culture of imperialism makes for an interesting case study of the relationship between power and myth-makers. With respect to British imperialism, the following studies are useful; Brian Street, *The Savage in Literature*, Routledge and Kegan Paul, London 1975; Jonah Raskin, *The Mythology of Imperialism*, Dell, New York, 1971; and L. P. Curtis, Jr., *Anglo-Saxons and Celts*, New York University Press, New York, 1968. Street, in summarizing Curtis's discussion of Anglo-Saxonism, points out that Curtis showed "how the historians of the day (Kemble, Green, Stubbs, Freeman, Charles Kingsley and Froude) constantly referred to this racial heritage to explain current history and created genealogies of English royalty, English families, and English customs to support their claims. Popular fiction was able to give dramatic life to these claims by presenting them in terms of concrete characters, whose abilities and actions brought home to the reader just what it meant to be an Englishman. These qualities are brought into vivid contrast with the 'baser' actions and qualities of the 'inferior' races of the world." Street, op. cit., p. 19. See also Daniel A. Offiong, "The Cheerful School and the Myth of the Civilizing Mission of Colonial Imperialism," *Pan-African Journal* 9, no. 1 (1976): 35–54.

5. Ferdinand Lundberg's *Cracks in the Constitution*, Lyle Stuart, New York, 1980, is the latest contribution to the literature that examines the American "Founding Fathers." In his review essay of Lundberg, Gore Vidal observed: "The state legislatures accredited seventy-four men to the convention. Fifty-five showed up that summer. About half drifted away. Finally, 'no more than five men provided most of the discussion with some seven more playing fitful supporting roles.' Thirty-three framers were lawyers (already the blight had set in); forty-four were present or past members of Congress; twenty-one were rated rich to very rich—Washington and the banker Robert Morris (soon to go to jail where Washington would visit him) were the richest; 'another thirteen were affluent to very affluent'; nineteen were slave owners; twenty-five had been to college (among those who had *not* matriculated were Washington, Hamilton, Robert Morris, George Mason—Hamilton was a Columbia drop-out). Twenty-seven had been officers in the war; one was a twice-born Christian—the others tended to deism, an eighteenth-century euphemism for agnosticism or atheism." Vidal, "The Second American Revolution?," *The New York Review of Books*, 5 February 1981, pp. 37–38. With respect to the Constitution, Vidal maintains: "The Framers wanted no political parties—or factions. It was their view that all right-minded men of property would think pretty much alike on matters pertaining to property. To an extent, this was—and is—true." Ibid., p. 41. See also Charles Beard, "Neglected Aspects of Political Science," *American Political Science Review* 43 (April 1948): 222.

6. See Frances Fitzgerald, *America Revised*, Vintage Books, New York, 1980.

7. "The removal of the Indians was explained by Lewis Cass—Secretary of War, governor of the Michigan territory, minister to France, presidential candidate: 'A principle of progressive improvement seems almost inherent in human nature. . . . We are all striving in the career of life to acquire riches of honor, or power, or some other object, whose possession is to realize the day dreams of our imaginations; and the aggregate of these efforts constitutes the advance of society. But there is little of this in the constitution of our savages.'" Howard Zinn, *A People's History of the United States*, Harper and Row, New York, 1980, p. 130. Cass, like his predecessor in what was termed at the time "Indian removal," was responsible for the expropriation of millions of acres from native Americans, thus promoting "their interest against their inclination." Moreover, "Cass—pompous, pretentious, honored (Harvard gave him an honorary doctor of laws degree in 1836, at the height of Indian removal) claimed to be an expert on the Indians. But he demonstrated again and again, in Richard Drinnon's words (*Violence in the American Experience: Winning the West*), a 'quite marvellous ignorance of Indian life'" (ibid.). Of the official legend surrounding Andrew Jackson, one of Cass's predecessors, Zinn writes: "The leading books on the Jacksonian period, written by respected historians (*The Age of Jackson* by Arthur Schlesinger; *The Jacksonian Persuasion* by Marvin Mayers), do not mention Jackson's Indian policy, but there is much talk in them of tariffs, banking, political parties, political rhetoric. If you look through high school textbooks and elementary school textbooks in American history you will find Jackson the frontiersman, soldier, democrat, man of the people—not Jackson the slaveholder, land speculator, executioner of dissident soldiers, exterminator of Indians." Ibid., pp. 128–29.

8. See Dee Brown, *Bury My Heart at Wounded Knee*, Holt, Rinehart and Winston, New York, 1971; Vine Deloria, Jr., *Custer Died for Your Sins*, Macmillan, New York, 1969; and David Bidney, "The Idea of the Savage in North American Ethnohistory," *Journal of the History of Ideas* 15, no. 2 (1954): 322–27.

9. Wesley Frank Craven, *White, Red, and Black*, University Press of Virginia, Charlottesville, 1971, p. 84.

10. For an excellent expose of the contemporary industry of pseudoscientific racism, see "Racism, Intelligence and the Working Class," published by the Party for Workers Power, Boston, n.d. (but after 1973); and Thomas Gossett, *Race: The History of an Idea in America*, Southern Methodist University Press, Dallas, 1963.

11. W. E. B. Du Bois, *Black Reconstruction in America, 1860–1880*, World Publishing, Cleveland, 1969 (original 1935), p. 718. Thirty years after Du Bois, the controversy surrounding the "Dunning school" was still unresolved. In 1967, Gerald Grob and George Billias would declare: "Underlying the interpretation of the Dunning school were two important assumptions. The first was that the South should have been restored to the union quickly and without being exposed to Northern vengeance. . . . Secondly, responsibility for the freedmen should have been entrusted to white Southerners. The Negro, these historians believed, could never be integrated into American society on an equal plane with whites because of his former slave status and inferior racial characteristics." Gerard N. Grob and George A. Billias (eds.), *Interpretations of American History*, Free Press, New York, 1967, 1:472. On the other hand, Dunning et al. still had their apologists. Wendell Holmes Stephenson suggested: "Southern enthusiasts brought sectional history into better balance, but they, like their predecessors ['north-easterners'], neglected the role of the Negro, and very early in their careers closed their minds to anthropological scholarship." Stephenson, *Southern History in the Making*, Louisiana State University Press, Baton Rouge, 1964, p. 250.

12. Du Bois, ibid., p. 723. In 1939, Francis Simpkins would echo Du Bois's judgment: "A biased interpretation of Reconstruction caused one of the most important political developments in the recent history of the South, the disfranchisement of the blacks. The fraud and violence by which this objective was first obtained was justified on a single ground: the memory of the alleged horrors of Reconstruction. Later, amid a flood of oratory concerned with this memory, the white rulers of the South, in constitutional

conventions of the 1890s and 1900s, devised legal means to eliminate the Negro vote. 'Reconstruction,' asserted the prime justifier of this act, 'was this villainy, anarchy, misrule and robbery, and I cannot, in any words that I possess, paint it.' These words of Ben Tillman were endorsed by all shades of white opinion from Carter Glass, Henry W. Grady, and Charles B. Aycock to Tom Watson, Hoke Smith, and James K. Vardaman." Simpkins in Grob and Billias, op. cit., p. 499. For Dunning's and Burgess's contributions to the development of American political science, see Bernard Crick, *The American Science of Politics*, Routledge and Kegan Paul, London, 1959, pp. 26–31, 135–37; and Albert Somit and Joseph Tannenhaus, *The Development of (American) Political Science: From Burgess to Behavioralism*, Allyn and Bacon, Boston, 1967, ch. 3. For an earlier lionization of Dunning, see Charles Merriam, "William Archibald Dunning," in Howard W. Odum (ed.), *American Masters of Social Science*, Holt, New York, 1927, pp. 131–45.

13. Quoted by Raphael Samuel, "British Marxist Historians," *New Left Review* 124 (March/April 1980): 28. Rainboro is also spelled Rainborough.

14. Zinn, op. cit., p. 247.

15. Nell Irwin Painter, *Exodusters: Black Migration to Kansas After Reconstruction*, Alfred Knopf, New York, 1976, pp. 15ff.

16. Douglas Daniels, *Pioneer Urbanites*, Temple University Press, Philadelphia, 1980, p. 44.

17. "The new cause was defined as 'white supremacy'—which in practice allowed Southern whites to reduce the freedmen to an inferior caste, as they had attempted to do by enacting the 'Black Codes' of 1865. To further this cause in 1868, [John Van Evrie simply reissued his book *Negroes and Negro 'Slavery'* with a topical introduction and under the new title *White Supremacy and Negro Subordination*. [Josiah] Nott also entered the Reconstruction controversy. In an 1866 pamphlet he reasserted the 'scientific' case for inherent black inferiority as part of an attack on the Freedmen's Bureau and other Northern efforts to deal with the Southern race question," and so on. George Frederickson, *The Black Image in the White Mind*, Harper and Row, New York, 1971, p. 187. Of course the new cause was not entirely monopolized by "Southern whites," as the ambiguous phrase goes; see Lawanda and John H. Cox, "Negro Suffrage and Republican Politics: The Problem of Motivation in Reconstruction Historiography," in Frank Otto Gatell and Allen Weinstein (eds.), *American Themes: Essays in Historiography*, Oxford University Press, New York, 1968, pp. 232–60. Forrest Wood also makes this clear in his study of the *post-bellum* period, *Black Scare: the Racist Response to Emancipation and Reconstruction*, University of California Press, Berkeley, 1968, pp. 30–36, though he is also capable of obfuscation on his own part: "The political exploitation of racism in the United States did not originate during the 1860s. But there was a difference between ante-bellum bigotry and the bigotry that followed the Emancipation Proclamation. Before the war there had been little reason for arousing hatred against Negroes because most of them had been slaves. Since, by law, they had been subordinate to whites, there had been little need to launch crusades for the purpose of keeping them in their 'place' " (p. 16). Implicit in Wood's casual absurdity is the assumption of Black passivity to oppression and more; the excision of the contradictions embodied in the exploitation of African and European labor; the dismissal of the political confrontation between agrarian capital and manufacturing capital in the late eighteenth century; the ignoring of the extensive period of rationalization of the slave trade; and the dropping of the Abolition movement from history. It was hardly the case, as Wood suggests, that the "Anglo-Saxon self-image was a sleeping giant that needed only to be aroused." Ibid., p. 16.

18. "Many of the most influential of our early university professors of American history were German-trained, and from their German professors they had taken over much of the Teutonic view of history. . . . This, of course, was a racist concept of history and it should be said that by no means all our historians accepted it. But many of them did." Wesley Frank Craven, *The Legend of the Founding Fathers*, Cornell University Press, Ithaca, 1956, p. 175. "At the turn of the century the American public and the academic community in general, moved by both international and domestic social trends that emphasized the progress of Western Teutonism as opposed to the backwardness of the colored races, had come to believe the extreme theories of black inferiority, and had accepted the disfranchisement and social regimentation of Southern Negroes. The allegedly sordid spectacle of black participation in Reconstruction was advanced as public exhibit number one that Negroes were incapable of political sophistication; social scientists and fiction writers presented a formidable array of racist material that convinced a receptive white America of the innate cultural and moral inferiority of blacks." William C. Harris in his introduction to John R. Lynch's *The Facts of Reconstruction*, Bobbs-Merrill, Indianapolis, 1970 (orig. 1913), pp. vi–vii.

19. For the earliest reactions of the Black petit bourgeoisie to racial fantasy and the Reconstruction, see the discussion of Charlotte Forten, Robert G. Fitzgerald, T. Thomas Fortune, John Wallace, and John Lynch in Daniel Savage Gray, "Bibliographic Essay: Black Views on Reconstruction," *Journal of Negro History* 58, no. 1 (January 1973): 73–85; and Allen W. Jones, "The Black Press in the 'New South': Jesse C. Duke's Struggle for Justice and Equality," *Journal of Negro History* 64, no. 3 (Summer 1979): 215–28. Duke, the editor of the Black newspaper, the Montgomery *Herald*, was not above swinging his cudgel at the most vulnerable appendage of racist white males. In one of his last editorials in Montgomery he attacked a recent lynching of a Black man by suggesting that the lynchers ask themselves: "Why is it that white women attract negro men now more than in former days?. . . . There is no secret to this thing, and we greatly suspect it is

the growing appreciation of the white Juliet for the colored Romeo, as he becomes more intelligent and refined." Ibid., p. 221. Having made his point, he promptly left town.

20. W. Augustus Low maintains that William C. Nell, writing in the mid-nineteenth century, was the first Afro-American to produce "nonslave" historical accounts, but that George W. Williams "was regarded as 'the most eminent Negro historian in the world' in his day. His book, *A History of the Negro Troops in the War of Rebellion, 1861–1865* (1888), for example, long remained distinctively in a class by itself." Low, "Historians," in W. Augustus Low and Virgil Cloft (eds.), *Encyclopedia of Black America*, McGraw-Hill, New York, 1981, p. 440. Williams is also discussed in more detail in Earl(ie) E. Thorpe, *Black Historians*, William Morrow, New York, 1970. Geiss discusses William W. Brown's earlier work; Geiss, op. cit., pp. 107–8.

21. John E. Bruce, for instance, in his address to a Philadelphia audience in October 1877, "Reasons Why the Colored American Should Go to Africa," spoke as a committed journalist: "For centuries the colored race has not been highly educated. This has not always been the fact, and history, which shows what has been done proves what may yet be. The Africans held possession of southern Egypt when Isaiah wrote, 'Ethiopia shall soon stretch out her hands unto God.' When the Queen of Sheba brought added wealth to the treasures of Solomon, and when a princely and learned Ethiopian became a herald of Christ before Paul the Hebrew, Cornelius, or the European soldiers were converted. The race to whom had been given the wonderful continent of Africa, can be educated and elevated to wealth, power and station among the nations of the earth." Philip S. Foner (ed.), *The Voice of Black America*, Capricorn, New York, 1972, 1:490. See also Moses, op. cit., p. 198.

22. George Washington Williams, *A History of the Negro Race in America from 1619 to 1880*, 2 vols., G. P. Putnam's Sons, New York, 1883.

23. This paradigm was already being vented with respect to the African continent; see the discussion of Alexander Crummell in Wilson Moses, op. cit., pp. 59–82; and David McBride, "Africa's Elevation and Changing Racial Thought at Lincoln University, 1854–1886," *Journal of Negro History* 62, no. 4 (October 1977): 363–77.

24. In an essay published in 1903 entitled "The Talented Tenth," Du Bois went to great pains to establish the fact of the existence of an educated and propertied Black elite in the United States. In it, he briefly described the history of the 34 Black colleges and universities in existence at that time, and gave some indication of the status of their curricula; he reported on the total number of Black graduates from white and Black colleges from 1876 to 1899, and gave a representative sampling of their occupations, and an estimate of their property. See Julius Lester (ed.), *The Seventh Son: The Thought and Writings of W. E. B. Du Bois*, Vintage, New York, 1971, 1:391–95; and for the beginnings of a post-Reconstruction entrepreneurial class in the South, Manning Marable, *Blackwater*, Black Praxis Press, Dayton, 1981, pp. 53–68; and Moses, op. cit., pp. 89–90.

25. A useful instance demonstrating the psychological distance traversed by the Black middle class is given by Jeremiah Moses in his discussion of the Black women's club movement in the late nineteenth century: "The club movement among Afro-American woman (*sic*) had its beginnings in the early 1800s with the formation of groups in those cities of the United States where the black middle class was large enough to provide a membership. 'As a general rule,' says Fannie Barrier Williams, 'those who, in the proper sense, may be called the best women in the communities where these clubs were organized, became interested and joined in the work of helpfulness.' Mrs. Williams saw this as a refutation of the charge that 'colored women of education and refinement had no sympathetic interest in their own race.' " Moses, op. cit., p. 105.

26. See Marable, op. cit., pp. 60–61; and Du Bois's description of the "Tuskegee Machine," in the text, note 43.

27. Of the early Ku Klux Klan, Allan Trelease writes: "Klan membership throughout the South resembled that in Tennessee; it was drawn from every rank and class of white society. . . . The maintenance of white supremacy, and the old order generally, was a cause in which white men of all classes felt an interest." *White Terror*, Harper Torchbooks, New York, 1971, p. 51. "Leadership within the organization more clearly belonged to the professional and planter class which had governed the region before the Radicals displaced them politically, but their economic and social power was hardly affected." Ibid., p. 296. On the level of Federal law and Constitutionally guaranteed rights, the story was the same: "If by 1890 it had become clear to the American Negro that he could not expect to obtain justice and fair play through the regular political processes of the national and state governments it would soon become equally clear to him that he could not expect much more from the courts of the land and especially the United States Supreme Court." Brisbane, op. cit., p. 25.

28. One Black spokesman, William Hooper Councill, expressed a mistaken notion that has long survived him: "Councill had a grotesquely exaggerated idea of white racial solidarity. He assumed that the whites had a great sense of loyalty to and respect for one another, and especially for the weaker members of their race. 'I honor the white man because he honors himself,' said Councill. 'I honor him because he places his mother, sister, wife and daughter on a platform up among the stars, gets a thousand Gatling guns, and

decrees death to him who seeks to drag them down. I honor him because he throws his powerful arms around every little red-headed freckled-face, poor white girl and boy in the land and makes the way possible for them to rise in the world.' This, of course, was pure nonsense in an age characterized by the degradation of labor and the exploitation of women and children by the forces of free enterprise." Moses, op. cit., p. 76.

29. The first draft of this chapter contained the term "Teutonic" here but it was thought it might misdirect rather than clarify. Still, Moses indicates that both Crummell and Edward Wilmot Blyden, the Americo-Liberian born in the Virgin Islands, were quite conscious of Germanic models. Moses, op. cit., p. 281 n. 24.

30. Ibid., pp. 70–71.

31. Ibid., p. 198.

32. Ibid., p. 73.

33. Ibid., pp. 103–31. Du Bois discusses his own and the relationship of other Boston Black intellectuals to Mrs. Ruffin in *The Autobiography of W. E. B. Du Bois*, International Publishers, n.p., 1968, pp. 136–37; he also discussed Margaret Murray, a classmate at Fisk and the third wife of Booker T. Washington, ibid., p. 112. See also for Margaret Washington, Bontemps, op. cit., pp. 137–38, 167.

34. "It was thinking on this order that led to the militarization of the black academic experience in such institutions as Hampton and Tuskegee, where not only were trades taught, but a thoroughgoing military-industrial organization of community life was enforced." Moses, op. cit., p. 75.

35. Ibid., pp. 214–15.

36. Ibid., p. 73.

37. The search for and designation of the seminal figure should have been by this time recognized as a frequently misconceived and reductionist venture. This seems particularly the case when ideas and ideology are the subject of investigation. Whether codified in a didactic or scholastic literature or manifest in social collectives, the elements of consciousness and thought are generally shared by force of circumstance, social and historical continuity, language, culture, and interest. Individual achievement may be seen as the culmination of a collective momentum marked by extraordinary circumstance (imagination, location, etc.). As such it is likely it is being replicated or in the process of coming into being elsewhere, either simultaneously or otherwise.

38. See Thorpe, op. cit.

39. "Blyden was one of a few Negroes to make a significant impact on the English-speaking literary and scholastic world in the nineteenth century. . . . Basically, his writings were designed to vindicate the Negro race. His major themes were: that the Negro race did have past achievements of which it could be proud, that it had special inherent attributes which it should strive to project in a distinctive 'African Personality,' that African culture—its customs and institutions—were basically wholesome and should be preserved; and finally, that Christianity had a retarding influence upon the Negro, while that of Islam had been salutary—his most controversial theme, and one on which he wrote at length." Hollis Lynch, *Edward Wilmot Blyden: Pan-Negro Patriot, 1832–1912*, Oxford University Press, London, 1970, pp. 54–55; see also Moses, op. cit., pp. 42–45.

40. Moses, op. cit., pp. 134–36; see also August Meier, "The Paradox of W. E. B. Du Bois," in Logan, op. cit., p. 83; and Broderick, op. cit., pp. 52–54. The "Conservation of Races" is republished in the collection of writings edited by Julius Lester, Du Bois, *The Seventh Son*, op. cit., pp. 176–87.

41. Du Bois, "The Talented Tenth," in *The Seventh Son*, op. cit., p. 385.

42. *The Autobiography of W. E. B. Du Bois*, op. cit., pp. 236–37.

43. Ibid., p. 239. Robert Brisbane, who as a political scientist at Morehouse College should know this history intimately, supports Du Bois: "[Washington's] opinions were widely publicized and his patrons, which included philanthropists such as Andrew Carnegie, Jacob Schiff, and Julius Rosenwald, contributed hundreds of thousands of dollars to Tuskegee Institute. In time, it became difficult for any Negro college or institution to obtain funds from philanthropists if Washington withheld his approval. . . . [T]his point was . . . driven home to John Hope during his first years as president of Morehouse College." Brisbane, op. cit., p. 32.

44. "[W]hen placed in their historical setting, it is easy enough to explain how it was that the social philosophy of the Negro historians, sadly lacking in a grasp of the dynamic forces, turned out to be the rather naive Emersonian gospel of self-reliance, simple optimism and patient regard for destiny. Notwithstanding all that has been said, let us not be misunderstood. We have little quarrel with these chroniclers gone by. They served their day and in that day few men in America realized what was going on . . . when we see the story of the Negro since Emancipation as the record of the clashes and rationalizations of individual and group impulse against an American social order of an unfolding capitalism, within which operates semi-articulate arrangements and etiquettes of class and caste, we begin to understand." Reddick, "A New Interpretation for Negro History," *Journal of Negro History* 21, no. 1 (January 1937): 26–27.

45. Washington, in any case, was not bound by any manner of class courtesy when his political position was threatened. He manipulated the Negro press through those newspapers he subsidized or owned

(which included the *New York Age*, the *Washington Colored American*, *Alexander's Magazine* and the Washington *Bee*—see Brisbane, op. cit., p. 38), and had resort to more insidious methods: "Washington began plotting the destruction of the Niagara Movement from the very day of its inception. He planted spies and informers within the group and actually sought to encourage dissension and division. And through the use of his considerable influence over the editors and publishers of Negro newspapers, he was able to effectuate at least a partial blackout of news of the Niagara Movement within the Negro press." Ibid., p. 41. Du Bois characterized the method of the Tuskegee-fronted structure of domination "monstrous and dishonest." Du Bois, *The Autobiography*, op. cit., p. 247.

46. Du Bois, *The Autobiography*, op. cit., p. 238. Some of the care with which Washington and his image were treated by American capitalism is apparent in most biographies of the man, generally inserted as a demonstration of influence over the capitalists who subsidized him! They made certain that a steady stream of publications, lectures, and letters were seen to come from his hand by subsidizing "ghost writers"; Carnegie insured an income for life for Washington and his third wife; and they set beside him as his personal secretary, Emmett Scott, a man schooled in Black political patronage. See Bontemps, op. cit., and Louis R. Harlan, *Booker T. Washington: The Making of a Black Leader*, Oxford University Press, New York, 1972. That their solicitousness with respect to Washington as an instrument of domination of the Black petit bourgeoisie intelligentsia was substantially well placed is perhaps proven by the directions taken by the next generation of that strata. Twelve years after Washington's death in 1915, Black students were in revolt at Negro institutions of higher education. See Brisbane, op. cit., pp. 101–11. By the 1930s, the scientist, George Washington Carver, the "folk saint" of Tuskegee and a large part of the substantiation of Washington's rationalizations on race, was embittered enough by his experiences in the South and elsewhere in the country to send some of his best students to the Soviet Union and prescribe poisons for radical activist friends who might use them as the less painful death in confrontation with white mobs. Linda O. Hines, "White Mythology and Black Duality: George W. Carver's Response to Racism and the Radical Left," *Journal of Negro History* 62, no. 2 (April 1977): 134–46.

47. "Populism had put in the minds of blacks certain higher expectations of life, and these could not be beaten out by the boots of any Secret Nine or Red Shirts or other terrorist groups. Incorporated into the blacks' past by 1900 were not only the heady power given to them and protected for them by Reconstruction governments but the more sober experience of Populism. In the Populist movement black people got a sense of being equal participants in the political process, rather than mere recipients of federal favors; of gaining their ends by the power of the vote. Numbers of blacks had worked and socialized with white people of similar interests on a level of relative equality if not actual integration; had had the experiences of organizing and campaigning, of committee work, party politics, national conventions; of listening to and talking and reading about advanced economic ideas such as co-operatives and unions. They could not have come out of the movement unchanged in their hopes and goals." Florette Henri, *Black Migration*, Anchor Press, Garden City, 1976, pp. 10–11. For Populism, see Zinn, op. cit., pp. 280–89; Henri, op. cit., pp. 3–12; and C. Vann Woodward, *Tom Watson: Agrarian Rebel*, Oxford University Press, New York, 1963.

48. See Ira Katznelson, *Black Men, White Cities*, Oxford University Press, London, 1973, pp. 106–8.

49. "In the 1880s, when data on lynching were first collected, reports showed more whites lynched than blacks; the figures for lynch victims from 1882 to 1888 showed 595 whites and 440 blacks. By 1889 the trend had reversed, and in the 1890s lynching of blacks soared as the ultimate expression of Jim Crow [segregation]" Henri, op. cit., p. 43. Henri continues, "Figures . . . show that of all Negroes lynched between 1889 and 1941, less than 17 per cent were even charged with rape. Murder and felonious assault were the most usual charges . . . with rape the second most frequent. Among other offenses for which blacks were lynched were . . . insulting a white woman, writing to or paying attention to white women, proposing to or eloping with a white woman . . . testifying in court for another black or against a white, practicing voodoo, slapping a child, throwing stones, rioting, introducing smallpox, or disobeying ferry regulations." Ibid. "From 1885 to 1927, according to figures published in the World Almanac, 3,226 Negroes were lynched in the United States. During the same period 1,047 white persons were lynched in the United States. From 1885 to 1889 Negro lynchings ranged from 71 to 95 per year. In 1891, 121 Negroes were lynched. From 1891 until 1895 Negro lynchings ranged from 112 to 155 (1892). Since 1901 there has been no single year in which as many as 100 Negroes were lynched." Scott Nearing, *Black America*, Schocken, New York, 1969 (orig. 1929), p. 206. For the use of racism in the destruction of the Populist movement, see Zinn, op. cit., p. 285; Henri, op. cit., pp. 9–10; and Woodward, *Tom Watson*, op. cit., chaps. 21–23.

50. Henri, op. cit., p. 51.

51. For opposition to the migration from Southern planters hit by the loss of significant portions of their cheap labor force, and for the remonstrations issued by Washington and other Black spokesmen to the migrants that the South was where they were at their "best," see Henri, ibid., pp. 73–79.

52. Trotter and George Forbes, graduates of Harvard and Amherst, respectively, in 1895, began the publication of the Boston Guardian in order to express their opposition to Booker T. Washington. This was in 1901, two years before Du Bois published his first public criticisms of Washington in his *The Souls of Black Folk*. Trotter and Forbes, along with their fellow Bostonians, Archibald Grimké and Clement Mor-

gan, established a formidable opposition to Washington, while in Chicago, the lawyers Ferdinand Barnett and E. H. Morris, and in Philadelphia, the physician Dr. N. F. Mossell, organized groups critical of the Tuskegee program in their communities. (See August Meier, "Radicals and Conservatives—A Modern View," in Logan, op. cit., pp. 42–44. "Meanwhile, at least as early as 1902, Washington had been utilizing his reservoirs of power to silence the opposition. He used personal influence to wean people away from the radicals, attempted to deprive opponents of their government jobs, where possible arranged to have his critics sued for libel, placed spies in radical organizations, employed his influence with philanthropists as an effective weapon in dealings with educators and others, deprived critics of participation and subsidies in political campaigns, and subsidized the Negro press to support him and to ignore or to attack the opposition." Ibid., p. 47. In July of 1903, Trotter and Forbes were finally able to arrange a personal confrontation with Washington at a meeting in Boston. The plan was to heckle Washington with barbed questions, aided by 30 or more others. Apparently the Boston police had been forewarned by Washington's attorney, William L. Lewis, and Trotter was arrested when he stood to address Washington. He was fined $50.00 and sentenced to thirty days in jail. Brisbane, op. cit., pp. 38–39, 253 n. 11. "The news of Trotter's imprisonment, in the summer of 1903, reached Du Bois at Atlanta University, where the latter was conducting classes in sociology. Like Trotter's other friends and followers, Du Bois became incensed. . . . It was here that Du Bois decided to abandon his efforts to improve the Negro's condition by 'Scientific study.' "Direct political and social action was to be the new strategy." Ibid., p. 39. Du Bois gave a similar account of these events; however, he put the events of the Boston meeting in 1905 and managed to suggest that the events that followed—namely the founding of the Niagara movement—were largely at his initiative rather than Trotter's. The Autobiography, op. cit., pp. 248–51. This tendency to reconstruct events with which he had been involved so that they revolved around himself is noted in Geiss (op. cit., pp. 232–33) and Brisbane, (op. cit., p. 253 n. 16). For examples of Trotter's critiques of Washington, see Francis Broderick and August Meier (eds.), Negro Protest Thought in the Twentieth Century, Bobbs-Merrill, Indianapolis, 1965, pp. 25–30.

53. According to Herbert Aptheker, the editor of Du Bois's papers, John Brown was Du Bois's favorite work, though he realized that his first historical monograph, The Suppression of the African Slave-Trade to the United States of America, 1638–1870 (Schocken, New York, 1969 [orig. 1896]), was "in the conventional sense," his most scholarly. Aptheker, "The Historian," in Logan, op cit., p. 262. Kelly Miller's assertion that Trotter wove a "subtle net" around Du Bois (see Meier, op. cit., p. 75) may be evidenced in the joint communique that Trotter and Du Bois wrote for the Niagara movement in 1906, when they said of John Brown: "We do not believe in violence, neither in the despised violence of the raid nor the lauded violence of the soldier, nor the barbarous violence of the mob; but we do believe in John Brown, in that incarnate spirit of justice, that hatred of a lie, that willingness to sacrifice money, reputation, and life itself on the altar of right." Du Bois, The Autobiography, op. cit., p. 251.

54. "A new theme in the pages of the Horizon and The Crisis was Du Bois's interest in the labor movement and in socialism. At one time he had viewed the white working class as the Negro's 'bitterest opponent.' By 1904 he had come to believe that economic discrimination was in large part the cause of the race problem, and to feel sympathetic toward the socialist movement. Three years later, he was writing favorably of the socialists in the Horizon. Elsewhere he advised the socialists that their movement could not succeed unless it included the Negro workers, and wrote that it was simply a matter of time before white and black workers would see their common economic cause against the exploiting capitalists. Though in 1908 Du Bois did not vote for the socialists because they had no chance of winning, in 1911 he joined the party. In a Marxist exegesis in the concluding pages of The Negro, Du Bois viewed both American Negroes and Africans, both the white workers and the colored races, as exploited by white capital which employed the notion of race differences as a rationalization of exploitation, segregation, and subordination. And he predicted that the exploited of all races would unite and overthrow white capital, their common oppressor." August Meier, "The Paradox of W. E. B. Du Bois," in Logan, op. cit., p. 82.

55. "The present world war is, then, the result of jealousies engendered by the recent rise of armed national associations of labor and capital whose aim is the exploitation of the wealth of the world mainly—outside the European circle of nations. These associations, grown jealous and suspicious at the division of the spoils of trade-empire, are fighting to enlarge their respective shares; they look for expansion, not in Europe but in Asia, and particularly in Africa." Du Bois, "The African Roots of War," in Clarke et al., op. cit., p. 280 (the original essay appeared in the Atlantic Monthly, May 1915, pp. 707–14.

56. See Du Bois, "Judging Russia," The Crisis 33 (February 1927): 189–90. Du Bois visited the Soviet Union in 1926, 1936, 1949, and 1959, visiting the Asian republics in his second and last trip. He was always critical of anti-Soviet propaganda and seems to have been hopeful that the revolution would succeed until his death. See Du Bois, The Autobiography, op. cit., pp. 29–43; and his criticism of the Nation's "wobblings in the case of Russia" in a letter to Freda Kirchwey, 13 December 1939, in The Correspondence of W. E. B. Du Bois, 2, Herbert Aptheker (ed.), University of Massachusetts Press, Amherst, 1976, pp. 202–3.

57. Du Bois's work in the Pan-Africanist movement is best reconstructed by Geiss, op. cit., pp. 229–62; see also Richard B. Moore, "Du Bois and Pan Africa," in Clarke et al., op. cit., pp. 187–212; and C. L. R. James, "W. E. B. Du Bois," in James, The Future in the Present, Allison and Busby, London, 1977, pp. 202–12.

58. In his own treatment of *Black Reconstruction*, Herbert Aptheker, the Marxist thinker most intimate with Du Bois's work, characterized him "as an idealist—philosophically speaking—in key areas of his thinking." Aptheker, "The Historian," op. cit., p. 261. Aptheker seemed to believe that Du Bois came too late to the works of Marx and Lenin for them to have had a profound impact on his conception of history. George Streator, described by Aptheker as a leader in the student strike at Fisk University in 1925 who later was asked by Du Bois to join him on the staff of *The Crisis*, was one of Du Bois's most informed critiques on the Black Left. Streator wrote a number of scathing letters to Du Bois in 1935 on the subjects of Marxism and the capabilities of the Black middle class. See Aptheker (ed.), *The Correspondence of W. E. B. Du Bois*, op. cit., 2:86–96. Streator wrote in 1941, according to Francis Broderick, "that he doubted that 'with all his talents Du Bois ever did more than turn to those vivid pages where Marx hammered with telling effect against the English society that gained its wealth through the African slave trade. All the rest to Du Bois was just so much Hegel, and I doubt that Du Bois did much to Hegel when he was a student in Germany.'" Broderick, op. cit., p. 148 note. Certain passages in *Black Reconstruction* might appear to confirm Aptheker's assessment (e.g., "The political success of the doctrine of racial separation, which overthrew Reconstruction by uniting the planter and the poor white, was far exceeded by its astonishing economic results," p. 700); but a close reading of the study and the fact that Du Bois taught seminars on Marx in 1904 and 1933 and was himself a student of German philosophy would seem to discredit Streator's criticisms. See Aptheker (ed.), *The Correspondence*, op. cit., p. 76; Broderick, op. cit., p. 148; and Eugene C. Holmes, "W. E. B. Du Bois: the Philosopher," in Clarke et al., op. cit., p. 79. In deference to Aptheker, whose interpretations of Marx have also come under attack (see Paul Buhle, "American Marxist Historiography, 1900–1940," *Radical America*, November 1970, pp. 5–35; and James O'Brien et al., " 'New Left Historians' of the 1960s," *Radical America*, November 1970, pp. 83–84), *Black Reconstruction* is hardly an idealist exercise in historiography. In the work, and on innumerable occasions, Du Bois stresses the underlying economic bases for the dismantling of the experiment in reconstruction and for the reconciliation between industrial capitalists and the southern agrarian capitalists who commanded labor and land in the antebellum period. The racial consciousness that prevented the development of democratic structures in America had begun as a concomitant to the slave system but ultimately acquired the character of a material force. But all along, it was economic forces that led to the unification of the nation's ruling classes: "It was not, then, race and culture calling out of the South in 1876; it was property and privilege, shrieking to its own kind, and privilege and property heard and recognized the voice of its own." (*Black Reconstruction*, op. cit., p. 630.)

59. The notion of American exceptionalism or "Americanism" emerged in the American Communist Party in the late 1920s as an explanation for the party's failures to attract a large following among American workers. The weakness of the party was attributed to the fact that unlike European capitalism, as Eugen Varga termed it, American capitalism was "still healthy." Since the "United States was an exception to the rule of capitalist decline," the Communist International's Eighth Plenum in 1927 suggested it "expected no great rise of the revolutionary labor movement 'in the nearest future.'" Theodore Draper, *American Communism and Soviet Russia*, Viking Press, New York, 1960, pp. 270–72.

60. Du Bois's lecture at the Rosenwald Conference was substantially reproduced in the *Baltimore Afro-American*, 20 May 1933, pp. 2–3. C. L. R. James made a similar point while discussing direct democracy before a Trinidadian audience in 1960. In contrasting the modern world with Athens during its democratic period some 2000 or more years ago, James argued: "Athens was divided into ten tribes or divisions, and every month they selected by lot a certain number of men from each division. . . . And these went into the government offices and governed the state for that month . . . I doubt if you could take thirty or forty people today from anywhere and put them into some government, however small it might be, and ask them to run it. It is not because government is so difficult. The idea that a little municipality, as we have them all over the world today, would have more difficult and complex problems than the city of Athens is quite absurd. *It is that people have lost the habit of looking at government and one another in that way*. It isn't in their minds at all." James, "What We Owe to Ancient Greece," in *Modern Politics*, bewick/ed, Detroit, 1973, p. 4.

61. Du Bois, op. cit.

62. In a letter to George Streator on 24 April 1935, Du Bois asserted: "I am convinced from wide contact with the working people of the United States, North, East, South and West, that the great majority of them are thoroughly capitalistic in their ideals and their proposals, and that the last thing that they would want to do would be to unite in any movement whose object was the uplift of the mass of Negroes to essential equality with them. . . . I regard with astonishment militarists who agitate against violence; and lovers of peace who want the class revolution immediately. It is quite possible that there have been times in the world when nothing but revolution made way for progress. I rather suspect that that was true in Russia in 1917. I do not think that it is true in the United States in 1935. But whether it is true or not, Negroes have no part in any program that proposes violent revolution. If they take part, they will make the triumph for such a program more difficult, and they will bring down upon the mass of innocent Negroes, the united vengeance of the white race. The result would be too terrible to contemplate. I am, therefore, absolutely and bitterly opposed to the American brand of communism which simply aims to stir up trouble and to make

Negroes shock troops in a fight whose triumph may easily involve the utter annihilation of the American Negro. I, therefore, attack and shall continue to attack American communism in its present form, while at the same time, I regard Russia as the most promising modern country." Aptheker (ed.), *The Correspondence*, op. cit., pp. 91–92. Streator, in his reply, agreed with Du Bois that "The cp of USA is led by stupid men." But, he continued, "it is nevertheless a working man's organization." He suggested Du Bois take more care in the future: "You attack American Communism, but you do not send any of your students out of Atlanta fired with the determination to work in the labor movement which you have talked about but never studied." "I can also attack the American Communist Party—get the distinction—but I can do my part in building the labor movement and in fighting Jim Crow in the labor movement." Streator to Du Bois, 29 April 1935, ibid., pp. 95, 94.

63. Du Bois's resignation from the NAACP and the editorship of *The Crisis* in 1935 was precipitated by his difficulties with the organization's executive secretary, Walter White, a man Du Bois did not trust or like. The substance of the quarrel, however, went far beyond personalities or administrative quirks. One factor was the impact that the emergence of the Universal Negro Improvement Association (UNIA) as a mass organization had on Du Bois's thinking. As a spokesman for the NAACP, Du Bois had been critical, sometimes viciously so, of the leadership of the UNIA. (See his "Marcus Garvey and the NAACP," *The Crisis*, 35, February 1928, p. 51, cited in D. Walden (ed.), *W. E. B. Du Bois: The Crisis Writings*, op. cit., pp. 307–10). But even in the early 1920s, Du Bois was receptive toward the UNIA program: "[S]horn of its bombast and exaggeration the main lines of the Garvey plan are perfectly feasible. What he is trying to say and do is this: American Negroes can, by accumulating and administering their own capital, organize industry, join the black centers of the Atlantic by commercial enterprise and in this way ultimately redeem Africa as a fit and free home for black men. This is true. This is feasible." ("Marcus Garvey," *The Crisis* 21 (January 1921): 112–15, cited in Walden, ibid., p. 325.) By the early 1930s, Du Bois had shorn the program of what he took to be its distracting elements and was presenting it as the core of his own program for the economic progress of American Blacks. This "sanitized" version of the UNIA program would prompt Harold Cruse, 30 years later, to remark: Du Bois upheld the idea of a separate black economy as 'not so easily dismissed' because 'in the first place we have already got a partially separate economy in the United States.' Yet he remarked in 1940 that his economic program for Negro advance 'can easily be mistaken for a program of complete racial segregation and even nationalism among Negroes . . . this is a misapprehension.' It seems not to have occurred to Du Bois that any thorough economic reorganization of Negro existence imposed from above, will not be supported by the popular masses unless an appeal is made to their nationalism." Cruse, *The Crisis of the Negro Intellectual*, William Morrow, New York, 1967, p. 309. It was Du Bois's advocacy of a Black co-operative commonwealth that the leadership of the NAACP opposed. See Broderick, op. cit., pp. 169–75. (For Du Bois's program, see his *Dusk of Dawn*, Schocken, New York, 1968 [orig. 1940], pp. 197–220.) While Henry Lee Moon suggests that Du Bois had fallen back to a position similar to Booker T. Washington's, it is clear that this was not the case since Du Bois was consciously basing his plans on the presumption of the "collapse of capitalism." *Dusk of Dawn*, op. cit., p. 198. (For Moon's characterization, see Moon, op. cit., pp. 28–29.)

64. For the UNIA and the African Blood Brotherhood, see Theodore Vincent, *Black Power and the Garvey Movement*, Ramparts, San Francisco, 1972 and the forthcoming publication of the Garvey Papers introduced and edited by Robert Hill, UCLA. For the Scottsboro case, see Dan T. Carter, *Scottsboro: A Tragedy of the American South*, Oxford University Press, London, 1968.

65. "Before our leaders can essay this new task they have a vast lesson to learn." "Our professional classes are not aristocrats and our masters—they are and must be the most efficient of our servants." Rosenwald Conference, op. cit.

66. As we shall see, Du Bois argued that the roots of the Depression of the third decade of the twentieth Century were to be found in the responses of white labor to the freeing of the slaves. See *Black Reconstruction*, op. cit., p. 30.

67. Rosenwald Conference, op. cit.

68. All quotations from *Black Reconstruction* are taken from the Meridian (the World Publishing Company) edition, 1969.

69. See Robert Fogel and Stanley Engerman, *Time on the Cross*, Little, Brown, Boston, 1974, 2:20–29.

70. This is very close to a paraphrase of Marx's description of primitive accumulation in *Capital*, a work to which Du Bois alludes frequently in *Black Reconstruction*.

71. See Philip Foner, *Organized Labor and the Black Worker, 1619–1973*, International Publishers, New York, 1976, pp. 4–16; and Robert Starobin, *Industrial Slavery in the Old South*, Oxford University Press, New York, 1970.

72. "[T]he white workingman has been asked to share the spoil of exploiting 'chinks and niggers.' It is no longer simply the merchant prince, or the aristocratic monopoly, or even the employing class, that is exploiting the world; it is the nation, a new democratic nation composed of united capital and labor." "Democracy in economic organization, while an acknowledged ideal, is today working itself out by admitting to a share in the spoils of capital only the aristocracy of labor—the more intelligent and shrewder

and cannier workingmen. The ignorant, unskilled, and restless still form a large, threatening, and, to a growing extent, revolutionary group in advanced countries." Du Bois, "The African Roots of War," op. cit., pp. 277, 281.

73. In the late 1860s and early 1870s, according to William Z. Foster (a historian who twice in his life headed the American Communist Party as its General Secretary), "There was much good will between the National Labour Union and the Colored National Labor Union, and if they could not establish closer working unity between Negro and white workers, this was due to their failure to overcome a number of serious obstacles. Chief among these was the NLU failure to combat the employers' Jim Crow policies in industry. The white workers tended to oust Negro workers from the skilled trades, to refuse to work with them in the shops, and to bar them from the trade unions. This white chauvinist trend which was to wreak such havoc in the labor movement in later decades, was already manifest among unions in the NLU." Foster, *The Negro People in American History*, International Publishers, New York, 1954, p. 351. A journalist observing the 1869 convention of the NLU wrote: "When a native Mississippian and an ex-confederate officer, in addressing a convention, refers to a colored delegate who has preceded him as 'the gentleman from Georgia' . . . when an ardent and Democratic partisan (from New York at that) declares with a rich Irish brogue that he asks for himself no privilege as a mechanic or as a citizen that he is not willing to concede to every other man, white or black . . . then one may indeed be warranted in asserting that time works curious charges." Quoted by Zinn, op. cit., pp. 236–37. See also Foner, *Organized Labor and the Black Worker*, op. cit., pp. 30–63 for the history of NLU, the CNLU, the Knights of Labor and other unions; and Herbert Gutman, "The Negro and the United Mine Workers of America," in Julius Jacobsen (ed.), *The Negro and the American Labor Movement*, Anchor Books, Garden City, 1968, pp. 119–20.

74. See Du Bois, "Organized Labor," in Julius Lester (ed.), *The Seventh Son*, op. cit., 2:301–2. The editorial originally appeared in *The Crisis*, July 1912.

75. Karl Marx and Friedrich Engels, *The German Ideology*, in Robert C. Tucker, *The Marx-Engels Reader*, W. W. Norton, New York, 1972, p. 128.

76. See Richard Lichtman, "The Fascade of Equality in Liberal Democratic Theory," *Socialist Revolution*, January 1970, pp. 85–126.

77. In 1925, one Black Marxist took stock of his society: "The slow growth of Marxism among negroes has been wholly due to the inability both of the social democrats and the Communists to approach the negro on his own mental grounds, and to interpret his peculiar social situation in terms of the class struggle. To-day the American negro has evolved his own bourgeoisie, even though as yet but petty. And more and more the lines sharpen in the conflict between the white and black bourgeoisies. The negro petty bourgeoisie rallies the negro masses to him in his struggle against the more powerful white bourgeoisie, and the negro masses are permeated with the belief that their social degradation flows from the mere fact that they are markedly of a different race, and are not white. . . . The negro is revolutionary enough in a racial sense, and it devolves upon the American Communist Party to manipulate this racial revolutionary sentiment to the advantage of the class struggle." James Jackson, "The Negro in America," *Communist International*, February 1925, p. 51. This was not the James E. Jackson who was active in the American Communist Party in the 1940s and later, and who edited *The Daily Worker*, for a time; this was L. Fort-Whiteman, described by the editors of the *Communist International* as "an emigrant [presumably to Great Britain] of the oppressed negro race." Ibid., p. 53. George Streator put the same thought to Du Bois, but much more simply: "There is no such thing as a Negro *loving* his race in the matter of capital investment and profit." 8 April 1935, in Aptheker (ed.), *The Correspondence of W. E. B. Du Bois*, op. cit., 2:90.

78. Rosenwald Conference lecture, op. cit.

79. During the first decade after the Russian Revolution, the crises confronting the Soviet Union and the world Communist movement were dramatized by leadership struggles in Russia and in the Comintern's national parties. In Russia, Lenin's long and increasingly incapacitating illness, and finally his death (1924) released the brake: "Although factions had existed in Lenin's lifetime, these had been transitory and their members had frequently changed sides. [By 1925] the emerging alignment represented hardened positions based on conflicting programs and slogans and was unresponsive to compromise or individual maneuver. . . . Above all, the sharp division among Russian leaders stemmed from the policy decisions, on socialism in one country and the interpretation and implementation of NEP. . . . Within the Politburo Zinoviev, Kamenev, and Trotsky assumed the left position Bukharin, Aleksei Rykov, and Mikhail Tomsky, the right; and Stalin, the center, although he invariably allied himself with the right." Helmut Gruber, *Soviet Russia Masters the Comintern: International Communism in the Era of Stalin's Ascendancy*, Anchor/Doubleday, Garden City, 1974, p. 21. Gruber discusses the policies in question and the political developments, ibid., pp. 20–25, 175–200; see also Fernando Claudin, *The Communist Movement: From Comintern to Cominform, Part I*, Monthly Review Press, New York, 1975, pp. 46–102. For the American factions in the leadership struggle, see Benjamin Gitlow, *I Confess*, E. P. Dutton, New York 1939, pp. 493–570; Theodore Draper, *American Communism and Soviet Russia*, Viking Press, New York, 1963, chaps. 16, 17, and 18; and for the political destinies of many of the participants, Daniel Bell, *Marxian Socialism in the United States*, Princeton University Press, Princeton, 1967, pp. 133–34 n. 220. For Black American Communists and the

leadership disputes, see Harry Haywood, *Black Bolshevik*, Liberator Press, Chicago, 1978, pp. 176–91. For examples of the discipline and opportunism shown by many leading Black Communists toward frequent changes in the party's "line" see William Nolan's polemically anti-Communist but often informative work, *Communism versus the Negro*, Henry Regnery Co., Chicago, 1951, passim; and Harry Haywood, *For a Revolutionary Position on the Negro Question*, Liberator Press, Chicago, 1975.

80. Du Bois mentioned Engels only rarely, and then he seemed to be entirely wedded to the phrase "Marx and Engels," suggesting an earlier critic of whom Marx had complained: "What is strange, is to see how he treats the two of us as a singular: 'Marx and Engels says.' " Letter to Engels, 1 August 1856, cited by S. S. Prawar, *Karl Marx and World Literature*, Oxford University Press, Oxford, 1976, p. 1. Marxist-Leninism, the conventional designation of the Comintern's theories and policies in the post-Lenin period is identified with the dogma and politics of Stalin rather than with Lenin. More recently, it is frequently termed "Stalinism." See Perry Anderson, *Considerations of Western Marxism*, Verso, London, 1979, pp. 19–21.

81. See Georg Lukács, "Class Consciousness," in *History and Class Consciousness*, Merlin Press, London, 1971.

82. *The Writings of Leon Trotsky*, Martin Secker and Warburg, London, 1964, 6:336.

83. Engels suggested that those who followed him and Marx—the Marxists—were subject to dogma and reductionism. For instance, Engels expressed his exasperation with "economistic" Marxists in his letter to Joseph Bloch in 1890, see Robert C. Tucker, op. cit., p. 642.

84. "The Marxist orthodoxy of the Third Communist International introduced considerable changes in the theory of class among socialists. Instead of deriving its theory from an examination of the actual division of social and technical labor within capitalist production, there was a tendency to regard the working class within a single dimension. The ideal typical revolutionary class was the factory and transportation manual worker, that is, the famous 'industrial working class.' Workers in basic industries, those which produced means of production were the critical base of revolutionary class action since they occupied the central position within the production system." "Part of the difficulty in the Old Left notion of the working class inheres in the broad two-class scheme of Marx himself . . . the concept of the great schism between bourgeois and proletarian constituting the structure of capitalist society found in the Manifesto was abstracted from concrete circumstances and transformed into dogma by the Marxism of both the Stalin era and the Social Democrats alike." Stanley Aronowitz, "Does the United States Have a New Working Class?," in George Fischer (ed.), *The Revival of American Socialism*, Oxford University Press, New York, 1971, pp. 188, 189. In the same volume, Paul Sweezy took on those critics of Marx's theory of revolution who "note that the proletariat of what has become the most advanced and powerful capitalist country, the United States of America, has never developed a significant revolutionary leadership or movement." "Workers and the Third World," ibid., pp. 154–68. Sweezy's position was that of these critics and the earlier American Marxists who had relied on industrial workers for revolution had neither read Marx carefully nor realized the true dimensions of capitalism: "In Marx's theory of capitalism, the proletariat is not always and necessarily revolutionary. It was not revolutionary in the period of manufacture, becoming so only as a consequence of the introduction of machinery in the industrial revolution. The long-run effects of machinery, however, are different from the immediate effects. If the revolutionary opportunities of the early period of modern industry are missed, the proletariat of an industrializing country tends to become less and less revolutionary. This does not mean, however, that Marx's contention that capitalism produces its own gravediggers is wrong." "If we consider capitalism as a global system . . . we see that it is divided into a handful of exploiting countries and a much more numerous and populous group of exploited countries. The masses in these exploited dependencies constitute a force in the global capitalist system which is revolutionary in the same sense and for the same reasons that Marx considered the proletariat of the early period of modern industry to be revolutionary." Ibid., p. 168. See also Daniel Bell, op. cit., pp. 106–16.

85. See Franz Borkenau, *World Communism*, University of Michigan Press, Ann Arbor, 1971, pp. 64–65, 84–93; and Bell, op. cit., pp. 102–6.

86. See Gruber, op. cit., chaps. 1 and 2; and Borkenau, op. cit., chaps. 6, 7, and 8.

87. This is the more popular rendering of the phrase found in Marx's "Contribution to the Critique of Hegel's Philosophy of Right," which began: "Just as philosophy finds its material weapons in the proletariat, so the proletariat finds its intellectual weapons in philosophy." In Tucker, op. cit., p. 23.

88. "International socialism was in fact motivated by conflicting impulses and its policy was characterized by ambiguities which socialists at the time preferred to ignore. They found refuge in short-term solutions and compromises, thereby avoiding the issues that would have forced them to take a stand. 'The International's total inability to oppose the war' had its roots in the organization's many contradictions in the foundations and in the theoretical weaknesses of a preventive strategy that determined the concrete forms of socialist attitudes and policies. Based on the majority's view of imperialism, on an interpretation which the facts belied, the International's pacifist strategy was characterized by marked contradictions: an awareness of new stages in the evolution of capitalism; an appreciation of the immediacy of the threat and a basic optimism as to the outcome of the crisis that ignored the possibility of a universal clash. The

International's activities on the world scene were therefore haphazard and dictated by the seriousness of the crises. Neither the equation 'war = revolution' nor the alternative 'war or revolution' was in the minds of the leaders of the International." "It is impossible to say whether the leaders of the International were the captives of their own myths or whether their reaction was the classical manifestation of that characteristic trait of the Second International: reformist practice screened behind verbal radicalism." Georges Haupt, *Socialism and the Great War*, Clarendon Press, Oxford, London, 1972, pp. 220–21.

89. See Borkenau, op. cit., pp. 161–70. For details on the rules of eligibility for the Comintern, see Nolan, op. cit., pp. 4–5.

90. Nolan, op. cit., p. 4.

91. Nathan Glazer, *The Social Basis of American Communism*, Harcourt, Brace and World, New York, 1961, pp. 25–26.

92. Theodore Draper, *The Roots of American Communism*, Viking, New York, 1963, p. 31.

93. Glazer, op. cit., p. 22.

94. See David Brody, *Steelworkers in America*, Harvard University Press, Cambridge, 1960, chap. 1. Even the militant Wobblies had difficulty with ethnic loyalties, see Melvyn Dubofsky, *We Shall Be All: A History of the Industrial Workers of the World*, Quadrangle/New York Times, New York, 1969, pp. 24–26, and esp. pp. 350–58.

95. Gabriel Almond, *The Appeals of Communism*, Princeton University Press, Princeton, 1965, pp. 141–47. Almond's study shared with many of those works written and published in the early 1950s—particularly those included in the Fund for the Republic series edited by Clinton Rossiter (David Shannon's *The Decline of American Communism*; Theodore Draper's *The Roots of American Communism* and *American Communism and Soviet Russia*; Daniel Bell's *Marxian Socialism in the United States*; and Nathan Glazer's *The Social Basis of American Communism*)—a degree of precautionary concern for the extent to which American Jews might be identified with radicalism in the highly repressive ambiance of McCarthyism. George Rawick, who worked as a research assistant for Bell, Glazer and Shannon while employed by the Fund, commented: "Nathan Glazer started with a thesis . . . the attempt of a whole group of people around the American Jewish Committee and elsewhere to so to speak 'clean up' the Red taint from the Jewish community. And that was a particular concern of Professor Glazer, it was a particular concern of Moshe Dechter (?) who worked in the same office, it was a particular concern of Daniel Bell. . . . They started out with a thesis . . . and the politics of that thesis and the politics of the fund for the Republic was very simple: We were going to do on the Liberal and anti-Communist Left, do it ourselves before McCarthy and the others got to do it, so we could prove that we had cleared our own house." "One of the things which constantly went on during this period—much more important than the publishing of the books—is that all the people who worked as part of this project were constantly engaged in the process of rehabilitation of people leaving the Communist Party, including Earl Browder." Interview with Rawick, Winter 1976. Almond's contribution was to transpose political issues into psychodynamic or psychopathic phenomenon. See for instance his treatment of "Alice," pp. 282–84.

96. "The Second Congress of the Comintern issued an ultimatum to force the unification of the American Communist and United Communist parties. When this did not help, the Comintern, in the spring of 1921, sent a delegation to the United States, consisting of Charles E. Scott (the party name of Carl Jansen or Charles Johnson, a Lettish Communist, formerly of Roxbury, Massachusetts), Louis C. Fraina, one of the American delegates to the Second Congress, and Sen Katayama, the Japanese exile who had become a Comintern official. This delegation brought the warring parties together into the Communist party of America in May 1921." Draper, *American Communism*, op. cit., p. 25; see also Draper, *The Roots of American Communism*, op. cit., pp. 148–281; for the pre-unification period, see Gitlow, op. cit., chap. 1.

97. "The most startling and significant aspect of the American Communist movement in 1919 was its national composition. For the Communist party, the Russian members represented almost 25 per cent of the total, and the entire East-European membership accounted for over 75 per cent. The English-speaking members represented only 7 per cent with the Michigan group and 4 per cent without it. Though the percentage of English-speaking members was higher in the Communist Labor party, it could not have been very high if 90 per cent of both parties came from the foreign-language federations." Draper, *The Roots of American Communism*, op. cit., p. 190.

98. In the late 1930s, Gitlow, one of the founding members of the American Communist movement and a "Communist candidate for Vice-President of the United States in 1924 and 1928," would write: "The determination of the Russian Federation to control the movement out of Russian nationalist considerations certainly characterized its early phases. When better contact was established with Soviet Russia and the Communist International, the Russian heritage was not cast off, the Party did not become more American, but instead more Russian." Gitlow, op. cit., p. 57.

99. See Bell, op. cit., pp. 108–11; Melech Epstein, *The Jew and Communism*, Trade Union Sponsoring Committee, New York, n.d., pp. 252–53; Arthur Liebman, op. cit., chap. 8; and Glazer, op. cit., chaps. 2, 3, and 4.

100. Florette Henri, op. cit., pp. 63–64; Theodore Vincent, having had some professional experience of

his own with a Black press (the Los Angeles Herald Dispatch), suggested: "[T]he UNIA press was virtually the only free press available to black people in the 1920s and 1930s. Other black publishing concerns were usually tied to white money." Vincent, *Black Power and the Garvey Movement*, Ramparts Press, San Francisco, 1972, p. 255.

101. Henri, ibid., pp. 89–90; and Vincent, ibid., p. 36.

102. "For a short time in the early 1920s, the Garveyites held together an unprecedented black coalition which included cultural nationalists, political nationalists, opponents of organized religion (atheists, separatists, or simply reformers), advocates of armed rebellion, pacifists, women's liberation fighters, participants in Democratic and Republican machine politics, a smattering of left-wingers, many who wanted no contact with whites, and a small but significant number who wanted the UNIA to cooperate with integrated civil rights organizations to end discrimination and segregation." Vincent, ibid., p. 20. See also Tony Martin, *Race First*, Greenwood Press, Westport, 1976.

103. The modification of capitalism that could be found in the UNIA ranged from retail businesses to co-operatives. Garvey, himself, had strong hostilities toward capitalists on the grande bourgeois scale and often seemed to publicly move toward a tentative commitment to socialism. "Much of Garvey's hold on the masses was due to ideas not very different from some espoused by communists. Despite his firm espousal of the race-first principle, for example, there was a persistent class component to Garvey's thinking. As against the white race, he saw the need for intraracial solidarity but within the race he demonstrated quite clearly that he identified with the oppressed masses against those with pretensions to more exalted status." Tony Martin, op. cit., p. 231.

104. "Garvey was exceedingly pessimistic about the future of the heavily outnumbered black man in the western hemisphere. Beyond the boundaries of the mother continent, he could see only "ruin and disaster" for his people. Consequently, he asked that Africa's scattered and abused children be restored to her. Garvey claimed that the 'legitimate, moral and righteous home of all Negroes' was Africa, but he did not favor an immediate wholesale exodus from the New World. . . . Not all blacks were wanted in Africa anyway. 'Some are no good here and naturally will be no good there.' Unwanted were the indolent and dependent." Robert Weisbord, *Ebony Kinship*, Greenwood Press, Westport, 1973, pp. 55–56.

105. Weisbord has indicated, in part, the extent to which the American and British governments colluded to destroy the UNIA's influence among Black Americans, inhabitants of the West Indies and Africa. Ibid., pp. 57–82. Robert A. Hill in discussions with this author has traced J. Edgar Hoover's sly obsession with the emergence of a "Black messiah" to his acquaintance with the UNIA in the 1920s. Hoover, as a young bureaucrat in the Department of Justice was instrumental in delaying Garvey's return to the United States from Central America in 1922.

106. Until quite recently, the most serious work on the UNIA and other Black radical movements during the 1920s and 1930s was done by governmental agents: "There are two anthologies of black radical publications of the World War I period; ironically, they were both compiled by right-wing government agents. Attorney General Mitchell Palmer's 'Radicalism and Sedition among the Negroes as Reflected in Their Publications' was published in 1919; and 'Revolutionary Radicalism: A Report of the Joint Legislative Committee of New York Investigating Seditious Activities' appeared in 1920." Vincent, op. cit., p. 254.

107. According to Weisbord, Du Bois may have gone a bit further in his opposition to Garvey. Garvey suspected Du Bois had helped to sabotage the relations between the UNIA and the Liberian regime. Weisbord suggests that this might have been the case, and that Du Bois may have been acting on behalf of both the American and British governments. Weisbord, op. cit., pp. 70–72.

108. Quoted in Jervis Anderson, *A. Philip Randolph*, Harcourt Brace Jovanovich, New York, 1973, p. 132.

109. Claude McKay, *Harlem: Negro Metropolis*, Harcourt Brace Jovanovich, New York, 1968 (orig. 1940), p. 143.

110. Vincent, op. cit., p. 19. Martin's work, *Race First*, has already been cited. Robert A. Hill, editor of the Marcus Garvey Papers at UCLA, is currently preparing the publication of what should stand as the definitive collection of UNIA documents.

111. For the Brotherhood, see Vincent, op. cit., pp. 74–85 and passim; Martin, op. cit., pp. 237–46; Draper, *American Communism and Soviet Russia*, op. cit., pp. 322–32; and Foner, *Organized Labor and the Black Worker*, op. cit., pp. 148–49; Draper and Vincent, though both were in personal contact with Briggs give different birthplaces for him—Nevis and St. Kitts, respectively. Theman Taylor's unpublished biography of Briggs (1981) should clarify several such discrepancies.

112. See Harry Haywood, *Black Bolshevik*, op. cit., pp. 122–31.

113. Vincent, op. cit., pp. 75–76.

114. Draper, *American Communism and Soviet Russia*, op. cit., p. 324.

115. Ibid., p. 506 n. 26.

116. Though the identity confusion of the early period of the Brotherhood ultimately came to be resolved through its "Race Catechism" (see Vincent, op. cit., pp. 46–47) and the CPUSA's "Black Belt Thesis," other contradictions, specifically programmatic ones, persisted. Briggs, himself, represents an interesting instance of the individual significance of the social contradictions of the United States and the West Indies.

Briggs was phenotypically European. Though once he and Garvey became political enemies Garvey would accuse Briggs of being a white men "passing" for a Black, this ironically was put to some good use by the UNIA. "Passing" as white, Briggs bought a ship for the UNIA in 1924. This was a part of an attempt by Briggs to reconcile the UNIA, the Brotherhood, and the CPUSA. This was three years after the Brotherhood had been expelled from the UNIA by convention vote. Briggs, reportedly, was quite sensitive about his complexion, which may account, in part, for his severe speech impediment and the difficulty he encountered earlier in locating a people with which to identify. Theodore Vincent described the Brotherhood as the "first left-wing Black nationalist organization and one of the first organizations to consider seriously a separate Black republic in the Southern United States." Ibid., p. 74. Draper, on the other hand, characterized it as "a small propagandist organization typical of the 'New Negro' period." *American Communism and Soviet Russia*, op. cit., p. 325. These are fundamentally different reconstructions. For example, Vincent begins his identification of the Brotherhood with a long description of its role in the 1921 race riot in Tulsa, Oklahoma. He stresses the role that the organization played in defending the Black community of that city and the pride with which the Brotherhood identified its participation in late 1921. (The ABB at first seemed to deny any role: "The African Blood Brotherhood, which is believed by the authorities in Tulsa, Okla. to have fomented the race riot in that city, yesterday issued a formal statement denying that this organization or members of its Tulsa branch were in any way the aggressors in that Tulsa disturbances. . . . 'An article in *The Times* of June 4 implies responsibility on the part of the African Blood Brotherhood for the unfortunate bloody occurrences in Tulsa, Okla. This organization has no other answer to make save to admit that the African Blood Brotherhood is interested in having negroes organized for self-defense against wanton attack.'" *The New York Times*, 5 June 1921, p. 21. Then, according to Vincent, several months later the ABB began to appeal to prospective members on the basis of its role: "What Other Organization Can Match That Brave Record?" Vincent, op. cit., p. 75. Draper, to the contrary, argues that the ABB "attracted national attention once in 1921 when it was falsely charged with responsibility for starting the "'race riots' in Tulsa, Oklahoma." Draper, ibid., p. 325. Draper finds it difficult to accept evidence of the Brotherhood's involvement in active struggle as opposed to propaganda. He goes on to describe the programs and aims of the Brotherhood: "a liberated race; absolute race equality—political, economic, social; the fostering of race pride; organized and uncompromising opposition to Ku Kluxism; rapprochement and fellowship within the darker masses and with the class-conscious revolutionary white workers; industrial development; higher wages for Negro labor, lower rents; a united Negro front." Ibid. This catalogue of purposes, however, does not make clear the emphasis found within the ABB for the establishment of a Black nation. Nor does it clarify the role that Briggs's notion of self-determination played in the formulation of nationalism in the American Communist Party.

117. Draper, ibid., p. 323.

118. For Thorne, see Robert A. Hill, "Zion on the Zambezi: Dr. J. Albert Thorne, 'A Descendant of Africa, of Barbados,' and the African Colonial Enterprise: The 'Preliminary Stage,' 1894–97," paper presented at the *International Conference on the History of Blacks in Britain*, Institute of Education, University of London, 28–30 September 1981.

119. See Haywood, *Black Bolshevik*, op. cit., pp. 123–24: "They espoused 'economic radicalism,' an oversimplified interpretation of Marxism which, nevertheless enabled them to see the economic and social roots of racial subjugation. Historically, theirs was the first serious attempt by Blacks to adopt the Marxist world view and the theory of class struggle to the problems of Black Americans."

120. Draper, *American Communism and Soviet Russia*, op. cit., pp. 328, 508 n. 42.

121. Ibid., pp. 343–46.

122. *Martin*, op. cit., p. 239.

123. Tony Martin discusses Garvey's reaction to the report of Lenin's death in January 1924: "Garvey's first response was a telegram to the all Soviet Congress which said in part, 'To us Lenin was one of the world's greatest benefactors. Long life to the Soviet Government of Russia.' This was followed by a lengthy speech at Liberty Hall entitled, 'The Passing of Russia's Great Man,' in which he called Lenin 'probably the greatest man in the world between 1917 and the hour of 1924 when he breathed his last.' He expressed the view also that the whole world was destined ultimately to assume Russia's form of government. He presumed that the UNIA's message of condolence would be treated with respect, even though 'unfortunately, we have not yet sent an ambassador to Russia.' He explained that Lenin represented the class that comprised the majority of mankind." Martin, op. cit., p. 252. For Garvey's antipathy toward American Communists, see ibid., pp. 253–65.

124. See Milton Cantor, *The Divided Left: American Radicalism, 1900–1975*, Hill and Wang, New York, 1978, p. 30; Draper, *American Communism and Soviet Russia*, op. cit., pp. 315–16. R. Laurence Moore summarized the history of American socialism and Blacks in the early period: "American socialists at the turn of the century appeared ready to champion the cause of economic and social justice for Negroes when all other elements in American society were turning increasingly against the former slaves." "Unhappily what happened subsequent to the 1901 convention quickly called this progressive and brave commitment into question. The Negro resolution [of 1901] which to many in the party seemed a natural declaration for

an organization dedicated to the brotherhood of all workers was never reaffirmed. At the 1904 convention the party rejected attempts to write a similar document; and through 1912, the year the socialists mustered their greatest strength in a national presidential election, the Negro problem was not again even discussed on the floor of a national convention." Moore, "Flawed Fraternity—American Socialist Response to the Negro, 1901–1912," *The Historian* 32, no. 1 (November 1969): 2–3. Draper's summary of the early American Communists and Blacks is almost identical: "The Negroes counted least of all in the early Communist movement. Not a single Negro delegate seems to have attended either [the Communist or Communist Labor parties' conventions]. So little was the Negro problem in the Communist consciousness that the Communist Labor program had nothing at all to say about it. The Communist party's program connected the 'problem of the Negro worker' with that of the unskilled worker. The basic analysis was inherited from the Socialist movement: 'The Negro problem is a political and economic problem. The racial oppression of the Negro is simply the expression of his economic bondage and oppression, each intensifying the other.' The American Communists did not depart from this traditional Marxist attitude until the next decade. In this area, as in so many others, the American Communists at first followed in the footsteps of the historic Left Wing." Draper, *The Roots of American Communism*, op. cit., p. 192.

125. The most analytically imaginative treatment of this issue is Harold Cruse's, *The Crisis of the Negro Intellectual*, William Morrow, New York, 1967, pp. 147–70. Cruse argues that in the first three decades of the movement, the party's most successful period, ethnic nationalism defeated the attempt at Americaniza-tion: "It evidently never occurred to Negro revolutionaries that there was no one in America who possessed the remotest potential for Americanizing Marxism but themselves. Certainly the Jews could not with their nationalistic aggressiveness, emerging out of Eastside ghettos to demonstrate through Marxism their intellectual superiority over the Anglo-Saxon *goyim*. The Jews failed to make Marxism applicable to anything in America but their *own* national-group social ambitions or individual self-elevation. As a result, the great brain-washing of Negro radical intellectuals was not achieved by capitalism or the capitalistic bourgeoisie, but by Jewish intellectuals in the American Communist Party" (p. 158). As Cruse, himself, suggests, Melech Epstein, a leading Jewish intellectual in the movement from the 1920s to 1939 (see Glazer, op. cit., pp. 205–6 n. 86), inadvertently confirms Cruse's reconstructions, see Epstein, op. cit., chaps. 30 and 31. Arthur Liebman also complements Cruse's views: "The attitudes and values that Jews and non-Jews held about themselves and each other, on the whole, proved to be significant impediments to the development of a 'successful' Left in the United States. Given the long-engrained tradition of ethnic antagonisms in a society where ethnic communities were and continue to be placed in the roles of rivals for scarce and desirable goods, services, and positions, no political movement in this country could be free from the debilitating tensions emanating from these ethnic rivalries. The problem of the Left was greatly exacer-bated in this regard because of the highly prominent and visible role of the Jews within it. The vicious cycle of anti-Semitism and Jewish chauvinism and defensiveness, divisive element emanating out of America's cultural and political history, proved to be especially onerous burdens for the Left in America." Liebman, op. cit., pp. 534–35.

126. See James Jackson (Lovett Fort-Whiteman), op. cit., p. 52. George Padmore was still using the phrase "Zionism" to refer to the UNIA when he wrote *Pan-Africanism or Communism*, op. cit., pp. 65–82. For Jews in the early American Communist Party, see Glazer, op. cit., pp. 42, 147–48; Liebman, op. cit., pp. 58–60; Gitlow, op. cit., pp. 157–61; and Draper, *The Roots of American Communism*, op. cit., pp. 188–93.

127. See Tony Martin, op. cit., pp. 249ff.

128. "Lenin was a mere name which had appeared so infrequently in the American Socialist press that scarcely a handful of non-Russians would have been able to identify him." "Lenin's name seems to have been mentioned for the first time in America in an article on 'The Evolution of Socialism in Russia' by William English Walling in the *International Socialist Review* of July 1907 . . . But Walling was far ahead of his time, and Lenin dropped completely out of sight for several more years. The next time, in the *New Review* toward the end of 1915, Lenin was listed as one of the signatories of the Zimmerwald Manifesto. Some excerpts from the pamphlet *Socialism and War* by Lenin and Zinoviev were published in tale *International Socialist Review* of January 1916, with favorable comment. It seems likely that this was the first American publication of anything written by Lenin." Draper, *The Roots of American Communism*, op. cit., pp. 72–73. "The earliest meeting of Lenin with an American of which we have any knowledge is the one in 1905 with Arthur Bullard, a journalist." "There is evidence in the Lenin archives in Moscow that would indicate that many other American workers had heard of Lenin and his activities before 1917. On December 1, 1913, the editorial board of *Appeal to Reason*, the *biggest* Socialist newspaper ever published in the United States, sent Lenin '16 two-page leaflets and eight 32-page pamphlets [which] comprise our list of publica-tions to date.' A working-class club in New York City, on March 30, 1914, sent 'the sum of 1437 kronen and 90 heller ($292.61), which is a contribution from the Workmen's Circle to the Russian Social-Democratic Party (Bolshevik)' to Lenin, then in exile in Cracow, Poland. Late in 1915, the Socialist Propaganda League, a left-wing group in Boston, sent Lenin a copy of its manifesto." Foreword from Daniel Mason and Jessica Smith (eds.), *Lenin's Impact on the United States*, reprinted in Philip Bart et al. (eds.), *Highlights of A Fighting History: 60 Years of the Communist Party, USA*, International Publishers, New York, 1979, p. 342.

129. Draper, *American Communism and Soviet Russia*, op. cit., p. 321.

130. V. Lenin, *"Left-Wing" Communism—An Infantile Disorder, Selected Works*, Progress Publishers, Moscow, 1967, 3:351.

131. For the context of Lenin's retreat from theory, see Claudin, op. cit., pp. 46–102; Roger Pethybridge, *The Social Prelude to Stalinism*, Macmillan Press, London, 1977, pp. 40ff; and Draper, *The Roots of American Communism*, op. cit., pp. 248–51. See also Almond, op. cit., pp. 27ff, for an antagonistic appraisal of the pamphlet as a party manual.

132. V. Lenin, *The State and Revolution, Selected Works*, Lawrence and Wishart, London, 1969, 3:281.

133. See V. Lenin, "The Tasks of the Proletariat in the Present Revolution," *Selected Works*, Progress Publishers, Moscow, 1970, pp. 41–47.

134. Lenin, *"Left-Wing" Communism*, op. cit., p. 350.

135. *Theses and Resolutions Adopted at the Third World Congress of the Communist International, July 12, 1921.*

136. See Alfred Meyer, *Leninism*, Praeger, New York, 1962, passim; and Arthur Rosenberg, *A History of Bolshevism*, Oxford University Press, London, 1934, and especially the introduction to the French edition by Georges Haupt, Grasset, Paris, 1967.

137. Draper, *American Communism and Soviet Russia*, op. cit., pp. 320–21.

138. Claude McKay, *A Long Way from Home*, Harcourt Brace and World, New York, 1970 (orig. 1937), p. 177.

139. See McKay, ibid., p. 180; and Draper, *American Communism and Soviet Russia*, op. cit., pp. 25, 67, 165–66.

140. Rose Pastor Stokes, "The Communist International and the Negro," *The Worker*, 10 March 1923. For Stokes, see Vincent, op. cit., p. 82 note.

141. Stokes, ibid.

142. Ibid.

143. See Harry Haywood, *Black Bolshevik*, op. cit., pp. 66–67, 217.

144. Jane Golden died on the day of Haywood's arrival in Moscow. Ibid., pp. 153–55.

145. Ibid., pp. 229–30.

146. For Nasanov, see Draper, *American Communism and Soviet Russia*, op. cit., pp. 170, 344–50; for Katayama and Nasanov in Russia, see Haywood, *Black Bolshevik*, op. cit., pp. 218–19. For Haywood's early opposition to Black nationalism, see ibid., pp. 134–38.

147. Draper, ibid., p. 349.

148. George Charney could recall that even in the late 1940s, the question was still unresolved in some party circles: "The debate at the conference was animated, especially on the part of a number of young Negro intellectuals who had emerged into recent leadership. They were men of brilliant capabilities, trained in the youth movement in the South, some of them war veterans who, stationed in India, had become avid students of its struggle for national independence. They spoke eloquently in support of the doctrine of self-determination. They used Stalin's 'classic' on the national question as their authority, as had Harry Heywood (*sic*), Cyril Briggs, and others who had represented the first Negro cadre in the party a generation ago. We never fully resolved whether this thesis originated in the Comintern and was applied to the U.S., or whether it was originally inspired by the early Negro nationalist groupings in the party and grudgingly accepted by the Comintern." Charney, *A Long Journey*, Quadrangle, Chicago, 1968, p. 193.

149. Pogany is consistently portrayed as an opportunist whose enunciation of the Comintern's "self-determination" fine was the first inkling of the position the American Party received in 1928. Haywood, *Black Bolshevik*, op. cit., pp. 256–68; and Draper, *American Communism and Soviet Russia*, op. cit., pp. 347–49. The phrase, however, was implied by William Z. Foster in his *Toward Soviet America*, Hyperion Press, Westport, 1932, pp. 300–306.

150. Unrepentant Zionists like Melech Epstein found this intolerable; see Cruse, op. cit., pp. 164–68.

151. Marx and Engels, *The Russian Menace to Europe*, Paul Blackstock (ed.), Free Press, Glencoe, 1952, pp. 99–100.

152. Engels, *The Role of Force in History*, International Publishers, New York, 1977, pp. 29–30.

153. See Chapter 1 for Marx and Engels on nationalism.

154. Draper, *American Communism and Soviet Russia*, op. cit., pp. 349–50.

155. J. Stalin, "Marxism and the National Question," cited in Draper, ibid., p. 344.

156. Draper, ibid., p. 355; and Haywood, *For a Revolutionary Position on the Negro Question*, op. cit., passim.

157. Stalin was a Georgian, and, according to Isaac Deutscher, began the development of his political consciousness as a Georgian nationalist; see Deutscher, *Stalin*, op. cit., p. 6

158. For whatever they are worth, see the figures produced in Glazer, op. cit., pp. 174–75. More useful is the excellent work of Mark Naison.

159. See Benjamin Quarles, *Allies for Freedom: Blacks and John Brown*, Oxford University Press, New York, 1974, pp. 168–69.

160. See Philip Foner, *Organized Labor and the Black Worker*, op. cit., pp. 6–10.

161. Raphael Samuel, "British Marxist Historians I," op. cit., pp. 22–26.

162. Ibid., p. 23.

163. Perry Anderson, op. cit., pp. 3–4, 50–53.

164. See Claudin, op. cit., passim.

165. Anderson, op. cit., pp. 19–20.

166. Milton Cantor, op. cit., p. 135.

167. Anderson, op. cit., p. 69.

168. See ibid., for one recent treatment of the divergence in Marxian thought. Also note that Anderson has restricted his survey to Western and Central Europe.

169. See Robert Tucker (ed.), *Marx-Engels Reader*, op. cit., for the appropriate references to *The Holy Family* (pp. 104–6); *The German Ideology* (pp. 111–64), and *The Communist Manifesto* (pp. 331–62).

170. See Marx's discussion of the French petit bourgeoisie in *The Eighteenth Brumaire of Louis Bonaparte*, in Tucker, ibid., passim.

171. Engels, *The German Revolutions*, University of Chicago Press, Chicago, 1967, p. 29.

172. Du Bois, *Black Reconstruction*, op. cit., p. 611.

173. For Lenin's sense of the peasantry, see George Lichtheim, *Marxism*, Praeger, New York, 1973, p. 334, or Meyer's *Leninism*, op. cit.; for Trotsky, see Isaac Deutscher, *The Prophet Armed*, op. cit., pp. 155–58.

174. Cited in Hamza Alavi, "Peasants and Revolution," *The Socialist Register*, 1965, p. 247.

175. Ibid., p. 249.

176. See Meyer, op. cit., pp. 126–43.

177. Marx, *The Eighteenth Brumaire of Louis Bonaparte*, op. cit., pp. 123–24.

178. Engels, *The German Revolutions*, op. cit., pp. 33, 131.

179. Du Bois, "The Negro and Radical Thought," in Moon, op. cit., pp. 265–68. This essay originally appeared in *The Crisis* as an editorial in July 1921.

180. "The Problem of Problems," address to the Ninth Annual Convention of the Intercollegiate Socialist Society, 27 December 1917, published in Philip Foner (ed.), *W. E. B. Du Bois Speaks*, Pathfinder Press, New York, 1970, p. 266.

181. Du Bois, "Judging Russia," in Moon, op. cit., p. 273; editorial in *The Crisis*, February 1927.

182. "The record of the Negro worker during Reconstruction presents an opportunity to study inductively the Marxian theory of the state. I first called this chapter 'The Dictatorship of the Black Proletariat in South Carolina,' but it has been brought to my attention that this would not be correct since universal suffrage does not lead to a real dictatorship until workers use their votes consciously to rid themselves of the dominion of private capital. There were signs of such an object among South Carolina Negroes, but it was always coupled with the idea of that day, that the only real escape for a laborer was himself to own capital." *Black Reconstruction*, op. cit., p. 381 note.

183. Du Bois, "Judging Russia," op. cit., p. 273.

184. Du Bois, "A Pageant in Seven Decades," Convocation, Atlanta University, in P. Foner (ed.), *W. E. B. Du Bois Speaks*, op. cit., pp. 65–66.

185. "Karl Marx and the Negro," in Daniel Walden, op. cit., p. 399; editorial in *The Crisis*, March 1933.

186. "Marxism and the Negro Problem," in Moon, op. cit., p. 292 (orig. appeared in *The Crisis*, May 1933).

187. Alfred Meyer, op. cit., p. 169.

188. The response to *Black Reconstruction* was mixed. (See Jessie Guzman, "W. E. B. Du Bois—The Historian," *Journal of Negro Education* [Fall 1961]: 377–85.) On one side, Du Bois was praised for his lyricism and scholarship and for having written a book that defied description by its grandness. Some of his critics, however, argued it was not history. With the American Communists, the range was more narrow. Abram L. Harris, a Black Marxist sociologist, critiqued Du Bois for an immature application of Marxism as well as for racialism. (See Harris, "Reconstruction and the Negro," *New Republic*, 7 August 1935, pp. 367–68.) Ben Stolberg entitled his review "Black Chauvinism," (*The Nation*, 15 May 1935, pp. 570–71) and would have agreed with Harris on the advisability of instructing Du Bois in Marxism. The official party view was presented by James S. Allen (or Sol Auerbach), for a time the head of International Publishers, the party publishing house. Harold Cruse writes of Allen's reaction: "Between 1932 and 1937, James S. Allen was commissioned to write four books and pamphlets on Negro affairs. The last one was *Reconstruction—The Battle for Democracy*. What inspired this hurriedly written Marxist study was the appearance, in 1935, of W. E. B. Du Bois's classic work on the same period . . . the most definitive study ever to be written on Reconstruction from the Negro point of view. A good part of the foreword to Allen's book is given over to a Marxist criticism of 'Du Bois in his praiseworthy *Black Reconstruction*' and his 'errors.'" *The Crisis of the Negro Intellectual*, op. cit., p. 163. Allen's task was to resurrect the working class movement from the criticisms that Du Bois had voiced in his attempt to analyze that movement's historical weaknesses. Allen's work quickly replaced that of Du Bois within the party nexus. He and others also successfully screened American Marxism from Du Bois's theoretical revisions. (See Paul Buhle's comments in "American Marxist Historiography, 1900–1940," *Radical America*, November 1970, pp. 5–35.) Thus the Left

picked at Black Reconstruction until nothing remained but the narrative of Black legislative achievement. The work of Herbert Aptheker, the leading Communist scholar on Negro Movements, began under this discipline. (See George Charney's comments on Aptheker's made-to-order work on the Hungarian Uprising, Charney, op. cit., p. 295.) The force of Du Bois's work was more than the ideologues of American Marxism required and, on the other hand, more than American academic history could accept. More than two decades would pass before *Black Reconstruction* would again receive serious attention in either circle. By that time, Du Bois was nearing his nineties and the American Communist Party had been reduced to a sect. By the third decade, the shadow of Du Bois lay across American historiography.

Chapter Ten

1. Hollis Lynch, writing while his historical judgment seemed to match that of his subject too closely, opened his study of Edward Blyden with the declaration that: "The nineteenth was probably the most humiliating century in the history of the Negro race." Hollis Lynch, *Edward Wilmot Blyden: Pan-Negro Patriot, 1832–1912*, Oxford University Press, Oxford, 1970, p. 1. Lynch's justification rested on the persistence of the African slave trade "despite the well-intentioned efforts of the British to stop it and the legal prohibitions imposed upon it by European and American nations" (ibid.); and Negro phobia: "[P]erhaps the greatest wrong inflicted on the Negro race in the nineteenth century was the successful building up of a myth that the Negro was inherently inferior to other races" (ibid., pp. 2–3). But even more debilitating to Lynch's comprehension of the period was his consistent belittling of Black resistance. Both the Haitian Revolution and the resistance to the Confederacy by Afro-Americans were submerged in Lynch's mind by fortuitous locations and developments. Of the first, he was satisfied to write: "West Indian Negroes were fortunate in being the first in the New World to gain their emancipation" (ibid., p. 2). And of the second, he claimed: "So entrenched was slavery in the southern United States that it took the Civil War (1861–1865) to bring about its downfall" (ibid., p. 1). Indeed, Lynch's depiction of "the Negro world in the nineteenth century and the making of a race champion," entirely devoid of any reference to collective Black radicalism, revolves around the dilemma of the Black petit bourgeoisie (the "free Negro") during the eras of slavery and the postemancipation. For them, no doubt, the period was an unpleasant one.

2. "It was . . . the absence of a manufacturing infra-structure after Independence, the development of essentially feudal relations in agriculture, the struggles of the peasantry to remain landed and self-subsistent, the growth of a landed rural middle class, the creation of a prebendary state bureaucracy, the inability of any of the dominant warring factions of the ruling class to achieve a decisive and long-lasting political and economic hegemony, and the penetration and dominance of foreign capital, which would seriously block all attempts at the capitalist transformation and development of Haiti during the nineteenth century." Alex Dupuy, "Class Formation and Underdevelopment in Nineteenth Century Haiti," 1981 (unpublished paper).

3. W. David McIntyre, *Colonies into Commonwealth*, Blandford Press, London, 1974, pp. 152–53.

4. For the Morant Bay Uprising in Jamaica in 1865, see Bernard Semmel, *Jamaican Blood and Victorian Conscience*, Houghton Mifflin, Cambridge, 1963; and Peter Abrahams, *Jamaica*, Her Majesty's Stationery Office, London, 1957, pp. 74–127.

5. McIntyre, op. cit., pp. 169–72; and Christopher Hibbert, *The Great Mutiny*, Viking Press, New York, 1978.

6. The Liberal Party, while in power, "had evacuated Afghanistan and the Transvaal, and had abandoned Cordon at Khartoum to a death they refused to avenge. They had gone further and attempted to break up the Empire. They wished to consolidate the Empire by granting the Irish Home Rule." Elie Halevy, *Imperialism and the Rise of Labour, A History of the English People in the Nineteenth Century*, Ernest Benn, London, 1961 (orig. 1926), 5:10; see also McIntyre, op. cit., pp. 124–28.

7. Immanuel Geiss, *The Pan-African Movement*, Methuen, London, 1974, p. 66.

8. Halevy, op. cit., p. 11.

9. "[A]n entire section of the Liberal leaders, the followers of Lord Rosebery, were imperialists, and during the three years of Liberal government the Foreign Office had pursued an imperialist policy." Halevy, ibid., p. 8.

10. "For the inhabitants of these islands at the beginning of this century the British Empire was for better or worse what Lord Curzon described as 'a great historical and political and sociological fact which is one of the guiding factors in the history of mankind.' Most of them (at least outside Ireland) seem to have thought it to be for the better. . . . They would have been brought up in the nursery on the patriotic verse of Robert Southey and Thomas Campbell. At school their minds would have been moulded by men with the robust and simple-minded patriotism of Charles Kingsley and of William Johnson Cory, that vehement enthusiast who taught so many future members of the ruling class at Eton, not least among them Lord Rosebery and Lord Esher. From schools . . . this generation passed to universities where they came in contact with professors like John Ruskin: Ruskin, who told the audience at his Inaugural Lecture as Slade Professor of Fine Art at Oxford in 1870 that it must be the task of Englishmen 'still undegenerate in race; a

race mingled of the best northern blood,' to 'found colonies as fast and as far as she is able formed of her most energetic and worthiest men;—seizing every piece of fruitful waste ground she can set her foot on, and there teaching these her colonists that their chief virtue is to be fidelity to their country, and that their first aim is to be to advance the power of England by land and sea.' If they were historians, they would be introduced to the works of Carlyle and Froude, who spread the same message." Michael Howard, "Empire, ,Race and War," *History Today* 31 (December 1981): 5. See also, Brian Street, *The Savage in Literature*, Routledge and Kegan Paul, London, 1975; Jonah Raskin, *The Mythology of Imperialism*, Delta, New York, 1971; V. G. Kiernan, *The Lords of Humankind*, Weidenfeld and Nicolson, London, 1969; and Halevy, op. cit., pp. 18–22.

11. Halevy, op. cit., pp. 11–12.

12. "The peons [backwoodsmen of mixed Spanish-Amerindian-African descent from Venezuela], the African immigrants, and the black ex-soldiers, and their descendants, were important groups in the island's peasantry in the nineteenth century. But the peasantry in Trinidad originated with the withdrawal of ex-slaves from the sugar plantations after 1838. Perhaps around 7,000 ex-slaves left the estates to become stallholders. Of these, about five-sixths became owners of between one and ten acres of land, growing chiefly provisions and cocoa, and often giving casual labour to the estates during crop." Bridget Brereton, *Race Relations in Colonial Trinidad 1870–1900*, Cambridge University Press, Cambridge, 1979, p. 138. Brereton's study has been of particular use in the following descriptions of nineteenth-century Trinidad. See also Donald Wood, *Trinidad in Transition: The Years after Slavery*, Oxford University Press (for the Institute of Race Relations), London, 1968, pp. 49ff.

13. The decline of sugar production in Trinidad during the 1840s and 1850s was also attributable to the neglect of the road systems that connected the plantations and ports in western Trinidad. This neglect was connected to the movement of ex-slaves—an attempt by the planters to keep their labor close by. Thirty years after emancipation, the new governor, A. H. Gordon (appointed in 1866) and his surveyor-general were confronted with the results: "During his early excursions Gordon saw at first hand the state of the roads. Everywhere he found neglect. As he was travelling on the main highway to San Fernando a rotten bridge collapsed beneath his party.... The Surveyor-General planned an ambitious programme of new roads, not without opposition from some planters who feared that an improvement in communications might drain off labourers from the estates." Wood, op. cit., pp. 268, 269.

14. Ibid., p. 63.

15. Ibid. Brereton reports: "Victorians were preoccupied with the need for 'steady industry,' 'reliable labour,' by the non-white races of the Empire—usually for a European employer. As the London *Spectator* said, steady industry was 'in English opinion, the single virtue, except reverence for white faces, to be demanded of black men.' The 'lazy nigger' myth performed a useful role: it justified the exploitation of black labourers by the planters, and the neglect of independent peasant cultivators by the government." Brereton, op. cit., p. 148.

16. For a fuller treatment of the attempt to recruit immigrant labor from the West Indies, Africa, the United States, and China, see Wood, op. cit., chaps. 4 and 8. Of the liberated Africans, J. J. (Jacob) Thomas (who will be discussed in the text) "listed the principal tribal groups sent to Trinidad as the 'Mandingoes, Foulahs, Houssas, Calvers, Gallahs, Karamenties, Yorubas, Aradas, Cangas, Kroos, Timnehs, Veis, Eboes, Mokoes, Bibis, Congoes.'" Brereton, op. cit., p. 134.

17. See Wood, op. cit., pp. 107–10.

18. Ibid., p. 158.

19. Brereton, "The Experience of Indentureship: 1845–1917," in John La Guerre (ed.), *Calcutta to Caroni: The East Indians of Trinidad*, Longman Caribbean, Trinidad, 1974, p. 32.

20. Ibid., p. 26.

21. J. C. Jha, "Indian Heritage in Trinidad, West Indies," *Caribbean Quarterly* 19, no. 2 (June 1973): 30. "Conditions like these were part of the fabric of life but the Mutiny depressed them even further. Many of the Bengal army were Brahmins and Rajputs from Oudh and the North-West Provinces; the campaign ebbed and flowed over their homelands and battles were fought in districts which were centres for colonial emigration. Sharp fighting took place, for example, in Jaunpur, Mirzapur, Arrah, and Allahabad; the 17th Native Infantry had risen in Azamgarh in the first months of the troubles; and Cawnpore and Lucknow were bitterly besieged. But worse for the peasantry than pitched battles and the sieges of towns were the mopping-up raids and skirmishes in the villages; for them it was more like an episode in the Thirty Years' War than a disciplined nineteenth-century campaign." Wood, op. cit., p. 148. See also Hibbert, op. cit., for other details of the atrocities committed by the British and the rebellious sepoys.

22. See Jha, op. cit., passim. Hindus dominated Muslims almost 9:1.

23. Extracted from a colonial petition of August 1919, requesting the permanent stationing of a white garrison in Trinidad, and cited by Brinsley Samaroo, "The Trinidad Workingmen's Association and the Origins of Popular Protest in a Crown Colony," *Social and Economic Studies* 21, no. 2 (June 1972): 213.

24. Ibid., p. 206.

25. Wood, op. cit., pp. 152–53. "The *Tazia* procession (Husain or Hose) was the biggest festival in which

Hindus also participated. In fact, from 1850s this festival became the annual demonstration of Indian national feeling which culminated in the Hose Riots of San Fernando in 1884. A big flag is raised at the start of the ceremony and the *tazias* (replicas of the tombs of Hasan and Husain, grandchildren of prophet Mohammed) are led by specially trained moon dancers to the accompaniment of drum beating and 'gatka' (stick) fighting. In the past fire rod dancing was also done, twirling a twelve foot pole with flaming rags secured to either end. Even non-Indians have been taking part in the procession." Jha, op. cit., p. 31. For the attitudes of Afro-Creoles and East Indians toward one another, see Brereton, *Race Relations*, op. cit., pp. 188–90.

26. One prominent member of the colored middle class, Dr. Stephen Moister Laurence wrote in his memoirs concerning the language of British colonials: "When however we analyse the term 'native' in relation to racial origin as well as place of birth, we discover the true explanation of many a mistake made alike by British people in general and the Colonial Office in particular. This special class division must have begun long ago when the East—that is, India—was *the* Colonial possession. Naturally, there were but few English, and these were mostly constantly back and forth, so that the whole Indian people were referred to as natives. This was perfectly correct, because they were both of pure Indian stock and of Indian birth. This justified use of the term 'native' would be extended to the entire East, and also to Africa." "But when one turns to the West Indies the whole question takes on a very different complexion, and calls for handling from a very different angle." "If, instead of presuming that these factors in the West Indies had the same significance or insignificance as in the East, British authorities had acquainted themselves with the difference, then Downing Street [the Secretary of State for the Colonies was once located there as well as the Prime Minister] at least—not to mention religious authorities—would have made fewer mistakes and most likely scored more numerous successes than recorded history has established." "The Trinidad Water Riot of 1903: Reflections of an Eyewitness," edited by L. O. Laurence, *Caribbean Quarterly*, 15, no. 4 (December 1969): 13–14.

27. See Samaroo, op. cit., p. 206.

28. Wood, op. cit., p. 127.

29. Brereton, *Race Relations*, op. cit., p. 148.

30. Ibid., p. 164.

31. Ibid., chap. 8; see also D. V. Trotman, "The Yoruba and Orisha Worship in Trinidad and British Guiana 1838–1870," *African Studies Review*, 19, no. 2 (September 1976): 1–17; and J. D. Elder, "The Yoruba Ancestor Cult in Gasparillo," *Caribbean Quarterly* 16, no. 3 (August 1970) (cited by Brereton).

32. Brereton, ibid., p. 162.

33. Wood, op. cit., p. 136.

34. Ibid., pp. 157–59. "[B]y late 1870s the Indians in Trinidad had some good horses which won prizes in races, and the best kept cows and between 1885 and 1909 they acquired 69,087 acres of land." Jha, op. cit., p. 30; see also Winston Dookeran, "East Indians and the Economy of Trinidad and Tobago," in John La Guerre, op. cit., pp. 69–83 for the persistence of poverty among East Indians.

35. Wood, op. cit., p. 276. These crops were developed by enterprising East Indians early on to substitute for imports of the foods familiar to the Indian diet.

36. See Brereton, *Race Relations*, op. cit., pp. 191–92.

37. Chinese immigration was halted in 1866 by the Kung Convention. See Wood, op. cit., pp. 160–67 for details of the Trinidad episode.

38. "The French Creoles dominated the white Creole elite. These were mainly whites of French descent, but the term was generally understood to include people of English Irish, Spanish, Corsican, and even German descent, born in the island, and almost invariably Roman Catholic. People born in Europe, but resident in Trinidad for many years, and linked by marriage to this group, were also by courtesy considered to be French Creoles." Brereton, *Race Relations*, op. cit., p. 35. Trinidad had served as a receptacle for French emigre aristocrats in the West Indies who fled Haiti and other French possessions in the wake of the French and Haitian revolutions.

39. Ibid., p. 204.

40. See Wood, op. cit., chap. 14.

41. This process is described in Brereton, *Race Relations*, op. cit., p. 47.

42. See Laurence, op. cit.; and Samaroo, op. cit.

43. Brereton, *Race Relations*, op. cit., p. 63.

44. Ibid., p. 86.

45. Ibid., translation mine.

46. Ibid., p. 99.

47. Ibid., p. 97.

48. Wood, op. cit., p. 249.

49. For Thomas's background, see Brereton, *Race Relations*, op. cit., pp. 91–96.

50. Quoted in C. L. R. James, "Discovering Literature in Trinidad: The 1930s," in *Sphere of Existence*, Allison and Busby, London, 1980, pp. 241–42.

51. Brereton, *Race Relations*, op. cit., pp. 94–95.

52. Ibid., pp. 92–97.

53. *Geiss*, op. cit., pp. 176ff. Williams's pan-Africanism was also anticipated in Thomas's experience: "J. J. Thomas wrote in 1889 that he was 'familiar since early childhood with members of almost every tribe of Africans . . . who were brought to the West Indies.'" Brereton, *Race Relations*, op. cit., p. 134. For his enumeration, see note 235.

54. "J. J. Thomas was one of those who expressed strong race pride. He was only too conscious of the extent of self-contempt and self-hatred among his fellow blacks in the West Indies. He saw how the values of white superiority had been internalised, with disastrous results. One factor in this process, in his view, was the education of young West Indians by white teachers. He thought their influence was 'to a very great degree subversive of the national sentiment,' by which he meant racial consciousness." "There were individually brilliant blacks. But there had to be 'some potential agency to collect and adjust them into the vast engine essential for executing the true purposes of the civilised African Race.'" Brereton, *Race Relations*, op. cit., pp. 104, 106.

55. Ibid., p. 94.

56. Both H. Sylvester Williams and R. E. Phipps raised the issue of the place of the West Indian middle classes in the governing of their societies at the Pan-African Conference in London in 1900; Geiss, op. cit., pp. 187, 193.

57. James, *The Case for West-Indian Self Government*, Hogarth, London, 1933, pp. 10–11. Colonial officials, apparently, were not the only ones who might be shocked by the discovery of "civilized" west Indians. Dr. Stephen Laurence observed: "Perhaps the best resume and the most fitting comment on this question is the reply said to have been given to her Majesty Queen Victoria at her Jubilee [in 1897] by the late Mr. Lazare [Emmanuel Mzumbo Lazare, a solicitor and conveyancer, born in Trinidad in 1864], himself of pure African stock: 'Do you speak English in Trinidad?' asked her Majesty. 'Madam in Trinidad we are all English.'" Laurence, op. cit., p. 15.

58. James, ibid., p. 31.

59. Richard Small, "The Training of an Intellectual, the Making of a Marxist," in Paul Buhle (ed.), *C. L. R. James: His Life and Work*, a special issue of *Urgent Tasks* 12 (Summer 1981): 13. James's paternal grandfather was the pan boiler, his maternal grandfather, Josh Rudder, was the engine driver. See James, *Beyond a Boundary*, op. cit., pp. 17–19, 22–25. Both grandfathers had achieved positions normally reserved for whites in the nineteenth century. Rudder, especially, achieved an expertise with locomotives that still put him in occasional demand even in his late retirement. He jealously husbanded his knowledge from whites. On one instance, having performed one of his miracles, James described the old man's reaction. "An enthusiastic crowd, headed by the manager, surrounded Josh, asking him what is was that had performed the miracle. But the always exuberant Josh grew silent for once and refused to say. He never told them. He never told anybody. The obstinate old man wouldn't even tell me. But when I asked him [one] day, 'Why did you do it?' he said what I had never heard before. 'They were white men with all their M.I.C.E. and R.I.C.E. and all their big degrees, and it was their business to fix it. I had to fix it for them. Why should I tell them?'" Ibid., p. 25.

60. Brereton, *Race Relations*, op. cit., p. 134.

61. Ibid., p. 167.

62. Small, op. cit., p. 13.

63. James, *Beyond a Boundary*, op. cit., pp. 25–26.

64. Small, op. cit., p. 13. "The game of cricket, therefore, in a real sense mirrored life in general in West Indian society, where a similar dichotomy existed. Whites were represented in the top echelons of West Indian Society, out of all proportion to their numbers in the population. They led and non-white West Indians were expected to follow. Decisions with respect to who should play, on which grounds test matches in the West Indies should be played, amount of entrance fee for games and hence profits, continued to be made by the whites." Maurice St. Pierre, "West Indian Cricket—A Socio-Historical Appraisal, Part I," *Caribbean Quarterly* 19, no. 2 (June 1973): 8.

65. James, *Beyond a Boundary*, op. cit., p. 13. See also J. A. Mangan, *Athleticism in the Victorian and Edwardian Public School*, Cambridge University Press, Cambridge, 1981.

66. Samaroo, op. cit., pp. 206–7.

67. For an account of the founding of the British Labour Party during the first three years of the present century, see Halevy, op. cit., pp. 261–81.

68. Samaroo, op. cit., p. 210.

69. McIntyre, op. cit., p. 132.

70. Ibid., pp. 133–34.

71. George Padmore, *Africa and World Peace*, Frank Cass, London, 1972, p. 235. For details of the African and Black troops used by the colonial powers in the nineteenth as well as the twentieth century (until the late 1920s), see Padmore, *The Life and Struggles of Negro Toilers*, Sun Dance Press, Hollywood, 1971, pp. 111–20. Elsewhere, Padmore had quoted General Smuts of South Africa on the French use of troops: "During

the first year of the war 70,000 black troops were raised in French West Africa. By 1918 Black Africa had furnished France 680,000 soldiers and 238,000 labourers in all. We have seen what we have never seen before, what enormously valuable material lay in the Black Continent." Padmore, *Pan-Africanism or Communism*, Doubleday, New York, 1972, p. 98.

72. See Padmore, Negro Toilers, op. cit., pp. 117–19, for figures. Harry Haywood was a veteran of the French campaigns and describes the experience of Black American troops in France in Haywood, *Black Bolshevik*, op. cit., pp. 53–78. See also W. E. B. Du Bois's treatment in "The Black Man in the Revolution of 1914–1918," and "An Essay Toward a History of the Black Man in the Great War," in *The Seventh Son*, Julius Lester (ed.), op. cit., pp. 107–15 and 115–57, respectively.

73. Samaroo, op. cit., pp. 211–12. James was underage but he attempted to volunteer for the war effort (but in the Merchants' and Planters' Contingent): "Young man after young man went in [to the volunteers' office], and I was not obviously inferior to any of them in anything. The merchant talked to each, asked for references and arranged for further examination as the case might be. When my turn came I walked to his desk. He took one look at me, saw my dark skin and, shaking his head vigorously, motioned me violently away." "What matters is that I was not unduly disturbed." James, *Beyond a Boundary*, op. cit., p. 40.

74. Samaroo, ibid., pp. 210–11. A more profound interpretation is provided by Fitz A. Baptiste: "The war produced a price spiral for commodities and the British Caribbean, the commodity producer par excellence, tried to cash in on the boom as best they could. Some statistics for Jamaica reveal that, despite the effects by 1917/18 of the British blockade and the German submarine warfare on Allied trade, export values were maintained, even though there were falls in volumes, owing to the general spurt in prices for commodities, especially cocoa and coffee." "While a factor in this was clearly sheer exploitative greed by the merchant categories in the colonial society, a more fundamental cause was the enforced shift of dependence for imports from Britain to the United States and to Canada as the blockade and the Battle of the Atlantic began to register themselves in the Caribbean.... The extraordinarily high percentage for imports from the United States [for Jamaica, 67.6 percent] clearly reflected some of the distortions effected by the war and which were still continuing into the post-war years." Baptiste, "The United States and West Indian Unrest: 1918–1939," Working Paper No. 18, Institute of Social and Economic Research, University of the West Indies, Jamaica, 1978, pp. 5–6.

75. Samaroo, ibid., pp. 211–16. "There were disturbances in British Honduras in July 1919 and again in 1920; in Jamaica on two occasions in 1918 and also in 1924; in Trinidad in late 1919/early 1920; in St. Lucia in February, 1920; and in the Bahamas in December, 1922. The list may well be shown to be longer." Baptiste, op. cit., p. 7.

76. See Small, op. cit., p. 16; and W. F. Elkins, "A Source of Black Nationalism in the Caribbean: The Revolt of the British West Indies Regiment at Taranto, Italy," *Science and Society* 34 (Spring 1970): 99–103 (cited by Small).

77. Samaroo, op. cit., p. 219; and James, *The Black Jacobins*, op. cit., appendix, pp. 403–4. A very different experience for Blacks in the various theaters of war was their own interaction: the discovery of their mutual oppression. Claude McKay recalled his own experience in London during the war: "One club was for colored soldiers. It was situated in a basement in Drury Lane. There was a host of colored soldiers in London, from the West Indies and Africa, with a few colored Americans, East Indians, and Egyptians among them . . . I went often and listened to the soldiers telling tales of their war experiences in France, Egypt and Arabia. Many were interested in what American Negroes were thinking and writing." McKay, *A Long Way From Home*, op. cit., p. 67.

78. McIntyre, op. cit., pp. 209–10. In his dispatches to Washington, the Acting American Consul, Henry D. Baker, wrote from Port of Spain in December 1919 of the racial concerns he shared with Trinidad's colonial officials: "[M]ention was made of an interview between the Governor of Trinidad and Tobago and the manager of the General Asphalt Company [where a strike was expected and Baker had in place 'a trusted coloured employee'] in the course of which the Governor allegedly stated that the Colonial Government had no confidence in the local police force which was predominantly black and advised the asphalt and oil companies to establish a white militia. As if to show that he meant business, the Governor provided 25 rifles and 11 rounds of ammunition for use by the militia. That by itself, is a remarkable index of the racist reaction of the authorities, backed by the expatriate and local white interests, to what was clearly perceived as a 'black power' movement." Baptiste, op. cit., p. 12. Baker recommended to Washington: "intervention, preferably at the invitation of the British authorities, but, 'in the threatened massacre of white people,' to use his own words in a separate message, without it." Ibid., p. 13.

79. James, *Beyond a Boundary*, op. cit., p. 71.

80. Ibid., pp. 70–71.

81. Of the many recollections James has published of his friendship with Padmore, perhaps the most poignant is the brief: "[W]e were boys together, and used to bathe in the Arima River, underneath the ice factory." James, "Discovering Literature in Trinidad: The 1930s," op. cit., p. 238, see also James Hooker, *Black Revolutionary*, op. cit., pp. 2–3.

82. Hooker, op. cit., pp. 3–4.

83. Ibid., p. 16.

84. Ibid., p. 31.

85. Small, op. cit., p. 17; see also James, *Beyond a Boundary*, op. cit., p. 117.

86. James, *Beyond a Boundary*, op. cit., p. 116.

87. "The ex-British colonials have got to break away from parliamentarism. I did it through becoming a Marxist." Alan J. MacKenzie interview with James, "Radical Pan-Africanism in the 1930s," *Radical History Review* 24 (Fall 1980): 71.

88. Ibid.

89. For the publication of James's first major works including the novel, *Minty Alley*, see Robert A. Hill, "In England, 1932–1938," *Urgent Tasks* 12 (Summer 1981): 19–27; and E. Elliot Parris, *"Minty Alley,"* ibid., pp. 97–98.

90. James, *Beyond a Boundary*, op. cit., pp. 118–19.

91. See Basil Wilson, "The Caribbean Revolution," *Urgent Tasks* 12 (Summer 1981): 47–54.

92. Halevy, op. cit., pp. 211–12.

93. Stuart MacIntyre, *A Proletarian Science: Marxism in Britain, 1917–1933*, Cambridge University Press, Cambridge, 1980, p. 23.

94. "This sour creed, imported from abroad, which refused to set before its adherents an ideal which made appeal to the heart but was content to prove by scientific arguments, or what purported to be such, the approach of a complete upheaval of society, at once violent in its methods, and beneficient in its effects, repelled many of those Englishmen who for the past twenty-five years or more [before 1884] had been approaching Socialism by other routes. In agreement with the Marxists to denounce a social order based on the unhappiness of the majority and the war of all against all, they did not share the Marxian interpretation of history. They did not invite the working classes to use violence. The formula of the class war was absent from their vocabulary. Neither Ruskin, the man whose spirit inspired British Socialism, nor William Morris himself, though he professed a species of anarchist Communism, was in the strict sense a revolutionary. England had passed through two revolutions—the Puritan revolution of the seventeenth century, the industrial revolution of the eighteenth—and their dark shadow still lay over the land. Without recourse to violence, Socialism must teach the nation the art of being good, and happy, the cult of beauty." Halevy, op. cit., pp. 221–22. Halevy's prejudice is his own, but the fact of the limited impact of Marxism in Britain in the late nineteenth and early twentieth centuries is generally established. See, for example, David Smith, *Socialist Propaganda in the Twentieth-Century British Novel*, Macmillan Press, London, 1978, pp. 4–10.

95. See Stanley Pierson, *Marxism and the Origins of British Socialism*, Cornell University Press, Ithaca, 1973, pp. 67–68.

96. Stuart MacIntyre, op. cit., p. 17.

97. For the Fabians, see Pierson, op. cit., pp. 106–39; and Halevy, op. cit., pp. 105–6 for Fabian imperialism.

98. Pierson, ibid., pp. 137–38.

99. Stuart MacIntyre, op. cit., p. 65.

100. Neal Wood, *Communism and British Intellectuals*, Victor Gollancz, London, 1959, p. 23; and MacIntyre, op. cit., pp. 4–11.

101. See L. J. MacFarlane, *The British Communist Party*, MacGibbon and Kee, Worcester and London, 1966, chap. 7.

102. "From the middle of 1924 until the General Strike, the party's membership doubled, largely as a result of its work in the industrial and trade union fields. During the miners' struggle of 1926 membership rocketed to over 10,000, only to start on a decline which became sharper as the party adopted a more and more uncompromising attitude towards the Labour Party and the trade unions. By the end of the twenties the membership had fallen back to 3,200, roughly the same figure as in the period 1922 to mid-1924. The adoption of the 'new line' was the main factor which accelerated the rate of decline after 1928." MacFarlane, ibid., p. 286; see also Wood, op. cit., p. 23.

103. Wood, op. cit., p. 51.

104. Ibid., pp. 27–28.

105. Stuart MacIntyre, op. cit., p. 19; see also Raphael Samuel, "British Marxist Historians I," *New Left Review* 120 (March–April 1980): 23–24.

106. "A British radical intelligentsia, comparable to the long-established continental intelligentsias, did not appear until the nineteen-thirties. In the main British intellectuals had always been Liberal or Conservative. Then between 1928 and 1933 a change occurred in their outlook. Just before the opening of the new decade, G. D. H. Cole sensed 'a disquieting insecurity' among young intellectuals. Their pursuit of pleasure ceased to be satisfying. A new seriousness came to the fore in the place of the former joie de vivre. Increasing attention was given to politics. Whereas sex and aesthetics had been the major topics of conversation, now everybody began to talk politics. As time passed the politics of the intellectual moved leftward to socialism and communism. What began as a political awakening became a great radicalization." Wood, op. cit., p. 37. For the impact of this movement on English historiography, see Eric Hobsbawm,

"The Historians' Group of the Communist Party," in Maurice Cornforth (ed.), *Rebels and Causes*, Lawrence and Wishart, London, 1978, pp. 21–47.

107. See Stuart MacIntyre, op. cit., pp. 47–65; Alan McKinnon, "Communist Party Election Tactics: A Historical Review," *Marxism Today* 24, no. 8 (August 1980): 20–26, Henry Pelling, "The Early History of the Communist Party of Great Britain 1920–29," *Transactions of the Royal Historical Society*, 5th ser., vol. 8 (1958): 41–57; John Strachey, "Communism in Great Britain," *Current History*, January 1939, pp. 29–31; and Hugo Dewar, *Communist Politics in Britain: The* CPCB from its Origins to the Second World War, Pluto Press, London, 1976, chaps. 7–10.

108. See Folarin Shyllon, "The Black Presence and Experience in Britain: An Analytical Overview," paper presented to the International Conference on the History of Blacks in Britain, University of London, 30 September 1981, p. 7; and Geiss, op. cit., p. 201.

109. In the post–World War I years, American and British officials worked closely to orchestrate the access of Black British colonials to the English-speaking metropoles: "According to U.S. immigration records, the United Kingdom used up 43.9 per cent of its quota between 1925 and 1929; 22.6 per cent between 1930 and 1934; and a mere 4.4 per cent in the 1936/40 period. This left room, technically, for considerable emigration to the United States from the British colonies in the Caribbean. However, this never occurred or, to be more direct, was never allowed to happen. Through the issuance of visas, and the requirement of substantial bonds, the United States, with the tacit approval of the British metropolitan and colonial authorities, exercised an extremely tight control over the flow of British West Indians. The result was a sharp decline in the numbers of British West Indians entering the United States after 1925. In comparison to the average of thousands a year up to and including 1924, the average for the rest of the 1920s and for the 1930s became hundreds a year. In 1932, for example, a mere 113 British West Indians entered the United States." Baptiste, op. cit., pp. 19–20. Recall that this was a period of Black political movement in the United States in which West Indians had played prominent parts: that is, the UNIA, the CPUSA, the student movements at Black colleges and universities, the ABB, and so on.

110. See Ian Duffield, "The Dilemma of Pan-Africanism for Blacks in Britain, 1760–1950," paper presented to the International Conference on the History of Blacks in Britain, op. cit., pp. 7–8. (Duffield's unpublished doctoral thesis, "Duse Mohamed Ali and the Development of Pan-Africanism, 1866–1945," Edinburgh University, 1971, is generally accepted as the definitive work on Mohamed Ali Duse.) See also Geiss, op. cit., pp. 226–27.

111. The histories of these organizations have been reviewed in Geiss, op. cit., chaps. 14 and 17; see also Nigel File and Chris Power, *Black Settlers in Britain, 1555–1958*, Heinemann Educational Books, London, 1981, pp. 72–77.

112. For Padmore, Chris Jones, and Arnold Ward, see Hooker, op. cit.; and MacKenzie, op. cit.; for Dutt and Saklatvala, see MacFarlane, op. cit.; information on Blackman has been obtained from interviews with him in London, December 1981. Geiss maintains that as early as 1898 the Liberal Party was having discussions about the possibility of a Black man standing for Parliament to represent "the Crown Colonies and Protectorates, West Africa, West Indies, etc. etc." Geiss, op. cit., p. 178.

113. See Geiss, op. cit., pp. 347–53; and Hooker, op. cit., pp. 48–49.

114. The most sympathetic interpretation of the actions taken by Stalin and the Comintern is that the dismantling of much of the propaganda apparatus in support of "world revolution" and national liberation struggles in the colonies was necessary in exchange for trade, entrance into the League of Nations for the Soviet Union, and the establishment of a loose antifascist front of "collective security" with the imperialist and capitalist states. The alternative, it continues, was the prospect of a German war, tacitly approved by those ruling classes in England, France, and America for whom the Sixth Congress of the Comintern had expressed resolute hostility. Padmore, who early in 1933 had spent several months imprisoned by Nazi authorities in Hamburg, either was unimpressed with this rationale (a certain incredulousness was warranted; less than a year later, on January 26, 1934, Stalin, at the Seventeenth Congress of the CPSU, dismissed the threat of fascism to the Soviet Union and reminded his party that the USSR had established "the best relations" with fascist Italy. Fernando Claudin, *The Communist Movement*, op. cit., 1:176–77), or was no longer capable of loyalty to a world movement led by a leadership characterized by Claudin (who was himself expelled from the Spanish Communist Party in 1965 after 32 years of active membership) as suffering from "a deep-going sickness: atrophy of the theoretical faculties, bureaucratization of the organizational structures, sterilizing monolithicity, unconditional subordination to the manoeuvres of Stalin's camarilla." Ibid., p. 166. Padmore's most credible statement—he was later seldom capable of the "political objectivity" regarding the Soviet Union with which he prided himself here—indicated a "betrayal of the fundamental interests of my people" (Hooker, op. cit., p. 31). Franz Borkenau suggested that a strong contributing factor to the Soviet Union's rapprochement to the imperialist powers were the struggles internal to the Soviet administration, Borkenau, *World Communism*, op. cit., pp. 388–93. Geiss maintains that "most coloured communists or fellow-travellers left the movement" at this time. He cites Padmore, Kouyaute, and Kenyatta as examples, Geiss, op. cit., p. 338. My own research suggests otherwise. Discussions with Afro-American veterans of the Spanish Civil War have indicated that even the

revelation of Soviet aid to Italy during the 1935 Italian invasion of Ethiopia (William Nolan in his *Communism Versus the Negro*, op. cit., pp. 135, 245 n. 90, cites articles in the New *York Times*, 8 and 10 September 1935), did not deter them. James Yates told me: "We didn't get a chance to go to Ethiopia much as many of us would have liked to gone. But when Ethiopia was invaded and Italy overran it, those same troops left there and went to Spain. This was a time and a chance for especially the Blacks to volunteer and get back at the fascists that had invaded Ethiopia." Interview, 26 April 1978, Binghamton. Harry Haywood has maintained the same position. Interview, Spring 1977, Binghamton; and see also his *Black Bolshevik*, op. cit., pp. 448–49, 459–60, and chap. 18.

115. James, *Beyond a Boundary*, op. cit., p. 114.

116. "When the war ended the black community in Britain was quite large, perhaps as numerous as 20,000 souls, and with the closing down of war factories they flocked to dockside areas, particularly Cardiff and Liverpool. During the war, black sailors had earned good money in the merchant navy, but with the demobilization of white sailors who had been serving in the Royal Navy, the blacks fell on hard times as they were discarded to make way for the demobilized whites. Blacks were expelled from jobs they had held for years just to make places for white men." "Resentment at blacks competing for jobs with white workers, and reaction to black men marrying white women, finally erupted into racial violence in 1919. Race riots swept such British cities and towns as Liverpool, Cardiff, Manchester, London, Hull, Barry, and Newport, Mon. Reporting the Liverpool incidents *The Times* of 10 May 1919, pointed out that the war had increased the black men in Liverpool until they then numbered about 5,000." Folarin Shyllon, op. cit., p. 8.

117. In Berlin and Paris, American Blacks, for example, Ethel Waters and Josephine Baker, joined French colonial dependents; in Britain, the prize-fighter Jack Johnson, and Paul Robeson, were contemporaries of Learie Constantine and the Sierra Leone actor, Robert Adams.

118. See Makonnen, op. cit., p. 133; Padmore, *Pan-Africanism or Communism*, op. cit., p. 95; and James, *Beyond a Boundary*, op. cit., pp. 128–29.

119. Interview with Mrs. Veronica Sankey, 20 July 1980, Brighton; Edward and Veronica Sankey founded the Sankey Printing Company in Ikeja, Nigeria.

120. Makonnen, op. cit., p. 152.

121. Ibid., p. xvii.

122. See Geiss, op. cit., pp. 355, 387–90.

123. "I became a bona fide member of the publishers' association, and proceeded to bring out a number of pieces that needed publicity. There was a pamphlet by Kenyatta [*Kenya: Land of Conflict*], and a kind of Socratic discussion between Nancy Cunard and George Padmore on the black man's burden [*White Man's Duty*], and a manuscript by Eric Williams [*The Negro in the Caribbean*]." Makonnen, op. cit., p. 145.

124. Ibid., p. 123.

125. Ibid., p. 159.

126. Ibid., p. 124.

127. Ibid., p. 126. In Africa, "Europeans who attempted to live native style quickly went to pieces. Some missionaries who tried this approach failed wretchedly. Many white men who let their standards fall in the immensity of the continent took to drink and self-despair, and some became so deranged they sought refuge from the immensity of the continent, like wild animals, in lairs under rocks or in caves. 'Going *shenzi*,' it was called." Jeremy Murray-Brown, *Kenyatta*, Fontana/Collins, London, 1974, p. 47. Murray-Brown maintains that Kenyatta while living in Britain was driven by similar strains, but resolved them by discovering a sacred tree in his garden in Storrington, and "maintained communion with the spirits of his people through libations and prayers." Ibid., pp. 214–15.

128. Makonnen, ibid., p. 155.

129. Ibid., p. 124.

130. See Julian Symons, *The Thirties: A Dream Revolved*, Faber and Faber, London, 1975, chaps. 5–10; Douglas Hill (ed.), *Tribune 40*, Quartet Books, London, 1977, pp. 1–24; Neal Wood, op. cit., pp. 53–63; and David Smith, op. cit., pp. 48–56.

131. Symons, ibid., pp. 56–57; and Smith, ibid., pp. 48–49.

132. Symons, ibid., p. 56.

133. Douglas Hill, op. cit., p. 3.

134. On Spain, Julian Symons recalled: "The rebels [under Franco] were being armed with German and Italian guns and rifles, so that the British Government's declaration in favour of a policy of non-intervention was in effect support of the rebellion." "The policy of non-intervention, Stephen Spender said, was 'more grotesquely, obviously and dangerously a support of interference by the Fascist powers than was the arms embargo in the Abyssinian conflict a present of munitions and victory to Italy.'" Symons, op. cit., pp. 107, 108.

135. See Folarin Shyllon, op. cit., p. 9. Presumably, Shyllon is relying on the unpublished Ph.D. thesis authored by Ian Duffield; see note 110.

136. Wayne Cooper and Robert C. Reinders, "Claude McKay in England, 1920," *New Beacon Reviews*, Collection One, 1968, pp. 3–21 (reprinted from *Race*, ix, 1967). Cooper and Reinders recount: "McKay

escaped arrest but his 'big black grin' [McKay's description] did not prevent the Home and/or Foreign Office from preparing a dossier on him. In 1930 McKay wrote to Max Eastman that the English government prevented him from visiting Gibraltar (McKay was still a British subject) and that a French official in Fez told him that the 'British Secret Service had me listed as a propagandist.' Two years later McKay was having trouble with the British Consul in Tangiers and was prevented from entering British territory—including his home island of Jamaica. And in the following year he complained to Eastman that 'those dirty British bastards working respectably in the dark' were blocking his re-entry into the United States." Ibid., p. 12.

137. See Hooker, op. cit., pp. 23, 43.

138. "In the Caribbean colonies, a clamp was placed on radicals. Butler spent much of the war locked up. In Jamaica, Bustamante was also interned for a while under the wartime defence regulations. Despatches from the American Consul in Kingston tell how the Colonial Government, in the face of local reactions, took advantage of the power vested in it by the Defence Regulations to detain persons who were noted as 'bitter critics' of British colonialism. One of those detained was Wilfred A. Domingo who was described as 'a native of Jamaica who for some years has been resident in New York from which place he has taken an active part in Jamaican politics.' He was removed from a ship taking him from the United States to Jamaica before it actually docked at Kingston and placed in an internment camp. . . . It is not inconceivable that the news that he was on his way to Jamaica was sent to the British authorities by the American and British intelligence networks in the United States. Intelligence was one facet and an important one of the developing Anglo-American wartime collaboration in Caribbean defence, with the Americans in the senior role." Fitz A. Baptiste, op. cit., pp. 45–46.

139. For a recent evaluation of British Marxist intellectuals, see E. P. Thompson's collection of essays, *The Poverty of Theory*, Merlin, London, 1978; and Perry Anderson's sometimes specious rejoinder, *Arguments Within English Marxism* Verso, London, 1980.

140. James, *Beyond a Boundary*, op. cit., p. 122.

141. Richard Small, op. cit., p. 17.

142. Robert A. Hill, "In England, 1932–1938," op. cit., pp. 23–24. Hill also provides a defense of James's Trotskyism: "[A] large body of Trotsky's followers, not just in France but throughout the European working-class movement, were genuine Leninists who, while not willing to tolerate Stalin's betrayal, went with Trotsky because he seemed to offer a possibility of sustaining the revolutionary political principles of Lenin. The cadres whom James became associated with in the Trotskyist movement were bearers of the political thought and practice of Lenin and Bolshevism at its prime. *Most of them could be classified as Trotskyists only secondarily.* From them James gained an immense knowledge of the internal make-up of the revolutionary socialist movement and the special role which outstanding workers came to play in its development" (ibid., p. 23). This interpretation of Trotskyism (and Hill indicates a debt to the work of Franz Borkenau—see Borkenau, op. cit., p. 396) is only partially sound. It implies, correctly, the cult of personality with which Stalinists were comfortable, and frequently attached to those they opposed (the history of the Communist movement in Western countries is replete with "deviations" known by the suffix "-ite"), but it also displaces Stalin and Trotsky with Lenin by the same logic ("bearers"). I can only guess at what "outstanding workers" means, and if I have surmised correctly it suggests one of the fundamental flaws in James's thought, one which will be explored in his treatment of the Haitian Revolution. Finally, James, in his "Notes On Dialectics" (Allison and Busby, London, 1980), a manuscript that Hill had a great deal to do with preserving, provides a much more historical interpretation of Trotskyism, one which places that "phenomenon" within the history of the progressive development of the working classes. That, too, I shall attempt to demonstrate later in the text.

143. Sylvia Wynter, "In Quest of Matthew Bondsman: Some Cultural Notes on the Jamesian Journey," *Urgent Tasks* 12 (Summer 1981): 54.

144. James, *Beyond a Boundary*, op. cit., p. 34.

145. Ibid., p. 47. For Thackeray, see Margaret Forster, *William Makepeace Thackeray: Memoirs of a Victorian Gentleman*, Quartet, London, 1980.

146. James, ibid., p. 37.

147. See J. A. Mangan, *Athleticism in the Victorian and Edwardian Public School*, Cambridge University Press, Cambridge, 1981. Mangan believes that Arnold's role has been overdone, but generally confirms James's earlier treatment of the public school phenomenon; see Mangan, chap. 1.

148. James, *Beyond a Boundary*, op. cit., pp. 158–60. Grace, James declares, was the best known Englishman of his time, that is the last quarter of the nineteenth century. And James deplores the fact that neither Trevelyan, nor Postgate or Cole in their histories of that century found a place for him. But when he declared that he could "no longer accept the system of values which could not find in these books a place for W. G. Grace" (ibid., p. 157), he was also, it would appear, coming to terms with a species of Marxism that possessed neither imagination or political relevance. He had come to terms with the relationship between culture, class power, and economic dominance that had reduced even Marx to a somewhat mumbled admission of perplexity (see Marx on the Western ideal in Greek art in his *A Contribution to the*

Critique of Political Economy). And James realized that he had gone quite far: "The conjunction hit me as it would have hit few of the students of society and culture in the international organization to which I belonged." Ibid., p. 151. Though it is difficult to get her to say it, Sylvia Wynter confirms James' self-assessment: "The co-evolution of new popular forms of social organization, i.e., trade union organizations, political parties, international organization, organizational forms of struggle for popular democracy with the rise of the desire for organized sports all within the decade 1860–1870 provide the basis for the Jamesian reflection on the complexity of human needs, for his implicit affirmation that the 'realization of one's powers' at both the individual and the group level is the most urgent imperative of all . . . [it] was a conjunction that hit James, only because unlike Trotsky he had moved outside the monoconceptual Labor frame to the wider frame of a popular theoretics." Wynter, op. cit., p. 58.

149. See Basil Wilson, op. cit., pp. 49–50; see also Eric Williams's few comments on James in his autobiography, *Inward Hunger*, op. cit.

150. See Thompson's "Foreword" and the title essay in *The Poverty of Theory*, op. cit.

151. E. P. Thompson, "The Politics of Theory," in Raphael Samuel (ed.), *People's History and Socialist Theory*, Routledge and Kegan Paul, London, 1981, p. 397.

152. James, *Beyond a Boundary*, op. cit., p. 150.

153. Ibid., p. 152. The residues of James's "Victorian" upbringing remain until this day and are given full rein at times in this volume. Witness: "The Greeks were the most politically minded and intellectually and artistically the most creative of all peoples." Ibid., p. 154. Hardly a considered or even possible judgment.

154. Ibid., p. 155.

155. Ibid., p. 153.

156. Ibid., p. 155.

157. "Wordsworth had said that England needed manners, virtue, freedom, power. Arnold saw that it had power. Freedom for him was embodied in the first Reform Act. But manners and virtue he was sure were absent and he was equally sure that their continued absence from the realm would end in the destruction of both power and freedom. Mealy-mouthed generations have watered him down as they have watered down Charles Dickens. Arnold was a man of tempestuous temperament. He was tormented all his life by the fear that England (in fact the whole modern world) would be cracked wide open by social revolution and end either in ruin or military dictatorship. It was to counter this that he did what he did. He aimed to create a body of educated men of the upper classes who would resist the crimes of Toryism and the greed and vulgarity of industrialists on the one hand, and the socialistic claims of the oppressed but uneducated masses on the other." Ibid., p. 160.

158. Ibid., p. 162.

159. John Rae, "Play Up, Play Up," *Times Literary Supplement*, 2 October 1981, p. 1120.

160. James, *Beyond a Boundary*, op. cit., p. 164.

161. Ibid.

162. Alan McKinnon, "Communist Party Election Tactics," op. cit., p. 23.

163. See Henry Pelling, *A History of British Trade Unionism*, Penguin, Harmondsworth, 1976.

164. See Alan McKinnon, op. cit., pp. 22–23. T. D. Burridge suggested one reason for the Labour Party's new vitality: "Though the Party never officially adopted an outright pacifist position, a dedicated pacifist, George Lansbury, was Leader of the Party from 1932–35. In addition, Socialist theory interpreted war in economic terms as a clash of rival imperialisms—the last, most decadent stage of capitalism. Even towards the end of the turbulent 1930s, the Party's advocacy of the collective security doctrine owed relatively little to the idea that the possession of allies would be the best means of fighting a war. Instead, much greater emphasis was placed on the argument that a collective security policy would be the most effective way of preventing a major war." *British Labour and Hitler's War*, Andre Deutsch, London, 1976, pp. 17–18. See also C. L. R. James's very insightful critique of Labour Party politics, "The British Vote for Socialism," in *The Future in the Present*, op. cit., pp. 106–18 (orig. published 1945).

165. Peter Blackman, who left Barbados in the early 1930s, recalls that Du Bois was an important figure to West Indian Blacks attempting to establish their racial identity in the post–World War I period. This largely resulted from the appearance of the *Crisis* magazine. Interview, London, 18 November 1981. James implies the influence of *Black Reconstruction* on his thinking in the 1930s in several places, cf. *Nkrumah and the Ghana Revolution*, Lawrence Hill, Westport, 1977, pp. 74–75; "The Making of the Caribbean People," loc. cit., p. 179; and "W. E. B. Du Bois," in *The Future in the Present*, op. cit., pp. 202–12. For Chilembwe, see George Shepperson and Tom Price, *Independent African*, Edinburgh University Press, Edinburgh, 1958, and C. J. Robinson, "Notes Toward a 'Native' Theory of History," *Review* 4, no. 1 (Summer 1980): 45–78 (Shepperson's response follows: "Ourselves as Others," ibid., pp. 79–87); for Lamine Senghor, see Geiss, op. cit., pp. 310ff; and for Kimbangu, Vittorio Lantenari, *Religions of the Oppressed*, Alfred Knopf, New York, 1963.

166. Makonnen, op. cit., p. 116. For the responses of Afro-Americans to the Italo-Ethiopian war, see S. K. B. Asante, "The Afro-American and the Italo-Ethiopia Crisis, 1934–1936," *Race* 15, no. 2 (October 1973):

167–84; and Haywood, *Black Bolshevik*, op. cit., pp. 448ff.; and for the Caribbean, Robert G. Weisbord, *Ebony Kinship*, Greenwood Press, Westport, 1973, pp. 102–10. For Italian imperialism, see J. L. Miege, *L'Imperialisme Colonial Italien de 1870 a Nos Jours*, SEDES, Paris, 1968, chaps. 13 and 14.

167. See Makonnen, op. cit., p. 114, for his impressions of James. James articulated his position in Fenner Brockway's *New Leader* in an article entitled "Is This War Necessary?," 4 October 1935, p. 3. For the ILP's position, see James Maxton and Fenner Brockway, "The War Threat," *New Leader*, 22 March 1935, pp. 1, 3; and Brockway, "What Can We Do about Mussolini?," *New Leader*, 19 July 1935, p. 2.

168. See James, "Is This War Necessary?," op. cit., p. 3; and the report of James's activity at the Spring Conference of the ILP, "The Abyssinian Debate," *New Leader*, 17 April 1936, p. 4. For James's opinion of Haile Selassie, see Makonnen, op. cit., pp. 114, 184.

169. Geiss, op. cit., pp. 280–81. Makonnen recalled: "It is said . . . that a number of the influential Ethiopians like [Workineh] Martin and Heroui. . . considered themselves as not being Negroes. In fact, Ethiopians were said to have betrayed the same attitude when, after Haile Selassie's coronation, a delegation came to America. Dr. Workineh Martin was on it, and he refused to lecture even at Howard University. And when the delegation took with them back to Ethiopia only two or three very fair-skinned Negroes, this again seemed to prove that they thought themselves to be white people." "This apparent preference for mulattoes, and the Emperor's refusal to receive the Garveyite delegation, made Garvey bitter about Haile Selassie until the time of the former's death. It was one of the issues that George Padmore and I used to fight him over, because at that time in London, Haile Selassie symbolized our unity in Europe. And yet from the time of the Emperor's arrival in England, Garvey castigated him as a man who, instead of dying on the battlefield in the tradition of Ethiopian leaders, had slunk away to England to find refuge; how could such a coward, Garvey alleged, be the leader of such a great nation?" Makonnen, op. cit., pp. 74–75; see also Weisbord, op. cit., pp. 100–101, 103.

170. James, "Fighting for the Abyssinian Empire," *New Leader*, 5 June 1936, p. 2.

171. Some colonial authorities would trace the disturbances of the late 1930s in the West Indies to the Italo-Ethiopian War. In 1938, Sir Selsyn Grier would inform his audience at an Oxford University seminar on colonial administration: "Repercussions of the Italo-Abyssinian War were profound and widespread. The people of the West Indies saw in it an unprovoked attack by the European upon the African, and this gave rise to a feeling of racial animosity." "Unrest in the West Indies," in Oxford University Summer School on Colonial Administration, op. cit., p. 61.

172. See Hugh Thomas, *The Spanish Civil War*, Harper and Row, New York, 1961; Fernando Claudin, op. cit., pp. 210–42; and Julian Symons, op. cit., pp. 106–22.

173. There were five brigades: the Eleventh, German, known as the Thaelmann Brigade the Twelfth, Italian, known as the Garibaldis; the Thirteenth, pan-Slavic, known as the Dombrowski Brigade; the Fourteenth, French and Belgian; and the Fifteenth, consisting of British (English, Canadians, and Irish), American (the Abraham Lincoln Battalion), Caribbean, Central and South American (59th Spanish Battalion) volunteers. See Joseph Brandt (ed.), *Black Americans in the Spanish People's War Against Fascism, 1936–1939*, New Outlook Publishers, New York, n.d. [1979?]; "A Negro Nurse in Republican Spain," The Negro Committee to Aid Spain, New York, 1938 (reissued by Veterans of the Abraham Lincoln Brigade, 1977); Salaria Kee (now O'Reilly) was the subject; Haywood, *Black Bolshevik*, op. cit., chap. 18; and interviews with Haywood (Santa Barbara, 6 February 1980) and James Yates (Binghamton, 26 April 1978), both Black veterans of Spain. Brandt estimates that between 80 and 100 Black Americans volunteered for the Spanish Civil War. For Nyabongo, a Ugandan who fought with the antifascists in Spain, see Kenneth King's note in Makonnen, op. cit., p. 176 n. 16.

174. For the disturbances in Trinidad, see Eric Williams, *History of the People of Trinidad and Tobago*, People's National Movement Publishing Co., Port-of-Spain, 1962, pp. 232–42, and Brinsley Samaroo, "Politics and Afro-Indian Relations in Trinidad" in J. La Guerre, op. cit., pp. 84–97; for Jamaica, see Ken Post, *Arise Ye Starvelings: The Jamaican Labour Rebellion of 1938 and Its Aftermath*, Martinus Nijhoff, The Hague, 1978.

175. Cited in Geiss, op. cit., p. 346.

176. This was the position that James would espouse in his meetings with Trotsky in Mexico in 1939. See James, "The Revolutionary Answer to the Negro Problem in the USA," in *The Future in the Present*, op. cit., pp. 119–27. For the discussions with Trotsky at Coyocan, see George Breitman (ed.), *Leon Trotsky on Black Nationalism and Self-Determination*, Merit Publishers, New York, 1972, pp. 24–48; Tony Martin, "C. L. R. James and the Race/Class Question," *Race* 2 (1972): 183–93; and Paul Buhle, "Marxism in the U.S.A.," in *Urgent Tasks* 12 (Summer 1981): 28–39.

177. James, " 'Civilising' the 'Blacks,' " *New Leader*, 29 May 1936, p. 5.

178. Robert Hill adds an interesting and provocative element to the analysis of James's development of consciousness: "At a very profound and fundamental level, Robeson as a man *shattered* James's colonial conception of the Black Physique. In its place the magnificent stature of Robeson gave to him a new appreciation of the powerful and extraordinary capacities which the African possessed, in both head and

body. Robeson broke the mould in which the West Indian conception of physical personality in James had been formed. That was a time when Black West Indians grew up with an unconscious prototype of the white Englishman and white Englishwoman as their absolute standards of physical perfection and development. James's encounter with Robeson was nowhere more profound than in its forcing him to abandon these inherited values." "Thus, it is the contention of the present writer that *The Black Jacobins* would have been significantly different in quality in the absence of James's relationship to Robeson." "In England, 1932–38," op. cit., pp. 24–25. James met Robeson in 1936 and the latter performed the title role in a production of James's play, *Toussaint L'Ouverture*. Dorothy Butler Gilliam, in her biography of Robeson, puts the meeting and the production of the play at Westminster Theatre in early 1936, see Gilliam, *Paul Robeson: All-American*, New Republic Books, Washington, D.C., 1976, pp. 87–88. For James's view of Robeson's Marxism, see ibid., p. 127; and James, "Paul Robeson: Black Star," in *Spheres of Existence*, op. cit., pp. 261–62.

179. See James's criticisms of Padmore on this issue, *Nkmah and the Ghana Revolution*, op. cit., p. 63; for Kenyatta, see Murray-Brown, op. cit., p. 221.

180. James, ibid., pp. 69, 71. For James in the United States, see Martin, "C. L. R. James and the Race/Class Question," op. cit., pp. 184–85; and Buhle, "Marxism in the U.S.A.," op. cit., passim.

181. These views were summarized in the final resolutions passed by the Fifth Pan-African Congress in Manchester, 1945: "The first of these, 'The Challenge to the Colonial Powers,' took an intermediate line between the revolutionary impatience of Padmore and Nkrumah on the one hand and Du Bois's more cautious conception of 1944 on the other. 'The delegates to the Fifth Pan-African Congress believe in peace. . . . Yet if the Western world is still determined to rule mankind by force then Africans, as a last resort, may have to appeal to force in the effort to achieve Freedom, even if force destroys them and the world.' The second general statement was the 'Declaration to the Colonial Workers, Farmers and Intellectuals,' drafted by Nkrumah, which expresses once again the limitless desire for independence: against imperialist exploitation the colonial peoples should concentrate upon winning political power, and for this an effective organization was essential. The tactics recommended were strikes and boycotts—non-violent methods of struggle." Geiss, op. cit., p. 407.

182. James, *Nkrumah and the Ghana Revolution*, op. cit., pp. 73–74.

183. As recently as 1977, James was declaring: "The man at the helm is the African intellectual. He succeeds—or independent Africa sinks: unlike Britain in the seventeenth and France in the eighteenth centuries, there is no class on which the nation falls back after the intellectuals have led the revolution as far as it can go." Ibid., p. 15.

184. Azinna Nwafor, in one of the most forceful critiques of the Pan-African movement, sees the Manchester conference as one of the more progressive moments in Pan-Africanism. Nevertheless, Nwafor concludes: "Pan-Africanism did not offer a revolutionary choice to the emancipation of Africa from its centuries of conquest, domination, and colonial exploitation. The necessarily progressive role which the movement played in the evolution of Africa to independent status should not be underestimated, but the severe limitations of the scope and method are such that it contributed in no small degree to the disarray of the contemporary African scene and the general disenchantment with the fruits of political independence. It would seem that the storm centres of popular uprising for African emancipation were in fact headed off with the aid of Pan-Africanists, who represented themselves to the colonial authorities as the only forces capable of curbing the violence of the masses." "In many respects the OAU [the Organization of African Unity] is the culmination and embodiment of that Pan-Africanism which Padmore has chronicled. Starting as a political movement in exile, and handed on to a group of aspiring and dedicated African leadership who led their several countries to political independence, Pan-Africanism had been a movement carried out over the heads and at the expense of the African peoples themselves. At Addis Ababa [in 1963] this breed of African leadership determined to constitute itself as a new kind of Holy Alliance to preserve the existing status quo which they had inherited from their colonial masters. Their abhorrence of political revolution is total. As one of them stated, with brutal frankness: 'Speaking for ourselves, we prefer things as they are.'" Nwafor's "Introduction" to the 1972 reissue of Padmore's Pan-Africanism or Communism, op. cit. pp. xxxvii–xxxviii, xxxix–xl.

185. James, *The Black Jacobins*, op. cit., pp. 375–76. Subsequent pagination during the discussion of the work will be cited in text.

186. Cabral, "The Weapon of Theory," in *Revolution in Guinea*, Monthly Review Press, New York, 1969, p. 102. Earlier in the same address (given at a Tricontinental Conference in Havana, Cuba, January 1966), Cabral had asked: "[D]oes history begin only with the development of the phenomenon of 'class,' and consequently of class struggle? To reply in the affirmative would be to place outside history the whole period of life of human groups from the discovery of hunting, and later of nomadic and sedentary agriculture, to the organisation of herds and the private appropriation of land. It would also be to consider—and this we refuse to accept—that various human groups in Africa, Asia and Latin America were living without history, or outside history, at the time when they were subjected to the yoke of imperialism.

It would be to consider that the peoples of our countries, such as the Balantes of Guinea, the Coaniamas of Angola and the Macondes of Mozambique, are still living today—if we abstract the slight influence of colonialism to which they have been subjected—outside history, or that they have no history." Ibid. p. 95.

187. Marx, Engels, Lenin, and Trotsky were bourgeois ideologists in terms of their social origins and educations. Marx and Engels had seemingly acknowledged this in *The Communist Manifesto*: "[S]o now a portion of the bourgeoisie goes over to the proletariat, and in particular, a portion of the bourgeois ideologists, who have raised themselves to the level of comprehending theoretically the historical movement as a whole." Furthermore, with the exception of Engels, none of them seems to have given over much time to the study of working classes. For the most part their works were concentrated on the bourgeoisies: their histories, their States and administrations, their organization of production, their ideologies and philosophies. All, of course, certainly looked closely at the historical and social processes of the breakdown of societies, viz. revolutions, but these were the contradictions of bourgeois societies. It was also the case that few proletarian intellectuals were ever attended to in their writings. This raises again the question: Is Marxism a theory for the proletariat or of the proletariat? One American Marxist has answered the question in this way: "While in their practice Marxists have often tried to take account of the praxis of the proletariat, their theory proves a hindrance." Dick Howard, *The Marxian Legacy*, Macmillan, London, 1977, p. 274. E. P. Thompson seems to have come to similar conclusions in *The Making of the English Working Class*, op. cit., and *The Poverty of Theory*, op. cit.

188. In 1949, Cornelius Castoriadis wrote in "The Relations of Production in Russia": "The dictatorship of the proletariat cannot be simply the political dictatorship; it must be above all the economic dictatorship of the proletariat, for otherwise it will only be a mask for the dictatorship of the bureaucracy." Cited by Dick Howard, op. cit., p. 266. Castoriadis has proven to be one of the most consistently critical Marxists. His conclusions followed those of James made ten years earlier in *World Revolution, 1917–1936: The Rise and Fall of the Communist International*, Martin Secker and Warburg, London, 1937. Interestingly enough, Oliver C. Cox, writing in 1948, had not yet found it possible to hone his considerably acute and critical eye on the Russian state: see *Caste, Class and Race*, Monthly Review Press, New York, 1948, chap. 11.

189. James, "The Making of the Caribbean People," op. cit., p. 180.

190. This is the position taken by Robert Lacerte, "Xenophobia and Economic Decline: The Haitian Case, 1820–1843," *The Americas* 37, no. 4 (April 1981): 499–515.

191. Marvin and Anne Holloway reissued the book in 1969 through their Drum and Spear Press. This version was entitled *A History of Pan-African Revolt* and included an "epilogue" which detailed Black movements between 1939 and 1969.

192. David Widgery notes: "As disaster overwhelmed the German Left, and Stalin switched to the desperate alliance-mongering of the Popular Front, James—now the editor of the Revolutionary Socialist League's paper, *Fight* made regular clandestine visits to the Paris exile grouping of revolutionaries around Trotsky. 'They were very serious days,' James admonishes, inflecting the adjective 'serious' as only an old-time Trotskyist can. 'There was a German boy very active in our movement. One day we found him at the bottom of Seine.' " "James was, with D. D. Harber, the British delegation to the founding conference of the Trotskyist Fourth International in 1938. This tiny body was established with the hope that, in the holocaust to come, a clearsighted International might find a way through the chaos. But Trotsky and, effectively, Trotskyism succumbed to the terrible repression." "A Meeting with Comrade James," *Urgent Tasks* 12 (Summer 1981): 116.

193. Tony Martin, for one, believes that James was disciplined by Trotsky on the "Negro Problem" to good purpose. See Martin, "C. L. R. James and the Race/Class Question," op. cit., pp. 27–28. What is purported to be three direct transcripts of the discussions between James, Trotsky, and others have been published as *Leon Trotsky on Black Nationalism and Self-Determination*, George Breitman (ed.), Merit Publishers, New York, 1967. Some flavor of the exchanges can be found in their remarks on Black self-determination:

"Johnson: I am very glad that we have had this discussion, because I agree with you entirely. It seems to be the idea in America that we should advocate it as the CP has done. You seem to think that there is a greater possibility of the Negroes' wanting self-determination than I think is probable. But we have a hundred percent agreement on the idea which you have put forward that we should be neutral in the development.

Trotsky: It is the word 'reactionary' that bothers me.

Johnson: Let me quote from the document [Johnson's position paper]: 'If he wanted self-determination, then however reactionary it might be in every other respect, it would be the business of the revolutionary party to raise that slogan.' I consider the idea of separating as a step backward so far as a socialist society is concerned. If the white workers extend a hand to the Negro, he will not want self-determination.

Trotsky: It is too abstract, because the realization of this slogan can be reached only as the 13 or 14 million Negroes feel that the domination by the whites is terminated. To fight for the possibility of realizing an independent state is a sign of great moral and political awakening. It would be a tremendous revolutionary step.

This ascendancy would immediately have the best economic consequences." Ibid., pp. 31–32. "Johnson" was of course James.

194. For some of his experience in the Missouri work, see James, "The Revolutionary Answer to the Negro Problem in the USA," and "Down with Starvation Wages in South-East Missouri," in *The Future in the Present*, op. cit.

195. *Notes on Dialectics* (Allison and Busby, London, 1980) was in the original a series of letters from James to his associates in the Johnson-Forest organization (see below). According to Robert A. Hill (personal communication) they were known as the "caretaker" papers. David Widgery quotes James as saying the letters were "written in Reno when I was seeing about a divorce." Widgery, op. cit., p. 116. Hill, in collaboration with the Detroit-based Friends of Facing Reality group (whose nucleus was the older members of the Johnson-Forest organization), edited the letters into book form in 1966. For some of the history of the Detroit group, see Dan Georgakas, "Young Detroit radicals, 1955–1965," *Urgent Tasks* 12 (Summer 1981): 89–94.

196. "Although the Communist Party reached its numerical peak of 80,000 during wartime, it had become a virtual agent of State Capitalism in Russia and America, as its bitter opposition to A. Philip Randolph's planned March On Washington, its avid support of the No Strike Pledge and of the Min-neapolis Trotskyists' prosecution by the government all attested. Interlocked with the Red Army invasion of postwar Eastern Europe—'Revolution from the Tank Turret' carried out with the imprisonment or murder of opposing radical and democratic forces as if no other form of liberation were now imaginable— the Communist direction showed something more than 'betrayal' had taken place. The Party's ethnic and race following, which had in a certain sense compensated for its limited cadre outside the leadership of industrial unions, drifted away. Whatever its future, American radicalism would be something very dif-ferent from what it had been." Paul Buhle, "Marxism in the U.S.A.," op. cit., p. 32.

197. See Stanley Weir, "Revolutionary Artist," *Urgent Tasks* 12 (Summer 1981): 87; and Tony Martin, "C. L. R. James and the Race/Class Question," op. cit., pp. 25–26.

198. See W. Jerome and A. Buick, "Soviet State Capitalism? The History of an Idea," *Survey* 62 (January 1967); and Martin, ibid. Daniel Bell has contributed a comic version of American Trotskyism, cf. *Marxian Socialism in the United States*, op. cit., pp. 153–57.

199. See Martin, ibid; and Georgakas, op. cit., passim.

200. James, *Notes on Dialectics*, op. cit., p. 7. Subsequent pagination will be indicated in the text.

201. "Lenin had a notion of socialism. It is noticeable that up to 1905 he thought of socialism always in terms of the Commune. And after 1917 he changed—he changed not for Russia but for the world. We have to do the same. We have not done it. For if we had we would recognize in Lenin's articles and methods in Russia of 1917–23 the greatest possible source of theoretical understanding and insight into the world of today." Ibid., p. 147.

202. On occasion, James came quite close to acknowledging this paradox: "The party is the knowing of the proletariat as being. Without the party the proletariat knows nothing. We are here at the climax of a development characteristic of class society. The proletariat is the only historical class to which the party, the *political party*, is essential . . . the bourgeoisie has never found a political party necessary to its existence. The characteristic form of bourgeois political power is the perfection of the state, and for long periods the bourgeoisie has been content and flourished even without control of the state power. The bourgeoisie has no need for a special organization of knowing. Bourgeois society is capitalist production, and by its position as agent of capital, the bourgeoisie automatically is in possession of capitalist knowing, science, art, religion, and the essence of bourgeois politics which is the maintenance of capitalist production." "Apart from its existence as wage-slaves, the proletariat has no history except the history of its political, i.e. revolutionary, organizations. No class in history except the proletariat (and this is by no means accidental) has ever openly, boldly, and both theoretically and practically, aimed at the seizure of state power. The history of the theory and practice of this unprecedented phenomenon in human history is the history of the proletarian political party." Ibid., pp. 172–73. For Castoriadis, see his "On the History of the Workers' Movement," *Telos* 30 (1976): 3–42; and Dick Howard, op. cit., chap. 10.

203. "[A] moment's (Marxist) reflection points to the inadequacy of Trotsky's notion of Russia as a 'degenerated workers' state . . . The 'degeneration' would concern only the form, not the essence, of the Russian social formation. But this confuses the juridical forms of property with the actual relations of production themselves. For Marx, it is precisely these relations of production which determine the forms of distribution and their (deformed) superstructural reflection. The vacillations in Trotsky's own analy-ses—for example on the question of 'Thermidor,' or on the tactics to be followed by the Opposition—stem from the identification of form and essence." Dick Howard, ibid., p. 265.

204. "It was the workers who did the theoretical work on the soviet. . . . *They* thought over the soviet. They analysed it and remembered it, and within a few days of the February revolution they organized in the great centres of Russia this unprecedented social formation. Lenin saw it this time." James, *Notes on Dialectics*, op. cit., p. 138.

205. Vincent Harding recalled: "One of the things I remember with a combination of sadness and humor

was a long conversation that C. L. R. and Harry Haywood had in our house in Atlanta. It was focused to a large degree—and I just found it somewhat ironic and, as I said, somewhat sad, even though a lot of the development of the conversation also had its humor to it—to see these two really experienced and gifted Black men literally arguing about which expression of Marxist ideology and organization was really best. I think with that experience it took both of them out of the mainstream of so much of Black life, and took their strengths away from that mainstream. I just have the feeling it would have been so much healthier if both of these men might have found some common ground and might have found ways of using their energy beyond those kinds of arguments that grew out of the experiences of the late twenties and thirties, that for them were very fresh wounds and very hard experiences . . . it was just very hard to feel the real significance of some of those ideological arguments that they were carrying on at that time." Interview with Harding by Ken Lawrence, published as "Conversation," *Urgent Tasks* 12 (Summer 1981): 124.

206. See John Bracey's "Nello," *Urgent Tasks* 12 (Summer 1981): 125.

207. Paul Buhle/Noah Ignatin/James Early/Ethelbert Miller interview with James, *Urgent Tasks* 12 (Summer 1981): 82.

Chapter Eleven

1. The social and literary critiques of H. L. Mencken and the radical novels of Sinclair Lewis and Theodore Dreiser were Wright's formative introduction to American thought. See Michael Fabre, *The Unfinished Quest of Richard Wright*, William Morrow, New York, 1973, pp. 67–69. He had, however, an earlier instruction that Addison Gayle recapitulates: "He discovered that the actions of whites were often precipitous; altercations with them might occur spontaneously, for seemingly illogical reasons or none at all. Among his earliest jobs was one as a porter in a clothing store owned by two white men, father and son. Both sported reputations for maltreatment of blacks. He witnessed several beatings and slappings of blacks who fell behind in their payments. One of the most despicable concerned a black woman. Unable to pay her bill, she was dragged into the store by the two men and herded toward the back room, where she was pummeled and kicked. Afterward, in a state of semiconsciousness, she was shoved out into the street. A white policeman appeared as if on call, stared contemptuously at the dazed woman, then arrested her for drunkenness. The two men washed their hands, gazed benevolently at Wright." Gayle, *Richard Wright: Ordeal of a Native Son*, Anchor Press, Garden City, 1980, p. 35. Among numerous instances like this, two others are enlightening: "He did not take [white] threats about murder lightly. The example of Bob, brother of one of his classmates, was too recent. Bob, who worked in a hotel frequented by white prostitutes, was rumored to have been involved with one of them. Some white folks warned him to end the relationship. For whatever reason, he did not do so and was lynched. When his classmate had rendered the episode to him, Wright had been moved by his friend's grief; but he had felt, too, something of the anxiety and fear that the act of murder produced in the entire black community. Such actions were designed to control behavior and to stem the desire for rebellion among blacks." Ibid., p. 36. Earlier, white terror had struck much closer. Wright's mother had taken her two sons to live with her sister Margaret and her husband, Silas. One night Silas did not return: "The atmosphere in the house was one of silent, desperate waiting. Food was kept hot on the stove. Each sound inside and outside the house rang with deafening clarity. The two sisters took turns peering into the early mist. Sometime later, they were called to attention by a knock on the door. It was not Silas' knock. It was the knock of the dreaded messenger, one of the unsung blacks who historically, sometimes in the dark of the night or the early morning, surreptitiously delivered messages of disaster. This one was short, precise: Hoskins had been killed by white men. His family was to stay away from town. There were to be no final rites." Ibid., p. 17. Experiences such as these, coupled with his father's abandonment of his family, his mother's breakdown and paralysis, his short but nightmarish stay in an orphanage, had predictable results on Wright's personality. But most can be directly and not too indirectly traced to their bases in American social history, particularly where Black labor had been employed. It is hardly to the point, as in the instance of Martin Kilson's pseudo-psychological and reductionist treatment of Wright, to frame them in terms of "marginality." Cf. Kilson, "Politics and Identity Among Black Intellectuals," *Dissent* (Summer 1981): 339–49.

2. See James Baldwin, "The Exile" and "Alas, Poor Richard," in *Nobody Knows My Name*, Dial, New York, 1961; and also Ellen Wright's accounts of Baldwin and Wright in Faith Berry, "Portrait of a Man as Outsider," *Negro Digest*, December 1968, pp. 27–37.

3. See James Ford, "The Case of Richard Wright," *Daily Worker*, 5 September 1944.

4. See Ben Burns, "They're Not Uncle Tom's Children," *The Reporter* 14, no. 8 (March 1956): 21–23; and Gayle, op. cit., p. 272.

5. See "Amid the Alien Corn," unidentified author, *Time*, 17 November 1958, p. 28; see also Gayle's speculations, op. cit., p. 287.

6. Gayle, who has had access to heavily censored documents from the American State Department, the Federal Bureau of Investigation, and the Central Intelligence Agency, reports that the CIA was "monitoring" talks by Wright as early as April 1951 (op. cit., pp. 219–21); that Wright's "leadership of the Franco-

American Fellowship angered agents of the military, the FBI, the CIA, and the State Department" (p. 221); that within the Black expatriate group, made up of "writers, artists, students, ex-GI's, composers, musicians, and representatives of various governmental agencies such as UNESCO and the United States Information Service . . . there were those, a growing number, who served as agents or informers for the CIA, the FBI, and the American Embassy" (p. 207); and that the agencies' files indicated an increasing traffic of correspondence, reports, and surveillance on Wright from 1956 until his death in 1960 (pp. 262–63; 277–86). Wright, himself dealt with the CIA's activities in the American Black movement and in the expatriate community in France in two works; his unpublished manuscript, "Island of Hallucination" (later published under the title *American Hunger*), and his speech to students and members of the American Church in Paris (8 November 1960), entitled "The Situation of the Black Artist and Intellectual in the United States." Wright's comments in the speech have been summarized by Fabre, op. cit., p. 518. For more on Wright and the CIA, see Constance Webb, *Richard Wright*, Putnam, New York, 1968, pp. 375–77, 396; and Faith Berry, op. cit. Paul Robeson, among others, was undergoing similar treatment by American agencies at this time. See Philip S. Foner (ed.), *Paul Robeson Speaks*, Brunner/Mazel, New York, 1978: "[B]eyond revoking Robeson's passport and forbidding him to leave the continental United States from 1950 to 1957, officials of the United States government also sought to influence public opinion against Robeson; to discourage another government 'from honoring Robeson as a great humanitarian and activist for human rights'; to prevent Robeson's employment abroad in a non-political area; and to undermine his political impact by issuing anti-Robeson news releases, and using or soliciting statements of other black leaders to discredit him" (p. 4).

7. See Hoyt Fuller's interview with Chester Himes in *Black World* 21 (March 1972): 93; Webb, op. cit., pp. 312, 417; and Gayle, op. cit., pp. 235–36. Schine was an investigator on the staff of Senator Joseph McCarthy's Senate Subcommittee on Investigations. Like Roy Cohn, Schine seems to have been one of several links between McCarthy and the "elites" whose support gave McCarthy power. Cf. Michael P. Rogin, *The Intellectuals and McCarthy*, MIT Press, Cambridge, 1967, p. 250.

8. Richard and Ellen Wright had few illusions concerning their enemies, but conclusive evidence was not easily obtained. See Berry, op. cit., pp. 34ff. Some of Wright's acquaintances were skeptical about a "campaign" against Wright but others found it quite reasonable to assume one was in place, see Ollie Harrington, "The Mysterious Death of Richard Wright," *Daily World*, 17 December 1977. Gayle's review of the "sanitized" files of the American intelligence agencies brings the pattern much closer to the surface. Still there are the worrying problems of missing documents and heavily censored ones: "In fact, the number of censored documents during these last, most troublesome years of Wright's life make it difficult to know just what areas of his life or activities were targeted." Gayle, op. cit., pp. 290–91.

9. Fabre published the following letter from Wright to Margit de Sabloniere on 30 March 1960: "You must not worry about my being in danger . . . I am not exactly unknown here and I have personal friends in the de Gaulle cabinet itself. Of course, I don't want anything to happen to me, but if it does, my friends will know exactly where it comes from. If I tell you these things, it is to let you know what happens. So far as the Americans are concerned, I'm worse than a Communist, for my work falls like a shadow across their policy in Asia and Africa. That's the problem; they've asked me time and again to work for them: but I'd die first. . . . But they try to divert me with all kinds of foolish tricks." Fabre, op. cit., p. 509. The files that Gayle has seen confirm Wright's assertions, even beyond Fabre's expectations: "Although he exaggerated the extent and intent of some attacks, I believe that many were expressly designed to make him lose his sense of reality. Whether caused by personal jealousy, political intrigue or racial malevolence, the desire to harm Wright was indisputable." Ibid., pp. 524–25. Seven years later, Gayle was more equivocal: "The temptation to draw conclusions in line with those who believe that the FBI and the CIA were directly involved in Wright's sudden death are great. To do so, however, based upon the facts of the documents, would be wrong. I did not find, *nor did I expect to find*, evidence to support this assertion, held by a great many of the writer's friends. What I found was a pattern of harassment by agencies of the United States Government, resembling at times a personal vendetta more so than an intelligence-gathering investigation" (my emphasis). Gayle, op. cit., p. xv. Gayle, however, believes that there is something amiss in the documents: "The role of the State Department, however, is another matter, for it was here that the seeming vendetta occurred. The only document that supposedly originated with the State Department casts Wright in an unfavorable position. Documents filtered through the State Department to the FBI show an inordinate amount of activity on the part of the Foreign Service during the last months of Wright's life. Most of the documents are heavily deleted, so their content is difficult to comprehend clearly. Whether there is any connection between this activity and Wright's death may be known only if the deleted sections of the documents are released." Ibid. In addition, of course, as John Stockwell, a former CIA operative has shown, the State Department by the early 1970s at least had developed communications procedures concerning covert operations that denied access to even its own communicators. See Stockwell, *In Search of Enemies*, Futura Publications, London, 1979, p. 93.

10. *American Hunger* (Harper and Row, New York, 1977) is the title Wright originally suggested (among others) for his unpublished manuscript, "Island of Hallucination." Fabre, op. cit., p. 616 n. 19. The mate-

rial published under the former title is in large measure the parts of *Black Boy* (Harper, New York, 1945), which Harper expunged from its 1945 edition. Darryl Pinckney would appear to be wrong when he suggests in his review of *American Hunger* that Wright himself was responsible for the deletion (see "Richard Wright: the Unnatural History of a Native Son," *Village Voice*, 4 July 1977, p. 80), since Wright had published much of the material in the *Atlantic Monthly* (August and September 1944) under the title "I Tried to be a Communist."

11. Robert Bone, *The Negro Novel in America*, Yale University Press, New Haven, 1965, p. 158.

12. Ibid., p. 160.

13. See Bone, ibid., and Addison Gayle, *The Way of the New World* (Doubleday, Garden City, 1976), for these characterizations of Wright's work. For good reasons Gayle does not cite his previous work in his biography of Wright.

14. For the Gold Coast (now Ghana), see Wright's report, *Black Power* (Harper, New York, 1954); and Cedric J. Robinson, "A Case of Mistaken Identity," paper presented to the African Studies Association Conference, Los Angeles, 1 November 1979.

15. Fabre, op. cit., p.xviii.

16. Harold Cruse, *The Crisis of the Negro Intellectual*, William Morrow, New York, 1971, p. 182.

17. Ibid., p. 188.

18. Richard Wright, "Blueprint for Negro Writing," New Challenge, Fall 1937, p. 61. This essay was reprinted in *Race and Class* 21, no. 4 (1980).

19. Quite early on in his party experience, Wright while reflecting on his mother's reaction of horror to Communist propaganda had come to the conclusion that: "They had a program, an ideal, but they had not yet found a language." Richard Crossman (ed.), *The God That Failed*, Harper, New York, 1965, p. 107.

20. See Fabre, op. cit., pp. 89–200; and Webb, op. cit., pp. 114–16.

21. Daniel Aaron, "Richard Wright and the Communist Party," *New Letters* (Winter 1971): 178.

22. Crossman, op. cit., pp. 107–8. For some other interesting attempts to deal with the development of American working-class thought, see Stanley Feldstein and Lawrence Costello (eds.), *The Ordeal of Assimilation*, Doubleday, Garden City, 1974; and the special issue, "The Origins of Left Culture in the US: 1880–1940," *Cultural Correspondence/Green Mountain Irregulars* 6–7 (Spring 1978).

23. Wright, "Blueprint," op. cit., p. 59.

24. See Alfred Meyer, *Leninism*, Praeger, New York, 1971, pp. 40–41; and Leonard Shapiro, "Two Years That Shook the World," *New York Review of Books*, 31 March 1977, pp. 3–4.

25. See Geiss, op. cit., pp. 163–75, 213.

26. Gayle, *The Way of the New World*, op. cit., chap. 8.

27. James Baldwin, "Everybody's Protest Novel," in *Notes of a Native Son*, Dial Press, New York, 1955, p. 22.

28. Sterling Brown's review in *Opportunity*, June 1940, p. 185.

29. Clifton Fadiman's review in the *New Yorker*, 2 March 1940, p. 6.

30. Crossman, op. cit., p. 106.

31. Ibid., p. 105

32. Ibid., p. 108.

33. See Benjamin Gitlow, *I Confess*, op. cit., chaps. 15 and 16; and Joseph Starobin, *American Communism in Crisis*, op. cit., p. 22.

34. See Wilson Record, *The Negro and the Communist Party*, op. cit.; and Roger Kanet, "The Comintern and the 'Negro Question': Communist Policy in the United States and Africa, 1921–1941," *Survey*, Autumn 1973, pp. 86–122.

35. Fabre, op. cit., p. 137.

36. Crossman, op. cit., pp. 141–42.

37. Ibid., p. 146.

38. Ibid.

39. See Earl Browder, "Democracy and the Constitution," in *The People's Front*, International Publishers, New York, 1938, pp. 235–48, and "Resolution on the Offensive of Fascism and the Tasks of the Communist International in the Fight for the Unity of Working Class Against Fascism," *Communist International*, 20 September 1935, p. 951.

40. Earl Browder, "The 18th Anniversary of the Founding of the Communist Party," in *The People's Front*, op. cit., p. 271.

41. Ibid., p. 275.

42. Browder, "Revolutionary Background of the United States Constitution," ibid., p. 266; and "Twenty Years of Soviet Power," ibid., p. 346.

43. See Wilhelm Reich's "What Is Class Consciousness?" in *Sex-Pol: Essays 1929–1934*, Lee Baxandall (ed.), Vintage Books, New York, 1972.

44. Wright to Michael Gold, reported in Fabre, op. cit., p. 185.

45. Wright, "How 'Bigger' Was Born," introduction to *Native Son*, Harper, New York, 1966, p. xix.

46. Ibid., p. xx.

47. Ibid., p. xxiv.

48. In April 1940, Wright had written to Gold: "[I]f I should follow Ben Davis's advice and write of Negroes through the lens of how the Party views them in terms of political theory, I'd abandon the Bigger Thomases. I'd be tacitly admitting that they are lost to us, that fascism will triumph because it alone can enlist the allegiance of those millions whom capitalism has crushed and maimed." Fabre, op. cit., pp. 185–86.

49. Wright, "How 'Bigger' Was Born," op. cit., p. xix.

50. Ibid., p. xviii.

51. Ibid., p. xvii.

52. Ibid., p. xxiv.

53. Wright, *Native Son*, op. cit., pp. 391–92.

54. See Fabre, op. cit., pp. 184–87, for a summary of the reactions of party leaders to *Native Son*.

55. Wright, "Blueprint," op. cit., p. 60.

56. Jean Baudrillard, *The Mirror of Production*, Telos Press, St. Louis, 1975.

57. See Cornelius Castoriadis, "On the History of the Workers' Movement," *Telos*, Winter 1976/77, pp. 3–42.

58. Wright, "Blueprint," op. cit., p. 54.

59. Ibid., p. 58.

60. Richard Wright, *The Outsider*, Harper, New York, 1953, pp. 118–19.

61. See W. E. B. Du Bois, *Black Reconstruction*, op. cit. passim.

62. See Theodore Draper, *American Communism and Soviet Russia*, op. cit.; Dan Carter, *Scottsboro*, op. cit.; and Wilson Record, *The Negro and the Communist Party*, op. cit.

63. Wright, "Blueprint," op. cit., pp. 62–63.

64. See Fabre, op. cit., pp. 365ff; and Webb, op. cit., p. 312.

65. See Cedric J. Robinson, "The Emergent Marxism of Richard Wright's Ideology," *Race and Class* 19, no. 3 (1978): 221–37.

66. Richard Wright, *White Man Listen!*, Doubleday, Garden City, 1957, pp. 34–35. For the function of myth, see Cedric J. Robinson, *The Terms of Order*, State University of New York Press, Albany, 1980.

67. See Giovanni Piana, "History and Existence in Husserl's Manuscripts," *Telos* 13 (Fall 1972): 86–164; Georg Lukács, "On the Responsibility of Intellectuals," *Telos* 2, no. 1 (Spring 1969): 123–31, William Leiss's review on Husserl and Paul Piccone's "Reading the Crisis," *Telos* 8 (Summer 1971): 110–21 and 121–29, respectively.

68. Karl Marx, "Contribution to the Critique of Hegel's Philosophy of Right: Introduction," in Robert Tucker (ed.), *The Marx-Engels Reader*, W. W. Norton, New York, 1972, p. 12.

69. Wright, *The Outsider*, op. cit., p. 129.

70. Daniel Aaron, op. cit., p. 180

71. Wright, *The Outsider*, op. cit., p. 227.

72. Ibid., p. 334.

73. Richard Wright, "The Voiceless Ones," *Saturday Review*, 16 April 1960, p. 22. Raman K. Singh's analysis of Cross may be applied (as he suggested) to Wright: "In opposing Communism, Cross is not giving up Marxism; he is merely seeking to abolish the tyranny of the Party. And in adopting Existentialism, he is not abandoning Marxism, but showing his awareness of both economic and cosmic consciousness." Singh, "Marxism in Richard Wright's fiction," *Indian Journal of American Studies* 4, nos. 1, 2 (June/December 1974): 33–34. This is decidedly not the position taken by other writers who came out from the Communist movement as John Diggins sees them; Diggins, "Buckley's Comrades: The Ex-Communist as Conservative," *Dissent*, Fall 1975, pp. 370–81.

74. Wright, *White Man Listen!*, op. cit., pp. 19–20.

75. Wright, *The Outsider*, op. cit., p. 334.

76. Karl Marx and Friedrich Engels, *The Communist Manifesto*, in Tucker, op. cit., p. 343.

77. Wright, *The Outsider*, op. cit., p. 221.

78. Marx and Engels, *The Communist Manifesto*, op. cit., p. 345.

79. Wright, *The Outsider*, op. cit., pp. 176–77.

80. Wright, "Blueprint," op. cit., p. 57.

BIBLIOGRAPHY

Aaron, Daniel. 1971. "Richard Wright and the Communist Party." *New Letters*, Winter.

Abrahams, Peter. 1957. *Jamaica*. Her Majesty's Stationery Office, London.

"Abyssinian Debate, The." 1936. *New Leader*, 17 April.

Adas, Michael. 1979. *Prophets of Rebellion: Millenarian Protest Movements against the European Colonial Order*. University of North Carolina Press, Chapel Hill.

Ajayi, J. F. A., and Michael Crowder (eds.). 1972. *History of West Africa*, vol. 1. Columbia University Press, New York.

Alavi, Hamza. 1965. "Peasants and Revolution." *The Socialist Register*.

Alho, Olli. 1976. *The Religion of the Slaves*. Finnish Academy of Science, Helsinki.

Alvares, Francisco. 1970. *Narrative of the Portuguese Embassy to Abyssinia during the Years 1520–1527*, ed. Lord Stanley of Alderley. Burt Franklin Publisher, New York.

Almond, Gabriel. 1965. *The Appeals of Communism*. Princeton University Press, Princeton.

"Amid the Alien Corn." 1958. *Time*, 17 November.

Anderson, James D. 1976. "Aunt Jemima in Dialectics: Genovese and Slave Culture." *Journal of Negro History* 61.

Anderson, Jervis. 1973. *A. Philip Randolph*. Harcourt Brace Jovanovich, New York.

Anderson, Perry. 1974. *Lineages of the Absolute State*. NLB, London.

———. 1979. *Considerations of Western Marxism*. Verso, London.

———. 1980. *Arguments within English Marxism*. Verso, London.

Anstey, Roger. 1975a. *The Atlantic Slave Trade and British Abolition, 1760–1810*. Humanities Press, Atlantic Highlands, N.J.

———. 1975b. "The Volume and Profitability of the British Slave Trade, 1761–1807." *Race and Slavery in the Western Hemisphere*, ed. Stanley Engerman and Eugene Genovese. Princeton University Press, Princeton.

Aptheker, Herbert. 1945. *Essays in the History of the American Negro*. International Publishers, New York.

———. 1964. *American Negro Slave Revolts*. International Publishers, New York (orig. 1943).

———. 1971. "The Historian." *W. E. B. Du Bois: A Profile*, ed. Rayford Logan. Hill and Wang, New York.

———. 1973. "Maroons within the Present Limits of the United States." *Maroon Societies*, ed. Richard Price. Anchor, Garden City.

——— (ed.). 1976. *The Correspondence of W. E. B. Du Bois*, vol. 11. University of Massachusetts Press, Amherst.

Arendt, Hannah. 1958. *The Origins of Totalitarianism*. Meridian Books, Cleveland.

Aronowitz, Stanley. 1971. "Does the United States Have a New Working Class?" *The Revival of American Socialism*, ed. George Fischer. Oxford University Press, New York.

Asad, Talal (ed.). 1973. *Anthropology and the Colonial Encounter*. Humanities Press, New York.

Asante, S. K. B. 1973. "The Afro-American and the Italo-Ethiopia Crisis, 1934–1936." *Race* 15, no. 2.

Atanda, J. A. 1974. "British Rule in Buganda." *Tarikh* 4, no. 4.

Austen, Ralph. 1979. "The Islamic Slave Trade Out of Africa (Red Sea and Indian Ocean)." *The Uncommon Market: Quantitative Studies in the Atlantic Slave Trade*, ed. Henry Gemery and Jan Hogendorn. Academic Press, New York.

Avineri, Shlomo. 1968. *The Social and Political Thought of Karl Marx*. Cambridge University Press, Cambridge.

——— (ed.). 1969. *Karl Marx on Colonization and Modernization*. Anchor, Garden City.

Ayalon, David. 1953. "Studies on the Structure of the Mamluk Army, Part 2." *Bulletin of the School of Oriental and African Studies* 15.

———. 1977. "Studies in Al-Jabarti." *Studies on the Mamluks in Egypt*. Variorum Press, London.

Azurara, G. E. de. 1896. *The Chronicle of the Discovery and Conquest of Guinea*, vol. 1, ed. C. R. Beazley and E. Prestage. Burt Franklin Publisher, New York.

Balandier, Georges. 1969. *Daily Life in the Kingdom of the Kongo*. Meridian Books, New York.

———. 1970. *Political Anthropology*. Pantheon, New York.

Baldwin, James. 1955. *Notes of a Native Son*. Dial Press, New York.

———. 1961. *Nobody Knows My Name*. Dial Press, New York.

Banton, Michael, and Jonathan Harwood. 1975. *The Race Concept*. Praeger, New York.

Baptiste, Fitz A. 1978. "The United States and West Indian Unrest 1918–1939." Working Paper No. 18, Institute of Social and Economic Research, University of the West Indies, Jamaica.

Bark, William C. 1958. *Origins of the Medieval World*. Stanford University Press, Stanford.

Barnett, Richard and Ronald Muller. 1974. *Global Reach*. Simon and Schuster, New York.

Barr, Stringfellow. 1959. *Mazzini, Portrait of an Exile*. Holt, New York.

Barraclough, Geoffrey. 1963. *The Origins of Modern Germany*. Capricorn Books, New York.

Barth, Heinrich. 1857. *Travels and Discoveries in North and Central Africa*. 5 vols. Longmans, Green and Co., London.

Batie, Robert Carlyle. 1976. "Why Sugar? Economic Cycles and the Changing Staples on the English and French Antilles, 1624–54." *Journal of Caribbean History* 8.

Baumer, Franklin L. 1944. "England, the Turk, and the Common Corps of Christendom." *American Historical Review* 50, no. 1.

Barzun, Jacques. 1932. *Race*. Harcourt Brace, New York.

———. 1966. *The French Race*. Kennirat, New York.

Baudrillard, Jean. 1975. *The Mirror of Production*. Telos, St. Louis.

Beach, D. N. 1979. " 'Chimurenga': The Shona Rising of 1896–97." *Journal of African History* 20, no. 3.

Beard, Charles. 1948. "Neglected Aspects of Political Science." *American Political Science Review* 43.

Beazley, C. Raymond. 1923. "Prince Henry of Portugal and His Political, Commercial and Colonizing Work." *American Historical Review* 17, no. 2.

Beckford, George. 1972. *Persistent Poverty*. Oxford University Press, Oxford.

Bell, Daniel. 1967. *Marxian Socialism in the United States*. Princeton University Press, Princeton.

Bell, Wendell. 1977. "Inequality in Independent Jamaica: A Preliminary Appraisal of Elite Performance." *Revista/Review Interamericana*, Summer.

Beltran, G. Aguirre. 1945. "Races in Seventeenth-Century Mexico." *Phylon* 6, no. 3.

Bender, Gerald. 1978. *Angola Under the Portuguese*. University of California Press, Berkeley.

ben-Jochannan, Yosef. 1971. *Africa: Mother of Civilization*. Alkebu-Lan, New York.

Bennett, Lerone. 1964. *Before the Mayflower*. Johnson Publications, Chicago.

Berlin, Ira. 1974. *Slaves without Masters*. Vintage, New York.

Berlin Isaiah. 1973. "Historical Materialism." *Karl Marx*, ed. Tom Bottomore. Prentice-Hall, Englewood Cliffs.

Bermant, Chaim. 1975. *London's East End*. Macmillan, New York.

Berry, Faith. 1968. "Portrait of a Man as Outsider." *Negro Digest*, December.

Berry, Mary F. 1971. *Black Resistance, White Law*. Appleton-Century-Croft, New York.

Bethell, Leslie. 1969. "The Independence of Brazil and the Abolition of the Brazilian Slave Trade: Anglo-Brazilian Relations, 1822–1826." *Latin American Studies* 1, no. 2.

Bidney, David. 1954. "The Idea of the Savage in North American Ethnohistory." *Journal of the History of Ideas*.

Bittle, William, and Gilbert Geis. 1964. *The Longest Way Home*. Wayne State University Press, Detroit.

Blackman, Peter. 1981. Interview with C. I. Robinson. London, 18 November.

Blackstock, Paul, and Bert Hoselitz (eds.). 1952. "Karl Marx and Friedrich Engels." *The Russian Menace to Europe*. Free Press, Glencoe.

Blake, John William. 1967. *Europeans in West Africa, 1450–1460*, vol. 1. Kraus, Nendeln.

Blassingame, John. 1972. *The Slave Community*. Oxford University Press, New York.

Bleby, Henry. 1853. *Death Struggles of Slavery*. William Nichols, London.

Bloch, Marc. 1966. *French Rural History*. University of California Press, Berkeley.

Bloom, Solomon. 1941. *The World of Nations*. Columbia University Press, New York.

Bone, Robert. 1965. *The Negro Novel in America*. Yale University Press, New Haven.

Bontemps, Arna. 1961. *100 Years of Negro Freedom*. Dodd, Mead and Co., New York.

Borkenau, Franz. 1971. *World Communism*. University of Michigan Press, Ann Arbor.

Bottomore, Tom (ed.). 1973. *Karl Marx*. Prentice-Hall, Englewood Cliffs.

Boxer, C. R. 1962. *The Golden Age of Brazil, 1695–1750*. University of California Press, Berkeley.

———. 1965. *Four Centuries of Portuguese Expansion, 1415–1825*. Witwatersrand University Press, Johannesburg.

———. 1975. *Women in Iberian Expansion, 1415–1815*. Oxford University Press, New York.

Boyd-Bowman, Peter. 1969. "Negro Slaves in Early Colonial Mexico." *The Americas* 26, no. 2.

Bracey, John. 1981. "Nello." *Urgent Tasks* 12.

Brandes, George. 1968. *Ferdinand Lassalle*. Bergman, New York (orig. 1874 and 1875).

Brandt, Joseph (ed.). n.d. *Black Americans in the Spanish People's War against Fascism 1936–1939*. New Outlook Publishers, New York.

Braudel, Fernand. 1973. *Capitalism and Material Life, 1400–1800*. Harper and Row, New York.

——. 1976. *The Mediterranean and the Mediterranean World in the Age of Philip II*, vols. 1 and 2. Harper and Row, New York.

Breitman, George (ed.). 1972. *Leon Trotsky on Black Nationalism and Self-Determination*. Merit Publishers, New York.

Brereton, Bridget. 1974. "The Experience of Indentureship: 1845–1917." *Calcutta to Caroni. The East Indians of Trinidad*, ed. John La Guerre. Longman Caribbean, Trinidad.

——. 1979. *Race Relations in Colonial Trinidad, 1811–1900*. Cambridge University Press, Cambridge.

Briggs, Asa. 1960. "The Language of 'Class' in Early Nineteenth-Century England." *Essays in Labour History*, ed. Asa Briggs and John Saville. Macmillan, London.

Brisbane, Robert. 1970. *The Black Vanguard*. Judson Press, Valley Forge.

Brockway, Fenner. 1935. "What Can We Do about Mussolini?" *New Leader*, 19 July.

Broderick, Francis. 1959. *W. E. B. Du Bois: Negro Leader in a Time of Crisis*. Stanford University Press, Stanford.

Broderick, Francis, and August Meier (eds.). 1965. *Negro Protest Thought in the Twentieth Century*. Bobbs-Merrill, Indianapolis.

Brody, David. 1960. *Steelworkers in America*. Harvard University Press, Cambridge.

Brook, G. L. 1958. *A History of the English Language*. W. W. Norton, New York.

Browder, Earl. 1935. "Resolution on the Offensive of Fascism and the Tasks of the Communist International in the Fight for the Unity of Working Class against Fascism." *Communist International*, 20 September.

——. 1938. *The People's Front*. International Publishers, New York.

Brown, Dee. 1971. *Bury My Heart at Wounded Knee*. Holt, Rinehart and Winston, New York.

Brown, Michael Barratt. 1974. *The Economics of Imperialism*. Penguin, Harmondsworth.

Brown, Sterling. 1940. Review of Richard Wright's *Native Son*. *Opportunity*, June.

Bucher, Carl. 1968. *Industrial Evolution*. August Kelley, New York, (orig. 1901).

Buckley, Roger Norman. 1979. *Slaves in Red Coats*. Yale University Press, New Haven.

Buhle, Paul. 1970. "American Marxist Historiography, 1900–1940." *Radical America*, November.

—— (ed.). 1981. *C. L. R. James: His Life and Work*, special issue of *Urgent Tasks* 12.

——. 1981. "Marxism in the U.S.A." *Urgent Tasks* 12.

Buhle, Paul, Noah Ignatin, James Early, and Ethelbert Miller. 1981. Interview with C. L. R. James. *Urgent Tasks* 12.

Buisseret, David, and S. A. G. Taylor. 1978. "Juan de Bolas and His Pelinco." *Caribbean Quarterly* 24, nos. 1, 2.

Burke, James. 1978. *Connections*. Little, Brown, Boston.

Burn, W. L. 1937. *Emancipation and Apprenticeship in the British West Indies*. Jonathan Cape, London.

Burns, Ben. 1956. "They're Not Uncle Tom's Children." *The Reporter* 14, no. 8.

Burridge, T. D. 1976. *British Labour and Hitler's War*. Andre Deutsch, London.

Butterfield, Herbert. 1957. *The Origins of Modern Science*. Free Press, New York.

Cabral, Amilcar. 1969. *Revolution in Guinea*. Monthly Review Press, New York.

——. 1973. *Return to the Source*. Africa Information Service.

Cairns, H. Alan. 1965. *Prelude to Imperialism*. Routledge and Kegan Paul, London.

Callinicos, Alex. 1976. *Althusser's Marxism*. NLB, London.

Calogeras, Joao Pandia. 1959. *A History of Brazil*. University of North Carolina Press, Chapel Hill.

Campbell, Mavis. 1974. "Aristotle and Black Slavery: A Study in Race Prejudice." *Race* 15, no. 3.

——. 1976. *The Dynamics of Change in a Slave Society*. Fairleigh Dickinson University Press, Rutherford.

Camporesi, Cristiano. 1972. "The Marxism of Sidney Hook." *Telos*, Summer.

Canetti, Elias. 1966. *Crowds and Power*. Viking Press, New York.

Canny, Nicholas. 1972. "The Ideology of English Colonization: From Ireland to America." *William and Mary Quarterly*, 3d ser., vol. 30, no. 4.

Cantor, Milton. 1966. "The Image of the Negro in Colonial Literature." *Images of the Negro in American Literature*, ed. Seymour Gross and John Edward Hardy. University of Chicago Press, Chicago.

——. 1978. *The Divided Left: American Radicalism, 1900–1975*. Hill and Wang, New York.

Cantor, Norman (ed.). 1963. *The Medieval World, 300–1300*. Macmillan, New York.

Carr, Edward H. 1961. *What Is History?* Vintage, New York.

Carter, Dan T. 1968. *Scottsboro: A Tragedy of the American South*. Oxford University Press, London.

Carus-Wilson, E. M., and Olive Coleman. 1963. *England's Export Trade, 1275–1547*. Oxford University Press, Oxford.

Casal, Lourdes. 1979. "Race Relations in Contemporary Cuba." *Minority Rights Group*, no. 7, London.
Case, Lynn. 1970. *Franco-Italian Relations, 1860–1865*. AMS Press, New York (orig. 1932).
Castles, Stephen. 1972. "The Function of Labour Immigration in Western European Capitalism." *New Left Review*, no. 73.
Castles, Stephen, and Godula Kosack. 1973. *Immigrant Workers and Class Structure in Western Europe*. Oxford University Press, London.
Castoriadis, Cornelius. 1976–77. "On the History of Workers' Movement." *Telos*, no. 30.
———. 1977. "The Relations of Production in Russia." *The Marxian Legacy*, ed. Dick Howard. Macmillan, London.
Castro, Americo. 1954. *The Structure of Spanish History*. Princeton University Press, Princeton.
Caute, David. 1964. *Communism and the French Intellectuals, 1914–1960*. Macmillan, New York.
Chace, William, and Peter Collier (eds.). 1970. *Justice Denied*. Harcourt, Brace and World, New York.
Chadwick, H. Munro. 1945. *The Nationalities of Europe and the Growth of National Ideologies*. Cambridge University Press, Cambridge.
Chamberlin, E. R. 1967. *Everyday Life in Renaissance Times*. Capricorn Books, New York.
Charney, George. 1968. *A Long Journey*. Quadrangle, Chicago.
Chilcote, Ronald. 1969. *Emerging Nationalism in Portuguese Africa*. Hoover Institution, Stanford.
Clammer, David. 1973. *The Zulu War*. St. Martin's Press, New York.
Clarke, John Henrik, Esther Jackson, Ernest Kaiser, J. H. O'Dell (eds.). 1970. *Black Titan: W. E. B. Du Bois*. Beacon Press, Boston.
Claudin, Fernando. 1975. *The Communist Movement: From Comintern to Cominform*. Penguin, Harmondsworth.
Clegg, Ian. 1971. *Workers' Self-Management in Algeria*. Monthly Review Press, New York.
Clough, Owen (ed.). 1933. *Report on African Affairs for the Year 1933*. Empire Parliamentary Association, Billings and Sons, Guildford.
Coffin, Joshua. 1970. "An Account of Some of the Principal Slave Insurrections." *Slave Insurrections, Selected Documents*. Negro University Press, Westport (orig. 1860).
Cohn, Norman. 1970. *The Pursuit of the Millennium*. Oxford University Press, New York.
Cole, G. D. H. 1953. *A History of Socialist Thought*, vol. 1, *Socialist Thought, The Firerunners, 1789–1850*. St. Martin's Press, New York.
———. 1954. *A History of Socialist Thought*, vol. 2, *Socialist Thought, Marxism and Anarchism, 1850–1890*. Macmillan, London.
Coleman, D. C. 1957. "Eli Heckscher and the Idea of Mercantilism." *The Scandinavian Economic History Review* 5, no. 1.
Conrad, Robert. 1972. *The Destruction of Brazilian Slavery, 1850–1888*. University of California Press, Berkeley.
Cook, M. A. (ed.). 1970. *Studies in the Economic History of the Middle East from the Rise of Islam to the Present Day*. Oxford University Press, London.
Cook, Sherburne, and Woodrow Borah. 1963. *The Aboriginal Population of Central Mexico on the Eve of the Spanish Conquest*. University of California Press, Berkeley.
Coolidge, Mary R. 1969. *Chinese Immigration*. Arno Press, New York (orig. 1909).
Cooper, Wayne, and Robert C. Reinders. 1968. "Claude McKay in England, 1920." *New Beacon Reviews*, Collection One (reprinted from *Race* 9, 1967).
Cornforth, Maurice (ed.). 1978. *Rebels and Causes*. Lawrence and Wishart, London.
Cox, Oliver. 1959. *The Foundations of Capitalism*. Philosophical Library, New York.
———. 1964. *Capitalism as a System*. Monthly Review Press, New York.
———. 1970. *Caste, Class and Race*. Modern Reader, New York (orig. 1948).
Craton, Michael. 1974. *Sinews of Empire*. Anchor, Garden City.
———. 1979. "Proto-Peasant Revolts: The Late Slave Rebellions in the British West Indies 1816–1832." *Past and Present*, no. 85.
———. 1980. "The Passion to Exist: Slave Rebellions in the British West Indies 1650–1832." *Journal of Caribbean History* 13.
Craven, Wesley Frank. 1956. *The Legend of the Founding Fathers*. New York University Press, New York.
———. 1971. *White, Red and Black*. University Press of Virginia, Charlottesville.
Crick, Bernard. 1959. *The American Science of Politics*. Routledge and Kegan Paul, London.
Cronon, E. David. 1955. *Black Moses: The Story of Marcus Garvey and the Universal Negro Improvement Association*. University of Wisconsin Press, Madison.
——— (ed.). 1972. *Marcus Garvey*. Prentice-Hall, Englewood Cliffs.
Crosby, Alfred W., Jr. 1977. *The Columbian Exchange*. Greenwood Press, Westport.
Crossman, Richard (ed.). 1965. *The God That Failed*. Harper, New York.
Crow, Jeffrey. 1980. "Slave Rebelliousness and Social Conflict in North Carolina, 1775–1802." *William and Mary Quarterly* 37.

Cruise-O'Brien, Rita. 1980. "Factors of Dependence." *Decolonization and After*, ed. W. H. Morris-Jones and Georges Fischer. Frank Cass, London.

Cruse, Harold. 1967. *The Crisis of the Negro Intellectual*. William Morrow, New York.

Cuffe, Paul. 1969. "A Brief Account of the Settlement and Present Situation of the Colony of Sierra Leone in Africa." *Apropos of Africa*, ed. Adelaide C. Hill and Martin Kilson. Frank Cass, London.

Cultural Correspondence/Green Mountain Irregulars. 1978. "The Origins of Left Culture in the US, 1880– 1940," nos. 6–7.

Cummings, Milton, and David Wise. 1977. *Democracy under Pressure*. Harcourt Brace Jovanovich, New York.

Curtin, Philip. 1964. *The Image of Africa*. University of Wisconsin Press, Madison.

———. 1969. *The Atlantic Slave Trade: A Census*. University of Wisconsin Press, Madison.

——— (ed.). 1971. *Imperialism*. Walker, New York.

———. 1972. "The Atlantic Slave Trade, 1600–1800." *History of West Africa*, vol. 1, ed. J. F. A. Ajayi and Michael Crowder. Columbia University Press, New York.

———. 1977. "Slavery and Empire." *Comparative Perspectives on Slavery in New World Plantation Societies, Annals of the New York Academy of Sciences*, vol. 292.

Curtis, L. P., Jr. 1968. *Anglo-Saxons and Celts*. New York University Press, New York.

Curwen, C. A. 1971. "China." *The Making of the Modern World: Europe Discovers the World*, vol. 1, ed. Douglas Johnson. Barnes and Noble, New York.

Daget, Serge. 1975. "La repression Britannique sur les Negriers Français du trafic illegal: Quelques conditions generales ou specifiques." Unpublished paper presented in Maine, 20–22 August.

Daniel, Norman. 1960. *Islam and the West*. Edinburgh University Press, Edinburgh.

———. 1979. *The Arabs and Medieval Europe*. Longman, London.

Dalfiume, Richard. 1971. "The 'Forgotten Years' of the Negro Revolution." *Black Liberation Politics: A Reader*, ed. Edward Greer. Allyn and Bacon, Boston.

Daniels, Douglas. 1980. *Pioneer Urbanites*. Temple University Press, Philadelphia.

Darkwah, R. H. Kofi. 1975. *Shewa, Menilek and the Ethiopian Empire, 1813–1889*. Heinemann, London.

Davidson, Basil. 1964. *The African Past*. Little, Brown, Boston.

———. 1981. *The People's Cause: A History of Guerrillas in Africa*. Longmans, Harlow.

Davidson, David. 1966. "Negro Slave Control and Resistance in Colonial Mexico, 1519–1650. *Hispanic American Historical Review* 46, no. 3.

Davies, Arthur. 1952. "Origins of Columbian Cosmography." *Studi Colombiana*, vol. 2, Stabilimento Arti Grafiche ed Affini, Genova.

Davies, K. G. 1962. "The Mess of the Middle Class." *Past and Present*, no. 22.

———. 1970. *The Royal African Company*. Atheneum, New York.

Davies, K. G. B. 1952. "The Origin of the Commission System in the West India Trade." *Transactions of the Royal Historical Society*, 5th ser., vol. 2.

Davis, David Brion. 1966. *The Problems of Slavery in Western Culture*. Cornell University Press, Ithaca.

Davis, Horace. 1965. "Nations, Colonies and Social Classes: The Position of Marx and Engels." *Science and Society* 29, no. 1.

———. 1967. *Nationalism and Socialism*. Monthly Review Press, New York.

Davis, Ralph. 1973. *The Rise of the Atlantic Economies*. Weidenfeld and Nicolson, London.

Dawley, Alan. 1978–79. "E. P. Thompson and the Peculiarities of the Americas." *Radical History Review*, no. 19.

Debbasch, Yvan. 1973. "Le Maniel: Further Notes." *Maroon Societies*, ed. Richard Price. Anchor, Garden City.

Debien, Gabriel. 1973. "Marronage in the French Caribbean." *Maroon Societies*, ed. Richard Price, Anchor, Garden City.

De Felice, Renzo. 1977. *Interpretations of Fascism*. Harvard University Press, Cambridge.

Deloria, Vine, Jr. 1969. *Custer Died for Your Sins*. Macmillan, New York.

Denham, Major, Capt. Clapperton, and the late Dr. Oudney. 1831. *Travels and Discoveries in Northern and Central Africa*. 4 vols. John Murray, London.

DePauw, Linda Grant. 1973. "Land of the Unfree: Legal Limitations on Liberty in Pre-Revolutionary America." *Maryland Historical Magazine* 68, no. 4.

Derry, T. K., and M. G. Blakeway. 1973. *The Making of Pre-Industrial Britain*. John Murray, London.

Deutscher, Isaac. 1979. *The Prophet Armed: Trotsky 1879–1921*. Oxford University Press, Oxford.

Dewar, Hugo. 1976. *Communist Politics in Britain: The CPCB from Its Origins to the Second World War*. Pluto Press, London.

Dickson, P. G. M. 1967. *The Financial Revolution in England*. Macmillan, London.

Diggins, John. 1975. "Buckley's Comrades: The Ex-Communist as Conservative." *Dissent*, Fall.

Diggs, Irene. 1953. "Zumbi and the Republic of Os Palmares." *Phylon* 14, no. 1.

Diop, Cheikh Anta. 1974. *The African Origin of Civilization*. Lawrence Hill, New York.

Dobbs, Maurice. 1946. *Studies in the Development of Capitalism*. Routledge, London.

Dookeran, Winston. 1974. "East Indians and the Economy of Trinidad and Tobago." *Calcutta to Caroni: The East Indians of Trinidad*, ed. John La Guerre. Longman Caribbean, Trinidad.

Douglas, Mary. 1966. *Purity and Danger*. Frederick Praeger, New York.

Draper, Theodore. 1957. *The Roots of American Communism*. Viking, New York.

——. 1960. *American Communism and Soviet Russia*. Viking, New York.

——. 1971. *The Rediscovery of Black Nationalism*. Secker and Warburg, London.

Drowser, Margaret S. 1965. "Egypt: Archaeology and History." *Encyclopedia Britannica*, vol. 8. University of Chicago Press, Chicago.

Du Bois, W. E. B. 1915. "The African Roots of the War." *Atlantic Monthly* 115.

——. 1920. *Darkwater*. Constable and Co., London.

——. 1921. "Marcus Garvey." *The Crisis* 21, January.

——. 1927. "Judging Russia." *The Crisis* 33, February.

——. 1928. "Marcus Garvey and the NAACP." *The Crisis* 35, February.

——. 1933. Lecture at the Rosenwald Conference. Reproduced in the *Baltimore Afro-American*, 20 May.

——. 1968a. *The Autobiography of W. E. B. Du Bois*. International Publishers, n.p.

——. 1968b. *Dusk of Dawn*. Schocken, New York (orig. 1940).

——. 1969a. *Black Reconstruction in America, 1860–1880*. World Publishing, Cleveland (orig. 1935).

——. 1969b. *The Suppression of the African Slave-Trade to the United States of America, 1638–1870*. Schocken, New York (orig. 1896)

——. 1970a. *Black Titan: W. E. B. Du Bois*, ed. John Hendrick Clarke et al. Beacon Press, Boston.

——. 1970b. *W. E. B. Du Bois Speaks*, ed. Philip Foner. Pathfinder Books, New York.

——. 1971. *The Seventh Son: The Thought and Writings of W. E. B. Du Bois*, vol. 1, ed. Julius Lester. Vintage, New York.

——. 1972a. *W. E. B. Du Bois: The Crisis Writings*, ed. Daniel Walden. Fawcett, Greenwich.

——. 1972b. *The Emerging Thought of W. E. B. Du Bois*, ed. Henri Lee Moon. Simon and Schuster, New York.

——. 1976. *The Correspondence of W. E. B. Du Bois*, vol. 2, ed. Herbert Aptheker. University of Massachusetts Press, Amherst.

Dubofsky, Melvyn. 1969. *We Shall Be All: A History of the Industrial Workers of the World*. Quadrangle/New York Times, New York.

Duffield, Ian. 1981. "The Dilemma of Pan-Africanism for Blacks in Britain, 1760–1950." Paper presented to the International Conference on the History of Blacks in Britain, University of London, September.

Dunn, Richard S. 1972. *Sugar and Slaves: The Rise of the Planter Class in the English West Indies, 1624–1713*. University of North Carolina Press, Chapel Hill.

Dupuy, Alex. 1976. "Spanish Colonialism and the Origin of Underdevelopment in Haiti." *Latin American Perspectives*, iss. 9, vol. 3, no. 2.

——. 1982. "Class Formation and Underdevelopment in Nineteenth-Century Haiti." *Race and Class* 24, no. 1.

Dzidzienyo, Anani. 1979. "The Position of Blacks in Brazilian Society." *Minority Rights Group*, no. 7, London.

Edwards, R. D. 1965. "The Tudors" (part of the essay, "Ireland"), *Encyclopaedia Britannica*, vol. 7.

Elder, J. D. 1970. "The Yoruba Ancestor Cult in Gasparillo." *Caribbean Quarterly* 16, no. 3.

Ellis, P. Berresford. 1973. *A History of the Irish Working Class*. George Braziller, New York.

Elkins, W. F. 1970. "A Source of Black Nationalism in the Caribbean: The Revolt of the British West Indies Regiment at Taranto, Italy." *Science and Society*, no. 34.

Eltis, D. 1975. "The Direction and Fluctuation of the Trans-Atlantic Slave Trade, 1821–43: A Revision of the 1845 Parliamentary Paper." Unpublished paper presented in Maine, 20–22 August.

Engels, Friedrich. 1950. *The Condition of the Working Class in England in 1844*. George Allen and Unwin, London (orig. 1845).

——. 1967a. "The Peasant War in Germany." *The German Revolutions*, ed. Leonard Kriegar. University of Chicago Press, Chicago.

——. 1967b. "Germany: Revolution and Counter-Revolution." *The German Revolutions*, ed. Leonard Kriegar. University of Chicago Press, Chicago.

——. 1972a. *The Role of Force in History*. International Publishers, New York.

——. 1972b. "History of Ireland." *Ireland and the Irish Question*, Karl Marx and Friedrich Engels. International Publishers, New York.

——. 1972c. Introduction to Karl Marx's *The Class Struggles in France, 1848 to 1850*. *Karl Marx and Friedrich Engels, Selected Works*, vol. 1. International Publishers, New York.

——. 1972d. "Socialism: Utopian and Scientific." *The Marx-Engels Reader*, ed. Robert Tucker. W. W. Norton, New York.

——. 1973. "The Magyar Struggle." *The Revolutions of 1848*, Karl Marx and Friedrich Engels. International Publishers, New York.

Engerman, Stanley L., and Eugene D. Genovese (eds.). 1975. *Race and Slavery in the Western Hemisphere*. Princeton University Press, Princeton.

Ennes, Ernesto. 1948. "The Palmares 'Republic' of Pernambuco: Its Final Destruction, 1697." *The Americas* 5, no. 2.

Enzensberger, Hans Magnus. 1974. Introduction. *The Devastation of the Indies: A Brief Account*, Bartolome de Las Casas. Seabury Press, New York.

Epstein, Melech. n.d. *The Jew and Communism*. Trade Union Sponsoring Committee, New York.

Escalante, Aquiles. 1973. "Palenques in Colombia." *Maroon Societies*, ed. Richard Price. Anchor, Garden City.

Espinosa, Antonio Vazquez de. 1942. *Compendium and Description of the West Indies*. Smithsonian Institution Press, Washington, D.C. (orig. 1629).

Essien-Udom, E. U. 1962. *Black Nationalism*. University of Chicago Press, Chicago.

Evans, William McKee. 1980. "From the Land of Canaan to the Land of Guinea: The Strange Odyssey of the 'Sons of Ham.'" *American Historical Review* 85, no. 1.

Fabre, Michel. 1973. *The Unfinished Quest of Richard Wright*. William Morrow, New York.

Fadiman, Clifton. 1940. Review of Richard Wright's *Native Son*. *New Yorker*, 2 March.

Fanon, Frantz. 1963. *The Wretched of the Earth*. Grove Press, New York.

Feldstein, Stanley, and Lawrence Costello (eds.). 1974. *The Ordeal of Assimilation*. Doubleday, Garden City.

Fernandes, Florestan. 1967. "The Weight of the Past." *Daedalus*, no. 96.

——. 1969. *The Negro in Brazilian Society*. Columbia University Press, New York.

File, Nigel, and Chris Power. 1981. *Black Settlers in Britain, 1555–1958*. Heinemann Educational Books, London.

Finley, M. I. 1964. "Between Slavery and Freedom." *Comparative Studies in Society and History* 6, April.

Finn, R. Weldon. 1963. *An Introduction to Domesday Book*. Longmans, London.

Fisch, Max. 1970. *The New Science of Giambattista Vico*. Cornell University Press, Ithaca.

Fischer, George (ed.). 1971. *The Revival of American Socialism*. Oxford University Press, New York.

Fishel, Leslie, Jr., and Benjamin Quarles (eds.). 1970. *The Black American*. Scott, Foreshaw, Morrow, Glenview.

Fitzgerald, Frances. 1980. *America Revisited*. Vintage, New York.

Fogel, Robert, and Stanley Engerman. 1974. *Time on the Cross*, vol. 2. Little, Brown, Boston.

Foner, Jack D. 1974. *Blacks and the Military in American History*. Praeger, New York.

Foner, Philip (ed.). 1970. *W. E. B. Du Bois Speaks*. Pathfinder Press, New York.

—— (ed.). 1972. *The Voice of Black America*, vol. 1. Capricorn Books, New York.

——. 1976. *Organized Labor and the Black Worker, 1619–1973*. International Publishers, New York.

—— (ed.). 1978. *Paul Robeson Speaks*. Brunner/Mazel, New York.

Forbath, Peter. 1979. *The River Congo*. D. P. Dutton, New York.

Ford, James. 1944. "The Case of Richard Wright." *Daily Worker*, 5 September.

Forster, Margaret. 1980. *William Makepeace Thackeray: Memoirs of a Victorian Gentleman*. Quartet, London.

Foster, William Z. 1932. *Towards Soviet America*. Hyperion Press, Westport.

——. 1970. *The Negro People in American History*. International Publishers, New York.

Franco, Jose L. 1973. "Maroons and Slave Rebellions in the Spanish Territories." *Maroon Societies*, ed. Richard Price. Anchor, Garden City.

Frankfort, Henri. 1961. *The Ancient Egyptian Religion*. Harper, New York.

Franklin, Benjamin. 1961. "Observations Concerning the Increase of Mankind, Peopling of Countries, etc." *The Papers of Benjamin Franklin*, ed. Leonard W. Labaree. Yale University Press, New Haven.

Franklin, John Hope. 1967. *From Slavery to Freedom*. Knopf, New York.

Fraser, W. H. 1970. "Trade Unionism." *Popular Movements c. 1830–1850*, ed. J. T. Ward. Macmillan, London.

Frazier, E. Franklin. 1947. "Human, All Too Human: The Negro's Vested Interest in Segregation." *Survey Graphic*, January.

——. 1957. *The Black Bourgeoisie*. Free Press, Glencoe.

Frederickson, George. 1971. *The Black Image in the White Mind*. Harper and Row, New York.

Fried, Albert and Ronald Sanders (eds.). 1964. *Socialist Thought*. Edinburgh University Press, Edinburgh.

Froude, James A. 1874. *The English in Ireland*, vols. 1–3. Scribner, Armstrong, New York.

Fuller, Hoyt. 1972. Interview with Chester Himes. *Black World*, no. 21.

Garrison, William Lloyd. 1968. *Thoughts on African Colonization*. Arno, New York (orig. 1832).

Gatell, Frank Otto, and Allen Weinstein (eds.). 1968. *American Themes: Essays in Historiography*. Oxford University Press, New York.

Gayle, Addison. 1976. *The Way of the New World*. Doubleday, Garden City.

——. 1980. *Richard Wright: Ordeal of a Native Son*. Anchor/Doubleday, New York.

Geggus, David. 1980. "Haitian Divorce." *Times Literary Supplement*, 5 December.

Geiss, Immanuel. 1974. *The Pan-African Movement*. Methuen, London.

Gemery, Henry, and Jan Hogendorn (eds.). 1979. *The Uncommon Market: Quantitative Studies in the Atlantic Slave Trade*. Academic Press, New York.

Genovese, Eugene. 1971. "The Legacy of Slavery and the Roots of Black Nationalism." *Black Liberation Politics: A Reader*, ed. Edward Greer. Allyn and Bacon, Boston.

——. 1975. *Roll, Jordan, Roll*. Deutsch, London.

——. 1979. *From Rebellion to Revolution*. Louisiana State University Press, Baton Rouge.

Genovese, Eugene, and Elizabeth Fox-Genovese. 1979. "The Slave Economies in Political Perspective." *Journal of American History* 66, no. 1.

Georgakas, Dan. 1981. "Young Detroit Radicals, 1955–1965." *Urgent Tasks* 12.

Gerber, David. 1981. "Can You Keep 'Em Down on the Plantation after They've Read Rousseau?" *Radical America* 15, no. 6.

Gerhard, Peter. 1978. "A Black Conquistador in Mexico." *Hispanic American Historical Review* 58, no. 3.

Giddings, Joshua. 1858. *The Exiles of Florida*. Follett, Foster and Co., Columbus.

Gilliam, Dorothy Butler. 1976. *Paul Robeson: All-American*. New Republic Books, Washington, D.C.

Gitlow, Benjamin. 1939. *I Confess*. E. P. Dutton, New York.

Glazer, Nathan. 1961. *The Social Basis of American Communism*. Harcourt, Brace and World, New York.

Goddard, David (ed.). 1973. *Ideology in Social Science*. Vintage, New York.

Gomperz, Theodor. 1906. *Greek Thinkers*, vol. 1. John Murray, London.

Gossett, Thomas. 1963. *Race: The History of an Idea in America*. Southern Methodist University Press, Dallas.

Gray, Daniel Savage. 1973. "Bibliographic Essay: Black Views on Reconstruction." *Journal of Negro History* 58, no. 1.

Greenfield, Sidney M. 1977. "Madeira and the Beginnings of New World Sugar Cane Cultivation and Plantation Slavery: A Study in Institution Building." *Comparative Perspectives on Slavery in New World Plantation Societies, Annals of the New York Academy of Sciences*, vol. 292, ed. Vera Rubin and Arthur Tuden.

Greer, Edward (ed.). 1971. *Black Liberation Politics: A Reader*. Allyn and Bacon, Boston.

Grier, Sir Selsyn. 1938. "Unrest in the West Indies." *Oxford University Summer School on Colonial Administration, Second Session, 27 June–8 July*. Oxford University Press, Oxford.

Griffith, G. O. 1932. *Mazzini, Prophet of Modern Europe*. Hodder and Stoughton, London.

Grimal Henri. 1978. *Decolonization: The British, French, Dutch and Belgian Empires, 1919–1963*. Routledge and Kegan Paul, London.

Grob, Gerald N., and George A. Billias (eds.). 1967. *Interpretations of American History*, vol. 1. Free Press, New York.

de Groot, Sylvia W. 1973. "The Bush Negro Chiefs Visit Africa: Diary of an Historic Trip." *Maroon Societies*, ed. Richard Price. Anchor, Garden City.

Gross, Izhak. 1980. "The Abolition of Negro Slavery and British Parliamentary Politics, 1832–3." *Historical Journal* 23, no. 1.

Gross, Seymour, and John Edward Hardy (eds.). 1966. *Images of the Negro in American Literature*. University of Chicago Press, Chicago.

Gruber, Helmut. 1974. *Soviet Russia Masters the Comintern: International Communism in the Era of Stalin's Ascendancy*. Anchor/Doubleday, Garden City.

Guiseppi, Montague. 1895. "Alien Merchants in England in the Fifteenth Century." *Transactions of the Royal Historical Society*, new ser., vol. 9.

Gutkind, Peter. 1974. "The Emergent African Urban Proletariat." Occasional Paper Series, no. 8, Center for Developing-Area Studies, McGill University, Montreal.

Gutman, Herbert. 1976. *The Black Family in Slavery and Freedom, 1750–1925*. Pantheon, New York.

Guzman, Jessie. 1961. "W. E. B. Du Bois—The Historian." *Journal of Negro Education*, Fall.

Halecki, Oscar. 1963. *The Millennium of Europe*. Notre Dame University Press, Notre Dame.

Halevy, Elie. 1961. *Imperialism and the Rise of Labour: A History of the English People in the Nineteenth Century*, vol. 5. Ernest Benn, London (orig. 1926).

Hall, Marie Boas. 1964. "Scientific Thought." *Shakespeare in His Own Age, Shakespeare Survey 17*. Cambridge University Press, Cambridge.

Hall, Raymond. 1978. *Black Separatism in the United States*. University Press of New England, Hanover.

Hamdani, Abbas. 1979. "Columbus and the Recovery of Jerusalem." *Journal of the American Oriental Society* 99, no. 1.

Hammond, J. L. 1930. "The Industrial Revolution and Discontent." *Economic History Review* 2, no. 2.

Haring, C. H. 1963. *The Spanish Empire in America*. Harcourt, Brace and World, New York.

Harlan, Louis R. 1972. *Booker T. Washington: The Making of a Black Leader*. Oxford University Press, New York.

Harrington, Ollie. 1977. "The Mysterious Death of Richard Wright." *Daily Worker*, 17 December.

Harris, Abram L. 1975. "Reconstruction and the Negro." *New Republic*, 7 August.

Harris, P. B. 1969. *The Withdrawal of the Major European Powers from Africa*. Monographs on Political Science, no. 2. University College of Rhodesia, Salisbury.

Harris, William C. 1970. Introduction. *The Facts of Reconstruction*, John R. Lynch. Bobbs-Merrill, Indianapolis (orig. 1913).

Harrison, Royden. 1964. "The British Labour Movement and the International in 1864." *The Socialist Register, 1964*, eds. Ralph Miliband and John Saville. Merlin Press, London.

Hart, Richard. 1980. *Slaves Who Abolished Slavery*, vol. 1, *Blacks in Bondage*. Institute of Social and Economic Research, University of the West Indies, Jamaica.

Haupt, George. 1967. Introduction to the French Edition. *A History of Bolshevism*, Arthur Rosenberg. Grasset, Paris.

———. 1972. *Socialism and the Great War*. Clarendon Press, Oxford.

Haupt, George, Michael Lowy, and Claudia Weill. 1974. *Les Marxistes et la question nationale*. François Maspero, Paris.

Havighurst, Alfred. 1958. *The Pirenne Thesis*. D. C. Heath, Boston.

Haward, W. I. 1951. "The Financial Transaction between the Lancastrian Government and the Merchants of the Staple from 1449 to 1461." *Studies in English Trade in the Fifteenth Century*, ed. Eileen Power and M. M. Postan. Routledge and Kegan Paul, London.

Hays, Denys. 1966. *Europe in the Fourteenth and Fifteenth Centuries*. Longman, London.

———. 1968. *Europe: The Emergence of an Idea*. Edinburgh University Press, Edinburgh.

Haywood, Harry. 1975. *For a Revolutionary Position on the Negro Question*. Liberator Press, Chicago.

———. 1978. *Black Bolshevik*. Liberator Press, Chicago.

Hechter, Michael. 1975. *Internal Colonialism*. University of California Press, Berkeley.

Heckscher, Eli. 1955. *Mercantilism*, vol. 1. George Allen and Unwin, London.

Hegel, G. W. F. 1956. *The Philosophy of History*, ed. C. J. Friedrich. Dover, New York.

Henderson, W. O. 1961. *The Industrial Revolution in Europe*. Quadrangle, Chicago.

———. 1976. *The Life of Friedrich Engels*, vol. 1. Frank Cass, London.

Henri, Florette. 1976. *Black Migration*. Anchor, Garden City.

Herder, Johann Gottfried Von. 1968. *Reflections on the Philosophy of the History of Mankind*. University of Chicago Press, Chicago (orig. 1784–91).

Hertz, Friedrich. 1970. *Race and Civilization*. KTAV, n.p.

Hetherington, Penelope. 1978. *British Paternalism and Africa, 1920–40*. Frank Cass, London.

Heyck, Thomas W. 1974. *The Dimensions of British Radicalism: The Case of Ireland*. University of Illinois Press, Urbana.

Hibbert, Christopher. 1978. *The Great Mutiny*. Viking Press, New York.

Higman, B. W. 1979. "Slavery Remembered: The Celebration of Emancipation in Jamaica." *Journal of Caribbean History* 12.

Hill, Adelaide C., and Martin Kilson. 1969. *Apropos of Africa*. Frank Cass, London.

Hill, Douglas (ed.). 1977. *Tribune 40*. Quartet Books, London.

Hill, Lawrence F. 1931. "The Abolition of the African Slave Trade to Brazil." *Hispanic American Historical Review* 11, no. 2.

Hill, Robert A. 1981a. "Zion on the Zambezi: Dr. J. Albert Thorne, 'A Descendant of Africa, of Barbados,' and the African Colonial Enterprise: The 'Preliminary Stage,' 1894–97." Paper presented at the International Conference on the History of Blacks in Britain, University of London, 28–30 September.

———. 1981b. "In England, 1932–1938." *Urgent Tasks* 12.

Hindus, Michael. 1976. "Black Justice under White Law: Criminal Prosecutions of Blacks in Antebellum South Carolina." *Journal of American History* 63, no. 3.

Hines, Linda O. 1977. "White Mythology and Black Duality: George W. Carver's Response to Racism and the Radical Left." *Journal of Negro History* 62, no. 2.

Hirschfield, Magnus. 1938. *Racism*. Victor Gollancz, London.

Hobsbawm, Eric. 1952. "Economic Fluctuations and Some Social Movements since 1800." *Economic History Review*, 2d ser., vol. 5, no. 1.

———. 1962. *The Age of Revolution: 1789–1848*. Mentor, New York.

———. 1964. *Labouring Men*. Weidenfeld and Nicolson, London.

———. 1968. *Industry and Empire*. Penguin, Harmondsworth.

———. 1972. "Some Reflections on Nationalism." *Imagination and Precision in the Social Sciences*, ed. T. J. Nossiter, A. H. Hanson, and Stein Rokkan. Faber and Faber, London.

———. 1976. "The Crisis of Capitalism in Historical Perspective." *Socialist Revolution*, no. 30.

——. 1978. "The Historians' Group of the Communist Party." *Rebels and Causes*, ed. Maurice Cornforth. Lawrence and Wishart, London.

Hofstadter, Richard. 1971. *America at 1750*. Knopf, New York.

Holmes, Jack D. L. 1970. "The Abortive Slave Revolt at Pointe Coupee, Louisiana 1795." *Louisiana History* 11, no. 4.

Holmes, Martin. 1965. "Evil May-Day 1517." *History Today* 15, no. 9.

Homze, Edward. 1967. *Foreign Labor in Nazi Germany*. Princeton University Press, Princeton.

Hook, Sidney. 1933. "Materialism." *Encyclopedia of Social Sciences*, vol. 10. New York.

——. 1962. *From Hegel to Marx*. University of Michigan Press, Ann Arbor.

Hooker, James R. 1970. *Black Revolutionary: George Padmore's Path from Communism to Pan-Africanism*. Praeger, New York.

Hopkins, Elizabeth. 1971. "The Nyabingi Cult of Southwestern Uganda." *Rebellion in Black Africa*, ed. R. Rotberg. Oxford University Press, London.

Horsman, Reginald. 1981. *Race and Manifest Destiny*. Harvard University Press, Cambridge.

Howard, Dick. 1977. *The Marxian Legacy*. Macmillan, London.

Howard, Michael. 1981. "Empire, Race and War." *History Today*, no. 31.

Hunter, G. K. 1964. "Elizabethans and Foreigners." *Shakespeare in His Own Age, Shakespeare Survey* 17, ed. Allardyce Nicoll. Cambridge University Press, Cambridge.

Hunwick, J. O. 1978. "Black Africans in the Islamic World: An Understudied Dimension of the Black Diaspora." *Tarikh* 5, no. 4.

Huttenback, R. A. 1976. *Racism and Empire*. Cornell University Press, Ithaca.

Ikime, Obaro. 1973. "Colonial Conquest and African Resistance in the Niger Delta States." *Tarikh* 4, no. 3.

Inalcik, Halil. 1966. *The Ottoman Empire*. Weidenfeld and Nicolson, London.

Inglis, Brian. 1971. *Poverty and the Industrial Revolution*. Hodder and Stoughton, London.

Inikori, J. E. 1976a. "Measuring the Atlantic Slave Trade: An Assessment of Curtin and Anstey." *Journal of African History* 17, no. 2.

——. 1976b. "Measuring the Atlantic Slave Trade: A Rejoinder by J. E. Inikori." *Journal of African History* 17, no. 4.

Irvine, Keith. 1970. *The Rise of the Colored Races*. W. W. Norton, New York.

Jackson, James. 1925. "The Negro in America." *Communist International*, February.

Jacobsen, Julius (ed.). 1968. *The Negro and the American Labor Movement*. Anchor, Garden City.

Jaffe, Philip. 1975. *The Rise and Fall of American Communism*. Horizon Press, New York.

James C. L. R. 1933. *The Case for West-Indian Self Government*. Hogarth, London.

——. 1935. "Is This War Necessary?" *New Leader*, 4 October.

——. 1936a. " 'Civilising' the 'Blacks.' " *New Leader*, 29 May.

——. 1936b. "Fighting for the Abyssinian Empire." *New Leader*, 5 June.

——. 1937. *World Revolution, 1917–1936: The Rise and Fall of the Communist International*. Martin Secker and Warburg, London.

——. 1963a. *The Black Jacobins*. Vintage, New York (orig. 1938).

——. 1963b. *Beyond a Boundary*. Hutchinson, London.

——. 1969. *A History of Pan-African Revolt*. Drum and Spear, Washington, D.C. (orig. 1938).

——. 1973. *Modern Politics*. bewick/ed, Detroit.

——. 1974. Interview with C. J. Robinson. Binghamton, New York, Spring.

——. 1977a. *Nkrumah and the Ghana Revolution*. Lawrence Hill, Westport.

——. 1977b. *The Future in the Present*. Lawrence Hill, Westport.

——. 1980a. *Spheres of Existence*. Allison and Busby, London.

——. 1980b. *Notes on Dialectics*. Allison and Busby, London.

——. 1980c. "Radical Pan-Africanism in the 1930s: Interview with Alan J. MacKenzie." *Radical History Review*, no. 24.

James, C. L. R., and George Padmore. 1977. "Revolts in Africa." *The Future in the Present*, C. L. R. James. Lawrence Hill, Westport (orig. 1938).

James, George. 1954. *Stolen Legacy*. Philosophical Library, New York (repr. 1976).

Jellema, Dirk. 1955. "Frisian Trade in the Dark Ages." *Speculum* 30, no. 1.

Jerome W., and A. Buick. 1967. "Soviet State Capitalism?: The History of an Idea." *Survey*, no. 62.

Jha, J. A. 1973. "Indian Heritage in Trinidad, West Indies." *Caribbean Quarterly* 19, no. 2.

Johnson, Douglas (ed.). 1971. *The Making of the Modern World: Europe Discovers the World*, vol. 1. Barnes and Noble, New York.

Joll, James. 1965. "The German Confederation, 1815–1866." *Encyclopaedia Britannica*, vol. 10.

Jones, Allen W. 1979. "The Black Press in the 'New South': Jesse C. Duke's Struggle for Justice and Equality." *Journal of Negro History* 64, no. 3.

Jordan, Winthrop. 1968. *White Over Black*. University of North Carolina Press, Chapel Hill.

Kanet, Roger. 1973. "The Comintern and the 'Negro Question': Communist Policy in the United States and Africa, 1921–1941." *Survey*, Autumn.

Karasch, Mary. 1974. "Black Worlds in the Tropics: Gilberto Freyre and the Woman of Color in Brazil." *Proceedings of the Pacific Coast Council on Latin American Studies*, no. 3.

Katz, William L. 1968. "Earliest Responses of American Negroes and Whites to African Colonization." Introduction to *Thoughts on African Colonization*, William Lloyd Garrison. Arno, New York.

Katznelson, Ira. 1973. *Black Men, White Cities*. Oxford University Press, London.

Kees, Hermann. 1961. *Ancient Egypt*. University of Chicago Press, Chicago.

Keita, Lanciany (Edward Philips). 1977–78. "African Philosophical Systems: A Rational Reconstruction." *Philosophical Forum* 9, nos. 2–3.

——. 1979. "The African Philosophical Tradition." *African Philosophy: An Introduction*, ed. Richard Wright. University Press of America, Washington, D.C.

Keller, Bonnie. 1978. "Millenarianism and Resistance: The Xhosa Cattle Killing." *Journal of Asian and African Studies* 13, nos. 1–2.

Kent, R. K. 1965. "Palmares: An African State in Brazil." *Journal of African History* 6, no. 2.

——. 1970. "African Revolt in Bahia: 24–25 January 1835." *Journal of Social History* 3, no. 4.

Kiernan, V. G. 1957. "Foreign Mercenaries and Absolute Monarchy." *Past and Present*, no. 11.

——. 1965. "State and Nation in Western Europe." *Past and Present*, no. 31.

——. 1969. *The Lords of Humankind*. Weidenfeld and Nicholson, London.

——. 1982. *European Empires from Conquest to Collapse*. Leicester University Press, Leicester.

Kilson, Martin. 1981. "Politics and Identity among Black Intellectuals." *Dissent*, Summer.

Kimble, David. 1963. *A Political History of Ghana: The Rise of Gold Coast Nationalism, 1850–1928*. Oxford University Press, London.

King, Johannes. 1973. "Guerrilla Warfare: A Bush Negro View." *Maroon Societies*, ed. Richard Price. Anchor, Garden City.

Kiple, Kenneth. 1976. *Blacks in Colonial Cuba, 1774–1899*. University of Florida Press, Gainesville.

Knecht, Robert. 1971. "The Discoveries." *The Making of the Modern World: Europe Discovers the World*, vol. 1. Barnes and Noble, New York.

Koning, Hans. 1976. *Columbus: His Enterprise*. Monthly Review Press, New York.

Kopytoff, Barbara Klamon. 1978. "The Early Development of Jamaican Maroon Societies." *William and Mary Quarterly* 35, no. 2.

Kranzberg, Melvin. 1965. "Industrial Revolution." *Encyclopaedia Britannica*, vol. 12.

Krieger, Leonard (ed.). 1967. *The German Revolutions*. University of Chicago Press, Chicago.

Krislov, Samuel. 1967. *The Negro in Federal Employment*. University of Minnesota Press, Minneapolis.

Kropotkin, Petr. n.d. *Mutual Aid*. Extending Horizon Books, Boston.

Kulikoff, Allan. 1978. "The Origins of Afro-American Society in Tidewater Maryland and Virginia, 1700–1790." *William and Mary Quarterly* 35, no. 2.

Labaree, Leonard W. (ed.). 1961. *The Papers of Benjamin Franklin*. Yale University Press, New Haven.

Lacerte, Robert. 1975. "The First Land Reform in Latin America: The Reforms of Alexander Potion, 1809–1814." *Inter-American Economic Affairs* 28, no. 4.

——. 1981. "Xenophobia and Economic Decline: The Haitian Case, 1820–1843." *The Americas* 37, no. 4.

La Guerre, John (ed.). 1974. *Calcutta to Caroni: The East Indians of Trinidad*. Longman Caribbean, Trinidad.

Lantenari, Vittorio. 1963. *Religions of the Oppressed*. Knopf, New York.

Las Casas, Bartolome de. 1974. *The Devastation of the Indies: A Brief Account*. Seabury Press, New York (orig. 1542).

Latouche, Robert. 1961. *The Birth of Western Economy*. Barnes and Noble, New York.

Laurence, Dr. Stephen Moister. 1969. "The Trinidad Water Riot of 1903: Reflections of an Eyewitness," ed. L. O. Laurence. *Caribbean Quarterly* 15, no. 4.

Lawrence, Ken. 1981. "Conversation: Interview with Vincent Harding." *Urgent Tasks* 12.

Lazersfeld, Paul, and Anthony Oberschall. 1965. "Max Weber and Empirical Research." *American Sociological Review* 30, no. 2.

Lazonick, William. 1978. "The Subjection of Labour to Capital: The Rise of the Capitalist System." *Review of Radical Political Economics* 10, no. 1.

Leiss, William. 1971. "Review on Husserl." *Telos*, no. 8.

LeMay, G. H. L. 1971. *Black and White in South Africa*. American Heritage Press.

Lenin, V. I. 1967a. *Selected Works*, vol. 1. International Publishers, New York.

——. 1967b. *What Is to Be Done? Selected Works*, vol. 1. International Publishers, New York.

——. 1967c. *"Left-Wing" Communism—An Infantile Disorder. Selected Works*, vol. 3. Progress Publishers, Moscow.

——. 1969. *The State and Revolution. Selected Works*, vol. 3. Lawrence and Wishart, London.

——. 1970. "The Tasks of the Proletariat in the Present Revolution." *Selected Works*. Progress Publishers, Moscow.

Leaner, Ralph, and Muhsin Mahdi (eds.). 1963. *Medieval Political Philosophy*. Free Press of Glencoe, New York.

Levine, Lawrence. 1977. *Black Culture and Black Consciousness*. Oxford University Press, New York.

Lewis, Bernard. 1970. *Race and Color in Islam*. Harper and Row, New York.

Lichtheim, George. 1969. *The Origins of Socialism*. Praeger, New York.

——. 1973. *Marxism: An Historical and Critical Survey*. Praeger, New York.

Lichtman, Richard. 1970. "The Facade of Equality in Liberal Democratic Theory." *Socialist Revolution*, January.

Liebman, Arthur. 1979. *Jews and the Left*. John Wiley, New York.

Livermore, Harold V. (ed.). 1963. *Portugal and Brazil*. Clarendon Press, Oxford.

——. 1965. "Portugal." *Encyclopaedia Britannica*, vol. 18.

Logan, Rayford (ed.). 1971. *W. E. B. Du Bois: A Profile*. Hill and Wang, New York.

London Times. 1816. Private letters published under "Negro Insurrection," 5 June.

Longmate, Norman. 1974. *The Workhouse*. St. Martin's Press, New York.

Lopez, R. S., H. A. Miskimin, and Abraham Udovitch. 1970. "England to Egypt, 1350–1500: Long-Term Trends and Long-Distance Trade." *Studies in the Economic History of the Middle East from the Rise of Islam to the Present Day*. Oxford University Press, London.

Lopez, Robert S. 1966. *The Birth of Europe*. Phoenix House, London.

Lopez, Robert S., and Irving Raymond (eds.). 1955. *Medieval Trade in the Mediterranean World*. Oxford University Press, Oxford.

Love, Edgar. 1967. "Negro Resistance to Spanish Rule in Colonial Mexico." *Journal of Negro History* 52, no. 2.

Low, W. Augustus. 1981. "Historians." *Encyclopedia of Black America*, ed. W. Augustus Low and Virgil Cloft. McGraw-Hill, New York.

Lowy, Michael. 1976. "Marxists and the National Question." *New Left Review*, no. 96.

Lukács, Georg. 1968. *History and Class Consciousness*. MIT Press, Cambridge.

——. 1969. "On the Responsibility of Intellectuals." *Telos* 2, no. 1.

Lundberg, Ferdinand. 1980. *Cracks in the Constitution*. Lyle Stuart, New York.

Luxemburg, Rosa. 1969. "The National Question." *Rosa Luxemburg*, ed. Peter Nettl. Oxford University Press, Oxford.

Lynch, Hollis. 1970. *Edward Wilmot Blyden: Pan-Negro Patriot, 1832–1912*. Oxford University Press, London.

Lynch, John R. 1970. *The Facts of Reconstruction*. Bobbs-Merrill, Indianapolis (orig. 1913).

McBride, David. 1977. "Africa's Elevation and Changing Racial Thought at Lincoln University, 1854–1886." *Journal of Negro History* 62, no. 4.

McDonald, Roderick. 1979. "The Williams Thesis: A Comment on the State of Scholarship." *Caribbean Quarterly* 25, no. 3.

——. 1980. "Measuring the British Slave Trade to Jamaica, 1789–1808: A Comment." *Economic History Review* 33, no. 2.

MacFarlane, L. J. 1966. *The British Communist Party*. MacGibbon and Kee, Worcester and London.

MacIntyre, Stuart. 1980. *A Proletarian Science: Marxism in Britain, 1917–1933*. Cambridge University Press, Cambridge.

McIntyre, W. David. 1974. *Colonies into Commonwealth*. Blandford Press, London.

McKay, Claude. 1968. *Harlem: Negro Metropolis*. Harcourt Brace Jovanovich, New York (orig. 1940).

——. 1970. *A Long Way from Home*. Harcourt, Brace and World, New York (orig. 1937).

MacKenzie, Norman. 1969. *Socialism: A Short History*. Harper Colophon, New York.

McKinnon, Alan. 1980. "Communist Party Election Tactics: A Historical Review." *Marxism Today* 24, no. 8.

McLellan, David. 1970. *Marx before Marxism*. Macmillan, London.

——. 1973. *Karl Marx: His Life and Thought*. Harper Colophon, New York.

McMillan, Duncan. 1965. "Charlemagne Legends." *Encyclopaedia Britannica*, vol. 5. University of Chicago Press, Chicago.

McNeill, William. 1977. *Plagues and People*. Anchor, Garden City.

Magubane, Bernard. 1971. "A Critical Look at Indices Used in the Study of Social Change in Colonial Africa." *Current Anthropology* 12, nos. 4–5.

Mair, Lucy. 1936. *Native Policies in Africa*. George Routledge, London.

——. 1975. "Anthropology and Colonial Policy." *African Affairs*, April.

Makonnen, Ras. 1973. *Pan-Africanism from Within*, ed. Kenneth King. Oxford University Press, London.

Makovic, Mihailo. 1977. "Stalinism and Marxism." *Stalinism*, ed. Robert Tucker. W. W. Norton, New York.

Malheiro, Agostinho Marques Perdigao. 1944. *A escravidao no Brasil*.

Maolwist, Marian. 1959. "The Economic and Social Development of the Baltic Countries from the Fifteenth to the Seventeenth Centuries." *Economic History Review*, 2d ser., vol. 12, no. 2.

Manchester, Alan. 1964. *British Preeminence in Brazil: Its Rise and Decline*. Octagon Books, New York.

Mangan, J. A. 1981. *Athleticism in the Victorian and Edwardian Public School*. Cambridge University Press, Cambridge.

Mannheim, Karl. 1936. *Ideology and Utopia*. Harcourt, Brace and World, New York.

Mansergh, Nicholas. 1965. *The Irish Question, 1840–1921*. University of Toronto Press, Toronto.

Manuel, Frank. 1956. Introduction. *The Philosophy of History*, G. W. F. Hegel, ed. C. J. Friedrich. Dover, New York.

Marable, Manning. 1981. *Blackwater*. Black Praxis Press, Dayton.

Marcus, Harold. 1975. *The Life and Times of Menelik II*. Clarendon Press, Oxford.

Marcuse, Herbert. 1968. *Reason and Revolution*. Beacon Press, Boston.

Marks, Shula. 1971. "The Zulu Disturbances in Natal." *Rebellion in Black Africa*, ed. Robert Rotberg. Oxford University Press, London.

Martin, Tony. 1972. "C. L. R. James and the Race/Class Question." *Race* 2.

——. 1976. *Race First*. Greenwood Press, Westport.

Marx, Karl. 1965. *Pre-Capitalist Economic Formations*. International Publishers, New York.

——. 1968a. "The Future Results of British Rule in India." *Karl Marx on Colonialism and Modernization*, ed. Shlomo Avineri. Doubleday, Garden City.

——. 1968b. *The Holy Family*, as quoted by Georg Lukács, *History and Class Consciousness*. MIT Press, Cambridge.

——. 1969. "Parliamentary Debate on India." *New York Daily Tribune*, 25 June 1853. Reprinted in *Karl Marx on Colonialism and Modernization*, ed. Shlomo Avineri. Anchor, Garden City.

——. 1970. *A Contribution to the Critique of Political Economy*. International Publishers, New York.

——. 1971a. *The Poverty of Philosophy*. International Publishers, New York.

——. 1971b. *The Class Struggles in France, 1848–50*. *Karl Marx: On Revolution*, ed. Saul Padover. McGraw-Hill, New York.

——. 1972a. *The German Ideology*. *The Marx-Engels Reader*, ed. Robert Tucker. W. W. Norton, New York.

——. 1972b. "Critique of the Gotha Program." *The Marx-Engels Reader*, ed. Robert Tucker. W. W. Norton, New York.

——. 1972c. "Theses on Feuerbach." *The Marx-Engels Reader*, ed. Robert Tucker. W. W. Norton, New York.

——. 1972d. "Confidential Communication, 28 March 1870." *Ireland and the Irish Question*, Karl Marx and Friedrich Engels. International Publishers, New York.

——. 1972e. "On the Jewish Question." *The Marx-Engels Reader*, ed. Robert Tucker. W. W. Norton, New York.

——. 1972f. "Outline of a Report on the Irish Question to the Communist Educational Association of German Workers in London." *Ireland and the Irish Question*, Karl Marx and Friedrich Engels. International Publishers, New York.

——. 1977. *Capital*, vol. 1. International Publishers, New York.

Marx, Karl, and Friedrich Engels. 1952. *The Russian Menace to Europe*, ed. Paul Blackstock and Bert Hoselitz. Free Press, Glencoe.

——. 1972a. *The Communist Manifesto*. *The Marx-Engels Reader*, ed. Robert Tucker. W. W. Norton, New York.

——. 1972b. *Ireland and the Irish Question*. International Publishers, New York.

——. 1972c. *The German Ideology*. *The Marx-Engels Reader*, ed. Robert Tucker. W. W. Norton, New York.

——. 1972d. *Karl Marx and Friedrich Engels, Selected Works*, vol. 1. International Publishers, New York.

——. 1973. *The Revolutions of 1848*. International Publishers, New York.

Mason, Daniel, and Jessica Smith (eds.). 1979. Foreword. *Lenin's Impact on the United States*. Reprinted in *Highlights of a Fighting History: 60 Years of the Communist Party, USA*, ed. Philip Bart et al. International Publishers, New York.

Mathieson, William Law. 1926. *British Slavery and Its Abolition*. Longmans, Green and Co., London.

Maxton, James, and Fenner Brockway. 1936. "The War Threat." *New Leader*, 17 April.

Mayhew, Arthur. 1938. "Education in the Colonies." *Oxford University Summer School on Colonial Administration, Second Session, 27 June–8 July 1938*. Oxford University Press, Oxford.

Mehlinger, Louis. 1916. "The Attitudes of the Free Negro toward African Colonization." *Journal of Negro History* 1, no. 3.

Mehring, Franz. 1969. *Karl Marx, The Story of His Life*. University of Michigan Press, Ann Arbor.

Meier, August. 1971a. "The Paradox of W. E. B. Du Bois." *W. E. B. Du Bois: A Profile*, ed. Rayford Logan. Hill and Wang, New York.

——. 1971b. " 'Radicals and Conservatives'—a Modern View." *W. E. B. Du Bois: A Profile*, ed. Rayford Logan. Hill and Wang, New York.

Melendy, Howard Brett. 1972. *The Oriental Americans*. Twayne Publishers, New York.

Mellon, Matthew. 1969. *Early American Views on Negro Slavery*. Bergman, New York.

Merivale, Herman. 1967. *Lectures on Colonization and Colonies*. Augustus Kelly, New York (orig. 1861).

Merriam, Charles. 1927. "William Archibald Dunning." *American Masters of Social Science*, ed. Howard W. Odum. Holt, New York.

Meyer, Alfred. 1962. *Leninism*. Praeger, New York.

Mez, Adam. 1937. *The Renaissance of Islam*. Luzac and Co., London.

Miege, J.-L. 1968. *L'Imperialisme colonial italien de 1870 nos jours*. SEDES, Paris.

——. 1980. "The Colonial Past in the Present." *Decolonization and After*, ed. W. H. Morris-Jones and Georges Fischer. Frank Cass, London.

Miliband, Ralph, and John Saville (eds.). 1964. *The Socialist Register, 1964*. Merlin Press, London.

Miller, Floyd. 1975. *The Search for a Black Nationality*. University of Illinois Press, Urbana.

Miller, John Chester. 1977. *The Wolf by the Ears*. New American Library, New York.

Miller, Stuart. 1969. *The Unwelcome Immigrant*. University of California Press, Berkeley.

Moon, Henri Lee (ed.). 1972. *The Emerging Thought of W. E. B. Du Bois*. Simon and Schuster, New York.

Moore, Richard B. 1966–67. "On Barbadians and Minding Other People's Business." *New World Quarterly* 3, nos. 1–2, Dead Season and Croptime.

——. 1970. "Du Bois and Pan-Africa." *Black Titan: W. E. B. Du Bois*, ed. John Henrik Clarke et al. Beacon Press, Boston.

Moore, R. Lawrence. 1969. "Flawed Fraternity—American Socialist Response to the Negro, 1901–1912." *The Historian* 32, no. 1.

Moreau de Saint-Mery, M. L. E. 1973. "The Border Maroons of Saint-Domingue: Le Maniel." *Maroon Societies*, ed. Richard Price. Anchor, Garden City.

Morgan, Edmund. 1975. *American Slavery, American Freedom*. W. W. Norton, New York.

Morgan, Gordon D. 1976. "In Memorium: Oliver C. Cox, 1901–1974." *Monthly Review*, May.

Morison, Samuel Eliot. 1942. *Admiral of the Ocean Sea*. 2 vols. Little, Brown, Boston.

——. 1952. "Columbus as Navigator." *Studi Colombiana*, vol. 2. Stabilimento Arti Grafiche ed. Affini, Genova.

Morris-Jones, W. H., and Georges Fischer (eds.). 1980. *Decolonization and After*. Frank Cass, London.

Moses, W. J. 1978. *The Golden Age of Black Nationalism, 1850–1925*. Archon Books, Hamden.

Mosse, George. 1978. *Toward the Final Solution*. J. M. Dent and Sons, London.

Mott, Frank L. 1939. *A History of American Magazines, 1741–1850*, vol. 1. Harvard University Press, Cambridge.

Mullin, Gerald (Michael). 1972. *Flight and Rebellion*. Oxford University Press, New York.

Murray, A. Victor. 1938. "Missions and Indirect Administration." *Oxford University Summer School on Colonial Administration, Second Session, 27 June–8 July 1938*. Oxford University Press, Oxford.

Murray, D. R. 1971. "Statistics of the Slave Trade in Cuba, 1790–1867." *Journal of Latin American Studies* 3, no. 2.

Murray, Margaret. 1964. *The Splendour That Was Egypt*. Sidgwick and Jackson, London (orig. 1949).

Murray-Brown, Jeremy. 1974. *Kenyatta*. Fontana/Collins, London.

Musson, A. E. 1975. "Continental Influences on the Industrial Revolution in Great Britain." *Great Britain and Her World, 1750–1914*, ed. Barrie Ratcliffe. Manchester University Press, Manchester.

Myers, Eugene A. 1964. *Arabic Thought and the Western World in the Golden Age of Islam*. Frederick Ungar Publishing, New York.

Nairn, Tom. 1975. "The Modern Janus." *New Left Review*, no. 94.

Naison, Mark. 1971. "Marxism and Black Radicalism in America: Notes on a Long (and Continuing) Journey." *Radical America* 5, no. 3.

——. 1974. "Communism and Black Nationalism in the Depression: The Case of Harlem." *Journal of Ethnic Studies*, Summer.

——. 1978a. "Harlem Communists and the Politics of Black Protest." *Marxist Perspectives* 1, no. 3.

——. 1978b. "Historical Notes on Blacks and American Communism: The Harlem Experience." *Science and Society* 42, no. 3.

——. 1981. "Communism and Harlem Intellectuals in the Popular Front: Anti-Fascism and the Politics of Black Culture." *Journal of Ethnic Studies* 9, no. 1.

Nash, A. E. Keir. 1979. "Reason of Slavery: Understanding the Judicial Role in the Peculiar Institution." *Vanderbilt Law Review* 32, no. 1.

Nearing, Scott. 1969. *Black America*. Schocken, New York (orig. 1929).

Negro in Virginia, The. n.d. Virginia Writers' Project, Hastings House, New York.

Negro Nurse in Republican Spain, A. 1977. The Negro Committee to Aid Spain, reissued by the Veterans of the Abraham Lincoln Brigade, New York (orig. 1938).

Nettl, Peter. 1969. *Rosa Luxemburg*. Oxford University Press, Oxford.

Newton, Arthur Percival (ed.). 1932. *The Great Age of Discovery*. University of London Press, London.

Nicholls, David. 1974. "A Work of Combat: Mulatto Historians and the Haitian Past, 1847–1867." *Journal of Interamerican Studies and World Affairs* 16, no. 1 .
———. 1979. *From Dessalines to Duvalier*. Cambridge University Press, Cambridge.
Nichols, Charles (ed.). 1972. *Black Men in Chains*. Lawrence Hill, New York.
Nichols, Roy. 1962. *The Disruption of American Democracy*. Collier Books, New York.
Nicoll, Allardyce (ed.). 1964. *Shakespeare in His Own Age, Shakespeare Survey 17*. Cambridge University Press, Cambridge.
Nolan, William. 1951. *Communism versus the Negro*. Henry Regnery, Chicago.
Norman, Edward. 1971. *A History of Modern Ireland*. Allen Lane/Penguin Press, London.
Nossiter, T. J. 1972. "Shopkeeper Radicalism in the Nineteenth Century." *Imagination and Precision in the Social Sciences*, ed. T. J. Nossiter, A. H. Hanson, and Stein Rokhan. Faber and Faber, London.
Nossiter, T. J., A. H. Hanson, and Stein Rokkan (eds.). 1972. *Imagination and Precision in the Social Sciences*. Faber and Faber, London.
Nwafor, Azinna. 1972. Introduction. *Pan-Africanism or Communism*, George Padmore. Doubleday, New York.
Nyerere, Julius. 1979. *Ujamaa: Essays on Socialism*. Oxford University Press, Dar es Salaam.
Oates, Stephen. 1970. *To Purge This Land with Blood*. Harper Torchbooks, New York.
Obichere, Boniface. 1969. "African History and Western Civilization." *Black Studies in the University*, ed. A. Robinson, C. Foster, and D. Ogilvie. Bantam, New York.
O'Brien, James, et al. 1970. " 'New Left Historians' of the 1960's." *Radical America*, November.
Odum, Howard (ed.). 1927. *American Masters of Social Science*. Holt, New York.
Offiong, Daniel A. 1976. "The Cheerful School and the Myth of the Civilizing Mission of Colonial Imperialism." *Pan-African Journal* 9, no. 1.
Okoye, Nwabueze F. 1980. "Chattel Slavery as the Nightmare of the American Revolutionaries." *William and Mary Quarterly* 37, no. 1.
Olela, Henry. 1979. "The African Foundations of Greek Philosophy." *African Philosophy: An Introduction*, ed. Richard A. Wright. University Press of America, Washington, D.C.
———. 1981. *From Ancient Africa to Ancient Greece*. Select Publishing, Atlanta.
Origo, Iris. 1955. "The Domestic Enemy: The Eastern Slaves in Tuscany in the Fourteenth and Fifteenth Centuries." *Speculum* 30, no. 3.
———. 1957. *The Merchant of Prato*. Knopf, New York.
Orum, Thomas T. 1975. "The Politics of Color: The Racial Dimension of Cuban Politics during the Early Republican Years, 1900–1912." Unpublished Ph.D. diss., Department of History, New York University.
Ott, T. O. 1973. *The Haitian Revolution*. University of Tennessee Press, Knoxville.
Owens, Leslie Howard. 1976. *This Species of Property*. Oxford University Press, New York.
Padmore, George. 1971. *The Life and Struggles of Negro Toilers*. Sun Dance Press, Hollywood.
———. 1972a. *Africa and World Peace*. Frank Cass, London (orig. 1937).
———. 1972b. *Pan-Africanism or Communism*. Doubleday, New York.
Padover, Saul (ed.). 1971. *Karl Marx: On Revolution*. McGraw-Hill, New York.
Painter, Nell Irvin. 1976. *Exodusters: Black Migration to Kansas after Reconstruction*. Knopf, New York.
Palmer, Colin. 1975. "Religion and Magic in Mexican Slave Society, 1570–1650." *Race and Slavery in the Western Hemisphere: Quantitative Studies*, ed. Stanley L. Engerman and Eugene Genovese. Princeton University Press, Princeton.
Palmer, R. R., with Joel Colton. 1959. *A History of Modern Europe*. Knopf, New York.
Pares, Richard. 1960. *Merchants and Planters, Economic History Review* Supplement, no.e.
Parker, William. 1972. "Fugitives Resist Kidnapping." *Black Men in Chains*, ed. Charles Nichols. Lawrence Hill, New York.
Parris, E. Elliot. 1981. "Minty Alley." *Urgent Tasks* 12.
Parry, Benita. 1972. *Delusions and Discoveries*. University of California Press, Berkeley.
Parry, J. H. 1966. *The Establishment of the European Hegemony: 1415–1715*. Harper and Row, New York.
Passmore, John. 1970. *The Perfectibility of Man*. Duckworth, London.
Patterson, H. Orlando. 1969. *The Sociology of Slavery*. Fairleigh Dickinson University Press, Rutherford.
———. 1973. "Slavery and Slave Revolts: A Sociohistorical Analysis of the First Maroon War, 1665–1740." *Maroon Societies*, ed. Richard Price, Anchor, Garden City.
Peires, J. B. 1979. "Nxele, Ntsidana and the Origins of the Xhosa Religious Reaction." *Journal of African History* 20, no. 1.
Pelling, Henry. 1958. "The Early History of the Communist Party of Great Britain, 1920–9." *Transactions of the Royal Historical Society*, 5th ser., vol. 8.
———. 1976. *A History of British Trade Unionism*. Penguin, Harmondsworth.
Perez, Louis A. 1976. *Army Politics in Cuba, 1898–1958*. University of Pittsburgh Press, Pittsburgh.
Perham, M. 1938. "British Native Administration." *Oxford University Summer School on Colonial Administration, Second Session, 27 June–8 July 1938*. Oxford University Press, Oxford.

Pethybridge, Roger. 1977. *The Social Prelude to Stalinism*. Macmillan, London.

Peyre, Henri. 1968. *Historical and Critical Essays*. University of Nebraska Press, Lincoln.

Peytraud, Lucien. 1897. "L'Esclavage aux Antilles Français avant 1789 d'après des documents inedits des Archives Coloniales." Thèse Presentée a la Faculté des Lettres de Paris, Paris.

Piccone, Paul. 1971. "Reading the *Crisis*." *Telos*, no. 8.

Pierson, Stanley. 1973. *Marxism and the Origins of British Socialism*. Cornell University Press, Ithaca.

Pinckney, Darryl. 1977. "Richard Wright: The Unnatural History of a Native Son." *Village Voice*, 4 July.

Pipes, Daniel. 1980. "Black Soldiers in Early Muslim Armies." *International Journal of African Historical Studies* 13, no. 1.

Pirenne, Henri. 1937. *Economic and Social History of Medieval Europe*. Harcourt, Brace and World, New York.

——. 1948. *Medieval Cities, Their Origins and the Revival of Trade*. Princeton University Press, Princeton.

——. 1968. *Mohammed and Charlemagne*. Unwin University Books, London.

Polanyi, Karl. 1957. *The Great Transformation*. Beacon Press, Boston.

Poole, Reginald. 1960. *Illustrations of the History of Medieval Thought and Learning*. Dover, New York.

Poppino, Rollie. 1968. *Brazil, the Land and People*. Oxford University Press, New York.

Post, Charles. 1982. "The American Road to Capitalism." *New Left Review*, no. 133.

Post, Ken. 1978. *Arise Ye Starvelings: The Jamaican Labour Rebellion of 1938 and Its Aftermath*. Martinus Nijhoff, The Hague.

Postan, M. 1939. "The Fifteenth Century." *Economic History Review* 9, no. 2.

Power, Eileen, and M. M. Postan (eds.). 1951. *Studies in English Trade in the Fifteenth Century*. Routledge and Kegan Paul, London.

Prawar, S. S. 1976. *Karl Marx and World Literature*. Oxford University Press, Oxford.

Prestage, Edgar. 1932. "Vasco da Gama and the Way to the Indies." *The Great Age of Discovery*, ed. Arthur Percival Newton. University of London, London.

——. 1934. "The Anglo-Portuguese Alliance." *Transactions of the Royal Historical Society*, 4th ser., vol. 17.

Price, Richard (ed.). 1973. *Maroon Societies*. Anchor, Garden City.

——. 1976. *The Guiana Maroons: A Historical and Bibliographical Introduction*. Johns Hopkins University Press, Baltimore.

Procacci, Giuliano. 1970. *The History of the Italian People*. Weidenfeld and Nicolson, London.

Proceedings of a General Court Martial Held at the Colony House in George Town on Monday the 13th Day of October 1823, *Edinburgh Review*, xl, 89, March 1824.

"Punishment for a Negro Rebel." 1902. Documents, *William and Mary Quarterly*, ser. 1, vol. 10, no. 3.

Quarles, Benjamin. 1958. "Lord Dunmore as Liberator." *William and Mary Quarterly* 15, no. 4.

——. 1961. *The Negro in the American Revolution*. University of North Carolina Press, Chapel Hill.

——. 1974. *Allies for Freedom: Blacks and John Brown*. Oxford University Press, New York.

"Racism, Intelligence and the Working Class." n.d. [post-1973]. Published by the Party for Workers Power, Boston.

Rae, John. 1981. "Play Up, Play Up." *Times Literary Supplement*, 2 October.

Ramos, Arthur. 1951. *The Negro in Brazil*. Associated Publishers, Washington D.C. (orig. 1939).

Ramsey, P. 1960. "The European Economy in the Sixteenth Century." *Economic History Review*, 2d ser., vol. 12, no. 3.

Ranger, T. O. 1967. *Revolt in Southern Rhodesia, 1896–7*. Heinemann, London.

——. 1977. "The People in African Resistance: A Review." *Journal of Southern African Studies* 4, no. 1.

Raskin, Jonah. 1971. *The Mythology of Imperialism*. Dell, New York.

Ratcliffe, Barrie. 1975. *Great Britain and Her World, 1750–1914*. Manchester University Press, Manchester.

Rau, Virginia. 1957. "A Family of Italian Merchants in Portugal in the Fifteenth Century: The Lomellini." *Studi in Onore de Armando Sapori*, vol. 1. Instituto Editoriale Cisalpino, Milano.

Rawick, George. 1976. Interview with C. J. Robinson, Winter.

Reckord, Mary. 1968. "The Jamaican Slave Rebellion of 1831." *Past and Present*, no. 40.

Record, Wilson. 1971. *The Negro and the Communist Party*. Atheneum, New York.

Reddick, Lawrence. 1937. "A New Interpretation for Negro History." *Journal of Negro History* 21, no. 1.

Redkey, Edwin. 1969. *Black Exodus*. Yale University Press, New Haven.

Reich, Wilhelm. 1972. "What Is Class Consciousness?" *Sex-Pol: Essays 1929–1934*, ed. Lee Baxandall. Vintage, New York.

Rensberger, Boyce. 1979. "Nubian Monarchy Called Oldest." *New York Times*, 1 March.

Return of Trials of Slaves: Jamaica, 1814–1818. Colonial Office 137–147, Public Records Office, London.

Richard, Jean. 1969. "The Mongols and the Franks." *Journal of Asian History* 3, no. 1.

Riva, Francisco Perez de la. 1973. "Cuban Palenques." *Maroon Societies*, ed. Richard Price. Anchor, Garden City.

Roark, James. 1977. *Masters without Slaves*. W. W. Norton, New York.

Robinson, Armstead, Craig Foster, and Donald Ogilvie (eds.). 1969. *Black Studies in the University*. Bantam, New York.
Robinson, Cedric J. 1978. "The Emergent Marxism of Richard Wright's Ideology." *Race and Class* 19, no. 3.
——. 1979. "A Case of Mistaken Identity." Paper presented at the African Studies Association Conference, Los Angeles, 1 November.
——. 1980a. *The Terms of Order*. State University of New York Press, Albany.
——. 1980b. "Notes Toward a 'Native' Theory of History." *Review* 4, no. 1.
——. 1981. "Amilcar Cabral and the Dialectic of Portuguese Colonialism." *Radical America* 15, no. 3.
Robinson, R. E., and J. A. Gallagher (with Alice Denny). 1961. *Africa and the Victorians*. Macmillan, London.
Rodinson, Maxime. 1974a. *Mohammed*. Vintage, New York.
——. 1974b. "The Western Image and Western Studies of Islam." *The Legacy of Islam*, ed. Joseph Schacht and C. E. Bosworth, Oxford University Press, London.
Rodney, Walter. 1965. "Portuguese Attempts at Monopoly on the Upper Guinea Coast, 1580–1650." *Journal of African History* 6, no. 3.
——. 1969. "Upper Guinea and the Significance of the Origins of Africans Enslaved in the New World." *Journal of Negro History* 54, no. 4.
——. 1972. *How Europe Underdeveloped Africa*. Bogle-L'Ouverture, London.
Rodrigues, Jose Honorio. 1965. *Brazil and Africa*. University of California Press, Berkeley.
Rogers, Francis M. 1964. "The Attraction of the East and Early Portuguese Discoveries." *Luso-Brazilian Review* 1, no. 1.
Rogin, Michael P. 1967. *The Intellectuals and McCarthy*. MIT Press, Cambridge.
Rosenberg, Arthur. 1934. *A History of Bolshevism*. Oxford University Press, London.
Rotberg, Robert (ed.). 1971. *Rebellion in Black Africa*. Oxford University Press, London.
Rotter, Gernot. 1967. "Die Stellung des Negers in der islamisch-arabischen Geselschaft bis XVI Jahrhundert." Unpublished dissertation.
Rougemont, Denis de. 1966. *The Idea of Europe*. Macmillan, New York.
Rout, Leslie R., Jr. 1976. *The African Experience in Spanish America*. Cambridge University Press, Cambridge.
Roux, Edward. 1964. *Time Longer Than Rope*. University of Wisconsin Press, Madison.
Roy, M. N. 1976. *Fascism*. Best Books, Jijnasa.
Royce, Edward. 1980. "Genovese on Slave Revolts and Weiner on the Postbellum South." *Insurgent Sociologist*, no. 10.
Rubin, Vera, and Arthur Tuden (eds.). 1977. *Comparative Perspectives on Slavery in New World Plantation Societies*. Annals of the New York Academy of Sciences 292.
Ruchames, Louis. 1969. *Racial Thought in America*. Grosset and Dunlap, New York.
Rude, George. 1964. *The Crowd in History*. John Wiley and Sons, New York.
Russell-Wood, A. J. R. 1968. *Fidalgos and Philanthropists*. University of California Press, Berkeley.
——. 1974. "Black and Mulatto Brotherhoods in Colonial Brazil: A Study of Collective Behavior." *Hispanic American Historical Review* 54, no. 4.
Said, Edward. 1978. *Orientalism*. Pantheon, New York.
Saignes, Miguel Acosta. 1973. "Life in a Venezuelan *Cumbe*." *Maroon Societies*, ed. Richard Price. Anchor, Garden City.
Samaroo, Brinsley. 1972. "The Trinidad Workingmen's Association and the Origins of Popular Protest in a Crown Colony." *Social and Economic Studies* 21, no. 2.
Samuel, Raphael. 1980. "British Marxist Historians." *New Left Review*, no. 120.
—— (ed.). 1981. *People's History and Socialist Theory*. Routledge and Kegan Paul, London.
Sanchez-Albornoz, Nicolas. 1974. *The Population of Latin America: A History*. University of California Press, Berkeley.
Sanderson, Lillian. 1975. "Education and Administrative Control in Colonial Sudan and Northern Nigeria." *African Affairs* 74, no. 297.
Sandford, Eva. n.d. *The Mediterranean World in Ancient Times*. Publisher unlisted.
Sankey, Veronica. 1980. Interview with C. J. Robinson. Brighton, England, 20 July.
Saunders, J. V. D. 1959. "The Brazilian Negro. *The Americas* 15, no. 3.
Scelle, Georges. 1906. *Histoire Politique de la Traite Negrière aux Indes de Castille*. 2 vols. Larose and Forcel, Paris.
——. 1910. "The Slave-Trade in the Spanish Colonies of America: The Assiento." *American Journal of International Law* 4, no. 3.
Schacht, Joseph, and C. E. Bosworth (eds.). 1974. *The Legacy of Islam*. Oxford University Press, London.
Schirokauer, Arno Lassalle. 1931. *The Power of Illusion and the Illusion of Power*. George Allen and Unwin, London.

Schuler, Monica. 1970. "Ethnic Slave Rebellions in the Caribbean and the Guianas." *Journal of Social History* 3, no. 4.

——. 1980. *Alas, Alas, Kongo: A Social History of Indentured African Immigration into Jamaica, 1841–1865.* Johns Hopkins University Press, Baltimore.

Schumpeter, J. A. 1965. *Capitalism, Socialism and Democracy.* Unwin, London.

Schwartz, Stuart. 1970. "The *Mocambo*: Slave Resistance in Colonial Bahia." *Journal of Social History* 3, no. 4.

Scott, Ian. 1978. "Middle Class Politics in Zambia." *African Affairs* 77, no. 308.

Seligman, Charles C. 1933. *Egypt and Negro Africa.* Routledge and Sons, London.

Sellin, J. Thorsten. 1976. *Slavery and the Penal System.* Elsevier, New York.

Semmel, Bernard. 1963. *Jamaican Blood and Victorian Conscience.* Houghton Mifflin, Cambridge.

Shapiro, Leonard. 1977. "Two Years that Shook the World." *New York Review of Books,* 31 March.

Sharp, William F. 1975. "The Profitability of Slavery in the Colombian Choco, 1680–1810." *Hispanic American Historical Review* 55, no. 3.

Shepperson, George. 1972. "Garvey as Pan-Africanist." *Marcus Garvey,* ed. E. David Cronon. Prentice-Hall, Englewood Cliffs.

——. 1980. "Ourselves as Others." *Review* 4, no. 1.

Shepperson, George, and Thomas Price. 1958. *Independent African.* Edinburgh University Press, Edinburgh.

Shillington, Violet. 1906. "The Beginnings of the Anglo-Portuguese Alliance." *Transactions of the Royal Historical Society* 20.

Shyllon, Folarin. 1981. "The Black Presence and Experience in Britain: An Analytical Overview." Paper presented to the International Conference on the History of Blacks in Britain, University of London, 30 September.

Silverberg, Robert. 1972. *The Realm of Prester John.* Doubleday, Garden City.

Singh, Raman K. 1974. "Marxism in Richard Wright's Fiction." *Indian Journal of American Studies* 4, nos. 1–2.

Skinner, Elliot. 1980. "The Persistence of Psychological and Structural Dependence after Colonialism." *Decolonization and Dependence,* ed. Aguibou Yansane. Greenwood Press, Westport.

Slave Insurrections, Selected Documents. 1970. Negro University Press, Westport (orig. 1860).

Slave Rebellion Trials: Jamaica. 1832. Colonial Office 137–185, Public Records Office, London.

Slessarev, Vsevolod. 1959. *Prester John: The Letter and the Legend.* University of Minnesota Press, Minneapolis.

Small, Richard. 1981. "The Training of an Intellectual, the Making of a Marxist." *Urgent Tasks* 12.

Smith, Abbot E. 1947. *Colonists in Bondage: White Servitude and Convict Labor in America, 1607–1776.* University of North Carolina Press, Chapel Hill.

Smith, Anthony. 1971. *Theories of Nationalism.* Harper and Row, New York.

Smith, David. 1978. *Socialist Propaganda in the Twentieth-Century British Novel.* Macmillan, London.

Smith, T. Lynn. 1966. "The Racial Composition of the Population of Colombia." *Journal of Inter-American Studies* 8, no. 2.

Snowden, Frank. 1970. *Blacks in Antiquity.* Harvard University Press, Cambridge.

Snyder, Louis. 1939. *Race.* Longmans, Green and Co., New York.

——. 1962. *The Idea of Racialism.* D. Van Nostrand, Princeton.

Soboul, Albert. 1974. *The French Revolution, 1787–1799.* Random House, New York.

Somit, Albert, and Joseph Tannenhaus. 1967. *The Development of (American) Political Science: From Burgess to Behavioralism.* Allyn and Bacon, Boston.

"Special Editorial Note for the People South of Mason and Dixon's Line, A." 1854. *Putnam's Monthly* 3, no. 15.

Stalin, J. V. 1953. "Marxism and the National Question." *Works,* vol. 11. Foreign Languages, Moscow.

Stampp, Kenneth. 1956. *The Peculiar Institution.* Vintage, New York.

Starobin, Joseph. 1972. *American Communism in Crisis, 1943–1957.* University of California Press, Berkeley.

Starobin, Robert. 1970. *Industrial Slavery in the Old South.* Oxford University Press, New York.

Stein, Robert. 1980. "Mortality in the Eighteenth-Century French Slave Trade." *Journal of African History* 21, no. 1.

Stockwell, John. 1979. *In Search of Enemies.* Futura Publications, London.

Stoddard, T. Lothrop. 1914. *The French Revolution in San Domingo.* Houghton Mifflin, Boston.

Stokes, Rose Pastor. 1923. "The Communist International and the Negro." *The Worker,* 10 March.

Stolberg, Ben. 1935. "Black Chauvinism." *The Nation,* 15 May.

Stone, Carl. 1973. *Class, Race and Political Behaviour in Urban Jamaica.* Press University of the West Indies, Mona.

Stone, Norman. 1980. "The Many Tragedies of Haiti." *Times Literary Supplement,* 15 February.

St. Pierre, Maurice. 1973. "West Indian Cricket—A Socio-Historical Appraisal, Part 1." *Caribbean Quarterly* 9, no. 2.

Strauss, Eric. 1951. *Irish Nationalism and British Democracy*. Columbia University Press, New York.

Street, Brian. 1975. *The Savage in Literature*. Routledge and Kegan Paul, London.

Stephenson, Wendell Holmes. 1964. *Southern History in the Making*. Louisiana State University Press, Baton Rouge.

Strachey, John. 1939. "Communism in Great Britain." *Current History*, January.

Stuart, James. 1913. *A History of the Zulu Rebellion*. Macmillan, London.

Studi Colombiana, vol. 2. 1952. Stabilimento Arti Grafiche (ed.) Affini, Genova.

Styron, William. 1978. "Hell Reconsidered." *New York Review of Books* 25, no. 11.

Sweezy, Paul. 1971. "Workers and the Third World." *The Revival of American Socialism*, ed. George Fischer. Oxford University Press, New York.

Sweezy, Paul, et al. 1976. *The Transition from Feudalism to Capitalism*. New Left Books, London.

Symons, Julian. 1975. *The Thirties: A Dream Revolved*. Faber and Faber, London.

Tassin, Algernon. 1916. *The Magazine in America*. Dodd, Mead, New York.

Taussig, Michael. 1979. "Black Religion and Resistance in Colombia: Three Centuries of Social Struggle in the Cauca Valley." *Marxist Perspectives* 2, no. 2.

Tawney, R. H. 1950. "A History of Capitalism." *Economic History Review*, 2d ser., vol. 2, no. 3.

Taylor, A. E. 1966. *Plato, the Man and His Work*. World Publishing, Cleveland.

Taylor, A. J. 1960. "Progress and Poverty in Britain." *History* 45, February.

Taylor, Theman. 1981. "Cyril Briggs and the African Blood Brotherhood: Effects of Communism on Black Nationalism, 1919–35." Unpublished Ph.D. diss.

Taylor, William B. 1970. "The Foundation of Nuestra Senora de Guadalupe de los Morenos de Amapa." *The Americas* 26, no. 4.

Thomas, Hugh. 1961. *The Spanish Civil War*. Harper and Row, New York.

Thomas, John L. 1963. *The Liberator: William Lloyd Garrison*. Little, Brown, Boston.

Thompson, E. P. 1966. *The Making of the English Working Class*. Vintage, New York.

——. 1967. "Time, Work-Discipline, and Industrial Capitalism." *Past and Present*, no. 38.

——. 1974. *Whigs and Hunters*. Pantheon, New York.

——. 1978. *The Poverty of Theory*. Monthly Review Press, New York.

——. 1981. "The Politics of Theory." *People's History and Socialist Theory*, ed. Raphael Samuel. Routledge and Kegan Paul, London.

Thomson, George. 1977. *The First Philosophers*. Lawrence and Wishart, London (orig. 1955).

Thorpe, Earl(ie) E. 1970. *Black Historians*. William Morrow, New York.

Thrupp, S. 1951. "The Grocers of London: A Study of Distributive Trade." *Studies in English Trade in the Fifteenth Century*, ed. Eileen Power and M. M. Postan. Routledge and Kegan Paul, London.

Tigar, Michael, and Madeline Levy. 1977. *Law and the Rise of Capitalism*. Monthly Review Press, New York.

Times Literary Supplement. 1973. Articles by E. E. Evans-Pritchard, M. Douglas, Edmund Leach, Lucy Mair, and Rodney Needham, 6 July.

Trelease, Allen. 1971. *White Terror*. Harper Torchbooks, New York.

Trevor-Roper, Hugh. 1963a. "The Rise of Christian Europe I: The Great Recovery." *The Listener*, 28 November.

——. 1963b. "The Rise of Christian Europe: The Dark Ages." *The Listener*, 12 December.

——. 1963c. "The Rise of Christian Europe: The Crusades." *The Listener*, 19 December.

——. 1963d. "The Rise of Christian Europe: The Medieval Renaissance." *The Listener*, 26 December.

——. 1965. *The Rise of Christian Europe*. Harcourt, Brace and World, New York.

Trotman, D. V. 1976. "The Yoruba and Orisha Worship in Trinidad and British Guiana, 1838–1870." *African Studies Review* 19, no. 2.

Trotsky, Leon. 1964. *The Writings of Leon Trotsky*, vol. 6. Martin Secker and Warburg, London.

Tuchman, Barbara. 1977. *A Distant Mirror*. Ballantine Books, New York.

Tucker, Robert. 1971. *Philosophy and Myth in Karl Marx*. Cambridge University Press, Cambridge.

—— (ed.). 1972. *The Marx-Engels Reader*. W. W. Norton, New York.

——. 1977. *Stalinism*. W. W. Norton, New York.

Tutuola, Amos. 1954. *My Life in the Bush of the Ghosts*. Faber and Faber, London.

Ullmann, Walter. 1965. *The Growth of Papal Government in the Middle Ages*. Methuen, London.

"Uncle Tom at Home." 1856. *Putnam's Monthly* 8, no. 43.

Uribe, Jaramillo. 1964. "La poblacion indigene de Colombia en el momento de la Conquista y sus transformaciones posteriores." *Anuario Colombiano de historia social y de la cultura* 1, no. 2.

Vansina, Jan. 1966. *Kingdoms of the Savanna*. University of Wisconsin Press, Madison.

Verlinden, Charles. 1953. "Italian Influence in Iberian Colonization." *Hispanic American Historical Review* 33, no. 2.

——. 1955. *L'esclavage dans l'Europe medievale*, vol. 1. Peninsule Iberique, Bugge, France.

——. 1958. "Navigateurs, marchands et colons italiens au service de la decouverte et de la colonisation portugaise sous Henri le Navigateur." *Le Moyen Age* 64, no. 4.

——. 1970. *The Beginnings of Modern Colonization*. Cornell University Press, Ithaca.

Vidal, Gore. 1981. "The Second American Revolution?" *New York Review of Books*, 5 February.

Vila, Enriqueta. 1977. "The Large-Scale Introduction of Africans into Veracruz and Cartagena." *Comparative Perspectives on Slavery in New World Plantation Societies*, ed. Vera Rubin and Arthur Tuden. *Annals of the New York Academy of Sciences* 292.

Vincent, Theodore. 1972. *Black Power and the Garvey Movement*. Ramparts, San Francisco.

Walden, Daniel (ed.). 1972. *W. E. B. Du Bois: The Crisis Writings*. Fawcett, Greenwich.

Wallerstein, Immanuel. 1974. *The Modern World System*. Academic Press, New York.

——. 1980. *The Modern World System II*. Academic Press, New York.

Ward, Sir Adolphus W. 1917. *Germany 1815–1890*, vol. 2. Cambridge University Press, Cambridge.

Ward, J. T. (ed.). 1970. *Popular Movements c. 1830–1850*. Macmillan, London.

——. 1974. *Chartism*. Harper and Row, New York.

Webb, Constance. 1968. *Richard Wright*. Putnam, New York.

Webb, R. 1971. *The British Working Class Reader*. Kelley, New York.

Weir, Stanley. 1981. "Revolutionary Artist." *Urgent Tasks* 12.

Weisbord, Robert. 1973. *Ebony Kinship*. Greenwood Press, Westport.

Westermann, William L. 1955. *The Slave Systems of Greek and Roman Antiquity*. American Philosophical Society.

Widgery, David. 1981. "A Meeting with Comrade James." *Urgent Tasks* 12.

Wiecek, William. 1978. "Slavery and Abolition before the United States Supreme Court, 1820–1860." *Journal of American History* 65, no. 1.

Wilks, Ivor. 1975. *Asante in the Nineteenth Century*. Cambridge University Press, London.

Williams, Eric. 1962. *History of the People of Trinidad and Tobago*. People's National Movement Publishing Co., Port-of-Spain.

——. 1966. *Capitalism and Slavery*. Capricorn Books, New York.

——. 1969. *Inward Hunger*. Andre Deutsch, London.

——. 1970. *From Columbus to Castro*. Harper and Row, New York.

Williams, George Washington. 1883. *A History of the Negro Race in America from 1619 to 1880*. G. P. Putnam's Sons, New York.

Williams, Raymond. 1971. "Literature and Sociology." *New Left Review*, no. 67.

Williams, William Appleman. 1980. "Empire as a Way of Life." *The Nation*, 2–9 August.

Wilson, Basil. 1981. "The Caribbean Revolution." *Urgent Tasks* 12.

Wilson, Carus. 1951. "The Overseas Trade of Bristol." *Studies in English Trade in the Fifteenth Century*, ed. Eileen Power and M. M. Postan. Routledge and Kegan Paul, London.

Wish, Harvey. 1970. "American Slave Insurrections before 1861." *Justice Denied*, ed. William Chace and Peter Collier. Harcourt, Brace and World, New York.

Wolin, Sheldon. 1960. *The Politics of Vision*. Little, Brown, Boston.

Wood, Donald. 1968. *Trinidad in Transition: The Years after Slavery*. Oxford University Press, for the Institute of Race Relations, London.

Wood, Forrest. 1968. *Black Scare: The Racist Response to Emancipation and Reconstruction*. University of California Press, Berkeley.

Wood, Neal. 1959. *Communism and British Intellectuals*. Victor Gollancz, London.

Wood, Peter. 1975. *Black Majority*. Norton, New York.

Woodward, C. Vann. 1963. *Tom Watson: Agrarian Rebel*. Oxford University Press, New York.

Wright, Irene. 1930. "The Spanish Resistance to the English Occupation of Jamaica, 1655–1660." *Transactions of the Royal Historical Society*, 4th ser., vol. 12.

Wright, Richard. 1944. "I Tried to Be a Communist." *Atlantic Monthly*, August and September.

——. 1945. *Black Boy*. Harper and Row, New York.

——. 1953. *The Outsider*. Harper, New York.

——. 1954. *Black Power*. Harper and Brothers, New York.

——. 1957. *White Man Listen!* Doubleday, Garden City.

——. 1960. "The Voiceless Ones." *Saturday Review*, 16 April.

——. 1977. *American Hunger*. Harper and Row, New York.

——. 1980. "Blueprint for Negro Writing." *Race and Class* 21, no. 4 (orig. 1937).

Wright, Richard R. 1902. "Negro Companions of the Spanish Explorers." *American Anthropologist* 4, no. 2.

Wynter, Sylvia. 1981. "In Quest of Matthew Bondsman: Some Cultural Notes on the Jamesian Journey." *Urgent Tasks* 12.

Yansane, Aguibou (ed.). 1980. *Decolonization and Dependence*. Greenwood Press, Westport.

Yates, Frances A. 1979. *The Occult Philosophy in the Elizabethan Age*. Routledge and Kegan Paul, London.

Yates, Names. 1978. Interview with C. J. Robinson. Binghamton, New York, 26 April.

Zambardino, Rudolph A. 1980. "Mexico's Population in the Sixteenth Century: Demographic Anomaly or Mathematical Illusion?" *Journal of Interdisciplinary History* 11, no. 1.

Zeller, Edward. 1948. *Outline of the History of Greek Philosophy*. Routledge and Kegan Paul, London.

Zinn, Howard. 1970. *The Politics of History*. Beacon Press, Boston.

——. 1980. *A People's History of the United States*. Harper and Row, New York.

INDEX

Abbott, Robert, 212–13
Abolition: of British slave trade, 157–58; of British slavery, 164
Absolute state, 21–22; and alien mercenaries, 22–23, 323 (n. 99); and banditry, 323 (n. 98)
Africa, 270; and Mediterranean civilizations, 83–85; and medieval Europe, 85–87; in European thought, 74–81, 342 (n. 53); origins of slave laborers, 117–20; and colonialism, 311–13
African Blood Brotherhood, 198, 213, 215–18, 227, 385 (n. 116)
African cultures: and Brazilian slave revolts, 153–55; and resistance, 165–66, 354 (n. 2)
African history: denial of, 336 (n. 6)
African resistance. *See* African cultures: and resistance
African slavery: and Islam, 88–89
African soldiers: in World War I, 253–54
Afro-Americans soldiers: in World War I, 253
Afro-West Indian Literary Society, 260
America: origins of nationalist myths, 186; and workers' consciousness, 200–203; and immigrant workers, 210–11; origins of socialism in, 210–11
—colonial: and Amerindians, 339 (n. 25); and concern with Black resistance, 340 (n. 45); racial characteristics in, 78–81
American Communist Party (CPUSA), 197, 198, 208, 217, 218, 223, 226–27, 231–32, 255, 279, 292–97, 380 (n. 59); and Comintern, 211–12; and Jews, 211–12, 384 (n. 95); and Blacks, 382 (n. 77), 386 (n. 124); and foreign-language federations, 384 (nn. 97, 98); and self-determination, 388 (n. 148)
American Indians, 77, 125–26, 130–31, 339 (n. 25), 356 (nn. 23, 26, 27, 28), 357 (n. 37), 374 (n. 7)
American Negro Academy, 191–93
American Revolution: and class, 339 (n. 29)
American Trotskyist movement. *See* Trotskyism: American
Anglo-Saxonism, 34, 36, 327 (n. 43), 328 (n. 71), 373 (n. 4); and Socialism, 258–60, 395 (n. 94)
Aptheker, Herbert, 369 (n. 1)
Argentina, 129–30
Arnold, Matthew, 255, 399 (n. 157)
Arnold, Thomas, 266, 268
Athleticism: in ancient Greece, 267–68; in Britain, 268–69

Australia, 253
Azikiwe, Nnamdi, 260

Babeuf, François-Noel (Gracchus), 49–51, 331 (nn. 25, 32)
Baldwin, James, 289, 305
"Baptist War" (Jamaica), 161–64
Barbados: slave revolts in, 158–60
Belgium, 253
Besant, Annie, 258
Beyond a Boundary, 266–69, 285
Black Belt thesis, 295
Black colleges and universities, 372 (n. 22), 377 (n. 33)
Black emigration, 335 (n. 3)
Black historiography. *See* Historiography: Black
The Black Jacobins, 265, 274–78, 285
Black labor: migration of, in America, 212–13. *See also* Slaves—labor
Blackman, Peter, 261, 308, 399 (n. 165)
Black migration, 194–95
Black petit bourgeoisie, 312; and colonialism, 178–81; and racial consciousness, 189, 376 (n. 25); and ideology, 191–95; and capitalism, 206–7; in Cuba and Brazil, 371 (n. 19)
Black radical intelligentsia, 287–88; in Britain, 260–70; and British Intelligence, 263–64; and socialism, 313
Black radicals: and Black petit bourgeoisie, 178–81; development of, 181–82
Black radical theory, 5
Black radical tradition, 3, 72–73, 238–40, 270, 272, 285–86, 287, 288, 309–18, 334 (n. 1); resistance in, 4–5; as negation of Western civilization, 72–73; and violence, 167–69, 368 (n. 1); and revolutionary consciousness, 167–71, 275–76; and intelligentsia, 170–71; misperceptions of, 175–76; and slavery, 177; and Du Bois, 194–95; in Trinidad, 245–46; and C. L. R. James, 272–74, 285–86; and Richard Wright, 297–301
Black Reconstruction, 228–31, 234–39, 270–71, 389 (n. 188)
Blassingame, John, 123–25, 354 (n. 7)
"Blueprint for Negro Writing," 291–92
Blyden, Edward Wilmot, 217, 377 (n. 39)
Boggs, Grace (Lee), 280, 285
Bone, Robert, 290

Boukman (maroon), 147, 148
Bourgeoisie: first development, 13–16; first destruction of, 17–18; rise of modern, 18–21; the state and modern, 20–21
Braudel, Fernand, 25, 102, 177, 323 (n. 88), 350 (n. 30)
Brazil, 140, 310, 311; and slave rebellions, 132–33, 152–55; slavery in, 149–55; and slave trade, 364 (nn. 195, 200); African origins of slaves, 364 (nn. 202, 204); and Black petit bourgeoisie, 371 (n. 19)
Briggs, Cyril, 216–18, 224, 385 (nn. 111, 116)
Britain, 260–70, 275; Blacks residing in, 260–70, 397 (nn. 116, 123, 127)
British colonialism: and capitalism, 112–14; and slave labor, 116; and slave trade, 117–20; and self-government, 241–42
British Colonial Office, 253, 264
British Communist Party (CPGB), 259, 261, 270, 395 (n. 102)
British imperialism, 242–43, 280–81, 390 (n. 10)
British Labour Party, 253–64 passim, 270, 399 (n. 164)
British Liberal Party, 390 (n. 6)
Brockway, Fenner, 261
Browder, Earl, 227, 296, 371 (n. 2)
Brown, John, 76, 229, 311
Burgess, John, 188, 374 (n. 12)
Bustamante, Alexander, 398 (n. 138)
Butler, Rab, 398 (n. 138)
Butterfield, Herbert, 343 (n. 78)

Cabral, Amilcar, 276, 401 (n. 186); on resistance, 122
Campbell, Grace, 216
Canada, 253
Capitalism: and slave labor, 4, 109–20, 200–203, 228–30; and feudalism, 9–10; and immigrant labor, 23–24; and Western civilization, 24–28; industrial, and poverty/unemployment, 31–33, 325 (n. 8); and Black labor, 308–9; and ethnic labor, 324 (n. 100); early trade networks, 321 (n. 31); and imperialism, 370 (n. 5)
Carnegie, Andrew, 194
Carver, George Washington, 378 (n. 46)
The Case for West-Indian Self Government, 250–51
Castoriadis, Cornelius, 326 (n. 29), 402 (n. 188)
Castro, Americo, 92
Central Intelligence Agency, 289, 404 (n. 6), 405 (n. 9)
Césaire, Aimé, 183–84
Ceylon, 254, 270
Cheng Ho, 105–6, 349 (n. 16)
Chile, 129–30
Chilembwe, John, 168, 254, 271
China, 270; explorations in Indian Ocean, 105–6, 349 (n. 26), 350 (n. 28)
Chinese workers: in Trinidad, 246
Cipriani, Arthur, 254, 255, 256, 265
Class consciousness: among white workers in United States, 201–3

Class formation: race and ethnicity, 26–27
Claudin, Fernando, 396 (n. 114)
Cockburn, Claud, 264
Cole, G. D. H., 258
Cole, Margaret, 258
Colombia, 130, 131, 132, 137–38, 166; and marronage, 360 (nn. 104, 107)
Colonial America. See American—colonial
Colonialism: documentation of, 164–65; resistance to, 165–66; contradictions of, 179–80. See also British colonialism; Spanish colonialism
Columbus, Christopher, 106–9, 125, 351 (n. 49)
Congress of Industrial Organizations (CIO), 232
Constantine, Learie, 255–56, 262, 265, 266
Cortes, Hernan, 130
Cox, Oliver, 110, 179, 182, 183, 288, 313, 315, 316, 341 (n. 47), 372 (n. 32), 402 (n. 188)
Creoles, French (Trinidad), 245–47, 247–48, 392 (n. 38)
Cricket: in Trinidad, 252, 266–69; in West Indies, 407 (n. 64)
Crummell, Alexander, 191, 192, 193, 217, 370 (n. 12)
Cruse, Harold, 291, 305, 381 (n. 63), 387 (n. 125)
Cuba, 140–41, 311; and Black petit bourgeoisie, 371 (n. 19)
Curtin, Philip, 110, 112, 117, 151, 338 (n. 21), 352 (n. 72)

Davis, David Brion, 75–76, 96, 338 (nn. 14, 16)
DeLeon, Daniel, 258, 373 (n. 2)
Dessalines, 168, 278
Dickens, Charles, 266–67
Dom Henrique (the Navigator), 93–94, 345 (n. 112)
Domingo, W. A., 215–16, 217, 398 (n. 138)
Doty, Edward, 216
Draper, Theodore, 334 (n. 2)
Du Bois, W. E. B., 149, 182, 217, 256, 262, 271, 287, 288, 291, 293, 300, 305, 313–14, 315–16, 354 (n. 15), 372 (n. 27), 378 (n. 52), 379 (n. 53), 399 (n. 165), 401 (n. 181); background of, 185–86; critique of American historiography, 187–88; and American Negro Academy, 192–93; and Black radical tradition, 194–95; at Rosenwald Conference, 197–99; and Marxism, 207–8, 228–31, 236–37, 380 (n. 58), 383 (n. 80); and UNIA, 214, 385 (n. 107); on the "General Strike," 235–36; on slave consciousness and rebellion, 237; and "labor aristocracy," 328 (n. 69); and American racism, 337 (n. 12); on Talented Tenth, 376 (n. 24); on socialism, 379 (n. 54); on working class and war, 379 (n. 55); and Soviet Union, 379 (n. 56); on American Communist Party, 380 (n. 62); and NAACP, 381 (n. 63); on labor aristocracy, 381 (n. 72); on dictatorship of proletariat, 389 (n. 182)
Dunayevskaya, Raya, 279–80
Dunning, William, 374 (nn. 11, 12)
Duse, Mohamed Ali, 260, 264
Dutt, Rajani Palme, 261

East Indians: in Trinidad, 244–46

Egypt: Blacks in, 82–84; and Mediterranean Europe, 83–84; and Nubia, 84; impact on Greek thought, 84, 342 (n. 63)

Engels, Friedrich: and Irish labor, 39; on history and the dialectic, 64–65; on Irish question, 328 (n. 57); on race, 328 (n. 65); on medieval rebellions, 330 (n. 7); on national state, 332 (n. 73). *See also* Marx, Karl—and Engels

English working class: and class consciousness, 29–30, 33–36; rebellions, 33; and trade unionism, 35–36; and ethnic divisions, 41–42; occupational divisions, 326 (n. 32)

Esteban (*ladino*), 129

Ethiopian Progressive Association, 260

Eurocentricism, 97–99

Europe, medieval: agriculture and trade in, 15–16; and slave trade, 16–17; peasant rebellions in, 17–18; decline of, 17–18, 320 (n. 27); and Africa, 85–86; and Islam, 87–89, 344 (n. 91), 347 (n. 119); and Mongol Empire, 90; and Black Death, 90–91; and Aristotle, 96–97; myths in, 343 (n. 75); and decline of knowledge, 343 (n. 78); and climatic changes, 344 (n. 89); and Crusades, 344 (n. 90)

European civilization: formation, 10–13, 27–28, 319 (n. 6), 320 (n. 21); early decline, 12–13

Fanon, Frantz, 168, 183, 298

Federal Bureau of Investigation, 404 (n. 6), 405 (n. 9)

Florida: slavery in, 141–42

Fort-Whiteman, Lovett, 216

Foster, William Z., 227

Fox-Genovese, Elizabeth, 341 (n. 48)

Franklin, Benjamin, 336 (n. 7), 339 (n. 26); racial consciousness of, 77

Froude, James, 36–38, 248

Fugitive Slave Law, 337 (n. 30)

Gallacher, Willie, 261

Garvey, Marcus, 213–24 passim, 254–55, 256, 261, 270–71, 334 (n. 2), 385 (nn. 103, 104, 105); on Lenin, 386 (n. 123)

Gayle, Addison, 293–94, 374 (nn. 6, 8, 9)

Genoa: merchant colonies in Portugal, 103–4; and English monarchy, 104–5; merchants in Spain, 106; role of merchants in Columbus expeditions, 108–9; rise of, 350 (n. 30); bankers in Spain, 351 (nn. 51, 55)

Genovese, Eugene, 168, 176, 341 (n. 48), 367 (n. 273), 369 (n. 1)

Germany, 253, 297–98; nationalism in, 53–58

Gold Coast, 254–55

Grace, W. G., 266–67, 398 (n. 148)

Greece, 268–69

Greek civilization: and Africa, 83–84

Grenada, 254–55

Guiana: slave revolts in, 160, 366 (n. 244); and marronage, 360 (n. 110)

Haiti, 274–78, 310, 311, 363 (n. 160), 390 (n. 2); slave society in, 144–49

Haitian Revolution, 146, 147–49, 363 (n. 176)

Hall, Otto, 215–16, 218, 223–24

Harding, Vincent, 403 (n. 205)

Haywood, Harry, 216, 217, 218, 223–24, 295, 396 (n. 114), 403 (n. 205)

Hegel, G. W. F., 280–85; and Eurocentrism, 73–74, 335 (n. 5)

Hill, Robert, 215, 385 (n. 105), 398 (n. 142), 400 (n. 178), 403 (n. 195)

Historiography: Black, 187–88, 189–90, 274, 377 (n. 44); racialism in American, 187–89, 374 (n. 11)

Hobsbawm, E. J., 31–32, 325 (n. 8), 326 (nn. 12, 21)

Hook, Sidney, 373 (n. 2)

Huiswoud, Otto, 216, 221, 223

Hyndman, Henry, 258

Imperialism. *See* British imperialism; Colonialism

Indentured servants, 78–81, 338 (n. 23), 339 (nn. 36, 37)

Independent Labour Party (Britain), 257–58, 258–60, 261, 271

India, 253, 254–55, 270

India Mutiny (1857), 391 (n. 21)

Indies: meaning in Middle Ages, 348 (n. 128)

Industrial Revolution, 30–31

Inikori, J. E., 111, 112–13, 352 (n. 72)

International African Friends of Ethiopia, 271–72

International African Service Bureau, 273, 274

International Brigade, 264, 272, 400 (n. 173)

International Trade Union Committee of Negro Workers, 261, 295

Ireland: conquest and colonization, 36–39, 41–42, 327 (n. 55); rebellions, 38–39; derationalization of economy, 39; emigration, 340 (n. 39)

Irish: labor, 39–40, 259–60; peasants, 116

Isabel, Alonzo, 216

Islam: and science, 87; and medieval Europe, 87–89, 346 (n. 117); and slavery, 94–95; and European racism, 346 (n. 117)

Italo-Ethiopian War, 261, 271–74; and West Indies, 400 (n. 171)

Jamaica, 141, 156–57, 310; and slave rebellions, 135–37, 366 (nn. 246, 249, 265), 367 (n. 268); and marronage, 160–64

James, C. L. R., 145, 146–49, 164–65, 177, 182, 183, 184, 188, 261, 262, 287, 288, 291, 305, 313, 314–16, 363 (n. 177), 365 (n. 232), 394 (n. 81), 399 (n. 165), 400 (n. 178), 401 (n. 183), 403 (nn. 195, 202, 205); on British colonials, 250–51; origins of social thinking, 251–52, 393 (n. 59); early political consciousness, 254–57; and Trotskyism, 265, 398 (n. 142); on English literature, 266; on connections between ancient Greece and British Empire, 267–68; and Italo-Ethiopian War, 271–72; and armed rebellion, 273–74; Pan-Africanism, 278–79; on Athenian democracy, 380 (n. 60); on athleticism, 398 (n. 148); on

Greeks, 399 (n. 153); on Stalinism, 402 (n. 192); and Trotsky, 402 (n. 193)
James, George, 342 (nn. 62, 63)
Japan, 270
Jefferson, Thomas, 355 (n. 17)
Jews, 211–12, 384 (n. 95)
Johnson-Forest Tendency, 279, 280
Jones, Chris, 261
Jordan, Winthrop, 323 (n. 89), 336 (n. 6), 338 (n. 17)

Katayama, Sen, 221, 223, 224
Kenya, 254–55
Kenyatta, Jomo, 262, 270, 273, 274, 397 (nn. 123, 127)
Kimbangu, Simon, 271
Ku Klux Klan, 376 (n. 27)

Labor. See Black labor; Slaves—labor
Las Casas, Bartolome de, 96–97, 126–27
Law, Oliver, 295
League of Coloured People, 260, 263
League of Struggle for Negro Rights, 295
Lenin, V. I., 207–8, 209, 217, 223, 224, 226, 227, 234, 237, 276, 277–78, 281–85, 373 (n. 2), 382 (n. 79), 403 (n. 201); on national question, 63; on Negro Question, 219–21; on origins of socialism, 330 (n. 18); and American socialism, 387 (n. 128)
Lincoln, Abraham, 238
Louisiana, 149
L'Ouverture, Toussaint, 148, 276–78, 369 (n. 9)
Lukács, Georg, 373 (n. 2)
Lynch, Hollis, 390 (n. 1)
Lynching, 378 (n. 49)

Mackandel (maroon), 147, 169
McKay, Claude, 215, 221, 223, 264, 394 (n. 77); and British Intelligence, 397 (n. 136)
Makonnen, T. Ras, 260, 262–63, 270–71, 400 (n. 169)
Marronage, 119–20, 310–11; in Spanish colonies, 130–32; in Jamaica, 135–37, 160–64; in Colombia, 137, 360 (nn. 104, 107); in Venezuela, 137–38; in Guianas and Suriname, 138–39, 360 (n. 110); in North America, 142–43; in Haiti, 146–47
Martin, Tony, 215
Marx, Karl: on Irish Question, 40–43, 329 (n. 72), 333 (n. 84); on the proletariat, 41–43, 48; and materialism, 51–52; on the state and capitalist development, 57–61; on necessity of bourgeois rule, 58–59; on capitalism as world system, 59–60; on nationalism, 60–61; on capitalism and slave labor, 81–82, 112–13, 341 (n. 47); on primitive accumulation, 121; on Irish immigration, 328 (n. 70); on social ideas, 329 (n. 82); and German communists, 331 (n. 40); on German workers, 332 (n. 74); on bourgeoisie, 332 (n. 75), 333 (n. 78); on France and class development, 333 (n. 81)
—and Engels: on the proletariat, 41–43, 48; write Communist Manifesto, 46–48; on petit bourgeoisie, 48; as German nationalists, 52–53,

55–57, 60–61, 332 (n. 53), 333 (n. 86); and Ferdinand Lassalle, 53–57; on national liberation movements, 60–61; on capitalist wars, 120; on nationalism, 224–26; on class struggle, 233–37; as bourgeois ideologists, 330 (n. 18); role of, 402 (n. 187)
Marxism, 207–12, 232–40, 259–60, 287–88, 313–16; as Western construct, 1–2; and consciousness, 62; and culture, 62–63; and theories of revolution, 274–78; and working classes and imperialism, 372 (n. 32)
Merchants' and Planters' Contingent, 253–54, 394 (n. 73)
Mexico, 129–30, 209; aboriginal population of, 126; slavery in, 128, 130–32
Miller, Kelly, 372 (n. 22)
Milliard, Peter, 262
Mocambos. See Palenques
Moody, Harold, 260, 263
Moore, Richard B., 215–16, 217, 218
Morgan, Edmund, 77, 336 (n. 7), 338 (n. 23), 339 (n. 25)
Mosley, Oswald, 264

Nasanov, N., 224
Nash, A. E. K., 340 (n. 46)
National Association for the Advancement of Colored People (NAACP), 197–98, 215, 221
Nationalism: in Europe, 3; and Marxism, 62–65; and racial myths, 324 (n. 108)
Nationalist movements, 254–55; for liberation, 270
Native Son, 293–99
Negro Commission (of Fourth Congress), 222–23
Nell, William C., 376 (n. 20)
New York, 141
Nkrumah, Kwame, 260, 262, 401 (n. 181)
Notes on Dialectics, 279–86
Nubia, 84, 343 (n. 67)
Nyerere, Julius, 183

Obeah, 136–37
Olivier, Sydney, 258
Opoba, Samuel, 262
Owen, Chandler, 214–15
Owens, Gordon, 216
Owens, Leslie H., 123–24, 354 (n. 7)

Padmore, George, 164–65, 182, 184, 249–74 passim, 287, 288, 305, 313, 315–16, 394 (n. 81), 396 (n. 114), 397 (n. 123), 400 (n. 169), 401 (nn. 181, 184)
Painter, Nell Irvin, 189
Palenques (quilombos, mocambos), 131–33, 358 (n. 75)
Palmares, 133–35, 136, 359 (nn. 84, 85, 99)
Pan-Africanism, 249, 254–55, 260, 262–63, 274, 401 (nn. 181, 184)
Panama, 131
Peasants: and revolution, 233–37
Pepper, John (Josef Pogany), 224